OXFORD EUROPEAN COMMUNITY LAW SERIES

General Editor: F. G. Jacobs
Advocate General, The Court of Justice
of the European Communities

European Community Law of State Aid

OXFORD EUROPEAN COMMUNITY LAW SERIES

The aim of this series is to publish important and original studies of the various branches of European Community Law. Each work will provide a clear, concise, and critical exposition of the law in its social, economic, and political context, at a level which will interest the advanced student, the practitioner, the academic, and government and Community officials.

Other Titles in this Series

The European Internal Market and International Trade: A Legal Analysis
P. Eeckhout

The Law of Money and Financial Services in the European Community
J. A. Usher

Legal Aspects of Agriculture in the European Community
J. A. Usher

European Community Sex Equality Law
Evelyn Ellis

European Community Competition Law
Second Edition
Dan Goyder

EC Tax Law
Paul Farmer and Richard Lyal

European Community Company Law
Vanessa Edwards (forthcoming)

Directives in European Community Law: A Study of Directives and their Enforcement in National Courts
Sacha Prechal

European Community Law of State Aid

ANDREW EVANS

CLARENDON PRESS · OXFORD
1997

Oxford University Press, Great Clarendon Street, Oxford OX2 6DP

Oxford New York

Athens Auckland Bangkok Bogota Bombay
Buenos Aires Calcutta Cape Town Dar es Salaam
Delhi Florence Hong Kong Istanbul Karachi
Kuala Lumpur Madras Madrid Melbourne
Mexico City Nairobi Paris Singapore
Taipei Tokyo Toronto
and associated companies in
Berlin Ibadan

Oxford is a trade mark of Oxford University Press

Published in the United States
by Oxford University Press Inc., New York

British Library Cataloguing in Publication Data
Data available

Library of Congress Cataloging in Publication Data
Data available
ISBN 0–19–876451–0

1 3 5 7 9 10 8 6 4 2

Typeset by Vera A. Keep, Cheltenham
Printed in Great Britain
on acid-free paper by
Biddles Ltd., Guildford and King's Lynn

General Editor's Foreword

The general prohibition in the EC Treaty of State aid or subsidies is an essential part of the internal market. It is closely related to the core freedoms, the free movement of goods and the freedom to provide services, since subsidies normally favour the national producer or supplier and are inherently liable to distort trade between Member States. In economic terms, subsidies to inefficient domestic industry offset the advantages which should result from the abolition of protectionist barriers. Subsidies distort the mechanisms of the market and can, unless given for legitimate purposes and subject to proper controls, amount to a massive misallocation of resources.

From another perspective—which is the principal perspective of the EC Treaty—the control of State aid falls within the field of competition policy. The provision by a Member State of a direct subsidy to its own industry may amount to the most blatant example of distortion of competition and, in effect, of rigging the market, often at the expense of the economies of other Member States. Thus, subsidies intended for apparently good reasons, such as to preserve jobs, will often have the effect of simply exporting unemployment, and if they do achieve their intended aims will give the domestic industry an unjustified competitive advantage.

The EC Treaty provisions on State aid, therefore, are included within the Treaty's 'Rules on competition'; the Treaty provides that State aid, whether granted by a Member State or through State resources in any form whatsoever, shall, if it distorts or threatens to distort competition, and subject only to narrowly drawn exceptions, be incompatible with the common market. The Treaty confers on the Commission, moreover, exceptionally broad and far-reaching powers to deal with State aid. The Commission is expressly empowered to keep under constant review all existing aid and, if it finds that aid is not compatible with the common market, or is being misused, to decide that the State concerned shall abolish or alter the aid within a period of time to be determined by the Commission. Proposals to grant new aid, or to alter existing aid, must be notified in advance to the Commission, and may be blocked if found objectionable.

The Court of Justice also is given special powers which reflect the importance and urgency of the matter. If a State does not comply with a Commission decision, the Commission, or another Member State, may seise the Court direct—thus short-circuiting the somewhat protracted requirements of the normal infringement procedure. Both the Commission and the Court may, in appropriate circumstances, prescribe interim measures. Member States may be required to recover any aid unlawfully granted.

What is necessary above all for the understanding of the subject of State aid is a systematic examination of the practice of the Commission. It is that examination which this book provides. The detailed analysis of the Commission's practice across the whole field of the economy provides an invaluable guide to a broad range of issues. The author explores the implications of privatization and nationalization of sectors of the economy, and the implications of liberalization of the markets on the one hand and of industrial policy on the other. He examines the limits of regional policy, which necessarily plays an important part in defining the contours of legitimate development aid. Of great importance also is the interaction of State aid as a component of competition policy with other policies—notably agriculture, transport and the environment.

Across the whole field, the book tackles problems both practical and conceptual. It considers the criteria to be used in assessing financial contributions from the State, such as the private investor test, and the ways in which those criteria are to be applied. It analyses the pervasive distinction between restructuring aid and operating aid.

This book admirably serves the objectives of the Oxford European Community Law Series by examining the law in its social, economic and political context, in an area which is ideally suited to that treatment. It also provides guidance to the practitioner and student which can properly be described as indispensable.

Francis G. Jacobs

November 1996

Preface

This book examines the control of state aid by EU law. Articles 92 to 93 of the EC Treaty require such aid to be controlled because of its capacity to distort competition in trade between Member States. In this sense the origin of state aid control lies in competition policy. However, in the elaboration of such control issues relating to a range of other policies, industrial policy, social policy, environmental policy, and so on, are raised.

In examining the relevant law, the book deals with issues having major social importance and involving use of substantial financial resources. The nature of the context in which the issues arise and of the procedures whereby they are tackled in Union practice means that reliance on traditional legal sources alone may be inadequate for effective examination. In this sense, judgments of the European Courts, on which most analysis of Union law focuses, constitute 'tips of icebergs'. Hence, the materials to which reference is made in the book include not only Union legislation and judgments of the European Courts. Above all, European Commission decisions under Articles 92 to 93 of the Treaty, the importance of which has only recently begun to be recognized by legal writers, have been systematically examined. The Commission's own descriptions of its decisions are used in the book, although pre-1973 decisions have been translated into English. These descriptions may sometimes be inelegant or inconsistent, but they are also informative, especially as to the way in which the Commission classifies a given aid measure or aid system.

The issues raised are topical because of the challenges to state aid policy entailed by German re-unification, creation of the European Economic Area, accession of Austria, Finland, and Sweden to the European Union, and likely future enlargement of the Union to include several countries of Central and Eastern Europe.

The book is written for students and teachers of EU law, officials, and decision-makers in Union, national, and regional institutions, and legal practitioners. Financial support for the research on which the book is based has been provided by the Tercentenary Fund of the Bank of Sweden and the European University Institute, in Florence.

ANDREW EVANS
European University Institute
and University of Umeå
May 1996

Table of Contents

Abbreviations

AiH	*Aktuellt i Handelspolitiken*
Bull. EC	Bulletin of the European Communities
BVS	Bundesanstalt fur vereinigungsbedingte Sonderaufgaben
BYIL	*British Yearbook of International Law*
CAP	Common Agricultural Policy
CCT	Common Customs Tariff
CDE	*Cahiers de Droit Européen*
CES	Comité Economique et Social
CMLR	Common Market Law Reports
CMLRev.	*Common Market Law Review*
Cmnd.	Command Papers (British Government Publication)
COM	Communication from the European Commission
Débs. PE	Débats du Parlement Européen
DN	*Dagens Nyheter*
EAGGF	European Agricultural Guidance and Guarantee Fund
ECLRev.	*European Competition Law Review*
ECR	European Court Reports
ECSC	European Coal and Steel Community
ECU	European Currency Unit
EG	Europeiska Gemenskaperna (European Communities)
EIB	European Investment Bank
EJIL	*European Journal of International Law*
ELRev.	*European Law Review*
EP Debs.	European Parliament Debates
EP Doc.	European Parliament Working Document
ERDF	European Regional Development Fund
ERU	Expertgruppen för Forskning om Regional Utveckling (Expert Group for Research on Regional Development)
ESF	European Social Fund
ETS	European Treaty Series
EuR	*Europa Recht*
Euratom	European Atomic Energy Community
Eurostat	Statistical Office of the European Communities
FT	*Förvaltningsrättslig Tidskrift*
GATT	General Agreement on Tariffs and Trade
HL	House of Lords
ICLQ	*International and Comparative Law Quarterly*
JCMS	*Journal of Common Market Studies*

JFT	*Tidskrift Utgiven av Juridiska Föreningen i Finland*
JO	Journal Officiel des Communautés Européennes
JT	*Juridisk Tidskrift*
JWT	*Journal of World Trade*
JWTL	*Journal of World Trade Law*
LIEI	*Legal Issues of European Integration*
MEPs	Members of the European Parliament
MLR	*Modern Law Review*
NORD	Nordiska Ministerrådets Utredningsserie (Nordic Council Reports)
NordREFO	Nordisk Institut för Regionalpolitik Forskning (Nordic Institute for Regional Policy Research)
NU	*Nordisk Utredningsserie* (E = English version)
OCT	Overseas Countries and Territories
OECD	Organization for Economic Co-operation and Development
OJ	Official Journal of the European Communities
PHARE	Poland and Hungary: Assistance for Economic Restructuring
Prop.	Regeringens Proposition
Rec.	Recueil de la Cour de Justice des Communautés Européennes
RFSP	*Revue Française de Science Politique*
RDE	*Rivista di Diritto Europeo*
RGDIP	*Revue Générale de Droit International Public*
RMC	*Revue du Marché Commun*
RTDE	*Revue Trimestrielle de Droit Européen*
SAF	Svenska Arbetsgivareföreningen
SEC	Internal Document from the Secretariat-General of the European Commission
SFS	Svensk författningssamling
SG	Secretariat-General of the European Commission
SOU	Sveriges Offentliga Utredningar
SvD	*Svenska Dagbladet*
SvDN	*Svenska Dagbladet, Näringsliv*
SvJT	*Svensk Juristtidning*
SÖ	Sveriges Överenskommelser med Främmande Makter
TfR	*Tidsskrift for Rettsvitenskap*
UU	Utrikesutskottets Betänkande
YBEL	*Yearbook of European Law*
ZaöRV	*Zeitschrift für Ausländisches Öffentliches Recht und Völkerrecht*

Tables

Treaties

Union Legislation and Administrative Decisions

Directives

EFTA Court Judgments

1

Introduction

Article 92(1) of the EC Treaty provides that, save as otherwise provided in this Treaty, any aid granted by a Member State or through state resources in any form whatsoever which distorts or threatens to distort competition by favouring certain undertakings or the production of certain goods[1] shall, in so far as it affects trade between Member States, be incompatible with the common market.[2]

The saving clause embodies the *lex specialis* principle. It recognizes that special rules may apply to aid in the agricultural sector, by virtue of Article 42 of the Treaty, and in the transport sector, by virtue of Article 80 of the Treaty. In addition, to the extent of the applicability of the ECSC Treaty, aid to the coal and steel sectors is unaffected by Article 92.[3] In other words, Article 92(1) only applies to coal and steel activities not covered by the ECSC Treaty.[4] Moreover, Article 112(1) of the EC Treaty provided that, without prejudice to obligations undertaken by them within the framework of other international organizations, Member States should, before the end of the transitional period, progressively harmonize the systems whereby they granted aid for exports to third countries (i.e. states which are not members of the European Union), to the extent necessary to ensure that competition between undertakings of the Union was not distorted. The implication is that such harmonization may affect the applicability of Article 92(1) to aid to exports to such countries. Finally, Article 92(1) is inapplicable where aid is compatible with the common market under Article 93(2) or (3).

In addition, aid may be permissible in connection with the production of, or trade in, arms, munitions, and war materials under Article 223(1)(b) of the EC Treaty,[5] though reliance on this provision may be challenged under Article 225

---

[1] Thus a change in ownership of industrial facilities does not affect the requirements of Art. 92. See Dec. 93/627 ([1993] OJ L309/21) concerning aid granted by the Spanish authorities on the occasion of the sale by Cenemesa/Cademesa/Conelec of certain selected assets to Asea-Brown Boveri.

[2] See, generally, A. Evans and S. Martin, 'Socially Acceptable Distortion of Competition: EC Policy on State Aid' (1991) 16 *ELRev.* 79–111.

[3] Art. 232(1) EC.

[4] Slynn AG in Case 238/85 *Deutsche Babcock Handel GmbH* v. *EC Commission* [1987] ECR 5119, 5131. The application of Art. 92 EC to aid to the nuclear industry is unaffected by Art. 232(2) EC, which merely states that provisions of the EC Treaty do not derogate from those of the Euratom Treaty. See Reischl AG in Joined Cases 188–190/80 *France, Italy and the UK* v. *EC Commission: transparency directive* [1982] ECR 2545, 2599.

[5] See, e.g., Dec. 89/633 ([1989] OJ L367/62) concerning aid provided or to be provided by the Spanish Government to Enasa, an undertaking producing commercial vehicles under the

of the Treaty. Aid might also be authorized to deal with balance-of-payments problems under Article 108 of the original version of the EEC Treaty.[6] Moreover, during the transitionary period[7] aid might be authorized under Article 226(1) where 'difficulties [arose] which [were] serious and liable to persist in any sector of the economy or which could bring about serious deterioration in the economic situation of a given area . . . in order to rectify the situation and adjust the sector concerned to the economy of the common market'. The difficulties covered included those which might arise from operation of the Treaty.[8]

Otherwise, the scope of application of Article 92(1) is broad. Although it refers only to 'goods', trade in services, such as tourism,[9] postal services,[10] television broadcasting,[11] banking[12] and other financial services,[13] publication of scientific abstracts,[14] and betting,[15] is also covered by this provision. On the other hand, assistance to 'non-profit-making activities (of a charitable, social, or cultural nature)' is not covered.[16]

Strictly speaking, Article 92(1) merely provides that aid covered thereby is incompatible with the common market. Unlike Article 4(c) of the ECSC Treaty, it does not expressly state that aid is prohibited. However, the Court of Justice, possibly having regard the general duty imposed on Member States by

brand 'Pegasus'; Notice C38/92 (ex NN128/92) ([1993] OJ C267/11) concerning aid which Italy had decided to grant to EFIM; and para. 9.2 of the Community Framework for state aids for research and development ([1986] OJ C83/1).

[6] See currently Art. 109h EC.

[7] Art. 8 of the EEC Treaty. See also the transitional arrangements regarding production aid for oil in para. 2 of the Protocol to the Treaty on mineral oils and certain of their derivatives.

[8] Joined Cases 73 & 74/63 *NV Internationale Crediet- en Handelsvereniging 'Rotterdam' and De Coöperatieve Suikerfabriek en Raffinederij G.A. 'Puttenhoek'* v. *Minister van Landbouw en Visserij* [1964] ECR 1, 25.

[9] See, regarding cut-price petrol for tourists in Italy, Commission Reply to Written Question 445/70 by Mr Vredeling ([1971] JO C22/10).

[10] Draft notice on the application of the competition rules to the postal sector and in particular on the assessment of certain state aid measures relating to postal services ([1995] OJ C322/3), para. 6.

[11] H. Morch, 'Summary of the Most Important Recent Developments' [1995] 6 *Competition Policy Newsletter* 41–7, 45–6.

[12] Dec. 95/547 ([1995] OJ C308/92) giving conditional approval to the aid granted by France to Crédit Lyonnais. See, earlier, Notice ([1984] OJ C15/20) of a proposal by the Netherlands Government to grant aid to an Amsterdam bank.

[13] Dec. 95/452 ([1995] OJ L264/30) on state aid in the form of tax concessions to undertakings operating in the Centro di Servizi Finanziari ed Assicurativi di Trieste pursuant to Art. 3 of Italian Law 19 of 9 Jan. 1991. See, regarding public credit institutions, Case 387/92 *Banco de Credito Industrial SA* v. *Ayuntamento Valencia* [1994] ECR I–877. See also Letter NN135/92 ([1995] OJ C262/11) informing the French Government of the decision not to regard as state aid the tax arrangements applicable to the French postal administration.

[14] Notice regarding aid for the publication of the scientific abstracts journal 'Physics Briefs' in Germany ([1981] OJ C319/4).

[15] Dec. 93/625 ([1993] OJ L300/15) concerning aid granted by the French Government to the Pari Mutuel Urbain and to the racecourse undertakings.

[16] *Sixth EEC General Report* (EEC Commission, Brussels,1963), 68.

Article 5 of the EC Treaty to refrain from any measures jeopardizing attainment of Community objectives, treats Article 92(1) as entailing a prohibition of the aid indicated therein.[17]

Indeed, there are said to be a 'basic principle stated in the Treaty that state aids are incompatible with the Common Market'[18] and even a 'rebuttable presumption' that aid covered by Article 92(1) is prohibited.[19] As the Court of First Instance puts it, this provision 'seeks in principle, as a rule of competition, to prevent aid granted by Member States from distorting competition or affecting trade between Member States'.[20] The prohibition is substantially extended to three EFTA States (Iceland, Liechtenstein, and Norway) by Article 62(1) of the European Economic Area (EEA) Agreement as well as to aid granted by Member States affecting trade with or between these EFTA States.[21]

In practice, however, it is stressed that the prohibition of aid is tempered by the Commission's power to take economic, social, and political considerations into account under Article 92(2) and (3) of the Treaty and also by the powers of the Council under Article 93(2).[22] The same point has been made in connection with the legislative power of the Council under Article 92(3)(e).[23]

In particular, Article 92(2) provides that three categories of aid are compatible with the common market. Such aid must be authorized by the Commission. However, according to Article 93(2), the Commission may act against aid which is incompatible with the common market or which is being misused. The implication is that 'misuse' of aid otherwise covered by Article 92(2) may preclude its authorization. Moreover, it has to be established that a particular aid does fall within the categories laid down in Article 92(2),[24] and that the requisite conditions of compatibility with the common market are met.[25]

[17] See the references to 'aid which is prohibited' in Joined Cases 6/69 & 11/69 *EC Commission* v. *France: preferential rediscount rate for exporters* [1969] ECR 523, 540; and to 'the prohibition in Article 92(1)' in Case 78/76 *Firma Steinike und Weinlig* v. *Germany* [1977] ECR 595, 608 and Case C–354/90 *Fédération Nationale du Commerce Extérieur des Produits Alimentaires and Syndicat Nationale des Négociants et Transformateurs de Saumon* v. *France* [1991] ECR I–5505, I–5528.

[18] *Tenth Report on Competition Policy* (EC Commission, Brussels, 1981), 111.

[19] Darmon AG in Case 248/84 *Germany* v. *EC Commission: regional aid* [1987] ECR 4013, 4028.

[20] Joined Cases T–447/93, T–448/93 & T–449/93 *Associazione Italiana Tecnico Economica del Cemento, British Cement Association and Titan Cement Company SA* v. *EC Commission* [1995] ECR II–1971, II–2017.

[21] Art. 92(2) and (3) EC are also substantially reproduced by Art. 61(2) and (3) EEA, espectively. See, generally, A. Evans, *European Community Law, including the EEA Agreement* (Kluwer, Deventer, 1994), chap. 16.

[22] Warner AG in Case 74/76 *Iannelli & Volpi SpA* v. *Ditta Paolo Meroni* [1977] ECR 557, 582.

[23] Case C–400/92 *Germany* v. *EC Commission: Cosco* [1994] ECR 4701, 4730; and Joined Cases C–356/90 & C–180/91 *Belgium* v. *EC Commission: aid to shipbuilding* [1993] ECR I–2323, I–2358. The EEA Joint Committee may adopt corresponding acts under Art. 63 EEA.

[24] Communic. C21/94 (ex N415/93) ([1994] OJ C325/8) concerning certain aids which the authorities of the Region of Abbruzzo had decided to grant in the fisheries sector.

[25] Notice on co-operation between national courts and the Commission in the state aid field ([1995] OJ C312/8), para. 14.

First, aid which has a social character[26] and is granted to individual[27] consumers,[28] provided that it is granted without discrimination related to the origin of the products concerned, is compatible with the common market under Article 92(2)(a).[29]

The acquisition of wheat by the state and its subsequent resale at a discount, which had the effect of reducing bread prices, might be an example of aid covered by this provision.[30] Certainly, the Commission considered that British aid to bring down the price of bread for consumers was covered.[31] Tax relief for individual consumers purchasing cars fitted with pollution reduction devices may also be covered.[32]

On the other hand, aid to make up the losses incurred by an airline in meeting its obligation to operate unprofitable routes may not be covered.[33] Similarly, state financing of the purchase from a ferry operator of travel vouchers for use by low-income groups falls outside the scope of Article 92(2)(a), at least where there is a commitment to purchase a set number of vouchers over a fixed period rather than on the basis of need.[34] Such an arrangement may only be authorized when relations between the operator and the public authorities are put on the basis of 'a normal commercial relationship with arm's length pricing for the services provided'.[35] Moreover, as a rule, such aid should cover only specific categories of passengers travelling on a given route, such as children, the handicapped, or low-income people. However, where an air route concerns an underprivileged region, such as an island, aid to transport facilities available to the whole population of the region may fall under Article 92(2)(a).[36]

[26] The Union itself may grant such aid. See, e.g., Reg. 3730/87 ([1987] OJ L352/1) laying down the general rules for the supply of food from intervention stocks to designated organizations for distribution to the most deprived persons in the Community.

[27] According to Reischl AG in Case 52/76 *Luigi Benedetti* v. *Munari F.lli s.a.s.* [1977] ECR 163, 190, price subsidies to the population as a whole may not be permissible.

[28] In the French, Italian, and Dutch versions respectively the terms '*consommateurs*', '*consumatori*', and '*verbruikers*'. These terms relate to the final consumer and are thus narrower than '*utilisateurs*', '*utilizzatori*', and '*gebruikers*' are found, which are found in Art. 85(3) EC.

[29] Cf. Case 415/85 *EC Commission* v. *Ireland: VAT zero rating* [1988] ECR 3097, 3120–1, regarding the possibility of zero rating goods and services to the final consumer for social reasons. Cf. also Art. 56 ECSC, which provides for 'readaptation aid' in favour of workers in the coal and steel industries.

[30] Reischl AG in Case 52/76 *Luigi Benedetti* v. *Munari F.lli s.a.s.* [1977] ECR 163, 190, though the fact that the aid went directly to certain mills rather than to individual consumers made it problematic.

[31] Bull. EC 7/8–1974, 2132. But cf., regarding quantitatively-based French aid to milk consumption, Commission Reply to Written Question 112/70 ([1970] OJ C123/2) by Mr Vredeling.   [32] *Europe* 5234 (31 Mar. 1990).

[33] Communic. C7/93 (N327/92) ([1993] OJ C178/2) on the future method of compensation of TAP's deficit related to the Atlantic autonomous regions of the Azores and Madeira.

[34] Communic. C32/93 (NN40/93) ([1994] OJ C70/5) on aids granted by Spain to Ferries Golfo de Vizcaya.   [35] *Ibid.*

[36] Application of Arts. 92 and 93 EC and Art. 61 EEA to state aids in the aviation sector ([1994] OJ C350/5), para. 24.

The proviso that the aid must not be discriminatory reflects a general principle of Union law that differentiation between undertakings will only be permissible where there is an objective justification.[37] In the absence of such a justification, aid which differentiates will be prohibited.[38] Thus Irish aid for the consumption of Irish bread could not be authorized, because it was discriminatory.[39] Only when Ireland agreed to extend the scheme to benefit imports and to promote restructuring was it authorized.[40] Similarly, aid benefiting a particular company and its workers cannot be authorized under this provision.[41]

Secondly, aid to make good the damage caused by natural disasters or exceptional occurrences[42] is compatible with the common market under Article 92(2)(b). Earthquakes and volcanic eruptions,[43] and weather of an exceptional and short-term character may be treated as such a disaster.[44]

Accordingly, aid to Liguria for reconstruction required as a result of floods in October 1977 and aid granted in response to flooding in the south-east of the Netherlands[45] and in North Rhine–Westphalia[46] were authorized, as was aid to Friuli–Venezia Giulia for reconstruction of industrial plant destroyed by the 1976 earthquake.[47] Similarly, French aid to make good damage caused to farming by frost, hail, and drought[48] and Italian aid to forestry damaged by 'bad weather' in the Trentino–Alto Adige region of Italy[49] were authorized, as was

[37] Case 8/57 *Groupement des Hauts Fourneaux et Aciéries Belges* v. *ECSC High Authority* [1957–8] ECR 245, 258; and Case 9/57 *Chambre Syndicale de la Sidérurgie Française* v. *ECSC High Authority* [1957–8] ECR 319, 330.

[38] Dec. 67/217 ([1967] OJ 1275) on the amendment of certain aids granted by the Netherlands for the processing of certain cereals in products for human consumption; and Dec. 67/218 ([1967] JO 1277) on the alteration of aid granted by Germany for the processing of hard wheat in products for human consumption. Where discrimination is present, there may also be a violation of Art. 90(1) taken together with Art. 6 EC. See, e.g., Dec. 87/359 ([1987] OJ L194/28) concerning reduction in air and sea transport fares available only to Spanish nationals resident in the Balearic Islands.

[39] Notice regarding the subsidy granted by the Irish Government on the consumption of standard bread ([1979] OJ C109/9).

[40] Bull. EC 10–1979, 2.1.33.

[41] *Twenty-Fourth Report on Competition Policy* (EC Commission, Brussels, 1995), 518.

[42] The Union itself may grant such aid. See, e.g., Reg. 1506/76 ([1976] OJ L168/11) on the Community contribution towards repairing the infrastructural damage caused by the earthquake in May 1976 in the region of Friuli–Venezia Giulia; and Dec. 88/561 ([1988] OJ L309/32) relating to exceptional Community aid for the reconstruction of areas stricken by earthquakes which took place in Greece in Sept. 1986. See, more generally, Art. 5(h) of Reg. 2085/93 ([1993] OJ L193/44) amending Reg. 4256/88 laying down provisions for implementing Reg. 2052/88 as regards the EAGGF, Guidance Section.

[43] Notice C11/92 (ex NN134/91) ([1993] OJ C59/7) concerning aid which Italy had decided to introduce by Law 34/1991 of the Sicilian region concerning the marketing and sale of Sicilian products.

[44] Cf. Dec. 82/743 ([1982] OJ L315/21) on the aids provided for in Campania to help producers of plums.

[45] *Twenty-Fourth Report on Competition Policy*, n. 41 above, 170.

[46] Bull. EC 7/8–1995, 1.3.154.

[47] *Eighth Report on Competition Policy* (EC Commission, Brussels, 1979), 118.

[48] Bull. EEC 9/10–1963, 53.

[49] Bull. EC 5–1969, 37

respect of losses of income for fishermen due to bad weather off
enland.[50] Later German aid to compensate fishermen for the
~~es of decreased temperatures in Greenland waters was more prob-
..auc, because the fishermen were not considered to have suffered any
damage.[51]

Apparently, temporary aid to re-establish the equilibrium disturbed is envisaged. Thus aid to irrigation, granted even during 'normal' weather conditions,
is not usually covered,[52] though aid not granted to individual farmers may be
unobjectionable.[53]

However, the damage suffered must 'attain a certain severity at individual
level'.[54] In the case of drought, only those farmers who have suffered damage
exceeding that to which they are liable as a normal risk of agricultural holdings
may receive aid. Hence, aid for the purchase of irrigation water, irrespective of
whether the purchaser has suffered production losses as a result of the drought,
is not covered.[55] A minimum threshold rate of losses suffered by each holder
(30 per cent of gross normal production—20 per cent in less-favoured regions)
has been set.[56] Accordingly, aid to Sardinian farmers who had suffered losses of
35 per cent based on their average production in the previous three years was
authorized, as was a 75 per cent reduction in the cost of water used for
irrigation as a result of the drought in respect of quantities of water exceeding
the normal average consumption over the previous three years.[57] Such aid must
not exceed the losses actually suffered,[58] and so there must be no overcompensation.[59]

Aid to insurance against damage by hail may be treated similarly,[60] at least
where the state bears part of the risk.[61] However, such treatment is problematic.
Since such aid presumably leads to a reduction in premiums, it may be said to

---

[50] *Sixteenth Report on Competition Policy* (EC Commission, Brussels, 1987), 197.
[51] Notice ([1988] OJ C291/4) as regards the granting of daily indemnities for fishing in
Greenland waters during 1988 by freezers sailing under the German flag.
[52] Communic. C6/90 (ex NN91/89) ([1994] OJ C19/4) concerning aid granted by the Region
of Sardinia (reduction of irrigation tariffs).
[53] Bull. EU 11–1995, 1.3.167.
[54] Communic. C16/91 ([1994] OJ C58/8) concerning aids which Italy had decided to grant to
agricultural holdings following drought.
[55] Communic. C30/95 (ex NN113/B/93) & E7/95 ([1995] OJ C295/8) concerning aid which
Italy (Sicily) had granted in the agricultural sector.
[56] Dec. 95/366 ([1995] OJ L218/20) on aid granted by Italy (Sardinia) in the agricultural
sector.
[57] Communic. C91/89 ([1990] OJ C111/3) concerning aids which Sardinia had decided to
grant.
[58] Communic. NN23/89 ([1990] OJ C169/9) concerning aids which Italy had decided to grant
for AIMA measures during 1986 and 1987.
[59] Notice C20/95 (ex N131/95) ([1995] OJ C289/14) concerning aid granted by the Abruzzo
region in the agricultural sector.
[60] *Eighteenth Report on Competition Policy* (EC Commission, Brussels, 1989), 208 and 210.
[61] Communic. ([1987] OJ C160/4) concerning an aid scheme intended to compensate farmers
whose orchards had been destroyed by hail.

have the same effect as assistance with the costs of paying the premiums. The Commission apparently prefers to examine such assistance under Article 92(3)(c), and only to authorize it where it goes beyond expenditure which farmers should reasonably be expected to bear as a normal commercial risk[62] or where it constitutes an element in the improvement of farm management.[63] As such, it may not exceed 50 per cent of the insurance premiums.[64] Generally, aid to preventive measures appears not to be favoured in Commission application of Article 92(2)(b). For example, while aid to winegrowers who had suffered loss because of vine disease was authorized, aid for the spreading of insecticide by helicopter was less acceptable.[65]

Exceptional occurrences for the purposes of this provision may cover 'man-made' damage,[66] such as that associated with a strike, war, serious internal political disturbances; extraordinary events at sea, or navigational accidents arising fortuitously or caused by *force majeure*;[67] explosions or catastrophic mine accidents; damage suffered because of World War II;[68] or social or religious persecution.[69] In such cases, irrespective of the extent of the damage, the Commission considers compensation for losses suffered by individuals to be justified, but causation must be established, and again there must not be overcompensation.[70]

The aid must be used to make good such damage.[71] Aid which is merely intended to favour the development of undertakings in areas affected by natural

---

[62] Communic. C48/95 (N295/95 & N296/95) ([1996] OJ C73/12) concerning aid which Belgium intended to grant in the form of aid and obligatory contributions to the Animal Health and Production Fund (poultry and dairy sectors).

[63] Dec. 72/251 ([1972] JO L163/19) on the grant of aid for the creation of a reserve fund to cover risks-damage caused by hail to producers of apples and pears in the Netherlands; and Communic. on certain Italian aids granted in the sectors of fruit and fruit-based preparations, excluding citrus fruits ([1972] JO C13/2).

[64] Communic. ([1987] OJ C96/3) concerning the application of aid measures for fruit growers covering a proportion of the cost of insurance against hail.

[65] Communic. E2/89—C34/89 ([1989] OJ C302/4) concerning aid supported by the Winegrowers Solidarity Fund.

[66] Cf. the argument that World War II, the division of Germany, and 'the disastrous effects of the socialist state economy' of the former GDR constituted such occurrences in M. Schütte and J.-P. Hix, 'The Application of the EC State Aid Rules to Privatizations: The East German Example' (1995) 32 *CMLRev*. 215–48, 226.

[67] Communic. C21/94 (ex N415/93) ([1996] OJ C42/3) concerning aid that Italy had decided to grant in the fisheries sector (Region of Abruzzi).

[68] Bull. EC 12–1968, 32. There may thus be an overlap between this subpara. and Art. 92(2)(c), which is discussed below.

[69] H. von der Groeben, H. von Boeckh, J. Thiesing, and C.-D. Ehlermann, *Kommentar zum EWG-Vertrag* (Baden-Baden, 1983), 1604. Cf. E. Wohlfarth, U. Everling, H. J. Glaesner, and R. Sprung, *Die Europäische Wirtschaftsgemeinschaft, Kommentar zum Vertrag* (Vahlen, Berlin, 1960), 276.

[70] Communic. C3/94 (ex N42/93/A, N41/93) ([1994] OJ C115/6) concerning aids which France had decided to grant to fruit growers affected by the road blockade in summer 1992.

[71] Notice ([1985] OJ C277/5) concerning the aid measures proposed by the region of Sicily for farms having suffered damage as a result of the bad weather of April/May 1984 and Dec. 1984/Jan. 1985 and emergency measures to assist cereal producers and poultry farmers.

disasters,[72] irrespective of whether or not the aid recipient has suffered any individual damage, is not covered;[73] nor is aid supporting productive activity in the region concerned, which goes beyond the simple reconstruction of enterprises destroyed or damaged by natural disasters.[74] Hence, aid granted ten to twelve years after an earthquake[75] and regional development aid as a measure accompanying reconstruction aid[76] may not be authorized.

Thirdly, aid to the economy of certain areas of the Federal Republic of Germany affected by the division of Germany,[77] in so far as such aid is required in order to compensate for the economic disadvantages caused by that division, is compatible with the common market under Article 92(2)(c).[78] Introduction of new aid schemes or the maintenance of existing schemes may be covered.[79] In particular, tax concessions for products and services supplied by Berlin firms to firms in the Federal Republic and investment aid of 25 per cent were authorized under this provision,[80] as was compensation for tolls levied by the Soviet Zone authorities on German hauliers going to and from West Berlin.[81] Even operating aid[82] to farmers may be authorized.[83]

However, the general preference of the Commission was to encourage conversion. Thus transport aid was only authorized in the *Zonenrandgebiet*, because it was designed to enable undertakings to change over to products less

[72] Dec. 91/175 ([1991] OJ L86/23) concerning aid provided for in Italian Law 120/87 to assist certain areas of the Mezzogiorno affected by natural disasters, which was partly annulled on procedural grounds in Case C–364/90 *Italy* v. *EC Commission: aid to areas in the Mezzogiorno affected by natural disasters* [1993] ECR I–2097. See, similarly regarding aid to an area which had suffered from flooding, Reply by Mr Van Miert to Written Question 2880/92 ([1993] OJ C155/21) by Mr Mauro Chiabrando.

[73] Notice C35/92 (ex N172/A/91) ([1994] OJ C78/2) concerning aid granted by the Region of Friuli–Venezia Giulia.

[74] Notice C31/92 (N454/91) ([1992] OJ C324/3) concerning aid granted by Italy for the reconstruction of the Valtellina.

[75] Notice C16/92 (NN24/92) ([1992] OJ C208/9) concerning aid granted by Italy to certain regions of the Mezzogiorno.

[76] Dec. 91/500 ([1991] OJ L262/29) concerning aid granted to enterprises in the Friuli–Venezia Giulia region.

[77] The categories of permissible aids were indicated in Bull. EEC 2–1965, 33. See also the *Ninth Report on Competition Policy* (EC Commission, Brussels, 1980), 89, but cf., regarding objections to aid in certain parts of the *Zonenrandgebiet*, the *Eleventh Report on Competition Policy* (EC Commission, Brussels, 1982), 160.

[78] Dec. 71/295 ([1971] JO L179/37) on tax concessions under the Law of 28 Dec. 1968 on the transport of goods by road, as prolonged on 23 Dec. 1970.

[79] Notice C59/91 (NN150/91) ([1992] OJ C35/27) concerning the investment premium granted by Germany under the 'Investitionszulagengesetz 1991'; Notice C63/91 (NN153/91) ([1992] OJ C35/30) concerning the tax-free reserves allowed by Germany under the 'Fördergebietsgesetz 1991'.

[80] *Sixth Report on Competition Policy* (EC Commission, Brussels, 1977), 102–3.

[81] *First EC General Report* (EC Commission, Brussels, 1968), 222. See, most recently, regarding the acceptability of transport aid under Art. 92(2)(c), Bull. EU 4–1994, 1.2.53.

[82] See sect. 3.5 below, regarding such aid.

[83] Communic. on aid granted by Germany (Bavaria) in the form of a production premium for piglets ([1970] JO C23/7).

sensitive to transport costs and to put an end to aid unlimited in time.[84] Most recently, aid was authorized on condition that recipients introduced an alternative, self-financed means of transport by the end of 1995.[85]

Drafts for the Treaty on European Union[86] envisaged deletion of Article 92(2)(c),[87] apparently because 'the economic justification for continuous subsidization of these regions has ceased to exist'.[88] However, the final version of the Treaty left this paragraph unaffected. In practice, the Commission has proved reluctant to take a position on the question whether this paragraph remains applicable following reunification[89] and is apparently content to secure its strict interpretation[90] and the gradual[91] phasing out of the aid concerned.[92]

Thus the Commission accepted a transitional period, until the end of 1992, for the phasing out of an existing investment aid scheme in West Berlin and the new *Länder*, but initiated the Article 93(2) procedure[93] in respect of aid to be granted after that deadline. According to the Commission, it was necessary to consider whether the overall level of aid was commensurate with the urgency of the problems concerned.[94] The Commission preference is generally to apply Article 92(3)(a) to aid to the new *Länder* and only to apply Article 92(2)(c) 'exceptionally . . . to deal with aid arising from the division of Germany'.[95]

According to the Court of Justice, the kinds of aid listed in Article 92(2) are not affected by the prohibition in Article 92(1).[96] However, aid is authorized

---

[84] Bull. EC 12–1968, 32.

[85] *Twenty-Fourth Report on Competition Policy* (n. 41 above, 495).

[86] *Europe Docs* 1709/10 (3 May 1991) and 1722/23 (5 July 1991).

[87] It was excluded from Art. 6(2) of the Agreement on Civil Aviation with Norway and Sweden ([1992] OJ L200/21), which otherwise reproduced Art. 92(2) EC.

[88] *The European Community and German Unification*, Bull. EC. Supp. 4/90, 75. See, similarly, the *Twentieth Report on Competition Policy* (EC Commission, Brussels, 1991), 131.

[89] Notice C60/91 (ex NN73/91, NN76/91) ([1993] OJ C43/14) regarding the proposal by the German Government to award state aid to the Opel group in support of its investment plans in the new *Länder*; and Notice C9/93 (NN22/93) ([1993] OJ C210/9) regarding aid which Germany had decided to grant to SST–Garngesellschaft mbH, Thüringen. See, regarding aid to an investment in Berlin made prior to unification, Dec. 92/465 ([1992] OJ L263/15) concerning aid granted by Berlin to Daimler-Benz.

[90] Dec. 94/266 ([1994] OJ L114/21) on the proposal to award aid to SST–Garngesellschaft mbH, Thüringen.

[91] The Economic and Social Committee considered that the transitional period was too long and should be considerably reduced. See the Opinion of 20 Nov. 1990 ([1991] OJ C41/14) on the Communication on the Community and German Unification, para. 8.5.

[92] Cf. the discussion of the possibility that this provision might continue to apply to aid to regions suffering from past division in T. Giegerich, 'The European Dimension of German Reunification: East Germany's Integration into the European Communities' [1991] *ZaöRV* 384–450, 444–5.

[93] See sect. 7.5.3 below, regarding this procedure.

[94] Notice C59/91 (NN150/91) ([1992] OJ C32/27) concerning the investment premium granted by Germany under the 'Investitionszulagengesetz 1991'; Notice C63/91 (NN153/91) ([1992] OJ C35/30) concerning the tax-free reserves allowed by Germany under the 'Fördergebietsgesetz 1991'.

[95] *Twenty-Fourth Report on Competition Policy* (n. 41 above, 170).

[96] Case 78/76 *Firma Steinike und Weinlig* v. *Germany* [1977] ECR 595, 608.

under Article 92(2)(c) only where the Commission recognizes that it is 're-quired' to compensate for the disadvantages concerned.[97] In the application of this subparagraph at least, the Commission does not accept aid otherwise covered thereby to be automatically exempt from monitoring in sectors subject to special rules, and aid to modernize and rationalize production may be prohibited, if the recipient belongs to such a sector. The reasoning of the Commission is that, in a sector suffering from overcapacity, aid which does not effect any basic changes is 'not appropriate to compensate any economic disadvantages . . . as no lasting economic development [is] being initiated'.[98] In relation to Article 92(2) generally, the power of the Commission to assess whether, in the light of economic factors, the conditions for authorization are met may effectively imply a degree of discretion.

Article 92(3) provides that further categories of aid may be considered to be compatible with the common market. Thus the Commission is formally empowered to exercise discretion, subject to possible review by the European Courts,[99] in deciding whether to authorize aid under this paragraph.[100] In exercising its discretion, the Commission considers whether the aid promotes a project that is in the Union interest as a whole and whether the aid is limited to that which is necessary for the achievement of the result.[101] According to the Commission, if the aid is so limited, the risk of trade distortion is kept to a minimum.[102]

In particular, Article 92(3)(a) provides that aid to promote the economic development of areas where the standard of living is abnormally low or where there is serious underemployment may be considered compatible with the common market. This paragraph concerns aid to the 'peripheral regions' of the Union and is considered in detail in Chapter 4.

Article 92(3)(b) provides that two kinds of aid may be considered compatible with the common market. The first kind of aid concerned is that to promote the execution of an important project of 'common European interest'. This language might suggest that the importance of a project is not to be assessed solely by reference to the Union interest. However, the Declaration annexed to the EEA Agreement on Article 61(3)(b) of the Agreement distinguishes be-

---

[97] Dec. 94/266 ([1994] OJ L114/21) on the proposal to award aid to SST–Garngesellschaft mhH, Thüringen.

[98] Dec. 86/509 ([1986] OJ L300/39) on aid granted by Germany and Bavaria to a producer of polyamide and polyester yarn situated in Deggendorf. See also Notice C9/93 (NN22/93) ([1993] OJ C210/9) regarding aid which Germany had decided to grant to SST–Garngesellschaft mbH, Thüringen.

[99] See sect. 7.6 below.

[100] Cf. the distinction which Darmon AG in Case C–189/91 *Petra Kirsammer-Hack* v. *Nurhan Sidal* [1993] ECR I–6185, I–6203 sought to make between explicit Treaty exceptions for certain categories of aid and other categories assessed by the Commission with 'realism and subtlety'.

[101] *Twelfth Report on Competition Policy* (EC Commission, Brussels, 1983), 160.

[102] Dec. 89/58 ([1989] OJ L25/92) concerning aid provided by the UK Government to the Rover Group.

tween the 'Community interest' and 'the interest of EFTA States' and implies that outside the scope of this Agreement Article 92(3)(b) of the EC Treaty only concerns the 'Community interest'. Moreover, according to the Court of Justice, the policy of the Commission, that under Article 92(3)(b) a project must form part of a transnational European programme supported jointly by a number of Member States or arise from concerted action by a number of Member States to combat a common threat such as environmental pollution, is justifiable.[103] Apparently, therefore, in the application of this provision account need not be taken of the interests of European states outside the EEA.

To be authorized, aid must promote the project, in the sense that without the aid the project would not go ahead, or only in such a manner that it would no longer be considered an important project of common European interest.[104] Similarly, Article 198e(c) of the Treaty provides for the European Investment Bank to assist the financing of projects of common interest to several Member States which are of such a size or nature that they could not be entirely financed by the various means available in the individual Member States. The implication may be that a state contribution to the financing of projects covered by the latter provision is compatible with the common market under Article 92(3)(b).

In practice, aid for projects jointly supported by Member States may be authorized under Article 92(3)(b).[105] For example, in February 1986 the French, Belgian, and Luxembourg Governments jointly notified to the Commission a proposal to establish a 'European Development Zone' in an area straddling the three countries' frontiers around Longwy, Aubange, and Rodange. At the centre of the zone it was planned to set up a business park, in which investors could receive aid up to 30 per cent nge (net grant equivalent)[106] of investment costs and special customs arrangements, involving the free-warehouse (*'magasin franc'*) system and simplified procedures for inward processing, would be applicable. Road and rail links would be improved, as would research and development facilities in high technology, and derelict land would be reclaimed. The Commission considered that the zone faced special problems of industrial redevelopment and that a joint, co-ordinated response to these problems held definite advantages from the point of view of European integration.[107]

---

[103] Joined Cases 62 & 72/87 *Exécutif Régional Wallon and SA Glaverbel* v. *EC Commission* [1988] ECR 1573, 1595.

[104] Notice C32/94 (N48/94) ([1994] OJ C293/6) with regard to the aid for the construction of a rape seed oil methylester pilot plan operated by the Raiffeisen Hauptgenossenschaft Nord AG, Kiel.

[105] Rec. 63/371 ([1963] JO 1796) to Belgium and France concerning an economic co-operation project at the regional level concerning the north of Lorraine and the south of the Belgian province of Luxembourg..

[106] i.e., the discounted post-tax value of total assistance from public sources expressed as a percentage of discounted fixed project costs.

[107] *Sixteenth Report on Competition Policy*, n. 50 above, 180–1.

Aid may also be authorized where it is provided, not necessarily to a joint project as such, but to certain participants in the project. For example, the Commission authorized: German aid for the production of the airbus, involving companies from different Member States and technical and economic features;[108] German aid to space projects, mostly carried out through international and European co-operation;[109] German aid to companies co-operating with others in France, the Netherlands, and the United Kingdom in a project concerning a terrestrial digital radio system;[110] German aid to companies co-operating with British companies in a project concerning high-definition television;[111] Italian aid for collaborative research and development with Boeing, which would entail the creation of jobs in the Mezzogiorno;[112] and Italian aid which enabled undertakings 'to engage in more balanced co-operation with other firms in the Community'.[113]

Even if the project is not a joint one, aid may still be authorized, because its execution is considered to be of common interest. Thus, for example, environmental aid[114] and aid to investment in energy-saving schemes[115] may be authorized, as were aid to the British nuclear industry[116] and aid granted by any Member State for the marketing of aircraft and aircraft parts.[117] However, aid limited to a single undertaking is unlikely to qualify as a project of common interest.[118]

There may be an overlap between treatment of aid to such projects under Article 92(3)(b) and its treatment under Article 92(3)(c).[119] For example, the Commission considered that aid to research and development concerning wind power could be authorized under either subparagraph.[120]

The second kind of aid which may be authorized under Article 92(3)(b) is aid to remedy a serious disturbance in the economy of a Member State.[121] For example, temporary aid provided by the Italian Government to small and medium-sized undertakings to offset the effects of a 'business slowdown' was authorized in 1972.[122]

---

[108] Bull. EC 4–1974, 2112 and Bull. EC 3–1989, 2.1.73.
[109] Bull. EC 12–1982, 2.1.46.
[110] Bull. EC 3–1989, 2.1.62.
[111] Bull. EC 3–1989, 2.1.64.
[112] Bull. EC 11–1975, 2.1.24.
[113] Bull. EC 5–1986, 2.1.58.
[114] See sect. 6.5 below.
[115] See sect. 6.6 below.
[116] *Twentieth Report on Competition Policy*, n. 88 above, 176.
[117] *Second Report on Competition Policy* (EC Commission, Brussels, 1973), 92.
[118] Dec. 89/254 ([1989] OJ L106/34) relating to aid which the Belgian Government had granted to a petrochemicals company at Ottignies/Louvain-la-Neuve (SA Belgian Shell).
[119] See 16–17 below.
[120] Bull. EC 10–1986, 2.1.70.
[121] Cf., regarding a disturbance for the purposes of Art. 2 ECSC, Joined Cases 27–29/58 *Compagnie des Hauts Fourneaux et Fonderies de Givors* v. *ECSC High Authority* [1960] ECR 241, 258.
[122] *Second Report on Competition Policy*, n. 117 above, 104–7; and Commission Reply to Written Question 585/71 ([1972] JO C68/4) by Mr Vredeling.

More generally, in response to the 1974–5 recession, the Commission decided that, to protect employment, any Member State could grant aid, including tax deductions or low interest loans, for a limited period. Aid could also be granted to ensure the survival of firms in difficulties, so as to avoid redundancies, but only in the case of undertakings which were basically sound and needed a respite to prepare and initiate restructuring programmes. Aid granted on the basis of investment only was more problematic, in that it might encourage firms to undertake labour-saving operations or at least to favour investments involving the creation of very few jobs.[123]

The Temporary Employment Subsidy in the United Kingdom was authorized in 1975 because of the 'very rapid increase in unemployment'.[124] Employment aid in Ireland, which was payable to employers over a twenty-four-week period, was also authorized.[125] However, the British scheme was expanded, and the Commission required the introduction of measures to avoid undue concentration in any one sector and the removal of the 'purely stop-gap' aspects of the scheme.[126]

In the case of a later, Greek, aid scheme, the Commission noted that the economic situation of Greece had been consistently deteriorating up to October 1985. Both internal and external balances had created a difficult situation which demanded firm policy measures. In particular, the Greek authorities were confronted with very serious external payments and pressures on the exchange rate in September 1985. Thus, on 11 October 1985, they introduced an economic stabilization and recovery programme. By this time many Greek companies had got into financial difficulties as a result of past government policies. Given the major effort of the Greek authorities to reverse such policies in this programme, aid to companies which, though basically viable, had run into difficulties threatening their survival could be authorized under Article 92(3)(b). However, the aid had to be for closure or restructuring[127] and limited to remedying the disturbance. It was not to induce the transfer of an investment which could have taken place in another Member State in a less favourable situation.[128] Moreover, the aid must not result in recipients being left in a stronger position than was necessary to ensure their viability[129] or in a stronger position *vis-à-vis* industries in other Member States than they would have had if the disturbance had not arisen in the first place. Consequently, the aid must

[123] *Fifth Report on Competition Policy* (EC Commission, Brussels, 1976), 93.
[124] *Seventh Report on Competition Policy* (EC Commission, Brussels, 1978), 167.
[125] Bull. EC 5–1978, 2.1.26.
[126] Bull. EC 1–1978, 2.1.16.
[127] Notice ([1988] OJ C124/4) and Communic. C2/88 (ex NN126/87) ([1992] OJ C1/4) concerning aid to Heracles General Cement Company in Greece; Dec. 91/144 ([1991] OJ L73/27) on aid granted by the Greek Government to a cement manufacturer (Halkis Cement Company).
[128] Cf. Case 730/79 *Philip Morris Holland BV* v. *EC Commission* [1980] ECR 2671, 2692.
[129] Case 2/88 (NN128/87) ([1996] OJ C84/3) regarding aid which the Greek authorities had decided to grant to Heracles General Cement Company.

not promote expansion of production capacity, nor must it merely shift the problem without finding a general solution to the social and industrial problems facing the Union as a whole.[130]

The Commission objected to aid granted in breach of these conditions[131] and, more particularly, to aid to facilitate the privatization of a firm which would not be attractive to private investors.[132] On the other hand, aid to a privatization programme, which involved the writing-off of debts and capital conversion of the companies to be privatized, was subsequently authorized.[133]

If such an authorization is to be granted, the disturbance must apparently be cyclical rather than structural and must be abnormal by reference to the cyclical fluctuations which may be expected in the sector concerned.[134] Hence, aid cannot be granted for as long as three years.[135] For example, Danish aid was authorized under Article 92(3)(b) in 1975,[136] but economic improvement meant that by the following year aid could only be authorized for industrial restructuring under Article 92(3)(c).[137]

Particular account, however, may be taken of the 'burden of the past'. For example, aid was approved for a Portuguese chemical firm, because it partially covered an unfavourable financial structure from which the company had suffered since its formation prior to Portuguese accession to the Union.[138] On the other hand, although German unification had 'negative effects' on the German economy, these effects were not considered sufficient to justify application of Article 92(3)(b).[139]

Apparently, the disturbance must have national significance. For example, a local unemployment rate around twice the national average does not involve such a disturbance where the national rate is low by Union standards.[140] Equally, a crisis 'confined to a clearly defined sector of the economy' does not constitute such a disturbance,[141] though a 'systemic crisis' in the banking sector

---

[130] Dec. 88/167 ([1988] OJ L76/18) concerning Law 1386/1983 by which the Greek Government granted aid to Greek industry.
[131] Bull. EC 12–1988, 2.1.136. [132] Bull. EC 3–1989, 2.1.67.
[133] *Twenty-First Report on Competition Policy* (EC Commission, Brussels, 1992), 158.
[134] Dec. 77/172 ([1977] OJ L54/39) concerning an aid for the pigmeat sector in the UK.
[135] Dec. 73/274 ([1973] OJ L254/14) on Art. 20 of Italian Law 1101 of 1 Dec. 1971 on the restructuring, reorganization, and conversion of the textile industry.
[136] Bull. EC 6–1975, 2120. [137] Bull. EC 7/8–1976, 2128.
[138] Bull. EC 10–1991, 1.2.32. Cf., in connection with Art. 92(3)(c), Dec. 92/321 ([1992] OJ L176/57) concerning aid awarded by Spain to Intelhorce SA, a state-owned producer of cotton textiles.
[139] Notice C58/91 (NN144/91) ([1993] OJ C97/7) concerning aid awarded by the German Government to Carl Zeiss Jena, Jenoptik and Jenaer Glaswerk; Communic. C60/91 (ex NN73/91, NN76/91) ([1993] OJ C43/14) regarding the proposal by the German Government to award state aid to the Opel group in support of its investment plans in the new *Länder*. It has been doubted whether the position of the Commission would be supported by the European Courts. See M. Schütte and J.-P. Hix, n. 66 above, 231.
[140] Case 730/79 *Phillip Morris Holland BV* v. *EC Commission* [1980] ECR 2671, 2692.
[141] Dec. 94/725 ([1994] OJ L289/26) on measures adopted by the French Government concerning pigmeat.

does so.[142] Where aid to the regions concerned has already been authorized under Article 92(3)(a), any additional aid can only be justified if the disturbance has provoked a grave deterioration in the socio-economic conditions of these regions.[143]

The disturbance must also be serious by Union standards. For example, in 1984 the Commission recognized that the Belgian economy faced social and economic difficulties, but also maintained that these difficulties were not the most serious in the Union. In this situation the danger of escalation of aids was most immediate, and any aid was most likely to affect trade between Member States. Hence, employment aid could not be authorized under Article 92(3)(b),[144] even though such aid in Belgium had previously been authorized under the same provision.[145] Similarly, 'disquieting' economic and social problems in the United Kingdom were not significantly more serious than those of other 'central regions' and thus did not amount to a disturbance for the purposes of Article 92(3)(b).[146]

At the same time, aid must be of such a scope and scale as to be capable of remedying the disturbance. Hence, aid to a particular sector of the economy is not covered by Article 92(3)(b),[147] unless sectoral problems are sufficiently serious to justify aid under this provision.[148]

Instead of resorting to Article 92(3)(b), the Commission might in the past have authorized aid to tackle balance-of-payments problems under Article 108(3) EEC,[149] as in the case of France in 1968.[150] Under the latter provision export aids and preferential rediscount rates,[151] which might be less acceptable under Article 92(3)(b),[152] could be authorized.

[142] Dec. 95/547 ([1995] OJ L308/92) giving conditional approval to the aid granted by France to Crédit Lyonnais.

[143] Case C–364/90 *Italy* v. *EC Commission: aid to areas in the Mezzogiorno affected by natural disasters* [1993] ECR I–2097, I–2124–5.

[144] Dec. 84/508 ([1984] OJ L283/42) on the aid granted by the Belgian Government to a producer of polypropylene and yarn.

[145] Dec. 82/829 ([1982] OJ L350/36) on a proposed aid by the Belgian Government in respect of certain investments carried out by an oil company at its Antwerp refinery.

[146] Dec. 84/94 ([1984] OJ L51/17) on the aid that the UK Government proposed to grant for an investment to expand production capacity for polypropylene film.

[147] Dec. 94/813 ([1994] OJ L335/82) concerning aid to French pig farmers—Stabiporc adjustment fund. See, earlier, Dec. 77/172 ([1977] OJ L54/39) concerning an aid for the pigmeat sector in the UK.

[148] Mayras AG in Joined Cases 31/77R & 53/77R *EC Commission* v. *UK* and *UK* v. *EC Commission: aid to pig producers* [1977] ECR 921, 934.   [149] See now Art. 109h EC.

[150] Dec. 68/301 ([1968] JO L178/15) authorizing France to take certain safeguard measures under Art. 108(3).

[151] Art. 7 of Dec. 85/594 ([1985] OJ L373/9) authorizing Greece to take certain safeguard measures under Art. 108(3). The phasing-out of the aid was required by Dec. 86/614 ([1986] OJ L357/28) amending Dec. 85/594. See, more particularly, regarding the prohibition of export aid for candied fruit peel, Dec. 88/612 ([1988] OJ L335/31) amending Dec. 86/614. The suspension of a decision requiring earlier termination of such aid to citrons was unsuccessfully sought in Case 111/88R *Greece* v. *EC Commission: aid to citrons* [1988] ECR 2591.

[152] Joined Cases 6 & 11/69 *EC Commission* v. *France: preferential rediscount rate for exporters* [1969] ECR 523, 540.

Article 92(3)(c) provides, in turn, that aid to facilitate the development of certain economic activities or of certain economic areas may be compatible with the common market. This subparagraph may cover sectoral aid, which is discussed in Chapter 5, and aid to the 'central regions', which is discussed in Chapter 4. Aid for restructuring of an enterprise, even in a disadvantaged region, is evaluated under the 'sectoral derogation' in this provision. Authorization is subject to the proviso that the aid does not adversely affect trading conditions to an extent contrary to the common interest.

Use of the term 'facilitate' rather than 'promote' (as in Article 92(3)(a)) suggests that a greater contribution to development from aid recipients is required for the purposes of Article 92(3)(c). In applying this requirement, the Commission may take into account 'historic and regional considerations',[153] as in the case of aid to a single undertaking which fell outside the scope of Article 92(3)(a).[154] Account may also be taken of considerations of international competitiveness[155] and of any Union policy for the relevant sector. For example, German loans for prospectors of new oil fields and non-repayable aid of up to 30 per cent of the costs of companies acquiring crude oil deposits or holdings in other companies working such fields were authorized under Article 92(3)(c),[156] as was extension of the aid to prospecting for natural gas,[157] because such aid was in line with Union energy policy.

The proviso in Article 92(3)(c) seems broader than that relating to 'the development of trade' in Article 90(2) of the Treaty.[158] Various considerations may be relevant to determination whether the former proviso is respected. For example, importance is attached to the scale on which aid recipients will be operating.[159]

The concept of the common interest in this proviso is not restricted to the sum of individual interests of undertakings or of categories of undertakings.[160] Thus, in assessing the compatibility of aid with the common market under Article 92(3)(c), the Commission takes account of sectoral characteristics, as where 'growth consumption has slackened'[161] or there is overcapacity.[162]

---

[153] Notice C58/91 (NN144/91) ([1993] OJ C97/7) concerning aid awarded by the German Government to Carl Zeiss Jena, Jenoptik, and Jenaer Glaswerk; and Dec. 93/627 ([1993] OJ L309/21) concerning aid granted by the Spanish authorities on the occasion of the sale by Cenemesa/Cademesa/Conelec of certain selected assets to Asea-Brown Boveri.

[154] Dec. 94/696 ([1994] OJ L273/22) on the aid granted by Greece to Olympic Airways.
[155] Bull. EC 1–1979, 2.1.36.
[156] Bull EC 12–1969, 28; Bull. EC 2–1975, 2109.   [157] Bull. EC 7/8–1973, 2113.
[158] Cf. Rozès AG in Case 78/82 *EC Commission* v. *Italy: tobacco monopoly* [1983] ECR 1955, 1989.   [159] Notice C58/91, n. 153 above.
[160] Case 9/57 *Chambre Syndicale de la Sidérurgie Française* v. *ECSC High Authority* [1958] ECR 319, 330.
[161] Dec. 79/743 ([1979] OJ L217/17) on a proposed Netherlands Government assistance to increase the production capacity of a cigarette manufacturer.
[162] Dec. 85/153 ([1985] OJ L59/21) concerning aid which the Belgian Government granted in 1983 to a ceramic sanitary ware and crockery manufacturer; and Dec. 86/366 ([1986] OJ L223/

Account may also be taken of whether the anti-competitive effects of the aid are likely to be magnified by other anti-competitive measures.[163] Aid will be found to be contrary to the common interest where it is 'irreconcilable with the general principles of the common market, particularly the free movement of goods'.[164]

Finally, Article 92(3)(d), as amended by the Treaty on European Union (TEU), provides that the Commission may authorize aid to promote culture and heritage conservation,[165] where such aid does not affect trading conditions and competition in the Union to an extent that is contrary to the common interest.[166] This amendment follows Commission practice under Article 92(3)(b) and (c) regarding aid to the press and the film industry. In 1962, for example, the Commission expressed the view that aid to film production might be authorized under Article 92(3)(b). However, fiscal aid had to be temporary and progressively reduced, to the extent that the industry attained results considered satisfactory,[167] and the preference seems to have been for aid harmonization.[168]

This approach was soon replaced by one according to which the Commission sought elimination of discrimination. For example, in Decision 76/574[169] concerning the Italian scheme of assistance for the press and paper-manufacturing industry granted through the Ente Nazionale per la Cellulosa e per la Carta (ENCC) the Commission authorized aid to publishers to purchase newsprint, provided that the aid was also made available in relation to newsprint which publishers wished to import directly without going through the ENCC.[170] The Commission also decided that Greek aid to the film industry could, in view of its combined economic and cultural function, be authorized under Article 92(3)(c). However, there had to be no discrimination contrary to

30) concerning aid which the Belgian Government had granted to a ceramic sanitary ware and crockery manufacturer.

[163] See, e.g., Dec. 94/696 ([1994] OJ L273/22) on the aid granted by Greece to Olympic Airways.

[164] Dec. 76/780 ([1976] OJ L270/39) concerning assistance granted by the Italian Government through the Istituto Nazionale per il Commercio Estero for advertising campaigns to expand the sale of exports by certain Italian industries.

[165] Aid to cultural or sports centres may constitute infrastructure provision falling outside the definition of aid for Art. 92(1) purposes. See sect. 2.2.4 below.

[166] The Union itself provides aid in the cultural field, such as that for translations of literary works. See, e.g., the pilot scheme to provide financial aid for translation of contemporary literary works ([1993] OJ C5/12). See now Art. 128 EC, as introduced by the TEU. However, distinguishing between culture and economic activity may be problematic. Cf. A. Evans, 'Freedom of Trade under the Common Law and European Community Law: The Case of the Football Bans' (1986) 102 *LQR* 510–42. Cf. also, regarding betting on horse races, Case T–471/93 *Tierce Ladbroke SA* v. *EC Commission* [1995] ECR II–2537.

[167] Reply to Written Question 72 ([1962] JO 154) by Mr Carboni.

[168] *Ninth EEC General Report* (EEC Commission, Brussels, 1966), 87.

[169] [1976] OJ L185/32.

[170] See also, regarding French, German and Italian aid, the *Sixteenth Report on Competition Policy*, n. 50 above, 159.

other Treaty provisions, notably those concerning the free movement of persons and services.[171] The Commission also sought extension of such aid to cover film production in other Member States, so as to further the growth of intra-Union competition in film production.[172] Cross-border financial, cultural, and economic co-operation in connection with production and distribution of national cultural works was generally favoured.[173]

Particular account may be taken of competition from other mass media, such as television, and from new forms of leisure activity[174] and of 'strong competitive pressures from third-country productions which [are] dominant in the market'.[175] The increasing significance of such factors may explain why early Commission opposition to export aid for films[176] has given way, at least in the case of books, to a more tolerant approach.[177]

Further categories of aid may be authorized by Council enactments under Article 92(3)(e). Such enactments may establish 'an abstract and general framework' to be applied by the Commission.[178] So far, the Council has only acted in the case of aid to shipbuilding, notably so as to permit the grant of operating aid.[179]

Particular aid measures may also be authorized by the Council, on application by the Member State concerned, under Article 93(2).[180] According to this provision, the Council may decide that aid which a Member State is granting or intends to grant shall be considered to be compatible with the common market in derogation from the provisions of Article 92, if such a decision is justified by exceptional circumstances. Applications for such authorization must be made before the Commission has adopted a decision under Article 93(2).[181]

Such applications are not always successful,[182] though authorizations are increasingly being granted in the agricultural sector.[183] They have been granted,

---

[171] Dec. 89/441 ([1989] OJ L208/3) on aid granted by the Greek Government to the film industry for the production of Greek films.

[172] *Fourth EC General Report* (EC Commission, Brussels, 1971), 30; and *Second Report on Competition Policy*, n. 122 above, 95–6.

[173] *Eighteenth Report on Competition Policy* (EC Commission, Brussels, 1989), 185.

[174] Bull. EC 7/8–1979, 2.1.37.

[175] *Eighteenth Report on Competition Policy* (EC Commission, Brussels, 1989), 185.

[176] *First Report on Competition Policy* (EC Commission, Brussels, 1972), 137.

[177] Dec. (NN127/92) to raise no objection to aid for the export of books ([1993] OJ C174/6; Bull. EC 5–1993, 1.2.48), which was annulled by the CFI in Case T–49/93 *Société internationale de diffusion et de l'édition (SIDE)* v. *EC Commission* [1995] ECR II–250.

[178] Darmon AG in Case C–400/92 *Germany* v. *EC Commission: Cosco* [1994] ECR I–4701, I–4708.   [179] See sect. 5.8 below.

[180] Analogies may be made with Art. 226 EC. See R. Quadri, R. Monaco, and A. Trabucchi, *Trattato Istitutivo della Comunità Economica Europea* (Giuffrè, Milan 1965), ii, 753.

[181] Mayras AG in Case 70/72 *EC Commission* v. *Germany: investments grants for mining* [1973] ECR 813, 835.

[182] See, e.g., regarding Italian textile aid, the *Second Report on Competition Policy*, n. 122 above, 89. See also Dec. 77/172 ([1977] OJ L54/39) concerning an aid for the pigmeat sector in the UK.

[183] See the figures given by Cosmas AG in Case C–122/94 *EC Commission* v. *EU Council: aid to wine producers* [1996] ECR I–881, I–887, n. 33.

for example, in relation to French aid to the paper industry, following a political commitment made during intergovernmental tariff negotiations;[184] aid in several Member States to wine producers faced with large market surpluses;[185] Danish aid for the slaughter of hens, also in the context of a market surplus;[186] British aid for sugar refining[187] and for beef farmers;[188] and German aid to compensate farmers because of loss of income following introduction of a common price for cereals.[189] Such practice reflects the Council function in Article 145 of the Treaty of ensuring co-ordination between general Union policy and the economic policies of the Member States, though the decisions are individual rather than of *caractère réglementaire*.[190]

In its decision-making the Council enjoys discretion not only as to the nature and scope of the aid measures to be authorized but also to some extent in the findings of basic fact, inasmuch as it is open to the Council to rely on general findings. For example, the Council could authorize aid to wine producers because the imbalance on the Union wine market, owing to the continued existence of such a situation, entailed the risk of serious economic and social repercussions in Italy and of engendering a critical situation in France.[191]

However, an authorization must be 'justified by exceptional circumstances'. Such circumstances, which may relate to the economy in general or to a particular sector, must be extraordinary and unforeseen, or at least not permanent, and thus not chronic.[192]

The circumstances must also be sufficiently serious. For example, when German farmers were already recovering under Union legislation[193] 80 per cent

---

[184] Decision of 19 Dec. 1960 ([1960] JO 1972) on the existing French aid system in favour of certain types of paper pulp. It was extended by Dec. 67/146 ([1967] JO 548) and Dec. 68/160 ([1968] JO L76/12).

[185] Dec. 88/415 ([1988] OJ L198/42) on the granting, by certain Member States, of aid for the short-term private storage of table wine and must. This measure followed previous measures on the same topic. See Dec. 75/249 ([1975] OJ L103/24), Dec. 76/306 ([1976] OJ L72/15), Dec. 84/230 ([1984] OJ L115/83), Dec. 84/258 ([1984] OJ L124/44), Dec. 85/213 ([1985] OJ L96/34), Dec. 85/272 ([1985] OJ L151/49), Dec. 86/196 ([1986] OJ L139/49), and Dec. 87/375 ([1987] OJ L200/17).

[186] Dec. 76/556 ([1976] OJ L168/12) on the system of aid applicable to the slaughter of hens in Denmark.

[187] Dec. 73/209 ([1973] OJ L207/47) concerning the present system of aid in the UK for the refining of raw sugar.

[188] Dec. 75/142 ([1975] OJ L52/35) concerning the system of aid in the UK for the slaughter of certain adult bovine animals intended for slaughter.

[189] Dec. 70/355 ([1970] JO L157/27) on the application of compensatory measures in favour of German cereal producers.

[190] Cosmas AG in Case C-124/94 *EC Commission* v. *EU Council: aid to wine producers* [1996] ECR I-881, I-901.

[191] *Ibid.*, I-924-5.

[192] Cosmas AG, *ibid.*, I-908.

[193] Reg. 855/84 ([1984] OJ L90/1) on the calculation and the dismantlement of the monetary compensatory amounts applying to certain agricultural products.

of their loss of income due to the dismantling of positive monetary compensatory amounts, the discovery of the shortfall did not constitute an exceptional circumstance such as to justify authorization[194] under Article 93(2).[195] Moreover, the Council may not authorize aid contrary to other Treaty provisions, such as those concerning taxation.[196] Hence, this provision does not empower the Council to develop its own 'aid policy'.[197]

Formally, therefore, the Treaty framework for state-aid control comprises a prohibition of aid in Article 92(1) and the possibility of its authorization under Article 92(2) or (3) or Article 93(2). In substance, these provisions embody various legal requirements—that competition should not be distorted, that regional development should be promoted or facilitated, that sectoral development should be facilitated and so on. Interactions between these requirements determine the real meaning of Articles 92 and 93.

These requirements may be expressed by reference to the concept of discrimination. On the one hand, aid distorting competition may be characterized as discriminatory.[198] On the other hand, it may be said to be the essential condition for authorization that the aid does not give rise to different advantages for undertakings placed in the same situation or to identical advantages for undertakings placed in appreciably different situations.[199] In other words, the Treaty recognizes the possibility that aid may be justified in the social interest, provided that it is granted in conditions of parity for all the Member States.[200]

Aid limited to purchases of domestically produced goods[201] and export aid[202] may readily be treated as discriminatory and hence incompatible with the common market.[203] Treatment of other kinds of aid may be more problematic. Differential treatment may not only be generally required for an optimal allocation of resources in 'real life situations',[204] but may also reflect the diversity of national situations.[205] It may not be assumed that aid associated

---

[194] Dec. 84/361 ([1984] OJ L185/41) concerning an aid granted to farmers in Germany.

[195] Slynn AG in Case 253/84 *Groupement agricole d'exploitation en commun (GAEC) de la Ségaude* v. *EC Council and EC Commission* [1987] ECR 123, 147.

[196] Jacobs AG in Case C–438/92 *Rustica Semences SA* v. *Finanzamt Kehl* [1994] ECR I–3519, I–3527; and Cosmas AG in Case C–124/94 *EC Commission* v. *EU Council: aid to wine producers* [1996] ECR I–881, I–889, I–908.

[197] E. Grabitz and M. Hilf, *Kommentar zum Europäische Union* (Beck, Munich, 1992), Art. 93, para. 36.

[198] Joined Cases 32 & 33/58 *Société Nouvelle des Usines de Pontlieue Aciéries du Temple (SNUPAT)* v. *ECSC High Authority* [1959] ECR 127, 143.

[199] Case 214/83 *Germany* v. *EC Commission: aid to the steel industry* [1985] ECR 3053, 3091.

[200] *Commissario dello Stato per la Regione Siciliana* v. *La Regione Sicilia* [1970] CMLR 35, 38.

[201] *Fifth EEC General Report* (EEC Commission, Brussels, 1962), 83.

[202] *Ibid.*, 81.

[203] *Eighth EEC General Report* (EEC Commission, Brussels, 1965), 80.

[204] L. Philips, *The Economics of Price Discrimination* (Cambridge University Press, Cambridge, 1983), 1.

[205] Dutheillet de Lamothe AG in Case 26/70 *Internationale Handelsgesellschaft mbH* v. *Einfuhr- und Vorratsstelle fur Getreide und Futtermittel* [1970] ECR 1125, 1153.

with such differential treatment amounts to discrimination incompatible with the common market.

At the same time, the limitations of language,[206] social demands,[207] and their status as elements in the legal system established by the Treaty imply that the meaning of the requirements embodied in Articles 92 and 93(2) does not depend simply on the wording of these provisions. It also depends on the selection of the various requirements[208] in the application of these provisions to individual cases[209] and on efforts to secure acceptance of such application through its articulation in policy terms.[210] Such efforts, which may be assisted as much by development of a 'statistical frame of reference' deriving from surveys of state aid[211] as from the formal legal framework, 'necessarily involve interpretation of the broad principles laid down in Articles 92 and 93'.[212] A consequence may be that the Commission 'no longer limits its action to the supervision and prohibition of illegal state aids, but enlarges its range of activities using quasi-regulatory tools'.[213]

The relevant Union practice, principally that of the Commission, is examined in detail in the following chapters. Account is taken of the relationship between the evolution of Commission practice and the case law of the European Courts and Union legislation. Particular attention is paid to interactions

---

[206] Even though it asserted that 'the tasks performed by rules are tasks for which the primary tool is the specific linguistic formulation of a rule' (F. Schauer, 'Formalism' (1988) 97 *Yale LJ* 509–48, 510), it is admitted that 'legal terms possess a core of settled meaning and a penumbra of debatable meaning' (*ibid.* 514) and that the choice of meaning may be determined by 'external factors' (*ibid.* 516).

[207] Cf. the view that early Commission successes in securing aid modifications may be attributed to the favourable economic conditions of the time. See A. Sacle, 'Les Aides d'état et la Communaute economique européenne' [1965] *RMC* 136–44, 142.

[208] The Commission may select differently from the Council (cf., in connection with Art. 39(1) EC requirements, Cosmas AG in Case C–124/94 *EC Commission* v. *EU Council: aid to wine producers* [1996] ECR I–881, I–907, by way of a reflection of the highly selective nature of the law's 'internal models of social reality'. See G. Teubner, 'Autopoiesis in Law and Society: A Rejoinder to Blankenburg' (1984) 18 *Law and Soc. Rev.* 291–301.

[209] It is said that aid cannot be defined in advance, because this is a field in which experience must prevail over imagination (A. Sacle, n. 207 above, 140), and that 'competition policy is preeminently pragmatic in character' (F. Andriessen, 'The Role of Anti-Trust in the Face of Economic Recession: State Aids in the EEC' [1983] *ECLR* 340–50, 350).

[210] See, e.g., application of Arts. 92 and 93 EC and Art. 5 of Dir. 80/723 to public undertakings in the manufacturing sector ([1991] OJ C273/2), para. 23. The CFI may be sympathetic. According to this Court in Joined Cases T–244/93 & T–486/93 *TWD Textilwerke Deggendorf GmbH* v. *EC Commission* [1995] ECR II–2265, II–2285, the 'operative' part of a Commission decision must be interpreted by having regard to the reasoning which led to its adoption.

[211] *Fourth Survey on State Aids in the European Community in the Manufacturing and Certain Other Sectors*, COM(95)365, 45.

[212] Submission of the Commission in Joined Cases 166 & 220/86 *Irish Cement Ltd* v. *EC Commission* [1988] ECR 6473, 6482.

[213] G. della Cananea, 'Administration by Guidelines: The Policy Guidelines of the Commission in the Field of State Aids' in I. Harden (ed.), *State Aid: Community Law and Policy* (Bundesanzeiger, Trier, 1993) 61–75, 68.

which may occur between Article 92 and various other provisions also forming part of the Treaty system.[214]

On the one hand, Article 3(g) requires the institution of a system ensuring undistorted competition within the Union.[215] This provision apparently implies that the prohibition in Article 92(1), which is examined in Chapter 2, should be broadly interpreted. Such an interpretation may seem consistent with completion of the internal market,[216] the requirements of which may, for example, be invoked against export aid.[217] The further implication is that the provisions for aid authorizations in Article 92(2) and (3) should be strictly interpreted. Such thinking is consistent with the idea that the Treaty 'starts from the principle of the market mechanism'[218] and with the general principle that 'derogations' from market freedoms should be strictly interpreted.[219] The thinking may be reinforced by the importance of compliance with the convergence criteria for Economic and Monetary Union,[220] which may imply a general preference for reducing overall aid levels.[221]

It may seem consistent with such implications to view Article 92 as envisaging liberal equality, that is, the type of equality which results from the prohibition of public intervention in the market.[222] Certainly, the grant of any aid to given undertakings may, depending perhaps on questions of the interchangeability of the goods concerned[223] and the state of the market,[224] be viewed as discrimination against other undertakings.[225] According to such

---

[214] An analogy might be drawn with the effect given to the express requirement in Art. 136 EC that association with the OCT be implemented 'on the basis of the principles set out in this Treaty' and of 'the experience acquired' in Joined Cases T–480/93 & T–483/93 *Antillean Rice Mills NV* v. *EC Council and EC Commission* [1995] ECR II–2305, II–2340.

[215] See also Arts. 3(1)(a) and 130 EC. Cf., regarding Arts. 4(c) and 95 ECSC, R. Quadri, R. Monaco and A. Trabucchi (eds.), *Trattato Istitutivo della Comunità Europea del Carbone e dell'Acciaió: Commentario* (Giuffrè, Milan, 1970), i, 103.

[216] See, e.g., the *Sixteenth Report on Competition Policy*, n. 50 above, 135; and *Completing the Internal Market*, COM(85)310, 39–40.

[217] Dec. 89/659 ([1989] OJ L394/1) relating to Ministerial Dec. E3789/128 of the Greek Government establishing a special single tax on undertakings. Cf., earlier, under the ECSC Treaty Joined Cases 27–29/58 *Compagnie des Hauts Fourneaux et Fonderies de Givors* v. *ECSC High Authority* [1960] ECR 241, 254.

[218] F. Andriessen, n. 209 above, 348.

[219] See, e.g. Capotorti AG in Case 730/79 *Philip Morris Holland BV* v. *EC Commission* [1980] ECR 2671, 2701.

[220] See, regarding the budgetary discipline envisaged in Art. 104c EC, A. Petersen, 'State Aid and the European Union: State Aid in the Light of Trade, Competition, Industrial and Cohesion Policies' in I. Harden (ed.), n. 207 above 20–5, 24. More generally, the need to prevent aid being used instead of devaluation is recognized (*ibid.* 20).

[221] *Fourth Survey on State Aids in the European Community in the Manufacturing and Certain Other Sectors*, COM(95)365, 42 and 45.

[222] Cf., F. Andriessen, n. 209 above, 344.

[223] Capotorti AG in Joined Cases 117/76 & 16/77 *Ruckdeschel* v. *Hauptzollamt Hamburg–St. Annen* [1977] ECR 1753, 1782.

[224] Case 1/54 *France* v. *ECSC High Authority: coal and steel prices* [1954–6] ECR 1, 7.

[225] F. Y. Jenny, 'Competition and State Aid Policy in the EU' [1994] *Fordham Corporate Law Institute* 75–98, 82.

views, whether aid is granted for regional objectives or to certain sectors of the economy, the intervention is likely to affect the conditions of competition by interfering with the principle of equal access to resources and by eventually destroying the principles of equality of opportunity for undertakings competing with each other in a single market.[226]

Support for such views may be sought in early case law concerning the ECSC Treaty. This Treaty has been said to seek the most rational distribution of production at the highest possible level of productivity based on the composition of production costs resulting from the physical and technical conditions peculiar to the various producers.[227] More particularly, equality before natural conditions is said to have been envisaged. Hence, natural advantages, such as those resulting from geographical conditions, constitute a fundamental element of competition which should not be distorted through the use of aid.[228]

Such thinking was elaborated in *Givors*,[229] where certain undertakings established in the South of France sought to retain the preferential transport tariffs which they enjoyed before the entry into force of the ECSC Treaty. It was argued that withdrawal of the preferential tariffs would provoke fundamental and persistent disturbances in the French economy.[230] In response to this argument, Advocate General Roemer maintained that such aid would drain the general economy of resources and thus reduce the opportunities of expansion for rationalized undertakings.[231] If it were possible to compensate for the special difficulties of an undertaking by means of special advantages, the situation would remain the same as that existing before the common market was established. However, it was the stated objective of the ECSC Treaty to allow for changes in the structure of the common market in the interest of a more rational distribution of production. Hence, aid to compensate undertakings for disadvantages arising from their location was incompatible with the prohibition of state aid in Article 4(c) of this Treaty.[232]

The Court of Justice itself ruled that product prices must comply with the fundamental principle of competition, which was the basis of the common market, and result from the natural production conditions to which producers were subject. The tariffs in question had precisely the effect of distorting those conditions and, for this reason were prohibited.[233]

---

[226] Mayras AG in Case 70/72 *EC Commission* v. *Germany: investments grants for mining* [1973] ECR 813, 834.

[227] Joined Cases 27–29/58 *Compagnie des Hauts Fourneaux et Fonderies de Givors* v. *ECSC High Authority* [1960] ECR 241, 258.

[228] Lagrange AG in Joined Cases 3–18, 25 & 26/58 *Barbara Erzbergbau AG* v. *ECSC High Authority* [1960] ECR 173, 211. See also Joined Cases 63–69/72 *Wilhelm Wehrhahn Hansamühle* v. *EC Council* [1973] ECR 1229, 1250.

[229] Joined Cases 27–29/58 *Compagnie des Hauts Fourneaux et Fonderies de Givors* v. *ECSC High Authority* [1960] ECR 241.

[230] According to Art. 2(2) ECSC, such disturbances are to be avoided.

[231] [1960] ECR 241, 273.

[232] *Ibid.*, 274.　　　　　　　　　　　　　　　　　　[233] *Ibid.*, 259.

In drawing up their tariffs, the Member States were to consider transport conditions alone and, therefore, the comparability of the different routes and locations from the point of view of transport.[234] Prohibition of preferential tariffs might result in a temporary reduction in employment and in the closure of some undertakings. However, their prohibition might be necessary to enable the common market to achieve its stated objectives, since the disappearance of undertakings which could not continue to exist by their own unaided efforts but only with the help of constant and massive subsidies would strengthen the resistance of the transport industry to crises.[235]

On the other hand, Article 92(2) and (3) of the EC Treaty reflects a basic feature of system established by this Treaty—that certain distortions of competition may be lawful, because the Treaty seeks more than simply the maximization of competition. In the context of aid control this feature is expressed by the principle of compensatory justification, which is examined in Chapter 3. According to this principle, certain aid may produce benefits for the Union[236] which compensate for the distortions of competition entailed and may thus justify the aid. Hence, the 'effects of so-called "normal competition" [may] be kept to some extent in proportion'.[237] The implication is that interventionist equality,[238] that is, the type of equality which results from public intervention in favour of 'the disadvantaged', may be envisaged in Article 92. In particular, the possibility is implied of 'application of particular rules designed to enable less productive undertakings to meet the requirements of competition in the common market'.[239] Reconciliation of such equality with liberal equality may be seen as the function of the compensatory justification principle. In other words, its function may be seen as that of 'striking a balance between the "minus" as regards competition as a result of the aid and the "plus" as regards industrialization and development'.[240]

The practical implications may owe much to various Treaty provisions. The latter may allow the Commission 'a lot of leeway to decide what kind of interference in market mechanisms (through state aids) should be legitimized'.[241] For example, treatment of regional aid, which is examined in Chapter

---

[234] Case 19/58 *Germany* v. *ECSC High Authority: transport tariffs for mineral fuels and ores* [1960] ECR 225, 235.

[235] *Ibid.* 237.

[236] See, in connection with the 'harmonious development of economic activities' sought by Art. 2 of the original version of the EEC Treaty, A. Sacle, n. 207 above, 136.

[237] Lagrange AG in Case 1/54 *France* v. *ECSC High Authority: coal and steel prices* [1954–6] ECR 1, 28.

[238] Cf., regarding Art. 92(3)(a) and pursuit of equality of opportunity, M. Caspari, 'EEC Competition Law and Industrial Policy' [1989] *Fordham Corporate Law Institute* 163–78, 173.

[239] Capotorti AG in Joined Cases 117/76 & 16/77 *Ruckdeschel* v. *Hauptzollamt Hamburg–St. Annen* [1977] ECR 1753, 1782.

[240] Darmon AG in Joined Cases 166 & 220/86 *Irish Cement Ltd* v. *EC Commission* [1988] ECR 6473, 6494.

[241] Jenny, n. 225 above, 87.

4, may be affected by cohesion objectives,[242] particularly the objective of reducing regional disparities, in Article 130a of the Treaty.[243] According to Article 130b, the formulation and implementation of Union policies, presumably including competition policy, shall take into account such objectives and contribute to their achievement. Treatment of aid granted to particular sectors, which is examined in Chapter 5, may similarly be affected by Treaty provisions other than Article 92. For example, Article 42 of the Treaty stipulates that the provisions on competition apply to the agricultural sector only to the extent decided by the Council, account being taken of the objectives of the common agricultural policy. Even treatment of 'horizontal aid', which is the subject of Chapter 6, may be affected by other Treaty provisions. For example, Article 130r(2) of the Treaty requires that environmental policy be integrated into the definition and implementation of other Union policies, implicitly including competition policy,[244] and provides that one of the principles of the former policy is the 'polluter pays' principle.

This formal classification of aid as regional, sectoral, or horizontal partly reflects interactions between Article 92 requirements and the Treaty system. However, as the Commission admits, aid classification may be partly dependent on which of the objectives declared by a Member State is considered to be the primary one.[245] As a result, procedures for application of Article 92, which are considered in Chapter 7, may be decisive for treatment of aid.

In establishing these procedures in Articles 93 and 94, the Treaty apparently tends towards formally separating these 'institutional law' procedures from the 'substantive economic law' of Article 92. In other words, the 'basic rules' in Article 92 and the 'implementation machinery' in Article 93[246] are formally separated. To the extent of this formal separation, the procedures concerned may appear to have the essential function of securing compliance with predetermined requirements in Article 92,[247] and the organic role really played by the procedures in the activation and development of these requirements may be concealed.[248]

Since these procedures determine those requirements of Article 92 which are articulated and developed, the former procedures play an organic role in

[242] Art. B TEU.

[243] Note the reference to this objective in the Communic. on the method for the application of Art. 92(3)(a) and (c) to regional aid ([1988] OJ C212/2).

[244] Note the reference to Art. 130r in Notice C2/93 (ex N505/92) ([1996] OJ C33/7) concerning environmental aid that Belgium had decided to grant under two decrees of the Walloon Regional Council.

[245] Cf. the *Fourth Survey on State Aids in the European Community in the Manufacturing and Certain Other Sectors*, COM(95)365, 20.

[246] Mayras AG in Case 70/72 *EC Commission* v. *Germany: investment grants for mining* [1973] ECR 813, 834.

[247] Art. 93 makes no reference to third parties.

[248] Cf. G. Teubner (n. 208 above), regarding 'environmental exchange mechanisms'. It was noted early on that the Commission sought to associate Member States with its *réflexions* in the state aid field. See A. Sacle, n. 207 above, 136.

the evolution of the effective meaning of this provision. In particular, according to the Court of Justice, the provisions of Article 92(1) are intended to take effect in the legal systems of Member States, so that they may be invoked before national courts, where they have been put into concrete form by acts having general application provided for by Article 94 or by decisions in particular cases envisaged by Article 93(2).[249] Hence, Article 92(1) cannot be interpreted in isolation, but only having regard to the scheme of Articles 92 to 94.[250]

Complex interactions can occur between the demands of institutional equality, that is, equality of participation in public decision-making, and pursuit of the types of equality envisaged in Article 92. Such interactions occur, for example, when views of other Member States and interest groups are treated by the Commission as demonstrating that aid distorts competition and affects trade between Member States.[251] Unless such interactions are explored, critically important changes at the systemic level may remain masked by continuities at the levels of formal legal and institutional discourse.[252]

In short, therefore, fundamental issues as to the relationship between law and policy and as to that between economic law and institutional law may arise in Union practice in the field of state aid. On the one hand, the content of policy may be affected by the institutional context in which it is formed and implemented. On the other hand, the way that the decision-making procedure operates may be affected by the content of policy.[253] On the basis of examination of this practice conclusions concerning these issues are drawn in Chapter 8.

[249] Case 77/72 *Carmine Capolongo* v. *Azienda Agricola Maya* [1973] ECR 611, 621–2; Case 78/76 *Firma Steinike und Weinlig* v. *Germany* [1977] ECR 595, 609.

[250] Case 77/72 *Carmine Capolongo* v. *Azienda Agricola Maya* [1973] ECR 611, 621.

[251] See, e.g., Notice C60/95 (NN 169/95) ([1996] OJ C124/5) regarding aid granted by the Austrian government to Head Tyrolia Mares, in the form of capital injections. See also sect. 7.6.3 below. Limitations to interactions of this kind explain why 'there may be valid legal rules really in existence which determine possibilities not yet realised by anyone's actions.' See N. MacCormick and O. Weinburger, *An Institutional Theory of Law* (Reidel, Dordrecht, 1986), 11.

[252] D. J. Gerber, 'The Transformation of European Community Competition Law' (1994) 35 *Harvard International Law Journal* 97–147, 98.

[253] Cf. R. Dehousse, 'Completing the Internal Market: Institutional Constraints and Challenges' in R. Bieber, J. Pinder, and J. H. H. Weiler, *1992: One European Market* (Nomos, Baden-Baden, 1988) 311–36, 311 and 324.

2

The Prohibition in Article 92(1)

The operation of the prohibition in Article 92(1) of the EC Treaty depends on the definition of state aid and on conditions relating to anti-competitive effects. The latter conditions require that there be favouritism in the grant of aid, that competition may be distorted, and that trade between Member States may be affected.

2.2 DEFINITION OF STATE AID

The EC Treaty does not define state aid, though the concept 'falls exclusively within the ambit of Community law'.[1] To provide such a definition would, it is said, have been neither feasible nor useful, since concrete definitions would have been liable to restrict the scope of the concept. It is considered necessary for the concept to have a broad scope, if Article 92 is to make a meaningful contribution towards ensuring that competition is not distorted, in accordance with Article 3(g) of the Treaty.[2]

In Union practice aid has been variously defined. Most definitions treat aid as simultaneously entailing benefits for undertakings and burdens for the state. Thus it may be defined as a measure 'representing a cost or a loss of revenue to the public authorities and a benefit to recipients';[3] an advantage entailing a burden to public finances in the form either of expenditure or of reduced revenue;[4] or as 'a contribution at the expense of public funds or the reduction of charges which an undertaking normally has to bear'.[5]

Some definitions may concentrate on the benefits for aid recipients,[6] and

[1] Submission of the Commission in Case T–459/93 *Siemens SA* v. *EC Commission* [1995] ECR II–1675, II–1698.

[2] Lenz AG in Case 234/84 *Belgium* v. *EC Commission: Meura* [1986] ECR 2263, 2269. Hence, the concept has been said to encompass all interventions which public bodies may effect to modify the establishment of prices within the competitive sphere (*Commissario dello Stato per la Regione Siciliana* v. *La Regione Sicilia* [1970] CMLR 35, 38).

[3] *Fourth Survey on State Aids in the European Community in the Manufacturing and Certain Other Sectors*, COM(95)365, 51.

[4] Capotorti AG in Case 82/77 *Openbar Ministerie* v. *Jacobus Philippus Van Tiggele* [1978] ECR 25, 52.

[5] Roemer AG in Case 9/70 *Franz Grad* v. *Finanzamt Traunstein* [1970] ECR 825, 853.

[6] According to E. Wohlfarth, V. Everling, H. J. Glaesner, and R. Sprung, *Die Europäische Wirtschaftsgemeinschaft, Kommentar zum Vertrag* (Vahlen, Berlin, 1960), 273, it covers all direct or

treat aid as: any grant or advantage from the public authorities;[7] 'certain unmarketlike advantages attributable to the state which are liable to improve the economic situation of the undertaking which benefits from them in comparison with that of other undertakings';[8] the payment of a proportion of the costs of production by someone other than the purchaser;[9] a benefit which the recipient would not otherwise have received 'in the normal course';[10] or interventions which mitigate the charges which are normally included in the budget of undertakings.[11]

The idea underlying such definitions is that a grant from the state for no consideration[12] or for inadequate consideration[13] may constitute aid. For example, in classifying tax credits to Italian road hauliers as aid, the Commission noted the absence of any evidence that the recipients of the credits were expected to provide anything in return.[14] The application of such thinking may be problematic. For example, if an undertaking incurs losses 'at the state's behest' and thus implicitly provides consideration, the covering of these losses by public money is still classified as aid.[15] On the other hand, aid to reduce the costs of waste paper collectors is not covered by Article 92(1), provided that the collected waste paper is subsequently made available to the paper industry as secondary raw material at prevailing market prices.[16] The rationale is that compensation for performance of a public service rather than aid is involved.[17]

indirect benefits granted by the state to individual undertakings or sectors. See, similarly, J. Mégret, J.-V. Louis, D. Vignes, M. Waelbroeck, J. L. Dewost, P. Brueckner, and A. Sacchettini, *Le Droit des Communautés Européennes* (Université Libre de Bruxelles, Brussels, 1972), iv, 380; and D. H. Scheuing, *Les Aides Financières Publiques* (Berger-Levrault, Paris, 1974), 268. W. G. Ganshof van der Meersch, *Le Droit des Communautés Européennes* (Larcier, Brussels, 1969), 863 is more elaborate. Here aid is defined as any measure which favours the competitive position of an undertaking and thus tends to compensate for an aspect of economic inferiority in a discriminatory way.

[7] Reischl AG in Joined Cases 188–190/80 *France, Italy, and the UK v. Germany: transparency directive* [1982] ECR 2545, 2595.

[8] Lenz AG in Case C–44/93 *Namur—Les Assurances du crédit v. Office national du Ducroire and Belgium* [1994] ECR I–3829, I–3847.

[9] Lagrange AG in Case 30/59 *De Gezamenlijke Steenkolenmijnen in Limburg v. ECSC High Authority* [1961] ECR 1, 44.

[10] Slynn AG in Case 84/82 *Germany v. EC Commission: Belgian aid to textiles* [1984] ECR 1451, 1501.

[11] Case 30/59 *De Gezamenlijke Steenkolenmijnen in Limburg v. ECSC High Authority* [1961] ECR 1, 19. See also Case C–301/87 *France v. EC Commission: Boussac* [1990] ECR I–307, I–362.

[12] Reischl AG in Case 61/79 *Amministrazione delle Finanze dello Stato v. Denkavit Italiana Srl* [1980] ECR 1205, 1235.

[13] Fenelly AG in Case C–56/93 *Belgium v. EC Commission: natural gas tariff* [1996] ECR I–723, I–733.

[14] Communic. C32/92 (ex NN67/92) ([1992] OJ C316/7) on aids granted by Italy to professional road hauliers.

[15] Slynn AG in Case 223/85 *Rijn-Schelde-Verolme (RSV) Maschinenfabriken en Scheepswerven BV v. EC Commission* [1987] ECR 4617, 4650.

[16] Reply by Sir Leon Brittan to Written Question 2057/92 ([1993] OJ C47/14) by Mr George Patterson.

[17] See regarding aid for the collection and disposal of used tyres in Denmark and of waste oil in Spain, H. Morch, 'Summary of the Most Important Recent Developments' [1994] 3 *Competi-*

Similarly, indemnities granted by a Member State to undertakings collecting or disposing of waste oils do not constitute aid within the meaning of Article 92, but rather consideration for services performed by such undertakings.[18] However, overcompensation for the costs of meeting public-service obligations may constitute aid.[19]

Other definitions concentrate on the burden undertaken by the state. Accordingly, aid may be defined as: assumption by the state of costs which normally fall on undertakings;[20] assumption by the state of part of the risk which is normally assumed by undertakings and for which the state is not responsible;[21] or compensation from the state to a company or receipt of less revenue by the state.[22]

Yet more definitions concentrate on state purposes. According to these definitions, aid is seen as: the grant of resources or advantages by the state designed to encourage attainment of economic or social objectives sought by the state;[23] any type of support granted by a Member State or through state resources other than for commercial purposes;[24] or funds made available by the state which in the normal course of events would not be provided by a private investor applying normal commercial criteria and disregarding other considerations of a social, political, or philanthropic nature.[25] However, where such action is objectively justified on commercial grounds, the fact that it also furthers a political aim does not necessarily mean that it constitutes aid.[26]

These definitions go beyond the strict concept of 'subventions', because they cover not only positive transfers of resources from the state but also relief from charges normally imposed by the latter.[27] More particularly, the definitions go

tion Policy Newsletter 61–6, 63. See also, regarding Dutch aid to encourage the purchase of low-pollution cars, Bull. EC 3–1989, 2.1.66. Cf., however, regarding tax relief to compensate users of recycled raw materials for the higher incidence of waste which was involved in the process and was taxable on disposal, the *Twenty-Third Report on Competition Policy* (EC Commission, Brussels, 1994), 246.

[18] Case 240/83 *Procureur de la République* v. *Association de Défense des Brûleurs d'Huiles Usagées* [1985] ECR 531, 550. See, earlier, Bull. EC 9/10–1969, 35.

[19] See, regarding public broadcasters, the *Twenty-Third Report on Competition Policy*, n. 17 above, 315.

[20] Darmon AG in Case 248/84 *Germany* v. *EC Commission: regional aid* [1987] ECR 4013, 4027.

[21] Dec. 90/70 ([1990] OJ L47/28) concerning aid provided by France to certain primary processing steel undertakings.

[22] Dec. 82/73 ([1982] OJ L37/29) on the preferential tariff charged to glasshouse growers for natural gas in the Netherlands.

[23] Case 61/79 *Amministrazione delle Finanze dello Stato* v. *Denkavit Italiana Srl* [1980] ECR 1205, 1228. See, similarly, H. Desterbecq-Fobelets, 'Le contrôle externe de l'octroi des aides étatiques aux entreprises privées en Belgique' [1979] *Administration Publique* 277–301, 278.

[24] Lenz AG in Case 234/84 *Belgium* v. *EC Commission: Meura* [1986] ECR 2263, 2269. The aim of state participation—one of public policy, such as social or structural policy, or to produce a return—may be decisive for the question whether aid is involved (*ibid.*, 2270).

[25] Jacobs AG in Joined Cases C–278/92, C–279/92 & C–280/92 *Spain* v. *EC Commission: Intelhorce* [1994] ECR I–4103, I–4113.

[26] Case C–56/93 *Belgium* v. *EC Commission: natural gas tariff* [1996] ECR I–723, I–790.

[27] Case C–387/92 *Banco de Crédito Industrial SA* v. *Ayuntamiento de Valencia* [1994] ECR I–877, I–907.

beyond that employed by the Union in the context of trade with third countries. For example, *Fediol*[28] concerned the question whether Brazilian producers of soya meal were receiving unlawful subsidies. According to the Court of Justice, it could be seen from the list of examples annexed to GATT that the concept of export subsidy had been understood as necessarily implying a financial charge borne directly or indirectly by public bodies. An advantage to the recipient in itself was not sufficient to constitute such a subsidy.[29]

A comprehensive definition of aid for the purposes of Article 92 is apparently attempted in paragraph 1.1 of the Guidelines for the examination of state aid to fisheries and aquaculture.[30] It treats as aid:

all measures entailing a financial advantage in any form whatsoever funded directly or indirectly from the budgets of public authorities (national, regional or provincial, departmental or local) . . . capital transfers, reduced-interest loans, interest subsidies, certain state holdings in the capital of undertakings, aid financed by special levies and aid granted in the form of state securities against bank loans or the reduction of or exemption from charges or taxes, including accelerated depreciation and the reduction of social contributions.

In reality, even this definition tends to exemplify[31] rather than exhaustively to define aid for the purposes of Article 92.

2.2.1 Financial Measures

Apart from the outright grant of funds, various financial measures may be treated as involving the grant of aid.

Credit

The provision of credit, particularly export credit,[32] may constitute aid where the costs of the credit are reduced,[33] interest rebates are paid,[34] a premium too

---

[28] Case 188/85 *EEC Seed Crushers and Oil Producers Federation (Fediol)* v. *EC Commission* [1988] ECR 4193, 4255.

[29] The Commission argued that Brazilian aid was not 'sectorally specific' because it was granted in respect of all the major basic agricultural commodities (27 products) without being of specific benefit to soya beans, which, although representing 31.9% of basic agricultural production, absorbed 31.7% of the financing. This argument was accepted by the ECJ (*ibid.*, 4227).

[30] [1994] OJ C260/3.

[31] See, earlier, Commission Replies to Written Question 48/63 ([1963] JO 2235) by Mr Burgbacher and to Written Question 110/82 ([1982] OJ C221/5) by Mr Welsh.

[32] See Joined Cases 6 & 11/69 *EC Commission* v. *France: preferential rediscount rate for exporters* [1969] ECR 523, 540, regarding French aid. See also Case 57/86 *Greece* v. *EC Commission: interest rebates on export credits* [1988] ECR 2855, 2871 and Bull. EC 9–1988, 2.1.54, regarding Greek aid.

[33] Reduced bank handling charges may involve aid. See Communic. C30/93 (ex N348/93) ([1993] OJ C336/9) concerning financing measures for the fisheries bank.

[34] *Eighth Report on Competition Policy* (EC Commission, Brussels, 1979), 153–6. See, e.g., Dec. 82/364 ([1982] OJ L159/44) concerning the subsidizing of interest rates on credits for exports from France to Greece after the accession of that country to the EEC.

low to reflect the risk actually involved is charged,[35] or the security required is inadequate[36] or non-existent.[37] The fact that the grant of a loan may be 'of a commercial nature' is not of itself sufficient to show that it does not amount to aid within the meaning of Article 92, since such a transaction may nonetheless be affected at a rate which gives the borrower a special advantage by comparison with its competitors.[38] The takeover by the state of the obligation of a private guarantor to pay debts covered by the guarantee also constitutes aid.[39]

The amount of the aid is equal to the difference between the interest rate which the borrower would have to have paid to a private sector creditor and the rate actually paid or the difference between the sum which could have been raised on the financial markets with the security provided and the sum actually borrowed.[40] However, where an unsecured loan is made to an undertaking which under normal circumstances would be unable to obtain credit, the whole amount of the loan is treated as aid.[41] In practice, rather than granting loans, Member States may prefer to limit budgetary burdens through reducing the cost of loans with interest subsidies.[42]

Guarantees

The provision of a state guarantee[43] and 'comfort letters . . . assuring the lenders that the Government is behind' an undertaking[44] may constitute aid,[45]

[35] Notice C17/93 (NN77/93) ([1994] OJ C71/3) concerning aid granted by Belgium to SA Forges de Clabecq in the form of a cash loan of 500 million Bfrs. The Commission may have regard to the average rate of indebtedness and conditions in the sector concerned. See Dec. 94/813 ([1994] OJ L335/82) concerning aid to French pig farmers.

[36] Communic. C26/93 (ex NN23/93) ([1993] OJ C235/6) concerning aid decided by the German Government in favour of Märkische Faser AG in Premnitz, Brandenburg. See, regarding acceptance as security of property already mortgaged to other creditors, Notice C9/95 (ex N121/94) ([1995] OJ C282/3) regarding aid which Spain has granted to Tubacex.

[37] Dec. 96/236 ([1996] OJ L78/31) concerning state aid granted by Hamburg to the ECSC steel undertaking Hamburger Stahlwerke GmbH, Hamburg.

[38] Case T–95/94 *Chambre Syndicale Nationale des Entreprises de Transport de Fonds et Valeurs (Sytraval) and Brink's France Sarl.* v. *EC Commission* [1995] ECR II–2651, II–2675.

[39] Notice C47/95 (ex NN61/95) ([1996] OJ C68/5) in connection with aid granted by the Italian Government and the Region of Sicily to agricultural co-operatives.

[40] T. Soames and A. Ryan, 'State Aid and Air Transport' [1995] *ECLR* 290–309.

[41] Application of Arts. 92 and 93 EC and of Art. 61 EEA to state aids in the aviation sector ([1994] OJ C350/5), para. 32.

[42] *Fourth Survey on State Aids in the European Community in the Manufacturing and Certain Other Sectors*, n. 3 above, 18.

[43] Letter to Member States SG(89)D/4328 (*Competition Law in the European Communities*, ii. *Rules Applicable to State Aids* (EC Commission, Brussels, 1990), 37); Letter SG(89)D12772 (*ibid.* 38). See, e.g., Notice C14/94 (NN133/92 & N514/93) ([1994] OJ C94/4) concerning the advantages given to Olympic Airways. A communication on aid granted in the form of guarantees has been drafted by the Commission. See the *Twenty-Fourth Report on Competition Policy* (EC Commission, Brussels, 1995), 166.

[44] Dec. 94/698 ([1994] OJ L279/29) concerning increase in capital, credit guarantees, and tax exemption in favour of TAP (Transportes Aéreos Portugueses).

[45] See, regarding a guarantee where the commission charged did not reflect the degree of risk involved, Bull. EC 12–1992, 1.3.80.

particularly where 'poorly ranked' undertakings are thereby enabled to obtain loans at market rates.[46] A guarantee may do so whether or not the state concerned later has to make good a loss,[47] because the provision of a guarantee removes the element of risk which the undertaking would otherwise have to bear. It is this effect, rather than the cost to the state, which is decisive. Alleged imperfections in the capital market do not affect such characterization of a guarantee.[48] Nor does the fact that the benefit represented by the guarantee is of a qualitative nature and cannot be quantified, save where a 'mishap' entails actual disbursement of state funds under the guarantee.[49]

More particularly, a guarantee in respect of the debts of companies becoming insolvent as a result of an obligation to repay aid previously granted in breach of Article 92 constitutes aid, because it is designed to restore the advantages conferred on the companies by the previous aid.[50] Where the legal status of a public enterprise precludes bankruptcy or where the state becomes the sole owner of an undertaking in difficulty and thereby assumes unlimited liability, the situation may be assimilated to that of the grant of a guarantee.[51]

There is a presumption that a state guarantee involves the grant of aid, if the guarantee is necessary for the survival of the company concerned, as an appropriate return is impossible in such a case.[52] There is a similar presumption where the guarantee lasts for an exceptional length of time or entails a very high risk.[53]

The mere publication of a decision to award a guarantee may constitute aid, because it gives the undertaking concerned an advantage in its relations with banks and suppliers.[54] Mobilization of a guarantee constitutes a new aid which has to be notified under Article 93(3),[55] if it is mobilized under different conditions from those initially approved at the granting stage.[56] Where

[46] *Fourth Survey on State Aids in the European Community in the Manufacturing and Certain Other Sectors*, n. 3 above, 5.

[47] Dec. 79/519 ([1979] OJ L138/30) concerning the 'special financing scheme for investments to increase exporting firms' production capacity' in France.

[48] Notice C49/91 (E15/90) ([1992] OJ C22/6) regarding a general aid scheme in the Netherlands entitled 'Regeling Bijzondere Financiering'.

[49] *Third Report on Competition Policy* (EC Commission, Brussels, 1973), 98.

[50] Notice C59/94 (NN125/94) ([1995] OJ C220/2) concerning the extraordinary administration of enterprises in a state of insolvency resulting from the obligation to repay aid incompatible with Arts. 92 and 93 EC.

[51] Application of Arts. 92 and 93 EC and of Art. 5 of Dir. 80/723 to public undertakings in the manufacturing sector ([1991] OJ C273/2), para. 38.1 and 2.

[52] Notice C26/95 (NN52/95) ([1995] C121/4) regarding aid which France had decided to grant to Crédit Lyonnais.

[53] Dec. 95/547 ([1995] OJ L308/92) giving conditional approval to the aid granted by France to Crédit Lyonnais.

[54] Communic. C29/92 (NN12/92) ([1992] OJ C234/8) concerning aid decided by the Basque country in favour of La Papelera Española.

[55] See sect. 7.5.2 below. According to the Letter of 12 Oct. 1989 SG(89)D12772 n. 43 above, guarantee schemes (but not guarantees within the terms of such schemes) must already have been notified.

[56] Notice C28/93 (N446/93) ([1993] OJ C286/2) concerning aid which Germany intended to grant to NINO Textil AG, Nordhorn.

an authorized guarantee is replaced by a grant, the latter must also be notified.[57]

The amount of aid involved is usually regarded as the difference between the interest rate payable under normal commercial conditions and that actually obtained because of the guarantee. Such conditions imply a risk premium, even if the lender had 'every assurance of recovering its claim'. Where the loan is not secured against movable or immovable property, the implied premium is greater.[58] If, however, the position of the undertaking concerned is so poor that it would be unable to borrow without the guarantee,[59] or if the guarantee is necessary for the survival of the company concerned and no return is to be expected,[60] the amount of aid involved may be equal to the amount of money borrowed with the help of the guarantee.

However, a guarantee may fall outside Article 92 where the charge for the guarantee is wholly met by the undertaking concerned, and the mobilization conditions are acceptable to the Commission.[61] In addition, the guarantee must be secured by mortgage rights on fixed assets which can reasonably be judged sufficient to cover the risks involved.[62] It must also be contractually linked to specific conditions allowing for the compulsory declaration of bankruptcy of the beneficiary and for the guarantee to be honoured only after the guaranteed creditor has recovered what he can of the debt through realization of the assets of the debtor.[63] In any receivership procedure the public guarantor must be treated as any other creditor.[64]

The importance of the control of guarantees is rendered all the greater by Article 104c of the EC Treaty and the Protocol on the Excessive Deficit Procedure, which concern budgetary discipline by Member States. These provisions cover state lending to public undertakings but presumably not borrowing by such undertakings on the financial markets guaranteed by the state. Thus they may encourage Member States to use guarantees to assist such undertakings.

[57] Dec. 88/174 ([1988] OJ L79/29) concerning aid which Baden-Württemberg had provided to BUG-Alutechnik GmbH, an undertaking producing semi-finished and finished aluminium products.

[58] Dec. 95/466 ([1995] OJ L267/49) concerning aid granted by the Flemish Region to the Belgian airline Vlaamse Luchttransportmaatschappij NV.

[59] Communic. C15/94 (N122/94, NN22/94 & E3/93) ([1994] OJ C93/12) concerning the existing tax exemption and planned recapitalization of TAP; Dec. 94/696 ([1994] OJ L273/22) on the aid granted by Greece to Olympic Airways.

[60] Notice C26/95 (NN52/95) ([1995] OJ C121/4) regarding aid which France had decided to grant to Crédit Lyonnais.

[61] See, e.g., Dec. 94/172 ([1994] OJ L79/24) concerning Italian Law 102 of 2 May 1990 providing for the reconstruction and regeneration of the Valtellina.

[62] Notice C28/92 (ex N199/92) ([1993] OJ C277/5) regarding aid which Spain had decided to grant to Esmaltaciones San Ignacio SA.

[63] *Twenty-Third Report on Competition Policy* (n. 17 above, 244).

[64] Notice C28/93 (N446/93) ([1995] OJ C327/8) regarding aid which Germany planned to grant to Nino Textil AG, Nordhorn, Lower Saxony.

Tax concessions

Aid may be found to be present where the state reduces the public charges generally imposed on undertakings through tax concessions. This is so, for example, where a bank is able to finance investments, which others are unable or unwilling to finance, because of such concessions.[65] Tax concessions for the formation of bank consortia set up to facilitate the financial reorganization of major industrial undertakings by taking over temporary holdings and consolidated loans may also be found to constitute aid to the undertakings concerned.[66] Imperfections in the capital market do not affect such a finding.[67] Equally, exemption of a particular undertaking from a tax on profits may constitute aid, even though the undertaking has never made any profits to be taxed, at least where it has prospects of being profitable in the future.[68] On the other hand, tax concessions compensating the French Post Office for the costs involved in performance of public service obligations relating to the provision of a rural postal service do not constitute aid, because the costs are greater than the tax concessions.[69]

More particularly, special depreciation rules,[70] failure by the public authorities to take proceedings to enforce tax debts,[71] or any divergence from the ordinary procedure for recovering tax debts[72] may constitute aid, as may exemption from rules requiring a delay in making VAT deductions. Such an exemption allows the beneficiary to deduct immediately the VAT it has paid to suppliers compared to the normal situation under which deduction can only be made later. It thus enables the recipient to earn extra interest at the expense of the state.[73] Moreover, while inadvertent adoption of a wrong valuation for tax-

---

[65] Dec. 73/263 ([1973] OJ L253/10) on the tax concessions granted, pursuant to Art. 34 of French Law 65–66 and to the Circular of 24 Mar. 1967, to French undertakings setting up business abroad. This position has support in the ECJ. See Mancini AG in Case 290/83 *EC Commission* v. *France: aid to poor farmers* [1985] ECR 439, 442; and Case C–387/92 *Banco de Crédito Industrial SA* v. *Ayuntamiento de Valencia* [1994] ECR I–877, I–908.

[66] Bull. EC 7/8–1982, 2.1.35. See also the *Tenth Report on Competition Policy* (EC Commission, Brussels, 1981), 153.

[67] Notice C49/91 (E15/90) ([1992] OJ C22/6) regarding a general aid scheme in the Netherlands entitled 'Regeling Bijzondere Financiering'. Cf. the argument advanced regarding such imperfections and state financing of public undertakings in K. Hellingman, 'State Participation as State Aid under Art. 92 of the EEC Treaty: The Commission Guidelines' (1986) 23 *CMLRev.* 111–31, 119.

[68] Aid E3/93 ([1993] OJ C163/5) proposing appropriate measures to abolish the tax exemptions in favour of TAP.

[69] Bull. EU 1/2–1995, 1.3.39.

[70] Letter E/93 ([1993] OJ C289/2) proposing action to be taken in respect of fiscal aid given to German airlines in the form of a depreciation allowance.

[71] Dec. 91/144 ([1991] OJ L73/27) on aid granted by the Greek Government to a cement manufacturer (Halkis Cement Company).

[72] Notice C20/92 (ex NN18/92) ([1992] OJ C198/9) concerning aid which Spain planned to grant to Fundix SA.

[73] Dec. 92/35 ([1992] OJ L14/35) requiring France to suspend the implementation of aid in favour of the Pari Mutuel Urbain, introduced in breach of Art. 93(3) EC.

assessment purposes may not constitute aid,[74] aid may be present where a state agency knowingly persists in a misapplication of a legislative provision having such a consequence.[75]

On the other hand, a Union arrangement for exemption under certain conditions from a charge of compulsory and uniform application throughout the Union is not treated as aid.[76] Certain tax repayments also fall outside Article 92 because they are covered by Article 96 of the Treaty, but the latter provision is to be narrowly interpreted.[77]

Relief from Social Security Charges

Assistance with,[78] or reduction of,[79] social security payments or the waiving by a social security institution of its preferential rights as a creditor[80] may constitute aid.[81] This may be so where the state assists an undertaking in meeting its obligations under employment legislation or collective agreements with trades unions to provide redundancy benefits and/or early-retirement pensions.[82] Coverage by the state of early-retirement costs involves the grant of aid equivalent to the total value of the minimum legal indemnities otherwise payable by the employer on dismissal of the workers concerned.[83] Aid may also

[74] But see D. Lasok, 'State Aids and Remedies under the EEC Treaty' [1986] *ECLR* 53–60.
[75] Lord Oliver of Aylmerton in *R.* v. *A-G, ex p. Imperial Chemical Industries PLC* [1987] 1 CMLR 72, 105–6.
[76] Dec. 90/197 ([1990] OJ L105/15) on an aid granted in France to cereal farmers and producers, financed by the reimbursement of specific fiscal and parafiscal charges.
[77] *Fifteenth Report on Competition Policy* (EC Commission, Brussels, 1986), 182. See, e.g., Dec. 92/129 ([1992] OJ L47/19) on aid granted by the Italian Government to the forestry, pulp, paper and board industry and financed by means of levies on paper, board and cellulose.
[78] Dec. 80/932 ([1980] OJ L264/28) concerning the partial taking-over by the state of employers' contributions to sickness insurance schemes in Italy; and Dec. 83/245 ([1983] OJ L137/24) on an aid scheme in favour of the textile and clothing industry in France.
[79] Notice ([1984] OJ C149/3) concerning the Greek Currency Committee Dec. 1574/80 and its amendments, in particular Dec. 350/82 and the reduction of the employer's share of social security charges attributable to exports which was unavailable to a small number of undertakings as an alternative aid measure.
[80] Notice C9/95 (ex NN121/94) ([1995] OJ C282/3) regarding aid which Spain had granted to Tubacex.
[81] During negotiation of the Treaty it was apparently considered that social security matters would not be covered by Art. 92. See S. Neri and H. Sperl, *Traité instituant la Communauté Économique Européenne* (ECJ, Luxembourg, 1960), 230–1. See also J. Mégret, n. 6 above, iv, 382.
[82] Community Guidelines on State Aid for Rescuing and Restructuring Firms in Difficulty ([1994] OJ C368/12), para. 3.2.5. See also Dec. 94/374 ([1994] OJ L170/36) on Sicilian Law 23/1991 concerning extraordinary assistance for industry and Art. 5 of Sicilian Regional Law 8/1991 concerning, in particular, financing for Sitas; Dec. 90/70 ([1990] OJ L47/28) concerning aid provided by France to certain primary processing steel undertakings; Notice C58/91 (NN144/91) ([1992] OJ C73/2) concerning aid awarded by the German Government to Carl Zeiss Jena, Jenoptik, and Jaener Glaswerks; and Notice ([1987] OJ C78/5) regarding aid which the Italian Government has decided to grant to ports.
[83] Dec. 93/627 ([1993] OJ L309/21) concerning aid granted by the Spanish authorities on the occasion of the sale by Cenemesa/Cademesa/Conelec of certain selected assets to Asea-Brown Boveri.

be involved where in particular industries the state covers the cost of benefits provided by undertakings to redundant workers going beyond the statutory or contractual obligations of the undertakings.[84] Thus aid is involved where the state covers the costs of paying wages to beneficiaries of social programmes between the time of acceptance of the programmes by the workers' council and their implementation.[85] Even payments made directly to workers may constitute aid, where the effect is to reduce the social charges otherwise payable by an undertaking,[86] as may aid paid to bodies other than the undertaking itself, where the latter benefits through the reduction in its social security charges resulting from the jobs cut.[87]

On the other hand, Member States' general social security schemes under which redundancy benefits and retirement pensions are paid directly to redundant workers do not involve aid.[88] Moreover, the Commission 'is not likely to object to [public finance] in respect of the salaries and indemnities that the workers would otherwise not have received'.[89] In such connections, the Commission recognizes the need to take account of disparities in Member States' social legislation as regards the obligations imposed on firms.[90] Where the assistance goes to workers employed by a firm which has ceased to exist and its liabilities are not taken over by a new firm,[91] or where assistance is provided in connection with payments to workers on a reduced working week,[92] no aid is present.

[84] Though such aid is usually authorized 'because the workers are then the primary beneficiaries of the aid'. See Notice C7/95 (N412/94) ([1995] OJ C262/16) concerning the aid the German Government intended to grant to Maschinenfabrik Sangerhausen i. K., Sachsen-Anhalt.

[85] Bull. EC 6–1989, 2.1.91. See, similarly, regarding the social costs related to closure of a steel plant, Bull. EC 9–1988, 2.1.59.

[86] Notice C19/91 (ex NN8/91) ([1993] OJ C68/3) concerning aid which the Spanish Government decided to grant to Victorio Luzuriaga SA (Vilusa); and Dec. 91/1 ([1991] OJ L5/18) concerning aids in Spain which the central and several autonomous governments had granted to Magefesa, producer of domestic articles of stainless steel and small electric appliances. But cf., regarding general aid schemes for recruitment and training, Dec. 93/193 ([1993] OJ L85/22) on the aid granted for the creation of industrial enterprises in Modane, Savoy (France).

[87] Notice C19/91 (NN8/91) ([1991] OJ C182/10) concerning aid which Spain planned to grant to Victorio Luzuriaga SA (Vilusa).

[88] H. Morch, 'Summary of the Most Important Recent Developments' (1994) 3 *Competition Policy Newsletter* 61–6, 63.

[89] Notice C1/95 (NN144/94) ([1995] OJ C144/13) concerning aid provided by the Spanish authorities to Suzuki-Santana Motor SA in support of the motor vehicle plant of that car manufacturer in Linares (Andalucia).

[90] *Twenty-Fourth Report on Competition Policy*, (n. 43 above, 173). See, e.g., regarding payments to redundant workers and to their pension fund, Notice C58/91 (NN144/91) ([1992] OJ C73/2) concerning aid awarded by the German Government to Carl Zeiss Jena, Jenoptik, and Jaener Glaswerk.

[91] Dec. 92/328 ([1992] OJ L182/94) concerning aid granted by the French Government for the disposal of the assets of the MFL Group (producer of heavy-duty machine tools).

[92] Communic. C43/86 (ex NN69/86) ([1990] OJ C162/10) concerning aid awarded by the French authorities to UFAM (Usines et Fonderies Arthur Martin), at Revin. In finding no aid to be present in Notice C35/91 (ex N658/90) ([1993] OJ C59/4) concerning aid which Italy had decided to grant to the alkaline salts industry, the Commission also noted that there was no legal obligation on the undertaking to pay the benefits.

Reduced Returns

Failure by the state to maximize the return on its capital may constitute aid. A normal rate of return is defined with reference where possible being made to that of comparable private companies.[93]

Thus a state commitment to place future public contracts with a particular company[94] may involve aid, as may free advertising made available by a public undertaking to a subsidiary;[95] provision of logistical and commercial assistance without 'the normal payment' being required;[96] the sale of land at a price below the market value;[97] and a contribution towards the cost of developing land to be sold to a private company where the expected selling price would not have covered even half the cost.[98] Similarly, the letting of plant at a rent too low to cover servicing costs or at a rent below the market rate[99] or abnormally low rents for airport infrastructure;[100] may involve aid.

The behaviour of a public authority in disposing of an asset to a commercial interest, trading in the Union, should correspond to the rationale of a private vendor operating under normal market economy conditions.[101] A 'break-even approach' on the part of the public authority does not exclude the possibility of aid being involved.[102] Unless the Member State has undertaken all efforts to sell the property in question comparable with an open bid procedure, acceptance of any sale price below the market price involves the grant of aid.[103]

Likewise, there may be aid where the state pays too much to purchase land from an undertaking, though 'obligatory compensation for . . . intrusion in

---

[93] Application of Arts. 92 and 93 EC and Art. 5 of Dir. 80/723 to public undertakings in the manufacturing sector ([1991] OJ C273/2), para. 43.

[94] *Twentieth Report on Competition Policy* (EC Commission, Brussels, 1991), 169. Cf. Lenz AG in Case C–21/88 *Du Pont de Nemours Italiana SpA* v. *Unità Sanitaria Locale 2 di Carrara* [1990] ECR I–889, I–913.

[95] *Twenty-Second Report on Competition Policy* (EC Commission, Brussels, 1993), 249–50.

[96] Jacobs AG in Case C–39/94 *Syndicat Français de l'Express International (SFEI)* v. *La Poste*, Opinion of 14 Dec. 1995.

[97] *First Report on Competition Policy* (EC Commission, Brussels, 1972), 126. Although land normally accounts for only a small part of investment costs, subsidized prices could upset the delicately balanced differentials in the level of regional incentives and so disrupt regional policy. See the *Twenty-Third Report on Competition Policy*, n. 17 above, 248.

[98] Bull EU 1/2–1995, 1.3.55. Notice C20/94 (N27/94) ([1995] OJ C283/2) concerning aid for the development of the site occupied by Kimberly-Clark Industries at Toul/Villey-Saint-Etienne (Meurthe-et-Moselle).

[99] Case T–95/94 *Chambre Syndicale Nationale des Entreprises de Transport de Fonds et Valeurs (Sytraval) and Brinks France SARL* v. *EC Commission* [1995] ECR II–2651, II–2672.

[100] Para. 44 of application of Arts. 92 and 93 EC and Art. 61 EEA to state aids in the aviation sector ([1994] OJ C350/5).

[101] Dec. 92/11 ([1992] OJ L6/36) concerning aid provided by the Derbyshire County Council to Toyota Motor Corporation.

[102] *Ibid.* See also Notice C66/91 (NN154/91) ([1992] OJ C48/3) regarding aid which Germany had decided to grant to Sony GmbH.

[103] Notice C36/92 (ex NN108/92) ([1994] OJ C21/4) concerning the terms of a land purchase agreement between the City of Friedberg/Hessen and Fresenius AG.

property rights' does not constitute aid.[104] In particular, the ratio of rent charged by a public body to private users to the price paid by the former body to purchase leases held by these users may be such as to involve aid, at least if the premises would have reverted to the public body without cost when the leases expired.[105]

A preferential tariff fixed by a public authority for a particular customer or class of customers can also constitute aid if it results in the state receiving less revenue.[106] The apparent implication is that the Commission can require that a minimum tariff necessary to eliminate the aid is fixed.[107] However, a preferential tariff may be objectively justified on commercial grounds, such as cost savings, the need to resist competition on the same market from other sources of supply,[108] or economies of scale, though the magnitude of the tariff reduction must be reasonably related to production costs.[109] Aid may also be found to be absent where tariff reductions benefit Union customers who are facing strong competition from third-country undertakings, regard being had to the trade deficit and liberalization of trade with third countries.[110] In this connection, account may be taken of 'downstream' competitive pressures on customers.[111]

In general, a tariff involves no aid where it covers costs and allows for a profit margin for the public authority concerned,[112] or at least for the authority to

[104] See, regarding aid to farmers alongside a meadowland nature reserve, *European Report* 2048 (10 June 1995). See also Bull. EU 6–1995, 1.3.60, regarding compensation for damage suffered as a result of a unilateral decision of the regional authorities.

[105] *Fifteenth Report on Competition Policy* (EC Commission, Brussels, 1986), 199. Cf. the *Tenth Report on Competition Policy* (EC Commission, Brussels, 1981), 123.

[106] Dec. 82/73 ([1982] OJ L37/29) on the preferential tariff charged to glasshouse growers for natural gas in the Netherlands; and Dec. 85/215 ([1985] OJ L97/49) on the preferential tariff charged to glasshouse growers for natural gas in the Netherlands. The latter decision was upheld by the ECJ in Case 213/85 *EC Commission* v. *Netherlands* [1988] ECR 281 and Joined Cases 67, 68 & 70/85 *Kwekerij Gebroeders van der Kooy BV, Johannes van Vliet, Landbouwschap and Belgium* v. *EC Commission* [1988] ECR 219.

[107] A. Evans, 'Energy Pricing and Community Law: *Kwekerij Gebroeders van der Kooy BV, Johannes Wilhelms van Vliet, the Landbouwschap and the Netherlands; Commission* v. *Netherlands* (1988/ 89) *OGLTR* 70–1. Cf., regarding the increases in French electricity prices required by the Commission, *Financial Times*, 12 Oct. 1989.

[108] [1988] ECR 219, 270. See also Case C–169/84 *Société CdF Chimie azote et fertilisants SA and Société chimique de la Grande Paroisse SA* v. *EC Commission* [1990] ECR I–3083; and Case C–56/93 *Belgium* v. *EC Commission: natural gas tariff* [1996] ECR I–723.

[109] Notice C38/92 (NN128/92) ([1993] OJ C75/2) regarding aid which Italy had decided to grant to EFIM.

[110] Dec. (N546/93 & N595/93) ([1994] OJ C35/6) concerning the price for gas used by industry as a raw material.

[111] *Ibid.*

[112] Case C–313/90 *Comité International de la Rayonne et des Fibres Synthétiques (Cirfs)* v. *EC Commission* [1993] ECR I–1125, I–1146. According to the Commission, there is no aid where prices cover 'both variable and fixed costs, once general profitability is ensured'. See Notice C50/93 ([1992] OJ C344/4) regarding a preferential tariff system applied to the Netherlands for supplies of natural gas to Dutch nitrate fertilizer products. However, discriminatory charges may be prohibited by Arts. 90(1) and 86 EC. See, regarding discounts from airport landing charges in Belgium, Dec. 95/364 ([1995] OJ L216/8) relating to a proceeding pursuant to Art. 90(3) EC.

which the profit must be remitted.[113] Extension of a preferential tariff to undertakings in other Member States may be taken to suggest that the tariff is a normal response to market needs and commercial pressures rather than a politically motivated aid.[114] It is also recognized that in the interests of long-term profits, short-term losses may be commercially justified.[115]

The underlying principle was expressed by the Commission in 1963. According to the Commission, the renunciation by the state of a return on capital would constitute aid where a private investor would not be willing to renounce, or would only partially renounce, his return. The renunciation would do so, because it would result not from commercial considerations but from those of a political character.[116]

In the above practice the aid definition applied sometimes takes as its starting-point the effects for the state. Sometimes the starting-point may be the effects for the recipient. Often the result may be unaffected by the choice of starting-point. For example, *Amministrazione delle Finanze dello Stato* v. *Denkavit Italiana Srl*[117] concerned the repayment of sums unlawfully levied by the Italian authorities as charges having equivalent effect to customs duties on products from other Member States. According to Advocate General Reischl, the repayment of the charges was not aid, because there was 'no distribution of state resources'.[118] On the other hand, the Court of Justice ruled in the same case that such a repayment was not aid, because undertakings received no advantages to encourage the attainment of the economic or social objectives sought.[119]

In some cases the choice of starting-point may be decisive for treatment of state action. For example, the Commission doubted whether a Dutch state participation scheme was covered by Article 92, because it was not clear that the undertakings in which the state participated would benefit.[120] Moreover, support for publicity campaigns to increase general environmental awareness and provide specific information about, for example, selective waste collection, conservation of natural resources or environmentally friendly products may fall outside this provision where the support is so general in scope and distant from the market place as not to confer an identifiable financial benefit on specific firms.[121] Similarly, measures to encourage final consumers (firms and

---

[113] Fenelly AG in Case C–56/93 *Belgium* v. *EC Commission: natural gas tariff* [1996] ECR I–723, I–728.

[114] *Ibid.*   [115] *Ibid.*

[116] Reply to Written Question 48 ([1963] JO 2235) by Mr Burgbacher.

[117] Case 61/79 [1980] ECR 1205. See also Case 811/79 *Amministrazione delle Finanze dello Stato* v. *Ariete SpA* [1980] ECR 2545, 2555.

[118] [1980] ECR 1205, 1235. See also, regarding the decisive significance of a 'cost' to the state, Jacobs AG in Joined Cases C–278/92, C–279/92 & C–280/92 *Spain* v. *EC Commission: Intelhorce* [1994] ECR I–4103, I–4112.

[119] [1980] ECR 1205, 1228. See also Case T–471/93 *Tierce Ladbroke SA* v. *EC Commission* [1995] ECR II–2537, II–2558.

[120] Bull. EC 9–1979, 2.1.28.

[121] Community guidelines on state aid for environmental protection ([1994] OJ C72/3), para. 3.3.

individuals) to purchase environmentally friendly products may fall outside, because they do not confer a tangible financial benefit on particular firms.[122]

The underlying issues may take on prominence in relation to damages which the national authorities may be ordered to pay to undertakings in compensation for harm they have caused to the latter. The Court of Justice has ruled that such damages do not constitute aid within the meaning of Article 92,[123] because the undertakings are not favoured thereby. Similar views have been expressed in relation to payment of legal costs[124] and damages awarded by arbitrators.[125] However, to hold that aid is never involved in such circumstances may be problematic.[126] If a recipient could successfully sue the national authorities for damages following their recovery of illegal aid, such recovery would be effectively frustrated.[127]

Further problems may arise, because it is not only the effects for direct beneficiaries which are to be taken into account. For example, the Commission considers that compensation for German electricity producers for using coal rather than oil falls outside Article 92(1), because these producers gain no advantage over other electricity producers.[128] However, the Commission recognizes that aid is implied for the coal industry.[129]

2.2.2 Coercive Measures

Whichever starting-point for definition of state aid is adopted, financial resources must be found to be involved. Apparently, Article 92 is interpreted as being exclusively concerned with state 'use'[130] of financial resources rather than with state regulation of the use of such resources by others.[131]

---

[122] *Ibid.* para. 3.5.

[123] Joined Cases 106 & 120/87 *Asteris AE* v. *Greece and the EEC* [1988] ECR 5515, 5540.

[124] Darmon AG in Case C–189/91 *Petra Kirsammer-Hack* v. *Nurhan Sidal* [1993] ECR I–6185, I–6201.

[125] Notice C35/91 (ex N658/90) ([1993] OJ C59/4) concerning aid which Italy had decided to grant to the alkaline salts industry.

[126] Slynn AG [1988] ECR 5515, 5530. Cf. also Dec. 95/524 ([1995] OJ L300/23) concerning aid granted by the Italian State to Iritecna SpA.

[127] Slynn AG in Joined Cases 106–120/87 *Asteris AE* v. *Greece and the EEC* [1988] ECR 5515, 5530. See also, regarding a claim for damages for negligent failure to apply for aid subsequently found by the Commission to be prohibited, *Lener Ignace* v. *Dominique Beauvois* [1994] 2 CMLR 419 (French Cour de Cassation).

[128] *Seventh Report on Competition Policy* (EC Commission, Brussels, 1978), 180.

[129] Dec. 89/296 ([1989] OJ L116/52) ruling on a financial measure taken by Germany in respect of the coal industry during 1988 and a supplementary financial measure in respect of the coal industry during 1987. See, later, Dec. 90/632 ([1990] OJ L346/18) and Dec. 90/633 ([1990] OJ L346/20).

[130] The expression 'use' is found in Case 259/85 *France* v. *EC Commission: aid to textiles and clothing* [1987] ECR 4393, 4418. Cf. the reference in S. Lehner and R. Meiklejohn, 'Fair Competition in the Internal Market' (1991) 48 *European Economy* 7–148, 53 to 'resources controlled' by public authorities.

[131] The concept of measures having equivalent effect to aid is not recognized by the ECJ (Case 290/83 *EC Commission* v. *France: aid to poor farmers* [1985] ECR 439, 450).

This interpretation does not preclude the possibility that use of Union resources may constitute aid,[132] at least in so far as the Member States have some discretion in the disbursement of such resources.[133] This possibility seems to be recognized in Regulation 2052/88.[134] Article 7(1) of this measure provides that 'measures financed by the Structural Funds . . . shall be in conformity with the provisions of the Treaties, with the instruments adopted pursuant thereto and with Community policies, including those concerning the rules on competition'.[135]

The situation may be more complicated where private resources are involved. According to the Court of Justice, aid need not necessarily be financed from state resources to be classified as aid.[136] More particularly, according to Article 1(2) of Decision 3632/93,[137] assistance to the coal industry may constitute aid, even if there is no 'burden on public budgets'. Assistance does not lose the character of an aid by the fact that it is wholly or partly financed by contributions imposed by the public authority and levied on the undertakings concerned.[138] Hence, state use of a levy may constitute aid. For example, Decision 89/296[139] concerned levies on sales of coal, which were used to compensate electricity producers in Germany for the higher costs of using Union coal rather than fuel oil or imported coal. Since the scheme, though 'not financed directly from public funds, [was] nevertheless paid for through levies that [were] obligatory as a result of government action',[140] it was treated as involving the grant of aid.[141]

---

[132] Notice on the *de minimis* rule for state aid ([1996] OJ C68/9).

[133] VerLoren van Themaat AG in Joined Cases 213–215/81 *Norddeutsches Vieh- und Fleischkontor Herbert Will Trawako, Transit-Warenhandels-Kontor GmbH & Co., and Gedelfi Grosseinkauf GmbH & Co.* v. *Bundesanstalt für Landwirtschaftliche Marktordnung* [1982] ECR 3583, 3617–8.

[134] On the tasks of the Structural Funds and their effectiveness and on co-ordination of their activities between themselves and with the operations of the European Investment Bank and the other existing financial instruments ([1988] OJ L185/9), as amended by Reg. 2081/93 ([1993] OJ L193/5).

[135] It has also been recognized by the ECJ that aid granted pursuant to Union legislation may have to be 'clawed back', to prevent artificial disparities in prices and distortion of competition. See Case 106/81 *Julius Kind KG* v. *EEC* [1982] ECR 2885. Cf. Case 12/57 *Syndicale de la Sidérurgie du Centre-Midi* v. *ECSC High Authority* [1957–8] ECR 374, 392, where the ECJ left open the question whether Art. 4(c) ECSC bound the Union.

[136] Case 290/83 *EC Commission* v. *France: aid to poor farmers* [1985] ECR 439, 449.

[137] Establishing Community rules for state aid to the coal industry ([1993] OJ L329/12).

[138] Case 78/76 *Firma Steinike und Weinlig* v. *Germany* [1977] ECR 595, 611.

[139] Ruling on a financial measure taken by Germany in respect of the coal industry during 1988 and a supplementary financial measure in respect of the coal industry during 1987 ([1989] OJ L116/52).

[140] See also Dec. 90/632 ([1990] OJ L346/18) concerning a financial measure taken by Germany in respect of the coal industry in 1988; and Dec. 93/66 ([1993] OJ L21/33) concerning financial measures by Germany in respect of the coal industry in 1990, 1991, and 1992 and also additional financial aid for the coal industry in 1989 and 1990.

[141] Hence, the transfer of the financial burden of a scheme to the state budget may be regarded merely as increasing aid transparency. See Dec. 93/147 ([1993] OJ L58/60) concerning the authorization of financial measures by Germany in respect of the coal industry in 1993.

In *Sloman Neptun*[142] the Commission sought to go further.[143] It argued that the exemption of non-residents employed on German-registered ships from German labour law, including minimum pay requirements, constituted aid.[144] The Court of Justice, however, ruled that no aid was present. The exemption conferred no advantage constituting a charge on the state, but only altered the framework for labour relations in the shipping industry.[145] Again, in *Kirsammer-Hack*[146] the Commission argued that exemption of small companies from unfair dismissal legislation constituted aid.[147] However, the Court of Justice ruled that no aid was present, because the exemption only concerned the legislative framework for labour relations in small companies.[148] In both cases state regulation of the use of resources by others rather than the use of resources by the state itself was apparently assumed to be present.[149]

Such distinctions between types of state intervention could find some support in the economics literature. The literature suggests that 'the closer the impact of the policy weapon to the source of the trouble, the more likely it is to be successful in curing it'.[150] In practice, however, to disassociate regulation of economic activity from the grant of aid may not always be easy.[151]

Minimum Price Controls

The Court of Justice ruled in *Van Tiggele*,[152] which concerned Dutch legislation regulating prices for spirits, that the fixing of minimum prices by the state did not involve the grant of state aid. The reason, according to the Court, was that advantages accruing to certain producers were 'not granted directly or indirectly through state resources in the meaning of Article 92(1)'.[153] According to Advocate General Capotorti, there was no aid because there was no 'burden on the public finances in the form either of expenditure or of reduced revenue'.[154]

However, subsequent Commission practice recognizes that 'regulatory subsidies' may be present where the state imposes minimum prices in a particular sector which are above market prices.[155] Thus a legislative power to align the

---

[142] Joined Cases C–72/91–C–73/91 *Sloman Neptun Schiffahrts AG* v. *Seebetriebsrat Bodo Ziesemer der Sloman Neptun Schiffahrts AG* [1993] ECR I–887.

[143] See, generally, M. M. Slotboom, 'State Aid in Community Law: Broad or Narrow Definition?' [1995] *ELR* 289–301.

[144] [1993] ECR I–887, I–900–1.   [145] *Ibid.*, I–934.

[146] Case C–189/91 *Petra Kirsammer-Hack* v. *Nurhan Sidal* [1993] ECR I–6185.

[147] *Ibid.*, I–6192–3.   [148] *Ibid.*, I–6220.

[149] Cf. the requirement that where the state is the main shareholder of a bank in crisis, its role as shareholder must be separated from its role as the supervisory authority required to safeguard confidence in the banking system in Dec. 95/547 ([1995] OJ L308/92) giving conditional approval to the aid granted by France to Crédit Lyonnais.

[150] R. H. Snape, 'The Importance of Frontier Barriers' in H. Kierzkowski (ed.), *Protection and Competition in International Trade* (Blackwell, Oxford, 1987) 215–32, 217.

[151] Cf. regarding the problems that may arise where a bank 'friendly' to a government pays an inflated price for state-owned assets, *European*, 28 Sept.–4 Oct. 1995.

[152] Case 82/77 *Openbar Ministerie* v. *Jacobus Philippus Van Tiggele* [1978] ECR 25.

[153] *Ibid.*, 41.   [154] *Ibid.*, 52.

[155] Lehner and Meiklejohn, n. 130 above, 17.

prices of newsprint purchased from several manufacturers in favour of the least competitive has been found by the Commission to involve aid.[156] The Commission also considered that the modification to the Danish Electricity Act to allow the national electricity company to cover past losses on certain commercial activities through higher electricity prices involved aid, as the electricity prices were controlled by the state and electricity consumers, due to the monopoly of this company on the supply of electricity, had no other choice but to accept the price increase.[157] Similarly, the coal reference price system, by which some Member States keep domestic prices above world market prices, has been treated as involving the grant of aid[158] or at least as having 'an effect equivalent to an aid',[159] as has the fixing of a minimum price for electricity generated from renewable energy sources.[160]

Maximum Price Controls

Maximum price controls[161] entail advantages for purchasers of the product concerned in the form of lower costs. Characterization of such advantages as aid is supported by the opinion of Advocate General VerLoren van Themaat in *BALM*,[162] though the question at issue in this case was whether allocation of a share in a Union tariff quota constituted state aid, and the Court of Justice answered the question in the negative. According to the Advocate General, the independent grant by the state of pecuniary advantages which were not paid for by the state might constitute aid.[163] Examples given by the Advocate General included reduced rates which a Member State might require private electricity companies or haulage contractors to apply, with reimbursement, to certain undertakings or in respect of certain products.[164]

French imposition of a ceiling on diesel fuel prices for fishermen, which involved compensation for the distributors to the extent that the market price exceeded the ceiling, was subsequently found by the Commission to entail aid

---

[156] Bull. EC 7/8–1987, 2.1.115. See also Communic. ([1988] OJ C306/6) regarding the aid measures of the Italian Government on the newsprint market comprising elements of aid for national manufacturers.

[157] H. Morch, 'Summary of the Most Important Recent Developments' [1995] 4 *Competition Policy Newsletter* 47–51, 49.

[158] *Second Survey on State Aids in the European Community in the Manufacturing and Certain Other Sectors* (EC Commission, Brussels, 1990), 21–2.

[159] *Fourth Survey on State Aids in the European Community in the Manufacturing and Certain Other Sectors*, n. 3 above, 37.

[160] *Twentieth Report on Competition Policy* (EC Commission, Brussels, 1991), 291.

[161] Cf. the non-committal reply of the Commission to the question whether differentiated limits on advertising by television companies could involve the grant of aid in the Reply by Mr Van Miert to Written Question E–2477/94 ([1995] OJ C196/1) by Fausto Bertinotti.

[162] Joined Cases 213–215/81 *Norddeutsches Vieh- und Fleischkontor Herbert Will Trawako, Transit-Warenhandels-Kontor GmbH & Co., and Gedelfi Großeinkauf GmbH & Co.* v. *Bundesanstalt für Landwirtschaftliche Marktordnung* [1982] ECR 3583.

[163] See, e.g., Dec. 89/296 ([1989] OJ L116/52) on financial measures taken by Germany in respect of the coal industry.

[164] [1982] ECR 3583, 3617.

for fishermen.[165] Selective authorizations of price rises have been similarly classified.[166] A Belgian scheme to allow pharmaceutical firms to raise prices (which were partly reimbursed to consumers under the social security system) in return for an undertaking to increase laboratory research, investment and employment in Belgium was similarly regarded.[167]

The Court of First Instance has gone further. In *Sytraval*[168] this Court found that fuel price reductions introduced 'at the behest of the government' constituted aid. The Court did not apparently treat the presence of aid as conditional on the compensation of undertakings which reduced their prices.

On the other hand, the possibility that maximum price controls also involve the grant of aid, because direct tax revenue may be reduced,[169] has been rejected by the Court of Justice. In *Sloman Neptune*[170] lower social security contributions were received by the state in the case of employees in respect of which exceptions from the minimum wage were permitted. The Court, reflecting the overlap between the definition of aid and the favouritism condition in Article 92(1), found no aid to be present because undertakings did not gain any specific advantage. Reduced receipts for the state were the result of decisions by individual workers and were in the nature of the system.[171]

Overlapping Treaty Provisions

The fact that regulation as well as state use of financial resources is involved does not prevent application of Article 92 to the latter. Even compatibility of regulation with the Treaty does not necessarily mean that associated aid falls outside Article 92.[172] For example, the fact that the system of imposition of tax may be compatible with Article 95 of the Treaty does not affect the Commission's appraisal of the aid funded by it having regard to Article 92.[173] Moreover,

---

[165] Dec. 86/592 ([1986] OJ L340/22) on the system of ceilings on the price of diesel fuel for fishermen introduced by the French Government.

[166] Dec. 92/327 ([1992] OJ L182/89) concerning aid granted by the Belgian Government to undertakings in the pharmaceutical industry in the form of programme contracts. Cf. the account taken of the fixed domestic price for cement in Communic. C2/88 (ex NN126/87) ([1992] OJ C1/4) concerning aid to Heracles General Cement Company in Greece.

[167] *Sixteenth Report on Competition Policy* (EC Commission, Brussels, 1987), 151. See also, regarding authorization of a price increase to enable a Danish utility to cover losses sustained through diversification activities, the *Twenty-Fourth Report on Competition Policy* (EC Commission, Brussels, 1995), 165.

[168] Case T–95/94 *Chambre Syndicale Nationale des Entreprises de Transport de Fonds et Valeurs (Sytraval) and Brinks France SARL* v. *EC Commission* [1995] ECR II–2651, II–2671.

[169] Cf. Slynn AG in Joined Cases 67, 68 & 70/85 *Kwekerij Gebroeders Van der Kooy BV* v. *EC Commission* [1988] ECR 219, 250, regarding the loss of revenue from corporate taxes suffered by the state, where a public body reduces its prices.

[170] Joined Cases C–72/91 & C–73/91 *Sloman Neptune Schiffahrts AG v. Seebetriebsrat Bodo Ziesemer der Sloman Neptune Schiffahrts SA* [1993] ECR I–887.

[171] *Ibid.*, I–934.

[172] Cf. Dec. 93/49 ([1993] OJ L20/14) relating to a proceeding pursuant to Art. 85 (IV/33.814—Ford/Volkswagen), para. 16, where the Commission referred to a decision not to raise any objections to proposed Portuguese aid to the joint venture concerned.

[173] Case 47/69 *France* v. *EC Commission: aid to textiles* [1970] ECR 487, 495. See also Dec. 91/

according to Article 54(3), the Council and Commission shall carry out their duties regarding the elimination of restrictions on freedom of establishment, in particular 'by satisfying themselves that the conditions of establishment are not distorted by aids granted by Member States'.[174] The apparent implication is that compatibility of national regulation with Articles 52–58, which concern freedom of establishment, does not preclude the possibility that aid contrary to Article 92 may be present.

Conversely, the mere fact that state use of financial resources may be involved does not prevent application to regulatory measures of the Article 30 prohibition of quantitative restrictions and measures having equivalent effect on imports between Member States,[175] the Article 13(2) prohibition of charges having equivalent effect to a customs duty on such imports,[176] the prohibition of discrimination by state trading monopolies in Article 37,[177] or the Article 95 prohibition of discriminatory taxation. Hence, discriminatory fiscal practices are not exempt from the application of Article 95 on the ground that they might be classified at the same time as a method of financing state aid.[178] Nor is the subjection of aid recipients to Article 85 or 86 precluded,[179] since the application of Article 92 must not produce a result which is contrary to specific provisions of the Treaty.[180]

Such provisions seek the same ends—the free movement of goods under 'normal' conditions of competition—as Article 92. However, they do not make the same provision for aid authorization as Article 92(2) and (3), and their

538 ([1991] OJ L294/43) on the animal health and production fund in Belgium: and Dec. 95/486 ([1995] OJ L227/10) concerning aid and compulsory contributions to promote market outlets for poultry and rabbit farming products in Belgium.

[174] See, e.g., Dec. 73/263 ([1973] OJ L253/10) on the tax concessions granted, pursuant to Art. 34 of French Law 65–566 of 12 July 1965 and to the Circular of 24 Mar. 1967, to French undertakings setting up abroad. Cf., regarding the free movement of workers and freedom to supply services, Dec. 89/441 ([1989] OJ L208/38) on aid granted by the Greek Government to the film industry for the production of Greek films.

[175] Case 74/76 *Iannelli and Volpi S.p.A.* v. *Ditta Paolo Meroni* [1977] ECR 557, 576. Case 249/81 *EC Commission* v. *Ireland: 'Buy Irish' campaign* [1982] ECR 4005, 4021; and Case 103/84 *EC Commission* v. *Italy: aid for the purchase of Italian vehicles* [1986] ECR 1759, 1774. See, similarly, Case 18/84 *EC Commission* v. *France: tax advantages for newspaper publishers* [1985] ECR 1339, 1348. See, most recently, Case C–21/88 *Du Pont de Nemours Italiana SpA.* v. *Unità Sanitaria Locale No. 2 di Carrara* [1990] ECR I–889, I–922.

[176] Case 77/72 *Carmine Capolongo* v. *Azienda Agricola Maya* [1973] ECR 611, 623.

[177] Case 91/78 *Hansen GmbH* v. *Hauptzollamt Flensburg* [1979] ECR 935, 953; Case 17/81 *Pabst and Richarz* v. *Hauptzollamt Oldenburg* [1982] ECR 1331, 1348; and Case 253/83 *Sektkellerei C.A. Kupferberg & Cie KG* v. *Hauptzollamt Mainz* [1985] ECR 157, 185.

[178] Case 277/83 *EC Commission* v. *Italy: tax concessions for production of Marsala* [1985] ECR 2049, 2058. See also Case 73/79 *EC Commission* v. *Italy: tax on sugar* [1980] ECR 1533, 1547; and Joined Cases 142 & 143/80 *Amministrazione delle Finanze dello Stato* v. *Essevi SpA and Carlo Salengo* [1981] ECR 1413, 1436.

[179] In Dec. 93/126 ([1993] OJ L50/14) (IV/33.151—VIK-GVSt) an agreement was exempted for the purposes of Art. 85 EC and Art. 65 ECSC, but this decision was expressed to be without prejudice to assessment of the compatibility of aid to the German coalmining industry with the ECSC Treaty (Art. 2 of the Dec.).

[180] Case C–225/91 *Matra SA* v. *EC Commission* [1993] ECR I–3203, I–3260.

application may not be prejudiced by any such authorization.[181] Hence, the technique employed by a state to provide support may affect its legality.[182] The role of national courts and their relations with the Commission may also be affected, given that provisions such as Articles 13(2), 30, and 95 of the Treaty, but not Article 92,[183] are directly effective before such courts. These results may reflect a general tendency of the Court of Justice to adopt a more strict approach to regulatory than to financial measures.[184]

2.2.3 General State Interventions

Problems may arise in distinguishing the grant of aid from the operation of general fiscal rules, social security measures, conjunctural policy measures,[185] and so on.[186] Ultimately, the problems raised may merge with those of determining whether state use of financial resources is involved.[187]

The established position of the Court of Justice is that Article 92 does not distinguish between measures of state intervention by reference to their causes or aims but requires evaluation of such measures in relation to their effects.[188] Thus, for example, according to the Court, aid may be present where a particular industrial sector is exempted from the normal application of a general social security system, without there being any justification for the exemption in the nature or general scheme of the system.[189]

In accordance with the case law, the Commission considers that measures which have neither as their object nor their effect the favouring of certain

---

[181] Dec. 88/167 ([1988] OJ L76/18) concerning Law 1386/1983 by which the Greek Government granted aid to Greek industry. See also Joined Cases C–134/91 & C–135/91 *Kerafina-Keramische und Finanz-Holding AG and Vioktimatiki AEVE* v. *Elliniko Dimisio and Organismos Oikonomikis Anasygkratissis Epicheirisseon AE* [1992] ECR I–5699, I–5720.

[182] This result may be controversial. See J. M. F. Martin and O. Stehmann, 'Product Market Integration versus Regional Cohesion in the Community' (1991) 16 *ELRev.* 216–43.

[183] See sect. 7.6.5 below.

[184] Cf. Case 72/83 *Campus Oil* v. *Minister for Industry and Energy* [1984] ECR 2727, 2754. However, where it is a question of influencing the choice of an undertaking as between different possible locations within the same Member State, regulatory measures may be preferred by the Commission. See Notice C1/93 (N724/92) ([1993] OJ C75/7) concerning aid granted by the Italian Government (autonomous province of Trento) to Cartiere del Garda.

[185] Darmon AG in Case 310/85 *Deufil GmbH & Co. KG* v. *EC Commission* [1987] ECR 901, 915.

[186] During negotiation of the Treaty France insisted that aid to compensate for the costs of pursuing general interest duties was not covered by Art. 92. See S. Neri and H. Sperl, n. 81 above, 231. Problems of distinguishing may be most pronounced where a general aid scheme (see sect. 3.6 below) is present.

[187] Case C–189/91 *Petra Kirsammer-Hack* v. *Nurhan Sidal* [1993] ECR I–6185, I–6220.

[188] Case 173/73 *Italy* v. *EC Commission: aid to textiles* [1974] ECR 709, 719. See also Case 310/85 *Deufil GmbH & Co. KG* v. *EC Commission* [1987] ECR 901, 924; and Slynn AG in Case 84/82 *Germany* v. *EC Commission: Belgian aid to textiles* [1984] ECR 1451, 1501.

[189] Case 173/73 *Italy* v. *EC Commission: aid to textiles* [1974] ECR 709, 719. See also Case 310/85 *Deufil GmbH & Co. KG* v. *EC Commission* [1987] ECR 901, 923–4. See, generally, the *Second Survey on State Aids in the Community in the Manufacturing and Certain Other Sectors* (EC Commission, Brussels, 1990), 4–5.

undertakings or the production of certain goods, or which apply to persons in accordance with objective criteria without regard to the location, sector, or undertaking in which the beneficiary is employed do not involve aid.[190] For example, the suspension of debt repayments in favour of a Spanish steel company did not in itself constitute aid, but a general measure taken within the framework of Spanish insolvency legislation applicable to all companies.[191] The generality of the measure concerned within the Union as a whole may be relevant in such evaluations. For example, exemptions from duty of imported materials used in shipbuilding 'are common in all Member States and therefore they constitute a part of the economic environment in the Community'. Hence, aid is not present.[192] On the other hand, a Finnish employment aid scheme available to all undertakings in every sector of industry and every region of the country did constitute aid within the meaning of Article 92(1), because the authorities could decide on a discretionary basis the level of aid and the length of the subsidized period for each unemployed person taken on by a company.[193] In practice, the evaluations may often be more problematic than such decisions suggest.

Taxation Systems

Tax concessions that apply throughout the tax system and are available automatically and without any exercise of discretion in the economy as a whole constitute general intervention outside the scope of Article 92(1).[194] For example, tax concessions for industrial investment in Portugal, covering a percentage of investment undertaken in a given year and the whole of retained profits reinvested in the business concerned, constituted general tax changes which did not fall under this provision.[195] Similarly, German assistance with social security charges based on a general measure, the application of which left no discretionary power to the public authorities, was not covered thereby.[196]

On the other hand, concessions limited to a very short period of time, involving restrictions as to the size of the beneficiary and allowing the government a wide discretion are likely to be treated as aid.[197] Accordingly, a

---

[190] Notice on co-operation between national courts and the Commission in the state aid field ([1995] OJ C312/8), para. 7.

[191] H. Morch, 'Summary of the Most Important Recent Developments' (1995) 4 *Competition Policy Newsletter* 47–51, 49.

[192] Notice C10/91, C11/91 & C12/91 (ex NN54/90, NN56/90 & NN58/90) ([1991] OJ C123/16) regarding aid which Greece has granted to shipbuilding in the period 1987 to 1990.

[193] Morch, n. 191 above, 49.

[194] Art. 99 provides for harmonization of tax rules affecting trade between Member States. Moreover, in Case 249/81 *EC Commission* v. *Ireland: 'Buy Irish' campaign* [1982] ECR 4005 the Commission argued that state action favouring all domestic products against imports was too general to be caught by Art. 92(1) (*ibid.*, 4015), though the Court avoided ruling on the issue.

[195] Bull. EC 2–1987, 2.1.56.

[196] Notice C7/95 (N412/94) ([1995] OJ C262/16) concerning aid the German Government intended to grant to Maschinenfabrik Sangerhausen, GmbH i.K., Sachsen-Anhalt.

[197] *Twentieth Report on Competition Policy* (EC Commission, Brussels, 1991), 180. See also Dec.

divergence from the general system for contributions to unemployment insurance funds;[198] tax relief in favour of export earnings;[199] selective reductions that favour certain firms compared with others, whether such selectivity is at individual, sectoral or regional level;[200] and tax relief applicable to products derived from certain agricultural materials, which bestows an advantage on a given product[201] have been so treated.

As the Commission puts it, a tax measure falls under Article 92(1) where it constitutes a departure from the generally accepted or benchmark tax system, which produces favourable tax treatment for particular types of activities or groups of taxpayers. Thus where, in accordance with normal national practice in relation to holdings, tax credits result from the before-tax losses of one part of the group being offset against profits of other parts, the credits do not constitute aid. Tax credits granted by way of exception from such practice constitute aid.[202] Again, tax reliefs granted in certain development areas are regarded as aid, whereas the rate structure is regarded as an integral part of the benchmark tax system.[203] Not only are enterprises in other Member States put at a competitive disadvantage by the aid, because the aided undertakings are favoured in a way outside the normal fiscal or social security systems that contribute to the equilibrium between Member States, but also undertakings not receiving aid in the same Member State are disadvantaged and pay higher taxes directly or indirectly.[204]

However, in some cases such departures from the benchmark system are on the borderline between aid within the meaning of Article 92(1) and general

93/625 ([1993] OJ L300/15) concerning aid granted by the French Government to the Pari mutuel urbain and to the racecourse undertakings; and Dec. 92/389 ([1992] OJ L207/47) concerning the state aid provided for in Decree–Laws 174 of 15 May 1989 and 254 of 13 July 1989 and in the draft Law 4230 regularizing the effects produced by these Decree–Laws.

[198] Case T–95/94 *Chambre Syndicale Nationale des Entreprises de Transport de Fonds et Valeurs (Sytraval) and Brinks France SARL* v. *EC Commission* [1995] ECR II–2651, II–2671.

[199] Dec. 89/659 ([1989] OJ L394/1) relating to Ministerial Dec. E3789/128 of the Greek Government establishing a special single tax on undertakings.

[200] Notice C21/92 (NN26/92) ([1992] OJ C240/7) concerning aid granted by Italy to certain regions of the Mezzogiorno. See, regarding selective reductions in Italy, Bull. EC 11–1972, 80.

[201] Communic. C43/94 (ex NN49/93) ([1994] OJ C365/3) concerning aids which Italy has decided to grant to producers and processors of oil-seeds with a view to encouraging the production of biofuels. Special taxation arrangements, such as Petroleum Revenue Tax in the UK, may apply to certain sectors and thus be problematic. See C. Quigley, 'The Notion of State Aid in the EEC' [1988] *ECLR* 242–56, 256. Cf. Capotorti AG in Case 249/81 *EC Commission* v. *Ireland: 'Buy Irish' campaign* [1982] ECR 4005, 4031.

[202] Notice C56/95 (N941/95) ([1996] OJ C75/2) concerning aid that Spain planned to grant its publicly-owned shipbuilding yards.

[203] See, e.g., in the case of aircraft acquisition, Communic. C41/93 (E4/93 & N640/93) ([1994] OJ C16/3) on fiscal aid given to German airlines in the form of a depreciation facility.

[204] *Second Survey on State Aids in the European Community in the Manufacturing and Certain Other Sectors* (EC Commission, Brussels, 1990), 7.

measures.[205] The Commission considers that further work has to be carried out in order to elucidate this 'grey area'.[206]

Training Systems

Assistance provided by the public authorities for education, including vocational training, does not usually constitute aid within the meaning of Article 92(1).[207] For example, training aid awarded not to undertakings but to employed persons or job seekers does not do so.[208] Moreover, an employment-grant scheme operated by local labour-market boards on a non-discretionary and non-selective basis falls outside the scope of Article 92(1).[209] More particularly, training aid for the unskilled and long-term unemployed is not covered, since it is 'intended to overcome the difficulties that some workers encounter when seeking employment because they have no training or else the wrong training'.[210] Such practice is supported by the Court of Justice, which accepts that assistance with training not for the exclusive benefit of an undertaking falls outside Article 92(1).[211]

However, where specific training is involved, falling outside the general system of education and vocational training and corresponding to the particular needs of a given undertaking, sector, or region, a contribution by the public authorities to training costs may constitute aid. It will do so, unless the training is mainly provided outside the firm by specialized bodies or leads to qualification levels recognized by industry agreements.[212]

The rationale for the distinction in the Treaty between aid and general state interventions and the greater willingness to tolerate the latter are based, according to the Commission, on a recognition to date that it is not the aim of competition policy to try to remove fundamental differences between national cost structures which contribute to the wider economic and social framework within which firms operate in each Member State. Where there are differences in the role of the state in the economy and the provision of public goods, there will also be differences in the overall level of taxation. To try to remove such

---

[205] Cf. the apparent finding that reductions in tax and social payments for Swedish seamen did not constitute aid of the kind covered by Art. 92. See *Sverige–EFTA–EG 1988* (Utrikes-departementets Handelsavdelning 1989), 52.

[206] *Second Survey on State Aids in the European Community in the Manufacturing and Certain Other Sectors*, n. 204 above, Technical Annex, 10; and *Fourth Survey on State Aids in the European Community in the Manufacturing and Certain Other Sectors*, COM(95)365, 58.

[207] Dec. 91/390 ([1991] OJ L215/11) on aid granted by the French Government to the undertaking Saint-Gobain (Eurofleet) at Salaisse-sur-Sanne (glass sector).

[208] Dec. 93/193 ([1993] OJ L85/22) on the aid granted for the creation of industrial enterprises in Modane, Savoy (France).

[209] Bull. EC 1/2–1993, 1.2.72.

[210] Bull. EC 7/8–1979, 2.1.31.

[211] Case C–225/91 *Matra SA* v. *EC Commission* [1993] ECR I–3203, I–3257.

[212] Notice C20/94 (NN27/94) ([1994] OJ C170/8) concerning aid for the development of the site occupied by Kimberly Clark Industries at Toul/Villey-St-Etienne (Meurthe-et-Moselle).

differences would undermine the basis for mutually beneficial trade.[213] Conversely, since social security costs in a Member State form part of that framework, differences in relative burdens for undertakings cannot in themselves justify the granting of aid.[214]

Commission thinking reflects that in the Spaak Report.[215] According to this Report, the varying burden on the economy of individual countries arising from, for example, taxation or social security systems did not in itself distort the terms of competition, since such differences tended to be balanced out by general foreign trade relations, in particular the rate of exchange.[216] In any case, an approximation of basic conditions would, it was expected, result from the development of the common market itself and from the interaction of market forces and the relations between the participants.

Commission thinking may also take account of Articles 101 and 102 of the Treaty.[217] Article 101 concerns differences between national provisions distorting conditions of competition in the common market and where the distortion needs to be eliminated. Article 102 concerns planned provisions of this kind. They thus concern provisions, such as those of tax and social security systems, having effects which are not specific to certain firms or products.[218] Specificity[219] or selectivity[220] is thus said to distinguish what is covered by Article 92 from the 'generic distortions of competition'[221] with which Articles 101 and 102 are concerned.[222]

However, provisions concerned only with the effects of general measures

---

[213] *Second Survey on State Aids in the European Community in the Manufacturing and Certain Other Sectors* (EC Commission, Brussels, 1990), 6–7. However, according to *Distortions of Competition in Hothouse Agriculture*, COM(80)306, 32, Art. 103 (conjunctural policy) or Art. 104 (balance of payments) in the original version of the EEC Treaty might be applicable.

[214] *Twelfth Report on Competition Policy* (EC Commission, Brussels, 1983), 127.

[215] Comité intergouvernemental créé par la conférence de Messine, *Rapport des Chefs de Délégation aux Ministres des Affaires Etrangères* (Secretariat of the Comité, Brussels, 1956), 64–5.

[216] For example, the Commission took view that aid to offset the high interest rates payable by shipbuilders in Italy was prohibited because the shipbuilders were compensated by the weakness of the Lire. See Dec. 88/281 ([1987] OJ L119/33) on aid for shipbuilding and ship repair in Italy—Art. 10 of Law 111 of 22 Mar. 1985.

[217] See, regarding these provisions, P. Collins and M. Hutchings, 'Articles 101 and 102 of the EEC Treaty: Completing the Internal Market' [1986] 11 *ELR* 191–9.

[218] *First Survey on State Aids in the European Community in the Manufacturing and Certain Other Sectors* (EC Commission, Brussels, 1989), 5–6. See also J.A. Winter, *Nationale Steuenmaatregeln en het Gemeenschapsrecht* (Kluwer, Deventer, 1981), 227.

[219] Darmon AG in Joined Cases 72 & 73/91 *Sloman Neptune Schiffahrts AG v. Seebetriebsrat Bodo Ziesemer der Sloman Neptune Schiffahrts SA* [1993] ECR I–887, I–916. See also H.-W. Rengeling, 'Das Beihilferecht der Europäischen Gemeinschaften' in B. Borner and K. Neundorfer (eds.), *Recht und Praxis der Beihilfen im Gemensamen Markt* (Heymann, Cologne, 1984), 23–54, 29.

[220] R. Barents, 'Recente ontwikkelingen in de rechtspraak over steunmaatregelen' [1988] *SEW* 352–64, 356.

[221] Case 173/73 *Italy* v. *EC Commission: aid to textiles* [1974] Raccoltà della Giurisprudenza della Corte 709, 720 (the English translation is wrong).

[222] See, similarly, regarding the distinction between aid and conjunctural policy measures under Art. 103 EC, Darmon AG in Case 310/85 *Deufil GmbH & Co. KG* v. *EC Commission* [1987] ECR 901, 915.

may have limited utility. For example, according to the Commission, Article 101 cannot apply to the distortions in horticulture which result from the fixing of prices for petroleum products at different levels. It would be arbitrary to take in isolation one of the general conditions under which undertakings operate in a Member State, such as fuel prices, while ignoring the impact of other general conditions affecting production, such as social security payments, direct taxation, and credit conditions.[223]

Division of Powers

Ultimately issues requiring determination of the relations between state powers and Union powers are raised.[224] For example, according to the Court of First Instance, the choice of the French legislature concerning the organization of the national market in taking bets on horse races could not itself be impugned as contrary to Article 92(1).[225] Moreover, according to the Commission, training aid is not covered by Article 92, where it is strictly limited to time spent in training and not in productive employment. As such, it constitutes performance of the responsibility of the state in the field of vocational education.[226] Again, monetary policy remains, at least for the moment, largely the province of Member States. The latter may implement this policy, provided they do not grant preferential interest rates[227] or other forms of aid.[228]

2.2.4 Infrastructure Provision

The provision by public authorities of infrastructure which is traditionally covered by the state budget does not constitute aid in the sense of Article 92.[229]

---

[223] *Distortions of Competition in Hothouse Agriculture*, COM(80)306, 33.

[224] Cf. the application of Art. 92 to aid to financial institutions, subject to the proviso that 'account [is] taken of the possible impact on financial markets' in Notice C26/95 (NN52/95) ([1995] OJ C121/4) regarding aid which France had decided to grant to the bank Crédit Lyonnais. See also the *Twenty-Fourth Report on Competition Policy* (EC Commission, Brussels, 1995), 188.

[225] Case T–471/93 *Tiercé Ladbroke SA* v. *EC Commission* ([1995] ECR II–2537, II–2560. Cf., as regards VAT harmonization and social policy, Case 415/85 *EC Commission* v. *Ireland: VAT zero-rating* [1988] ECR 3097, 3120. Cf. also, regarding sport, A. Evans, 'Freedom of Trade under the Common Law and European Community Law: The Case of the Football Bans' (1986) 102 *LQR* 510–42.   [226] *Ninth Report on Competition Policy* (EC Commission, Brussels, 1980), 121.

[227] Joined Cases 6/69 & 11/69 *EC Commission* v. *France: preferential rediscount rate for exporters* [1969] ECR 523, 539–40. See also Dec. 86/187 ([1986] OJ L136/61) on aids granted by Greece in the form of interest rebates in respect of exports of all products with the exception of petroleum products.

[228] Case 57/86 *Greece* v. *EC Commission: interest rebates on export credits* [1988] ECR 2855, 2872. Cf., the rejection of the German argument based on Art. 104 EC by Darmon AG in Case 248/84 *Germany* v. *EC Commission: regional aid* [1987] ECR 4013, 4030–1 and by the Commission in Dec. 87/15 ([1987] OJ L12/17) on the compatibility with the common market of aid under the German Federal/*Land* Government Joint Regional Aid Programme in six labour market regions. Cf., earlier, Case 95/81 *EC Commission* v. *Italy: advanced payments for imported goods* [1982] ECR 2187, 2199, regarding Arts. 104 and 30 EC.

[229] *Seventeenth Report on Competition Policy* (EC Commission, Brussels, 1988), 143; Bull. EC

Thus support for hospitals,[230] the building of schools, prisons and public offices,[231] housing construction,[232] transport infrastructure,[233] port administration,[234] decontamination,[235] logistic supply bases for oil exploration rigs,[236] or for fundamental research, designed generally to increase scientific and technical knowledge and not carried out in an undertaking,[237] falls outside Article 92. Similarly, research contracts put out to tender,[238] and the financing of agencies engaged in research on a non-profit-making basis, such as universities, are not covered by Article 92.[239] Thus, for example, low-interest loans for the importation of scientific instruments and 'high tech' goods by research institutes do not constitute aid.[240] Nor is aid present where assistance is for infrastructural improvements not intended to benefit a particular undertaking[241] or where the company will contribute to the costs through local taxes.[242] Such practice is supported by the Court of Justice, which considers that provision of infrastructure not for the exclusive benefit of a given undertaking falls outside Article 92.[243]

However, assistance to private operators who provide the infrastructure may be covered by Article 92(1). Thus assistance for the protection of parks and

3–1987, 2.1.80; *Second Survey on State Aids in the European Community in the Manufacturing and Certain Other Sectors* (EC Commission, Brussels, 1990), Annex II, para. 2.1.

[230] Commission Reply to Written Question 564/91 ([1991] OJ C227/29) by Mr Antony.

[231] Notice C27 & 28/90 (ex NN71 & 73/89) ([1992] OJ C181/5) concerning interest subsidies on loans to small and medium-sized industrial and commercial enterprises and works projects and miscellaneous assistance schemes.

[232] *Sixth EEC General Report* (EEC Commission, Brussels, 1963), 68.

[233] See, regarding aid for airports, motorways, and bridges aimed at meeting planning needs or implementing national environmental and transport policies, Application of Arts. 92 and 93 EC and Art. 61 EEA to state aids in the aviation sector ([1994] OJ C350/5), para. 12.

[234] Dec. 94/374 ([1994] OJ L170/36) on Sicilian Law 23/1991 concerning extraordinary assistance for industry and Art. 5 of Sicilian Regional Law 8/1991 concerning, in particular, financing for Sitas.

[235] Communic. C62/91 (NN75, 77, 78, 79/91) ([1992] OJ C68/14) concerning the proposal by the German Government to award state aid to the Volkswagen group in support of its investment plans in the new *Länder* and Communic. C60/91 (NN73/91 & 76/91) ([1992] OJ C68/2) concerning the proposal by the German Government to award state aid to the Opel group in support of its investment plans in the new *Länder*.

[236] *Ibid.*

[237] Dec. 91/500 ([1991] OJ L262/29) concerning aid granted to enterprises in the Friuli–Venezia Giulia region.

[238] Bull. EC 3–1988, 2.1.72.

[239] *Second Report on Competition Policy* (EC Commission, Brussels, 1973), 105.

[240] Dec. 72/261 ([1972] JO L166/12) on aids for the importation of scientific instruments and advanced technology goods, granted under Italian Law 471 of 14 July 1969; and Notice C52/91 (N484/91) ([1992] OJ C22/8) concerning the Belgian Government's notification of a draft order of the Brussels region on economic growth and scientific research.

[241] Dec. 91/390 ([1991] OJ L215/11) on aid granted by the French Government to the undertaking Saint-Gobain (Eurofleet) at Salaisse-sur-Sanne (glass sector).

[242] *Seventeenth Report on Competition Policy* (EC Commission, Brussels, 1988), 220.

[243] Case C–225/91 *Matra SA* v. *EC Commission* [1993] ECR I–3203, I–3257. Van Gerven AG (*ibid.*, I–3235) also relied on the fact that the undertaking would, like other undertakings, pay for the infrastructure services in the future.

nature reserves falls under this provision, when it is granted to farmers to carry out the work.[244] Aid may also be present where infrastructure is provided for the benefit of one or more particular undertakings or productive activities[245] rather than being open to all potential users who pay the charges prescribed by legislation,[246] or where assistance is provided to specific companies when using the infrastructure.[247] Thus aid to enable local authorities to buy sites for industrial building may be covered by Article 92.[248]

Where infrastructures, such as the connection of an industrial site to the public railway system,[249] renewal of a sewage system and site preparation prior to the start of construction work,[250] usually have to be built by the private sector,[251] their provision by public authorities may also be covered.[252] In principle, the purchaser of the site should bear the costs of such work.[253] Hence, soil replacement, pile-driving, and filling-in should be paid by the site purchaser, but the local authority may provide sewerage, energy, and water supply services.[254] In practice, the Commission may distinguish between external and internal development of a site and only treat assistance with the latter as aid.[255]

Moreover, aid may be present where state-supported research is carried out by,[256] or in collaboration with, firms[257] or under contracts with firms,[258] the

[244] Notice C31/92 (N454/91) ([1992] OJ C324/3) concerning aid granted by Italy for the reconstruction of the Valtellina.

[245] Commission Reply to Written Question 28 ([1967] JO 2311) by Mr Dehousse; Notice C20/94 (NN27/94) ([1994] OJ C170/8) concerning aid for the development of the site occupied by Kimberly Clark Industries at Toul/Villey-St-Etienne (Meurthe-et-Moselle). The criterion may be expressed as that of discrimination. See *Sixth EEC General Report* (EEC Commission, Brussels, 1963), 71.

[246] Notice C35/91 (ex N658/90) ([1993] OJ C59/4) concerning aid which Italy had decided to grant to the alkaline salts industry.

[247] Cf., regarding assistance for the second Munich airport, the Reply by Mr Kinnock to Written Question E–1347/95 ([1995] OJ C222/68) by Wolgang Kreissl-Dorfer.

[248] Bull. EC 2–1970, 66.

[249] Where a public railway company assists with the costs of building or maintaining railway sidings but recoups its losses through the freight rates later charged and there are no cross-subsidies, aid is not involved. See the *Twenty-Third Report on Competition Policy* (EC Commission, Brussels, 1994), 246.

[250] Communic. C60/91 (ex NN73/91, NN76/91) ([1993] OJ C43/14) regarding the proposal by the German Government to award state aid to the Opel group in support of its investment plans in the new *Länder*.

[251] See, regarding port, electricity, and rail services, the summary of the Commission Decision not to raise objections to the aid which the Portuguese Government planned to grant to the joint venture of Ford and Volkswagen to establish a multipurpose vehicle plant in the Setubal peninsula ([1991] OJ C257/5).

[252] C. Quigley, n. above, 253.   [253] Bull. EC 7/8–1986, 2.1.72.

[254] *Seventeenth Report on Competition Policy* (EC Commission, Brussels, 1988), 166; and the *Sixteenth Report on Competition Policy* (EC Commission, Brussels, 1987), 185.

[255] Notice C41/94 (ex NN37/94) ([1994] OJ C369/6) concerning aid which Germany had granted to Fritz Egger Spanplattenindustrie GmbH & Co. KG at Brilon.

[256] Case 47/69 *France* v. *EC Commission: aid to textiles* [1970] ECR 487, 502.

[257] Notice C53/91 (N529/91) ([1992] OJ C10/4) regarding aid which Germany had decided to grant in the laser research sector. See, regarding joint financing of a research institute, where the

[*See p. 54 for n. 257 cont. and n. 258*]

agencies act on a contract basis[259] or research services are provided at prices which do not reflect their real costs.[260] The fact that services may be provided at market prices does not necessarily eliminate any aid element.[261]

2.2.5 Nationalization

Serious definitional problems[262] may arise from exercise by a Member State of its freedom under the Treaty to nationalize.[263] The implication is that state investment is not automatically contrary to Article 92.[264] Not only capital injections but also 'other forms of public funds' provided to public undertakings, such as loans, guarantees,[265] and the waiver of debts, may be involved.[266] Although such investment is normally dictated by exigencies going beyond the profit motive, this factor is inherent in public ownership, the 'existence and special nature of which are confirmed' by Article 222 of the Treaty,[267] and it cannot alone justify the bringing into play of Article 92.[268] For example, as the Commission recognizes, the provision of capital, loans, or guarantees by a government to an airline which it owns may constitute an aid, a normal commercial transaction between the owner of an enterprise, and that enterprise or a mixture of the two.[269] Such provision is only covered by Article 92 where it has 'the effect of aids'.[270] Disputes may arise between Directorate General IV

---

company concerned could exercise an option for an exclusive licence for developing and commercially exploiting any invention that might result from these activities, H. Morch, 'Summary of the Most Important Recent Developments' (1994) 3 *Competition Policy Newsletter* 61–6, 62.   [258] Bull. EC 5–1993, 1.2.40.

[259] Notice C52/91 (N484/91) ([1992] OJ C22/8) concerning the Belgian Government's notification of a draft order of the Brussels region on economic growth and scientific research. See, generally, the *Twentieth Report on Competition Policy* (EC Commission, Brussels, 1990), 238.

[260] In Communic. ([1990] OJ C239/10) regarding aid which Italy had decided to grant in order to compensate the losses of the state-owned yard Fincantieri for 1987 and 1988 and Law 234/89 providing for aid to shipbuilding, state financing of R & D was allowed, pending the outcome of a studies of conditions under which research contracts were awarded to universities.

[261] Notice C48/94 (NN104/94 (ex N514/92)) ([1995] OJ C161/5) regarding aid which the French Government had decided to grant to 'Institut Français du Pétrole'.

[262] *Second Report on Competition Policy* (EC Commission, Brussels, 1973), 127.

[263] This freedom is respected by the Commission. See Commissioner Andriessen (EP Debs., No. 1–275, 121, 14 Oct. 1981) and the Reply to Written Question 1156/81 ([1982] OJ C38/10) by Mr Damseaux.

[264] Case 323/82 *S.A. Intermills* v. *EC Commission* [1984] ECR 3809, 3830.

[265] Application of Arts. 92 and 93 EC and of Art. 5 of Dir. 80/723 to Public Undertakings in the Manufacturing Sector ([1991] OJ C273/2), paras. 1 and 23 (n. 24).

[266] Communic. C26/86 & C43/87 ([1990] OJ C198/2) regarding aid which France had decided to grant to the chemical undertaking CDF Chimie (Orkem).

[267] *Second Report on Competition Policy* (EC Commission, Brussels, 1973), 127.

[268] The Italian Government, in particular, apparently objects to the treatment of capital injections in industry as aid. See the *Second Survey on State Aids in the European Community in the Manufacturing and Certain Other Sectors* (EC Commission, Brussels, 1990), 9.

[269] *Progress towards the development of a Community air transport policy*, COM(84)72, 38.

[270] *Second Report on Competition Policy* (EC Commission, Brussels, 1973), 109.

and the Directorate for Transport, which is responsible for controlling aid to airlines, about whether such an effect is involved.[271]

Attempts to clarify the applicability of Article 92 may be made in Union legislation. In particular, Article 1(4) of Decision 3632/93[272] defines as aid 'financing measures taken by Member States in respect of coal undertakings which are not regarded as risk capital provided to a company under standard market-economy practice'. Similarly, Article 1(2) of Decision 3855/91[273] defines as aid state financing measures in respect of steel undertakings which the state directly or indirectly owns, where they 'cannot be regarded as a genuine provision of risk capital according to usual investment practice[274] in a market economy'.

The Commission has sometimes gone further and referred to a presumption of aid, where the state invests in a company,[275] or at least where the financial situation of the company concerned is such as to preclude a normal return[276] from the invested capital within a reasonable time.[277] This presumption can only be rebutted where the behaviour of the state is found to be compatible with that of a private investor operating under normal market conditions,[278] and is 'compelling' where the sector concerned is in difficulties or suffering from structural overcapacity.[279]

Whether or not such a presumption is fully reflected in Commission practice, the latter seeks to distinguish between state investment,[280] which may be made without being subject to Union supervision, and the granting of aid by public authorities to promote the public good, which is supervised under

[271] See, e.g., regarding a French capital injection in Air France, the *Financial Times*, 11 July 1992. See also the Resolution of the European Parliament of 20 Apr. 1993 ([1993] OJ C150/34) on the Commission's report on the evaluation of aid schemes established in favour of Community air carriers, para. 17.

[272] Establishing Community rules for state aid to the coal industry ([1993] OJ L329/12).

[273] Establishing Community rules for aid to the steel industry ([1991] OJ L362/57).

[274] Art. 1(2) of Dec. 322/89 ([1989] OJ L38/8) establishing Community rules for aid to the steel industry referred to 'standard company practice', as does Art. 1(d) of Dir. 90/684 ([1990] OJ L380/27) on aid to shipbuilding.

[275] Dec. 96/75 ([1996] OJ L15/31) concerning aid granted by the Flemish region of Belgium to the truck producer DAF; and Dec. 96/76 ([1996] OJ L15/37) concerning aid granted by the Netherlands to the truck producer DAF.

[276] The Commission may quantify what it considers would be an acceptable return to a private investor. See Dec. 96/278 ([1996] OJ L104/25) concerning the recapitalization of the Iberia company.

[277] Notice C39/94 (ex NN55/94) ([1994] OJ C328/2) regarding aid which Italy had decided to grant to Iritecna SpA.

[278] Notice C3/92 (ex N645/91) ([1992] OJ C105/16) concerning possible state aid elements contained in agreements between the Dutch State, Volvo Car Corporation, and Mitsubishi Motors Corporation.

[279] Community guidelines on state aid for rescuing and restructuring firms in difficulty ([1994] OJ C368/12), para. 2.3.

[280] A grant which does not affect the level of equity capital cannot be regarded as an investment. See Dec. 89/633 ([1989] OJ L367/62) concerning aid provided or to be provided by the Spanish Government to Enasa, an undertaking producing commercial vehicles under the brand 'Pegasus'.

Article 92.[281] However, although the Union has special rules designed to facilitate detection of the grant of aid to public undertakings,[282] problems of distinguishing state investment from state aid may remain.

Private-Investor Test

To distinguish between state investment and state aid covered by Article 92, the Commission considers whether the provision of state finance is necessitated by the unwillingness of the private sector to provide it. Hence, the concept of necessity is said to be 'inherent in that of aid'.[283] The same test is used to quantify the aid. According to paragraph 11 of a 1991 Communication,[284] 'the aid must be assessed as the difference between the terms on which the funds were made available by the state to the public enterprise and the terms which a private investor would find acceptable in providing funds to a comparable private undertaking when the private investor is operating under normal market conditions'.

In the view of the Commission, this test—the private-investor test—is necessary to uphold the principle of neutrality with regard to the system of property ownership and the principle of equal treatment[285] between public and private undertakings.[286] This view is accepted by the Court of Justice.[287]

In application of the test reliance may be placed on objective criteria, such as that of scale.[288] According to this criterion, state investment has to be regarded as aid where its scale is greater than that which would be acceptable to the private sector. In the view of the Commission, the scale of a state investment may be evidence that the undertaking concerned would have been unable to

---

[281] Lenz AG in Case 40/85 *Belgium* v. *EC Commission: Boch* [1986] ECR 2321, 2328 and in Case 234/84 *Belgium* v. *EC Commission: Meura* [1986] ECR 2263, 2270.

[282] Dir. 80/723 ([1980] OJ L195/35, as amended by Dir. 85/413, [1985] OJ L229/20 and Dir. 93/84, [1993] OJ L254/16) on the transparency of financial relations between Member States and public undertakings. Even when an aid scheme is authorized, any acquisition of share-holdings pursuant to the scheme may have to be specially notified to the Commission. See, in the case of a Belgian scheme, Bull. EU 11–1995, 1.3.51.

[283] Darmon AG in Case C–400/92 *Germany* v. *EC Commission: Cosco* [1994] ECR 4701, 4717.

[284] Application of Arts. 92 and 93 EC and of Art. 5 of Dir. 80/723 to public undertakings in the manufacturing sector ([1991] OJ C273/2).

[285] *Ninth Report on Competition Policy* (EC Commission, Brussels, 1980), 103.

[286] Application of Arts. 92 and 93 EC and of Art. 5 of Dir. 80/723 to public undertakings in the manufacturing sector ([1991] OJ C273/2), para. 11. See, earlier, the *Second Report on Competition Policy* (EC Commission, Brussels, 1973), 125–7. In relation to credit institutions, the principle is embodied in Art. 104(2) EC, as amended by the TEU. See also Art. 90(2) EC, regarding undertakings entrusted with the operation of services of general economic interest or having the character of a revenue-producing monopoly.

[287] Joined Cases 188–190/80 *France, Italy, and the UK* v. *EC Commission: transparency directive* [1982] ECR 2545, 2577–8. See also Case 304/85 *Acciaierie e Ferriere Lombarde Falck* v. *EC Commission* [1987] ECR 871, 896.

[288] VerLoren van Themaat AG in Case 323/82 *S.A. Intermills* v. *EC Commission* [1984] ECR 3809, 3841.

raise the sums concerned on the capital market.[289] The length of the investment may also be important,[290] it being supposed that the private sector would not be attracted by such long-term investments as the state might be prepared to make.[291] On the other hand, temporary state funding of losses of a publicly owned undertaking may be unobjectionable where the losses reflect conjunctural problems of the sector concerned.[292] However, such criteria merely enable inferences to be drawn about the central question—whether the return on the investment would have been such as to attract private investors.[293]

Efforts squarely to face this question may proceed on the basis of simplified conceptions as to the aims of private investors. Thus, for example, a distinction may be made between 'the purchase of shares by the state . . . as an investment for the purposes of obtaining income or capital appreciation, the aim of the ordinary investor' and their purchase 'merely [as] a vehicle for providing financial support for a particular company'.[294] Similarly, it is said that 'private undertakings determine their industrial and commercial strategy by taking into account in particular requirements of profitability. Decisions of public undertakings, on the other hand, may be affected by factors of a different kind within the framework of the pursuit of objectives of public interest'.[295]

The underlying rationale for the practice is that state financing of public undertakings does not, like financial contributions by private persons to an undertaking, derive from the private property of such persons, which is in all respects subject to commercial risk, but rather directly or indirectly from the resources of the state budget. Hence, the state has resources on a scale unavailable to private businessmen.[296] At the same time, there is the danger

---

[289] Notice C46/94 (NN60/94 and NN92/94) ([1994] OJ C373/5) concerning aid which Italy proposed to grant to Seleco SpA, Pordenone. See also Communic. C65/94 (NN79/93) ([1995] OJ C261/2) on aid granted by Italy to Viamare SpA di Navigazione.

[290] Reischl AG in Joined Cases 188–190/80 *France, Italy, and the UK* v. *EC Commission: transparency directive* [1982] ECR 2545, 2591.

[291] See also Slynn AG in Case 84/82 *Germany* v. *EC Commission: Belgian aid to textiles* [1984] ECR 1451, 1501.

[292] Dec. 88/454 ([1988] OJ L220/30) concerning aid provided by the French Government to the Renault group.

[293] Case 323/82 *S.A. Intermills* v. *EC Commission* [1984] ECR 3809, 3842; Case 234/84 *Belgium* v. *EC Commission: Meura* [1986] ECR 2263, 2286; Case 40/85 *Belgium* v. *EC Commission: Boch* [1986] ECR 2321, 2345; Case C–301/87 *France* v. *EC Commission: Boussac* [1990] ECR I–307, I–361; and Case C–142/87 *Belgium* v. *EC Commission: Tubemeuse* [1990] ECR I–959, I–1012. See also Dec. 87/515 ([1987] OJ L295/25) on aid granted by Germany for the purchase and lease of the Seeadler factory manufacturing fish products in Cuxhaven, Lower Saxony.

[294] Slynn AG in Joined Cases 296 & 318/82 *Netherlands and Leeuwarder Papierwarenfabriek BV* v. *EC Commission* [1985] ECR 809, 811. The Commission had earlier distinguished between *considerations d'ordre économique* and *motifs d'ordre publique* in its Reply to Written Question 48 ([1963] JO 2235) by Mr Burgbacher.

[295] Joined Cases 188–190/80 *France, Italy and the UK* v. *EC Commission: transparency directive* [1982] ECR 2545, 2577.

[296] Lenz AG in Case 234/84 *Belgium* v. *EC Commission: Meura* [1986] ECR 2263, 2271.

that in the use of those resources commercial considerations which a business-man would take into account do not always come into play.[297]

Ultimately, simplified conceptions of the relationship between state and market may be revealed. For example, *Belgium* v. *EC Commission: Meura*[298] concerned capital subscriptions by public authorities in a Belgian producer of equipment for the food industry. Here the Court of Justice accepted Commission characterization of the subscriptions as aid. The Court ruled that any such subscription would constitute aid unless a private shareholder, having regard to the foreseeability of obtaining a return and leaving aside all social, regional-policy, and sectoral considerations, would have made it.[299]

Consistently with this ruling, the Commission has found aid to be involved where the state subscribes capital to support restructuring[300] or acquires holdings in firms to help them until such time as they overcome temporary difficulties, or to achieve regional policy goals.[301] For example, in Decision 95/466,[302] the Commission acknowledged that Flemish authorities might 'wish to take account of the advantage to the Flemish economy of a direct connection between Antwerp and London City airport: but that has nothing whatsoever to do with the behaviour of a rational investor operating in a market economy'. Hence, state financing of an airline providing this connection was treated as aid. In such practice a test based on the conduct of a 'model' investor acting competitively, given what was foreseeable at the time,[303] seems to be envisaged.[304]

This model underlies Commission consideration of the position of the undertaking concerned. In the case of an undertaking under mixed ownership, the conduct of private shareholders, and even that of creditors, may be considered.[305]

---

[297] Reischl AG in Joined Cases 188–190/80 *France, Italy, and the UK* v. *EC Commission: transparency directive* [1982] ECR 2545, 2591.

[298] Case 234/84 [1986] ECR 2263, 2286.

[299] See also Jacobs AG in Joined Cases C–278/92, C–279/92 & C–280/92 *Spain* v. *EC Commission: Intelhorce* [1994] ECR I–4103, I–4113 and I–4139.

[300] Dec. 90/224 ([1990] OJ L118/42) on aid granted by the Italian Government to Aluminia and Comsal, two state-owned undertakings in the aluminium industry.

[301] *Second Report on Competition Policy* (EC Commission, Brussels, 1973), 108.

[302] Concerning aid granted by the Flemish Region to the Belgian airline Vlaamse Lucht-transportmaatschappij NV ([1995] OJ L267/49).

[303] Van Gerven AG in Case C–261/89 *Italy* v. *EC Commission: Aluminia* [1991] ECR I–4437, I–4451.

[304] However, private investors do not act in accordance with written or unwritten rules. See, e.g., M. Dony 'La Participation des pouvoirs publics au capital des entreprises et le droit de la concurrence' [1986] *CDE* 161–84, 169. More fundamentally, according to J. Habermas, *Legitimation Crisis* (Polity Press, Cambridge, 1988), 66, 'large corporations have such a broad temporal and material range of alternatives in which to arrive at their decisions that an investment *policy* (which requires additional premises for its foundation) takes the place of rational choice determined by external data'.

[305] For example, French state investment in a company which had taken over a bankrupt trailer manufacturer was considered to fall outside Art. 92. 40% of the new company was privately owned, and the receiver of the old company had closed part of the latter, rationalized

Position of the Undertaking Concerned

In examining the position of the undertaking concerned, the Commission considers its financial performance, economic and technical efficiency, and commercial strategy for different markets.[306] State financing of an undertaking which is basically viable and only has temporary problems pending conversion,[307] whose financial and economic position is sound, and which has good development potential[308] or which is undergoing a rapid financial recovery[309] is not treated as aid.[310] Such factors as the 'goodwill' enjoyed by an undertaking, the size of its network, and a 'strong presence' on the markets of third countries may also be taken into account.[311] The rationale is that a private shareholder could also be expected to subscribe the capital necessary to secure the survival of an undertaking which is experiencing temporary difficulties but is capable of becoming profitable again, possibly after reorganization. Acceptability of state subscriptions from the perspective of a private shareholder may be confirmed where the undertaking will develop new activities of high technological quality[312] or by subsequent sale of public shares at a profit.[313]

However, state investment involves aid, where, because of its inadequate cash flow, the company would be unable to raise the funds needed on the capital market. Thus aid is present where, in view of the duration and volume of the losses of the recipient, a normal return in dividends or capital gains cannot be expected for the capital provided by the state.[314] Account may also be taken of such factors as an obligation to repay aid previously found by the Commission to be prohibited by Article 92,[315] 'risky' investments made by the company concerned, and its failure to use earlier aid to solve its problems.[316] In the case of a loss-making company, there may be serious doubts whether a

the remainder and reached a settlement with creditors to convert short-term borrowing into medium and long-term loans. See Bull. EC 5–1987, 2.1.82 and the *Seventeenth Report on Competition Policy* (EC Commission, Brussels, 1988), 167.

[306] Application of Arts. 92 and 93 EC and Art. 61 EEA to state aids in the aviation sector ([1994] OJ C350/5), para. 29.

[307] Commission Reply to Question 7 put by the Court in Case 84/82 *Germany* v. *EC Commission: Belgian aid to textiles* [1984] ECR 1451, 1484.

[308] *Eighteenth Report on Competition Policy* (EC Commission, Brussels, 1989), 168.

[309] *Ibid.*, 186.

[310] But cf., where the scale of the investment is regarded as being greater than would have been available on the capital market, Slynn AG in Case 84/82 *Germany* v. *EC Commission: Belgian aid to textiles* [1984] ECR 1451, 1501 and VerLoren van Themaat AG in Case 323/82 *S.A. Intermills* v. *EC Commission* [1984] ECR 3809, 3841.

[311] Notice C14/95 (NN774/94) ([1995] OJ C114/7) concerning a Pta 130 billion capital injection into the Spanish company Iberia.

[312] *Ninth Report on Competition Policy* (EC Commission, Brussels, 1980), 112–3.

[313] *Sixteenth Report on Competition Policy* (EC Commission, Brussels, 1987), 155.

[314] Dec. 89/43 ([1989] OJ L16/52) on aids granted by the Italian Government to ENI–Lanerossi.

[315] Dec. 87/48 ([1987] OJ L20/30) concerning aid in Belgium in favour of the brewery equipment industry.

[316] Notice C14/95 (NN774/94) ([1995] OJ C114/7) concerning a Pta 130 billion capital injection into Iberia.

private investor would make an investment both covering the company's past losses and restoring the company's capital to its pre-existing level without taking remedial actions in the form of restructuring the company's activities or running down the size of its investment to a level commensurate with the risk and return from the investment.[317] If state financing is not expected to render the undertaking concerned profitable, it is likely to be treated as aid.[318] Thus public funds cannot be used regularly to offset the losses of firms.[319] In the case of a company in a 'hopeless' financial position, a private investor would be expected to accept the bankruptcy of the company concerned, if no purchaser for the latter could be found,[320] and would do so at a time when its 'assets/liabilities position still showed a surplus'.[321] For a state shareholder to do otherwise is likely to be treated as constituting the grant of aid.

For example, in Decision 82/312[322] the Commission examined the legality of an acquisition by the Belgian Government of a holding of Bfrs 120 million in a group whose combined balance-sheet showed a deficit of Bfrs 500 million. The Commission concluded that the acquisition of the holding could not be justified by reference to the book value of the group concerned. In another case the Commission considered that a private investor would not have paid almost eleven times his original investment in five years in order to dispose of half of the investment at its nominal price. For the state to do so involved the grant of aid.[323] Again, in view of the accumulated debts and the costs of the restructuring programme, the Commission considered that no investor apart from the state would be prepared to take part in the restructuring of the Belgian airline, Sabena. Hence, state participation in the airline was found to have constituted aid within the meaning of Article 92.[324]

---

[317] Communic. C6/92 (ex NN149/91) ([1992] OJ C122/6) concerning contributions by Italimpianti to CMF SUD SpA.

[318] Dec. 93/133 ([1993] OJ L55/54) concerning aid granted by the Spanish Government to Merco (an agricultural processing company). This practice has the support of the ECJ. See Case C–142/87 *Belgium* v. *EC Commission: Tubemeuse* [1990] ECR I–959, I–1012.

[319] *Ninth Report on Competition Policy* (EC Commission, Brussels, 1980), 93.

[320] Notice C42/94 (ex NN149/94) ([1994] OJ C377/4) with respect to the intended injection of public capital to the equity of Neue Maxhütte Stahlwerke GmbH, Meitingen-Herbertshofen and the intended granting of investment aid to Neue Maxhütte Stahlwerke GmbH.

[321] Notice C6/92 (ex NN149/91) ([1995] OJ C120/4) regarding aid which Italy granted to CMF SUD SpA and CMF SpA; and Dec. 95/524 ([1995] OJ L300/23) concerning aid granted by the Italian State to Iritecna SpA.

[322] Concerning the aid granted by the Belgian Government to an industrial and commercial group manufacturing wall coverings ([1982] OJ L138/18).

[323] Dec. 92/329 ([1992] OJ L183/30) on aid granted by the Italian Government to a manufacturer of ophthalmic products (Industrie Ottiche Riunite).

[324] Dec. 91/555 ([1991] OJ L300/48) on aid to be granted by the Belgian Government in favour of Sabena. See, similarly, Lenz AG in Case 40/85 *Belgium* v. *EC Commission: Boch* [1986] ECR 2321, 2330, regarding state participation in an undertaking in 'a hopeless financial situation' and where 94% of the new capital came from public funds.

Such thinking was summarized in a Commission Communication of 17 September 1984.[325] According to this Communication, aid is present where:

— the financial structure and, in particular, the debt structure of the undertaking concerned mean that a normal return cannot be expected within a reasonable time;[326]

— the undertaking would be unable, because of the lack of its own financing capacity, to raise on the market the capital needed for investment;

— the participation involves the taking over or the continuation of non-viable activity of an undertaking in difficulty through the creation of a new legal entity;[327]

— the holding is a short-term one, with the duration and selling price fixed in advance, so that the return to the provider of capital is considerably less than he could have expected from a capital market investment for a similar period;

— there is an obvious imbalance between public and private participation and the relative disengagement of private shareholders is largely due to the company's poor profit outlook;

— the participation exceeds the real value of the undertaking concerned.[328]

However, in the last two cases, there is no aid where the undertaking concerned is a small or medium-sized one which cannot offer sufficient guarantees for the capital market but whose prospects justify the participation. Equally, there is no aid where the strategic nature of the investment means that the participation can be regarded as normal, even though profitability is delayed; or where the development potential of the company means that the participation may be regarded as involving a special risk but as likely to pay off ultimately.[329]

Account may also be taken of the viability of restructuring plans for the undertakings concerned. For example, *Belgium* v. *EC Commission: Boch*[330] concerned a capital subscription to a Belgian producer of ceramics. At the time when the capital was subscribed, the producer had for several years been making very substantial losses relative to its turnover, its survival had already

---

[325] Public Authorities' Holding in Company Capital: the Commission's Position (Bull. EC 9–1984, 3.5.1). See, earlier, the *Tenth Report on Competition Policy* (EC Commission, Brussels, 1981), 144.

[326] Account may be taken not only of a decision as such to invest but also of the nature of the investment. See, regarding an advance on a future capital injection at a low-risk interest rate, Notice C33/93 (NN32/93) ([1993] OJ C346/7) regarding aid which France had decided to grant to Groupe Bull.

[327] See, e.g., Notice C32/95 (NN59/95) ([1995] OJ C295/17) regarding aid which Nidersachsen had decided to grant to ASL Lemwurder.

[328] Para. 3.3 of the 1984 Communication.

[329] *Ibid.*, para. 3.2.

[330] Case 40/85 [1986] ECR 2321.

necessitated several injections of capital by the public authorities in order to restore its depleted capital, and its products had to be sold on a market in which there was excess capacity.[331] There was no indication that the restructuring plan for the producer was likely to guarantee profitable operations in the future and hence to provide a sufficient basis to attract the requisite private capital. Indeed, the plan had already failed when the capital at issue was subscribed, since the Bfr 475 million constituting the first stage of the plan had been almost entirely absorbed by the trading losses incurred in the meantime. Accordingly, the new capital subscription had to be regarded as aid.[332]

Similarly, if the state invests in a company 'without a full and thorough study of [its] accounts',[333] or on the basis of a restructuring plan a key aspect of which can no longer be achieved because of developments which should have been known at the time of the investment, and no alternative strategy has been adopted,[334] aid may be involved. On the other hand, where a restructuring plan is considered realistic and the net present value of future cash flows over the 'normal life time' of an investment equals the amount of the investment, the latter is not treated as aid.[335]

Decisive importance may be attached to the conditions in the sector where the company is operating, though there may be problems in defining the relevant sector.[336] Thus state injection of capital in a financially sound company for new investment and expenditure directly related thereto will not normally constitute aid where there is no structural overcapacity in the sector concerned.[337] Where the overcapacity is cyclical rather than structural, state financing may be treated as the kind of investment which would be made by a private investor.[338] Where, however, the overcapacity is structural, the latter may be treated as entailing such handicaps that the company would have been unable to raise on the private capital markets the funds essential to its survival. Thus, for example, in the case of ceramic sanitary ware,[339] crockery,[340] con-

---

[331] *Ibid.*, 2345. See, similarly, Case 234/84 *Belgium* v. *EC Commission: Meura* [1986] ECR 2263, 2286.

[332] See, similarly, Case C–301/87 *France* v. *EC Commission: Boussac* [1990] ECR I–307, I–361; and Case C–42/93 *Spain* v. *EC Commission: Merco* [1994] ECR I–4175, I–4193.

[333] Notice C26/95 (NN52/95) ([1995] OJ C121/4) regarding aid which France had decided to grant to Crédit Lyonnais.

[334] Notice C22/92 (N727/91) ([1992] OJ C257/4) concerning aid which Italy planned to grant to Ilva SpA.

[335] Notice C12/94 (ex NN11/94 ([1994] OJ C330/7) regarding aid which Italy had decided to grant to Enichem SpA.

[336] Notice C17/94 (ex N102/93, ex N335/91 & ex N337/92) ([1995] OJ C319/4) concerning aid which Italy planned to grant to Tubificio di Terni Srl and Ilva Lamiere e Tubi Srl.

[337] Dec. 87/418 ([1987] OJ L227/45) concerning aid to a Belgian steel pipe and tube manufacturer.

[338] Notice C17/94 (ex N102/93, ex N335/91 & ex N337/92) ([1995] OJ C319/4) concerning aid which Italy planned to grant to Tubificio di Terni Srl and Ilva Lamiere e Tubi Srl.

[339] Dec. 83/130 ([1983] OJ L91/32) on aid granted by the Belgian Government to a firm manufacturing ceramic sanitary ware.

[340] Dec. 86/366 ([1986] OJ L223/30) concerning aid which the Belgian Government had granted to a ceramic sanitary ware and crockery manufacturer.

sumer electronics,[341] printing,[342] zinc, and lead[343] state participation has been treated as amounting to the grant of state aid. Account may also be taken of the low profitability of the sector and difficulties of making forecasts of future developments therein.[344] In crisis sectors state participation is usually treated as aid,[345] unless the undertaking concerned is highly competitive[346] or a restructuring plan likely to lead to viability is entailed.[347] For example, the Commission took the view in 1982 that the financial circumstances of virtually all publicly-owned steel companies and the market prospects of the sector as a whole were such that state provision of equity and quasi-equity finance to these companies inevitably contained aid elements.[348] More generally, a distinction may be made between a company in a 'traditional industrial sector' and a company developing new technologies or seeking to capture new markets.[349]

Conduct of Private Shareholders

Consideration may be given to the conduct of private shareholders, actual or potential, in companies partly owned or established by public authorities.[350] Where public authorities in other Member States are shareholders, their conduct is assimilated to that of private shareholders.[351]

As regards potential shareholders, aid will be involved where the state purchases shares at a higher price than they would be prepared to pay. Thus if the undertaking is quoted on the stock exchange, the purchase of its shares by the state at a price above the quoted one involves the grant of aid.[352] According to the Commission, the stock market price of a share 'represents a genuine market evaluation of the share value, as it reflects supply and demand

[341] Notice C46/94 (NN60/94 & NN92/94) ([1994] OJ C373/5) concerning aid which Italy proposed to grant to Seleco SpA, Pordenone.

[342] Notice C43/93 (ex NN97/93) ([1995] OJ C309/4) concerning aid granted by the French Government to Avenir Graphique, a printing firm.

[343] Notice C55/95 (ex NN46/95) ([1996] OJ C102/11) concerning state aid to the Enirisorse group.

[344] Notice C14/95 (NN774/94) ([1995] OJ C114/7) concerning a Pta 130 billion capital injection into Iberia.

[345] See, regarding the presumption to this effect, para. 3.4 of the 1984 Communication.

[346] *Twelfth Report on Competition Policy* (EC Commission, Brussels, 1983), 120.

[347] *Eighteenth Report on Competition Policy* (EC Commission, Brussels, 1989), 163. See also *ibid.*, 165 and Van Gerven AG in Case C–305/89 *Italy* v. *EC Commission: Alfa Romeo* [1991] ECR I–1603, I–1626.

[348] *Twelfth Report on Competition Policy* (EC Commission, Brussels, 1983), 120.

[349] Dec. 96/236 ([1996] OJ L78/31) concerning state aid granted by Hamburg to the ECSC steel undertaking Hamburger Stahlwerke GmbH, Hamburg.

[350] Notice C35/91 (ex N658/90) ([1993] OJ C59/4) concerning aid which Italy had decided to grant to the alkaline salts industry.

[351] Notice C2/94 (ex N40/94) ([1994] OJ C390/1) concerning aid that might be involved in an intended injection of public capital into the equity capital of Klöckner Stahl GmbH, Duisberg.

[352] Dec. 91/555 ([1991] OJ L300/48) on aid to be granted by the Belgian Government in favour of Sabena.

equilibrium in a fully public, transparent environment'.[353] Where the state already owns virtually all the shares in a quoted company, determination of the presence of aid cannot relate to its share price. Instead, the determination is based on the prospective return to the extra finance made available by the state.[354] In one case the purchase price paid by the state was based on the average of the net value of the company's assets and of the present value of its expected future earnings. The Commission considered that the state thereby overvalued the shares, since a company's stock exchange valuation was normally based on the present and expected yield of its shares. On the other hand, payment of a higher price than the one quoted may be considered normal for the purchase of a blocking minority, and thus may not be treated as involving the grant of aid.[355]

More usually, account is taken of the conduct of actual shareholders. Their conduct not only indicates the expectations of private investors as regards the profitability of an investment but may also affect its likely profitability. Hence, according to the Commission, the willingness of a private shareholder to provide financial liquidity to a company in difficulties may depend on the preparedness of fellow shareholders to contribute in line with their participation in the equity.[356] The implication is that where private shareholders so contribute, contributions by the state are less likely to involve aid.

For example, in April 1990 the Commission decided to accept the Italian Government's injection of ECU 92 million of new capital in the steel-tube producer, Dalmine, a subsidiary of the publicly-owned Ilva group. The Government had agreed to reduce its share of the capital increase to an amount such that the public and private shareholders would contribute equally to it in proportion to their original shareholdings, and had put forward additional measures for restructuring the company to restore its viability and ensure a satisfactory return for investors. Also, throughout the period, Dalmine's share price had held up well. The Commission, therefore, took the view that the transaction was in line with what a private investor would do under normal market economy conditions and did not involve aid.[357]

Similarly, the Commission accepted a capital injection of ECU 2.36 million and a participatory loan of ECU 2.36 million by the Wallonia Region in favour

[353] Dec. 93/412 ([1993] OJ L185/43) concerning aid awarded by the German Government to Hibeg and by Hibeg via Krupp GmbH to Bremer Vulkan AG, facilitating the sale of Krupp Atlas Elektronik GmbH from Krupp GmbH to Bremer Vulkan AG.

[354] Cf., where the state becomes the sole shareholder, Dec. 92/329 ([1992] OJ L183/30) on aid granted by the Italian Government to a manufacturer of ophthalmic products (Industrie Ottiche Riunite).

[355] *Fourteenth Report on Competition Policy* (EC Commission, Brussels, 1985), 137.

[356] Dec. 96/178 ([1996] OJ L53/41) on state aid that Bavaria granted to Neue Maxhütte Stahlwerke GmbH, Sulzbach-Rosenberg.

[357] *Twentieth Report on Competition Policy* (EC Commission, Brussels, 1991), 153–4. See, similarly, regarding a capital injection in a German steel company, Bull. EU 9–1994, 1.2.65, and regarding grants and debt write-offs for Volvo Car BV in the Netherlands, the *Tenth Report on Competition Policy* (EC Commission, Brussels, 1980), 144.

of Donnay, a company in which the Region was a minority shareholder. As the majority shareholder was also putting money into the company, the Commission concluded that the action of the Region was consistent with that of a private investor and did not involve aid.[358] On the other hand, aid may be present where a capital subscription by the government in a company under mixed ownership takes the government holding significantly above that which it had under the original distribution.[359]

Such decisions embody the general principle that aid will not be regarded as present where the subscription of funds by the state is in proportion to its existing holding and is matched by subscriptions by private shareholders, though the latter subscription must be on comparable terms[360] and must be 'substantial',[361] or have 'economic significance',[362] 'genuine economic significance',[363] 'real economic significance',[364] or 'economic relevance'.[365] Thus, for example, if 94 per cent of the new capital injected into an undertaking comes from public funds, the injection is likely to be regarded as aid.[366] However, the test is not only quantitative.[367] Accordingly, an investment designed merely to diversify the portfolio of a bank may be insufficient to justify application of the general principle, as may an investment which exposes private investors to risk which is 'overall very limited'.[368] Doubts about whether the state is acting commercially may also arise where 'not all other shareholders' act in the same way.[369]

The possibility that the conduct of private shareholders may itself be affected by state participation receives limited, though increasing, consideration. In

---

[358] *Twentieth Report on Competition Policy* (EC Commission, Brussels, 1991), 171.

[359] Dec. 87/418 ([1987] OJ L227/45) concerning aid to a Belgian steel pipe and tube manufacturer.

[360] Dec. 96/236 ([1996] OJ L78/31) concerning state aid granted by Hamburg to the ECSC steel undertaking Hamburger Stahlwerke GmbH, Hamburg.

[361] Notice C26/95 (NN52/95) ([1995] OJ C121/4) regarding aid which France had decided to grant to Crédit Lyonnais.

[362] Communic. C39/93 (NN87/93) ([1993] OJ C334/7) concerning the subscription by CDC Participations to two bond issues of Air France.

[363] Dec. 94/662 ([1994] OJ L258/26) concerning the subscription by CDC Participations to bonds issued by Air France.

[364] A shareholding of 4.43%, which has no effect on the management structure of the group concerned and does not enable important decisions to be opposed, lacks such significance. See Notice C33/B/93 (NN12/94) ([1994] OJ C80/4) regarding aid which France has decided to grant to Groupe Bull. On the other hand, a shareholding of 15% does apparently have the necessary significance. See Bull. EU 3–1994, 1.2.44.

[365] Dec. 94/118 ([1994] OJ L54/30) concerning aid to be provided by the Irish Government to the Aer Lingus group.

[366] Lenz AG in Case 40/85 *Belgium* v. *EC Commission: Boch* [1986] ECR 2321, 2330.

[367] See, e.g., Notice C36/93 (NN27/93) ([1994] OJ C31/4) regarding aid which the Flemish region of Belgium intended to grant to truck producer DAF.

[368] Dec. 94/662 ([1994] OJ L258/26) concerning the subscription by CDC Participations to bonds issued by Air France.

[369] Notice C41/95 (ex NN83/95) ([1995] OJ C312/19) with respect to loans totalling DM 24,1125 million Bavaria granted to Neue Maxhütte Stahlwerke GmbH between July 1994 and Mar. 1995.

Boussac,[370] which concerned capital subscriptions to a producer of textiles, clothing, and paper products, the Court of Justice noted that private capital subscriptions followed those of the state. The state subscriptions might be perceived by other shareholders and actual or potential creditors as reducing the risks of investing in, or dealing with, the company and, in this sense, constitute aid. According to the Commission, such subscriptions may entail 'an implicit state guarantee to creditors';[371] 'signals' to other interested parties;[372] or the possibility that 'the risk element of their investment is artificially alleviated by the extremely favourable participatory loans granted by the public authorities'.[373] In such circumstances, the fact that state participation is accompanied by private participation does not preclude the possibility of aid being involved.

State aid may also be involved where private shareholders are attracted by special privileges and guarantees.[374] Provision of such guarantees could only be taken as indicating a lack of confidence of private investors in the possibility of re-establishing long-term viability. Only the provision of genuine risk capital would sufficiently indicate the commercial viability of planned restructuring.[375] Similarly, indirect inducements, such as tax exemptions on sums used by companies to repurchase shares from public bodies,[376] and provision of capital prior to the subsidized takeover through privatization of the undertaking concerned may themselves be treated as aid.[377]

Reasonableness

In *Italy* v. *EC Commission: Lanerossi*,[378] which concerned capital injections by the Italian authorities in a nationalized producer of clothing, it was argued that the test whether aid was involved should relate to the actions of the private entrepreneur[379] rather than those of the private investor.[380] This argument

[370] Case C–301/87 *France* v. *EC Commission: Boussac* [1990] ECR I–307, I–361.
[371] Dec. 94/343 ([1994] OJ L154/37) concerning aid granted by the Spanish Government to Merco.
[372] Notice C38/93 (NN43/93 & NN58/93) ([1994] OJ C31/9) regarding aid which the Netherlands intended to grant to truck producer DAF.
[373] Notice C1/95 (NN144/94) ([1995] OJ C144/13) concerning aid provided by the Spanish authorities to Suzuki-Santana Motor SA in support of its motor vehicle plant in Linares (Andalucia).
[374] Notice ([1986] OJ C312/5) regarding aid planned by the Belgian Government for the textiles and glass-container industries: tax exemptions for sums allocated by private undertakings for repurchase of shares previously acquired by public investment bodies.
[375] Dec. 91/555 ([1991] OJ L300/48) on aid to be granted by the Belgian Government in favour of Sabena.
[376] *Sixteenth Report on Competition Policy* (EC Commission, Brussels, 1987), 148 and 162.
[377] Dec. 96/178 ([1996] OJ L53/41) on state aid that Bavaria granted to Neue Maxhütte Stahlwerke GmbH, Sulzbach-Rosenberg.
[378] Case C–303/88 [1991] ECR I–1433.
[379] The High Authority originally applied a test based on the conduct of a private *owner*. See the Reply to Written Question 170 by Mr Nederhorst ([1963] OJ 973). See also the Reply to Written Question 74 by Mr Burgbacher ([1963] JO 2546).
[380] [1991] ECR I–1433, I–1475.

seems to have been influential.[381] Advocate General Van Gerven accepted that, the relationship between the public and private sectors being so close, a private holding company could not ignore social and regional considerations.[382] The state could also reasonably take account of such considerations in its investment decisions, though it could not continue to support a loss-making subsidiary in a sector suffering from overcapacity without adopting a restructuring plan.[383] According to the Court of Justice itself, state investment in pursuit of a structural policy, general or sectoral, guided by long-term profitability perspectives would not constitute aid. However, aid would be present where the investment was made without any regard to the question of returns, even in the long term.[384]

The need for a 'more concrete' evaluation of state participation is implicit in such case law,[385] and is partly reflected in the evolution of Commission practice,[386] particularly its Communication of 1991.[387]

In this Communication the Commission recognizes that investors, public or private, must engage in risk-analysis. Such analysis requires the exercise of managerial skills, which necessarily implies a wide margin of judgement by the investor. Within that wide margin the exercise of judgement cannot be regarded as involving the grant of aid, though the Commission excludes the possibility that a public authority may happen to be better at foreseeing future market developments than anyone else.[388] Only where there are no objective grounds reasonably to expect that an investment will give an adequate rate of return that would be acceptable to a private investor in a comparable undertaking operating under normal market conditions is aid involved.[389] No distinction is now made between projects which have short or long-term pay-back periods, as long as the risks are adequately and objectively assessed and discounted at the time the decision to invest is made, in the way that a private investor would

---

[381] F. Minneci, 'Le partecipazioni pubbliche al capitale di imprese' [1991] *Diritto Comunitario e degli Scambi Internazionali* 365–72.

[382] This point seems already to have been recognized by Reischl AG in Joined Cases 188–190/80 *France, Italy, and the UK* v. *EC Commission: transparency directive* [1982] ECR 2545, 2591.

[383] [1991] ECR I–1433, I–1459.

[384] *Ibid.* I–1476; [1991] ECR I–1603, I–1640. See also Van Gerven AG (*ibid.*, 1626) and Case C–261/89 *Italy* v. *EC Commission: Aluminia* [1991] ECR I–4437, I–4449.

[385] F. Minneci, n. 381 above, 371.

[386] In other words, the case law of the Court 'enriches' Commission practice. See R. Kovar, 'Les Prises de participation publiques et le régime communautaire des aides d'état' [1992] *RTDE* 109–57, 122.

[387] Application of Arts. 92 and 93 EC and of Art. 5 of Dir. 80/723 to public undertakings in the manufacturing sector ([1991] OJ C273/2). Although the Communication relates only to aid to manufacturing undertakings, the Commission may apply the principles contained therein to other undertakings, such as airlines (*ibid.* para. 3).

[388] Communic. C18/89 (ex N121/87–63/89) ([1991] OJ C45/3) regarding aid which Germany had decided to grant to Bremen and Niedersachsen.

[389] Para. 27 of the 1991 Communication.

do.[390] In determining whether aid is involved, the Commission bases itself on the data available to the public authorities at the time of the investment.[391]

Moreover, it is accepted that a Member State may have 'a legitimate interest in the long-term viability' of the undertaking concerned.[392] Equally, it is recognized that a private undertaking may engage in cross-subsidization when it has a strategic plan with good hopes of long-term gain or where the cross-subsidy has a net benefit to the group as a whole. The Commission takes account of similar strategic goals where there is cross-subsidization in public holding companies.[393] Such cross-subsidization is treated as aid only where the Commission considers that there is no reasonable explanation for the flow of funds other than that aid is involved.[394]

Finally, the Commission recognizes the differences in approach a private investor may have between his minority holding in a company on the one hand and full control of a large group on the other. The former relationship may often be characterized as more of a speculative or short-term interest, whereas the latter usually involves a longer-term interest. Hence, transfers within a group of public bodies are, in principle, unobjectionable, but aid may be involved where a transfer takes place 'at rather symbolic terms that do not represent its intrinsic economic value in the light of its economic prospects'.[395] Similarly, where a public authority controls an individual undertaking or group of undertakings, it will normally be less motivated by purely short-term profit considerations than if it had merely a minority/non-controlling holding, and its time horizon will correspondingly be longer. Accordingly, the Commission takes account of the nature of the public authority's holding in comparing its behaviour with the benchmark of the equivalent private investor. More particularly, where a decision is made to abandon a line of activity because of its lack of medium/long-term commercial viability, the Commission accepts that a public group, like a private group, can be expected to decide the timing and scale of its run-down in the light of the impact on the overall credibility and structure of the group.[396]

---

[390] *Ibid.* para. 28. See, e.g., Notice C13/95 (NN9/95) ([1995] OJ C293/8) concerning aid granted by the Italian Government to Breda Fucine Meridionali.

[391] Notice C37/91 (ex N292/91 & N316/91) ([1992] OJ L244/2) regarding aid which France had decided to grant Compagnie des Machines Bull. Subsequent events may be taken into account in the determination of the compatibility of aid with the common market.

[392] *Twenty-Fourth Report on Competition Policy* (EC Commission, Brussels, 1995), 491.

[393] See also, beyond the manufacturing sectors, *Development of the Single Market for Postal Services*, COM(91)476, 219–20.

[394] Para. 29 of the 1991 Communication.

[395] Notice C6/92 (ex NN141/91) ([1993] OJ C282/5; [1995] OJ C120/4) regarding aid which Italy granted to CMF SUD SpA and CMF SpA. See also Notice C60/95 (NN 169/95) ([1996] OJ C124/5) regarding aid granted by the Austrian government to Head Tyrolia Mares, in the form of capital injections.

[396] Para. 30 of the 1991 Communication. See, e.g., Dec. 92/266 ([1992] OJ L138/24) on the conversion activities of French public industrial groups outside the steel and coal industries and excluding the Compagnie Générale Maritime. See, generally, C.-D. Ehlermann, 'Les Entreprises publiques et le contrôle des aides d'état' [1992] *RMC* 613–20; *Report of the Committee on Economic and Monetary Affairs and Industrial Policy on the Twentieth Report on Competition*

Nevertheless, there must be a possibility of a return within 'the foreseeable future'.[397]

As a result, state financing of conversion operations, including redeployment of workers and mitigation of the regional effects of a cutback, may not be treated as aid for the purposes of Article 92. Such operations involve a number of benefits, such as 'redirection of activities',[398] 'indirect material profit', and 'image maintenance'.[399]

However, there must be a 'coherent' restructuring plan,[400] sufficient restructuring must be taking place,[401] and financing of 'regional development operations' may still be treated as aid. At the same time, where capital injections coincide with the sale of publicly owned shares in the company concerned, the prospect of profit from the injections is removed, and so they constitute aid.[402] Moreover, arguments relating to image maintenance may be rejected, where a 'massive scaling down' of state investment in the group concerned is already apparent,[403] where a complete withdrawal is envisaged from the sector in which the ailing undertaking is active,[404] or where a private investor would have intervened earlier.[405] More generally, the Commission not only continues to compare state conduct with that of a private investor rather than private entrepreneur,[406] and, indeed, with that of a private investor 'without any particular relationship' with the undertaking concerned.[407] The Commission also seems reluctant to abandon all references to the conduct of the 'model'

Policy, EP Doc. A3–0338/91, 17. See also *The Measurement of the Aid Element of State Acquisitions of Company Capital* (Evolution of Concentration and Competition Series: Collection: Working Papers 87).

[397] Communic. C38/90 (NN76/89) ([1991] OJ C3/3) regarding aid which the Netherlands had decided to grant to the shipyard van der Giessen de Noord.

[398] Dec. 92/266 ([1992] OJ L138/24) on the conversion activities of French industrial groups outside the steel and coal industries and excluding the Compagnie Générale Maritime.

[399] See also Joined Cases C–278/92, C–279/92 & C–280/92 *Spain* v. *EC Commission: Intelhorce* [1994] ECR I–4103, I–4154.

[400] Communic. C39/93 (NN87/93) ([1993] OJ C334/7) concerning the subscription by CDC-participations to two bond issues of Air France.

[401] Notice C55/95 (ex NN46/95) ([1996] OJ C102/11) concerning state aid to the Enirisorse group.

[402] H. Morch, 'Summary of the Most Important Recent Developments' [1995] 5 *Competition Policy Newsletter* 43–9, 45.

[403] Notice C55/95 (ex NN46/95) ([1996] OJ C102/11) concerning state aid to the Enirisorse group.

[404] Notice C60/95 (NN 169/95) ([1996] OJ C124/5) regarding aid granted by the Austrian government to Head Tyrolia Mares, in the form of capital injections.

[405] Notice C6/92 (ex NN141/91) ([1993] OJ C282/5; [1995] OJ C120/4) regarding aid which Italy granted to CMF SUD SpA and CMF SpA. See also Notice C60/95 (NN 169/95) ([1996] OJ C124/5) regarding aid granted by the Austrian government to Head Tyrolia Mares, in the form of capital injections.

[406] Dec. 95/422 ([1995] OJ L253/22) concerning state aid that Bavaria intended to grant to the ECSC steel undertakings Neue Maxhütte Stahlwerke GmbH, Sulzbach-Rosenberg, and Lech Stahlwerke GmbH, Meitingen-Herbertshofen.

[407] Dec. 96/236 ([1996] OJ L78/31) concerning state aid granted by Hamburg to the ECSC steel undertaking Hamburger Stahlwerke GmbH, Hamburg.

investor,[408] even though such references are of doubtful compatibility with the case law of the Court of Justice.[409]

In the view of the Commission, such references may remain justified. Not to treat state participation based on considerations of social, regional-policy, and sectoral factors as aid 'would amount to granting Member States the power to rescue companies in difficulties on the basis of pure national interest [and] . . . would amount to emptying the market-economic private-investor principle of its meaning'.[410] Accordingly, the Commission may invoke 'traditional' public/private distinctions[411] in its findings that state participation involves the grant of aid.[412]

As a result, it continues to be disputed whether Commission practice accommodates 'normal behaviour in a social market economy'.[413]

2.2.6 Privatization

A reduction in the size of the public sector may not merely render aid more transparent. More fundamentally, since privatized undertakings will no longer be able to 'rely on privileged public assistance',[414] it may also be expected to lead to reduced use of aid.[415] However, unless a public undertaking is sold as a 'going concern', the sale takes place through an open bid or an equivalent procedure and the highest bid is honoured,[416] aid may be involved. The underlying principle is that the state must seek to maximize the recovery of its claims 'as any private creditor . . . setting aside all social, regional policy and sectoral considerations'. The fact that the purchaser may pay a 'reasonable price' does not in itself affect this requirement.[417] Moreover, where one such

---

[408] See, e.g., Dec. 93/133 ([1993] OJ L55/54) concerning aid granted by the Spanish Government to Merco (an agricultural processing company).

[409] Van Gerven AG in Case C–305/89 *Italy* v. *EC Commission: Alfa Romeo* [1991] ECR I–1603, I–1640.

[410] Dec. 92/317 ([1992] OJ L171/54) on state aid in favour of Hilaturas y Tejidos Andaluces SA and its buyer.

[411] Joined Cases 188–190/80 *France, Italy and the UK* v. *EC Commission: transparency directive* [1982] ECR 2545, 2577–8.

[412] Notice C50/90 (ex E/10/90) ([1991] OJ C105/5) concerning the conversion activities of public industrial groups outside the steel and coal industries and excluding the Compagnie Générale Maritime.

[413] Dec. 96/178 ([1996] OJ L53/41) on state aid that Bavaria granted to Neue Maxhütte Stahlwerke GmbH, Sulzbach-Rosenberg.

[414] Dec. 96/115 ([1996] OJ L28/18) on the aid granted by the Italian State to Enichem Agricoltura SpA.

[415] See, regarding privatization as a solution to 'recidivism', the *Twenty-Fourth Report on Competition Policy* (EC Commission, Brussels, 1995), 173.

[416] Communic. on the privatization of Stahl- und Walzwerk Brandenburg and Henningsdorfer Stahlwerk ([1992] OJ C161/10). Account was taken of the 'ample international publicity which preceded the sale'. See also the *Twenty-Second Report on Competition Policy* (EC Commission, Brussels, 1993), 225.

[417] Dec. 93/627 ([1993] OJ L309/21) concerning aid granted by the Spanish authorities on the occasion of the sale by Cenemesa/Cademesa/Conelec of certain selected assets to Asea–Brown Boveri.

undertaking is sold at a loss, the aid is not eliminated by the fact that other sales within the same privatization programme are profitable.[418]

Transformation

The Commission accepts that privatization in the former German Democratic Republic must follow a realistic path and that book values may be a poor guide to the real value of assets. On the other hand, the possibility is recognized that aid may be involved in privatization.[419] Thus the Commission requires that the process should be open and transparent. More particularly, it should not lead to the economy being dominated by a few giant firms, including some of Western European origin.[420] For example, the Commission is concerned that companies such as Opel[421] and Volkswagen[422] should not acquire some valuable productive assets at unrealistically low prices.

To tackle the problems raised, the Commission applied special criteria and procedures to the privatizing activities of the *Treuhandanstalt* (THA).[423] Accordingly, the Commission had to be notified of privatizations where more than 1,000 jobs after sale were involved. The Commission also had to be notified where companies that did not belong together historically were sold as a group. Such artificial groupings of companies might mean that the sale did not take place through unconditional bidding procedures and might involve aid. Moreover, if no bidder was willing to pay a positive price for a company and the THA still opted for sale, aid might be involved where closure of the company would have been a less costly option. Such sales, as well as other cases where a company was not sold to the highest bidder as the result of an open and unconditional bid, were to be notified to the Commission.[424]

On the other hand, the Commission accepted that compensation could be granted to the former owners of East German companies who resumed

[418] Dec. 95/422 ([1995] OJ L253/22) concerning state aid that Bavaria intended to grant to the ECSC steel undertakings Neue Maxhütte Stahlwerke GmbH, Sulzbach-Rosenberg, and Lech Stahlwerke GmbH, Meitingen-Herbertshofen.

[419] See, e.g., Notice C58/91 ([1992] OJ C73/2) concerning aid awarded by the German Government to Carl Zeiss Jena Jenoptik and Jenaer Glaswerk.

[420] Cf. the *Report of the Committee on Economic and Monetary Affairs and Industrial Policy on the Twentieth Report on Competition Policy*, EP Doc. A3–0338/91, 19. The European Parliament itself, in its Resolution of 15 July 1993 ([1993] OJ C255/201) on the Community response to the problem of restructuring in East Germany and the economic and social crisis, called on the THA to give priority to 'safeguarding the industrial base and key industries' in the former GDR (para. 31), but also considered that the Commission should ensure that there were no detrimental effects in the rest of the Union (para. 35).

[421] Communic. C60/91 (NN73/91 & 76/91) ([1992] OJ C68/2) concerning the proposal of the German Government to award state aid to the Opel group in support of its investment plans in the new *Länder*.

[422] Communic. C62/91 (NN75, 77, 78, 79/91) ([1992] OJ C68/14) concerning the proposal of the German Government to award state aid to the Volkswagen group in support of its investment plans in the new *Länder*.

[423] Bull. EU 1/2–1995, 1.3.35.

[424] H. Morch, 'Summary of the Most Important Recent Developments' (1995) 4 *Competition Policy Newsletter* 47–51, 50.

operations (reprivatizations), in view of the loss in value of these companies. It felt that this kind of compensation did not constitute aid, but rather an indemnity. The Commission had to be informed only if the compensation was not calculated on the basis of the usual criteria but was negotiated individually and amounted to DM 50 million or more, or if it was granted in sensitive sectors, including steel, shipbuilding, synthetic fibres, and motor vehicles, or to fisheries and/or agriculture.[425] Writing-off of debts contracted under the political and economic centralized system imposed by the former German Democratic Republic and exemption from responsibility for environmental damage before 1 July 1990 were also treated as falling outside Article 92, because they entailed no advantages for the undertakings concerned.[426]

The application of these special principles to privatization in the former German Democratic Republic was supposed to cease at the end of 1995.[427] Henceforth, such privatization is to be treated in the same way as privatization elsewhere in the Union.

Guidelines

Guidelines have been formulated regarding privatization in the Union generally.[428] According to these Guidelines, aid may be present where an undertaking is sold at a price below its market value[429] or where its debts are reduced prior to sale. However, privatization by means of a stock market flotation is generally presumed to involve no aid. Moreover, disposals made by unconditional invitation to tender involve no aid, if:

—the company is sold to the highest bidder;
—the terms and conditions of the invitation to tender are non-discriminatory[430] and transparent;[431] and
—interested parties are given ample time to prepare their offer and are

---

[425] *European Report* 1817 (2 Dec. 1992).

[426] *Twenty-First Report on Competition Policy* (EC Commission, Brussels, 1992), 157. See, e.g., Notice C16/95 (NN50/94) ([1995] OJ C215/8) concerning aid the German Government intended to grant to SKET Schwermaschinenbau Magdeburg GmbH.

[427] H. Morch, 'Summary of the Most Important Recent Developments' [1995] 3 *Competition Policy Newsletter* 41–7, 44.

[428] *Twenty-Third Report on Competition Policy* (EC Commission, Brussels, 1994), 255–6.

[429] Though a 'negative price' sale does not necessarily involve the grant of aid. See Notice C6/92 (ex NN141/91) ([1993] OJ C282/5; [1995] OJ C120/4) regarding aid which Italy granted to CMF SUD SpA and CMF SpA. See also Notice C60/95 (NN169/95) ([1996] OJ C124/5) regarding aid granted by the Austrian government to Head Tyrolia Mares, in the form of capital injections.

[430] In particular, the acquisition of shares offered for sale must be non-discriminatory in respect of non-national interested parties. See the Reply by Mr Van Miert to Written Question 423/93 ([1993] OJ C288/7) by Mrs Cristiana Muscardini.

[431] Otherwise, a presumption of aid is applied. See Communic. C31/93 (NN97/91) ([1993] OJ C293/4) on aid measures involved in the acquisition by KLM of the pilot school RLS. See also Notice C60/95 (NN169/95) ([1996] OJ C124/5) regarding aid granted by the Austrian government to Head Tyrolia Mares, in the form of capital injections.

given all the information they need in order to be able to carry out a correct evaluation.

Where two prospective purchasers of an undertaking make 'broadly comparable' offers, the acceptance of one offer rather than the other does not necessarily entail the grant of aid. Moreover, acceptance of an offer at a price lower than the net book value of the assets transferred may not involve aid because of estimated future operating losses of the undertaking sold and the significant amounts of investment and rationalization costs necessary to restore its viability.[432]

However, the following may involve aid:

—disposals made through restricted procedures or direct sales;
—disposals preceded by a debt write-off by the state, public enterprise or any other public body;
—disposals preceded by conversion of debts into capital or by a capital increase;[433] and
—disposals subject to conditions which would not be acceptable for a transaction between market-economy investors.[434]

In the case of an ailing company sold for its liquidation value, aid may also be involved,[435] unless employees are dismissed with only their legal entitlement to redundancy pay and creditors and lenders receive less than their outstanding monies, and only as far as the liquidation proceeds allow. However, state owners may not privatize rather than liquidate, where the former is the more costly option.[436] More particularly, state injection of capital into an ailing company in anticipation of, and with a view to, privatization constitutes aid, because there is no possibility of future profitability.[437] In detailing the liquidation costs, the state must separate itself as the owner/shareholder of a company and as a body responsible for the payment of unemployment/social

---

[432] Dec. 89/661 ([1989] OJ L394/9) concerning aid provided by the Italian Government to Alfa Romeo.

[433] See, e.g., Dec. 92/317 ([1992] OJ L171/54) on state aid in favour of Hilaturas y Tejidos Andaluces SA and its buyer.

[434] Notice C42/92 (NN140/91) ([1993] OJ C253/3) concerning Law 11/90 of 5 Apr. 1990 on the programme for the reprivatization of enterprises nationalized after 25 Apr. 1974. See also para. 43 of Application of Arts. 92 and 93 EC and Art. 61 EEA to state aids in the aviation sector ([1994] OJ C350/5). All undertakings that are to be sold under special conditions must be valued by independent experts, who are to give both a 'going concern' and a liquidation value. See the Reply by Mr Van Miert to Written Question 423/93 ([1993] OJ C288/7) by Mrs Cristiana Muscardini.

[435] Dec. 92/321 ([1992] OJ L176/57) concerning aid awarded by Spain to Intelhorce SA, a state-owned producer of cotton textiles.

[436] Dec. 94/996 ([1994] OJ L379/13) concerning the transfer by the Netherlands of a pilot school to the Royal Dutch Airline.

[437] Joined Cases C–278/92, C–279/92 & C–280/92 *Spain* v. *EC Commission: Intelhorce* [1994] ECR I–4103.

security benefits.[438] In comparing such costs with those of privatization, the Commission notes that 'under normal commercial conditions no shareholder is obliged to pay more, in case of the liquidation of a public limited company, than is covered by the assets'.[439] Moreover, state owners must exercise diligence and make a 'timely disposal' of their holding, by liquidating the company as soon as it becomes clear that no improvement in a poor financial situation can be expected.[440] The argument that restructuring may be less costly than liquidation may be rejected where this is only the case because the state, in contrast to the action which would have been expected of a private shareholder, failed to take timely action.[441]

The Rover *Case*

The technically complicated issues which may arise in efforts to identify the use of state aid to assist privatization are illustrated by the Commission assessment of the sale of the Rover Group by the UK Government to British Aerospace. In 1988 the grant of aid up to a limit fixed by the Commission had been authorized.[442] In the event, the Government provided three further 'incentives', which the Commission found to constitute aid exceeding the limit.

First, £9.5 million was paid to British Aerospace to cover part of the costs incurred in acquiring Rover shares from minority shareholders. According to the Commission, it was inconceivable that under normal market conditions a majority shareholder who sold his stake in a company would be prepared, without financial consideration, to cover such costs.

Secondly, £1.5 million was paid to Rover to cover the costs it incurred as a result of the sale. The Commission considered that this, too, was an expense which normally should be met by the acquiring company. In the absence of any binding stipulation to that effect in the contract of sale, the Commission could see no good reason why such an expense should be borne gratuitously by the vendor.

Finally, the Government agreed to defer payment of the £150 million purchase price from 12 August 1988 to 30 March 1990. The notional benefit to the purchaser was assessed as being £33.4 million. Unless such a deferment formed part of the sale contract and was reflected in the sale price, which was not the case, the Commission considered that a prudent investor, operating in

---

[438] Dec. 92/318 ([1992] OJ L172/76) on aid granted by Spain to Industrias Mediterraneas de la Piel SA. This view was accepted by the ECJ in Joined Cases C–278/92, C–279/92 & C–280/92 *Spain* v. *EC Commission: Intelhorce* [1994] ECR I–4103, I–4153.

[439] Communic. C23/94 (N258/94) ([1994] OJ C152/2) with regard to the notified capital increase of Air France.

[440] Notice C38/92 (NN128/92) ([1993] OJ C75/2) regarding aid which Italy had decided to grant to EFIM.

[441] Notice C22/A/92 (NN53/93) ([1993] OJ C213/6) regarding aid which Italy planned to grant to Ilva SpA.

[442] Dec. 89/58 ([1989] OJ L25/92) concerning aid provided by the UK Government to the Rover Group.

normal market conditions, would not, and would have no good reason to, agree to such a deferment of payment when selling his shareholding in the company.

In these circumstances, the Commission decided that the three incentives constituted unlawful state aid and ordered repayment. The Court of Justice annulled this decision on procedural grounds,[443] though Advocate General Van Gerven accepted the characterization of the concessions as aid.[444]

The Volvo *Case*

The Netherlands and Volvo Car Corporation, the principal shareholders in Volvo Cars BV in the Netherlands, had advanced interest-free loans to the latter company. The loans were to be repaid by way of a royalty payment of Dfl 600 on all cars of a particular model (the 400 Series model) sold, which would be placed in a separate fund for the shareholders held outside the company. In concluding that this arrangement did not constitute aid, the Commission noted that participation by the Dutch state and Volvo Cars Corporation in the use of the fund and any future reuses would always be in proportion to their shareholdings in the company. It was also noted that the risk of a shortfall in the repayment of the loans was matched by the possibility of a bonus of surplus repayments. In other words, the participation by the state would be consistent with that of a private investor.

However, these arrangements were revised, because the Dutch state wanted to reduce its holding from 70 per cent to 33.3 per cent by selling 33.3 per cent to Mitsubishi Motors Corporation and 3.3 per cent to Volvo Cars Corporation. Volvo Cars BV was to be restructured and renamed Nedcar. These revised arrangements involved termination of the production of the cars on the basis of which the royalty payments were to be made some two years earlier than planned. This termination was taken to imply a shortfall in repayments. Volvo Cars Corporation would be compensated by its interest as a shareholder in the new and, presumably, more profitable model. There was nothing, however, to suggest that the Dutch state would be compensated. Moreover, the Dutch state planned to sell the remainder of its holdings in equal shares to Volvo Cars Corporation and Mitsubishi in 1998 at 1992 prices.[445] Mitsubishi was to have no financial responsibility for the 400 Series.

The Commission objected that the price for the state holdings was based on the net book value of the assets of Volvo Cars BV in 1990. While the net book

---

[443] Case C–294/90 *British Aerospace plc and Rover Group Holding plc* v. *EC Commission* [1992] ECR I–493, I–522.

[444] *Ibid.*, I–514–5. The Commission initiated a new procedure. See Communic. C5/92 (ex NN23/92) ([1992] OJ C122/3) concerning aid provided by the UK Government to British Aerospace for its purchase of the Rover Group, subsequent to conditional Dec. 89/58 limiting the aid to this operation.

[445] Notice C3/92 (ex N645/91) ([1992] OJ C105/16) concerning possible state aid elements contained in agreements between the Dutch state, Volvo Car Corporation, and Mitsubishi Motors Corporation.

value should not be disregarded, it could be a very crude and misleading measure of the real value of a company.[446] This applied particularly in a case, such as the one at issue, where assets had been rapidly depreciated for accounting purposes but had never been revalued. The net book value also excluded any immaterial assets or goodwill.

Moreover, the exclusion of Mitsubishi responsibility for the 400 Series arguably warranted a premium on the price per share to be paid *vis-à-vis* that paid by Volvo Cars Corporation for its additional 3 per cent holding from the state, given that it would retain its 30 per cent responsibility for the 400 Series. The freezing of the price was also difficult to defend in view of the considerable investments and restructuring of the company planned for the coming years as well as the benefits and synergies likely to arise from the strong presence of an important Japanese producer such as Mitsubishi.

Finally, the Dutch state, like the other two shareholders, planned to provide Nedcar with an interest free loan of Dfl 700 million. It was difficult to see the justification for the loan when the terms of the arrangement excluded the possibility of the state achieving a return on the loan by way of, for example, a capital appreciation of its holding which would be realizable on sale, interest payments, or repayments of principal exceeding Dfl 700 million in the event that the new car sold particularly well. Moreover, the loan repayments would be made over the years 1998 to 2004. By this time the real value of the repayments would have eroded considerably. The other two shareholders would, on the other hand, as continuing shareholders with a clear interest in the new car series, enjoy exclusively whatever return was earned on the total Dfl 2,100 million interest-free loan.

On these grounds the Commission initially considered that the grant of state aid was involved. Subsequently, however, the Commission came to the conclusion that a profitable commercial transaction for the Dutch state was involved and, therefore, lifted its objections.[447]

2.3 ANTI-COMPETITIVE EFFECTS

Where aid of the kind covered by the above definitions is granted on a scale other than the purely negligible, competition within the common market will usually be different from what it would be if left to market forces. In exceptional cases the effects of aid may be 'nullified' by a requirement that the aid recipient lodge funds with the national authorities,[448] or where the recipient has never

---

[446] Communic. C62/91 (NN75, 77, 78, 79/91) ([1992] OJ C68/14) concerning the proposal by the German Government to award state aid to the Volkswagen group in support of its investment plans in the new *Länder*.

[447] Bull. EU 9–1994, 1.2.64.

[448] Dec. 93/625 ([1993] OJ L300/15) concerning aid granted by the French Government to the Pari Mutuel Urbain and to the racecourse undertakings.

operated on the market, so that the receipt of aid cannot distort competition.[449] Again, in one case the Commission found that aid to complete contracts, granted after the contracts had been made, did not help the recipients to win the contracts in competition with other Union undertakings and thus had no anti-competitive effects. The Commission also noted that one recipient operated only in third countries in an industry not in serious recession and that the other recipient specialized in the construction of drilling platforms, which was a 'depressed sector'.[450] However, in a later case the Commission considered that such aid did have anti-competitive effects, because without it other undertakings could have picked up the unfinished orders of the aid recipient.[451]

In general, any aid granted to an undertaking is treated as giving it an advantage in relation to others and as by its nature affecting competition.[452] Even if an aid recipient has ceased trading, anti-competitive effects may still arise, because the economic advantage is transferred to investors in the recipient and the entrepreneurial risk for such investors may be reduced or removed.[453] There may, indeed, be said to be a presumption that aid granted to undertakings distorts or threatens to distort competition, unless exceptional circumstances exist,[454] and affects trade between Member States.[455] The view was once expressed that statistics showing that trade flows had been affected by the aid should be produced,[456] but this view has not been followed in Commission practice.

Nevertheless, Article 92(1) stipulates that aid is only incompatible with the common market where, first, certain undertakings or the production of certain goods are favoured, secondly, there is a distortion of competition or threat thereof and, thirdly, trade between Member States is affected.[457] Hence, aid contrary to Article 92(1) is only present where these conditions are met.

---

[449] Dec. 95/524 ([1995] OJ L300/23) concerning aid granted by the Italian State to Iritecna SpA.

[450] Dec. 87/506 ([1987] OJ L290/21) concerning aid granted by the French Government to two steel groups.

[451] Notice C7/95 (N412/94) ([1995] OJ C262/16) concerning aid the German Government intended to grant to Maschinenfabrik Sangerhausen GmbH i.K., Sachsen-Anhalt.

[452] Case 304/85 *Acciaerie e Ferriere Lombarde Falck* v. *EC Commission* [1987] ECR 871, 895.

[453] Dec. 95/366 ([1995] OJ L218/20) on aid granted by Italy (Sardinia) in the agricultural sector; Notice C47/95 (ex NN61/95) ([1996] OJ C68/5) in connection with aid granted by the Italian Government and the Region of Sicily to agricultural co-operatives.

[454] Capotorti AG in Case 730/79 *Philip Morris Holland BV* v. *EC Commission* [1980] ECR 2671, 2698.

[455] Slynn AG in Case 57/86 *Greece* v. *EC Commission: interest rebates on export credits* [1988] ECR 2855, 2867. See also Lenz AG in Case 234/84 *Belgium* v. *EC Commission: Meura* [1986] ECR 2263, 2274–5.

[456] Reischl AG in Case 52/76 *Luigi Benedetti* v. *Munari Flli s.a.s.* [1977] ECR 163, 191.

[457] Provision for control of planned aid in Art. 93(3) implies that a potential effect on trade is sufficient. See R. Kovar, n. 386 above, 131.

2.3.1 Favouritism

The requirement of favouritism in Article 92(1) may imply that the 'balancing of burdens imposed by the state' is compatible with the Treaty,[458] and may reflect the idea that aid which is not limited to specific industries will result in offsetting exchange-rate adjustments rather than distortion of competition in international trade. In Commission practice the requirement is treated as meaning that if this provision is to be applied, there must be an element of selection or discrimination in the grant of aid.[459]

For example, German aid for companies taking on new staff, which was granted automatically and without being targeted at particular sectors, regions or categories of company, was held to fall outside Article 92(1).[460] Again, Dutch tax incentives were provided for the purchase of buses and lorries complying with strict standards for noise and exhaust emissions. All major European manufacturers were capable of making vehicles meeting the standards, and the tax relief covered only part of the additional costs. Consequently, Article 92(1) was inapplicable.[461] On the other hand, Italian aid for the selective collection and recycling of polyethylene waste was considered to entail favouritism for the purposes of this provision.[462]

Such practice does not imply that only aid to individual sectors or regions is covered by Article 92(1). For example, the grant of export aid to undertakings generally in a Member State is covered thereby.[463] It would be incongruous for such aid to be permitted and for sectoral aid to be prohibited.[464] Similarly, tax concessions generally available to firms in difficulty are treated as aid covered by Article 92(1).[465] Such treatment may be supported by the wording of Article 92. In particular, Article 92(2) and (3) allows for aids other than those limited to particular sectors or regions to be authorized and thus implies that aids not so limited may be covered by Article 92(1).

Moreover, determination whether favouritism is present relies on more than

---

[458] Reischl AG in Case 40/75 *Société des Produits Bertrand SA* v. *EC Commission* [1976] ECR 1, 15–6.

[459] *Twenty-Third Report on Competition Policy* (EC Commission, Brussels, 1994), 246–7. See, more particularly, regarding job-creation aid, *ibid.*, 267 and Guidelines on aid to employment ([1995] OJ C334/4), para. 6.

[460] *Twentieth Report on Competition Policy* (EC Commission, Brussels, 1991), 172.

[461] *Ibid.*, 174.

[462] Bull. EU 5–1995, 1.3.43.

[463] Roemer AG in Joined Cases 6 & 11/69 *EC Commission* v. *France: preferential rediscount rate for exporters* [1969] ECR 523, 552. See also, regarding Greek export aid, Bull. EC 3–1984, 2.1.54. See, regarding exports to third countries, Dec. 79/519 ([1979] OJ L38/30) concerning the 'special financing scheme for investments to increase exporting firms' production capacity' in France.

[464] Capotorti AG in Case 249/81 *EC Commission* v. *Ireland: 'Buy Irish' campaign* [1982] ECR 4005, 4031.

[465] Dec. 95/547 ([1995] OJ L308/92) giving conditional approval to the aid granted by France to Crédit Lyonnais.

purely formal examination of the aid concerned. Hence, aid which is formally available to undertakings generally may be treated as effectively favouring a particular sector[466] or a particular undertaking,[467] contrary to Article 92(1). Tax measures which are structured in such a way as to apply to only a very small number of operations, if not just to a single operation, are limited in time, only apply to large companies, and depend on the exercise of discretion may be similarly treated.[468]

Such practice entails a sufficiently broad conception of favouritism to raise serious doubts about what this condition adds to the condition implicit in aid definitions that exclude general state interventions.[469] Certainly, the two conditions may appear difficult to separate, as in the case, for example, of 'measures to encourage public health activities relatively far from the market'[470] and unemployment and other social security payments to workers.[471] The conclusion may be drawn that the very essence of state aid may be to distort competition through favouring certain undertakings.[472]

2.3.2 Distortion of Competition

In determining whether there is a distortion of competition or threat thereof for the purposes of Article 92(1), the Commission may have regard not only to the direct and immediate effects of aid on the market position of the recipient. The Commission may also consider the effects for potential competitors of the recipient as well as for his purchasers and suppliers.[473] Hence, consideration may be given to the 'downstream' effects[474] on competition in industries which

---

[466] Case C–169/84 *Société CdF Chimie et Fertilisants SA* v. *EC Commission* [1990] ECR I–3083, I–3116.

[467] Dec. 80/932 ([1980] OJ L264/29) concerning the partial taking-over by the state of employers' contributions to sickness insurance schemes in Italy. Cf. ESA Notice 95–002 ([1995] OJ C212/6) concerning aid which Norway proposed to grant in the form of a tax exemption for glass packaging from a basic tax on non-reusable beverage packaging.

[468] Dec. 92/389 ([1992] OJ L207/47) concerning the state aid provided for in Decree–Laws 174 of 15 May 1989 and 254 of 13 July 1989 and in draft Law 4230 regularizing the effects produced by these Decree–Laws.

[469] V. Coussirat-Coustère, 'Les Aides locales aux entreprises face au droit communautaire' [1985] *AJDA* 171–86, 174 does not attempt to distinguish between the two conditions.

[470] Dec. 95/456 ([1995] OJ L265/30) concerning a Greek aid scheme in the pharmaceutical sector, financed by means of levies on pharmaceutical and other related products.

[471] Reply to Written Question 110/82 ([1982] OJ C221/5) by Mr Welsh.

[472] Jacobs AG in Joined Cases C–278/92, C–279/92 & C–280/92 *Spain* v. *EC Commission: Intelhorce* [1994] ECR I–4103, I–4129.

[473] Dec. 67/217 ([1967] JO 1275) on the amendment of certain aids granted by the Netherlands for the processing of certain cereals in products for human consumption; and Notice C40/90 (ex N511/90) ([1992] OJ C290/5) concerning a draft aid which Germany had decided to grant in favour of Chukyo Europe GmbH.

[474] See, generally, regarding 'upstream' and 'downstream' subsidies and 'cross-subsides', G. M. Roberti, 'Le Contrôle de la Commission des Communautés européennes sur les aides nationales' [1993] *AJDA* 397–411, 404–5.

purchase goods from the aided recipient[475] or the effects of aid to the production of raw materials on the costing and profit margins on the final product.[476] In particular, account is taken of the indirect benefits for an undertaking which is currently the only purchaser of the output of the aided undertaking.[477] Similarly, 'upstream' effects may be considered where aid affects competition between suppliers of the recipient.[478]

The economic theory of the 'second best' might be thought relevant to the determinations made by the Commission. According to this theory, a distortion of competition reduces welfare because it results in a shift of resources to the production of goods that are, from a social point of view, less desirable. If there is only one distortion of competition, such theory holds that removing the distortion will improve welfare. If, on the other hand, there is more than one distortion, removing only one of them need not necessarily improve welfare. Its removal may mean that the misallocation of resources resulting from remaining distortions is increased. In other words, the effect of partial elimination of distortions may be to reduce overall welfare.[479] In such circumstances, as in the case of other market imperfections,[480] such as externalities[481] or economies of scale, aid can in theory restore efficiency and increase welfare. Since competition requires efficient allocation of resources, aid which merely corrects inefficient allocation associated with market failure may not be regarded as distorting competition.[482]

The Commission preference, however, is to seek elimination of all distortions.[483] According to Decision 86/592[484] on the system of ceilings on the price

[475] See, e.g., Dec. 72/253 ([1972] JO L164/22) on the grant of aid to encourage the rationalization of the growing and processing of fodder plants as well as co-operation between agricultural operators in the Netherlands.

[476] Dec. 84/508 ([1984] OJ L283/42) on the aid granted by the Belgian Government to a producer of polypropylene fibre and yarn.

[477] Communic. C61/91 (NN74/91 & 80/91) ([1992] OJ C68/8) concerning the proposal by the German Government to award state aid to Mercedes-Benz in support of its investment plans in the new *Länder*.

[478] Dec. 66/556 ([1966] JO 3141) on the aid system established by the French Government for the purchase of gliders; and Dec. 79/496 ([1979] OJ L127/50) on the UK scheme of assistance in the form of interest-relief grants in favour of the off-shore supplies industry. See, regarding aid to the press and the benefits for newsprint producers, the *Seventeenth Report on Competition Policy* (EC Commission, Brussels, 1988), 173.

[479] R. G. Lipsey and K. Lancaster, 'The General Theory of the Second Best' (1956) 23 *Review of Economic Studies* 11–32.

[480] See, regarding lack of information in the case of SMEs, 'State Aid Control in the Context of Other Community Policies' [1994] *European Economy*, Supp. A, No. 4, 4.

[481] Externalities may be negative, as in the case of pollution, or positive, as in the case of R & D or vocational training (*ibid.*, 3).

[482] Cf., for example, H. Mueller and H. van der Ven, 'Perils in the Brussels–Washington Steel Pact of 1982' (1982) 5 *The World Economy* 259–78.

[483] *Sixth Report on Competition Policy* (EC Commission, Brussels, 1977), 126. See also Dec. 79/496 ([1979] OJ L127/50) on the UK scheme of assistance in the form of interest relief grants in favour of the off-shore supplies industry.

[484] [1986] OJ L340/22.

of diesel fuel for fishermen introduced by the French Government, the existence of similar aids in other Member States can never affect the incompatibility
of an aid with the common market.

A few Commission decisions may seem more consistent with the above
theory. For example, no distortion of competition was found in the case of
French and German aid which did not lower the price of electricity produced
from Union coal below the price at which the electricity could be obtained from
other fuels, but only prevented or slowed down the changeover to supplies of
imported coal or fuel oil.[485] Similarly, a reduction in the Dutch gas price for
ammonia producers which did not bring the price paid by such producers
below that paid by ammonia producers in several other Member States was
found not to distort competition.[486] Again, according to *Distortions of Competition
in Hothouse Agriculture*,[487] 'exemption from, or refunds of, excise duty constitute
aid within the meaning of Articles 92 and 93. However, the Commission has
not taken exception to these practices in view of the comparable conditions in
the Member States.'

Such aid may entail the risks that a country operates below its production-
possibility boundary and that the state is merely a conduit for inefficient inter-
industry reallocation. On the other hand, the aid could also cause changes in the
quantities of factors of production which are in variable supply and, thereby, shift
the production-possibility frontier. If additional quantities of one or more factors
of production become available to the economy as a result of the aid, it is
conceivable that overall output levels may be increased.[488]

A political economy view[489] would imply that Commission control of aid
could play a critical role in countering such risks. Specifically, such control
might prevent special-interest groups securing aid detrimental to the economy
as a whole. In other words, it might distinguish between aid designed to correct
market failure and aid which merely increased distortion of competition.
Hence, some Member States may, ostensibly at least, favour rigorous control.[490]
However, the importance attached by the Union institutions to market integration[491] allegedly jeopardizes realization of the potential of supranational control. Indeed, it is said that the economic foundations of the criteria employed
by the Commission to control aid are unclear. Commission practice is not
consistently based on the above distinction, and there is no evidence that it is
primarily concerned with ensuring that aid does not increase the welfare of a

---

[485] *Fourth Report on Competition Policy* (EC Commission, Brussels, 1975), 95–6.

[486] Notice C50/83 ([1992] OJ C344/4) regarding a preferential tariff system applied to the
Netherlands for supplies of natural gas to Dutch nitrate fertilizer producers.

[487] COM(80)306, 33–4.

[488] J. D. Gaisford and D. L. McLachlan, 'Domestic Subsidies and Countervail: The Treacherous Ground of the Level Playing Field' [1990] JWT 55–77.

[489] R. E. Baldwin, 'Assessing the Fair Trade and Safeguards Laws in Terms of Modern Trade
and Political Economy Analysis' (1992) 15 *The World Economy* 185–202, 195.

[490] *The Regional Impact of Community Policies* (European Parliament, Luxembourg, 1991), 83.

[491] H. G. Johnson, *Aspects of the Theory of Tariffs* (Allen and Unwin, London, 1971), 402.

Member State at the expense of other Member States by altering the terms of trade.[492]

Market Unification

Questions of the function of the condition for application of Article 92(1) that there be a distortion of competition arose in *Italy* v. *EC Commission: aid to textiles*,[493] which concerned a reduction of social charges on Italian textile firms. Here the Court of Justice ruled that in the application of Article 92(1) the appropriate reference point for deciding whether there was a distortion must necessarily be the competitive position existing within the common market before the grant of the aid in question.[494] In so ruling, the Court implicitly followed Advocate General Warner. The latter, approving an early characterization[495] of the relationship between the prohibition of aid and the establishment of the common market, observed that there would be no real common market in an industry straddling several countries if one of those countries subsidized its own industry.[496]

In accordance with such thinking, aid may be regarded as distorting competition because it calculably improves the recipient's return on his investment, thereby strengthening his financial position compared with competitors who do not receive such assistance.[497] Such effects of aid may be regarded as being rendered increasingly serious by completion of the internal market.[498]

More particularly, distortions of competition may result from the impact of regional aid on the international mobility of investments.[499] The institution of a system ensuring that competition in the common market is not distorted implies that firms should be allowed to make up their own minds where to locate and that their choice should therefore not be swayed or guided by financial inducements.[500] In so far as aid induces firms to choose another location[501] or to remain in a given location,[502] a distortion of competition is

---

[492] J. S. Chard and M. J. Macmillan, 'Sectoral Aids and Community Competition Rules: the Case of Textiles' [1979] *JWTL* 132–57, 155.

[493] Case 173/73 [1974] ECR 709.   [494] *Ibid.*, 720.

[495] Case 30/59 *De Gezamenlijke Steenkolenmijnen in Limburg* v. *ECSC High Authority* [1961] ECR 1, 41 (Lagrange AG).   [496] [1974] ECR 709, 722.

[497] Dec. 87/15 ([1987] OJ L12/17) on the compatibility with the common market of aid under the German Federal/*Land* Government Joint Regional Aid Programme in six labour market regions.

[498] Dec. 93/133 ([1993] OJ L55/54) concerning aid granted by the Spanish Government to Merco (an agricultural processing company).

[499] Bull. EC 12–1992, 2.1.42. See regarding the undesirable social consequences of relocations, the Resolution of the European Parliament of 17 Feb. 1995 ([1995] OJ C56/197) on relocation of businesses in the European Union, especially recital B in the Preamble and para. 3.

[500] Dec. 87/573 ([1987] OJ L347/64) on the redesignation of assisted areas in Denmark on 1 Jan. 1987. See also Darmon AG in Case 248/84 *Germany* v. *EC Commission: regional aid* [1987] ECR 4013, 4031.

[501] Dec. 91/500 ([1991] OJ L262/29) concerning aid granted to enterprises in the Friuli–Venezia Giulia region.

[502] Dec. 87/99 ([1987] OJ L40/22) on aid proposed by Rheinland-Pfalz for a fibre processing

entailed.[503] When a firm relocates from one Member State to another, both the relocation itself and the production at, and the supply of output from, the new location change trade patterns.[504] At the same time, freedom of establishment may also be jeopardized.[505]

It might be objected that aid to offset the disadvantages of a region should not be regarded as distorting competition,[506] since such aid simply compensates undertakings for the disadvantages faced there. According to the Economic and Social Committee, regional aid which tackles problems of regions which are peripheral, sparsely populated, poorly endowed with infrastructure, or disadvantaged in terms of economic structure and corresponds to the intensity of the need causes no distortion of competition but compensates for existing distortions.[507]

However, the Commission considers that, strictly speaking, such aid still distorts competition, since it reduces the costs of the recipient in the area concerned, and may thus increase the profit margins of the recipient.[508] Even if the aid only represents the additional investment cost in an area, the recipient company is still favoured, because it is enabled to carry out its investment there without having to bear all the costs thereof.[509] Moreover, in most cases it is doubtful whether the disadvantages of an area can be quantified with sufficient accuracy to fix aid at a level which exactly compensates for them. In practice, regional aid is usually set by Member States at so high a level that it provides firms with a positive financial inducement to locate and invest in certain areas.[510]

Commission practice in the automobiles sector seems, at least at present, to be exceptional. In this sector the Commission accepts that regional aid may be

---

firm in Scheuerfeld; and Dec. 87/98 ([1987] OJ L40/17) on aid proposed by Rheinland-Pfalz for a metalworking firm in Betzdorf.

[503] See the early statement in the *First EC General Report* (EC Commission, Brussels, 1968), 70; and Roemer AG in Joined Cases 27–29/58 *Compagnie des Hauts Fourneaux et Fonderies de Givors v. ECSC High Authority* [1960] ECR 241, 275.

[504] Dec. 88/565 ([1988] OJ L310/29) on planned aid by the French Government for certain areas of Haute-Normande, Franche-Comté, and Sarthe, in the conversion centres of Dunkirk, Le Creusot, Fos, Caen, and the area of Roubaix-Tourcoing.

[505] Cf. Dec. 73/263 ([1973] OJ L253/10) on the tax concessions granted, pursuant to Art. 34 of French Law 65–566 and to the Circular of 24 Mar. 1967, to French undertakings setting up businesses abroad.

[506] B. Balassa, 'Subsidies and Countervailing Measures: Economic Considerations' in B. Balassa (ed.), *Subsidies and Countervailing Measures: Critical Issues for the Uruguay Round* (World Bank Discussion Paper No. 55, Washington, DC, 1989), 27–46.

[507] Opinion of 29 Jan. ([1986] OJ C75/12) on national regional development aid, para. 2.1.

[508] Dec. 92/465 ([1992] OJ L263/15) concerning aid granted by Berlin to Daimler-Benz.

[509] Dec. 93/564 ([1993] OJ L273/51) concerning aid the Italian Government intended to grant to Cartiere del Garda. See also Dec. 95/253 ([1995] OJ L159/21) on aid awarded by the French Government to Allied Signal Fibres Europe SA, Longwy, Meurthe-et-Moselle.

[510] Dec. 86/509 ([1986] OJ L300/34) on aid granted by Germany and Bavaria to a producer of polyamide and polyester yarn situated in Deggendorf.

'almost entirely utilized to cover the net regional disadvantages. As such, the regional aid will not create any noticeable trade distortion in a market segment where there is no structural overcapacity'.[511]

Beyond the automobiles sector such thinking has had little impact on Commission practice. In general, the Commission maintains its view that regional aid distorts competition for the purposes of Article 92(1). This view may be maintained, even if higher levels of aid are provided in neighbouring areas, where unemployment is lower,[512] and even if the amount involved is small and it is clear that the recipient would have gone ahead with a project in a particular locality without the aid.[513]

It was argued in *Philip Morris Holland* v. *EC Commission*[514] that a more developed economic analysis was necessary under Article 92(1) than is entailed by such practice. In this case a Dutch investment aid scheme had been approved by the Commission, subject to the condition of prior notification of individual grants. One such grant involved a project of Philip Morris to close a cigarette factory at one location in the Netherlands, while expanding capacity at another. There was substantial Union trade in cigarettes, and the Netherlands was one of the largest importers and exporters of cigarettes. Philip Morris, the second largest group of tobacco manufacturers in the world, expected the investment programme to give it half of Dutch manufacturing of cigarettes and anticipated that more than 80 per cent of its Dutch production would be exported to other Member States. On the basis of this information, the Commission found that the proposed aid was likely to distort competition by favouring the recipient within the meaning of Article 92(1).[515]

Philip Morris contested this finding before the Court of Justice on the ground that the economic analysis performed by the Commission was insufficient to justify it. According to the applicant, the Commission should apply the criteria for deciding whether there were any distortions of competition under Articles 85 and 86 of the Treaty, which concern restrictive practices by undertakings. The Commission ought, first, to determine the relevant market, and in order to do so ought to take account of the product, the territory, and the period of time in question. It ought then to consider the 'pattern' of this market in order to be able to assess how far the aid affected relations between competitors.[516]

---

[511] Summary of the Commission's decision not to oppose the aid which the UK Government intended to provide to Leyland Daf Vans Ltd in support of an investment project ([1993] OJ C281/7).

[512] Dec. 91/389 ([1991] OJ L215/1) on aid granted by the city of Hamburg. See also Dec. 91/305 ([1991] OJ L156/39) concerning investment aid which the Belgian Government planned to grant to Mactac SA, Soignies.

[513] Dec. 92/11 ([1992] OJ L6/36) concerning aid provided by the Derbyshire County Council to Toyota Motor Corporation.

[514] Case 730/79 [1980] ECR 2671.

[515] Dec. 79/743 ([1979] OJ L217/17) on proposed Netherlands Government assistance to increase the production capacity of a cigarette manufacturer.

[516] [1980] ECR 2671, 2688.

However, the Court simply noted that the aid strengthened the position of an undertaking compared with other undertakings competing in intra-Union trade.[517] It reduced the cost of converting the production facilities and thereby gave the recipient a competitive advantage over manufacturers who had completed or intended to complete at their own expense a similar increase in the production capacity of their plant. The Court considered these effects sufficient to justify the Commission finding that the aid threatened to distort competition.

In accordance with such thinking, the argument that state-subsidized loans do not distort competition under Article 92(1) where loans at lower rates are granted on the capital markets of other Member States has been rejected by the Commission.[518] Similarly, aid taking the form of tax credits for road hauliers in Italy did not escape this provision simply because the tax burden in Italy on diesel fuel was particularly high and this was a major cost factor for the undertakings concerned.[519]

On the other hand, Article 46 of the Treaty might permit a Member State to impose countervailing charges on imports from other Member States where there was no common organization of the agricultural market for the product concerned and, hence, no Council measure empowered the Commission to apply Article 92 to aid granted by other Member States.[520] According to the Commission, the imposition of such charges might be justified to prevent safeguards for employment and the standard of living of producers from being rendered meaningless.[521]

In *COFAZ*,[522] where the question at issue was whether the tariff structure of natural-gas prices in the Netherlands involved the grant of aid to Dutch manufacturers of ammonia, Advocate General VerLoren van Themaat considered that Member States also retained more general powers to introduce counterbalancing aid. According to the Advocate General, a Member State could counterbalance distortions of competition resulting from aid granted by another Member State by introducing aid having the same effect for the benefit of its own undertakings. However, in certain sectors or for certain purposes, such as environmental protection or regional development or for the realization of an important project in the interests of the Union, it might be considered

---

[517] *Ibid.*, 2688–9. Capotorti AG stressed the 'export bias' of Philip Morris (*ibid.*, 2697).

[518] *Eighth Report on Competition Policy* (EC Commission, Brussels, 1979), 155–6. However, in assessing a Dutch tariff in Dec. 82/73 ([1982] OJ L37/29) on the preferential tariff charged to glasshouse growers for natural gas in the Netherlands, the Commission noted that there was no specific tariff for gas used as a fuel or for any other forms of energy used in horticulture in any other Member State for the horticultural sector or for any other industrial category.

[519] Communic. C32/92 (ex NN67/92) ([1992] OJ C316/7) on aids granted by Italy to professional road hauliers.

[520] Case 337/82 *St Nikolaus Brennerei* v. *Hauptzollamt Krefeld* [1984] ECR 1051. See also Case 181/85 *France* v. *EC Commission: countervailing charges on imports of ethyl alcohol* [1987] ECR 689.

[521] [1984] ECR 1051, 1055.

[522] Case 169/84 *Cie Française de l'Azote (COFAZ) SA* v. *EC Commission* [1986] ECR 391, 407.

desirable to remove the distortion either wholly or in part by harmonizing aid.

An alternative solution was suggested by Advocate General Fennelly in *Belgium* v. *EC Commission: natural gas tariff*,[523] which also concerned natural-gas prices in the Netherlands. According to the Advocate General, if aid granted by a Member State were extended to undertakings in other Member States, any distortion of competition within the meaning of Article 92(1) would be eliminated, and this provision would be rendered inapplicable.

The Commission, nevertheless, maintains its preference for seeking the abolition of all aid which distorts competition. Otherwise, the Commission argues, Article 92 could not take effect until complete harmonization of all conditions affecting undertakings had been achieved within the Union.[524]

Sectoral Characteristics

Sectoral characteristics may be decisive for a finding that aid distorts competition.[525] This was so, for example, in the case of textile industries experiencing marketing difficulties both in Europe and in their traditional external markets owing to increasing competition from manufacturers in Eastern Europe and those with cheap labour sources; they were also having to deal with a drop in demand caused by the recession.[526]

Again, in the construction and engineering sector the work-load of companies is normally acquired in a limited number of open tenders where the price offered is the 'main orientative indicator' for placing the orders amongst the companies fulfilling the required specifications. The projects normally have a life of more than one year, and their budgets are generally of considerable value. Therefore, aid is likely to distort competition.[527]

Particular account may be taken of questions whether the sector concerned is characterized by overcapacity,[528] though definition of the relevant sector may be problematic;[529] poor prospects of growth in demand;[530] outlets that are

---

[523] Case C–56/93 ([1996] ECR I–723, I–735).

[524] *Eighth Report on Competition Policy* (EC Commission, Brussels, 1979), 155–6.

[525] Van Gerven AG in Case 305/89 *Italy* v. *EC Commission: Alfa Romeo* [1991] ECR I–1603, I–1622 and the Court itself (*ibid.*, I–1642).

[526] *Sixth Report on Competition Policy* (EC Commission, Brussels, 1977), 125.

[527] Notice C39/94 (ex NN55/94) ([1994] OJ C328/2) regarding aid which Italy had decided to grant to Iritecna SpA. See also Notice C6/92 (ex NN141/91) ([1995] OJ C120/4) regarding aid which Italy granted to CMF SUD SpA and CMF SpA.

[528] In such a sector the resulting 'intense pressure on prices and volume' may increase the likelihood that aid to suppliers may distort competition. See Notice C29/93 (ex N431/93) ([1993] OJ C306/3) regarding aid, which Baden-Württemberg intended to grant to the Aluminium Giesserei Villingen GmbH.

[529] Dec. 95/438 ([1995] OJ L257/45) concerning investment aid granted by Spain to Piezas y Rodajes, a steel foundry located in Teruel, Spain.

[530] Notice C5/94 (N24/94) ([1994] OJ C150/5) regarding aid which Germany planned to grant to Gebrüder Welger GmbH & Co. KG, Niedersachsen.

difficult to find and resulting redundancies;[531] low profit margins;[532] an 'atomized' structure;[533] capital-intensive investments;[534] or import penetration from third states.[535] In sectors with such characteristics aid may result in exportation of unemployment and/or retaliation,[536] or it may prevent the disappearance of an undertaking in difficulties which would have led to increased opportunities for other undertakings.[537] Even where the market is in balance and capacity is being 'utilized to a proper extent', aid to introduce new capacity may distort competition.[538] Any such distortion may be amplified where the sector concerned is 'highly regulated'.[539]

Overcapacity, or even the mere possibility of overcapacity,[540] has been a decisive consideration in the evaluation of the effects of aid to such sectors as synthetic fibres,[541] butyl acetate,[542] chemicals,[543] household appliances,[544] finished aluminium frames,[545] mechanical engineering,[546] computer

---

[531] Joined Cases 62 & 72/87 *Exécutif Régional Wallon and SA Glaverbel* v. *EC Commission* [1988] ECR 1573, 1593.

[532] Case 259/85 *France* v. *EC Commission: aid to textiles and clothing* [1987] ECR 4393, 4409 and 4419.

[533] Darmon AG in Case 310/85 *Deufil GmbH & Co. KG* v. *EC Commission* [1987] ECR 901, 915; Jacobs AG in Joined Cases 278/92, C–279/92 & C–280/92 *Spain* v. *EC Commission: Intelhorce* [1994] ECR I–4103, I–4128. The Court itself in the latter ruling referred to the 'specific difficulties' (*ibid.*, I–4158–9) of the sector concerned.

[534] Joined Cases T–244/93 & T–486/93 *TWD Textilwerke Deggendorf GmbH* v. *EC Commission* [1995] ECR II–2265, II–2295.

[535] Dec. 89/456 ([1989] OJ L223/22) on the French Government's aid proposal in favour of Caulliez Frères, cotton yarn producer located in Prouvy, France.

[536] *Thirteenth Report on Competition Policy* (EC Commission, Brussels, 1984), 144.

[537] *Twelfth Report on Competition Policy* (EC Commission, Brussels, 1983), 114.

[538] Dec. 82/4 ([1981] OJ L5/13) on proposed assistance by the Belgian Government for investments by an Antwerp chemical firm for the production of polyether-polyol.

[539] Dec. 92/327 ([1989] OJ L182/89) concerning aid granted by the Belgian Government to undertakings in the pharmaceutical industry in the form of programme contracts.

[540] Notice C37/94 (NN 10/93) ([1994] OJ C338/18) concerning aid included in a loan guarantee granted by Spain (Basque Government) to Guascor SA.

[541] Dec. 81/716 ([1981] OJ L256/22) on a proposal by the Netherlands Government to grant aid for increasing the production capacity by an undertaking in the chemical industry (polyethylene); Dec. 82/295 ([1982] OJ L132/53) on an aid scheme by the Belgian Government in respect of certain investments carried out by a Belgian undertaking to increase its production capacity for high-density polyethylene; and Dec. 84/498 ([1984] OJ L276/40) on an aid proposed by the Irish Government in favour of a producer of polyester yarn situated in Letterkenny.

[542] Notice C43/92 (NN131/92) ([1994] OJ C16/6) concerning aid awarded by the German Government to Buna AG.

[543] Communic. NN50/89 ([1989] OJ C281/9) concerning aid which the Italian Government had decided to grant to promote the reorganization of manufacturing industry.

[544] *Sixteenth Report on Competition Policy* (EC Commission, Brussels, 1987), 158.

[545] Dec. 88/174 ([1988] OJ L79/29) concerning aid which Baden-Württemberg had provided to BUG-Alutechnik GmbH, an undertaking producing semi-finished and finished aluminium products; Dec. 88/283 ([1988] OJ L121/57) on French Government aid to Pechiney, a company producing mainly aluminium; and Notice C38/92 ([1995] OJ C292/10) regarding a capital injection made by the Italian Government to Alumix, an aluminium producer.

[546] *Twenty-Fourth Report on Competition Policy* (EC Commission, Brussels, 1995), 515–6.

hardware,[547] crockery and ceramic sanitary ware,[548] flat glass,[549] chipboard,[550] particle board,[551] clothing,[552] equipment for the food industry,[553] cauldrons and brewery equipment,[554] pigmeat,[555] starch,[556] apples and pears,[557] ball-bearings,[558] steel pipes and tubes,[559] railway crossing frogs,[560] marine diesel engines,[561] industrial trucks,[562] trailers,[563] farm machinery,[564] aircraft main-

[547] Notice C33/B/93 (NN12/94) ([1994] OJ C80/4) regarding aid which France had decided to grant to Groupe Bull.

[548] Dec. 83/130 ([1983] OJ L91/32) on aid granted by the Belgian Government to a firm manufacturing ceramic sanitary ware; Dec. 85/153 ([1985] OJ L59/21) concerning aid which the Belgian Government granted in 1983 to a ceramic sanitary ware and crockery manufacturer; and Dec. 86/366 ([1986] OJ L223/30) concerning aid which the Belgian Government has granted to a ceramic sanitary ware and crockery manufacturer.

[549] Dec. 84/497 ([1984] OJ L276/37) on a proposal by the Netherlands Government to grant aid for an investment by a flat-glass manufacturer at Tiel; Dec. 84/507 ([1984] OJ L283/39) concerning aid which Luxembourg proposed to grant in respect of investment carried out by a flat-glass manufacturer at Bascharage; Dec. 86/593 ([1986] OJ L342/32) on a proposal by the Belgian Government to grant aid for investments by a flat-glass producer at Auvelais; Dec. 87/195 ([1987] OJ L77/47) on a proposal by the Belgian Government to grant aid for investments by a flat-glass producer at Moustier.

[550] Notice C40/95 (ex N353/95) ([1995] OJ C295/20) concerning aid which Germany intends to grant to Glunz AG, a wood-processing firm.

[551] Notice C41/94 (ex NN37/94) ([1994] OJ C369/6) concerning aid which Germany had granted to Fritz Egger Spanplattenindustrie GmbH & Co. KG at Brilon.

[552] Notice ([1985] OJ C51/4) of financial support equivalent to state aid given by the Italian Government to a number of state-owned ready-to-wear men's clothing manufacturers.

[553] Dec. 84/496 ([1984] OJ L276/34) on aid which the Belgian Government had granted to an undertaking at Tournai manufacturing equipment for the food industry.

[554] Dec. 87/48 ([1987] OJ L20/30) concerning aid in Belgium in favour of the brewery equipment industry.

[555] Dec. 77/172 ([1977] OJ L54/39) concerning an aid for the pigmeat sector in the UK.

[556] Dec. 91/474 ([1991] OJ L254/14) concerning aids granted by the Italian Government to Italgrani SpA for the setting up of an agri-foodstuffs complex in the Mezzogiorno.

[557] Dec. 72/251 ([1972] JO L163/19) on the grant of aid for the creation of a reserve fund to cover risks-damage caused by hail to producers of applies and pears in the Netherlands.

[558] Notice C58/94 (N541/94, N582/94, N604/94 & N627/94) ([1995] OJ C96/4) regarding aid which Germany had decided to grant to Unternehmensgruppe Müller/Loesch, FAG Kugelfischer AG, Steinbock Boss GmbH Fördertechnik and Jungheinrich AG, and INA Werk Schaeffler KG.

[559] Dec. 87/418 ([1987] OJ L227/45) concerning aid to a Belgian steel pipe and tube manufacturer; and Notice C4/93 (ex N652/92) ([1993] OJ C122/5) regarding aid which the German Government had decided to grant to Berg-Spezial-Rohr, Siegen.

[560] Notice C13/95 (NN9/95) ([1995] OJ C293/8) concerning aid granted by the Italian Government to Breda Fucine Meridionali.

[561] Notice C37/94 (NN10/93) ([1995] OJ C313/2) concerning aid included in a loan guarantee granted by Spain (Basque Government) to Guascor SA.

[562] Notice C58/94 (N541/94, N582/94, N604/94 & N627/94) ([1995] OJ C96/4) regarding aid which Germany had decided to grant to Unternehmensgruppe Müller/Loesch, FAG Kugelfischer AG, Steinbock Boss GmbH Fördertechnik and Jungheinrich AG, and INA Werk Schaeffler KG.

[563] Notice ([1986] OJ C276/7) regarding the provision of capital that the French Government had provided to an undertaking involved in the production of trailers and semi-trailers in France.

[564] Dec. 84/364 ([1984] OJ L192/35) concerning the proposal of the Italian Government to award aid to an engine and tractor manufacturer; and Dec. 88/468 ([1988] OJ L229/37) on aids

tenance,[565] oil refining,[566] and road haulage.[567] Even the risk of overcapacity, which is 'always present . . . in a dynamic market, characterized by intense competition', may be an influential consideration.[568]

In the case of aid which entails no increase in production capacity and leads to the viability of the recipient, consideration must still be given to the question whether the anti-competitive effects in the sector concerned are such as to render the aid prohibited.[569] At least in the context of overcapacity, where the output of the assisted company is used chiefly within the company itself, the damage is no less to other companies within the Union. Faced with rigid consumption patterns, the latter companies might be forced to make additional cuts.[570]

It seems from *Alfa Romeo*,[571] which concerned capital contributions to a car manufacturer, that Commission practice is supported by the Court of Justice. According to the Court, where an undertaking operates in a sector where there is surplus production capacity and producers from various Member States compete, any aid which it may receive from the public authorities is liable to distort competition inasmuch as its continuing presence on the market prevents competitors from increasing their market share and reduces their chances of increasing exports.[572]

'Aid War' Risks

Commission practice recognizes that integration in other respects can exaggerate the effects of any remaining distortions. According to the Commission, the

granted by the French Government to a farm machinery manufacturer at St Dizier, Angers and Croix.

[565] Notice C32/95 (NN59/95) ([1995] OJ C295/17) regarding aid which Niedersachsen had decided to grant to ASL Lemwerder.

[566] Dec. 73/293 ([1973] OJ L270/22) on aid which the Belgian Government intended to grant for extending an oil refinery at Antwerp and for setting up a new refinery at Kallo (province of East Flanders); Dec. 77/260 ([1977] OJ L80/23) concerning aid planned by the Belgian Government towards the extension of capacity of an oil refinery at Antwerp; Dec. 80/1157 ([1980] OJ L343/38) on a scheme of aid by the Belgian Government in respect of certain investments carried out by the Belgian subsidiary of an international oil group at its Antwerp refinery; and Dec. 81/984 ([1981] OJ L361/24) on a Belgian Government proposal to aid certain investments in a refinery at Antwerp.

[567] Communic. C32/92 (ex NN67/92) ([1992] OJ C316/7) on aids granted by Italy to professional road hauliers.

[568] Dec. 94/118 ([1994] OJ L54/30) concerning aid to be provided by the Irish Government to the Aer Lingus group.

[569] Joined Cases T–447/93, T–448/93 & T–449/93 *Associazione Italiana Tecnico Economica del Cemento, British Cement Association and Titan Cement Company SA* v. *EC Commission* [1995] ECR II–1971, II–2020.

[570] Dec. 84/509 ([1984] OJ L283/45) concerning assistance by the UK Government to a manufacturer of polyester yarn; and Dec. 86/509 ([1986] OJ L300/34) on aid granted by Germany and Bavaria to a producer of polyamide yarn situated at Deggendorf. See also Notice C9/93 (NN22/93) ([1993] OJ C210/9) regarding aid which Germany had decided to grant to SST-Garngesellschaft mbH, Thüringen.

[571] Case C–305/89 *Italy* v. *EC Commission: Alfa Romeo* [1991] ECR I–1603.

[572] *Ibid.*, I–1642.

'distortive effect of aid is magnified as other government-induced distortions are eliminated and markets become more open and integrated'.[573] For example, liberalization of air transport makes aid to this sector more objectionable.[574]

Ultimately, the Commission may be concerned to prevent 'aid wars' within the Union.[575] For example, in 1978 Ireland introduced an Employment Maintenance Scheme for the clothing and footwear industries. The aid entailed by this scheme responded to difficulties in this sector, which had been accentuated by the effect of the Temporary Employment Subsidy in the United Kingdom. The Irish scheme was objectionable because 'it smacked too much of a retaliatory measure with all the inherent dangers of such a situation, that is, an aid war'.[576] More generally, the Commission may seek to justify the prohibition of an aid measure on the ground that to permit it would 'set a precedent for the future and could lead to the growth of state aid on a large scale' in the sector concerned.[577]

Such practice is apparently supported by the Court of Justice, notably by its ruling in *Firma Steinike und Weinlig* v. *Germany*.[578] This case concerned a German fund, partly financed by the state, which promoted the agricultural and forestry industries in Germany, in particular by financing market research and advertising. It was argued that such assistance to German industry did not distort competition, because similar support was provided in other Member States. The Court, however, ruled that the breach by a Member State of Article 92(1) could not be justified by the fact that other Member States were also failing to respect this provision. The effects of more than one distortion of competition did not cancel one another out[579] but accumulated, and the damaging consequences for the common market were increased.[580] The ultimate consequence would be general use of operating aid.[581]

The result of such practice is that aid otherwise covered by Article 92(1) will

---

[573] Community Guidelines on State Aid for Rescuing and Restructuring Firms in Difficulty ([1994] OJ C368/12), para. 1.1.

[574] See, e.g., Letter E3/93 concerning tax privileges in favour of TAP ([1993] OJ C163/5).

[575] Cf. the British response to French poultry aid, which was condemned in Case 40/82 *EC Commission* v. *UK: poultry products* [1982] ECR 2793.

[576] *Eighth Report on Competition Policy* (EC Commission, Brussels, 1979), 165.

[577] Dec. 89/456 ([1989] OJ L223/22) on the French Government's aid proposal in favour of Caulliez Frères, cotton yarn producer located in Prouvy, France. See also Dec. 79/496 ([1979] OJ L127/50) on the UK scheme of assistance in the form of interest-relief grants in favour of the off-shore supplies industry.

[578] Case 78/76 [1977] ECR 595.

[579] See also Darmon AG in Case 310/85 *Deufil GmbH & Co. KG* v. *EC Commission* [1987] ECR 901, 917; and Dec. 79/519 ([1979] OJ L138/30) concerning the 'special financing scheme for investments to increase exporting firms' production capacity' in France.

[580] [1977] ECR 595, 612. See also Joined Cases 6 & 11/69 *EC Commission* v. *France: preferential rediscount rate for exporters* [1969] ECR 523, 540; and the *Eighth Report on Competition Policy* (EC Commission, Brussels, 1979), 155–6. Cf. Case 171/83R *EC Commission* v. *France: aid to textiles and clothing* [1983] ECR 2621, 2629.

[581] Dec. 82/364 ([1982] OJ L159/44) concerning the subsidizing of interest rates on credits for exports from France to Greece after the accession of that country to the EEC.

usually be found to distort competition. A 'degree of cross-border competition' is sufficient for such a finding.[582] Only exceptionally will aid escape this provision on the ground that no distortion is entailed. For example, aid to the sole supplier of an information-technology service was found not to distort competition, because there was no other firm within the Union providing such a service or in a position to do so.[583] Aid to the press was also found to fall outside Article 92(1), because there was 'no real competition' between newspapers published in different Member States.[584] Again, Danish aid for the collection and recycling of cadmium and lead batteries[585] and Dutch aid for the 'ecological' disposal of car wrecks[586] were found to fall outside Article 92(1), because the market was not yet capable of sustaining such activities on a commercial basis.

However, such findings presuppose a determination that there is no competition with similar goods, and such a determination may be problematic.[587] For example, Italian aid to municipal transport undertakings to encourage them to make use of energy-saving vehicles was not covered by Article 92, because the recipients did not compete with each other and so there could be no distortion of competition for the purposes of this provision. It was also difficult to say that manufacturers were aided because they received consideration for goods supplied.[588] On the other hand, whilst there may be only limited competition between the coal industries in different Member States, the impact of aids on the wider energy market cannot be ignored,[589] especially as the energy market becomes increasingly integrated with the completion of the internal market.[590]

The conclusion is often drawn that aid is presumed to distort competition, unless exceptional circumstances exist, such as the total absence in the common market of products which are identical to, or may be substituted for, those manufactured by the aid recipient.[591]

[582] Notice C43/93 (ex NN97/93) ([1995] OJ C309/4) concerning aid granted by the French Government to Avenir Graphique, a printing firm.

[583] *Sixteenth Report on Competition Policy* (EC Commission, Brussels, 1987), 168. But cf. Dec. 94/266 ([1994] OJ L114/21) on the proposal to award aid to SST-Garngesellschaft mbH, Thüringen.

[584] Communic. C24/90 (E9/89) ([1990] OJ C304/3) regarding aids to forestry, pulp, and paper production in Italy financed by means of quasi-fiscal levies.

[585] Bull. EU 11–1995, 1.3.49.   [586] *Ibid.*, 1.3.50.

[587] See, in the case of small four-wheeled-drive sports utility vehicles, Notice C1/95 (NN144/94) ([1995] OJ C144/13) concerning aid provided by the Spanish authorities to Suzuki-Santana Motor SA in support of its plant in Linares (Andalucia).

[588] Lenz AG in Case 103/84 *EC Commission* v. *Italy: aid for the purchase of Italian vehicles* [1986] ECR 1759, 1765–6.

[589] *Second Survey on State Aids in the European Community in the Manufacturing and Certain Other Sectors* (EC Commission, Brussels, 1990), 22.

[590] *Fourth Survey on State Aids in the European Community in the Manufacturing and Certain Other Sectors*, COM(95)365, 37. Similar considerations may apply in relation to railways and the wider transport market (*ibid.*).

[591] Capotorti AG in Case 730/79 *Philip Morris Holland BV* v. *EC Commission* [1980] ECR 2671, 2698.

2.3.3 Effect on Trade between Member States

Aid may be found to affect trade between Member States for the purposes of Article 92(1) simply because the recipient is engaged in such trade[592] or because the sector concerned has 'cross-border characteristics'[593] or is one where producers from different Member States are in significant[594] or effective competition.[595] Aid to large enterprises is 'normally' found likely to affect such trade,[596] as is aid which strengthens the position of all national undertakings in a particular sector involved in intra-Union trade[597] or all undertakings in an area such as the Mezzogiorno.[598] The likelihood of trade being affected may be increased by the 'intensity' of competition;[599] 'strong crowding out competition';[600] 'the progressive construction of the single market,'[601] as in the case of air transport,[602] road transport,[603] and financial services;[604] or

---

[592] Case C–42/93 *Spain* v. *EC Commission: Merco* [1994] ECR I–4175, I–4194. See also Dec. 84/364 ([1984] OJ L192/35) concerning the proposal by the Italian Government to award aid to an engine and tractor manufacturer; and Dec. 88/565 ([1988] OJ L310/28) on planned aid by the French Government for certain areas of Haute-Normande, Franche-Comté, and Sarthe, in the conversion centres of Dunkirk, Le Creusot, Fos, Caen, and the area of Roubaix-Tourcoing.

[593] See, regarding aid to airlines, Communic. C34/93 (N557/93) ([1993] OJ C291/4) on equity injections by the Irish Government in favour of Aer Lingus; Notice C14/94 (NN133/92 and N514/93) ([1994] OJ C94/4) concerning the advantages given to Olympic Airways; and Communic. C15/94 (N122/94, NN22/94 & E3/93) ([1994] OJ C93/12) concerning the existing tax exemption and planned recapitalization of TAP.

[594] Dec. 95/253 ([1995] OJ L159/21) on aid awarded by the French Government to Allied Signal Fibres Europe SA, Longwy, Meurthe-et-Moselle.

[595] However, if capacity utilization by others is not adversely affected, problems will not necessarily be shifted to other Member States. See Dec. 89/58 ([1989] OJ L25/92) concerning aid provided by the UK Government to the Rover Group.

[596] Notice C59/94 (NN125/94) ([1995] OJ C220/2) concerning the extraordinary administration of enterprises in a state of insolvency resulting from the obligation to repay aid incompatible with Arts. 92 and 93 EC.

[597] Communic. C32/92 (ex NN67/92) ([1992] OJ C316/7) on aids granted by Italy to professional road hauliers.

[598] Notice C34/92 (N615/92) ([1994] OJ C99/3) regarding aid which Italy had decided to grant under the form of reductions in and taking over by the state of social security contributions paid by firms in the Mezzogiorno.

[599] See, regarding Belgian aid to the chemicals industry, Bull. EC 5–1991, 1.2.40.

[600] Notice C64/94 (NN2/94) ([1995] OJ C113/17) regarding aid which Germany had decided to grant to Grundstücksverwaltungsgesellschaft Fort Malakoff Mainz mbH & Co. KG, a subsidiary of Siemens AG/Siemens Nixdorf Informationssysteme AG.

[601] Dec. 93/627 ([1993] OJ L309/21) concerning aid granted by the Spanish authorities on the occasion of the sale by Cenemesa/Cademesa/Conelec of certain selected assets to Asea-Brown Boveri.

[602] Liberalization is said to have led to intense competition. See Notice C14/94 (NN133/92 & N514/93) ([1994] OJ C94/4) concerning the advantages given to Olympic Airways; and Communic. C15/94 (N122/94, NN22/94 & E3/93) ([1994] OJ C93/12) concerning the existing tax exemption and planned recapitalization of TAP.

[603] Communic. C45/95 (NN48/95) ([1996] OJ C3/2) on tax credit for professional road hauliers in Italy.

[604] Dec. 95/547 ([1995] OJ L308/92) giving conditional approval to the aid granted by France to Crédit Lyonnais.

even 'advances in modern telecommunications and the processing power of computers'.[605]

Although it may not be 'possible to say exactly where the recipients' markets are since the prospective recipients are not known, past experience [may] indicate that some of the aided firms will be active in intra-Community trade' and, hence, that such trade may be affected.[606] Moreover, according to the Commission, if the investigation of the effect on trade is not to be restricted to a purely static or retrospective approach, account must be taken of the potential competition which could reasonably be expected to affect trade flows.[607] Thus the mere fact that the market shares of aid recipients may not have increased is not decisive for the question whether trade between Member States is affected for the purposes of Article 92(1).[608]

Domestic Activities

Early practice took little account of the impact of aid on domestic activities. In particular, in *Société des Produits Bertrand SA* v. *EC Commission*[609] an Italian public body had sold durum wheat for less than the market price to Italian producers of pasta and semolina. A French producer sought damages for the failure of the Commission to prohibit the aid implied for these producers. Presumably, in response to the arguments of the applicant that its French sales had been adversely affected, the Court of Justice concentrated on the question whether Italian exports had benefited.

However, as is now recognized, the grant of aid to one undertaking may mean that undertakings in the same Member State are 'disadvantaged and pay higher taxes directly or indirectly'.[610] Moreover, *France* v. *EC Commission: a brewery loan*[611] concerned French aid in the form of a subsidized loan for the modernization of a brewery. Here the Court of Justice ruled that aid to an undertaking may be such as to affect trade between Member States where that undertaking competes with products coming from other Member States, even if it does not itself exports its products. The aid may enable the undertaking to maintain or increase its domestic production, with the result that undertakings established in other Member States have less chance of exporting their products

---

[605] Dec. 92/35 ([1992] OJ L14/35) requiring France to suspend the implementation of aid in favour of the Pari Mutuel Urbain, introduced in breach of Art. 93(3) EC.

[606] Dec. 87/15 ([1987] OJ L12/17) on the compatibility with the common market of aid under the German Federal/*Land* Government Joint Regional Aid Programme in six labour market regions.

[607] *Fourteenth Report on Competition Policy* (EC Commission, Brussels, 1985), 129.

[608] Dec. 79/496 ([1979] OJ L127/50) on the UK scheme of assistance in the form of interest relief grants in favour of the off-shore supplies industry.

[609] Case 40/75 [1976] ECR 1, 8.

[610] *Second Survey on State Aids in the European Community in the Manufacturing and Certain Other Sectors* (EC Commission, Brussels, 1990), 7. See, earlier, the *Eleventh Report on Competition Policy* (EC Commission, Brussels, 1981), 124.

[611] Case 102/87 [1988] ECR 4067, 4087–8. See, earlier, Case 259/85 *France* v. *EC Commission: aid to textiles and clothing* [1987] ECR 4393, 4418.

to that Member State. Such aid is therefore likely to affect trade between Member States.[612]

Accordingly, even if the aid is directed towards activity within a Member State, the Commission may, as in the case of tax credits for road hauliers in Italy, find trade between Member States to be affected. The vehicles used for international road haulage are not inherently different from those used for national haulage. It is thus easy for hauliers to move resources between their national and international operations depending on the state of their respective markets.[613]

The Commission has also found that aid to an undertaking which does not itself export may affect trade between Member States, because it lowers the cost of domestic products[614] or favours the establishment of a plant which will substitute imports with its production.[615] Even aid which alters deliveries within a group of companies may be found to affect such trade.[616] As a result, there is claimed to be a presumption, not easily rebuttable, that aid affects trade between Member States.[617]

It is said to be only on markets for products where there exists no international trade, by reason of high transport costs, the scarcity of Union production,[618] or other particular circumstances, that in the present state of integration of the markets aid will not affect trade between Member States.[619] For example, although the production of graphic goods in the Member States is generally determined by domestic demand and the level of exports is generally below 10 per cent, the fact that there is some trade and cross-frontier competition in this industry means that aid to the printing industry may be covered by Article 92(1).[620] Again, in the *Twenty-Fourth Report on Competition Policy*[621] the Commis-

---

[612] See also Dec. 87/98 ([1987] OJ L40/17) on aid proposed by Rheinland-Pfalz for a metalworking firm in Betzdorf; Dec. 87/99 ([1987] OJ L40/22) on aid proposed by Rheinland-Pfalz for a fibre processing firm in Scheuerfeld; and Dec. 87/533 ([1987] OJ L313/24) on an Italian Government aid scheme to support Italian sugar traders.

[613] Communic. C32/92 (ex NN67/92) ([1992] OJ C316/7) on aids granted by Italy to professional road hauliers.

[614] Dec. 79/496 ([1979] OJ L127/50) on the UK scheme of assistance in the form of interest relief grants in favour of the off-shore supplies industry. See also Dec. 77/172 ([1977] OJ L54/39) concerning an aid for the pigmeat sector in the UK.

[615] Dec. 84/497 ([1984] OJ L276/37) on a proposal by the Netherlands Government to grant aid for an investment by a flat-glass manufacturer at Tiel.

[616] Darmon AG in Case 310/85 *Deufil GmbH & Co. KG* v. *EC Commission* [1987] ECR 901, 916. Cf., regarding the requirement of autonomy for the purposes of application of Art. 85 EC to relations between undertakings, Joined Cases 15 & 16/74 *Centrafarm* v. *Sterling Drug, Centrafarm* v. *Winthrop* [1974] ECR 1147, 1183.

[617] J. Biancarelli, 'Le Contrôle de la Cour de Justice des Communautés européennes en matière d'aides publiques' [1993] *AJDA* 412–36, 420.

[618] Reischl AG in Case 40/75 *Société des Produits Bertrand SA* v. *EC Commission* [1976] ECR 1, 16.

[619] Van Gerven AG in Case C–303/88 *Italy* v. *EC Commission: Lanerossi* [1991] ECR I–1433, I–1464.

[620] Notice C43/93 (ex NN97/93) ([1994] OJ C85/8) concerning aid granted by the French Government to Avenir Graphique, a printing firm.

[621] (EC Commission, Brussels, 1995), 522

sion found trade between Member States to be affected where the aid recipient exported all its products outside the Union and the only trade within the Union concerned trade between two other Member States.

On the other hand, in the *Sixth Report on Competition Policy*[622] the Commission considered that aids to the press were not generally contrary to Article 92(1), because this was not a sector where there was trade between Member States.[623] Similarly, since French essence of lavender represented 95 per cent of Union production and trade between Member States was almost non-existent, the Commission considered that aid to producers was not covered by Article 92(1).[624] Again, the European Parliament has argued that since there is scarcely any trade in coal between Member States, aid to this industry does not distort competition.[625] However, even in such circumstances trade might still be affected, in that there might be producers of substitute products or in that an undertaking might be artificially induced to invest in one Member State rather than another.[626] Otherwise, 'global' aid to the coal industry might not distort competition for the purposes of the ECSC Treaty and might thus escape Union control.[627]

Again, the lack of a trading infrastructure, which obliges aid recipients to operate almost exclusively on the local market, may mean that trade between Member States is found not to be affected.[628] In the case of the foundry industry, the need for customers to be in close contact with foundries and the relatively high transport costs of castings mean that there is little trade between Member States to be affected, and so aid to this industry is unlikely to be covered by Article 92(1).[629] Aid to small and medium-sized enterprises in Sicily to use quarry waste as inert filling material also fell outside Article 92(1). Given that the market for the materials was almost entirely local, the danger of trade between Member States being affected was remote.[630]

Likewise, aid for a dock serving an almost exclusively local fishing fleet and ships providing a link between Sicily and mainland Italy and the Lipari Islands was not regarded as affecting trade between Member States.[631] Aid granted to

---

[622] (EC Commission, Brussels, 1977), 123.

[623] The limited trade in Union-produced pulp was a factor relevant to authorization of aid to this sector under Art. 92(3)(c). See the *Sixteenth Report on Competition Policy* (EC Commission, Brussels, 1986), 104. [624] Bull. EC 4–1979, 2.1.27.

[625] Resolution of 11 Mar. 1992 ([1992] OJ C94/146) on Coal and the Internal Energy Market, para. 5.

[626] Dec. 85/275 ([1985] OJ L152/21) on the proposal of the French Government to grant regional aid to an undertaking engaged in the watch-making and optical and electronic engineering industries at Besançon, Doubs, France.

[627] Cf. R. Quadri, R. Monaco, and A. Trabucchi (eds.), *Trattato Istitutivo della Comunità Europea del Carbone e dell'Acciaio: Commentario* (Giuffrè, Milan, 1970), i, 104.

[628] *Sixteenth Report on Competition Policy* (EC Commission, Brussels, 1987), 173.

[629] *Seventh Report on Competition Policy* (EC Commission, Brussels, 1978), 155.

[630] *Twentieth Report on Competition Policy* (EC Commission, Brussels, 1990), 171.

[631] Bull. EC 12–1988, 2.1.126. See also, regarding aid to short-distance rail transport in the south-east of the UK, the *Twenty-Fourth Report on Competition Policy* (EC Commission, Brussels, 1995), 525.

purely domestic airlines, which do not have any direct or indirect links with international airlines is also considered unlikely to affect such trade. Such aid would only be caught if it had the effect of diverting significant volumes of international traffic into the Member State in question or of allowing carriers to cross-subsidize their international operations.[632]

However, trading conditions may have to be fully considered.[633] For example, Sicily was not considered 'isolated' as regards fisheries and had commercial links for fishery products with the rest of Italy and other countries. Hence, aid to Sicilian fishermen was found to affect trade between Member States.[634] Moreover, changes in trading conditions may be significant. For example, Irish aid to bakeries to enable them to lower the price of bread was accepted in 1975, because there did not seem to be trade between Member States in this product. Later such trade between Ireland and Northern Ireland developed, and was found likely to be affected by such aid.[635]

Extra-Union Activities

The Commission, with some support from the Court of Justice,[636] has tended to regard aid to the extra-Union activities of recipients as unobjectionable. For example, aid for promotional and marketing activities of the Scottish wool industry outside the Union;[637] Dutch aid for co-operative associations of small and medium-sized enterprises to promote extra-Union exports;[638] aid to Daimler-Benz in Bremen, much of the Bremen output being for export outside the Union;[639] and Belgian aid for investment designed to enable an undertaking to take advantage of a 'captive' market outside the Union[640] have been so regarded.[641]

However, even though aid for exports to third states is dealt with in Article 112 of the Treaty, which provides for its progressive harmonization, the

---

[632] Civil Aviation Memorandum No 2: Progress Towards the Development of a Community Air Transport Policy, COM(84)72, 38.

[633] See, regarding aid to domestic airlines, Evaluation des Régimes d'Aides Institués en Faveur des Transporteurs Aériens de la Communauté, SEC(92)431, 8.

[634] Dec. 87/419 ([1987] OJ L227/50) on a Regional Law providing for special measures for sea fishing in Sicily introduced by the Italian Government.

[635] Bull. EC 4–1979, 2.1.28.

[636] Case 259/85 France v. EC Commission: aid to textiles and clothing [1987] ECR 4393, 4419. See also Van Gerven AG in Case C–294/90 British Aerospace plc and Rover Group Holdings plc v. EC Commission [1992] ECR I–493, I–516.

[637] Bull. EC 7/8–1982, 2.1.42.

[638] Ibid., 2.1.50.

[639] Bull. EC 5–1988, 2.1.69.

[640] Dec. 87/418 ([1987] OJ L227/45) concerning aid to a Belgian steel pipe and tube manufacturer. See also Notice C9/93 (NN22/93) ([1993] OJ C210/9) regarding aid which Germany had decided to grant to SST-Garngesellschaft mbH, Thüringen.

[641] See also, regarding acceptance of aid to the export of witloof chicory to Japan and the United States, N323/93 ([1994] OJ C42/16); and, regarding aid to investments in Central and East European countries, the Twenty-Third Report on Competition Policy (EC Commission, Brussels, 1994), 264.

application of Article 92 to such aid, including tied development aid,[642] is not precluded. Equally, decisions under Article 113 of the Treaty, which provides for establishment of the common commercial policy, regarding aid to exports to third states do not imply the acceptability of such aid in intra-Union trade.[643] Given the interdependence of markets,[644] the possibility of trade between Member States being affected cannot be ruled out *a priori*.[645]

For example, a depression in the Union market for a particular product[646] is likely to sharpen competition between producers and lead them to seek additional outlets on the world market, which may itself be saturated. In such a context, aid reducing the production costs of one producer would inevitably affect the competitive capacity of others, both outside and inside the Union, and, therefore, trade between Member States.[647]

Equally, the existence of world overcapacity may mean that aid is likely to affect trade between Member States, even if the aid recipient has previously exported almost all its output outside the Union.[648] This is particularly so where a country such as the United States imposes import restrictions and there is increasing competition from other third states. Similarly, a slump in third-country markets may mean that increased trade between Member States is foreseeable and that trade between Member States is likely to be affected.[649]

More generally, the Commission has come to the view that the operations of an aid recipient in a third country may be relevant to the application of Article 92(1), because these operations could strengthen the position of the recipient in intra-Union markets and trade.[650] This will be particularly so when the aid

[642] Commission Reply to Written Question 1140/91 ([1991] OJ C259/41) by Mr Hughes. Cf. the objections to aid to 'dummy' undertakings in third states to re-export to the Union in the *Sixteenth Report on Competition Policy* (EC Commission, Brussels, 1987), 174.

[643] Note the Commission statement in the Council when the Decision of 4 Apr. 1978 (Bull. EC 4–1978, 2.2.46) on the OECD Arrangement on Guidelines for Officially Supported Export Credits was adopted. This statement was quoted in Dec. 82/364 ([1982] OJ L159/44) concerning the subsidizing of interest rates on credits for exports from France to Greece after the accession of that country to the European Economic Community. See also the *Seventh Report on Competition Policy* (EEC Commission, Brussels, 1978), 170–1.

[644] The Commission now assesses aid granted by Member States for compatibility with the EEA Agreement as well as the EC Treaty. See, e.g., Communic. C15/94 (N122/94, NN22/94 & E3/93) ([1994] OJ C93/12) concerning the existing tax exemption and planned recapitalization of TAP.

[645] Case 142/87 *Belgium* v. *EC Commission: Tubemeuse* [1990] ECR I–959, I–1013–4.

[646] Cf. the significance of the absence of a 'serious recession' in Dec. 87/506 ([1987] OJ L290/21) concerning aid granted by the French Government to two steel groups.

[647] Darmon AG in Case 310/85 *Deufil GmbH & Co. KG* v. *EC Commission* [1987] ECR 901, 916.

[648] Submission of the Commission (*ibid.*, 908).

[649] Joined Cases T–447/93, T–448/93 & T–449/93 *Associazione Italiana Tecnico Economica del Cemento, British Cement Association, and Titan Cement Company SA* v. *EC Commission* [1995] ECR II–1971, II–2021–2.

[650] Dec. 92/35 ([1992] OJ L14/35) requiring France to suspend the implementation of the aid described below in favour of the Pari Mutuel Urbain.

recipient is 'the largest world producer' in the relevant sector.[651] In the case of aid to direct investments in third states, the result could be increased domestic production in these states, which could lead to reduced imports, including imports from Member States.[652] Trade between Member States may also be affected, in that the aid recipients may be competing directly with companies in other Member States in the identification and follow-through of investments in third countries.[653] Accordingly, the Commission is examining aid schemes in all Member States in support of exports to third countries in order to determine their compatibility with Article 92.[654] At the same time, the Union institutions seem increasingly active in opposing aid granted by third countries.[655]

Non-Union Competition

The impact of non-Union producers[656] may be found to increase the likelihood of trade between Member States being affected, particularly given that there may be 'a global market for a mass commodity'.[657] For example, in the case of aid to a Spanish footwear producer, the Commission noted that the Union footwear industry faced steadily increasing import penetration from the developing and newly industrialized countries. Moreover, the industry was extremely fragmented, the average manufacturer being only about a sixtieth of the size of the aid recipients. In these circumstances, the Commission considered that the aid was likely to affect trade between Member States.[658]

At the same time, the fact that the production of an aided undertaking may serve mainly to replace goods imported from a third country does not preclude

[651] Dec. 93/627 ([1993] OJ L309/21) concerning aid granted by the Spanish authorities on the occasion of the sale by Cenemesa/Cademesa/Conelec of certain selected assets to Asea-Brown Boveri.

[652] Notice C49/95 (ex N76/95) ([1996] OJ C71/4) concerning aid which Germany intended to grant to Brandenburg for investment projects in Poland; Notice C50/95 (ex N317/95) ([1996] OJ C71/6) concerning aid which Austria intended to grant to the ERP programme for the internationalization of Austrian firms; and Notice C51/95 (ex N320/95) ([1996] OJ C71/9) concerning aid which Austria intended to grant to the ERP programme for investments in Eastern Europe.

[653] *Ibid.*

[654] Dec. 92/129 ([1992] OJ L47/19) on aid granted by the Italian Government to the forestry, pulp, paper, and board industry and financed by means of levies on paper, board, and cellulose.

[655] See, e.g., Reg. 3697/93 ([1993] OJ L343/1) withdrawing tariff concessions in accordance with Arts. 23(2) and 27(3)(a) of the Free Trade Agreement between the Community and Austria (General Motors Austria); and Dec. 92/169 ([1992] OJ L74/47) suspending the examination procedure concerning illicit practices within the meaning of Reg. 2641/84 consisting of the imposition in Japan of a port charge or fee used for the creation of a Harbour Management Fund.

[656] Account may also be taken of the impact of inward investment on Union capacity. See Dec. 96/257 ([1996] OJ L88/7) concerning the aid granted by Spain to Seat SA, a member of the Volkswagen group.

[657] Notice C32/95 (NN59/95) ([1995] OJ C295/17) regarding aid which Nidersachsen had decided to grant to ASL Lemwerder.

[658] *Twentieth Report on Competition Policy* (EC Commission, Brussels, 1991), 168. See, regarding market participation by companies from EFTA States, Dec. 91/305 ([1991] OJ L156/39) concerning investment aid which the Belgian Government planned to grant to Mactac SA, Soignies.

the possibility of trade between Member States being affected.[659] In one case aid for the establishment of a wood-processing plant in Germany would have meant that Belgian demand for the processed products would have been met by Germany. Since exports from Germany would have increased and imports from third States into Belgium would have decreased,[660] the Commission considered that trade between Member States could have been affected.

2.3.4 *De Minimis* Issues

Application of a *de minimis* rule in relation to Article 92(1) would mean that aid otherwise covered thereby would escape prohibition because of its limited effect on competition.[661] Such a rule may be seen as incorporating the subsidiarity principle in Article 3b of the Treaty.[662]

Objections to a de minimis *Rule*

It may be argued that the formal structure of Article 92 excludes application of a *de minimis* rule. According to this argument, in view of the availability of 'exceptions' from the Article 92(1) prohibition, minor hindrances to competition and trade between Member States cannot be allowed.[663] Objections to application of the rule may also emphasize qualitative considerations. It is said, for example, that 'the very idea of a state ignoring Treaty obligations is intrinsically more destructive to political harmony and market unity than occasional restrictive practices between firms'.[664]

At the same time, stress may be placed on practical considerations. According to Advocate General Warner in *Italy* v. *EC Commission: aid to textiles*,[665] this was a field where the difficulties of positive proof must often be insurmountable. Once it was clear that the natural consequence of the grant of an aid to an industry in a Member State must be to increase the competitiveness of that industry *vis-à-vis* its competitors in other Member States, the inference could

---

[659] Dec. 81/626 ([1981] OJ L229/12) on a scheme of aid by the Belgian Government in respect of certain investments carried out by a Belgian undertaking to modernize its butyl rubber production plant.

[660] Dec. 92/129 ([1992] OJ L47/19) on aid granted by the Italian Government to the forestry, pulp, paper and board industry and financed by means of levies on paper, board, and cellulose.

[661] Case 234/84 *Belgium* v. *EC Commission: Meura* [1986] ECR 2263, 2287–8. See regarding this ruling and *de minimis* issues, R. Barents, 'Recente ontwikkelingen in de rechtspraak over steumaatregeln' [1988] *SEW* 352–64, 356.

[662] A. Petersen, 'State Aid and European Union: State Aid in the Light of Trade, Competition, Industrial and Cohesion Policies' in I. Harden (ed.), *State Aid: Community Law and Policy* (Bundesanzeiger, Trier, 1993), 20–5, 22.

[663] Lenz AG in Case 102/87 *France* v. *EC Commission: a brewery loan* [1988] ECR 4067, 4078.

[664] Compliance with aid notification requirements in Art. 93(3) (sect. 7.5.2 below) might be rendered more difficult to secure by application of such a rule. See, more generally, regarding the significance of the Art. 5 obligation, Joined Cases 62 & 72/87 *Exécutif Régional Wallon and SA Glaverbel* v. *EC Commission* [1988] ECR 1573, 1583.

[665] Case 173/73 [1974] ECR 709.

properly be drawn that the aid did (or would if introduced) distort competition and affect trade between Member States.[666]

More particularly, to require that the effects of aid already granted be demonstrated would favour Member States which granted unnotified aid.[667] Thus the Commission denies that it is obliged 'to identify how an undertaking's commercial behaviour differed after receiving a state aid from what it would have been without such an aid'.[668]

Support for such positions might be found in the fact that the Commission does not have means of investigation comparable to those which it has in antitrust cases.[669] However, sympathy for the Commission in its efforts to overcome obstacles associated with its limited investigatory means is not unlimited. For example, in *Pleuger* the Court of Justice annulled a Commission decision for its failure to demonstrate that the series of aids granted by the City of Hamburg in pursuit of the same policy constituted what the decision described as an aid programme.[670] The consequence of the annulment was that the Commission would have to investigate each individual aid measure.

There may, however, be said to be a rationale for rejection of a *de minimis* rule which goes beyond legal form, intrinsic legal demands, or practical considerations. Whereas it is in the nature of a market with a competitive structure that conduct of undertakings with a limited effect on this structure is tolerable,[671] the same may be less true of state action. For example, in *France* v. *EC Commission: aid to textiles and clothing* the Court noted that profit margins in the sector concerned were always very narrow. Hence, the Commission did not exceed the limits of its discretion in taking the view that even relatively little aid would adversely affect trading conditions to an extent contrary to the common interest.[672]

This rationale may be thought to have support in *France* v. *EC Commission: aid to textiles*,[673] which concerned an aid scheme, financed by a tax on all textiles sold in France and used to assist reorganization of that industry. Although the goals of the scheme might have been acceptable, the Commission had found it prohibited by Article 92(1), because the tax extended to imports from other Member States, whereas the benefits went mainly to French firms.[674] In

---

[666] *Ibid.*, 728.

[667] Darmon AG in Joined Cases C–324/90 & C–342/90 *Germany and Pleuger Worthington GmbH* v. *EC Commission* [1994] ECR I–1173, I–1184.

[668] Dec. 93/349 ([1993] OJ L143/7) concerning aid provided by the UK Government to British Aerospace for its purchase of Rover Group Holdings over and above those authorized in Dec. 89/58 authorizing a maximum aid to this operation subject to certain conditions.

[669] Darmon AG in Joined Cases C–324/90 & C–342/90 *Germany and Pleuger Worthington GmbH* v. *EC Commission* [1994] ECR I–1173, I–1180.　　　　　　　[670] *Ibid.*, I–1206.

[671] Case C–62/86 *AKZO Chemie BV* v. *EC Commission* [1991] ECR I–3359, I–3455.

[672] Case 259/85 [1987] ECR 4393, 4419.

[673] Case 47/69 [1970] ECR 487.

[674] Dec. 69/266 ([1969] JO L220/1) concerning the French aid system to encourage research and modernization of industrial and commercial structures in the textiles industry. See also Dec. 74/8 ([1974] OJ L14/23) on para-fiscal taxes financing the 'Technical Centres' for leather and

challenging this finding before the Court of Justice, the French Government stressed the relatively small size of the tax. The rate, initially fixed at 0.20 per cent, had been raised to 0.44 per cent.

Advocate General Roemer accepted the assertion of the French Government that such low rates could lead only to a small increase in prices. However, he also doubted whether the situation should really be assessed in such quantitative terms. If it was considered from a qualitative point of view, the Advocate General had no doubt that imposing handicaps on foreign producers to the detriment of their competitive position, especially as a result of tax measures taken within the framework of an aid system, would distort trading conditions. The extent to which such negative effects were translated into reality was therefore irrelevant.[675]

The Court itself ruled that the rate of tax was not the essential element in finding a distortion of competition. According to the Court, the Commission rightly decided that this aid, whatever might be the rate of tax, had the effect, because of its method of financing, of distorting competition contrary to Article 92(1).[676]

Therefore, a quantitative analysis of the effects of aid on competition is unnecessary. The fact that the aid is relatively insignificant or that the recipient undertaking is relatively small does not necessarily preclude the possibility that competition may be distorted for the purposes of Article 92(1).[677] At least, the possibility is not excluded *a priori* by such factors.[678]

As the Commission has put it,[679] there is a distortion if aid 'calculably improves the recipient's return on his investment'.[680] The fact that market shares may not have altered is irrelevant.[681] There exists no critical market share accepted by the Commission below which possible distorting effects

for the clock and watchmaking industry; and, most recently, Dec. 91/255 ([1991] OJ L123/51) concerning aid and the parafiscal charge collected for the Comité national interprofessionnel de l'horticulture florale, ornamentale et des pépinières (CNIH)—draft decree introducing a parafiscal charge for the benefit of the CNIH. Similar objections may be made in relation to the practices of third states.

[675] Case 47/69 [1970] ECR 487, 501–2.   [676] *Ibid.*, 495.

[677] Case C–142/87 *Belgium* v. *EC Commission: Tubemeuse* [1990] ECR I–959, I–1015. See also Darmon AG in Joined Cases C–324/90 & C–342/90 *Germany and Pleuger Worthington GmbH* v. *EC Commission* [1994] ECR I–1173, I–1186.

[678] Joined Cases C–278/92, C–279/92 & C–280/92 *Spain* v. *EC Commission: Intelhorce* [1994] ECR I–4103, I–4159.

[679] Dec. 87/15 ([1987] OJ L12/17) on the compatibility with the common market of aid under the German Federal/*Land* Government Joint Regional Aid Programme in six labour market regions.

[680] Cf. Dec. 73/274 ([1973] OJ L254/14) on Art. 20 of Italian Law 1101 of 1 Dec. 1971 on the restructuring, reorganization and conversion of the textile industry. Even if aid does not directly reduce manufacturing costs, it may still be found to distort competition.

[681] Dec. 79/496 ([1979] OJ L127/50) on the UK scheme of assistance in the form of interest-relief grants in favour of the off-shore supplies industry; and Dec. 79/519 ([1979] OJ L138/30) concerning the 'special financing scheme for investments to increase exporting firms' production capacity' in France.

should be overlooked. Hence, aid may be found to be contrary to Article 92(1) where the exports of the aided undertaking to other Member States constitute only 0.03 per cent of all trade within the Union,[682] or where only 5 per cent of output is exported to other Member States.[683]

Practical Considerations

Practical considerations may constrain the Commission in its aid control efforts,[684] which it may seek to concentrate on 'cases of real importance to the Community'.[685] In particular, such considerations may affect the need for negligible alterations in aid to be notified to the Commission[686] under Article 93(3).[687] Indeed, the Commission proposed in 1965 that the Council should enact under Article 94 a regulation exempting from the notification requirement aid which was compatible with Article 92(2) or incapable of affecting trade between Member States. The Council failed to adopt the proposal. However, in Commission practice no notification was required of aid measures within general aid schemes which had already been authorized, provided that the aid measures were below thresholds fixed by the Commission.[688] More generally, the Commission has drawn up Guidelines regarding waiver of the requirement in the case of 'minor' aids.[689]

The Guidelines entail that outside sectors covered by specific Union 'policy statements' (steel, shipbuilding, synthetic fibres, and motor vehicles[690]) and the agricultural (as defined in Annex II to the Treaty), fishery, transport, and coal sectors the Commission will not, in principle, object to the grant of small-scale aid. Such aid is defined as that which is present where:

> —the recipient does not employ more than 250 people, has an annual turnover of not more than ECU 20 million or a balance sheet total not

[682] Dec. 88/174 ([1988] OJ L79/29) concerning aid which Baden-Württemberg had provided to BUG-Alutechnik GmbH, an undertaking producing semi-finished and finished aluminium products.

[683] Dec. 87/98 ([1987] OJ L40/17) on an aid proposal by Rheinland-Pfalz for a metalworking firm in Betzdorf.

[684] See, regarding such constraints, C.-D. Ehlermann, 'The Contribution of EC Competition Policy to the Single Market' (1992) 29 *CMLRev.* 257–82.

[685] Notice on the *de minimis* rule for state aid ([1996] OJ C68/9).

[686] Warner AG in Case 177/78 *Pigs and Bacon Commission* v. *McCarren Co. Ltd* [1979] ECR 2161, 2204.

[687] See sect. 7.5.2 below, regarding Art. 93(3) notification requirements. See also para. 50 of Application of Arts. 92 and 93 EC and Art. 61 EEA to state aids in the aviation sector ([1994] OJ C350/5).

[688] Letter SG(79)D/10478 (*Competition Law in the European Communities,* ii: *Rules Applicable to State Aids* (EC Commission, Brussels, 1990), 150–1).

[689] Community Guidelines on state aid for small and medium-sized enterprises ([1992] OJ C213/2); and the Explanatory Note on the use of the *de minimis* rule provided for in the Community framework for aids to SMEs (Letter of 23 Mar. 1993 (*Competition law in the European Communities,* ii: *Rules Applicable to State Aids* (EC Commission, Brussels, 1995), 68)).

[690] The reference to synthetic fibres and motor vehicles is omitted in the Notice on the *de minimis* rule for state aid ([1996] OJ C68/9).

exceeding ECU 10 million and is not more than 25 per cent owned by one or more companies falling outside this definition, except public investment corporations, venture capital companies or, provided no control is exercised, institutional investors, and

—the aid intensity does not exceed 7.5 per cent,

or

—the aid is designed to lead to job creation and amounts to no more than ECU 3,000 per job created

or

—in the absence of specific investment or job creation objectives, the total volume of aid a recipient may receive is not more than ECU 200,000.[691]

Aid to exports to other Member States and operating aid are unaffected by the Guidelines. The former kind of aid is treated as that which is directly linked to quantities exported, to the establishment and operation of a distribution network, or to current expenditure linked to the export activity. It does not include aid towards the cost of participating in trade fairs, or of studies or consultancy services needed for the launch of a new or existing product on a new market.[692]

Aid of the kind covered by these Guidelines could originally be granted, without having to be notified, up to a ceiling of ECU 50,000 over a three-year period.[693] This ceiling has now been raised to ECU 100,000.[694] Any decision granting *de minimis* aid or the rules of any scheme providing for aid of this kind must include an explicit stipulation that any additional aid granted to the same recipient under the *de minimis* rule must not raise the total *de minimis* aid received by the enterprise to a level above the ceiling over a three-year period.[695]

The 'Appreciability' Test

Commission practice may reflect considerations of substance as well as administrative convenience. According to the Commission, while all aid alters competitive conditions to some extent, it does not always have a perceptible impact on trade between Member States. This is especially so in the case of aid provided within the limits stipulated in the above Guidelines, mainly, though not exclusively, to small and medium-sized enterprises and often under schemes run by local or regional authorities.[696]

Thus, for example, in August 1985 the Commission did not object to an aid scheme of 26,000 million Lire in Sicily in favour of the local brick and tile industry, as the recipients were small and the products almost exclusively

---

[691] Para. 5 of the 1992 Guidelines.
[692] Notice on the *de minimis* rule for state aid ([1996] OJ C68/9), n. 3.
[693] Para 3.2 of the 1992 Guidelines.
[694] Notice on the *de minimis* rule for state aid ([1996] OJ C68/9).
[695] *Ibid.*
[696] See, e.g., Dec. 94/172 ([1994] OJ L79/24) concerning Italian Law 102 of 2 May 1990 providing for the reconstruction and regeneration of the Valtellina.

destined for the local market.[697] Similarly, aid to set up purely local services, such as 'neighbourhood care services' and certain local employment initiatives,[698] may be found not perceptively to affect trade between Member States.[699] Moreover, the Commission initially objected to German aid to companies for the purchase of other companies likely to go out of business,[700] but the objections were lifted because of the small scale of the aid.[701] Account may also be taken of the size of other undertakings in the sector[702] and the directness of the link between the products subject to the charge and the product aided. For example, aid for reafforestation was compatible with the common market, since the levying of the parafiscal charge on paper and cardboard of Italian or imported origin was not such as to aggravate the effect on competition and trade, because the link was very indirect.[703]

As the Commission puts it, 'below a certain level, aid cannot affect trade between Member States and does not therefore distort competition at Community level'.[704] More particularly, limited differences in the levies imposed on bets on horse races may not entail aid contrary to Article 92(1).[705] Apparently, aid must be such as to be capable of having real rather than purely theoretical effects[706] on trade between Member States.[707] The view that no *de minimis* rule applies to ECSC aid may be consistent with such thinking, given that the prohibition of such aid in Article 4(c) of the ECSC Treaty does not require that trade between Member States be affected.[708]

The Court of Justice may have initially been reluctant to embrace such thinking. According to the Court in 1970, aid might be contrary to Union law, even though trade between Member States was not substantially affected.[709]

---

[697] *Fifteenth Report on Competition Policy* (EC Commission, Brussels, 1986), 171.

[698] Guidelines on aid to employment ([1995] OJ C334/4), para. 7.

[699] H. Morch, 'Summary of the Most Important Recent Developments', n. 427 above, 41–7, 43.

[700] Bull. EC 1–1983, 2.1.23.   [701] Bull. EC 4–1983, 2.1.47.

[702] Dec. 94/374 ([1994] OJ L170/36) on Sicilian Law 23/1991 concerning extraordinary assistance for industry and Art. 5 of Sicilian Regional Law 8/1991 concerning, in particular, financing for Sitas.

[703] *Fourth Report on Competition Policy* (EC Commission, Brussels, 1975), 93. See also, regarding a levy not charged on imports from other Member States, the *Twentieth Report on Competition Policy* (EC Commission, Brussels, 1991), 164–5.

[704] *Twenty-Second Report on Competition Policy* (EC Commission, Brussels, 1993), 79. See also Notice on co-operation between national courts and the Commission in the state-aid field ([1995] OJ C312/8), para. 14; and Notice on the *de minimis* rule for state aid ([1996] OJ C68/9).

[705] See the Commission decision at issue in Case T–471/93 *Tierce Ladbroke SA* v. *EC Commission* [1995] ECR II–2537.

[706] Analysis of the effect of aid is not made in the abstract. See R. Kovar, n. 386 above, 132.

[707] See, e.g., Dec. 93/193 ([1992] OJ L85/22) on the aid granted for the creation of industrial enterprises in Modane/Savoy (France).

[708] Notice C39/95 (ex NN47/95) ([1995] OJ C344/8) concerning aid granted by Italy to Acciaierie di Bolzano. However, the question whether such trade is likely to be affected may be relevant to the possibility of aid being authorized under Art. 95 ECSC. See Dec. 96/269 ([1996] OJ L94/17) on aid to be granted by Austria to Voest-Alpine Erzberg Gesellschaft mbH.

[709] Case 47/69 *France* v. *EC Commission: aid to textiles* [1970] ECR 487, 495.

However, Advocate General Reischl subsequently took the view that, if aid has effects 'of such small dimension as to be of interest to only a very limited section of the market', such effects may be disregarded for the purposes of Article 92(1).[710] More particularly, according to Advocate General Capotorti, this provision does not apply where trade is affected at a purely national level, though there is no need to consider the volume of aid.[711] According to Advocate General Jacobs, it only applies where the activities of the recipient are 'important'.[712] According to the Court itself, in 1987, aid is only covered by Article 92(1), if 'it gives an appreciable advantage to recipients in relation to their competitors and is likely to benefit in particular undertakings engaged in trade between Member States'.[713]

Even so, the Commission may assess the effects of an aid not in isolation but as part of an overall package of assistance to the undertaking concerned.[714] For example, while the likelihood of trade between Member States being affected is relatively minor in the case of aid limited to a single locality and occurring at times of an international shortage,[715] aid to all undertakings in a region is liable to affect such trade.[716]

2.4 CONCLUSION

The prohibition in Article 92(1) is interpreted as covering any state aid which is capable of impeding or endangering the integration of national markets.[717] Such integration may be regarded as a condition for maintaining the competitive structure of the common market, and Article 92(1) may be said to have the function of securing for the Commission control over any aid which

[710] Reischl AG in Case 40/75 *Société des Produits Bertrand SA* v. *EC Commission* [1976] ECR 1, 17. See also J. A. Winter, n. 218 above, 238.

[711] Capotorti AG in Case 730/79 *Philip Morris Holland BV* v. *EC Commission* [1980] ECR 2671, 2697. Cf. assessment under Art. 86 with regard to 'the consequences for the effective competitive structure in the common market' in Case 30/87 *Corinne Bodson* v. *Pompes Funèbres des Régions Libérées SA* [1986] ECR 2479, 2514. Cf. also the exclusion in favour of public undertakings with a turnover of less than EUA 40 million in Dir. 80/723 ([1980] OJ L195/35) on the transparency of financial relations between Member States and public undertakings, Art. 4(d).

[712] Case C–42/93 *Spain* v. *EC Commission: Merco* [1994] ECR I–4175, I–4182. Cf., in connection with assessment of the effects of regional aid on competition, the Resolution of the European Parliament of 15 Oct. 1987 ([1987] OJ C305/128) on the effects of Arts. 92 and 93 EC on regional policy, paras 18–9.

[713] Case 248/84 *Germany* v. *EC Commission: regional aid* [1987] ECR 4013, 4041.

[714] Dec. 84/496 ([1984] OJ L276/34) on aid which the Belgian Government had granted to an undertaking at Tournai manufacturing equipment for the food industry.

[715] Reischl AG in Case 52/76 *Benedetti* v. *Munari F.lli sas* [1977] ECR 163, 190–1.

[716] Notice C21/92 (NN26/92) ([1992] OJ C240/7) concerning aid granted by Italy to certain regions of the Mezzogiorno.

[717] Both efficiency (see the *Eighteenth Report on Competition Policy* (EC Commission, Brussels, 1989), 13 and 16) and market unification (*ibid.*, 17) are sought. Cf., regarding the 'ratio legis' of Art. 92, Darmon AG in Case C–189/91 *Petra Kirsammer-Hack* v. *Nurhan Sidal* [1993] ECR I–6185, I–6201.

is capable of altering this structure. Through application of this provision the Commission seeks to maintain 'the right amount of competition in order for the Treaty's requirements to be met and its aims attained'.[718] Ultimately, competition policy is seen as a fundamental factor in European integration.[719] Accordingly, 'the monitoring of state aid must be viewed first and foremost in terms of the integration objective and only secondarily in terms of the optimum allocation of resources and economic efficiency'.[720]

Even so, maintenance of the competitive structure of the common market, which is the apparent concern of Commission practice,[721] may be seen as the best guarantee of efficiency. Certainly, the approach of the Commission is said to be 'refreshingly pragmatic' and to be concerned with securing a market structure in which there are sufficient companies to provide competition.[722] Therefore, it may be an oversimplification to argue that Commission practice entails the sacrifice of efficiency[723] in favour of market integration, though such practice may appear to show insufficient concern even to investigate possible efficiency losses.[724]

[718] *Ninth Report on Competition Policy* (EC Commission, Brussels, 1980), 10. Although free competition has to be maintained, it 'must not be allowed to go to extremes in a period of social need exacerbated by the economic crisis, thereby bringing about its own destruction by accentuating the oligopolistic character of many markets, as this would prove disastrous for small and medium-sized firms'. See G. Bernini, 'The Rules of Competition' in *Thirty Years of Community Law* (EC Commission, Luxembourg, 1983), 323–73, 370.

[719] F. Andriessen, 'The Role of Anti-Trust in the Face of Economic Recession: State Aids in the EEC' [1983] *ECLR* 340–50, 342.

[720] *Europe Doc.* 1848 (9 July 1993).

[721] Cf. the position of the ECJ that trade between Member States is affected for the purposes of Art. 86 EC where the 'structure of competition' in a market consisting of one Member State and part of another Member State is modified in Joined Cases C–241/91P & C–242/91P *Radio Telefis Eireann (RTE) and Independent Television Publications Ltd* (ITP) v. *EC Commission* [1995] ECR I–743, I–828.

[722] M. Pemberton, *Europe's Motor Industry after 1992* (Economist Intelligence Unit, London, 1991), 122.

[723] Cf. R. A. Posner, *Antitrust Law: an Economic Perspective* (University of Chicago Press, Chicago, Ill., 1976). Note, however, the argument that Posner relies on an unduly narrow conception of efficiency and that the US Congress envisaged a 'competitive process' rather than a 'quantitative concept of competition' in J. H. Flynn, 'Legal Reasoning, Antitrust Policy and the Social "Science" of Economics' (1988) 33 *The Antitrust Bulletin* 713–43.

[724] See, e.g., B. Hawk, 'The American (Anti-trust) Revolution: Lessons for the EEC' [1988] *ECLR* 53–87. Cf., however, regarding the undesirable consequences for welfare of exclusive concern for efficiency, W. J. Curran, 'On Democracy and Economics' (1988) 33 *Antitrust Bulletin* 753–77.

3

Compensatory Justification

Article 92(2) and (3) provide for authorization of certain aid covered by Article 92(1). In so doing, they reflect an idea running throughout the EC Treaty.[1] According to this idea, to secure objectives compatible with Union concerns other than maximization of competition,[2] what would otherwise be condemned as distortions or even restrictions of competition may be permitted. Thus, for example, Article 90(2) permits certain relaxation of Union competition law in the case of public undertakings entrusted with tasks of general interest.[3] Moreover, Article 85(3) permits exemption of certain restrictive agreements from the prohibition in Article 85(1), provided that the benefits of such agreements exceed those which would result from undistorted competition.[4]

Viewed against this background, Article 92(2) and (3) may be seen as providing for authorization of aid which will promote Union objectives,[5] such as economic and social cohesion,[6] outlined in Article 2 of the Treaty[7] and the

---

[1] Cf., regarding the considerations to be taken into account by the Commission when deciding whether or not to authorize a merger, the 13th recital in the Preamble to Reg. 2367/90 ([1990] OJ L219/5) on the notifications, time limits, and hearings provided for in Reg. 4064/89 ([1989]) OJ L395/1 on the control of concentrations between undertakings.

[2] Capotorti AG in Case 730/79 *Philip Morris Holland BV* v. *EC Commission* [1980] ECR 2671, 2701. The same idea underlies the case law of the Court of Justice recognizing 'mandatory requirements'. See, e.g., A. Evans, *European Community Law* (Kluwer, Deventer, 1994), sect. 8.7.

[3] See, regarding the relevance of this provision for the operation of Art. 92, Case 78/76 *Firma Steinike und Weinlig* v. *Germany* [1977] ECR 595, 611; and Letter NN135/92 ([1995] OJ C262/11) informing the French Government of the Commission decision not to regard as state aid the tax arrangements applicable to the French postal administration. See also H. von der Groeben, H. von Boeckh, J. Thiesing, and C.-D. Ehlermann, *Kommentar zum EWG-Vertrag* (Nomos, Baden-Baden, 1991), ii, 2566.

[4] See, e.g., Dec. 76/172 ([1976] OJ L30/13) relating to a proceeding under Art. 85 EC (IV/27.073—Bayer/Gist-Brocades).

[5] Art. 92 accepts that some aids may be 'normal' and contribute to development. See G. Palmeri, *Gli Aiuti di stato alle attività produttive ed il loro regime comunitario* (Maggioli, Rimini, 1989), 19.

[6] *Sixteenth Report on Competition Policy* (EC Commission, Brussels, 1987), 178; *Eighteenth Report on Competition Policy* (EC Commission, Brussels, 1989), 150. Cf. the references to Arts. 2 and 130a EC in the 13th recital in the Preamble to Reg. 4064/89 ([1989] OJ L395/1) on the control of concentrations between undertakings. Cf. also Case 136/86 *Bureau National Interprofessionnel du Cognac* v. *Yves Aubert* [1987] ECR 4789, 4814, where the Court did not rule out the possibility that an agreement might escape prohibition under Art. 85(1) and qualify for exemption under Art. 85(3) where it was intended to deal with a situation of stagnating sales and increasing stocks of cognac and to ensure balanced economic conditions in a region in which 63,000 wine-growers

[*See p. 108 for* n. *6 cont. and* n. 7].

Preamble thereto.[8] According to the Court of First Instance, in its application of these two paragraphs the Commission must have regard to 'considerations of Community policy'.[9] In practice, the Commission considers that aid authorization depends on the contribution of the aid 'to the achievement of the Community's general policy'.[10] Hence, the national interest of a Member State or the benefits obtained by the aid recipient in contributing to the national interest do not in themselves justify authorization.[11]

Rather, the acceptability of aid is dependent on the 'common European interest',[12] 'the Community's interest',[13] the 'common interest',[14] or the 'interest of the Community as a whole'.[15] Only if, from such a perspective, there is a 'compensatory justification'[16] may Article 92(2) or (3) apply. If the aid would lead to nothing more than a distortion of competition, with undue advantages accruing to the Member State concerned, it may not be authorized.[17] Authorization of such aid could lead to a 'subsidy race', which would strain national budgets and so impede the economic convergence required for monetary union.[18]

It may be inferred that through the principle of compensatory justification the Treaty and practice thereunder have absorbed ideas of neoclassical economics. In particular, Article 92(2) and (3) may be thought to recognize

and approximately 9,000 persons employed by wine dealers earned their living from wine growing.

[7] Cf., in connection with the ECSC Treaty, Dec. 89/218 ([1988] OJ L86/76) concerning aid that the Italian Government proposed to grant to the public steel sector.

[8] See, e.g., the *First Report on Competition Policy* (EC Commission, Brussels, 1972), 113.

[9] Joined Cases T–447/93, T–448/93 & T–449/93 *Associazione Italiana Tecnico Economia del Cemento, British Cement Association and Titan Cement Company SA* v. *EC Commission* [1995] ECR II–1971, II–2016.

[10] *The European Aircraft Industry: First Assessment and Possible Community Actions*, COM(92)164, 28.

[11] Dec. 79/743 ([1979] OJ L217/17) on proposed Netherlands Government assistance to increase the capacity of a cigarette manufacturer. See also the *Tenth Report on Competition Policy* (EC Commission, Brussels, 1981), 151; and the *Twelfth Report on Competition Policy* (EC Commission, Brussels, 1983), 160.

[12] Dec. 93/155 ([1993] OJ L61/55) concerning an aid measure proposed by the German authorities (Rhineland-Palatinate) for the distillation of wine.

[13] Dec. 93/154 ([1993] OJ L61/52) concerning an AIMA national programme on aid which Italy plans to grant for the private storage of carrots.

[14] Lenz AG in Case 234/84 *Belgium* v. *EC Commission: Meura* [1986] ECR 2263, 2275. See also Dec. 93/133 ([1993] OJ L55/54) concerning aid granted by the Spanish Government to Merco (an agricultural processor).

[15] Dec. 92/465 ([1992] OJ L263/15) concerning aid granted by Berlin to Daimler Benz AG.

[16] See, generally, K. Mortelmans, 'The Compensatory Justification Criterion in the Practice of the Commission in Decisions on State Aids' (1984) 21 *CMLRev.* 405–34.

[17] Dec. 81/626 ([1981] OJ L229/12) on a scheme of aid by the Belgian Government in respect of certain investments carried out by a Belgian undertaking to modernize its butyl rubber production plant. See, similarly, regarding French computer aid and Italian consumer electronics aid, the *Fifteenth Report on Competition Policy* (EC Commission, Brussels, 1986), 168–9.

[18] Community guidelines on state aid for rescuing and restructuring firms in difficulty ([1994] OJ C368/12), para. 1.1. 'Convergence criteria' are laid down by Art. 109j(1) EC and the Protocol on the Convergence Criteria.

that certain investments by undertakings have 'positive externalities'. Such investments generate positive economic effects for society, such as increased employment or regional development, which cannot be appropriated by the undertaking itself. Since the rational behaviour for the undertaking concerned would be to make these investments on a smaller scale than would be optimal for society, aid may be a justifiable means of ensuring that investments take place on the optimal scale. Aid may also be employed to tackle 'negative externalities', such as pollution. If the market does not penalize polluters, aid may be employed to provide undertakings with an incentive to reduce pollution.

In other words, aid may be authorized to accomplish Union objectives in the presence of market failure.[19] The implication is that a distinction should be sought between aid designed to correct market failure and aid designed to enable a company to exploit its trading position at the expense of its trading partners. According to such thinking, aid should only be authorized if market forces alone would fail to accomplish the relevant Union objective.[20] Only to the extent that the aid is strictly necessary to alleviate macroeconomic problems should the microeconomic inefficiency associated with the grant of aid be accepted.

Application of this principle involves 'more rigorous' application of Article 92 than in early Commission practice. In particular, evolution of economic conditions in the Union has rendered the Commission less willing to authorize aid to capacity-increasing investments which are likely to be profitable.[21]

This evolution in Commission practice was challenged in *Philip Morris Holland BV* v. *EC Commission*,[22] which concerned a decision prohibiting aid to a manufacturer of tobacco products in the Netherlands. The applicant argued that the role of the Commission in controlling aid should be much more limited than was implied by the principle of compensatory justification. In particular, the applicant objected to the Commission position that aid should only be authorized if the market, unaided, would not produce the desired effect. Rather, it was argued, the Treaty should be interpreted as requiring approval of all aid that fell within the categories laid down in Article 92(3). This argument was rejected by the Court of Justice.[23] Apparently, therefore, application of the compensatory justification principle is supported by the Court.

[19] J. S. Chard and M. J. Macmillan, 'Sectoral Aids and Community Competition Policy: The Case of Textiles' [1979] *JWTL* 132–57, 137.

[20] Dec. 82/776 ([1982] OJ L323/37) on a Belgian Government aid scheme concerning the expansion of the production capacity of an undertaking manufacturing mineral water, hot spring water, and soft drinks.

[21] Dec. 82/775 ([1982] OJ L323/34) on a Belgian Government aid scheme concerning the expansion of the production capacity of an undertaking manufacturing mineral water and soft drinks.

[22] Case 730/79 [1980] ECR 2671.

[23] *Ibid.*, 2690.

In applying this principle, the Commission considers the necessity for the aid and the nature of the aid, which must be such as to entail development.[24] In considering the nature of the aid, the Commission usually classifies aid as belonging to one of three types: restructuring aid, rescue aid, or operating aid. Such distinctions may be approved by the Court of Justice. According to the Court, the distinction between restructuring aid and operating aid at least is 'based on an objective and substantial criterion with regard to the aims which the Commission may lawfully pursue as part of its industrial policy'.[25]

3.2 NECESSITY

Aid must be necessitated by the seriousness of the problems faced[26] and by the requirements of a solution to these problems.[27] The latter element of necessity may be expressed by reference to the principle of proportionality.[28] Thus, for example, aid which 'exceeds significantly' the needs of a restructuring plan may be contrary to the common interest and prohibited.[29] The aid must also be necessary, in the sense that the objectives sought might otherwise be unattainable. Hence, the Commission, with the apparent support of the Court of Justice,[30] is likely to refuse authorization of aid to an investment which would be undertaken in any case.[31] Similarly, retrospective aid to an investment already undertaken,[32] at least in part;[33] aid for the production of goods for which demand is unsatisfied;[34] aid for investment in a sector not suffering from overcapacity;[35] or aid to conversion to a segment of the sector which does not

[24] Cf. C. Garbar, 'Aides d'état: pratique décisionnelle de la Commission de la Communauté européenne (1990–1994)' [1995] *RMC* 36–45, 44.

[25] Case 250/83 *Finsider* v. *EC Commission* [1985] ECR 131, 153.

[26] *Medium-term Economic Policy Programme (1966–1970)*, [1967] JO 1513, para. 6.6.

[27] Dec. 69/266 ([1969] JO L220/1) concerning the French aid system to encourage research and modernization of industrial and commerical structures in the textiles industry.

[28] Garbar, n. 24 above, 44.

[29] Dec. 90/224 ([1990] OJ L118/42) on aid granted by the Italian Government to Aluminia and Comsal, two state-owned undertakings in the aluminium industry.

[30] Capotorti AG in Case 730/79 *Philip Morris Holland* v. *EC Commission* [1980] ECR 2671, 2691. Cf. Case C–400/92 *Germany* v. *EC Commission: Cosco* [1994] ECR I–4701, I–4732.

[31] Dec. 84/364 ([1984] OJ L192/35) concerning the proposal by the Italian Government to award aid to an engine and tractor manufacturer.

[32] Dec. 88/173 ([1978] OJ L74/44) on the Belgian Government's aid proposal in favour of Roger Vanden Berghe NV, a polypropylene yarn and carpet producer located in Desselgem, Belgium; and Dec. 80/1157 ([1980] OJ L343/38) on a scheme of aid to the Belgian Government in respect of certain investments carried out by the Belgian subsidiary of an international oil group at its Antwerp refinery. See also Bull. EU 6–1995, 1.3.175, regarding retroactive aid for investment and start-up in farming in Wallonia.

[33] Dec. 83/468 ([1983] OJ 253/18) on a proposal to grant aid to an undertaking in the textile and clothing sector (undertaking 111).

[34] Dec. 90/379 ([1990] OJ L186/21) on aid to SA Sucrerie Couplet, Brunehaut-Wez, Belgium.

[35] Dec. 84/417 ([1984] OJ L230/28) on a proposed aid by the Netherlands Government in

suffer from overcapacity[36] may not be authorized,[37] because market forces would in any case lead to such investments. The necessity for further aid may also be doubted where an employment-aid scheme already applies;[38] regional aid has already been granted to the project in question;[39] or the Union itself has already provided aid for the project concerned.[40]

The essential questions considered in such practice relate to the adequacy of the recipient's own resources and the profitability of the aided investment.

3.2.1 Own Resources

Where an undertaking would be able to finance an investment from its own resources, aid to the investment may be regarded as unnecessary.[41] Hence, aid to an investment increasing the capacity of a firm will only be authorized where the financial position of the firm is such that the investment would be out of the question without aid, the situation of the sector concerned is such that any profits likely to be earned from the sums invested will be small or non-existent, and the Union interest in the investment is manifest.[42] Authorization is particularly likely to be refused where the financial situation of the aid recipient is not fundamentally different from that of other undertakings in the same industry which do not enjoy similar aid.[43]

respect of certain investments to be carried out by an oil company at its refinery in Borsele; Dec. 84/418 ([1984] OJ L230/31) on a proposal by the Netherlands Government in respect of certain investments to be carried out by an oil company at its refinery in the area of Rotterdam-Europoort.

[36] Dec. 82/829 ([1982] OJ L350/36) on a proposed aid by the Belgian Government in respect of certain investments carried out by an oil company at its Antwerp refinery.

[37] Treatment of retroactive aid in the agricultural sector is exceptional. See Notice C16/94 (ex N550/93) ([1994] OJ C159/3) concerning aid which Italy (the Region of Liguria) intended to grant for agricultural co-operatives.

[38] Dec. 81/626 ([1981] OJ L229/12) on a scheme of aid by the Belgian Government in respect of certain investments carried out by a Belgian undertaking to modernize its butyl rubber production plant.

[39] Dec. 79/743 ([1979] OJ L217/17) on proposed Netherlands Government assistance to increase the production capacity of a cigarette manufacturer; Dec. 81/716 ([1981] OJ L256/22) on a proposal by the Netherlands Government to grant aid for increasing the production capacity of an undertaking in the chemical industry (polyethylene).

[40] Dec. 88/318 ([1988] OJ L143/37) on Law 64 of 1 Mar. 1986 on aid to the Mezzogiorno; Notice C32/94 (N48/94) ([1994] OJ C293/6) with regard to the aid for the construction of a rape seed oil methylester pilot plant operated by the Raiffeisen Hauptgenossenschaft Nord AG, Kiel.

[41] Dec. 92/328 ([1992] OJ L182/94) concerning aid granted by the French Government for the disposal of the assets of the MFL Group (Machines françaises lourdes), producer of heavy-duty machine tools; Notice ([1985] OJ C51/3) of a proposal by the Luxembourg Government to award aid for an investment aimed at creating polyester film production capacity; and Communic. C12/90 ([1990] OJ C169/11) regarding aid which the Brussels Regional Authorities had decided to grant to Volkswagen SA.

[42] Notice N115/91 ([1991] OJ C200/13) concerning aid which Belgium had decided to grant to Belbottling, a firm located at Ghent, to help it carry out an investment aimed at increasing its bottling capacity.

[43] Dec. 82/776 ([1982] OJ L323/27) on a Belgian Government aid scheme concerning the expansion of the production capacity of an undertaking manufacturing mineral water, hot spring water and soft drinks.

In the case of a subsidiary, even one having separate legal personality,[44] account may be taken of the financial position of the parent company and its interest in the aided investment.[45] For example, where the aid recipient is a subsidiary of a much larger parent company, whose financial strength is considerable, market forces may be regarded as sufficient in themselves to secure normal development and the investment in question without aid.[46]

3.2.2 Profitability

Where the investment is expected to be profitable,[47] particularly having regard to the economic potential of the sector concerned,[48] or responds to anticipated demand,[49] aid is likely to be considered unnecessary. In the view of the Commission, such an investment may be carried out under normal market conditions alone, which could thus adapt the structures of the industry and the firm concerned to the latest demand trends.[50]

Accordingly, the Commission has refused to authorize aid to renew the research laboratories of a petrochemicals firm;[51] aid to the production of petrol without lead additives;[52] aid for the production of industrial gas;[53] aid to update the research facilities of an electrical and electronic engineering firm;[54] aid to an undertaking producing mineral water and soft drinks;[55] aid to the foodstuffs

---

[44] Case 323/82 *SA Intermills* v. *EC Commission* [1984] ECR 3809, 3826.

[45] Dec. 88/468 ([1988] OJ L229/37) on aids granted by the French Government to a farm machinery manufacturer at St Dizier, Angers, and Croix (International Harvester/Tenneco); Dec. 89/254 ([1989] OJ L34/106) relating to aid which the Belgian Government had granted to a petrochemicals company at Ottignies/Louvain-La-Neuve (SA Belgian Shell).

[46] Dec. 86/509 ([1986] OJ L300/34) on aid granted by Germany and Bavaria to a producer of polyamide and polyester yarn situated in Deggendorf.

[47] Dec. 84/499 ([1984] OJ L276/43) on the proposal by the Netherlands Government to grant aid for the building of a petrol additive production plant in the Rotterdam Europoort area.

[48] Communic. C46/89 ([1990] OJ C5/5) regarding aid which Belgium had decided to grant to the pharmaceutical undertaking, Smith Kline Biological SA, which concerned aid to an investment in biotechnology.

[49] Dec. 82/774 ([1982] OJ L323/31) on a Belgian Government aid scheme concerning the setting up of a new factory by a soft drinks manufacturer.

[50] Dec. 81/984 ([1981] OJ L361/24) on a Belgian Government proposal to aid certain investments in a refinery at Antwerp.

[51] Dec. 81/717 ([1981] OJ L256/26) on a proposal by the Netherlands Government to grant aid for investment in the petrochemical industry.

[52] Dec. 82/829 ([1982] OJ L350/36) on a proposed aid by the Belgian Government in respect of certain investments carried out by an oil company in its Antwerp refinery.

[53] Dec. 81/945 ([1981] OJ L338/39) on a Belgian Government proposal to aid certain investments to be carried out by a Belgian undertaking for the establishment of production capacity of argon.

[54] Dec. 81/767 ([1981] OJ L276/35) on a proposal by the Netherlands Government to grant aid for investment by an electrical and electronic engineering firm.

[55] Dec. 82/776 ([1982] OJ L323/37) on a Belgian Government aid scheme concerning the expansion of the production capacity of an undertaking manufacturing mineral water, hot spring water and soft drinks.

packaging industry;[56] aid to improvement of product quality and publicity by a ceramics producer;[57] and aid for provision of financial and insurance services.[58]

The rationale for such practice is that aid granted unnecessarily does not facilitate the development of certain economic activities. On the contrary, it accentuates disparities between trading conditions in the Member States to an extent contrary to the common interest.[59]

3.3 RESTRUCTURING AID

Restructuring aid is defined by the Commission as aid which is part of a feasible, coherent, and far-reaching plan to restore the long-term viability of the recipient.[60] In other words, it is aid which promotes adjustments to changing economic conditions by capital and labour.[61]

The Commission is said not to treat restructuring aid as *per se* contrary to the common interest, because such treatment would entail the introduction of an industrial policy for the sector concerned.[62] At the same time, there is also said to be the possibility that, if restructuring aid were so treated, undertakings or Member States might claim to be suffering discrimination in relation to undertakings and Member States where restructuring aid had previously been authorized.[63]

There may also be more positive reasons for authorizing restructuring aid.[64] Restructuring aid may lead to economies of scale and reduced labour costs per unit of production.[65] At the same time, such aid may reduce the social costs of

---

[56] Dec. 81/718 ([1981] OJ L256/29) on a proposal by the Netherlands Government to grant aid for investment in the foodstuffs packaging industry.

[57] Notice C39/92 (NN129/92) ([1993] OJ C46/3) concerning aid granted by Italy to the ceramics sector in Lazio.

[58] Notice C35/92 (ex N172/A/91) ([1994] OJ C78/2) concerning aid granted by the Region of Friuli–Venezia Giulia.

[59] Mancini AG in Case 259/85 *France* v. *EC Commission: aid to textiles and clothing* [1987] ECR 4393, 4410.

[60] Para. 2.1 of the Community guidelines on state aid for rescuing and restructuring firms in difficulty ([1994] OJ C368/12). Cf. the view of Slynn AG in Case 223/85 *Rijn-Schelde-Verolme (RSV) Maschinenfabrieken en Scheepswerven NV* v. *EC Commission* [1987] ECR 4617, 4651.

[61] See, regarding assistance to workers affected by restructuring, para. 3.2.5 of the Community guidelines on state aid for rescuing and restructuring firms in difficulty ([1994] OJ C368/12).

[62] C.–D. Ehlermann, 'State Aid Control in the European Union: Success or Failure' (1994–5) 18 *Fordham Intl. LJ* 1212–29, 1228.

[63] *Ibid.*, 1229. Cf. the complaint of the Spanish Industry Minister that stricter treatment of restructuring aid in the case of Air France than in the case of Iberia constituted 'discriminatory treatment' (*European*, 7–13 Dec. 1995).

[64] See, e.g., the *Second Programme de Politique Economique à Moyen Terme* ([1969] JO L129/7).

[65] *Les Aspects économiques de la conversion industrielle* (ECSC High Authority, Luxembourg, 1966), 102. Cf. Dec. 84/380 ([1984] OJ L207/17) relating to a proceeding under Art. 85 EC (IV/30.810—Synthetic fibres); Dec. 87/3 ([1987] OJ L5/13) in proceedings under Art. 85 EC (IV/31.55—ENI/Montedison); and Dec. 88/87 ([1988] OJ L50/18) relating to a proceeding under Art. 85 EC (IV/31.846—Enichem/ICI).

restructuring an undertaking in difficulty, and so bring economic benefits above and beyond the interests of the undertaking concerned.[66] The aid may thus be consistent with Article 130(1) of the EC Treaty, as amended by the Treaty on European Union. According to this provision, the Union and the Member States are to aim at speeding up the adjustment of industry to structural change.

However, the aid must facilitate development by re-establishing the competitiveness of the recipient[67] and remedying structural problems of sectors rather than merely those of the recipient.[68] Aid which does not meet these conditions cannot lead to the development of the economic activities in which the recipients are engaged.[69] At the same time, aid which does not guarantee the viability of the recipients without further aid may be regarded as affecting trading conditions to an extent contrary to the common interest under Article 92(3)(c).[70]

Restructuring aid may also be treated as adversely affecting trading conditions to an extent contrary to the common interest under this provision because of overcapacity in the sector concerned. Aid has been so treated, for example, in the tractor,[71] washing machines,[72] aluminium,[73] and synthetic fibres sectors.[74] More particularly, aid may be so treated where the sector is facing a sharp drop in demand[75] or simply because the aid is for modernization purposes.[76]

Moreover, such aid should not have the effect of shifting an unfair share of

[66] H. Morch, 'Summary of the Most Important Recent Decisions' (1994) 3 *Competition Policy Newsletter* 61–6, 64.

[67] Case C–301/87 *France* v. *EC Commission: Boussac* [1990] ECR I–307, I–336. See also Joined Cases C–278/92, C–279/92 & C–280/92 *Spain* v. *EC Commission: Intelhorce* [1994] ECR I–4103.

[68] Case C–303/88 *Italy* v. *EC Commission: Lanerossi* [1991] ECR I–1433, I–1480.

[69] Slynn AG in Case 84/82 *Germany* v. *EC Commission: Belgian aid to textiles and clothing* [1984] ECR 1451, 1504–5. See, similarly, Notice C37/91 (ex N292/91 and N316/91) ([1992] OJ C244/2) regarding aid which France had decided to grant to Compagnie des Machines Bull.

[70] See, e.g., Notice ([1985] OJ C37/3) regarding the Italian Government's proposal to provide aids to the state-owned aluminium industry.

[71] Dec. 64/651 ([1964] JO 3257) concerning the prohibition of Belgian aid granted to Ford Tractors (Belgium) Ltd, in Antwerp.

[72] Notice ([1986] OJ C310/6) regarding four different aid measures that the French Government intended to provide to an undertaking involved in the production of washing machines and cookers in Revin and Reims respectively.

[73] Notice ([1986] OJ C27/2) regarding the new capital of 650 billion lire that the Italian Government had decided to provide to a state-owned holding for the restructuring of its aluminium activities and on aid of unspecified form to the same holding for maintaining in operation a primary aluminium plant in the province of Bolzano.

[74] Notice ([1986] OJ C332/2) regarding aid planned by the UK Government for a synthetic yarn texturing company located at Abergoed, Wales.

[75] Notice ([1986] OJ C293/3) regarding aid which the Belgian Government intended to grant to a manufacturer of steel tubes. See, similarly, Notice ([1986] OJ C293/4) of a proposal by the Italian Government to grant aid to steel pipes and tubes producers.

[76] Notice ([1984] OJ C219/2) regarding a grant of DM 7.5 million that the German Government had provided to an undertaking producing semi-finished aluminium products in Germany. See also Notice ([1982] OJ C177/2) regarding an individual case of application of a Luxembourg aid scheme to assist a new firm manufacturing thin aluminium foil.

the burden of structural adjustment and the attendant social and industrial problems on to other producers who are managing without aid and to other Member States. Hence, the aid must not result in the company's having surplus cash which could be used for aggressive market-distorting activities, or new investment unrelated to restructuring,[77] or to sell at artificially low prices.[78] Unless such conditions are met, trade may be adversely affected to an extent contrary to the common interest.[79]

The legitimacy of aid meeting such conditions was recognized by Advocate General Mayras in *EC Commission* v. *Germany: investment grants for mining*,[80] which concerned German aid to regions affected by the 'coal crisis'. According to the Advocate General, it was reasonable that temporary aid be granted to facilitate the adaptation or conversion of an industry suffering from a recession caused by its structure.[81]

The criteria according to which such aid would be authorized were elaborated in the *Eighth Report on Competition Policy*,[82] and Guidelines were published in 1994.[83] The *Eighth Report* recognized that adjustment took time, and accepted that limited aid could be used to reduce the social and economic costs of change in certain circumstances and subject to strict conditions. Such aid was to be limited to cases where it was justified by circumstances in the industry concerned, for example, in order to overcome a structural or cyclical crisis. Time to 'learn by doing' might also be needed, though restructuring aid might be questioned where no profits were forecast for ten years.[84] However, if the aid recipient was not regarded as being in difficulty, the aid might be treated as unnecessary for restructuring purposes.[85] If the aid was unnecessary, trade might be affected to an extent contrary to the common interest.[86]

As formulated in the 1994 Guidelines, the conditions for authorization of restructuring aid are that:

—viability is restored;

---

[77] Notice C1/95 (NN144/94) ([1995] OJ C144/13) concerning aid provided by the Spanish authorities to Suzuki-Santana Motor SA in support of its plant in Linares (Andalucia).

[78] See, e.g., Notice C16/95 (NN50/94) ([1995] OJ C215/8) concerning aid the German Government intended to grant to SKET Schwermaschinenbau Magdeburg GmbH.

[79] Dec. 95/524 ([1995] OJ L300/23) concerning aid granted by the Italian State Iritecna SpA; and Dec. 96/115 ([1996] OJ L28/18) on the aid granted by the Italian Government to Enichme Agricoltura SpA.

[80] Case 70/72 [1973] ECR 813.

[81] *Ibid.*, 834. See also Lenz AG in Case 40/85 *Belgium* v. *EC Commission: Boch* [1986] ECR 2321, 2336.

[82] EC Commission, Brussels, 1979, 125–6.

[83] Community guidelines on state aid for rescuing and restructuring firms in difficulty ([1994] OJ C368/12).

[84] Bull. EC 7/8–1992, 1.3.65.

[85] Notice 58/94 (N541/94, N582/94, N604/94 & N627/94) ([1995] OJ C96/4) regarding aid which Germany had decided to grant to Unternehmensgruppe Müller/Loesch, FAG Kugelfischer AG, Steinbock Boss GmbH Fördertechnik and Jungheinrich AG, and INA Werk Schaeffler KG.

[86] Cf. VerLoren van Themaat AG in Case 214/83 *Germany* v. *EC Commission: aid to the steel industry* [1985] ECR 3053, 3072.

—aid is in proportion to the restructuring costs and benefits;[87]

—undue distortions of competition are avoided, and so, if there is sectoral overcapacity, the aid recipient must reduce its capacity proportionally to the aid received;

—the restructuring plan is fully implemented by the aid recipient, and other conditions imposed by the Commission[88] are respected; and

—annual reports are made to the Commission.[89]

In restoring the viability of an undertaking, the aid should not preserve the *status quo*[90] or postpone decisions or changes which are inevitable. Aid which does not entail any incentive towards, or lasting guarantee of, rationalization in the sector concerned cannot be authorized.[91] It must normally seek restructuring, which is sufficiently radical[92] as to render the recipient[93] or sector[94] able in the longer term to compete without fresh aid. In other words, the viability must be sustainable.[95] Accordingly, restructuring must go beyond minor modifications to product lines or organizational changes.[96] It must do so in relation to the company as a whole and not simply in relation to the plant receiving aid.[97] For example, German aid was authorized, because it contributed to a real restructuring of a production process relating to high specification products intended for very demanding defence requirements in the aircraft industry.[98] However, restructuring to the same extent as competitors may be insufficient where these competitors continue their restructuring efforts.[99] Moreover, the grant of further aid after less than a year may raise doubts whether the restructuring plan is capable of restoring the viability of the undertaking

---

[87] Thus aid may have to be reduced. See, e.g., Dec. 89/633 ([1989] OJ L367/62) concerning aid provided or to be provided by the Spanish Government to Enasa, an undertaking producing commercial vehicles under the brand 'Pegasus'.

[88] A commitment may also be required from the government concerned that it will not jeopardize implementation of such plans by acting differently from 'a normal shareholder'. See Dec. 94/653 ([1994] OJ L254/73) concerning the notified capital increase of Air France.

[89] Para. 3.2.2 of the 1994 Guidelines.

[90] See, e.g., Communic. C31/93 (NN97/91) ([1993] OJ C293/4) on aid measures involved in the acquisition by KLM of the pilot school RLS.

[91] Dec. 72/248 ([1972] JO L156/18) on the grant of aid by Belgium for the production of lucerne. See also Dec. 72/253 ([1972] JO L164/22) on the grant of aid to encourage the rationalization of the growing and processing of fodder plants as well as co-operation between agricultural operators in the Netherlands.

[92] *Thirteenth Report on Competition Policy* (EC Commission, Brussels, 1984), 144.

[93] *Eighth Report on Competition Policy* (EC Commission, Brussels, 1979), 157.

[94] *Fifth Report on Competition Policy* (EC Commission, Brussels, 1976), 85.

[95] Notice C33/B/93 (NN12/94) ([1994] OJ C80/4) regarding aid which France has decided to grant to Groupe Bull.

[96] *Twelfth Report on Competition Policy* (EC Commission, Brussels, 1983), 144.

[97] Notice C40/95 (ex N353/95) ([1995] OJ C295/20) concerning aid which Germany intended to grant to Grunz AG, a wood processing firm.

[98] *Fifteenth Report on Competition Policy* (EC Commission, Brussels, 1986), 170.

[99] Communic. C15/94 (N122/94, NN22/94 and E3/93) ([1994] OJ C93/12) concerning the existing tax exemption and planned recapitalization of TAP.

concerned.[100] Finally, aid will not be authorized simply because it may indirectly promote the restructuring of another industry.[101]

Proportionality implies that the intensity of aid should be strictly limited to the amount necessary to achieve the restructuring,[102] so that the main restructuring effort is made by the undertaking itself[103] and distortions of competition are kept to a minimum.[104] Proportionality may also imply that liquidation should be preferred to the grant of restructuring aid.[105]

To avoid undue distortions of competition, recipients will normally be expected to make a significant contribution to the restructuring plan from their own resources or from external financing on commercial conditions.[106] Moreover, aid should not be granted to the same sector over a long period,[107] though account may be taken of the 'burden of the past'.[108] More particularly, a firm should not normally receive restructuring aid more than once,[109] and further aid will be prohibited when restructuring has taken place successfully.[110]

The imposition of conditions of this kind on the use of restructuring aid may have the support of the Court of Justice. For example, *France* v. *EC Commission: Boussac*[111] concerned French aid to a textiles producer. Here the Court considered that the aid adversely affected trading conditions to an extent contrary to the common interest. According to the Court, the aid lowered the recipient's costs and thereby reduced the competitiveness of other manufacturers within the Union at the risk of forcing them to withdraw from the market, even though the latter had hitherto been able to continue their activity by virtue of restructuring and improvements in productivity and quality, financed by their own resources.

In practice, restructuring aid may be treated as adversely affecting trade

---

[100] Notice C29/93 (ex N431/93) ([1995] OJ C282/10) regarding aid which Germany intended to grant to Aluminium Giesserei Villingen GmbH.

[101] Dec. 81/797 ([1981] OJ L296/41) on a proposal by the Netherlands Government to grant aid for the creation of new production capacity by an undertaking in the chemical industry (magnesium oxide).

[102] Dec. 91/555 ([1991] OJ L300/48) on aid to be granted by the Belgian Government in favour of Sabena.

[103] Dec. 95/547 ([1995] OJ L308/92) giving conditional approval to the aid granted by France to Crédit Lyonnais.

[104] See, e.g., Dec. 90/70 ([1990] OJ L47/28) concerning aid provided by France to certain primary processing steel undertakings.

[105] Dec. 95/547 ([1995] OJ C308/92) giving conditional approval to the aid granted by France to Crédit Lyonnais.

[106] See, e.g., Notice C16/95 (NN50/94) ([1995] OJ C215/8) concerning aid the German Government intended to grant to SKET Schwermaschinenbau Magdeburg GmbH.

[107] *Twenty-Fourth Report on Competition Policy* (EC Commission, Brussels, 1995), 520.

[108] See, e.g., Dec. 92/317 ([1992] OJ L171/54) on state aid in favour of Hilaturas y Tejidos Andaluces SA and its buyer.

[109] Notice C1/95 (NN144/94) ([1995] OJ C144/13) concerning aid provided by the Spanish authorities to Suzuki-Santana Motor SA in support of its plant in Linares (Andalucia).

[110] Bull. EC 9–1984, 2.1.32, regarding a Belgian aid scheme for textiles.

[111] Case C–301/87 [1990] ECR I–307, I–364.

unless capacity reductions are entailed or some other aid 'counterpart' associated with compliance with other restructuring requirements is provided.

3.3.1 Capacity Reductions

In sectors suffering from overcapacity, which should be determined at the Union rather than the national level,[112] aid must not increase capacity,[113] and there may be a preference for aid to assist capacity reductions,[114] particularly the closure of unprofitable production lines or the elimination of idle capacities.[115] The rationale, according to the Code on aid to the synthetic fibres industry, is that 'a high rate of capacity utilization by synthetic fibres producers is an effective means of enhancing their international competitiveness'.[116] At the same time, such reductions are designed to 'alleviate the adverse effects on competitors who do not receive any aid'.[117] In some sectors all aid must lead to capacity reductions.[118] The reduction must be 'irreversible',[119] and so the sale of capacity to competitors within the EEA is not normally sufficient. Restructuring aid may be more acceptable where assets of the recipients are to be sold on markets not in competition with the Union.[120] The capacity reduction required may, however, be relaxed for firms in assisted areas and for small and medium-sized enterprises.[121]

Aid which does not lead to a capacity reduction may be regarded as incapable

---

[112] Dec. 70/304 ([1970] OJ L128/33) on a draft Italian law for the restructuring, reorganization, and conversion of the textiles industry.

[113] See, e.g., Dec. 84/498 ([1984] OJ L276/40) on an aid proposed by the Irish Government in favour of a producer of polyester yarn situated in Letterkenny. See, regarding aid for the production of washing machines, Bull. EC 7/8–1986, 2.1.81. Even if the aided investment itself will not lead to a capacity increase, the aid may still be prohibited because it is part of a more general plan to increase capacity. See Communic. C11/93 (ex N590/92) ([1994] OJ C99/6) concerning aids which Germany had decided to grant to the construction of a slaughterhouse in Kronach. However, aid which creates an additional market for the surplus production may be authorized. See Dec. 92/330 ([1992] OJ L183/36) on aid by Germany to the Deggendorf textile works.

[114] Dec. 83/475 ([1983] OJ L261/29) on an aid proposal in favour of two textile and clothing firms in Belgium.

[115] Notice C6/92 (ex NN149/91) ([1995] OJ C120/4) regarding aid which Italy granted to CMF SUD SpA and CMF SpA.

[116] [1992] OJ C346/2.

[117] EC Commission, 'State Aid Control in the Context of Other Community Policies' [1994] *European Economy*, Supp. A, No. 4, 8.

[118] *Commission policy on sectoral aid schemes*, COM(78)221, 9.

[119] Notice C1/95 (NN144/94) ([1995] OJ C144/13) concerning aid provided by the Spanish authorities to Suzuki-Santana Motor SA in support of its plant in Linares (Andalucia).

[120] Notice C6/92 (ex NN141/91) ([1995] OJ C120/4) regarding aid which Italy granted to CMF SUD SpA and CMF SpA. See also, regarding aid to increase the capacity of the recipient to sell in a 'captive market', Dec. 87/418 ([1987] OJ L227/45) concerning aid to a Belgian steel pipe and tube manufacturer.

[121] H. Morch, 'Summary of the Most Important Recent Decisions' (1994) 3 *Competition Policy Newsletter* 61–6, 61.

of improving the structure of the sector concerned[122] and thereby of facilitating its development for the purposes of Article 92(3)(c). The likelihood of sectoral development is assessed from a Union perspective.[123] At the same time, aid for an investment which increases production capacity in a sector in which there is already considerable overproduction is regarded as contrary to the common interest for the purposes of the same provision. It may be so regarded, even if regional development is acknowledged to be facilitated.[124] However, controversy may arise where it is claimed that the aid recipient is active in a subsector which does not suffer from overcapacity.[125] Moreover, aid which is granted pursuant to a regional aid scheme authorized by a Commission decision and which falls within the scope of the decision cannot be prohibited, so long as the decision remains in force, merely because it conflicts with sectoral policy requirements.[126]

The validity of such thinking was recognized by the Court of Justice in *Deufil GmbH & Co. KG* v. *EC Commission*,[127] which concerned German aid to a producer of synthetic fibres. According to Advocate General Darmon, the aid was contrary to the common interest. The latter required, in order to restore the balance between production and consumption of synthetic fibres in the Union, if not a reduction, at least a stabilization of production capacity, but certainly not an increase in it. At the same time, because there was structural overproduction, the aid was clearly short-term. It would not provide a permanent guarantee of profitability for the undertaking and would be of doubtful advantage for development of the region concerned, even in terms of employment generated.[128] The Court agrees that aid is particularly objectionable in a sector suffering from overcapacity.[129] Aid to encourage reduction of activities in crisis sectors or redirection therefrom may be more acceptable.[130]

For example, French[131] and Italian aid measures[132] in the shipbuilding sector were objectionable because they were not matched by restructuring to reduce excess capacity. On the other hand, another French scheme to assist ship-

---

[122] Dec. 89/456 ([1989] OJ L223/22) on the French Government's aid proposal in favour of Caulliez Frères, cotton yarn producer located in Prouvy, France.

[123] Case C–42/93 *Spain* v. *EC Commission: Merco* [1994] ECR I–4175, I–4196.

[124] See also Dec. 95/253 ([1995] OJ L159/21) on aid awarded by the French Government to Allied Signal Fibres Europe SA, Longwy, Meurthe-et-Moselle.

[125] Notice C4/93 (N652/92) ([1996] OJ C33/12) regarding aid which the German Government had decided to grant to Berg-Spezial Rohr GmbH, Siegen (North Rhine-Westphalia).

[126] Case C–47/91 *Italy* v. *EC Commission: aid to the Mezzogiorno* [1994] ECR I–4635.

[127] Case 310/85 [1987] ECR 901, 926.

[128] *Ibid.*, 918–19.

[129] Joined Cases 62 & 72/87 *Exécutif Régional Wallon and Glaverbel* v. *EC Commission* [1988] ECR 1573, 1597.

[130] Joined Cases C–278/92, C–279/92 & C–280/92 *Spain* v. *EC Commission: Intelhorce* [1994] ECR I–4103, I–4167.

[131] Notice ([1985] OJ C18/4) of additional aid given to the French shipbuilding industry in 1984.

[132] Notice ([1984] OJ C290/2) of the Italian Government's proposed aid scheme for the shipbuilding and ship-repair industries covering the period 1 July 1984 to 31 Dec. 1986.

building was authorized, because the Government agreed to reduce the level of aid originally planned and because the aid was 'linked to restructuring measures entailing an accelerated decrease of capacity in shipbuilding and ship repair'.[133] Irish aid was also authorized 'in order to enable the sole Irish shipyard, in Cork, to withstand the crisis. The granting of the subsidy [would] go hand in hand with conversion to ship repair and mechanical engineering.'[134]

Another Commission decision concerned the grant of aid to assist the winding up of Boch and the creation, in its place, of Noviboch. The Commission noted that Noviboch produced and marketed quality ceramic sanitary ware on a fairly modest scale, with 269 employees. Its output was currently 20 to 30 per cent lower than that of its predecessor. The restructuring stemming from the winding up of Boch had, therefore, contributed to the reorganization of a Union industry suffering from surplus production capacity. Accordingly, aid in the form of a subscription of Bfrs 400 million of share capital granted in connection with the starting-up of Noviboch was authorized under Article 92(3)(c).[135]

Similarly, aid designed to produce a reduction in the workforce may be authorized, though temporary lay-offs may be insufficient.[136] For example, in the case of aid to an Italian shipyard, the Commission noted that the yard concerned was undertaking an extensive restructuring programme aimed at converting almost half of its workforce to non-shipbuilding activities. Accordingly, the aid was authorized.[137] A German scheme, which was meant to underpin a major restructuring effort involving the closure of yards with the loss of 4,000 jobs and promoting medium-sized facilities specializing in building sophisticated vessels, was also authorized.[138]

The reduction requirement may depend on the extent of the overcapacity. For example, the Commission doubted whether a reduction of approximately 30 per cent in civil-aircraft maintenance capacity was a sufficient counterpart for aid in a sector with an overcapacity of some 25 to 30 per cent.[139] In manufacturing companies capacity depends to a large extent on the technical

---

[133] *Sixteenth Report on Competition Policy* (EC Commission, Brussels, 1987), 135–46. See, similarly, regarding an earlier French scheme, the *Tenth Report on Competition Policy* (EC Commission, Brussels, 1981), 128–9.

[134] *Eighth Report on Competition Policy* (EC Commission, Brussels, 1979), 130–1. However, ship repair was also a troubled sector (*ibid.*, 133–4). Irish officials apparently 'had anxious moments in negotiation with the Commission'. See R. O'Donnell, 'Industrial Policy' in P. Keatinge (ed.), *Ireland and EC Membership Evaluated* (Pinter, London, 1991), 96–103, 102. The yard's operations and workforce were substantially reduced in 1983. See the *Thirteenth Report on Competition Policy* (EC Commission, Brussels, 1984), 164.

[135] Dec. 87/423 ([1987] OJ L228/39) concerning aid which the Belgian Government had granted to a ceramic sanitary ware manufacturer at La Louvière.

[136] Cf. Dec. 92/317 ([1992] OJ L171/54) on state aid in favour of Hilaturas y Tejidos Andaluces SA and its buyer.

[137] *Tenth Report on Competition Policy* (EC Commission, Brussels, 1981), 130.

[138] *Fourteenth Report on Competition Policy* (EC Commission, Brussels, 1985), 146.

[139] Notice C32/95 (NN59/95) ([1995] OJ C295/17) regarding aid which Niedersachsen had decided to grant to AS Lemwerder.

throughput of the plant. When the aid recipient provides labour-intensive services and activities, greater importance is attached to factors such as staff trends in determination of capacity changes.[140]

The contribution of such practice to promoting efficiency is questionable. On the one hand, the consequence of the requirement of a capacity reduction may be that a company using aid to acquire the most advanced equipment and, hence, to become potentially amongst the most efficient in the Union may be compelled to surrender market share to less efficient Union or non-Union undertakings.[141] Indeed, the sale of profitable subsidiaries or branches to finance restructuring by the recipient may also be required.[142] More particularly, new entrants having no capacity to reduce may be denied aid to assist them in entering the market,[143] and so definition of the relevant sector or subsector may be decisive.[144] The fact that Commission practice may have such consequences implies that the practice is misconceived. Confirmation of the implication may be found in the economics literature. According to this literature, asymmetrical distribution of excess capacity may, in certain cases, enhance competition.[145]

On the other hand, in a sector suffering from overcapacity market forces may be expected to secure capacity reductions through inducing the contraction or bankruptcy of the intended aid recipient.[146] It is acknowledged that where there is a fall in demand in a market economy, undertakings not in receipt of aid may also be expected to adapt their capacity to demand.[147] However, political constraints may make the Commission willing to accept aid for capacity reductions.[148] State aid policy is said to be about fairness as well as economic efficiency. Firms that receive aid to help them restructure and stay in business must sacrifice some of their productive capacity for the benefit of their competitors who are denied the chance to gain from the disappearance of the

[140] Dec. 95/524 ([1995] OJ L300/23) concerning aid granted by the Italian state to Iritecna SpA.

[141] F. Y. Jenny, 'Competition and State Aid Policy in the European Community' (1994–5) 18 *Fordham Intl. LR.* 525–54, 549.

[142] Dec. 95/547 ([1995] OJ L308/92) giving conditional approval to the aid granted by France to Crédit Lyonnais.

[143] But cf. in relation to the former GDR, Dec. 94/266 ([1994] OJ L114/21) on the proposal to award aid to SST–Garngesellschaft mbH, Thüringen.

[144] See, regarding 'monospace' passenger cars, Summary of the Decision not to raise objections to the aid which the Portuguese Government plans to grant to the joint venture of Ford and Volkswagen to establish a multipurpose vehicle plant in the Setubal peninsula ([1991] OJ C257/5).

[145] Jenny, n. 141 above.

[146] Aid to eliminate excess capacity is said to be difficult to justify in terms of market failure arguments. See S. Rottenburg, 'Adjustment to Senility by Induced Contraction' [1964] *Journal of Political Economy* 575–83.

[147] VerLoren van Themaat AG in Case 214/83 *Germany* v. *EC Commission: aid to the steel industry* [1985] ECR 3053, 3071.

[148] See, in the field of air transport, T. Soames and A. Ryan, 'State Aid and Air Transport' [1995] *ECLR* 290–309, 301.

firm that would have failed without state aid.[149] However, the real concern of the Commission may be to avoid the grant of retaliatory aid by other Member States.

More particularly, the methodology of the Commission has been questioned. The Commission refers to the need to increase the rate of utilization of existing capacities to make Union industry more competitive and uses capacity utilization ratios to determine whether or not excess capacity has increased or decreased in a particular sector. Capacity utilization is calculated by the ratio of actual sales by Union undertakings to their total capacity. Overcapacity is calculated by the ratio of total Union demand for a product at a competitive price, whether this demand is met by Union undertakings or third-country undertakings. Except under strong assumptions, such as the absence of imports from third countries and perfect competition among Union undertakings, these two ratios are unrelated. Indeed, the value of capacity utilization ratios, as opposed to excess capacity ratios, is heavily dependent on the market strategy of the undertakings.[150]

Even so, the importance of capacity reductions has been stressed by the Court of Justice. *Netherlands and Leeuwarder Papierwarenfabriek BV* v. *EC Commission*[151] concerned a Commission decision prohibiting Dutch aid to a paperboard processor.[152] As the Court noted, the decision merely stated that the aid would not facilitate the development of certain economic areas within the meaning of Article 92(3)(c); that developments in the paperboard-processing industry showed that to maintain production capacity through the grant of aid would not be in the common interest; and that the paperboard-processing industry's future prospects ruled out the conclusion that the aid envisaged would not adversely affect trading conditions to an extent contrary to the common interest. However, there was no indication whatsoever in the decision that the Commission took into consideration the essential fact, which might have caused it to make a different assessment, that the aid in question was accompanied by a restructuring of the recipient undertaking which, by diverting its production to high-quality products, led to a reduction in its production capacity and in its market share. Partly on this ground the decision was annulled for inadequate reasoning.

Importance has continued to be attached to capacity reductions in the case law. In *Lanerossi*, which concerned Italian aid to textiles, the Court of Justice ruled that, if there is overcapacity in the relevant sector, development can only be facilitated through a reduction in the production capacity of the aid recipient

---

[149] C.–D. Ehlermann, 'State Aids under European Community Competition Law' (1994–5) 18 *Fordham Intl. LR.* 410–36, 425.

[150] Jenny, n. 141 above, 548.

[151] Joined Cases 296 & 318/82 [1985] ECR 809, 825.

[152] Dec. 82/653 ([1982] OJ L277/15) on aid granted by the Netherlands Government to a paperboard processing firm.

and an overall readjustment of the total production capacity for the sector as a whole.[153]

Similarly, *Spain* v. *EC Commission: Intelhorce*[154] concerned Spanish aid in the form of capital contributions to a public undertaking in the textile and footwear sectors. Here the Court confirmed that, as a counterpart to restructuring aid for undertakings in difficulty, the aid must be linked to a reduction or redirection of the recipient's commercial activities. In this case the sole purpose of the aid was to allow the recipient to continue its activities on a larger scale. Hence, the Commission was justified in finding Article 92(3)(c) to be inapplicable.

3.3.2 Other Restructuring Requirements

In the absence of overcapacity, aid maintaining the capacity of the recipient may be authorized.[155] Even aid entailing a capacity increase may be authorized, if the increase is essential for restoration of viability.[156] However, the Commission still requires that some contribution be made to the common interest.[157] For example, the Commission may require the elimination of arrangements limiting the competition to which the aid recipient is subject.[158] Imposition of such requirements is said to illustrate the use of aid control to protect not the Member States, but competitors against distortions of competition.[159]

Restructuring requirements may be laid down in legislation. For example, Article 3(2) of Directive 72/273[160] made the authorization of Italian aid to shipyards conditional upon implementation of a rehabilitation programme securing the competitiveness of Italian shipbuilding at the European level by the end of 1976 at the latest. Similarly, Article 2(b) of Directive 75/432[161] only authorized shipbuilding aid in Ireland and Italy after 1975 on such a condition. More generally, Article 6(1) of Directive 78/338[162] provided that shipbuilding aid had to be linked to the attainment of industrial restructuring objectives with a view to making the industry competitive and able to operate without aid or intervention.[163] Article 5(1) of Decision 2320/81[164] was rather more

---

[153] Case C–303/88 *Italy* v. *EC Commission: Lanerossi* [1991] ECR I–1433, I–1480.

[154] Joined Cases C–278, 279 & 280/92 [1994] ECR I–4103, I–4167.

[155] Case C–225/91 *Matra SA* v. *EC Commission* [1993] ECR I–3203, I–3257.

[156] H. Morch, 'Summary of the Most Important Recent Decisions' (1994) 3 *Competition Policy Newsletter* 61–6, 61.

[157] *Twenty-Third Report on Competition Policy* (EC Commission, Brussels, 1994), 270.

[158] Dec. 94/698 ([1994] OJ L279/29) concerning increase in capital, credit guarantees and tax exemption in favour of TAP (Transportes Aereos Portugueses).

[159] Ehlermann, n. 149 above, 1224. Cf. Jenny, n. 141 above, 527.

[160] On shipbuilding ([1972] JO L169/28).

[161] [1975] OJ L192/27.

[162] On aid to shipbuilding ([1978] OJ L98/19).

[163] *Eighth Report on Competition Policy* (EC Commission, Brussels, 1979), 129.

[164] Establishing Community rules for aids to the steel industry ([1981] OJ L228/14).

demanding and stipulated that in the steel sector restructuring aid must 'form an integral part of a restructuring programme'. In practice, however, compliance with such requirements might prove difficult to secure.[165]

Restructuring Plans

The existence of a restructuring plan may be decisive for a finding whether state support to an undertaking entails the grant of aid and for a finding whether aid may be authorized under Article 92(3).[166] Plans prepared, or at least verified, by independent experts tend to be favoured by the Commission.[167] Long-term restructuring aid without a viable restructuring plan is unlikely to be authorized.[168]

For example, in 1977 the Commission authorized a Dutch aid scheme, because the aid would be granted in the framework of the general plan for restructuring the shipbuilding industry and would be progressively reduced so as to provide an incentive to the preparation and implementation of more detailed plans by groups of shipyards.[169]

In practice, as in the case of a British aid scheme for shipbuilding, the Commission might experience difficulty in obtaining details of the planned restructuring measures. Accordingly, the Article 93(2) procedure[170] was opened against this scheme in 1984.[171] Subsequently the Government was able to satisfy the Commission as to the restructuring measures involved, and, in view of the fact that the losses of nationalized shipyards would be stemmed, the Commission authorized the scheme.

In some cases the Commission authorized the grant of aid, even before a restructuring plan had been produced. An early Commission decision[172] concerned an Italian draft law altering the system of aids to shipbuilding with the aim of ensuring adequate activity in Italian yards during the period considered necessary for them to become competitive. This arrangement was authorized by the Commission under Article 92(3)(c) as facilitating development of the industry, on condition that the Italian Government implemented a restructuring plan, which was to be submitted to the Commission within six months of the draft becoming law.[173]

[165] See Ch. 5.
[166] Van Gerven AG in Case C–305/89 *Italy* v. *EC Commission: Alfa Romeo* [1991] ECR I–1603, I–1630. See, e.g., regarding machine tools, Notice C61/95 (ex NN69/94) ([1996] OJ C101/7) regarding aid which had been granted to Gildemeister AG, Bielefeld.
[167] Dec. 90/70 ([1990] OJ L47/28) concerning aid provided by France to certain primary processing steel undertakings.
[168] Case 234/84 *Belgium* v. *EC Commission: Meura* [1986] ECR 2263, 2285; Case 40/85 *Belgium* v. *EC Commission: Boch* [1986] ECR 2321, 2346.
[169] *Seventh Report on Competition Policy* (EC Commission, Brussels, 1978), 143–4.
[170] See sect. 7.5.3 below.
[171] Notice regarding the UK proposal to assist shipbuilding during the period 1 July 1984 to 1 July 1986 ([1984] OJ C219/3).
[172] Dec. of 8 Mar. 1961 ([1961] JO 582) on an amendment to the Italian system of shipbuilding aid.
[173] See also the *EEC Ninth General Report* (EEC Commission, Brussels, 1966), 86.

The Commission objected in 1980 to a new Italian scheme, because the restructuring plan developed by the Italian Government had not been approved by the Parliament. The plan thus had no official status, and it was not clear that its targets would be worked towards in return for the aid.[174] The scheme was subsequently authorized, however, when the Government convinced the Commission of its firm intention to present to Parliament the restructuring plan discussed with the Commission and in view of social and regional considerations.[175]

Aid Degressivity

Aid degressivity—the process whereby aid is subject to successive decreases—is sought by the Commission when authorizing aid for restructuring.[176] For example, a United Kingdom aid scheme for shipbuilding was authorized, because it was degressive and in view of the restructuring already achieved.[177] A French scheme was also authorized, because it was degressive in character and was linked to restructuring efforts.[178]

However, Commission efforts to secure degressivity may be hampered by developments in international market conditions. For example, in 1984 the Commission objected to aid schemes for shipbuilding in the United Kingdom, Italy, and the Netherlands, which were said to involve inadequate restructuring arrangements.[179] In the following year, however, these schemes were authorized. The Commission was even able to authorize the Dutch scheme, which envisaged additional aid with no further restructuring being involved, because of the 'acute worsening of the state of the industry'.[180]

Procedural Expedients

In doubtful cases the Commission may seek to rely on procedural expedients.[181] For example, the Commission authorized an Italian aid scheme for shipbuilding, because it would 'be tied to some adaptation of the industry for it [would] be adjusted by reference to such criteria as the state of the order books of the yard concerned, its specialization and the types of vessel to be subsidised'. However, a requirement of prior notification of each individual application of the scheme was imposed.[182]

---

[174] *Tenth Report on Competition Policy* (EC Commission, Brussels, 1981), 131.

[175] *Eleventh Report on Competition Policy* (EC Commission, Brussels, 1982), 145.

[176] Art. 6(1) of Dir. 78/338 ([1978] OJ L98/19) on aid to shipbuilding. See the objections to an increase in the maximum rate of French aid in Bull. EC 11–1979, 2.1.34.

[177] *Eleventh Report on Competition Policy* (EC Commission, Brussels, 1982), 146.

[178] *Ibid.* 145.

[179] *Fourteenth Report on Competition Policy* (EC Commission, Brussels, 1985), 146.

[180] *Fifteenth Report on Competition Policy* (EC Commission, Brussels, 1986), 156–7.

[181] See, regarding a requirement that the results of a restructuring plan be notified to the Commission on a regular basis, Dec. 91/555 ([1991] OJ L300/48) on aid to be granted by the Belgian Government in favour of Sabena.

[182] *Eighth Report on Competition Policy* (EC Commission, Brussels, 1979), 131.

In the case of a UK scheme providing up to 30 per cent of the contract price, the Commission recognized that it had not been possible to prepare a plan to restructure the UK shipbuilding industry, because it had only just been nationalized. However, the Commission considered that the criteria for selecting the yards to be aided were not sufficiently restrictive to ensure that aid would be limited to yards with a real chance of becoming competitive in the future. In order to ensure that aid was granted on a sufficiently selective basis and that competition between shipyards in the Union was not distorted, the Commission decided to authorize the scheme on condition that each case was notified for prior approval. This approval would be reviewed after six months.[183] Again, the Commission considered that a French cost-escalation scheme, which made no provision for a link with restructuring, could only be authorized for a short period.[184]

Whether or not such procedural expedients have really assisted the Commission in securing respect for restructuring requirements, the practical difficulties for the Commission remain considerable. The Commission preference, as in the steel industry, may be to authorize restructuring aid only when it covers closure costs or is justified by reference to environmental policy or the promotion of research and development.[185]

3.3.3 Privatization

Where restructuring is linked with privatization, aid may be authorized as remedying a disturbance for the purposes of Article 92(3)(b),[186] or on sectoral grounds under Article 92(3)(c), provided it is not excessive.[187] A mere commitment to privatize an aid recipient in the future may be sufficient to secure authorization.[188] Such authorizations may extend to aid to permit transition from monopoly arrangements to a free market[189] or removal of protection for a national airline.[190]

More particularly, in the former German Democratic Republic certain guarantees and 'in exceptional cases' loans may be authorized, pending privat-

---

[183] *Seventh Report on Competition Policy* (EC Commission, Brussels, 1978), 141–2.

[184] *Ibid.*, 144–5.

[185] See sect. 5.6.1 below.

[186] See, e.g., Notice C2/88 (ex NN126/87) ([1992] OJ C1/4) concerning aid to Heracles General Cement Company in Greece.

[187] Dec. 89/58 ([1989] OJ L25/92) concerning aid provided by the UK Government to the Rover Group.

[188] Dec. 94/698 ([1994] OJ L279/29) concerning increase in capital, credit guarantees, and tax exemption in favour of TAP (Transportes Aéreos Portugueses); Notice C6/92 (ex NN141/91) ([1995] OJ C120/4) regarding aid which Italy granted to CMF SUD SpA and CMF SpA.

[189] Communic. C45/93 (N663/93) ([1994] OJ C100/9) concerning the England and Wales Milk Marketing Board reorganization scheme. See also Communic. 232/94 ([1994] OJ C229/8) concerning aids which the UK had decided to grant under the England and Wales Milk Marketing Reorganization Scheme.

[190] Dec. 94/653 ([1994] OJ L254/73) concerning the notified capital increase of Air France.

ization. However, aid may not be granted to cover losses arising from sales below the prevailing market price or from continued manufacturing of products for which no profitability can be expected at the prevailing market price because of a situation of general market overcapacity.[191]

The reasoning of the Commission is that a commitment to privatization offers the best guarantee available that the restructuring of the company concerned will enable it to return to full viability and obviate the need for aid in the future.[192] In other words, privatization is seen as a solution to 'recidivism'.[193] Through the condition that restructuring aid must lead to viability a commitment to privatization may even become a binding requirement in a Commission decision[194] or, as in the case of aid to Greek shipyards, in Union legislation.[195] The Article 93(2) procedure[196] may be employed to secure compliance with the requirement.[197]

At the same time, privatization may provide the company with the necessary funds to make a significant contribution to implementation of the restructuring plan,[198] and can reduce the amount of aid necessary for restructuring. In these circumstances, a smaller capacity reduction may be required, which may be vital for the survival of the undertaking concerned.[199]

3.4 RESCUE AID

Rescue aid is defined by the Commission as aid temporarily maintaining the position of a firm 'facing a substantial deterioration in its financial position reflected in an acute liquidity crisis or technical insolvency, while an analysis of the circumstances giving rise to the company's difficulties can be performed

[191] Notice C43/92 (NN131/92) ([1993] OJ C35/2) concerning aid granted by Germany to Buna AG; and Notice C14/93 (ex NN36/93) ([1993] OJ C220/31) regarding aid which Germany granted to Leuna AG. In the case of continued financing of companies still held by the THA, notification was required whenever the financial obligations *vis-à-vis* the THA of a company with more than 1,500 workers reached a total of DM 150 million or a multiple thereof. Thresholds for notification have now been lowered in respect of the institutions, which replaced the THA. See Bull. EU 1/2–1995, 1.3.35.

[192] Dec. 96/115 ([1996] OJ L28/18) on the aid granted by the Italian Government to Enichme Agricoltura SpA.

[193] *Twenty-Fourth Report on Competition Policy* (EC Commission, Brussels, 1995), 173.

[194] Ehlermann, n. 149 above, 1224. See, e.g., Dec. 89/218 ([1989] OJ L86/76) concerning aid that the Italian Government proposed to grant to the public steel sector; Dec. 95/524 ([1995] OJ L300/23) concerning aid granted by the Italian state to Iritecna SpA; Dec. 94/653 ([1994] OJ L254/73) concerning the notified capital increase of Air France.

[195] Art. 10 of Dir. 90/684 ([1990] OJ L380/27) on aid to shipbuilding.

[196] Sect. 7.5.3 below.

[197] Notice C10/94 (ex NN126/93) ([1996] OJ C68/4) concerning aid which Greece had granted to Neorion Shipyard of Syros.

[198] H. Morch, 'Summary of the Most Important Recent Decisions' (1995) 5 *Competition Policy Newsletter* 43–9, 48.

[199] Ehlermann, n. 149 above, 1225.

and an appropriate plan to remedy the situation devised'.[200] Such aid is tightly controlled by the Commission,[201] and even in regions covered by Article 92(3)(a) or (c)[202] it must be justified on sectoral grounds under the latter subparagraph.[203] Such aid is not treated as being covered by Article 92(2) at all.[204]

3.4.1 Authorization Conditions

The conditions under which rescue aid may be authorized were elaborated in a Commission letter to the Member States of 24 January 1979[205] and confirmed in Guidelines published in 1994.[206] Such aid cannot be granted simply to make the recipient a worthwhile acquisition by investors[207] and, since it must have no adverse effects on industrial activity in other Member States,[208] is more problematic in a sector facing a structural crisis than in a sector facing conjunctural problems.[209] It must be designed only to keep a firm in business while the causes of its difficulties are discovered and a remedy is devised[210] or pending definition of an industrial strategy by a Member State for a particular sector.

---

[200] Para. 2.1 of the Community guidelines on state aid for rescuing and restructuring firms in difficulty ([1994] OJ C368/12).

[201] See, e.g., Dec. 82/312 ([1982] OJ L138/18) concerning the aid granted by the Belgian Government to an industrial and commercial group manufacturing wall coverings; and Dec. 82/653 ([1982] OJ L277/15) on aid granted by the Netherlands Government to a paperboard-processing firm.

[202] Dec. 89/43 ([1989] OJ L16/52) on aids granted by the Italian Government to ENI–Lanerossi.

[203] Dec. 93/627 ([1993] OJ L309/21) concerning aid granted by the Spanish authorities on the occasion of the sale by Cenemesa/Cademesa/Conelec of certain selected assets to Asea-Brown Boveri.

[204] Dec. 88/174 ([1988] OJ L79/29) concerning aid which Baden-Württemberg had provided to BUG-Alutechnik GmbH, an undertaking producing semi-finished and finished aluminium products.

[205] _Eighth Report on Competition Policy_ (EC Commission, Brussels, 1979), 157–8.

[206] Community guidelines on state aid for rescuing and restructuring firms in difficulty ([1994] OJ C368/12), para. 3.1. In the agricultural sector Member States can 'choose' between these Guidelines and special principles regarding aid to agricultural holdings in difficulty as a result of financial burdens connected with past investments. See Communic. C33/95 (ex NN35/95) ([1995] OJ C293/12) concerning aid which Spain had granted to the company Carnicas el Sadar.

[207] Dec. 88/174 ([1988] OJ L79/29) concerning aid which Baden-Württemberg had provided to BUG-Alutechnik GmbH, an undertaking producing semi-finished and finished aluminium products.

[208] Dec. 87/585 ([1987] OJ L352/42) on aid granted by the French Government to a producer of textiles, clothing and paper products—Boussac Saint Frères.

[209] Dec. 82/670 ([1982] OJ L280/30) on aid granted by the Belgian Government to a paper-manufacturing undertaking. According to VerLoren van Themaat AG in Case 323/82 _SA Intermills_ v. _EC Commission_ [1984] ECR 3809, 3847, rescue aid had come to be more tightly controlled than in the years following the 1973–4 oil shock, when the crisis was conjunctural rather than structural.

[210] See, regarding Greek aid to restore undertakings in difficulties to financial health, Bull. EC 10–1986, 2.1.68.

There must also be a clear link between receipt of aid and realization of a restructuring programme,[211] and the programme must be capable of restoring viability.[212] The latter condition may not be met in the case of successive aid grants to the same undertaking.[213] The Court of Justice agrees that, in the absence of a genuine restructuring plan, rescue aid cannot bring about the lasting development of regions or sectors.[214]

Moreover, so as not to frustrate any necessary capacity reductions, the aid should be limited to cases where it is required to cope with acute social problems. This condition may be met where the undertaking concerned is 'a significant employer' in a region, even though the region is not covered by Art. 92(3)(a) or (c).[215]

Finally, the 1994 Guidelines added the express condition that the aid must be granted as a 'one-off operation'.[216] The repeated granting of aid must be restricted to exceptional cases justified solely by external factors which cannot be foreseen by the firm.[217]

Such practice might be embodied in legislation. In the case of the steel industry, Article 6 of Decision 2320/81[218] provided that 'emergency aid' was permissible for a maximum period of six months pending a restructuring plan or the closure of an undertaking. The amount and intensity of aid had to be justified by the restructuring effort involved, account being taken of general structural problems in the region where the investment was to take place.

Again, Article 4 of Directive 81/363,[219] on aid to shipbuilding, provided for authorization of aid to maintain an undertaking 'pending definitive solution of the problems confronting the undertaking concerned, in order to deal with acute social problems and the regional effects which may arise'.

3.4.2 Aid Forms

According to the Commission, rescue aid may only be provided in the form of loan guarantees or loans. Aid grants are not permissible even to rescue companies in the former German Democratic Republic,[220] nor are capital

---

[211] *Seventh Report on Competition Policy* (EC Commission, Brussels, 1978), 149.

[212] See, e.g., Notice ([1989] OJ C38/2) regarding aids that in Spain the central and autonomous governments had granted in favour of Magefesa, a producer of domestic articles of stainless steel for table use and other domestic appliances.

[213] *Seventh Report on Competition Policy* (EC Commission, Brussels, 1978), 150.

[214] Case 305/89 *Italy* v. *EC Commission: Alfa Romeo* [1991] ECR I–1603, I–1644.

[215] Notice C56/94 (NN86/93) ([1995] OJ C253/3) regarding certain measures undertaken or proposed in favour of La Seda de Barcelona SA, located in Cataluña and Madrid.

[216] Para. 3.1 of the 1994 Guidelines.

[217] Notice C24/95 (ex N682/93) ([1995] OJ C294/13) concerning Saarland's scheme of state guarantees.

[218] Establishing Community rules for aids to the steel industry ([1981] OJ L228/14).

[219] [1981] OJ L137/39.

[220] Bull. EU 1/2–1995, 1.3.50.

injections.[221] The loans must bear normal interest rates[222] and must be limited to a relatively short period—generally six months or less.[223]

The permissible forms of such aid were at issue in *SA Intermills* v. *EC Commission*,[224] which concerned a decision[225] prohibiting Belgian aid to a paper-manufacturing firm. The aid was linked to a restructuring programme that included a reduction in output, conversion from mass production to high value-added speciality papers, closure of two factories, and creation of three independent companies to manage the remaining factories. The aid took the form of equity investment by the Walloon Regional Executive in Intermills and in the three new companies and a low-interest loan to finance an investment programme by these companies.

The Commission found a justification for the loan under Article 92(3)(c). The Union paper industry had in the past faced strong competition from manufacturers in third states producing under particularly favourable natural conditions. This competition threatened to grow in the near future. Hence, it was in the Union interest that the paper industry should adapt to the new situation in particular by reducing the share of bulk-production paper in its output and converting to special papers.

However, the Commission distinguished between the loan and aid in the form of equity investment. The loan was considered to be directly related to the conversion toward speciality paper, whereas the equity investment, which amounted to Bfr 2,350 million in an enterprise whose capital and reserves were Bfr 1,250 million, was regarded as being intended mainly to allow the firm to meet its debt-servicing obligations. The Commission decided that this equity investment entailed the grant of unacceptable aid.

In challenging the Commission decision, Intermills argued that the Commission had not adequately explained why it was appropriate to distinguish between the two forms of aid. The Court of Justice agreed and ruled that the settlement of an undertaking's existing debts in order to ensure its survival did not necessarily adversely affect trading conditions to an extent contrary to the common interest under Article 92(3), where the aid was, for example, accompanied by a restructuring plan.[226] In this case, the Commission had not shown

---

[221] Dec. 89/661 ([1989] OJ L394/9) concerning aid provided by the Italian Government to Alfa Romeo; and Notice ([1988] OJ C295/3) concerning aid which Portugal had decided to grant to a chemical undertaking—Quimigal-Quimica de Portugal EP.

[222] Dec. 84/489 ([1984] OJ L273/26) on the FF 200 million of aid in the form of equity loans which the French Government granted to a newsprint producer in 1981 and 1982. In 1974, however, low-interest loans had been accepted on condition that they were linked with restructuring. See Bull. EC 6–1974, 2120.

[223] See, regarding guarantees, the *Twenty-Second Report on Competition Policy* (EC Commission, Brussels, 1993), 211.

[224] Case 323/82 [1984] ECR 3809. See also M. Dony, 'La Participation des pouvoirs publics au capital des entreprises et le droit de la concurrence' [1986] *CDE* 161–84.

[225] Dec. 82/670 ([1982] OJ L280 L280/30) on aid granted by the Belgian Government to a paper-manufacturing undertaking.

[226] In the absence of any such limitation on the utilization of new resources (as represented by

why the applicant's activities on the market, following the conversion of its production with the assistance of the aid granted, were likely to have such an adverse effect on trading conditions that its disappearance would have been preferable to its rescue.[227] On this ground, the Court annulled the Commission's decision. Apparently, the Court does not favour differential treatment of rescue aid according to its form.

3.5 OPERATING AID

From the perspective of competition policy the most objectionable type of aid is that which is classified as operating aid. According to the Court of First Instance, such aid does not in principle fall within the scope of Article 92(3). It cannot in any circumstances be considered compatible with the common market pursuant to Article 92(3)(c), as its very nature is such that it may affect trading conditions to an extent contrary to the common interest.[228] Authorization may thus be refused, even if the result is closure of the prospective recipient.[229]

3.5.1 Definition

Operating aid has been defined in Commission decisions as aid which has a direct effect on production costs and selling prices of recipients,[230] aid not associated with any investment or job creation,[231] and aid not requiring the recipient to provide anything in return.[232] It has been defined by the Court of Justice as aid which is granted without any specific condition and solely by reference to the quantities of the aided product used[233] and by the Court of First Instance as aid intended to relieve an undertaking of the expenses it would itself normally have had to bear in its day-to-day management or its usual activities.[234] According to the latter court, such aid involves no technical

the increase in capital), aid which could be used to finance operating expenditure may be present and may be prohibited. See Dec. 95/366 ([1995] OJ L218/20) on aid granted by Italy (Sardinia) in the agricultural sector.

[227] [1984] ECR 3809, 3832.

[228] Case T–459/93 *Siemens SA* v. *EC Commission* [1995] ECR II–1675, II–1696.

[229] Dec. 88/174 ([1988] OJ L79/29) concerning aid which Baden-Württemberg had provided to BUG-Alutechnik GmbH, an undertaking producing semi-finished and finished aluminium products.

[230] Dec. 82/744 ([1982] OJ L315/23) concerning Italian national Law 423/81 of 1 Aug. 1981 on measures for agriculture.

[231] Notice C29/95 (NN93/94) ([1995] OJ C290/5) concerning aid granted by Italy for polyethylene recycling.

[232] Dec. 90/554 ([1990] OJ L314/13) on the Spanish draft ministerial order on logistic support for the fishing fleet in 1988.

[233] Case C–86/89 *Italy* v. *EC Commission: aid for use of grape must* [1990] ECR I–3891, I–3909.

[234] Case T–459/93 *Siemens SA* v. *EC Commission* [1995] ECR II–1675, II–1696.

or structural change or development of the recipient 'otherwise than in an exclusively commercial way'. It merely enables it to offer its clients artificially favourable terms and to increase its profit margin without any justification.[235]

A more elaborate definition is contained in the *Guidelines for the examination of state aid to fisheries and aquaculture*.[236] According to these Guidelines, it is aid which is granted without imposing any obligation on the part of recipients and which is intended to improve the situation of undertakings and increase their business liquidity or is calculated on the basis of the quantity produced, or marketed, product prices, units produced or the means of production, and which has the effect of reducing the recipient's production costs or improving the recipient's income.[237]

The forms and purposes of such aid are various. It may, for example, take the form of 'soft credit', including the partial defrayal of interest payable on bank loans in favour of a certain category of producers[238] or exporters generally;[239] credit without any obligation to pay interest for nine months;[240] aid in respect of investments already made;[241] guarantees against movements in exchange rates[242] or in economic indicators such as labour costs or the cost of materials;[243] guarantees to an undertaking in such poor financial circumstances as to be unable to borrow from a credit institution, even at a very high rate of interest;[244] guarantees granted on terms which do not reflect market conditions;[245] and aid for orders received by firms in the form of an advance of 30 per cent of the contract amount at a subsidized rate of 4 per cent.[246]

---

[235] Case T–459/93 *Siemens SA* v. *EC Commission* [1995] ECR II–1675, II–1696.

[236] Guidelines for the examination of state aid to fisheries and aquaculture ([1994] OJ C260/3). [237] *Ibid.*, para. 1.3.

[238] Communic. C9/94 (ex NN116/93) ([1994] OJ C107/4) concerning aids which France had decided to grant in the pigmeat sector.

[239] Dec. 81/167 ([1986] OJ L136/61) on aids granted by Greece in the form of interest rebates in respect of exports of all products with the exception of petroleum products.

[240] Communic. ([1985] OJ C258/3) regarding credit without obligation to pay interest for 9 months to semolina millers in Greece for the purchase of raw material (durum wheat) to be used in the production of pasta.

[241] Communic. C6/94 (ex NN115/B/93) ([1994] OJ C155/4) concerning aid which the region of Marche (Italy) intended to grant for investments in the agricultural product processing and marketing sector; and Communic. C38/95 (NN70/95, ex N510/94) ([1995] OJ C294/22) concerning aid which the Walloon Government had decided to grant to encourage investment and installation in the agricultural sector.

[242] Dec. 84/416 ([1984] OJ L230/25) concerning the French Government's intention to accord special exchange risk cover to French exporters in respect of a tender for the construction of a power station in Greece.

[243] Notice C37/93 (NN 63/93) ([1994] OJ C170/5) concerning Art. 29*ter* of the Walloon decree of 25 June 1992 on support for Walloon firms participating in Community industrial programmes which were the subject of specific international agreements.

[244] Notice C14/94 (NN133/92 & N514/93) ([1994] OJ C94/4) concerning the advantages given to Olympic Airways.

[245] Notice C24/95 (ex N682/93) ([1995] OJ C294/13) concerning Saarland's scheme of state guarantees.

[246] Notice C12/92 (NN113/A/93) ([1994] OJ C113/3) concerning aid granted under Regional Laws 23/1991 and 25/1993 for orders obtained by firms operating in Sicily.

It may also take the form of tax relief or related concessions, such as a reduced rate of corporation tax in a particular sector;[247] a ten-year tax exemption on returns from approved investments;[248] tax concessions granted not on the basis of the initial investment but instead on the profits recorded by the recipient undertaking;[249] and relief from social charges.[250]

It may even take the form of state participation, such as capital injections by public authorities in an undertaking in difficulties not linked to a restructuring plan for the restoration of the economic viability of the undertaking;[251] capital injections to cover losses incurred in continually offering unrealistically low prices for public contracts;[252] aid to remedy a financial imbalance brought about by the management of the recipient or for 'any management needs';[253] or state provision of working capital.[254]

Such aid may be designed to alleviate the day-to-day costs of undertakings, as in the case of aid to finance early-retirement schemes or to reduce wage costs;[255] aid for transportation and storage;[256] aid for financing shipyard stocks of semi-finished products and finished products, as opposed to raw materials;[257] aid

---

[247] Communic. C1/94 (E2/93) ([1994] OJ C94/13) concerning aid which Ireland granted to mushroom growers. Tax credits determined by reference to investments made may be more acceptable. See the *Twenty-Second Report on Competition Policy* (EC Commission, Brussels, 1993), 265–6. See, more particularly, Dec. 93/254 ([1993] OJ L117/22) on Italian Decree–Law of 14 Jan. 1992 relating, *inter alia*, to the overall refinancing of the aid measures provided for by Law 64 of 1 Mar. 1986 on special aid to the Mezzogiorno.

[248] Dec. 70/304 ([1970] JO L128/33) on a draft Italian law for the restructuring, reorganization, and conversion of the textiles industry.

[249] Dec. 95/452 ([1995] OJ L264/30) on state aid in the form of tax concessions to undertakings operating in the Centro di Servizi Finanzieri ed Assicurativi di Trieste pursuant to Italian Law 19 of 9 Jan. 1991.

[250] Dec. 91/500 ([1991] OJ L262/32) concerning aid granted to enterprises in the Friuli–Venezia Giulia region.

[251] Notice C38/92 ([1995] OJ C292/10) regarding a capital injection made by the Italian Government to Alumix, an aluminium producer; and Notice C18/90 ([1990] OJ C229/6) regarding aid which Greece had decided to grant to Neorion Shipyards of Syros SA.

[252] Notice C6/92 (ex NN149/91) ([1992] OJ C122/6) concerning contributions by Italimpianti to CMF SUD SpA.

[253] Dec. 95/366 ([1995] OJ L218/20) on aid granted by Italy (Sardinia) in the agricultural sector.

[254] Dec. 89/58 ([1989] OJ L25/92) concerning aid provided by the UK Government to the Rover Group.

[255] Dec. 94/374 ([1994] OJ L170/36) on Sicilian Regional Law 23/1991 concerning extraordinary assistance for industry and Art. 5 of Sicilian Regional Law 8/1991 concerning, in particular, financing for Sitas.

[256] Communic. C25/91 ([1991] OJ C189/5) concerning aids by means of which the Netherlands intended to stimulate an environmentally acceptable disposal of surplus manure; and Notice C25/92 (N99/92) ([1992] OJ C283/6) on the AIMA programme for 1992 under which Italy planned to grant aid for the private short-term storage of table wine and grape must.

[257] Dec. 88/281 ([1988] OJ L119/33) on aid for shipbuilding and ship repair in Italy—Art. 10 of Law 111 of 22 Mar. 1985. See, similarly, the *Sixth Report on Competition Policy* (EC Commission, Brussels, 1977), 119–20 and the *Eighth Report on Competition Policy* (EC Commission, Brussels, 1979), 118.

granted by reference to the number of hectares under cultivation;[258] aid for a publicity campaign;[259] aid for advertising campaigns[260] and market surveys and for the purchase of equipment for leasing to clients;[261] and aid for the treatment and recovery of industrial waste.[262]

It may also entail assistance with modernization, as in the case of aid for the renovation of a float line at a flat-glass factory, which had to be carried out every six to nine years;[263] aid for replacement investment;[264] aid for the 'normal modernization' of plant;[265] and aid for the straightforward modernization of telecommunications equipment.[266] The Court of Justice seems to accept Commission characterization of aid to support periodic renovation as operating aid.[267]

Commission thinking is that where an investment is nothing more than a normal modernization of an out-of-date plant in order to enable the undertaking concerned to remain competitive, it should be made using the financial resources of the undertaking.[268] This view has been taken, for example, in the

---

[258] Dec. 84/224 ([1984] OJ L105/16) on the aid provided for in Campania to support the production of apricots.

[259] Dec. 93/508 ([1993] OJ L238/38) concerning aid decided by the Italian Government in favour of the ceramics industry of Lazio; and Case 249/81 *EC Commission* v. *Ireland: 'Buy Irish' campaign* [1982] ECR 4005, 4021.

[260] See, regarding advertising related directly to the products of one or more specific undertakings, the Community framework for national aids for the advertising of agricultural products ([1987] OJ C302/6), para. 2.2; and, regarding aid for advertising to promote exports to another Member State, Notice regarding assistance granted by the Italian Government to the Italian toy industry to promote sales in France ([1976] OJ C68/2). See also Dec. 76/780 ([1976] OJ L270/39) concerning assistance granted by the Italian Government through the Istituto Nazionale per il Commercio Estero for advertising campaigns to expand the sale of exports by certain Italian firms.

[261] Dec. 92/483 ([1992] OJ L288/25) concerning aid provided by the Brussels Regional Authorities in favour of the activities of Siemens SA in the data-processing and telecommunications sectors. The Commission view was approved by the CFI in Case T–459/93 *Siemens SA* v. *EC Commission* [1995] ECR II–1675, II–1706.

[262] Dec. 94/172 ([1994] OJ L79/24) concerning Italian Law 102 of 2 May 1990 providing for the reconstruction and regeneration of the Valtellina.

[263] Dec. 87/195 ([1987] OJ L77/47) on a proposal by the Belgian Government to grant aid for investments by a flat-glass producer at Moustier; Dec. 86/593 ([1986] OJ L342/32) on a proposal by the Belgian Government to grant aid for investments by a flat-glass producer at Auvelais.

[264] *Tenth Report on Competition Policy* (EC Commission, Brussels, 1981), 122–3; and *Eleventh Report on Competition Policy* (EC Commission, Brussels, 1982), 161–2.

[265] Case 310/85 *Deufil GmbH & Co. KG* v. *EC Commission* [1987] ECR 901, 926. See, similarly, regarding 'routine aid for straightforward modernization', Lenz AG in Case 234/84 *Belgium* v. *EC Commission: Meura* [1986] ECR 2263, 2276. See also, regarding aid for industrial and commercial renovation, Notice regarding the application of two existing aid schemes in favour of the textile and clothing industries in France ([1982] OJ C25/2).

[266] Bull. EC 12–1986, 2.1.66.

[267] Joined Cases 62 & 72/87 *Exécutif Régional Wallon and Glaverbel* v. *EC Commission* [1988] ECR 1573, 1597. See also Lenz AG (*ibid.*, 1586); and Slynn AG in Case 84/82 *Germany* v. *EC Commission: Belgian aid to textiles and clothing* [1984] ECR 1451, 1502.

[268] Dec. 86/509 ([1986] OJ L300/34) on aid granted by Germany and Bavaria to a producer of polyamide and polyester yarn situated in Deggendorf.

case of modernization aid to the motor industry;[269] the production of rubber goods;[270] aluminium processing;[271] production of television sets;[272] production of microprocessors;[273] production of telecommunications equipment;[274] production of computers;[275] and to production of electrical and electronic equipment.[276] Investments aimed at modernizing and expanding production plant are necessary to enable undertakings to respond effectively to demand for their products, and it is only natural and in their own interests to make such investments.[277] Hence, aid to such investments is not authorized under Article 92(3)(c), even where the recipient makes an exceptional effort to help its former employees by, for example, setting up a job-creation fund.[278]

A similarly broad definition of operating aid seems to be favoured by the Union legislature. For example, Directive 90/684[279] treated as operating aid to shipbuilding: aid to shipowners and to third parties which was available as aid for the building or conversion of ships; aid in the form of credit facilities for the building or conversion of vessels;[280] contract-related production aid, whether granted under sectoral, general, or regional-aid schemes, to the shipyards themselves; aid related to shipbuilding and ship conversion granted as development assistance to a developing country; any aid to facilitate the continued operation of shipbuilding and ship-conversion companies, including loss-compensation, rescue-aid, and all other types of operating aid[281] not directly supporting particular restructuring measures.

[269] Notice regarding three FIM loans that the French Government had provided or would provide to a group involved in the production of passenger cars, sets of tools and cycles and two of its subsidiaries involved in the production and marketing of passenger cars ([1986] OJ C144/3).

[270] Notice regarding a FIM loan that the French Government had provided to an undertaking involved in the production of rubber goods ([1986] OJ C144/3).

[271] Notice regarding a FIM loan that the French Government had provided to an undertaking involved in the transformation of aluminium in France ([1986] OJ C144/5).

[272] Notice regarding a FIM loan that the French Government had provided to an undertaking involved mainly in the production of television sets, sound equipment and their spare parts ([1986] OJ C144/6).

[273] Notice regarding a FIM loan that the French Government had provided to an undertaking involved in the production of CMOS microprocessors ([1986] OJ C144/6).

[274] Notice ([1986] OJ C159/3) regarding a FIM loan that the French Government had provided to an undertaking involved in telecommunications equipment.

[275] Notice (1986] OJ C128/12) regarding a FIM loan that the French Government had provided to an undertaking involved in computers and auxiliary equipment.

[276] Notice ([1986] OJ C128/13) regarding a FIM loan that the French Government had provided to an undertaking involved in the electrical equipment sector; and Notice ([1986] OJ C128/14) regarding a FIM loan that the French Government had provided to an undertaking involved in electronic equipment material.

[277] Dec. 87/194 ([1987] OJ L77/43) on a FIM loan to a mineral-water and glass-bottle manufacturer.

[278] Dec. 86/593 ([1986] OJ L342/32) on a proposal by the Belgian Government to grant aid for investments by a flat-glass producer at Auvelais.

[279] On aid to shipbuilding ([1990] OJ L380/27).

[280] Such aid might be permitted if it met OECD conditions (*ibid.*, Art. 4(6)).

[281] Including financial support to nationalized shipyards (Art. 1(d) of Dir. 90/684).

Even the possibility that aid may have such characteristics may render it objectionable. Therefore, the minimum investment level for aid supposedly for 'fundamental rationalization investment' must be set at a sufficiently high level to rule out the possibility of such aid being used for normal replacement investment.[282] For example, the Commission objected that the initial investment level for German aid was too low to preclude the possibility that the aid would be used to fund normal replacement investment. The Federal Government had to meet this objection by raising the minimum level of investment from 150 per cent to 200 per cent of the average depreciation of the previous three years.[283]

On the other hand, where aid is granted as part of a restructuring programme of particular importance from the point of view of economic policy, the practicality of the programme has been reviewed and attested to by independent auditors and the aid is liable to be refunded in certain circumstances if the recipient fails to close down plant or reduce capacity, the aid concerned may be found to lack operating character[284] and may be authorized.

However, aid must be 'directly connected' with a restructuring programme.[285] Aid supposedly for restructuring may be treated as operating aid where the link with restructuring is tenuous;[286] when it follows earlier aid and no restructuring plans have been prepared;[287] or simply when it is of 'long-standing nature'. Aid has been so treated, for example, where it has been granted to the furniture industry;[288] the leather and shoe industries;[289] the construction materials industry;[290] and the ports of Liverpool and London.[291]

The repetitive character of an aid[292] or its continuation after its objectives

---

[282] *Thirteenth Report on Competition Policy* (EC Commission, Brussels, 1983), 177.

[283] *Ibid.*, 102.

[284] Case 103/85 *Stahlwerke Peine-Salzgitter AG* v. *EC Commission* [1988] ECR 4131, 4153.

[285] Dec. 90/554 ([1990] OJ L314/13) on the Spanish draft ministerial order on logistic support for the fishing fleet in 1988.

[286] *Eighth Report on Competition Policy* (EC Commission, Brussels, 1979), 140.

[287] *Ibid.*, 141.

[288] Notice regarding aid which the French Government was reported to have decided to grant to the furniture industry ([1986] OJ C272/2).

[289] Notice (1986) OJ C261/11) regarding aid which the French Government was reported to have decided to grant to the leather, leather goods, and shoe industries.

[290] Notice ([1987] OJ C13/3) regarding aid which the French Government was reported to have decided to grant to the construction materials industry. Similar aid schemes had operated since 1975.

[291] Notice ([1987] OJ C96/4) regarding aid granted by the UK Government to the ports of London and Liverpool. Aid to early retirement had been provided since 1979 and the problem of surplus workers had not been settled. Cf. Notice C20/91 ([1992] OJ C166/6) concerning aid which Italy had granted to the electronic consumer goods and related components industry (REL).

[292] Bull. EC 10–1980, 2.1.29. See also Notice C19/94 (ex NN127/93) ([1994] OJ C206/7) concerning aid granted by the French Government to Cellulose du Rhône et de l'Aquitaine (CDRA).

have been sufficiently achieved[293] may also result in its being treated as operating aid. The fact that the aid finances the purchase of equipment which may be subject to depreciation for accounting and fiscal purposes under national legislation is irrelevant, because aid is to be examined in a Union context.[294] While the Commission once accepted that temporary aid for modernization might be justified, there was considered to be a risk that the continued grant of such aid over a long period might assist normal replacement and thus amount to operating aid.[295] Hence, regional development grants in the United Kingdom were objectionable, because they were granted in respect of all investment, including routine replacement of capital goods, and were granted for an unlimited period.[296]

The treatment of such aid may be affected by the innovatory nature of an aided investment. Thus aid may be authorized where modernization involves a fundamental change in the product or the production process.[297] For example, in a decision[298] concerning aid to a car manufacturer the Commission noted that certain aided investments were not simply aimed at modernization, the costs of which would have had to have been borne by the undertaking without aid, even if introduction of the latest technology were involved.[299] Rather, they aimed at developing genuinely innovatory products, which were 'totally new' and were linked to a change in manufacturing technology. One investment aimed at the design of a new type of headlight using new technology (replacement of metal technology by plastics technology) entailing total conversion of the production facilities. In the other case the innovation involved the launching of a totally new product (heavy-lorry pull-type clutches) with robotization of production forming part of a complete reorganization of production management. Therefore, the aid concerned was authorized under Article 92(3)(c) for the development of certain economic activities.[300]

---

[293] Dec. 87/417 ([1987] OJ L227/41) prohibiting an aid consisting of a subsidy on the sale of animal feed granted by the region of Abruzzi.

[294] Case T–459/93 *Siemens SA* v. *EC Commission* [1995] ECR II–1675, II–1699.

[295] *Tenth Report on Competition Policy* (EC Commission, Brussels, 1981), 146.

[296] Bull. EC 3–1981, 2.1.27.

[297] Bull. EC 7/8–1981, 2.1.35; *Eleventh Report on Competition Policy* (EC Commission, Brussels, 1982), 165.

[298] Dec. 89/348 ([1988] OJ L143/44) on aid granted by the French Government to an undertaking manufacturing equipment for the motor vehicle industry—Valéo.

[299] See, e.g., Dec. 87/303 ([1987] OJ L152/27) on an FIM (Industrial Modernization Fund) loan to a brewery.

[300] See, similarly, Dec. 89/305 ([1989] OJ L123/52) concerning aid from the French Government to an undertaking in the motor vehicle sector—Peugeot SA. See also Dec. 85/275 ([1985] OJ L152/21) on the proposal of the French Government to grant regional aid to an undertaking engaged in the watch-making and optical and electronic engineering industries at Besançon, Doubs, France.

3.5.2 Commission Objections

Operating aid may, it is feared, encourage undertakings to continue uncompetitive activities[301] rather than to tackle their problems through restructuring.[302] Such aid may thus hamper structural adaptation[303] rather than providing an incentive to the 'durable development'[304] required by Article 92(3).[305] More particularly, if it is not likely to render the beneficiary viable without permanent aid, it will not be regarded as contributing to the regional[306] or sectoral development[307] required under Article 92(3)(c).

For example, in Decision 88/281[308] the Commission considered the acceptability of aid for the building-up of stocks by shipbuilders. By its very nature, such aid, which should go primarily to yards without orders so as to enable them to anticipate new work, was tantamount to aid for continued operation pending new orders and would have the effect of delaying capacity cuts and implementation of restructuring measures. Hence, it was prohibited by the Commission.

At the same time, such aid may adversely affect trading conditions to an extent contrary to the common interest within the meaning of Article 92(3)(c).[309] According to the Court of Justice, the disappearance of undertakings which cannot continue to exist by their own unaided efforts, but only with the help of constant and massive subsidies, will strengthen the resistance of the common market to crises.[310] Hence, constant aid for undertakings as compensation for disadvantages arising from their operation or location is considered contrary to the common interest.[311]

---

[301] *Medium-term Economic Policy Programme (1966–70)* ([1967] JO 1513), para. 6.6. In principle, aid must not be purely conservatory. See Dec. 72/34 ([1972] JO L10/22) prohibiting Belgian aid to undertakings in difficulty. See also the *Eighth Report on Competition Policy* (EC Commission, Brussels, 1979), 140.

[302] Dec. 73/274 ([1973] OJ L254/14) on Art. 20 of Italian Law 1101 of 1 Dec. 1971 on the restructuring, reorganization, and conversion of the textile industry. See also Case 250/83 *Finsider* v. *EC Commission* [1985] ECR 131, 152.

[303] Dec. 79/496 ([1979] OJ L127/50) on the UK scheme of assistance in favour of the offshore supplies industry.

[304] Dec. 72/253 ([1972] JO L166/22) on the grant of aid to encourage the rationalization of the growing and processing of fodder plants as well as co-operation between agricultural operators in the Netherlands.

[305] *Fourteenth Report on Competition Policy* (EC Commission, Brussels, 1984), 169.

[306] Dec. 93/496 ([1993] OJ L233/10) concerning state-aid procedure C32/92 (ex NN67/92)—Italy (tax credit for professional road hauliers). The ECJ did not query this approach in Case C–142/87 *Belgium* v. *EC Commission: Tubemeuse* [1990] ECR I–959, I–1018.

[307] Cf. Slynn AG in Case 84/82 *Germany* v. *EC Commission: Belgian aid to textiles and clothing* [1984] ECR 1451, 1502.

[308] On aid for shipbuilding and ship repair in Italy—Art. 10 of Law 111 of 22 Mar. 1985 ([1988] OJ L119/33).

[309] Case T–459/93 *Siemens SA* v. *EC Commission* [1995] ECR II–1675, II–1706.

[310] Case 19/58 *Germany* v. *ECSC High Authority: transport aid* [1960] ECR 225, 237. See, similarly, Joined Cases 27–29/58 *Compagnie des Hauts Fourneaux et Fonderies de Givors* v. *ECSC High Authority* [1960] ECR 241, 257.   [311] See, regarding Art. 4(c) ECSC, *ibid.*, 274.

Apart from the fact that it permanently immobilizes factors of production in less productive and, therefore, less remunerative employment than that to which these factors could be assigned, such aid also encourages inflation directly by burdening national budgets and indirectly by correspondingly saddling industries with extra costs in fiscal terms.[312] It drains the general economy of resources and thus reduces the opportunities of expansion for rationalized undertakings.[313]

Moreover, if such aid were authorized, other Member States might be tempted to adopt similar measures,[314] or difficulties might be transferred from one Member State to another.[315] At the same time, such aid may be particularly damaging to competitors in that, in extreme cases, the recipient may be enabled to undertake projects with negative profit margins[316] and to undercut the prices of its competitors.[317]

In more practical terms it is difficult for the Commission to assess and quantify the scope of operating aid, which can often conceal the precarious circumstances of the recipient and the need for corrective action. The lack of transparency makes it impossible to check whether benefits are being granted to viable firms capable in time of facing up to competition. Hence, such aid may create regional or sectoral problems in the medium term.[318]

3.6 PRACTICAL PROBLEMS

Practical problems in the application of the compensatory justification principle may arise, notably in the case of general aid schemes, because the benefits of such schemes can no more readily be determined[319] than their adverse effects.[320] Accordingly, aid granted to all undertakings within an industry, whether it is affected by structural problems or not, cannot be authorized

---

[312] *Second Report on Competition Policy* (EC Commission, Brussels, 1973), 76. Aid harmonization may be seen as a means to reduce them to the level justified by the seriousness of the problems to be solved and to prevent budgetary costs rising as a result of senseless bids and counter-bids (*ibid.*).

[313] Roemer AG in Joined Cases 27–29/58 *Compagnie des Hauts Fourneaux et Fonderies de Givors* v. *ECSC High Authority* [1960] ECR 241, 273.

[314] Dec. 93/496 ([1993] OJ L233/10) concerning state aid procedure C32/92 (ex NN67/92)—Italy (tax credits for professional road hauliers).

[315] Communic. C32/92 (ex NN67/92) ([1992] OJ C316/7) on aids granted by Italy to professional road hauliers.

[316] See, e.g., the *Twenty-Second Report on Competition Policy* (EC Commission, Brussels, 1993), 242.

[317] Notice C6/92 (ex NN141/91) ([1993] OJ C282/5) regarding aid which Italy granted to CMF SUD SpA and CMF SpA.

[318] *Tenth Report on Competition Policy* (EC Commission, Brussels, 1981), 115.

[319] *Second Report on Competition Policy* (EC Commission, Brussels, 1972), 102.

[320] *Seventh EEC General Report* (EEC Commission, Brussels, 1964), 81. A working group to consider which methods of examination could be applied was established in 1961 (*Fifth EEC General Report* (EEC Commission, Brussels, 1962), 80–1). An early Commission memorandum

under Article 92(3)(c).[321] Certainly, sub-paragraphs (a) to (c) of Article 92(3) seem too specific to cover such schemes.[322] Thus, for example, the Commission objected to an aid scheme which lacked any specific definition of the kind of technology eligible for aid or of the activities carried out by recipients,[323] and only authorized the scheme on condition that it would be limited to undertakings producing new processes.[324]

On the other hand, the Commission was persuaded that it would be unreasonable to prohibit the existence of general aid schemes,[325] in view of the perceived need of Member States to have at their disposal general powers permitting them to act rapidly in circumstances where they considered the grant of aid to be necessary.[326] The solution adopted by the Commission, in the case of Belgian,[327] Dutch,[328] French,[329] Greek,[330] and Italian schemes,[331] was to authorize such schemes on condition that sectoral or regional plans drawn up thereunder or, failing this, significant individual grants were notified.[332] Threshold levels for notification under schemes authorized by the Commis-

was drafted and discussed at a multilateral meeting with senior government officials. See the *Ninth EEC General Report* (EEC Commission, Brussels, 1966), 84.

[321] Dec. 73/274 ([1973] OJ L254/14) on Art. 20 of Italian Law 1101 of 1 Dec. 1971 on the restructuring, reorganization, and conversion of the textile industry.

[322] Dec. 75/397 ([1975] OJ L177/13) on the aids granted by the Belgian Government pursuant to the Law of 17 July 1959 introducing and co-ordinating measures to encourage economic expansion and the creation of new industries; and Dec. 81/227 ([1981] OJ L103/43) on a proposal by the Netherlands Government to grant aid for the creation of new production capacity by an undertaking in the chemical industry (polypropylene).

[323] Bull. EC 7/8–1983, 2.1.40.

[324] Bull. EC 12–1983, 2.1.49.

[325] According to G. Bernini, 'The Rules of Competition' in *Thirty Years of Community Law* (EC Commission, Luxembourg, 1983) 323–73, 395, the Commission was influenced by 'problèmes politiques insurmontables'.

[326] *Tenth Report on Competition Policy* (EC Commission, Brussels, 1981), 147. See, earlier, the *Second Report on Competition Policy* (EC Commission, Brussels, 1973), 102.

[327] Dec. 72/173 ([1972] JO L105/13) on aid granted under the Belgian Economic Expansion Law of Dec. 1970; Dec. 76/22 ([1975] OJ L5/28) amending Dec. 72/173; Dec. 75/397 ([1975] OJ L177/13) on the aids granted by the Belgian Government pursuant to the Law of 17 July 1959 introducing and co-ordinating measures to encourage economic expansion and the creation of new industries; and Dec. 81/626 ([1981] OJ L229/12) on a scheme of aid by the Belgian Government in respect of certain investments carried out by a Belgian undertaking to modernize its butyl rubber production plant.

[328] Dec. 81/523 ([1981] OJ L196/1) on a proposal by the Netherlands to grant aid for certain investments by a manufacturer of insulating material (Rockwool).

[329] Dec. 79/519 ([1979] OJ L138/30) concerning the 'special financing scheme for investments to increase exporting firms' capacity' in France; and Dec. 85/378 ([1985] OJ L216/12) on the French system of assistance to industry comprising special investment loans to enterprises, additional refinancing loans and FIM (Industrial Modernization Fund) loans.

[330] Dec. 88/167 ([1988] OJ L76/18) concerning Law 1386/1983 by which the Greek Government granted aid to Greek industry.

[331] Dec. 87/16 ([1987] OJ L12/27) on a proposal by the Italian Government to grant aid to a firm in the chemical industry (producing industrial auxiliaries, intermediates, and pesticides).

[332] Dec. 85/18 ([1985] OJ L11/28) on the French regional planning grant scheme (*Prime d'aménagement du territoire*).

sion[333] were fixed in 1979 by reference to the proportion of aid in the total investment and by reference to the amount of the investment.[334] The question whether a threshold was met was apparently to be determined by reference to figures applying at the moment the authorities received the aid application.[335] It might be met where individual aid grants related to 'a homogeneous body of expenditure to be made at the same time'.[336]

However, since only the most prosperous Member States can afford general aid schemes, such schemes may thwart the effects of regional development policies and attract 'footloose investment' at the expense of other Member States.[337] Hence, their operation is now regarded by the Commission as contrary to the requirements of economic and social cohesion.[338] Accordingly, in June 1991 the Commission decided that general aid schemes in Belgium, Luxembourg, the Netherlands,[339] and the United Kingdom[340] should be discontinued. Indeed, the Commission has recently adopted the position that, in principle, aid is only permissible under Article 92(3)(c), where it is confined to the areas and ceilings for national regional aid or meets the guidelines for aid to small and medium-sized enterprises.[341] At the same time, the existence of general aid schemes is said to be increasingly difficult to reconcile with completion of the internal market.[342] On the other hand, a general aid scheme for investment in the former German Democratic Republic has been authorized,[343] and such schemes may also be authorized in the case of small and medium-sized enterprises.[344]

---

[333] See, e.g., Dec. 88/174 ([1987] OJ L79/29) concerning aid which Baden-Württemberg had provided to BUG-Alutechnik, an undertaking producing semi-finished and finished aluminium products.

[334] Letter to Member States SG(79)D/10478 (*Competition Law in the European Communities*, ii, *Rules Applicable to State Aids* (EC Commission, Brussels, 1990), 142–3).

[335] Communic. C28/92 (N199/92) ([1992] OJ C246/6) concerning aid decided by the Basque Government in favour of Esmaltaciones San Ignacio SA.

[336] Dec. 92/483 ([1992] OJ L288/25) concerning aid provided by the Brussels Regional Authorities in favour of the activities of Siemens SA in the data-processing and telecommunications sectors.

[337] Dec. 93/134 ([1993] OJ L55/61) concerning a draft order of the Brussels region providing for aid to promote economic growth and scientific research.

[338] *Europe* 5432 (15 Feb. 1991).

[339] Notice C49/91 (E15/90) ([1992] OJ C22/6) regarding a general aid scheme in the Netherlands entitled 'Regeling Bijzondere Financiering'.

[340] *Europe* 5301 (23/24 July 1990). The Commission secured the elimination of two such schemes in Belgium and the Netherlands. See the *Twentieth Report on Competition Policy* (EC Commission, Brussels, 1991), 182. See, regarding the UK, the *Twenty-Second Report on Competition Policy* (EC Commission, Brussels, 1993), 254.

[341] Dec. 93/337 ([1993] OJ L134/25) concerning a scheme of tax concessions for investment in the Basque country.

[342] *Fourth Survey on State Aids in the European Community in the Manufacturing and Certain Other Sectors*, COM(95)365, 21.

[343] Notice C59/91 (NN150/91) ([1992] OJ C35/27) concerning the investment premium granted by Germany under the *Investitionszulagengesetz 1991*.

[344] Guidelines on state aid for small and medium-sized enterprises ([1992] OJ C213/2), para. 4.1.

3.7 CONCEPTUAL PROBLEMS

The conceptual framework for Commission practice, which may not be unequivocally supported by the terms of Article 92 alone,[345] may appear to be one composed of a general prohibition in Article 92(1) and the possibility of exceptions[346] under Article 92(2) and (3). It has been said, for example, that the basic idea of the Treaty is the *prohibition in principle* of aid, emphasis being laid on its incompatibility with the common market.[347] Similarly, the Commission has expressed the view that state aid is *per se* incompatible with the common market[348] and with transparency demands.[349]

However, Commission practice may not readily be reduced to a two-stage test, according to which a finding of the presence of a distortion of competition is followed by a finding on the acceptability of an exception from the general prohibition of such distortions. Such a reduction may be difficult to reconcile with the concern of Union practice with market structure.[350]

Even the wording of Article 92 does not always support such a test. In particular, assistance covered by Article 92(2) may not always distort competition so as to be caught by Article 92(1) in the first place.[351] Rather, the issues involved may, in substance, be merged within a finding as to the compatibility of aid with underlying Treaty requirements. According to the European Parliament, 'state aid is not intrinsically positive or negative, but must be evaluated according to its objective and the effects it may have on economic and social cohesion'.[352] As Advocate General Capotorti maintained in *Philip Morris Holland BV* v. *EC Commission*,[353] in authorizing aid otherwise prohibited by Article 92(1), 'the Commission must strive to coordinate national policies towards aids on the basis of common criteria and in terms of the general interests of the

---

[345] J.-Y. Cherot, 'La Discipline des aides nationales dans la Communauté européenne' [1993] *Revue d'Economie Industrielle* 222–41, 236.

[346] Or one based on recognition of the limits to negative integration. See J. Biancarelli, 'Le Contrôle de la Cour de Justice des Communautés européennes en matière d'aides publiques' [1993] *AJDA* 412–36, 412.

[347] Roemer AG in Case 47/69 *France* v. *EC Commission: aid to textiles* [1970] ECR 487, 499.

[348] *Tenth Report on Competition Policy* (EC Commission, Brussels, 1980), 106 and 216.

[349] Application of Arts. 92 and 93 EC and Art. 5 of Dir. 80/723 to public undertakings in the manufacturing sector ([1991] OJ C273/2), para. 10.

[350] In implementing competition policy, the Commission has not chosen the way of '*splendide isolement*'. See J.-L. Cardieux, 'Restructuration industrielle et politique communautaire vis-à-vis des aides nationales' in J. Dutheil de la Rochère and J. Vandamme (eds.), *Interventions Publiques et Droit Communautaire* (Pedone, Paris, 1988), 77–88, 84.

[351] Cf., in connection with Art. 4(c) ECSC, R. Quadri, R. Monaco, and A. Trabucchi, *Trattato Istitutivo della Comunità Europea del Carbone et dell'Acciaio* (Giuffrè, Milan, 1970), i, 104.

[352] Resolution of 20 Apr.1993 ([1993] OJ C150/34) on the Commission's report on the evaluation of aid schemes established in favour of Community air carriers, para. 6.

[353] Case 730/79 [1980] ECR 2671.

Community'.[354] Compensatory justification issues may be subsumed within such coordination.

As the Court of Justice puts it, the prohibition in Article 92(1) 'is neither general nor absolute'.[355] In fact, this prohibition is concerned with integration and, as an element of the common market, is a means of achieving Article 2 objectives. Hence, trade-offs between competition in the static sense and competition in the dynamic sense may be expected.[356]

Accordingly, at least under Article 92(3)(c), the Commission considers that it must balance the beneficial effects of the aid against the adverse effects on trading conditions and the maintenance of undistorted competition.[357] For example, a region may suffer from geographical remoteness from major market outlets and relative economic backwardness, which may entail increased transport, inventory, overseas personnel, and infrastructure costs. Such handicaps, even though they may be partly offset by lower costs than those in more central locations, together with the need to give an additional incentive to attract investment to a disadvantaged region, may be treated as relevant both to the impact of aid on competition and to its acceptability on regional policy grounds.[358]

This approach was questioned by Advocate General Slynn in *Germany* v. *EC Commission: Belgian aid to textiles and clothing*.[359] According to the Advocate General, the proviso in Article 92(3)(c) requires an inquiry only into whether trading conditions are affected to an extent contrary to the common interest. It does not require the adverse effect to be balanced against the beneficial effects of the aid.[360] In taking this view, the Advocate General relied on the ruling of the Court of Justice in *France* v. *EC Commission: aid to textiles*.[361] Here the Court had ruled that aid might be contrary to the common interest because of its method of financing, 'despite the useful nature of the aid properly so-called and the fact that it conformed with the common interest'.[362] However, this

---

[354] *Ibid.*, 2702. See also VerLoren van Themaat AG in Case 169/84 *Cie Française de l'Azote (COFAZ) SA* v. *EC Commission* [1986] ECR 391, 404.

[355] Case 78/76 *Firma Steinike und Weinlig* v. *Germany* [1977] ECR 595, 609. See also G. Stammati, 'Disciplina degli aiuti' in A. Valsecchi and G. Stammati, *L'Integrazione Economica Europea* (Jardi Sapi, Rome, 1960), 274; and J. Flynn, 'State Aids and Self-Help' [1983] ELR 298–312.

[356] F. Y. Jenny, 'Competition and State Aid Policy in the European Community' (1994–5) 18 *Fordham Intl. LR.* 525–54.

[357] *Fourteenth Report on Competition Policy* (EC Commission, Brussels, 1984), 130. It may also be seeking to extend this approach to its practice under Art. 92(2) aid. See the *Fourth Survey on State Aids in the European Community in the Manufacturing and Certain Other Sectors*, COM(95)365, 31.

[358] Summary of the Decision not to raise objections to the aid which the Portuguese Government planned to grant to the joint-venture of Ford and Volkswagen to establish a multipurpose vehicle plant in the Setubal peninsula ([1991] OJ C257/5).

[359] Case 84/82 [1984] ECR 1451.

[360] *Ibid.*, 1506–7.

[361] Case 47/69 [1970] ECR 487.

[362] *Ibid.*, 496.

ruling was specifically concerned with the relationship between an aid and the method of its financing, and may not necessarily have been intended to apply to interpretation of this Article 92(3)(c) generally. Therefore, the case law does not unambiguously preclude Commission efforts to balance the various requirements of Article 92 in its practice under this provision.

3.8 CONCLUSION

The Commission once sought to draw a distinction between the various subparagraphs of Article 92(3) in terms of the common interest. According to the Commission, aid falling within Article 92(3)(a) or (b) was warranted by the pursuit of an objective which could be assumed to be in the common interest.[363] Article 92(3)(c) alone was subject to the further condition that trade must not be adversely affected to an extent contrary to the common interest.[364] Now, however, the Commission considers this condition to be implicit in Article 92(3)(b).[365] Hence, the Commission may require that the benefits deriving from aid granted under this provision outweigh the negative effects of the aid on competitors.[366] It is also said that the Commission cannot disregard the common interest in the application of Article 92(3)(a).[367] Thus restructuring aid is only permissible under the latter provision where it restores the recipient's viability without having unacceptable negative effects on conditions of competition within the Union.[368] The apparent implication in such practice is that aid authorization depends on far more than simply consideration of whether competition policy requirements can admit of an exception. Hence,

---

[363] *Fourteenth Report on Competition Policy* (EC Commission, Brussels, 1985), 130. But cf. Dec. 86/187 ([1986] OJ L136/61) on aids granted by Greece in the form of interest rebates in respect of exports of all products with the exception of petroleum products.

[364] During negotiation of the Treaty it was agreed, at the request of Germany, that a proviso equivalent to that in Art. 92(3)(c) should be removed from Art. 92(2)(c). See S. Neri and H. Sperl, *Traité instituant la Communauté Economique Européenne* (Court of Justice of the European Communities, Luxembourg, 1960), 231.

[365] Dec. 93/154 ([1993] OJ L61/52) concerning an AIMA national programme on aid which Italy plans to grant for the private storage of carrots; Dec. 93/155 ([1993] OJ L61/55) concerning an aid measure proposed by the German authorities (Rhineland-Palatinate) for the distillation of wine; Dec. 94/813 ([1994] OJ L335/82) concerning aid to French pig farmers; and Dec. 94/814 ([1994] OJ L335/90) on aid in respect of exports of mushrooms, granted in connection with the Market Development Fund in Ireland.

[366] Notice C2/88 (NN128/87) ([1996] OJ C84/3) regarding aid which the Greek authorities had decided to grant to Heracles General Cement Company.

[367] Jacobs AG in Joined Cases C–278/92, C–279/92 & C–280/92 *Spain* v. *EC Commission: Intelhorce* [1994] ECR I–4103, I–4117.

[368] Notice C1/95 (NN144/94) ([1995] OJ C144/13) concerning aid provided by the Spanish authorities to Suzuki-Santana Motor SA in support of its plant in Linares (Andalucia); and Dec. 92/321 ([1992] OJ L176/57) concerning aid awarded by Spain to Intelhorce SA, a state-owned producer of cotton textiles.

questions arise whether conceptions of aid control based on ideas of market failure adequately reflect Commission treatment of the various legal requirements relevant to such control. These questions are pursued in the following chapters.

4

Regional Aid

4.1 INTRODUCTION

Regional aid is aid granted on the basis of regional criteria. Article 92(3)(a) provides that aid to promote the economic development of areas where the standard of living is abnormally low or where there is serious under-employment (that is, 'peripheral regions') may be authorized. Moreover, Article 92(3)(c) provides that aid to facilitate the development of certain economic areas (that is, 'central regions') may be authorized, where such aid does not adversely affect trading conditions to an extent contrary to the common interest.[1] The implication is that aid control is to take into account not only competition-policy requirements but also those of regional development.

From the perspective of competition-policy requirements, regional aid may be seen as distorting competition. In particular, the geographical distribution of productive activities, which ought to be one of the most natural consequences of European integration, may be upset by escalating offers of aid by different Member States or regions. Hence, the Commission seeks to ensure that the scale of regional aid is related to the gravity of the problems involved, having regard to the situation in the industry concerned, the characteristics of the firm receiving aid, and its location.[2] The Commission also seeks to ensure that aid is only granted where market forces alone will not eliminate the difficulties of the region concerned and that the aid will not unduly distort competition in particular sectors.[3] Apparently, such practice is designed to ensure that the impact of regional aid on competition is 'neutralized'.

The importance of regional development requirements is underlined by Article 130a of the Treaty. It provides that in order to promote its overall harmonious development, the Union shall develop and pursue its actions leading to the strengthening of its economic and social cohesion. In particular, the Union shall aim at reducing disparities between the various regions and the backwardness of the least-favoured regions, including rural areas.[4]

---

[1] A distinction between central regions and other regions may also be made in relation to aid to remedy a serious disturbance under Art. 92(3)(b). See Lenz AG in Case 40/85 *Belgium* v. *EC Commission: Boch* [1986] ECR 2321, 2335.

[2] *First EC General Report* (EC Commission, Brussels, 1968), 70.

[3] See, e.g., Dec. 91/500 ([1991] OJ L262/29) concerning aid granted to enterprises in the Friuli–Venezia Giulia region.

[4] The reference to rural areas was added by the TEU.

From the perspective of such requirements, regional aid is assessed in terms of its effectiveness as a means of coping with regional problems. It may be argued that such aid will lead to lower productivity,[5] though dynamic conceptions suggest that distributional reforms and economic growth mutually support each other by circular causation.[6] It may also be argued that undue regional concentration of this action may result in neglect of more prosperous but 'under-producing' regions.[7] However, the principal concern of the Commission is that inadequate co-ordination of regional aid at the Union level may have a doubly unfavourable effect: on national budgets, which risk being involved in a kind of competitive supply of aid,[8] especially to frontier regions; and on the regions themselves, either because undertakings may find themselves almost encouraged to take things easy for a time in the expectation that the public authorities will increase the amount of aid given, or because the different regions receive greater or smaller aid not so much in accordance with the economic and social problems which they have to solve, but on the basis of an assessment of the competition between regions on either side of a frontier.[9]

The relationship between the two types of requirements is usually thought of in terms of conflict between liberalism and interventionism,[10] between free competition and solidarity,[11] or between the logic of the market and the demands of integration policy.[12] In accordance with such thinking, the Commission stated in the 1977 *Guidelines for Community Regional Policy*[13] that, in assessing the acceptability of regional aid under Article 92, it would balance the need to maintain competition against regional development considerations.

[5] In other words, such efforts at equalization conflict with liberal ideas of exploitation of comparative advantage. See V. Curzon Price, *1992: Europe's Last Chance? From Common Market to Single Market* (Institute of Economic Affairs, London, 1988), 27–8. See also, regarding the distinction between 'efficiency-oriented' and 'equity-oriented' integration, R. J. Langhammer, *EC Integration Widening Towards Eastern Europe* (Kiel Working Paper No. 524, 1992), 12.

[6] G. Myrdal, *Economic Theory and Under-Developed Regions* (Duckworth, London, 1957), 120–1.

[7] However, it has been argued that, to the extent that undertakings outside the aided regions are competitively disadvantaged, such undertakings will be forced to strengthen their position through technological development. Hence, their regions will also benefit. See D. Karsten, 'Regional Policy' in C.-C. Schweitzer and D. Karsten (eds.), *The Federal Republic of Germany and EC Membership Evaluated* (Pinter, London, 1990), 94–101, 99.

[8] J. Atik, 'Investment Contests and Subsidy Limitations in the EC' (1992) 32 *Virginia Journal of Intl Law* 837–69; A. Dixit and A. Kyle, 'The Use of Protection and Subsidies for Entry Protection and Deterrence' (1985) 75 *American Economic Rev.* 139–52.

[9] *First EC General Report* (EC Commission, Brussels, 1968), 234.

[10] See, e.g., *New Regional Policy Guidelines and Priorities*, Bull. EC, Supp. 4/81, 57–61; and C. Garbar, 'Aides d'état: pratique décisionnelle de la Commission de la Communauté européenne (1990–1994)' [1994] RMC 665–74.

[11] Darmon AG in Case 248/84 *Germany* v. *EC Commission: regional aid* [1987] ECR 4013, 4028.

[12] E. Grabitz, 'Réglementation nationale des aides aux entreprises et droit communautaire' in J. Dutheil de la Rochere and J Vandamme (eds.), *Interventions Publiques et Droit Communautaire* (Pedone, Paris, 1988), 72–6, 72. See also T. Frazer, 'The New Structural Funds, State Aids and Interventions on the Single Market' [1995] ELR 3–19, 9.

[13] Bull. EC, Supp. 2/77, 10.

Under the ECSC Treaty the search for such a balance was originally seen as a limited and temporary challenge. Member States could pursue regional-policy objectives outside the coal and steel sectors, but measures in pursuit of this policy which endangered liberalization of these sectors were to be restricted. Article 2 of the ECSC Treaty did require the Community institutions to take care not to provoke fundamental and persistent disturbances in the economies of Member States,[14] and the inference was drawn that Member States could grant aid to prevent the closure of undertakings on a large scale.[15] However, there was no justification for aid for individual undertakings the closure of which did not jeopardize the regional policy of a Member State. Moreover, aid in the form of 'support tariffs', designed 'to avoid any serious economic disturbance', was only permissible under Article 10 of the Convention on the Transitional Provisions for limited periods. If after the expiry of those periods it could not be expected that the undertakings which benefited therefrom could exist in the common market by their own efforts, such aid was no longer justified even from the point of view of regional policy.[16]

More particularly, Article 70 of the ECSC Treaty permitted preferential tariffs for inland transport of coal and steel products with Commission authorization. Such tariffs were regarded as permissible only where they were necessary for the attainment of Treaty objectives.[17] Thus they could be justified by the unusual situation of one or more undertakings or regional problems associated with developments in the coal and steel sectors, which made a reduction in the general tariff indispensable for the attainment of these objectives. However, since the integration aimed at by this Treaty was only partial, all the factors upon which regional policy depended could not be taken into account.[18] Therefore, this provision was regarded as permitting aid to enable recipients to overcome their difficulties rather than to offset them for as long as they existed or remained unchanged.[19]

Even so, special rates and conditions in favour of certain German undertakings situated close to the interzonal frontier might be permitted on the ground of the disadvantages created by factors of a non-economic nature 'and in particular by political contingencies which have separated these undertakings from their natural market, with the result that they need support either to be

[14] Art. 23(3) of the Convention on the Transitional Provisions also provided for measures of readaptation which could even take the form of the setting-up of new undertakings not subject to the ECSC Treaty and for assistance both to undertakings and to workers (Case 19/58 *Germany* v. *ECSC High Authority* [1960] ECR 225, 236).

[15] See, regarding employment surveys that were made, the *ECSC Sixth General Report* (ECSC High Authority, Luxembourg, 1958), ii, 180–3.

[16] Joined Cases 27–29/58 *Compagnie des Hauts Fourneaux et Fonderies de Givors* v. *ECSC High Authority* [1960] ECR 241, 276–7.

[17] *Sixth ECSC General Report* (ECSC High Authority, Luxembourg, 1958), i, 68–9.

[18] Joined Cases 27–29/58 *Compagnie des Hauts Fourneaux et Fonderies de Givors* v. *ECSC High Authority* [1960] ECR 241, 255.

[19] Case 28/66 *Netherlands* v. *EC Commission: preferential rail tariffs* [1968] ECR 1, 13.

able to adjust themselves to the new conditions or to be able to overcome this accidental disadvantage'.[20]

The position is more complicated under the EC Treaty. This Treaty seeks the integration of the economies of the Member States generally[21] Hence, in the application of this Treaty account must inevitably be taken of the requirements of regional policy, which are a component of the economic policy of each Member State. More particularly, the Preamble refers to reducing the differences existing between the various regions and the backwardness of the less favoured regions.[22]

On the other hand, the EEC Treaty did not originally require establishment of a regional policy,[23] and the conclusion might be drawn that the Treaty authors regarded the liberal equality implied by establishment of the common market as offering in itself an adequate solution to regional problems.[24] Such a conclusion might be justified to the extent that systematic intervention to compensate for differences in natural conditions would frustrate the objective of securing through effective competition the most efficient possible utilization of resources within the Union and, at the same time, would involve a degree of uniformity incompatible with the kind of integration sought by the Treaty. Hence, liberal equality might be expected to play a central role in Union approaches to regional problems.

Traditional trade theory would suggest that such equality could play this role effectively. According to this theory, the pattern of trade among regions is determined by their differing endowments of factors of production. Free trade permits industrial activity to adapt itself to the localization of natural and population resources in different regions. An uneven growth process must lead to a movement of factors out of high cost regions and into low cost regions, until cost differences are minimized. In other words, differences in the relative scarcities of labour and capital are reduced, and factor prices are equalized.

However, such theory deals with perfectly competitive markets and relies on various assumptions. It is assumed, for example, that regions have access to the same technologies, that transport costs are negligible, and that institutional impacts are neutral. In practice, such assumptions do not always hold good.[25]

[20] Joined Cases 3–18, 25 & 26/58 *Barbara Erzbergbau AG* v. *ECSC High Authority* [1960] ECR 173, 195.

[21] See, e.g., Art. 2 EC.

[22] 5th recital in the Preamble.

[23] Cf. Art. 130(a) EEC.

[24] P. S. R. F. Mathijsen, 'The Role of Regional Policy in the European Economic Integration Process' in S. Bates, W. Finnie, J. A. Usher, and H. Wildberg, *In Memoriam JDB Mitchell* (Sweet and Maxwell, London, 1983), 171–83.

[25] P. Krugman, 'Introduction: New Thinking About Trade Policy' in P. Krugman (ed.), *Strategic Trade Policy and the New International Economics* (MIT Press, Cambridge, Mass. 1986), 8 and L. Tsoukalis, *The New European Economy: The Politics and Economics of Integration* (Oxford University Press, Oxford, 1991), 204–5.

Trade may reflect absolute advantage,[26] and market failures mean that market mechanisms do not lead to the establishment of an equilibrium in which the prices of goods and of the factors of production are equalized. Such considerations explain the close similarity between the literature on regional economics and the new theories of international trade, which both emphasize the role of economies of scale, imperfect competition, differential products, and innovations.[27]

The regional impact of market imperfections may be exaggerated by integration. According to an early argument, 'space in large free-trade areas would be discriminatory against certain regions of a union and . . . we need some sort of artificial discrimination to neutralize that natural one'. Measures recommended included aid to 'firms in locations with potential advantages which would become actual in connection with a certain degree of agglomeration', differentiation of transportation charges, and the development of transport infrastructures.[28] Aid of this kind might, it was thought, prevent cumulative decline, particularly in less favoured regions.[29]

The Spaak Report maintained that aid should be acceptable for certain regions, so as to avoid excessive urban concentrations or to maintain a balance between different social groups. Aid to such ends would merely compensate for disadvantages imposed in the common good.[30] This approach was embodied in the EC Treaty.

In the original version of the Treaty Article 104 provided that in their pursuit of economic policy Member States were to take care to ensure a stable level of employment. Although this provision was not interpreted as implying for Member States a right to implement regional development programmes free of Commission control,[31] their implementation is by no means precluded by the Treaty. In this connection, regard may be had to the opinion of Advocate General Warner in *Procureur du Roi* v. *Debauve*.[32] This ruling concerned Belgian legislation on cable television advertising. One point at issue was whether the legislation discriminated against transmissions from other Member States by failing to take account of conditions there. According to the Advocate General, the Treaty acknowledges differences in regional conditions and in Articles 42 and 92 authorizes 'exceptional aids' to handicapped undertakings.[33] While the

---

[26] Freedom of factor movements and national collective bargaining mean that regional trade is based on absolute advantage. Weaker regions thus suffer unemployment and the outflow of factors of production.

[27] See, for example, M. N. Jovanovic, *International Economic Integration* (Routledge, London, 1992), 228–41.

[28] H. Giersch, 'Economic Union Between Nations and the Location of Industries' (1949–50) 16 *Review of Economic Studies* 87–97.

[29] G. Myrdal, n. 6 above, 25.

[30] Comité Intergouvernemental Créé par la Conférence de Messine, *Rapport des Chefs de Délégation aux Ministres des Affaires Etrangères* (Comité Secretariat, Brussels, 1956), 58.

[31] Darmon AG in Case 248/84 *Germany* v. *EC Commission: regional aid* [1987] ECR 4013, 4030.

[32] Case 52/79 [1980] ECR 833.   [33] *Ibid.*, 869.

grant of state aid is not justified by a failure of the Union to provide aid necessary to equalize competitive conditions,[34] the Commission may take account of the distance of a region from main markets and its economic backwardness in authorizing aid under Article 92(3)(a). In the view of the Court itself, such conditions entail increased costs in terms of transport, storage, and infrastructure, which are only partly offset by lower labour and construction costs.[35] Provided that differential treatment of regions, as regards the grant of regional aid, is 'based only on objective "economic and social" factors, such treatment accords with the legal requirements of the equality principle'.[36] Indeed, in so far as regional aid is given merely to compensate 'footloose' firms for higher costs in a second-best location, there may be claimed to be no distortion of competition, since the costs of such firms are no lower than if they had established themselves in the area of their first choice without the benefit of aid.

On the other hand, criteria for defining the existence of a regional problem are inadequate to determine the acceptability of aid from the perspective of competition policy, since the latter depends on the relative incidence of regional aid on competing industries. Where regions share either the same problem industries or the same new industries attracted by incentives, the failure of regional policy in one Member State may be related to the aid provided to their regions by other Member States.

Particularly controversial may be ideas of 'growth poles'.[37] The *Medium-Term Economic Policy Programme for 1966 to 1970*[38] recognized the acceptability of aid for the creation in the less-favoured regions of centres with *'un ensemble cohérent d'entreprises industrielles et d'activités de services, susceptibles de se développer spontanément après les interventions initiales'* ('a coherent group of industrial enterprises and service activities capable of spontaneous development after initial interventions'). Such thinking has been embodied in competition policy. According to the 1979 Commission Communication on Regional Aids,[39] the principle of regional specificity implied that regional aids should not be granted in a pinpoint manner. Hence, they should not be granted to isolated geographical points having virtually no influence on the development of a region. Only in respect of aid to support growth poles was an exception from this prohibition permissible.[40]

---

[34] Case C–86/89 *Italy* v. *EC Commission: aid for the use of grape must* [1990] ECR I–3891, I–3908–10.

[35] Case C–225/91 *Matra SA* v. *EC Commission* [1993] ECR I–3203, I–3257.

[36] Darmon AG in Joined Cases C–324/90 & C–342/90 *Germany and Pleuger Worthington GmbH* v. *EC Commission* [1994] ECR I–1173, I–1192. Aid control may thus become an instrument of Union policy. See C. Blumann, 'Régime des aides d'état: jurisprudence récente de la Cour de Justice (1989–1992)' [1992] *Revue du Marché commun et de l'Union européenne* 721–39, 730.

[37] See, generally, O. Vanneste, *The Growth Pole Concept and Regional Economic Policy* (De Tempel, Bruges, 1971).

[38] [1967] JO 1513, para. 6.6.

[39] [1979] OJ C31/9.   [40] Point 9(iii).

However, while growth centres may offer focal points for regional services and new forms of employment, they may be less successful in diffusing economic growth into their hinterlands. The result may even be to increase the scale of local socio-economic differences. For example, the attractiveness of coastal areas may have negative effects on the economic development of the regions immediately inland, which face a danger of 'desertification'.[41] In other words, growth centres may contribute to a shift of disparities from the inter-regional to the intra-regional level.[42]

Even so, the balancing of competition policy requirements with those of regional development does not necessarily imply attempts to reconcile the irreconcilable. Appropriate use of aid may counter the tendency for resources in certain regions to be under-utilized and may thus improve the structure of competition.[43] At the very least, aid may reduce the social costs of regional adaptation to international market conditions[44] and the threats of social instability—in themselves unfavourable to economic efficiency[45]—which might otherwise accompany such adaptation. Hence, cohesion may be seen as a prerequisite for structural adjustment of Union industry.[46] At the same time, strict aid control in more developed regions may increase the relative impact of authorized aid in less developed regions, and so cohesion may be promoted.[47] What seems critical for the balance sought in Commission practice is that, in accordance with the principle of compensatory justification, regional aid is effectively directed towards tackling development problems.[48]

In relation to regional aid, the principle implies essentially two requirements: aid should be concentrated on the most needy regions, and it must be of such a kind as to contribute to their development. The former requirement primarily reflects the general principle in Article 3(g) opposing distortion of competition and the specific opposition in Article 92(3)(c) to aid which affects

---

[41] *Europe 2000: Outlook for the Development of the Community's Territory*, COM(91)452, 185.

[42] Nevertheless, the idea of growth centres is not universally unpopular. See, e.g., G. Aldskogius, 'Regionalpolitikens utmaningar' (1991) 4 *Nordrevy* 7–11.

[43] Report of the Committee on Economic and Monetary Affairs on the *Second Report on Competition Policy* and on the *Communication on the Implementation of the Principles of Co-ordination of Regional Aid* (EP Doc. 264/73), 17; and *Industrial Policy in an Open and Competitive Environment*, COM(90)556, 9. See also the *Twenty-First Report on Competition Policy* (EC Commission, Brussels, 1992), 47.

[44] See, e.g., the Opinion of the Economic and Social Committee of 29 Jan. 1986 ([1986] OJ C75/12) on national regional development aid, para. 2.3; and the Opinion of the same Committee of 27 Nov. 1991 on industrial policy in an open and competitive environment ([1992] OJ C40/31), para. 3.2.3.

[45] W. Molle, *Regional Disparity and Economic Development in the European Community* (Saxon House, London, 1980), 1–4.

[46] *European Industrial Policy for the 1990s*, Bull. EC, Supp. 3/91, 13.

[47] *Ibid.*, 12.

[48] Cf., regarding the effects of political pressures for redistribution on the efforts of regulatory bodies to ensure allocative efficiency, G. Stigler, 'Toward an Economic Theory of Regulation' (1971) 2 *Bell Journal of Economics and Management Science* 3–21 and S. Peltzman, 'Toward a More General Theory of Regulation' (1976) 19 *Journal of Law and Economics* 211–40.

trading conditions to an extent contrary to the common interest. The latter requirement reflects the explicit condition for aid authorization in Article 92(3)(a) and (c) that development must be entailed. The underlying concern is with 'total welfare creation, measured in terms of an increase in development capacity'.[49]

4.2 CONCENTRATION

The need for aid concentration is expressed by the Commission in terms of the 'principle of regional specificity', and is considered to be consistent with both regional policy and competition policy.[50] Application of this principle is supported by the Court of Justice. In *EC Commission* v. *Germany: investment grants for mining*[51] the legality of a Commission decision of February 1971,[52] which prohibited German aid to improve the economic structure of regions affected by the crisis in the coal industry, was being challenged. Possibly in response to the challenge, 'co-ordination principles' for regional aid were published in October 1971.[53] The Court implicitly confirmed the need for their publication. It ruled that the Commission should clarify its criteria for determining areas in which aid was prohibited and in which it was authorized.[54]

According to the principle of regional specificity in Commission practice, aid may only be authorized where it is granted with due regard to the relative economic situation in the different regions concerned (or parts thereof)[55] and to the real advantages offered by the localities chosen by the investors.[56] Aid must be limited to regions suffering from problems that are sufficiently serious to require the grant of aid at the level proposed if investment is to be attracted,[57] and the objectives specified in Article 92(3)(a) or (c) are to be attained. Unless this limitation is respected, the Commission considers that the aid does not serve the objectives specified in these clauses. Rather, it furthers the private interests of the recipient,[58] and at the same time contributes to increased

---

[49] T. Frazer, n. 12 above, 11.

[50] *Medium-term Economic Policy Programme (1966–1970)* ([1967] JO 1513), 1565.

[51] Case 70/72 [1973] ECR 813.

[52] Dec. 71/121 ([1971] JO L57/19) on aid granted under Art. 32 of the Law on the Adaptation of German Coal-mining Undertakings and Coal-mining Areas.

[53] [1971] JO C111/1.　　　　　　　　　　　　　　　　[54] [1973] ECR 813, 831.

[55] Dec. 93/337 ([1993] OJ L134/25) concerning a scheme of tax concessions for investment in the Basque country.

[56] Bull. EC 3–1967, 28. See also the Reply to Written Question 28 by Mr Dehousse ([1967] JO 2311), where the Commission maintained that Belgian aid should be limited to regions of the greatest need, notably those suffering from problems of conversion from coal mining.

[57] See, e.g., Dec. 87/98 ([1987] OJ L40/17) on aid proposed by Rhineland-Pfalz for a metalworking firm in Betzdorf; and Dec. 91/305 ([1991] OJ L156/39) concerning investment aid which the Belgian Government planned to grant to Mactac SA, Soignies.

[58] Dec. 84/428 ([1984] OJ L241/20) on the proposal by the French Government to grant regional aid to a textile undertaking at La-Chapelle-Saint-Luc, Aube, France; and Dec. 85/18

regional disparities.[59] In the language of Article 92(3)(c) trading conditions are affected to an extent contrary to the common interest.

Hence, the Commission has prohibited aid schemes applicable to any undertaking in difficulties anywhere in the Member State concerned.[60] More particularly, when the Belgian Government sought to treat forty-one of its forty-three *arrondissements* as eligible for regional aid,[61] in Decision 72/173[62] the Commission drew up a list of regions in which such aid could be authorized. Such regions were divided into two categories, with a different ceiling being set for each category, depending on the severity of their problems.[63] The Commission also insisted that schemes in Italy,[64] Luxembourg,[65] and the Netherlands[66] respect the principle of regional specificity, and authorized a German aid scheme of tax exemptions only in respect of West Berlin and the *Zonenrand-gebiet.*[67]

There may, however, be some flexibility in the application of the principle of regional specificity. For example, French regional aid to an undertaking across the river from an assisted area was authorized. The authorization was based on the expectation that the aided investment would contribute to the development of the assisted area,[68] which was also eligible for Union aid under the Resider programme.[69] On the other hand, a German claim that a large proportion of

1984 ([1985] OJ L11/28) on the French regional planning grant scheme (*Prime d'aménagement du territoire*).

[59] Dec. 72/173 ([1972] JO L105/13) on aid granted under the Belgian Economic Expansion Law of Dec. 1970.

[60] Dec. 72/34 ([1972] JO L10/22) prohibiting Belgian aid to undertakings in difficulty.

[61] See, similarly, Communic. concerning a new regional aid scheme established in France ([1972] JO C77/2); Communic. in respect of a new system of regional grants introduced in France ([1973] OJ C32/2); and Communic. relating to the modifications which the French Government intends to make—with retroactive effect from 1 Jan. 1972—in the geographical scope of the tax concessions provided for the benefit of regional development ([1973] OJ C33/3). See also Notice regarding aid granted by the Netherlands Government to regional development ([1989] OJ C309/2).

[62] On aid granted under the Belgian Economic Expansion Law of Dec. 1970 ([1972] JO L105/13).

[63] See also objections to geographical scope in Notice concerning the regional aids system instituted by the Economic Expansion Law of 30 Dec. 1970 ([1981] OJ C316/4).

[64] *Second Report on Competition Policy* (EC Commission, Brussels, 1973), 84.

[65] Bull. EC 3–1973, 2115.

[66] Notice regarding the Dutch Investment Account Bill (*Wet Investeringsrekening*) introducing investment premiums ([1977] OJ C129/5). This scheme was also objectionable, because aid might be granted in respect of replacement investment.

[67] Dec. 71/295 ([1971] JO L179/37) on tax concessions under the Law of 28 Dec. 1968 on the Transport of Goods by Road, as prolonged on 23 Dec. 1970. Cf. the objections to geographical coverage in the Notice regarding the regional aid system introduced by the tenth general plan under the joint task for the improvement of regional economic structure in Germany ([1981] OJ C316/5).

[68] Bull. EC 5–1989, 2.1.90. See also Bull. EC 7/8–1989, 2.1.84.

[69] Reg. 328/88 ([1988] OJ L33/1) instituting a Community programme to assist the conversion of steel areas.

the workforce in the recipient area came from neighbouring assisted areas was discounted, as this proportion was only 6 per cent of the total workforce.[70]

The underlying economic and political tensions[71] are illustrated by a Resolution of the European Parliament.[72] According to this Resolution, the more developed Member States should concentrate their regional aid in their weakest regions both to avoid distortion of competition and to promote more efficient use of funds. However, such concentration would in itself be inadequate to tackle regional disparities within the Union. The more developed Member States, whose national economies may reflect less regional disparity, tend to allocate relatively more aid for regional development than the economically less developed Member States.[73] The latter tend to be unable to provide the aid needed to reduce their regional disparities.[74] While the developed Member States must have a certain latitude to pursue their own independent national regional policies, the overriding need to promote investment in the Union's least favoured regions must take precedence where it is in conflict with such latitude.[75] The implication is that the regional development efforts of the more developed Member States may have to be curbed in the interests of reducing regional disparities at the Union level.[76]

Such tensions have also received some recognition in the Court of Justice. *Germany* v. *EC Commission: regional aid* concerned a Commission decision prohibiting aid in certain German regions.[77] Here Advocate General Darmon described Article 92(3)(a) and (c) as introducing 'two derogations from freedom of competition based on Community solidarity (taking into account national solidarity)'.[78] In other words, a balance was envisaged between regional development efforts within Member States and reduction of disparities at Union level. The practical consequence is that while priority may be accorded to the problems of the peripheral regions of the Union, those of the central regions are not to be disregarded. Indeed, according to the Commission, sectoral considerations may mean that the question whether Article 92(3)(a) or (c) applies 'does not make any difference'.[79]

---

[70] Dec. 87/98 ([1987] OJ L40/17) on aid proposed by Rhineland-Pfalz for a metalworking firm in Betzdorf.

[71] Apparently, Commission efforts to control regional aid in Germany has led to 'considerable acrimony'. See 'Regional Policy and the European Community' [1992] *Journal of Regional Policy* 557–600, 583.

[72] Of 15 Oct. 1987 ([1987] OJ C305/128) on the effects of Arts. 92 and 93 EC on regional policy. [73] *Ibid.*, para. 4.

[74] *Ibid.*, para. 5. [75] *Ibid.*, para. 6.

[76] *Ibid.*, para. 7. Accordingly, the Commission should pay more attention to the effects on competition of combined forms of aid, particularly those applying outside assisted areas.

[77] Dec. 85/12 ([1985] OJ L7/28) on the North Rhine-Westfalia regional economic development programme.

[78] Case 248/84 [1987] ECR 4013, 4031.

[79] Notice C60/91 (ex NN/73/91, NN76/91) ([1993] OJ C43/14) regarding the proposal by the German Government to award state aid to the Opel group in support of its investment plans in the new *Länder*.

4.2.1 Peripheral Regions

In the 1971 *Principles for the Co-ordination of Regional Aid*[80] the Commission recognized the 'specific problems' of peripheral regions. In so doing, the Commission relied on a narrower conception of the periphery than that which may now be considered appropriate, particularly in view of successive enlargements of the Union.

'Traditional' Periphery

According to the *First Report on Competition Policy*,[81] the peripheral regions were large geographical areas, which were far from the consumer and industrial centres of the Union, where agriculture was still important, living standards still relatively low, and unemployment still an acute problem. A decision concerning proposed employment aid for three provinces in Sicily gives an idea of the kind of information considered by the Commission when evaluating aid for such regions. The Commission noted that net *per capita* incomes in the three provinces ranged between 54 per cent and 66 per cent of the national average and between 35 per cent and 42 per cent of the Union average. The population of the three provinces had declined considerably. Between 1961 and 1971 a net fall of between 4 per cent and 12 per cent was recorded. The population of Sicily as a whole declined by 1 per cent as against an increase of some 7 per cent in the total population of Italy. Emigration rates from the three provinces for the period 1961–71 were with a few exceptions higher than in any other Italian provinces. The employment situation was poor. In 1973 the percentage of persons in employment in Sicily amounted to only 25 per cent of the total population, as against an Italian average of 32 per cent. On the basis of these considerations, the Commission authorized the aid, even though the authorization meant that total aid to the areas concerned would exceed the levels usually authorized.[82]

Such practice might be thought consistent with the terms of Article 92(3)(a). As the Court of Justice ruled in *Germany* v. *EC Commission: regional aid*,[83] the use of the words 'abnormally' and 'serious' in this provision showed that this clause concerned only areas where the economic situation was extremely unfavourable in relation to the Union as a whole. The Court does not apparently share the view of the Economic and Social Committee that Article 92(3)(a) should apply not only to regions that are underdeveloped in relation to the Union average but also to 'regions that are extremely seriously dis-

---

[80] [1971] JO C111/1, para. 1.   [81] (EC Commission, Brussels, 1972), 119.

[82] *Sixth Report on Competition Policy* (EC Commission, Brussels, 1977), 108. See also the *Eighth Report on Competition Policy* (EC Commission, Brussels, 1979), 117. Cf. the exception from the aid ceiling in the case of Northern Ireland (Bull. EC 10–1977, 2.1.18; *Seventh Report on Competition Policy* (EC Commission, Brussels, 1978), 138).

[83] Case 248/84 [1987] ECR 4013, 4042.

advantaged in relation to the national average or the majority of regions in a Member State'.[84]

To identify areas covered by Article 92(3)(a), the Commission has now devised a simple statistical test, which has apparently led to the exclusion of certain parts of the Mezzogiorno from the scope of this provision.[85] According to a Commission Communication of 1988,[86] as amended in 1990,[87] Article 92(3)(a) may apply to NUTS[88] level III regions, reference being made to the situation of the level II region as a whole in which the level III region is located, which have a *per capita* gross domestic product of 75 per cent or less of the Union average. These regions, to which Northern Ireland and Teruel have been added for special reasons, are listed in Annex I to the Communication.

Analysis of regional problems by reference to NUTS level III regions is controversial. The Commission will, however, use smaller geographical units in 'justified exceptional circumstances'[89] and, in particular, admits that the labour market area is a unit of analysis far superior to that of the NUTS level III region.[90]

The 75 per cent threshold is also controversial. This threshold follows that used to identify Objective 1 regions (that is, 'regions whose development is lagging behind') in legislation on the Structural Funds.[91] It has been alleged, however, that having established a ranking of regions by gross domestic product, the Commission chose the threshold for Article 92(3)(a) purposes 'on the basis of empirical evidence of regions deemed to be underdeveloped'.[92]

Even reliance on gross domestic product data at all may be problematic. Such data are regarded as a composite measure of three factors: productivity, the rate of participation in the labour force and unemployment. They, therefore, constitute a measure both of the standard of living and of under-employment.

[84] Opinion of 29 Jan. 1986 ([1986] OJ C75/12) on national regional development aid, para. 3.2.

[85] Bull. EC 4–1987, 2.1.62. More particularly, Abruzzi has now come to be classified as an Art. 92(3)(c) region rather than as an Art. 92(3)(a) region. See Bull. EU 3–1995, 1.3.44.

[86] Communic. on the method for the application of Art. 92(3)(a) and (c) to regional aid ([1988] OJ C212/2), para. I.1.

[87] Communic. on the method of application of Art. 92(3)(a) to regional aid ([1990] OJ C163/5).   [88] Nomenclature of Territorial Units for Statistical Purposes.

[89] Para. II.1 of the 1988 Communic. See, e.g., Dec. 93/353 ([1993] OJ L145/25) concerning the application of the national regional aid scheme in an area in the north of the Province of Madrid.

[90] Notice 39/90 (ex N453/90) ([1992] OJ C290/2) concerning aid which Germany had decided to grant in favour of Nefab GmbH in Hueckelhoven; and Notice C40/90 (ex N511/90) ([1992] OJ C290/5) concerning a draft aid which Germany had decided to grant in favour of Chukyo Europe GmbH.

[91] Arts. 1 and 8 of Reg. 2052/88 ([1988] OJ L185/9) on the tasks of the Structural Funds and their effectiveness and on the co-ordination of their activities between themselves and with the operations of the EIB and the other existing financial instruments.

[92] 'Regional Policy and the European Community' [1992] *Journal of Regional Policy* 557–600, 592.

Under-employment concerns all those who are not fully employed in some way. In general, where under-employment is great, productive output will tend to be low and as such will also be reflected in gross domestic product data. For the areas concerned—predominantly rural areas with an underdeveloped industrial base or a limited level of service activities—unemployment statistics are not a satisfactory measure of under-employment. The general low level of technology in the industrial infrastructure and the unsophisticated range of service activities lead to a relative emphasis on labour in the production process. As a result, significant levels of under-employment may be unrecorded by unemployment data.[93]

On the other hand, under-employment also exists in regions where high unemployment or a low participation rate is combined with high productivity. In such cases *per capita* gross domestic product data may not fully reflect the extent of under-employment. However, application of Article 92(3)(a) is intended to be reserved for the most extreme cases of regional disadvantage, and it is felt that such cases can only be identified by examining the combined working of the three contributory factors, not by considering each one separately.[94]

Nevertheless, rigid application of a statistical test may not always be considered feasible. For example, paragraph I.1 of the 1988 Communication originally provided that the majority of level III regions within a level II region must be below the threshold. In accordance with this provision, Teruel, which was within the Level II region of Aragon,[95] would have been excluded from the scope of Article 92(3)(a). However, Teruel was treated as an Article 92(3)(a) region, because it bordered on other Article 92(3)(a) regions and was one of the most underdeveloped regions in Spain with a sparse population and a high degree of dependence on agriculture.[96] In practice, the Commission now seems willing to treat *zones* as eligible for aid under Article 92(3)(a), where they have 'particularly serious socio-economic problems', even if the *areas* to which they belong are not eligible under this provision.[97] Again, Northern Ireland was treated as eligible for aid under Article 92(3)(a) 'because of its particularly difficult situation'.[98] The fact that the former German Democratic Republic is treated as covered by this provision[99] highlights the erosion of the traditional link between application of Article 92(3)(a) and dependence on agriculture.

---

[93] Para. I.2 of the 1988 Communic.

[94] S. Lehner and R. Meiklejohn, 'Fair Competition in the Internal Market: Community State Aid Policy' (1991) 48 *European Economy* 58.

[95] 'State Aid Control in the Context of Other Community Policies' [1994] *European Economy*, Supp. A, No. 4, 9, n. 2.   [96] Para. I.4 of the 1988 Communication.

[97] H. Morch, 'Summary of the Most Important Recent Developments' (1995) 6 *Competition Policy Newsletter* 41–7, 44.

[98] Para. I.4 of the 1988 Communication.

[99] *Twenty-Fourth Report on Competition Policy* (EC Commission, Brussels, 1995), 496; Communic. C4/94 (ex NN103/93) ([1994] OJ C206/10) concerning aid decided by the German Government in favour of Leuna AG, Sachsen Anhalt.

In principle, for regions covered by this provision an aid ceiling of 75 per cent nge (net grant equivalent) applies. However, even in such regions, 'excessive' aid levels may render the aid incompatible with the common market because of negative effects on competition and trade.[100] Therefore, in accordance with the requirement in the 1979 Co-ordination Principles for Regional Aid[101] that ceilings must be adapted to the kind, intensity or urgency of the regional problems,[102] the Commission may impose ceilings lower than 75 per cent.[103]

Nordic Periphery

Challenges to established Commission practice regarding identification of peripheral regions may be entailed by the European Economic Area (EEA) Agreement and the latest enlargement of the Union. The challenges were illustrated in the *Opinion on Norway's Application for EU Membership*.[104] Here the Commission raised objections to the level of regional aid granted in Norway as well as to the operating character of some such aid.[105] On the other hand, given the accession of Finland and Sweden to the Union, the Commission recognizes that the climatic and demographic features specific to arctic and subarctic regions need to be taken into account in Union structural policies.[106] To the extent that these policies and competition policy must be consistent,[107] the implication is that such features might also have to be taken into account in the application of Article 92.

Confirmation of this implication is provided by a Joint Declaration annexed to the EEA Agreement. This Declaration concerns Article 61(3)(a) and (c) of the Agreement, which reproduce respectively Article 92(3)(a) and (c) of the EC Treaty. In the Declaration the Contracting Parties note that even if eligibility of a region for state aid has to be denied in the context of Article 61(3)(a) of the Agreement and according to the first stage of analysis under subparagraph (c),[108] examination according to other criteria, such as very low population density, is possible.

---

[100] Notice C32/94 (N48/94) ([1994] OJ C293/6) with regard to the aid for the construction of a rape seed oil methylester pilot plan operated by the Raiffeisen Hauptgenossenschaft Nord AG, Kiel.

[101] [1979] OJ C31/9.   [102] *Ibid.*, para. 9(iv).

[103] Para. I. 5. of the 1988 Communic. See, e.g., Dec. 93/254 ([1993] OJ L117/22) on Italian Decree–Law of 14 Jan. 1992 relating, *inter alia*, to the overall refinancing of the aid measures provided for by Law 64 of 1 Mar. 1986 on special aid to the Mezzogiorno.

[104] Bull. EC, Supp. 2/93.

[105] *Ibid.*, 24.

[106] See, regarding Sweden, the *Opinion on Sweden's Application for EU Membership*, Bull. EC, Supp. 5/92, 16.

[107] See, e.g., Art. 7(1) of Reg. 2052/88 ([1988] OJ L185/9) on the tasks of the Structural Funds and their effectiveness and on the co-ordination of their activities between themselves and with the operations of the EIB and the other existing financial instruments, as amended by Reg. 2081/93 ([1993] OJ L193/1).

[108] See sect. 4.2.2 below, regarding the 'two-stage' analysis.

The Swedish Government viewed the Declaration as indicating Union recognition of the particular nature of regional problems in Sweden, which would affect future Union treatment of regional aid in this country.[109] Partial confirmation of this view was provided by the outcome of negotiations for the fourth enlargement of the Union. In connection with distribution of Union aid, these negotiations led to establish a new Objective 6 for the Structural Funds, which concerns regions with a population density of less than 8 inhabitants per square kilometre.[110]

The EFTA Surveillance Authority (ESA) draws the conclusion from the Declaration that 'a very low population density' may qualify a region under Article 61(3)(a) of the Agreement.[111] This conclusion may not necessarily be acceptable to the Commission.[112] The latter now treats Teruel as being covered by Article 92(3)(c) of the EC Treaty, despite its low population density.[113] Moreover, rural areas in Scotland, which may have much in common with those in Norway (though not necessarily in terms of *per capita* gross domestic product), have traditionally been treated as being covered by Article 92(3)(c) rather than Article 92(3)(a). Only as their *per capita* gross domestic product has fallen towards the 75 per cent level have they come to be treated as Objective 1 regions for the purposes of the Structural Funds,[114] the possible implication being that they will now also be treated as regions covered by Article 92(3)(a).[115] In the case of rural Norwegian areas having a higher *per capita* gross domestic product[116] than rural areas of Scotland, it is uncertain whether authorization of aid under Article 61(3)(a) of the EEA Agreement would be compatible with established Commission practice.[117]

[109] *Europeisk Ekonomiska Samarbetsområdet. (European Economic Co-operation Area)*, prop. 1991/92:170, *del* (pt.) 3, *bil.* (app.) 9, 34.

[110] Prot. 6 to the Accession Agreement, as substituted by Art. 52 of Dec. 95/1 ([1995] OJ L1/1) adjusting the instruments concerning the accession of new Member States to the European Union.

[111] Para. 28.1.3 of Dec. 4/94/COL ([1994] OJ C231/1) on the adoption and issuing of the procedural and substantive rules in the field of state aid (guidelines on the application and interpretation of Arts. 61 and 62 EEA and Art. 1 of Prot. 3 to the Surveillance and Court Agreement).

[112] Cf. changes to the method for the application of Art. 92(3)(a) EC to regional aid ([1994] OJ C364/8), para. 1.1.

[113] Notice N463/94 ([1996] OJ C25/3) regarding the new Spanish map of assisted regions; Reply by Mr Van Miert to Written Question E–2402/95 ([1996] OJ C9/39) by Josu Imaz Miguel.

[114] Reg. 2081/93 ([1993] OJ L193/5) amends Annex I to Reg. 2052/88, so as to classify them as Objective 1 regions for the purposes of allocations from the Structural Funds.

[115] However, Hainault, in Belgium, has also come to be covered by Objective 1, though it is still classified as an Art. 92(3)(c) region: *Twenty-Fourth Report on Competition Policy* (EC Commission, Brussels, 1995), 495–6. Again, Flevoland in the Netherlands is covered by Objective 1, but the authorized aid intensity is only 25%. See Bull. EU 5–1995, 1.3.44.

[116] Cf. the Swedish figures published in *Norbotten inför EG-förhandlingen* (Länstyrelsen Norbottens län, Lulea, 1992).

[117] Only Finnmark and the four most northerly municipalities of Troms have been found by the ESA to be covered by Art. 61(3)(a) EEA. See *European Report* 1994 (19 Nov. 1994); [1995] OJ C14/4.

4.2.2 Central Regions

The central regions 'are generally fairly industrialized, even if sometimes rather out-of-date, and face as a result serious reconversion problems'.[118] The EC Treaty does not preclude the grant of aid in the central regions. However, the Commission considers that in such regions there is 'the greatest danger of escalating subsidies' and that aid to such regions may lead to increased regional disparities contrary to Article 2 of the Treaty.[119]

Consequently, opposition to aid in the central regions is well established in Commission practice.[120] For example, in 1964 the Commission found that the situation of Antwerp, which was prosperous in comparison with numerous other Union regions, did not justify the grant of aid under Article 92(3)(c).[121] Even where Belgian regional aid could be authorized under that provision, the highest levels of aid should be reserved for regions with the greatest need,[122] notably those where problems of conversion from coal-mining were present.[123] Similarly, in 1971 the Commission decided that a regional aid scheme could not be authorized under Article 92(3)(c) for German regions with a very high degree of industrialization, a good level of *per capita* gross domestic product and high rate of employment.[124] This decision was the first instance of a rejection of a regional aid scheme based on the economic and social conditions prevailing in the regions concerned. Agreement was subsequently reached with Germany on demarcation of the areas which could receive aid.[125]

Such practice may be consistent with the terms of Article 92(3)(c). The very requirement that aid under this provision should facilitate development implies that the region should have serious development problems.[126] Thus aid to a German region could not be authorized under Article 92(3)(c), because the unemployment rate was less than 30 per cent above the national average.[127] An analogy might be drawn with the refusal of the Commission to authorize aid under Article 92(3)(c) on sectoral grounds, where the aid is granted to all

---

[118] *First Report on Competition Policy* (EC Commission, Brussels, 1972), 119.

[119] Ibid.

[120] In 1966 the Commission objected to the 'scale' of Dutch aid to reduce employment difficulties arising from the conversion of coalmining areas in southern Limburg. See the *First EC General Report* (EC Commission, Brussels, 1967), 69.

[121] Dec. 64/651 ([1964] JO 3257) concerning the prohibition of Belgian aid granted to Ford Tractors (Belgium) Ltd at Anvers.

[122] Such need may be assessed in terms of cyclical problems: see Bull. EC 5–1984, 2.1.54.

[123] Commission Reply to Written Question 28/67 ([1967] JO 2311) by Mr Dehousse.

[124] Dec. 71/121 ([1971] JO 57/19) on aid granted under art. 32 of the Law on the Adaptation of German Coal-mining Undertakings and Coal-mining Areas.

[125] *First Report on Competition Policy* (EC Commission, Brussels, 1972), 125.

[126] Para. II.2 of the 1988 Communication.

[127] Dec. 85/12 ([1985] OJ L7/28) on the North Rhine–Westfalia regional economic development programme. See, similarly, regarding a British scheme to encourage the transfer of service undertakings to assisted areas, Bull. EC 7/8–1973, 2116.

undertakings in a given sector 'without distinguishing between those which have structural difficulties and those which do not'.[128]

At the same time, it would be against the common interest within the terms of Article 92(3)(c) to increase existing differences between regions and the backwardness of less favoured areas. Accordingly, the Commission insists that regional aid should not have the effect of diverting investment from less well-placed Member States.[129] To preclude this effect, the Commission prohibits aid, unless it is established that the aided region suffers from difficulties that are relatively severe within the Union context; that without the aid market forces would not eliminate these difficulties; and that the grant of aid does not unduly distort competition in particular sectors.[130]

The importance attached to the Union context has grown in Commission practice. In 1971 the Commission was willing to authorize aid in coalmining areas of North Rhine–Westphalia where *per capita* gross domestic product was 10 per cent below the average for the *Land*.[131] Moreover, in 1979[132] and 1980[133] the Commission was content to check the acceptability of aid to German regions well below the thresholds employed by the German Government. However, in 1981 unemployment and *per capita* gross domestic product were used by the Commission to identify German regions worse off than the Union average.[134]

Such practice may have support in the Court of Justice. In *Philip Morris Holland BV* v. *EC Commission*,[135] where the intended aid beneficiary was located in Bergen-op-Zoom in the Netherlands, the Court ruled that Commission assessments under Article 92(3)(c) must be made in a Union context, and not that of a single Member State. The local unemployment rate was 7 per cent, whereas the national average was 3.8 per cent, which was the lowest in the

---

[128] Dec. 73/274 ([1973] OJ L254/14) on Art. 20 of Italian Law 1101 of 1 Dec. 1971 on the restructuring, reorganization, and conversion of the textile industry. See also Dec. 84/472 ([1984] OJ L268/27) on the extension until 30 June 1983 of the regional aid supplement provided for in Art. 2(b) of the Belgian Economic Expansion Act of 30 Dec. 1970.

[129] See, e.g., Dec. 81/716 ([1981] OJ L256/22) on a proposal by the Netherlands Government to grant aid for increasing the production capacity by an undertaking in the chemical industry (polyethylene).

[130] Dec. 88/318 ([1988] OJ L143/37) on Law 64 of 1 Mar. 1986 on aid to the Mezzogiorno. See also Dec. 87/15 ([1987] OJ L12/17) on the compatibility with the common market of aid under the German Federal/*Land* Government Joint Regional Aid Programme in six labour market regions.

[131] Case 70/72 *EC Commission* v. *Germany: investment grants for mining* [1973] ECR 813.

[132] Notice regarding Germany's regional aid system pursuant to the 'joint task of improving regional economic structures' ([1979] OJ C36/22); *Ninth Report on Competition Policy* (EC Commission, Brussels, 1980), 89.

[133] *Tenth Report on Competition Policy* (EC Commission, Brussels, 1981), 116.

[134] *Eleventh Report on Competition Policy* (EC Commission, Brussels, 1982), 160. See also, regarding Belgium, *Ibid.* 161. A different method was used by Germany. See the *Thirteenth Report on Competition Policy* (EC Commission, Brussels, 1984), 176.

[135] Case 730/79 [1980] ECR 2671.

Union.[136] The Court considered that the Commission had with good reason assessed the standard of living and unemployment in the Bergen-op-Zoom area, not with reference to the national average in the Netherlands but in relation to the Union level.[137] It was also reasonable for the Commission to take the view that the investment to be effected in this case was not 'an important project of common European interest' and that the aid could not be likened to aid 'intended to remedy a serious disturbance in the economy of a Member State' within the meaning of Article 92(3)(b), since the proposed aid would have permitted the transfer to the Netherlands of an investment which could be effected in other Member States in a less favourable economic situation than the Netherlands. The Commission finding that market conditions in the sector concerned seemed apt, without state intervention, to ensure a normal development and that the aid could not therefore be regarded as 'facilitating' such development within the meaning of Article 92(3)(c) was also justified, when the need for aid was assessed from the stand-point of the Union rather than that of a single Member State.[138]

On the other hand, in *Germany* v. *EC Commission: regional aid*[139] the Court recognized that Article 92(3)(c) covered aid for the development of certain areas without being restricted by the economic conditions laid down in Article 92(3)(a). It empowered the Commission to authorize aid intended to further the economic development of areas of a Member State which were disadvantaged in relation to the national average.

This ruling may be consistent with the Commission view that national economic problems do not justify regional aid under Article 92(3)(c), unless the problems are more severe in the assisted areas than elsewhere in the Member State concerned.[140] In accordance with this view, the Commission objected to the absence of social or economic evidence to show that Belgian areas receiving regional aid were suffering more from the recession than the rest of the country.[141] Similarly, the Commission objected to Danish regional aid to areas which economic indicators showed to be little worse off than the national average.[142] However, the further implication of the ruling is that where there are serious disparities within the Member State, aid may be authorized under Article 92(3)(c).[143]

---

[136] Aid may, however, be authorized in an area where employment is increasing rapidly. See Bull. EC 9–1981, 2.1.31.

[137] [1980] ECR 2671, 2691–2

[138] *Ibid.*, 2692. See also Slynn AG in Joined Cases 296 and 318/82 *Netherlands and Leeuwarder Papierwarenfabrik BV* v. *EC Commission* [1985] ECR 809, 815.

[139] Case 248/84 [1987] ECR 4013, 4042.

[140] Cf. the *Fourteenth Report on Competition Policy* (EC Commission, Brussels, 1985), 171.

[141] Notice ([1983] OJ C122/4) regarding the additional regional aid scheme under Art. 2(b) of the Law of 30 Dec. 1970 on economic expansion.

[142] Bull. EC 12–1986, 2.1.114.

[143] Dec. 82/691 ([1982] OJ L290/39) on the designation of areas eligible for regional aid in Denmark from 1 Jan. 1982.

In short, the Commission must take account of both the Union context and the national context in evaluating regional aid under Article 92(3)(c). To this end, the Commission has devised a 'two-stage' test of eligibility under this provision.

'Two-stage' Test of Eligibility

Eligibility for regional aid under Article 92(3)(c) is determined on the basis of a two-stage test, which is designed to ensure a Union-related assessment that is systematic and objective.[144] It is alleged, however, that the Commission 'uses so-called quantitative criteria to provide a spurious "scientific" justification for decisions which are often subjective and the net result of extensive negotiations with Member States'.[145]

In a decision concerning a regional aid scheme in Belgium[146] the Commission described its approach to consideration whether there were regional problems which were serious enough to warrant the grant of aid. First, the Commission placed the Belgian regions in question in a Union context by comparing gross domestic product and the employment situation in those regions with the corresponding Union averages. Then the Commission sought to establish whether there were disparities between the regions at the national level which might justify the grant of regional aid. For this purpose, the Commission used certain indicators of economic development and employment, such as taxable income, unemployment, employment trends, net migration, demographic factors, and structure of economic activities. According to the Commission, this approach made it possible to identify the nature of the economic problems of the regions concerned and to establish whether they were structural. It was found that the Belgian scheme was not compatible with the principle of regional specificity as it would confer hardly any compensating benefits on regions suffering from real structural handicaps.[147] Such handicaps must result from industrial problems threatening the social fabric; changes in employment figures reflecting structural change rather than cyclical

[144] See, e.g., Dec. 85/12 ([1985] OJ L7/28) on the North Rhine–Westphalia regional economic development programme.

[145] 'Regional Policy and the European Community' [1992] *Journal of Regional Policy* 557–600, 592; F. G. Wishade, 'Competition Policy, Cohesion and the Co-ordination of Regional Aids in the European Community' [1993] *ECLR* 143–50.

[146] Dec. 82/740 ([1982] OJ L312/18) on the designation of development areas pursuant to Art. 11 of the Belgian Law of 30 Dec. 1970. See, later, Notice ([1983] OJ C241/3) regarding proposals by the Belgian Government to create employment zones at the Westhoek: Ieperkanaal, the arrondissement Oudenaarde, Kruishoutem, and the Kempen: Genk Sud; and Dec. 88/612 ([1988] OJ L335/31) amending for the second time Dec. 82/740, regarding the continued eligibility of certain parts of Limburg.

[147] See, similarly, Dec. 84/428 ([1984] OJ L241/20) on the proposal by the French Government to grant regional aid to a textile undertaking at La Chapelle-Saint-Luc, Aube, France; and Dec. 85/275 ([1985] OJ L152/21) on the proposal of the French Government to grant regional aid to an undertaking engaged in the watch-making and optical and electronic engineering industries at Besançon, Doubs, France.

trends;[148] or fluctuations in economic activity which have had the effect of increasing the structural disparities between regions.[149]

The same approach was adopted in relation to Danish regional aid, though in assessing regional disparities at the national level the Commission used as indicators: taxable income, unemployment, employment in the services sector, employment in the primary sector, population density, and net migration.[150] In relation to a German scheme, the Commission also took account of infrastructure provision and special structural problems such as a one-sided industrial structure or restructuring in the steel industry.[151] The Commission endeavoured in such decisions to develop the same method of analysis for all the Member States, despite differences in national selection methods and in the national statistics available.[152]

Refinement of this method was found to be necessary. In Decision 87/15,[153] which concerned German regional aid, the Commission had compared the *per capita* gross domestic product of the regions concerned with that of the six most developed Member States, but not with the German average, when opening the Article 93(2) procedure. However, in a letter of 31 July 1985 the Commission informed Germany of eligibility thresholds expressed by reference to national averages for gross domestic product and unemployment. In the final decision reference was made to these thresholds in the first stage of assessment of eligibility. Thus the first stage of the test was no longer limited to a simple comparison with Union averages. This stage was now based on thresholds of aid eligibility, expressed for each region in terms of structural employment and of *per capita* gross domestic product relative to Union and national averages.[154]

Such practice was challenged in *Germany* v. *EC Commission: regional aid*.[155] The German Government argued that it was solely at a national level and on the basis of indicators drawn up by the competent national authorities (criteria which were said to be more reliable and more comparable, especially in relation to the rate of unemployment) that the aid needs of the various regions of a Member State should be determined. The use of Union averages might be acceptable, in spite of the methodological reservations[156] with regard to the use

---

[148] Dec. 85/18 ([1985] OJ L11/28) on the French regional planning grant scheme (*Prime d'aménagement du territoire*).

[149] Dec. 84/472 ([1984] OJ L268/27) on the extension until 30 June 1983 of the regional aid supplement provided for in Art. 2(b) of the Belgian Economic Expansion Act of 30 Dec. 1970.

[150] Dec. 82/691 ([1982] OJ L290/39) on the designation of areas eligible for regional aid in Denmark from 1 Jan. 1982.

[151] Dec. 85/12 ([1985] OJ L7/28) on the North Rhine–Westphalia regional economic development programme.

[152] *Twelfth Report on Competition Policy* (EC Commission, Brussels, 1983), 139.

[153] On the compatibility with the common market of aid under the German Federal/*Land* Government Joint Regional Aid Programme in six labour market regions ([1987] OJ L12/17).

[154] *Fourteenth Report on Competition Policy* (EC Commission, Brussels, 1985), 168.

[155] Case 248/84 [1987] ECR 4013.

[156] In practice, problems may arise, as in the case of aid to the Twente region in the Netherlands, because of differences in statistical methods. See *European Report* 1691 (6 July 1991).

of two relatively crude criteria of assessment adopted by the Commission (GDP per inhabitant in 1978 and average rate of unemployment for 1975, 1977, and 1979), as a basis for allotting Union resources from the European Regional Development Fund (ERDF), but not for assessing the regional-policy requirements of a Member State, which could not be assessed on the basis of values which were fixed 'in relation to the economic level of Community regions whose development was unsatisfactory'. Their use would lead to a levelling downwards of regional aid, which would exclude regions of the Federal Republic from the benefit of such aid by reason of the economic situation in other Member States.

Advocate General Darmon did not accept that Commission assessment under Article 92(3)(a) and (c) could be equated with a process of levelling downwards. Aid intended to encourage the development of a region where there was, for example, serious under-employment (Article 92(3)(a)) could not be regarded as incompatible with the common market *solely* because that region was situated in a Member State where the general level of development was considered to be high. There would have to be other reasons, perhaps based on the situation of the region by reference to certain indicators or threshold values drawn up, if necessary on a differentiated basis, at a Union level. As regards Article 92(3)(c), the decision in question showed by the example, *inter alia*, of the labour market region of Aachen that aid might be granted on the basis of that provision even to regions situated in Member States with a high level of development.

Moreover, the Commission had examined whether there were any disparities between the areas in which it had prohibited aid and other areas in Germany such as to warrant the grant of regional aid. For that purpose it used several indicators covering, in particular, income and the level of economic activity, unemployment, labour supply, migration, and infrastructure provision. Then the Commission investigated whether the aid to the areas could be said to be compatible with the common market on account of special structural problems, such as a one-sided industrial structure or restructuring in the steel industry.

However, in relation to the Borken-Bocholt labour market region, the German Government had supplied information concerning not only the recorded and foreseeable increase in unemployment but also gross domestic product, which it said was 17 per cent below the national average. The statement of the reasons for the contested decision dealt only with the first indicator and did not refer to the second at all. It was, therefore, insufficient, and the Advocate General considered that the decision should be declared void on that ground.[157]

The Court of Justice itself ruled that in its decision the Commission confined itself to quoting the words of Article 92(1) without discussing the character-

---

[157] [1987] ECR 4013, 4034.

istics of the aid programme in order to show that it was incompatible with the common market within the meaning of that provision. Hence, the decision had to be declared void for lack of reasoning.[158]

Following this judgment, the Commission detailed its method, as refined in Decision 87/15, in the 1988 Communication.[159] According to this Communication, the Commission examines, in the first stage of the eligibility test, the situation of the region, usually identified as a NUTS level III region, by reference to thresholds of *per capita* gross domestic product[160] and unemployment. The basic thresholds are 85 per cent of average national *per capita* gross domestic product and 110 per cent of average national unemployment. These figures are adjusted by 'European indices'.[161] The indices express the Member State's position with respect to *per capita* gross domestic product and structural unemployment as a percentage of the corresponding Union average. The adjustment produces 'modified' thresholds. In principle, aid may be granted to a region which is found to have a *per capita* gross domestic product below the modified threshold or unemployment above the modified threshold.

According to this method, aid may be granted to a region with a 'negative regional disparity' in the national context, notwithstanding the relative situation of the Member State within the Union.[162] On the other hand, it is against the common interest to increase existing differences between regions and the backwardness of less-favoured areas. Hence, aid may only be granted to regions in Member States with a more favourable situation than the Union average, where the national regional disparities are correspondingly greater.[163]

However, in the light of the Joint Declaration concerning Article 61(3)(c) of the EEA Agreement, a further criterion is to be applied by the EFTA Surveillance Authority (ESA) and the Commission in the first stage of the test. According to the ESA, a region where the population density is less than 12.5 per square kilometre may, on this ground alone, be found eligible for aid under the first stage of the test applied under Article 61(3)(c) of the Agreement.[164] The Commission has similarly adapted its own practice under Article 92(3)(c) of the EC Treaty.[165] These adaptations are justified by the fact that the other indicators used in the first stage do not properly reflect regional problems specific to the Nordic countries. These problems result from geography—the remote northern location of some areas, harsh weather conditions and very

---

[158] *Ibid.*, 4042.

[159] [1988] OJ C212/2.

[160] Account is now taken of gross value added at factor cost (GVA). See the Commission Dec. of 1 June 1994, Bull. EU 6–1994, 2.1.59.

[161] Corresponding thresholds have been adopted by the ESA for EFTA States within the EEA ([1994] OJ C158/5).

[162] Para. II.2 of the 1988 Communic.   [163] *Ibid.*

[164] Dec. 88/94/COL ([1994] OJ L240/33) on the second amendment of the procedural and substantive rules in the field of state aid, para. 28.2.3.1.

[165] Changes to the method for the application of Art. 92(3)(c) EC to regional aid ([1994] OJ C364/8), paras. 2.5–6.

long distances inside the borders of the country concerned and from the very low population density in some parts.[166]

In the second stage of the test other indicators are considered. According to the 1988 Communication,[167] the indicators include: the trend and structure of unemployment,[168] development of employment, net migration, demographic pressures, population density,[169] activity rates, productivity, the structure of economic activity,[170] in particular the importance of declining sectors,[171] investment, geographic situation,[172] topography,[173] and infrastructure. Broader considerations, including the percentage of the national population covered by the regional aid scheme concerned and the need to achieve 'greater consistency between structural policy and competition policy' may also be taken into account.[174] Such indicators and considerations may lead the Commission to reverse the finding on aid eligibility reached in the first stage. Thus the result of the first stage 'is taken only as a *prima facie* presumption'.[175]

The operation of the two-stage test is illustrated by Decision 88/318[176] concerning aid to the Mezzogiorno. Italian modified thresholds for the purposes of application of Article 92(3)(c) were 85 per cent of gross domestic product and 116 per cent of unemployment. It was found that the NUTS Level III area of Frosinone had an unemployment rate above the threshold of 116 per cent. To decide what rate of aid was justified in this area, average gross domestic product and structural unemployment in the area were compared with those in Level III areas in France and the United Kingdom where the Commission had accepted the highest aid intensity allowed pursuant to Article

---

[166] Recognition of the significance of the last factor only in respect of the Nordic periphery may in itself be controversial. For example, France also considers that the two basic criteria are inadequate for identifying problems of its rural regions. See 'Regional Policy and the European Community' [1992] *Journal of Regional Policy* 557–600, 586–7.

[167] Para. II.3 of the 1988 Communic.

[168] An increase in unemployment may be too recent and coincide too closely with a general economic crisis to be definitely acknowledged as structural. Hence, aid may only be granted for a limited period. See the *Seventh Report on Competition Policy* (EC Commission, Brussels, 1978), 135.

[169] Rural depopulation might be decisive, even where new jobs were being created in the areas concerned. See, regarding the acceptability of French rural aid, the *Eighth Report on Competition Policy* (EC Commission, Brussels, 1979), 116.

[170] Dependence on net transfers from the national budget is not specifically covered.

[171] The Commission takes account of the particular difficulties faced by certain industrial areas whose decline needs to be halted by setting up new activities. See the *Seventeenth Report on Competition Policy* (EC Commission, Brussels, 1988), 174.

[172] See, regarding geographic isolation, Dec. 91/500 ([1991] OJ L262/29) concerning aid granted to enterprises in the Friuli–Venezia Giulia region.

[173] See, e.g., regarding the significance of mountainous topography, *Eleventh Report on Competition Policy* (EC Commission, Brussels, 1982), 166–7.

[174] Reply by Mr Van Miert to Written Question E–3031/93 ([1994] OJ C240/45) by Nora Mebrak-Zaidi. See also, regarding the French regional aid scheme, H. Morch, 'Summary of the Most Important Recent Developments' [1994] 3 *Competition Policy Newsletter* 61–6, 63.

[175] Dec. 87/98 ([1987] OJ L40/17) on aid proposed by Rhineland-Pfalz for a metalworking firm in Betzdorf.

[176] On Law 64 of 1 Mar. 1986 on aid to the Mezzogiorno ([1988] OJ L143/37).

92(3)(c) and with those in the provinces of the Centre-North of Italy. On the basis of this comparison the Commission decided that aid could be granted up to the ceiling of 30 per cent, which was provided for in point 2(iii) of the 1979 Communication on Regional Aid Systems[177] for the *Zonenrandgebiet* and certain Danish regions.

On the other hand, the Level III areas of Ascoli–Piceno, Riete, Rome, and Latina were found to have a *per capita* gross domestic product above 85 per cent of the national average and unemployment rates below 116 per cent of the national average. As the areas did not qualify for aid under the first stage, the Commission examined the economic data to assess whether they could, nevertheless, be deemed eligible for regional aid. Their gross domestic product and unemployment rates were compared with those in provinces of the Centre-North and with those in Level III areas in other Member States where the Commission had authorized regional aid. The Commission also examined the following data presented by the Italian authorities: changes in resident population, net migration, population density, activity rate (active population/resident population), changes in the levels of employment and unemployment, youth unemployment, number of income supplement claimants, potential unemployment, labour force forecasts, gross domestic product per employee, active population by economic sector, agricultural and manufacturing employment, industrialization, employment in the advanced technology industries, services dependent on specific industries, management services, growth of investment, degree of internationalization of the economy, infrastructure provision, and commercial interest rates. The comparisons and evaluation of these data did not lead the Commission to change its view that regional aid was unjustified in these regions.

The Italian authorities objected that the Commission failed to take into account the great variations in conditions within each province. These variations meant that some areas did suffer from an abnormally low standard of living or serious under-employment. In reply, the Commission maintained that, for assessing the social and economic situation of regions, the NUTS Level III areas used by the Commission were the smallest of the three units agreed upon between Eurostat and the Member States to serve as a uniform reference framework for regional statistics. In Italy the Level III unit was the province, and it was this which the Italian authorities themselves used to divide the Mezzogiorno into three zones of less, intermediate, and developed regions.

The second stage in the assessment made by the Commission may sometimes be decisive. For example, the Spanish Government proposed to grant aid up to a level of 45 per cent in the areas of Madrid and the Asturias.[178] Such a

---

[177] [1979] OJ C31/9.
[178] Notice E8/90 ([1991] OJ C32/5) concerning the review of the national scheme of regional incentives in the areas of Madrid and Asturias.

level was more in accordance with Article 92(3)(a) than Article 92(3)(c), under which it was only permissible as an exception. However, these areas did not qualify under the former clause. Consequently, that level could only be permitted under Article 92(3)(c) if the situation in these areas was exceptionally unfavourable. Their situation was much too favourable to meet the thresholds for application of Article 92(3)(c). Nevertheless, the rate of structural unemployment in the Asturias had risen in recent years, and the Structural Funds provided assistance there in pursuit of Objective 1 (that is, promoting the development and structural adjustment of regions whose development is lagging behind[179]) until 1993. For these reasons and taking into account the restructuring of the region's mining industry, the Commission decided, as an exception, to authorize aid under Article 92(3)(c) up to a level of 45 per cent in the outlying and central mining areas in the Asturias region until 1 June 1993.[180] On the other hand, the socio-economic situation of the Madrid region, in so far as *per capita* gross domestic product and the unemployment rate were concerned, had not worsened in recent years and was at present appreciably more favourable than the national average. Hence, the Commission found that the same aid level could not be authorized there. This finding reflects a general Commission tendency to prohibit aid where a recent decline in employment has been halted,[181] though aid may still be authorized where the regional economy may still be vulnerable to any cyclical reversal.[182]

Again, in examining a French regional aid scheme, the Commission considered that the specific industrial problems to which the French Government referred in defence of its inclusion of certain departments in the scheme were in such a wide range of industries that it was not possible to identify areas where the weakness of key local industry so threatened the social fabric as to justify regional aid. Moreover, the number in employment in 1980–1 was not a major criterion for the selection of assisted areas in the French scheme and in any case would have to be observed over a longer period. The rise in unemployment in the departments concerned between 1976 and 1980 could be an important pointer to eligibility for assisted-area status under the scheme. However, in considering the rise in unemployment, particular account should be taken of the level of unemployment reached by the end of the period. Apparently, the concern of the Commission was to establish whether there was 'high structural unemployment'.[183]

---

[179] Art. 1.1 of Reg. 2052/88 ([1988] OJ L185/9), as amended by Reg. 2081/93 ([1993] OJ L193/5).

[180] The Commission reminded the Spanish Government that it must be informed, under Art. 93(3), of any plans to continue the application of the national scheme of regional incentives in these areas beyond that date. See also the *Twentieth Report on Competition Policy* (EC Commission, Brussels, 1991), 183–4.

[181] Dec. 91/389 ([1991] OJ L215/1) on aid granted by the city of Hamburg.

[182] Dec. 91/500 ([1991] OJ L262/29) concerning aid granted to enterprises in the Friuli–Venezia Giulia region.

[183] Cf. Dec. 85/12 ([1985] OJ L7/28) on the North Rhine–Westfalia regional economic development programme.

Further information from the French Government established that the departments of Loire and Meurthe-et-Moselle were suffering from problems associated with industrial decline. In Loire the employment situation was bad, and there was substantial outward migration owing to the decline of traditional industries. In Meurthe-et-Moselle the decline of the steel industry had created structural problems throughout the local economy. Nièvre, Haute-Marne, and Maine-et-Loire had problems of underdevelopment. Nièvre was suffering from rural depopulation and incomes were very low. Haute-Marne was very thinly populated and suffering further rapid depopulation because of the constant loss of local job opportunities. In Maine-et-Loire population growth was outstripping the increase in jobs and leading to a growing imbalance. For these reasons, the Commission amended its initial assessment and authorized aid in these departments.[184]

Particular account may be taken of anticipated job losses. In the case of a German aid scheme for the labour market regions of Aachen and Julich, unemployment levels in these regions were currently below the modified threshold for Germany. However, since the closure of the local coal mine was expected to result in significant job losses (around 7,700),[185] the Commission decided to approve the scheme.[186] Similarly, aid to the Plymouth Travel to Work Area was authorized, having regard to possible future job losses. The authorization was limited to a period of three years, and before the end of that period the Commission would examine whether the predicted job losses and their negative effects on the labour market situation had actually occurred.[187]

Conversely, a decrease in unemployment relative to the national or Union average and a rise in earnings levels may mean that regional aid is no longer acceptable. Thus regional aid had to be eliminated in parts of Belgium which witnessed a decrease in unemployment relative to the national and Union averages and a rise in earnings levels.[188]

Account may also be taken of the need for aid to secure the investment concerned. One decision concerned aid to the German subsidiary of a Swedish company in Hueckelhoven. This area had been seriously affected by job losses in coal mining, with consequential effects for jobs in the field of supplies and services.[189] It also had a low *per capita* gross domestic product and was in an

---

[184] Dec. 85/18 ([1985] OJ L11/28) on the French regional planning grant scheme (*Prime d'aménagement du territoire*).

[185] See, similarly, regarding the importance attached to job losses resulting from the virtual disappearance of steelmaking in a French region, Bull. EC 7/8–1989, 2.1.84.

[186] Though approval was only for a limited period and the operation of the scheme would be monitored closely: see the *Eighteenth Report on Competition Policy* (EC Commission, Brussels, 1989), 191.

[187] *Fourteenth Report on Competition Policy* (EC Commission, Brussels, 1985), 174–5. See also, regarding Lolland in Denmark, Dec. 82/691 ([1982] OJ L290/39) on the designation of areas eligible for regional aid in Denmark from 1 Jan. 1982.

[188] *Fifteenth Report on Competition Policy* (EC Commission, Brussels, 1986), 189.

[189] Although Hueckelhoven did not constitute a *Kreis*, these job losses justified evaluation of aid by reference to an area smaller than a level III region.

area covered by Objective 2 of the Structural Funds (that is, converting regions seriously affected by industrial decline)[190] and by the Rechar programme.[191] Moreover, it would have been possible for the Swedish parent company to obtain investment aid from the Swedish authorities, to increase its production capacity in Sweden, and to export the finished product from there to the Union. In such circumstances, it seemed that, without the planned German aid, the investment would not take place in Hueckelhoven. For these reasons, the aid could be authorized under Article 92(3)(c).[192]

Ceilings

Even if a region is eligible for aid, the level of aid granted must facilitate development and must not be such that trading conditions are affected to an extent contrary to the common interest.[193] According to the Commission, establishment of undertakings by means of excessive aid entails a risk that such undertakings will not be viable and will be unable to exist without further aid.[194] Such aid may thus aggravate the structural weaknesses of the region.[195] Hence, the Commission introduced an aid ceiling for central regions eligible for aid in the 1971 Principles.[196] This ceiling, designed to define the limits which might be regarded as compatible with the common market,[197] was originally set at 20 per cent, though it was not envisaged that the ceiling would be applied without flexibility.[198]

The ceiling was extended to the new Member States in 1973, as follows:

—in Denmark the central regions included the entire territory with the exception of Greenland, the islands of Bornholm, Aero, Samsö, and Langeland and the special development area in Northern Denmark. Other areas were peripheral, and at a later stage the Faroes would be considered peripheral;

[190] Art. 1.2 of Reg. 2052/88, as amended by Reg. 2081/93 ([1993] OJ L193/5).

[191] Notice laying down guidelines for operational programmes in the framework of a Community initiative concerning the economic conversion of coal-mining areas, which Member States are invited to establish ([1990] OJ C20/3). It has been followed by Rechar II ([1994] OJ C180/26).

[192] Notice C39/90 (ex N453/90) ([1992] OJ C290/2) concerning aid which Germany had decided to grant in favour of Nefab GmbH in Hueckelhoven. See, similarly, Notice C40/90 (ex N511/90) ([1992] OJ C290/5) concerning a draft aid which Germany had decided to grant in favour of Chukyo Europe GmbH.

[193] Van Gerven AG in Case C–225/91 *Matra SA* v. *EC Commission* [1993] ECR I–3203, I–3230 acknowledged that the Commission had to seek to ensure that aid intensity was no greater than necessary to overcome regional handicaps.

[194] Dec. 85/11 ([1985] OJ L7/24) concerning aids provided for under Law 86 of the Region of Sicily of 5 Aug. 1982 on emergency measures in agriculture.

[195] Dec. 84/557 ([1984] OJ L305/40) concerning the state aids provided for by Law 97 of the Region of Sicily of 6 May 1981 on measures to encourage productive sectors of agriculture and various agricultural standards.

[196] Principles for the Co-ordination of Regional Aid ([1971] JO C111/1).

[197] Commission submission in Case 248/84 *Germany* v. *EC Commission: regional aid* [1987] ECR 4013, 4018.

[198] Para. 4 of the 1971 Principles.

—the whole of Ireland was peripheral;[199]

—in the United Kingdom the central regions were that part of the country not classified as assisted or intermediate areas. The other areas of the United Kingdom were to be classified at a later date, when aids would be co-ordinated throughout the enlarged Union.[200]

A rather more differentiated approach was adopted in the 1975 Principles,[201] which divided Union regions into four groups with different aid ceilings:

—Ireland, the Mezzogiorno, Northern Ireland, West Berlin:[202] aid ceilings were frozen at the level of aid prevailing on 1 January 1975;[203]

—regions of France benefiting from industrial development premiums, assisted areas (except intermediate areas) in the United Kingdom, and certain Italian regions outside the Mezzogiorno: aid ceilings of 30 per cent;

—the *Zonenrandgebiet*, the special development area in the North of Denmark and certain Danish Islands: aid ceilings of 25 per cent;

—all other regions: aid ceilings of 20 per cent, on the understanding that the trend should, as far as possible, be towards a reduction in the level of aids.[204]

Modifications were found necessary in the 1979 Principles,[205] when aid ceilings were expressed in two ways: either as a percentage of the amount of initial investment or in terms of aid per job created.[206] The ceilings were now:

—75 per cent of initial investment or EUA 13,000 per job for Ireland, the Mezzogiorno, and the French Overseas Departments;

—30 per cent of initial investment or EUA 5,500 per job created (with an

---

[199] Increases in the ceiling, from 45% to 50% (60% in the case of small firms) in the Greater Cork area, were later accepted under Art. 92(3)(a), in view of the serious deterioration in the employment situation and the generally unfavourable socio-economic situation in Ireland. See the *Fourth Report on Competition Policy* (EC Commission, Brussels, 1975), 177.

[200] COM(73)1110, para. II.2.

[201] COM(75)77.

[202] The ceiling did not cover aid granted under Art. 92(2)(c). See the *Sixth Report on Competition Policy* (EC Commission, Brussels, 1977), 103.

[203] This meant that there were 8 ceilings for Ireland, divided into 4 categories (designated areas, non-designated areas, the Shannon, and the Gaeltach). Each category had two ceilings: one for the setting up and one for the modernization or conversion of firms (*ibid.*). However, the Commission reserved the right, except in the case of Berlin, to carry out a prior examination of individual cases of application where there were specific sectoral problems or where it was necessary to do so for reasons relating to the functioning of the common market. The Commission might, therefore, ask to be informed of investment projects involving more than 25 million units of account where the proposed aid exceeded 35%.

[204] No ceiling was fixed for Greenland, which was regarded as facing a special situation.

[205] Communic. of 21 Dec. 1978 ([1979] OJ C31/9).

[206] Problems might arise from fixing ceilings in terms of the amount of aid per job created. In the first place, the amount would vary depending on labour costs in the region concerned. More aid might, therefore, be available in regions were labour costs were highest. Moreover, in the case of labour-intensive projects, the amount of aid permitted might be greater than the total cost of the investment.

absolute ceiling of 40 per cent[207]) for regional development premium areas in France, assisted areas in Italy outside the Mezzogiorno, and assisted areas in the United Kingdom (except intermediate areas and Northern Ireland);[208]

—25 per cent of initial investment or EUA 4,500 per job created (with an absolute ceiling of 30 per cent) for the *Zonenrandgebiet*, North Jutland, and the islands of Bornholm, Aero, Samsö, and Langeland in Denmark;

—20 per cent of initial investment or EUA 3,500 per job created (with an absolute ceiling of 25 per cent) in the most central regions, where the trend had to be towards reduction of aid levels.

In the Netherlands a ceiling of 25 per cent was imposed for some areas and a ceiling of 15 per cent for others.[209] Subsequently ceilings of 15 per cent, 25 per cent and 35 per cent were accepted and then replaced by one of 25 per cent.[210] There was a freeze on operating aid. Ceilings for aid to the transfer of an establishment were also introduced. There remained no ceiling for Greenland.

These arrangements were regarded as appropriate for simple extension to Greece. Thus in 1984 a ceiling of 75 per cent was introduced for all assisted areas in this country (except part of Corinthia and Lavreotiki, where it was 30 per cent).[211]

The third Union enlargement was seen as demanding greater differentiation of ceilings. For Spain ceilings were initially set at 75 per cent, 45 per cent, 30 per cent or 20 per cent. A ceiling of 45 per cent was set for three years in Sierra Norte de Madrid, the farming and mining areas of the Asturias, and the area of Campóo in Cantabria.[212] Subject to possible exceptions, the other ceilings were to be reduced from 75 per cent to 50 per cent and 45 per cent to 40 per cent over the same period.[213] For Portugal the ceiling was 65 per cent, 55 per cent, or 45 per cent, according to the location of the aided investment. Sectors undergoing restructuring (spinning, weaving, wool, and mixed finishing) were not covered. Regional aid could be cumulated with other aid up to a ceiling of 75 per cent.[214]

These ceilings indicated the maximum amount of aid which could normally

---

[207] The absolute ceilings did not apply to aid to the tertiary sector or to aid for the transfer of workers.

[208] This ceiling is to be generally applied by the ESA in the EFTA States. See Dec. 4/94/COL ([1994] OJ L231/1) on the adoption and issuing of the procedural and substantive rules in the field of state aid (guidelines on the application and interpretation of Arts. 61 and 62 EEA and Art. 1 of Prot. 3 to the Surveillance and Court Agreement).

[209] *Fifteenth Report on Competition Policy* (EC Commission, Brussels, 1986), 190.

[210] *Eighteenth Report on Competition Policy* (EC Commission, Brussels, 1989), 194.

[211] Athens did not receive regional aid (*Fourteenth Report on Competition Policy* (EC Commission, Brussels, 1985), 178).

[212] *Seventeenth Report on Competition Policy* (EC Commission, Brussels, 1988), 176.

[213] *Eighteenth Report on Competition Policy* (EC Commission, Brussels, 1989), 187–8.

[214] *Seventeenth Report on Competition Policy* (EC Commission, Brussels, 1988), 183.

be considered for authorization in regions eligible for aid.[215] The 1979 Principles stated that where problems different in kind, intensity or urgency occurred, the actual aid level must be adapted accordingly.[216]

Aid complying with the applicable ceiling would still have to be justified. In practice, such aid might be prohibited,[217] or the Commission might require its level to be reduced. For example, in Decision 72/173[218] the Commission authorized aid in certain Belgian regions only up to a level of 15 per cent, subject to a ceiling of Bfr 100 million for each investment. The only eligible regions were those where the Commission found a justification in national disparities, examined in the light of taxable income, unemployment, employment trends, the structure of economic activities, net migration, and demographic factors.

On the other hand, aid above the ceiling might exceptionally be authorized. Factors taken into account in authorizations of aid above the ceiling included: unemployment,[219] employment in the services sector, employment in the primary sector, and population density[220] and depopulation problems.[221] Again, a Dutch aid scheme with an aid intensity of 25 per cent was authorized in the case of investments involving the transfer of economic activity from the Randstad to a small number of selected growth centres.[222]

Such exceptions seem to have been particularly important for Scotland. For example, although the applicable ceiling for the region concerned was fixed at 30 per cent in the 1975 Principles, the Commission was willing to allow higher levels of aid to be granted by the Highlands and Islands Development Board (HIDB). The Commission took account of the fact that the region was undeniably lagging behind in development, that the HIDB provided assistance for small projects only, and that there were strict limits on aid grants. However,

---

[215] See the objections to likely breaches of the ceilings in certain areas of northern and eastern France in the *Ninth Report on Competition Policy* (EC Commission, Brussels, 1980), 92.

[216] Para. 9(iv) of the 1979 Principles.

[217] See, e.g., Dec. 73/293 ([1973] OJ L270/22) on aid which the Belgian Government intended to grant for extending an oil refinery at Antwerp and for setting up a new refinery at Kallo (province of East Flanders).

[218] On aid granted under the Belgian Economic Expansion Law of Dec. 1970 ([1972] JO L105/13). See also Dec. 75/397 ([1975] OJ L177/13) on the aids granted by the Belgian Government pursuant to the Law of 17 July 1959 introducing and co-ordinating measures to encourage economic expansion and the creation of new industries.

[219] *Ninth Report on Competition Policy* (EC Commission, Brussels, 1980), 93–4; *Tenth Report on Competition Policy* (EC Commission, Brussels, 1981), 123. See also the exception from the ceiling permitted in the case of Corby (Bull. EC 2–1980, 2.1.21) and the raising of the ceiling to 30% in the case of Scunthorpe, Newport and Pontypool (Bull. EC 7/8–1980, 2.1.135) in the UK.

[220] Dec. 82/691 ([1982] OJ L290/39) on the designation of areas eligible for regional aid in Denmark from 1 Jan. 1982.

[221] Dec. 85/18 ([1984] OJ L11/28) on the French regional planning grant scheme (*Prime d'aménagement du territoire*).

[222] *First Report on Competition Policy* (EC Commission, Brussels, 1972), 127; *Eighth Report on Competition Policy* (EC Commission, Brussels, 1979), 119; and *Tenth Report on Competition Policy* (EC Commission, Brussels, 1981), 125.

the Commission asked the British authorities to report annually on HIDB aid activities, since the socio-economic situation of the region was likely to improve as a result of the benefits of exploiting the oil fields in the North Sea.[223]

In 1980 the Commission decided that the HIDB could grant assistance of up to 75 per cent of initial investment or ECU 10,000 per job created to undertakings employing not more than ten persons. For other undertakings the limits were 50 per cent of initial investment or ECU 5,500 per job created.[224] The Commission took account of the genuine economic difficulties of the region attributable to its peripheral location, harsh physical environment, low population in dispersed areas, transport problems, unbalanced industrial structure, outward migration, and unemployment.[225] This Decision was later extended to Forres and Upper Moray, which exhibited similar 'social and economic characteristics of fragile rural communities'.[226]

In the case of assistance of £10 million for training workers for a fork-lift trucks factory at Irvine, also in Scotland, the Commission found the assistance acceptable, subject to the need for monitoring of implementation to ensure that the aid was paid only for genuine training costs. The Commission considered that it should, however, express its general concern at the level of aid in this case. Apart from the fact that the training aid was of an unusually large amount, it was offered cumulatively with a regional investment aid (with a maximum intensity of 29 per cent) which was in itself already close to the ceiling of 30 per cent fixed by the Commission. Moreover, there was over-capacity in the fork-lift trucks sector. In deciding not to raise any objections to the proposed aid, the Commission emphasized that it only took this position because of the benefit which the project would bring to an area suffering from Irvine's exceptional combination of difficulties. Irvine was a relatively small and isolated area on the periphery of the Union. Its unemployment rate over the years 1978–82 averaged over twice the figure for the United Kingdom. At the same time, account was taken of the agreement by the United Kingdom to a general reduction in its regional assistance of £300 million per year and to elimination of operating aid.[227]

An exception was also allowed in favour of a French aid scheme for craft and small industry in rural areas. The Commission took account of the relatively

---

[223] *Third Report on Competition Policy* (EC Commission, Brussels, 1974), 78. See also the *Fifth Report on Competition Policy* (EC Commission, Brussels, 1976), 75. Note the later acceptance of aid up to an intensity of 78% (Bull. EC 4–1978, 2.1.25; and the *Eighth Report on Competition Policy* (EC Commission, Brussels, 1979), 121–2).

[224] However, in Nairn, Lerwick and Kirkwall assisted-area ceilings applied.

[225] *Tenth Report on Competition Policy* (EC Commission, Brussels, 1981), 123–4; and Bull. EC 5–1980, 2.1.19.

[226] *Sixteenth Report on Competition Policy* (EC Commission, Brussels, 1987), 182.

[227] Notice ([1983] OJ C168/3) concerning aids to be granted to a company in respect of a training programme for a project to manufacture and market a new and enhanced range of fork-lift trucks in Scotland; *Fourteenth Report on Competition Policy* (EC Commission, Brussels, 1985), 176–7.

small size of the investments involved, the structural character of the aid and the limited size of the budget.[228]

Even Luxembourg benefited from certain exceptions. In Wiltz, Clervaux, Grevenmacher, and Luxembourg a nominal cumulated aid ceiling of 17.5 per cent of the investment was agreed. In Esch-sur-Alzette and Capellen the ceiling would generally be 20 per cent, though in the old industrial areas, especially the steel areas of Esch-sur-Alzette, it would be 25 per cent. In approving the aid in these areas, the Commission took account of the fall in earnings levels and the increase in unemployment that had occurred throughout the country during the previous decade and of the wide variations in the country, with the mainly agricultural areas requiring development and the old industrial areas requiring new industry to replace those in decline. With regard to the areas in the south, the Commission noted their extreme vulnerability due to their almost exclusive dependence on the steel industry.[229]

The practice of making or refusing such exceptions seems to have been replaced, at least partly, by the supposedly more flexible approach of fixing more differentiated ceilings. For example, in fixing a ceiling of 15 per cent for the provinces of Gorizia and Trieste, the Commission took particular account of the fact that the level of 30 per cent, which was the maximum intensity authorized under Article 92(3)(c), was applicable from 1991 in the province of Frosinone, which was experiencing far more serious socio-economic problems than the two provinces in question.[230]

The 1988 Communication[231] went further. A list of eligible regions was contained in Annex III to this Communication,[232] with differentiated ceilings being set for each such region. In principle, the ceilings ranged from 36 per cent to 75 per cent in Article 92(3)(a) regions and from 5.4 per cent to 30 per cent in Article 92(3)(c) regions.[233] However, according to the Annex, the ceiling was 75 per cent or ECU 10,000 per job created (for enterprises with no more than ten employees and where fixed investment did not exceed ECU 600,000) in the Highlands and Islands of Scotland, even though the areas concerned were treated as being covered by Article 92(3)(c).

In the case of the former German Democratic Republic, the Commission subsequently authorized aid up to 23 per cent and an extra 12 per cent in case of cumulation with other aid, such as investment tax relief on equipment and environmental aid. Higher aid levels might be applied in the case of small and

---

[228] *Eleventh Report on Competition Policy* (EC Commission, Brussels, 1982), 164–5.

[229] *Fifteenth Report on Competition Policy* (EC Commission, Brussels, 1986), 187–8.

[230] Dec. 91/500 ([1991] OJ L262/29) concerning aid granted to enterprises in the Friuli–Venezia Giulia region.

[231] [1988] OJ C212/2.

[232] Note the revisions in the Communications on the application of Art. 92(3)(c) to regional aid ([1989] OJ C78/5; [1990] OJ C163/5) and the Communic. on the application of Art. 92(3)(a) to regional aid ([1990] OJ C163/6).

[233] A. Marques, 'Community Competition Policy and Economic and Social Cohesion' [1992] *Regional Studies* 404–7, 405.

medium-sized undertakings. This authorization was subject to respect for the various aid frameworks in operation in the Union.[234]

These differentiated ceilings seem generally to be enforced. For example, in October 1990 the Commission objected to two aid awards with an intensity of 15 per cent which North Rhine–Westphalia intended to make to firms setting up in the district of Heinsberg, where a ceiling of 7.5 per cent applied.[235] Even so, the ceilings may be modified as conditions change. For example, as a result of industrial decline in the steel and shipbuilding sectors, the ceiling for Setubal in Portugal was raised from 37 per cent to 49.4 per cent to 53.3 per cent.[236] Conversely, improvements in regional conditions may demand lower ceilings.[237]

In practice, however, the aid levels approved by the Commission when it takes individual decisions on regional aid are often lower, and frequently significantly lower, than those set in the 1988 Communication.[238] Moreover, approved aid levels may vary, depending on the size of the recipient. For example, in regions in the Centre-North of Italy that qualify under Article 92(3)(c) aid is limited to 20 per cent for small enterprises, 15 per cent for medium-sized enterprises, and 10 per cent for large companies.[239] Consequently, it is said that 'maximum intensities' are effectively replacing the ceilings.[240] The intensities are determined 'in such a way that they can be considered to neutralize the handicaps involved in investing in the relevant regions, without giving them an undue advantage over the other regions'.[241]

However, concern has been expressed that, even where aid intensity as a percentage of investment is equivalent, distortions of competition are greater the more capital intensive the investment is, without any apparent additional contribution being made to regional development. Hence, the Commission has considered introducing a framework setting a ceiling linked to capital intensity for eligible investment.[242]

---

[234] State guarantees of 80% of a loan or project by undertakings in the new *Länder* or East Berlin were also authorized, as well as training aids. However, the last aids to East Berlin were to be eliminated by the end of 1994, and non-regional aids were to be limited to 8%. See the *Twenty-First Report on Competition Policy* (EC Commission, Brussels, 1992), 170.

[235] *Twentieth Report on Competition Policy* (EC Commission, Brussels, 1991), 183.

[236] Bull. EC 6–1988, 2.1.114. See, similarly, regarding the significance attached to the decline of the steel industry in the UK, the *Tenth Report on Competition Policy* (EC Commission, Brussels, 1981), 123.

[237] See, regarding Denmark, the *Eleventh Report on Competition Policy* (EC Commission, Brussels, 1982), 162–3.

[238] Para. II.4 of the 1988 Communic.

[239] Bull EU 3–1995, 1.3.44.

[240] *Report of the Committee on Regional Policy and Regional Planning on the effects of Arts. 92 and 93 EC on regional policy*, EP Doc. A2–114/87, 10.

[241] F. Andriessen, 'The Role of Anti-Trust in the Face of Economic Recession: State Aids in the EEC' [1983] *ECLR* 340–50, 343.

[242] *Twenty-First Report on Competition Policy* (EC Commission, Brussels, 1991), 123.

'Regressive' Principle

The level of aid authorized by the Commission may be affected by application of the 'regressive' principle. This principle, first introduced in the 1971 Principles,[243] means that the general trend regarding aid to the central regions should be downwards.[244] Accordingly, the Commission has frequently objected to the coverage of regional aid schemes, as in the case of schemes in France,[245] the Netherlands,[246] and Germany.[247] No increase in regional aid will usually be authorized where the socio-economic situation has not worsened,[248] and the Commission seeks to secure general reductions in the geographical coverage and levels of such aid.[249] For example, in 1991 the Commission secured a reduction in the coverage of Danish regional aid, from 20.7 per cent[250] to 19.9 per cent of the population, and a reduction in the budgetary allocation from ECU 17.8 million to ECU 3.1 million.[251] In the case of Germany, successive reductions were secured:[252] from 45 per cent to 38 per cent in 1987,[253] to 29 per cent in 1991 and to 22 per cent of the population of the western *Länder*. The maximum aid level has also been reduced from 23 per cent to 18 per cent.[255] However, following unification 38 per cent of the population of the whole of Germany lives in assisted areas.[256] In the case of France, a reduction from 41.21 per cent to 39.88 per cent of the population covered has been secured.[257]

Such practice follows the requirement in Article 93(1) of the Treaty that the

[243] [1971] JO C111/1, para. 4.

[244] See also the *Fourteenth Report on Competition Policy* (EC Commission, Brussels, 1984), 167–8.

[245] Notice ([1982] OJ C175/3) regarding the plan to introduce a regional aid scheme to be known as the *Prime à l'aménagement du territoire* (Regional Planning Premium).

[246] Notice ([1982] OJ C175/2; [1985] OJ C51/3) concerning the project communicated by the Dutch authorities on a reorganization of regional economic and social policies for the period 1981 to 1985.

[247] Notice ([1985] OJ C28/2) of amendments to the North Rhine–Westphalia regional economic development programme.

[248] See, in the case of the Netherlands, Bull. EC 7/8–1980, 2.1.37.

[249] See, e.g., Notice ([1985] OJ C166/6) concerning the proposed retention of certain areas within the German joint Federal/State regional aid programme.

[250] Dec. 87/573 ([1987] OJ L347/64) on the redesignation of assisted areas in Denmark on 1 Jan. 1987.

[251] *Twenty-First Report on Competition Policy* (EC Commission, Brussels, 1992), 170.

[252] In 1980 the Commission had compared regional aid in Germany with regional aid in other Member States and had come to the conclusion that the former was excessive. See the *Tenth Report on Competition Policy* (EC Commission, Brussels, 1981), 117.

[253] Bull. EC 12–1987, 2.1.114 and the *Seventeenth Report on Competition Policy* (EC Commission, Brussels, 1988), 176–7.

[254] *European Report* 1939 (1 Apr. 1994); Bull. EU 3–1994, 1.2.52.

[255] See also, regarding reductions in the regional aid granted by the *Länder*, the *Eighteenth Report on Competition Policy* (EC Commission, Brussels, 1989), 192.

[256] *Nineteenth Report on Competition Policy* (EC Commission, Brussels, 1990), 178; Bull. EU 3–1994, 1.2.52; *Twenty-Fourth Report on Competition Policy* (EC Commission, Brussels, 1995), 496.

[257] H. Morch, 'Summary of the Most Important Recent Developments' (1994) 4 *Competition Policy Newsletter* 61–6, 63–4.

Commission should, in co-operation with the Member States, keep under constant review existing systems of aid and should propose to the Member States any appropriate measures required by the progressive development or by the functioning of the common market. Such practice might also be thought to meet demands of the European Parliament that the Commission should supplement the initial co-ordination principles by 'provisions' for gradually reducing maximum aid levels.[258]

In the context of its reviews the Commission takes account of regional improvements. Such improvements may mean that extended coverage is prohibited,[259] though a year may be allowed to determine whether the improvement is caused by exceptional circumstances.[260] Thus, for example, the Commission took account of the changes, in terms of relative economic performance and unemployment, that had occurred in the French regions since 1984 (when the Commission last adopted a decision on the French regional aid scheme). In view of these changes, the Commission proposed in 1990 that the French authorities exclude from the scheme the areas currently eligible for aid in the departments of Charente, Cher, Indre, Landes, Mayenne, Orne, Bas-Rhin, Haut-Rhin, Ille-et-Vilaine, Vienne, and Indre-et-Loire.[261]

On the other hand, general compliance with the regressive principle by a Member State may affect Commission willingness to authorize aid to particular regions. For example, in 1983 the Commission raised objections to a Dutch regional aid scheme. The Dutch Government agreed to a reduction of 40 per cent in the total regional-aid budget. In view of this substantial reduction and the more detailed information supplied by the Dutch Government, the Commission amended its original position on four areas by accepting a smaller reduction than initially suggested in two of them and agreeing to the retention of the former level in the two others.[262] In subsequently accepting amendments to the scheme, the Commission took into particular consideration the fact that the changes would make the system more transparent and that only 22.5 per cent of the Dutch population would live in assisted areas in 1989–90, as compared with 27 per cent previously.[263]

---

[258] Resolution of 12 Feb. 1973 ([1973] OJ C14/8) on the first report on competition policy, para. 9.

[259] See, e.g., Notice regarding the extension of the areas eligible for the granting of the investment premium provided for by the Netherlands' Investment Premiums (*Investeringspremieregeling*) to the growth points of Goes, Vlissingen-Oost, and Terneuzen in the province of Zeeland ([1977] OJ C129/3). The Commission position was subsequently accepted by the Dutch authorities. See Communic. with regard to the changes made by the Netherlands Government to the regional aid scheme (*Investeringspremieregeling*) ([1978] OJ C141/2).

[260] *Tenth Report on Competition Policy* (EC Commission, Brussels, 1981), 119.

[261] *Twentieth Report on Competition Policy* (EC Commission, Brussels, 1991), 184. See also the reduction of population coverage reported in the *Twenty-Fourth Report on Competition Policy* (EC Commission, Brussels, 1995), 498.

[262] *Thirteenth Report on Competition Policy* (EC Commission, Brussels, 1984), 178.

[263] *Eighteenth Report on Competition Policy* (EC Commission, Brussels, 1989), 194. It now covers only 17.26% of the Dutch population. See H. Morch, 'Summary of the Most Important Recent Developments' (1995) 5 *Competition Policy Newsletter* 43–9, 46.

Slight increases in coverage might also be authorized.[264] Thus an increase from 26 per cent to 27 per cent of the working population of the United Kingdom was accepted in 1982.[265] Moreover, the requirements of the regressive principle seem not to be merely quantitative. For example, in 1984 the Commission noted that assisted areas in Great Britain now covered 35 per cent of the working population as opposed to 27.5 per cent prior to the changes accepted by the Commission. However, only 15.4 per cent of the population were in areas eligible for the relatively automatic Regional Development Grant aid (the Development Areas), whereas previously the figure was 21.9 per cent.[266] Hence, the new aid arrangements were authorized.

4.3 DEVELOPMENT

Even where Union law recognizes the aid eligibility of a region and the acceptability of the aid level involved, the targeting and the nature of the aid must be of such a kind that there is a sufficient impact on regional problems. Otherwise, the development required by Article 92(3)(a) and (c) may not be entailed.

4.3.1 Targeting

Targeting requirements mean that aid must not be individualized or even too localized. Rather, the Commission considers that the aid must be granted within the framework of a regional aid scheme.

Individualized Aid

It appears that aid to one undertaking alone will not normally be regarded as having a sufficient regional impact to be authorized under Article 92(3)(a) or (c).[267] For example, although Ireland was covered by Article 92(3)(a), aid to Aer Lingus was not granted under a general scheme from which all the airlines based in Ireland linking it with the rest of the world might benefit. Rather, it was an *ad hoc* measure which helped the state-owned carrier to overcome its financial crisis and maintained the latter on the market.[268] Therefore, Article

---

[264] See also, in the case of 'the worsening in the economic situation' in Spain, Bull. EU 7/8–1995, 1.3.67.

[265] *Twelfth Report on Competition Policy* (EC Commission, Brussels, 1983), 148.

[266] *Fourteenth Report on Competition Policy* (EC Commission, Brussels, 1985), 174–5.

[267] Dec. 82/740 ([1982] OJ L312/18) on the designation of development areas pursuant to Art. 11 of the Belgian Law of 30 Dec. 1970; and Dec. 87/585 ([1987] OJ L352/42) on aid granted by the French Government to a producer of textiles, clothing and paper products—Boussac Saint Frères. Cf., under the ECSC Treaty, Roemer AG in Joined Cases 27–29/58 *Compagnie des Hauts Fourneaux et Fonderies de Givors* v. *ECSC High Authority* [1960] ECR 241, 276–7.

[268] See also Notice C10/96 (NN142/95) ([1996] OJ C121/8) concerning the granting of various financial benefits to certain companies using Oseten airport.

92(3)(a) was inapplicable. Only in exceptional cases might the favourable impact of the aid on other companies, other investments, and employment in a region covered by Article 92(3)(a) lead to authorization under this paragraph.[269] However, account was taken of the peripherality of Ireland in the authorization of the aid on sectoral grounds under Article 92(3)(c).[270]

More particularly, aid in the form of a capital injection in an undertaking in an Article 92(3)(c) region may only be authorized, if the aid is intended to stimulate diversification activities and is not merely direct aid to the undertaking.[271] Similarly, aid in favour of a single undertaking[272] or sector[273] is normally regarded as inadequate to remedy a serious disturbance in the economy of a Member State for the purposes of Article 92(3)(b).

Localized Aid

According to the Commission, 'highly localized phenomena' cannot qualify a region under Article 92(3)(a) or (c).[274] Thus, for example, in Decision 82/691,[275] which concerned regional aid in Denmark, the Commission noted that the grouping of municipalities as carried out by the Danish authorities resulted in many groups with such a small population that to rule them as eligible for aid would be tantamount to approving aid to resolve local problems. In accordance with point 9(iii) of the 1979 Co-ordination Principles,[276] regional aid was not to be granted in a pin-point manner, that is, to isolated geographical points having virtually no influence on the development of the region as a whole. Hence, the Commission combined these municipalities into larger

---

[269] Notice C61/94 (N375/94) ([1995] OJ C113/5) concerning aid which the German Government intended to grant to Buna GmbH.

[270] Dec. 94/118 ([1994] OJ L54/30) concerning aid to be provided by the Irish Government to the Aer Lingus group. See also Communic. C15/94 (N122/94, NN22/94 and E3/93) ([1994] OJ C93/12) concerning the existing tax exemption and planned recapitalization of TAP; and Dec. 94/696 ([1994] OJ L273/22) on the aid granted by Greece to Olympic Airways.

[271] Dec. 92/318 ([1992] OJ L172/76) on aid granted by Spain to Industrias Mediterraneas de la Piel SA.

[272] Dec. 88/173 ([1978] OJ L74/44) on the Belgian Government's aid proposal in favour of Roger Vanden Berghe NV, a polypropylene yarn and carpet producer located in Desselgem, Belgium; Dec. 88/174 ([1988] OJ L79/29) concerning aid which Baden-Württemberg had provided to BUG—Alutechnik GmbH, an undertaking producing semi-finished and finished aluminium products; Dec. 88/468 ([1988] OJ L229/37) on aids granted by the French Government to a farm machinery manufacturer at St Dizier, Anges and Croix; and Dec. 89/456 ([1989] OJ L223/22) on the French Government's aid proposal in favour of Caulliez Frères, cotton yarn producer located in Prouvy, France.

[273] Dec. 77/172 ([1977] OJ L54/39) concerning an aid for the pigmeat sector in the UK; and Dec. 94/725 ([1994] OJ L289/26) on measures adopted by the French Government concerning pigmeat.

[274] Dec. 82/740 ([1982] OJ L312/18) on the designation of development areas pursuant to Art. 11 of the Belgian Law of 30 Dec. 1970. See, earlier, Dec. 72/173 ([1972] JO L105/13) on aid granted under the Belgian Economic Expansion Law of Dec. 1970.

[275] On the designation of areas eligible for regional aid in Denmark from 1 Jan. 1982 ([1982] OJ L290/39).

[276] [1979] OJ C31/9.

groups for the purposes of scrutiny as to whether Article 92(3)(c) was applicable.

However, aid to 'growth poles' might be authorized.[277] Moreover, areas of urban deprivation can often be isolated pockets within cities which are relatively prosperous. Hence, it has been argued by the European Parliament that local decentralized projects should be eligible for aid.[278]

Arguments such as the latter seem to have had little impact on Commission practice. According to the Commission, the requirement that aid must be available in the whole of a given region, rather than being limited to undertakings in isolated geographical points of a region, is not simply an administrative necessity. It is also a response to the need for action throughout the region in question, in accordance with the spirit and the letter of Article 92(3)(c). In so far as such aid is not granted to all undertakings located in the region experiencing the socio-economic difficulties required, an individual award to a single undertaking located at a given geographical point, such as a town, in the region would necessarily have a very limited effect and would not contribute to the development of the region. Hence, the aid would not be sufficiently in the Union interest to be authorized.[279]

However, problems of inadequate differentiation may arise.[280] For example, in Decision 82/691[281] Denmark argued that in the case of the municipalities in the County of Sönderjylland, a distinction should be made between the eastern and western parts of the county.[282] In the west the high level of employment in agriculture, the poor soil, and the low population density all warranted the granting of aid. This argument was less impressive to the Commission than the fact that the western municipalities bordered on assisted areas of Germany.

Apparently, then, the requirement of regional impact and the need to take account of local diversity may not always be readily reconcilable. Similar

---

[277] Bull EC 8–1966, 20; *Medium-term Economic Policy Programme (1966–70)* ([1967] JO 1513), para. 6.6; and the *Third EC General Report* (EC Commission, Brussels, 1970), 151.

[278] Resolution of 3 May 1994 ([1994] OJ C205/114) on the draft notice laying down guidelines for operational programmes which Member States are invited to establish in the framework of a Community initiative concerning urban areas, para. 15.

[279] Dec. 91/305 ([1991] OJ L156/39) concerning investment aid which the Belgian Government planned to grant to Mactac SA, Soignies.

[280] To prohibit the targeting of regional aid to areas considered too small in population terms may be particularly problematic in sparsely populated Northern Scandinavia. See *Sveriges Positionspapper om Regionalpolitik—Allmänna Kommentarer* (Sweden's Position Paper on Regional Policy—General Comments), 17 June 1993. Apparently Eurostat methods for defining regions are unacceptable to Finland. See *Commission Opinion on Finland's Application for Membership*, Bull. EC, Supp. 6/92, 34.

[281] On the designation of areas eligible for regional aid in Denmark from 1 Jan. 1982 ([1982] OJ L290/39).

[282] Cf. Dec. 82/740 ([1982] OJ L312/18) on the designation of development areas pursuant to Art. 11 of the Belgian Law of 30 Dec. 1970; and Dec. 88/318 ([1988] OJ L143/37) on Law 64 of 1 Mar. 1986 on aid to the Mezzogiorno.

problems of reconciliation may arise in the case of aid to 'narrowly-based reconversion areas' in France[283] and 'unemployment blackspots' in Spain.[284]

Regional Aid Schemes

The requirement of a regional impact may be difficult to satisfy where aid does not fall within a regional aid scheme. For example, the Commission objected to French aid to a farm machinery manufacturer,[285] Dutch aid to the petrochemical industry,[286] and to regional incentives in Germany[287] and Greece[288] outside the scope of such schemes. Similarly, the Commission objected to aid not generally granted to undertakings operating in regions defined in advance[289] and to aid to an undertaking with diverse locations,[290] because it did not facilitate the development of certain areas for the purposes of Article 92(3)(c).[291]

More particularly, the Commission objected that French regional aid might be granted, in exceptional circumstances, outside regions with assisted status.[292] The aid might be granted to projects located in the proximity of an assisted region which helped the region to overcome its economic and social problems. It might also be granted to firms introducing schemes apt to solve the serious problems arising in a non-assisted region from the closure of one or more firms or by serious disturbances in the employment situation. These arrangements, the effects of which were hard to assess, could divert regional aid from its objective, for they could be used to solve local, economic, or sectoral problems

[283] 'Regional Policy and the European Community' [1992] *Journal of Regional Policy* 557–600, 587.

[284] *Ibid.*, 591.

[285] Dec. 88/468 ([1988] OJ L229/37) on aids granted by the French Government to a farm machinery manufacturer at St Dizier, Angers, and Croix (International Harvester/Tenneco).

[286] Dec. 81/738 ([1981] OJ L262/22) on a proposal by the Netherlands Government to grant aid for the creation of new production capacity by an undertaking in the petrochemical industry (aromatic solvents).

[287] Notice ([1984] OJ C340/3) regarding the regional aid schemes of the *Länder* of Germany—schemes outside the joint programme; and Notice ([1985] OJ C220/2) of the proposal by Rhineland–Pfalz to grant regional aid outside the areas assisted by the Joint Federal/State Regional Aid Programme.

[288] Notice ([1985] OJ C75/4) concerning certain aspects of the system of incentives in support of regional and economic development in Greece. Cf., however, where the areas are covered by Objective 5b of the Structural Funds, Notice C35/92 (ex N172/A/91) ([1994] OJ C78/2) concerning aid granted by the Region of Friuli–Venezia Giulia.

[289] Dec. 89/348 ([1989] OJ L143/44) on aid granted by the French Government to an undertaking manufacturing equipment for the motor vehicle industry—Valéo.

[290] Notice C13/94 (NN13/94) ([1994] OJ C151/7) regarding aid which Italy had decided to grant to Enichem Agricoltura SpA.

[291] See, e.g., Dec. 89/254 ([1989] OJ L34/106) relating to aid which the Belgian Government had granted to a petrochemicals company at Ottignies/Louvain-La-Neuve (SA Belgian Shell).

[292] Cf., regarding authorization of inner-city regeneration measures outside the assisted areas of the UK, the *Eighth Report on Competition Policy* (EC Commission, Brussels, 1979), 122.

to the consequent detriment of regions classed as priority assisted areas on account of their structural weakness.[293]

However, such Commission practice was not fully supported by the Court of Justice in *Spain* v. *EC Commission: Intelhorce*,[294] which concerned aid to a state-owned producer of textiles. According to this ruling, the Commission cannot deny the application of Article 92(3)(a) to restructuring aid to individual undertakings in regions eligible for aid under that provision simply because the aid is granted on the basis of *ad hoc* decisions rather than under the relevant regional aid scheme. Aid granted on the basis of such a decision may qualify as regional aid under Article 92(3)(a), on condition that it contributes to the long-term development of the region without adversely affecting the common interest and competitive conditions within the Union.

The Commission has apparently sought to limit the impact of this ruling. According to the Commission, the condition stipulated by the Court is not met where the aid is for capacity-increasing investment in a sector already suffering overcapacity at Union level.[295]

Further controversy may arise because the impact of aid depends not only on the areas to benefit but also on the nature of the aid. The requirement that aid should contribute to the development of the regions concerned implies the conditions that it should be temporary,[296] and that it should render the beneficiary undertaking viable.[297] In determining whether regional aid meets these conditions, the Commission tends to rely on distinctions between infra-structure aid, restructuring aid, rescue aid, and operating aid.

4.3.2 Infrastructure Aid

Infrastructure involves the production of public goods, and, according to economic theory, the market will not provide such goods in large enough quantities, because they convey interdependencies.[298] Hence, infrastructure aid can render the market more competitive by reducing 'sunk costs'.[299]

The need of less-developed regions for infrastructure aid, such as for

---

[293] *Seventh Report on Competition Policy* (EC Commission, Brussels, 1978), 132. See, earlier, the *Second Report on Competition Policy* (EC Commission, Brussels, 1973), 83.

[294] Joined Cases C–278/92, C–279/92 & C–280/92 [1994] ECR I–4103, I–4161.

[295] See, e.g., Dec. 95/438 ([1995] OJ L257/45) concerning investment aid granted by Spain to Piezas y Rodajes, a steel foundry located in Teruel.

[296] *Medium-term Economic Policy Programme (1966–1970)* ([1967] JO 1513), para. 6.6.

[297] Case C–142/87 *Belgium* v. *EC Commission: Tubemeuse* [1990] ECR I–959, I–1018.

[298] F. Snickars, 'Infrastructure: A Treat for Regional Science Research' [1989] *The Annals of Regional Science* 251–3, 253.

[299] K. Bhaksar,*The Effect of Different State Aid Measures on Intra-Community Trade* (EC Commission, Brussels, 1990), 103–4. However, for regional development purposes, the value of infrastructure spending in itself has been doubted, unless there is a bottleneck. See D. Biehl, *The Contribution of Infrastructure to Regional Development: Final Report* (EC Commission, Brussels, 1986).

distribution networks[300] or, more generally, for an infrastructure which will enable them to make use of their resources,[301] is recognized in Union practice.[302] For example, Decision 87/15[303] concerned a German aid scheme with an emphasis on small, mainly family, businesses in the tourism sector. According to the Commission, it could be assumed that the aid did not affect tourist-trade flows to an extent contrary to the common interest, if at all. In arriving at this conclusion, the Commission took into account the fact that parts of the regions concerned had the natural amenities for tourism but lacked the facilities. Aid could enable the facilities to be improved and the natural amenities of the areas to be utilized and, therefore, could be considered compatible with the common market under Article 92(3)(c).

However, the Commission may seek to ensure that infrastructure aid will lead to major expansions or conversions of the undertakings involved, and that it is not merely a form of disguised rescue aid for undertakings in financial difficulties.[304] Moreover, even if the Commission considers that an aid will lead to substantial improvements in the infrastructure of the region concerned, it may still check to ensure that the intensity of the aid is in proportion to the problems it seeks to address.[305]

4.3.3 Restructuring Aid

The aim of industrial restructuring aid and regional development might be thought naturally compatible, though the regional objectives of a restructuring plan must not 'materially prejudice' its viability[306] and regional conditions must be favourable to future viability.[307]

Certainly, aid for regional conversion may be authorized. For example, the Commission authorized Italian aid to promote the start-up of alternative activities in an area (Genoa) hard hit by the decline of the steel and ship-building industries.[308] Again, the rundown of the Nakskor shipyard, the largest

---

[300] Thus the Commission authorized Italian aid to develop the distribution network in Sicily (Bull. EC 10–1986, 2.1.69).

[301] *Rapport sur la Situation Économique dans les Pays de la Communauté* (EC Commission, Brussels, 1958), 54.

[302] *Fourth Periodic Report on the Economic and Social Situation and Development of the Regions of the Community*, COM(90)609, 37.

[303] On the compatibility with the common market of aid under the German Federal/*Land* Government Joint Regional Aid Programme in six labour market regions ([1987] OJ L12/17).

[304] Dec. 88/167 ([1988] OJ L76/18) concerning Law 1386/1983 by which the Greek Government granted aid to Greek industry.

[305] Communic. C45/91 (ex N255/91) ([1991] OJ C299/4) concerning the proposal by the Italian Government to award state aid to the Fiat Group in support of its Second Mezzogiorno Improvement Plan.

[306] Communic. C34/93 (N557/93) ([1993] OJ C291/4) on equity injections by the Irish Government in favour of Aer Lingus.

[307] Notice NN56/94 and C4/94 (ex NN103/93) ([1995] OJ C227/8) concerning aid the German Government intended to grant to Leuna-Werke GmbH, Leuna/Merseburg.

[308] Bull. EC 6–1987, 2.1.82.

employer in Lolland (Denmark), led to a sharp rise in unemployment, which justified the grant of regional aid there.[309] Similarly, the Commission authorized French aid in areas of Lorraine directly affected by redundancies in the steel industry with a view to creating alternative employment to replace the jobs lost. Such aid was not to be granted to industries with excess capacity.[310]

Moreover, aid for the restructuring of industries important for a particular region may be authorized. For example, aid to a privatized fertilizer producer in the former German Democratic Republic was found to be justified by the large-scale reductions in capacity on the urea and ammonia market due to privatization and by the acute difficulties facing the region.[311] Aid for the restructuring of the second-largest chemicals producer in the former German Democratic Republic was authorized, because it would entail 'protection of a basic level of employment in the region'.[312] Aid for the construction of a new oil refinery, to be accompanied by the subsequent closure of two old refineries, was authorized, because of the major contribution which the operation would make to the restructuring of the same region.[313]

At the same time, restructuring aid associated with relocation may be favoured. For example, aid to encourage relocation to less developed areas such as the Mezzogiorno, counterbalancing the closure of capacity in the rest of Italy, was authorized.[314]

However, the Commission is studying the possibility of limiting regional aid towards capital-intensive investment 'whose contribution to regional development is sometimes insufficient to justify high rates of assistance'.[315] If the aid is to make the contribution to the long-term development of the region required by Article 92(3)(a) and (c), the Commission considers that it must at the very least re-establish the profitability of the recipient,[316] without producing any unacceptable negative effects on competition within the Union. As the Court of Justice acknowledges, such effects may be present where aid is granted in a sector suffering from overcapacity.[317] Particularly in such sectors, aid may be prohibited because it enables the recipient to increase or maintain its market

---

[309] Dec. 84/112 ([1984] OJ L62/23) amending Dec. 82/691.

[310] *Fourteenth Report on Competition Policy* (EC Commission, Brussels, 1985), 172–3.

[311] Bull. EC 6–1993, 1.2.61.

[312] *Ibid.*, 1.2.62.

[313] *Ibid.*, 1.2.63. Similarly, the sale of state-owned industrial sites at 50% of their value was authorized 'in view of the development problems of the region'. See *ibid.*, 1.2.64.

[314] Bull. EC 3–1983, 2.1.35.

[315] *Twenty-Second Report on Competition Policy* (EC Commission, Brussels, 1993), 58. See, more particularly, Dec. 89/456 ([1989] OJ L223/22) on the French Government's aid proposal in favour of Caulliez Frères, cotton yarn producer located in Prouvy, France.

[316] Similarly, Art. 19(2) of Reg. 1787/84 ([1984] OJ L169/1) on the European Regional Development Fund provided that where the ERDF assisted investment projects with the aim of preserving jobs, the investment had to fall within the framework of a conversion or restructuring plan ensuring that the recipient would be competitive.

[317] Case C–198/91 *William Cook plc* v. *EC Commission* [1993] ECR I–2486, I–2531.

share at the expense of competitors not receiving such aid.[318] Even in the Mezzogiorno, such considerations may render aid objectionable.[319] Hence, the grant of restructuring aid often has to be accompanied by capacity reductions. Nevertheless, the Commission, mindful of the obligation in Articles 130a and 130b of the Treaty to take account of the cohesion objective,[320] may require a smaller capacity reduction on the part of the aid recipients where regional development needs justify such flexibility.[321]

4.3.4 Rescue Aid

Rescue aid which is unlikely to bring about the lasting recovery of a firm may be found unable to contribute to the regional development required by Article 92(3)(a) and (c).[322] The fact that without the aid an undertaking may go out of business may not affect such a finding.[323]

For example, in a decision concerning regional aid in Germany the Commission found that this aid prevented market forces from having their normal consequences—the disappearance of a loss-making uncompetitive undertaking —kept the undertaking in business artificially, and facilitated its take-over by a large integrated aluminium group. This aid was of a rescue nature and, by artificially improving its profitability, favoured the recipient undertaking and its purchaser compared with other undertakings competing in this sector. Hence, the aid was prohibited.[324] Similarly, the Commission refused to authorize aid for the modernization of a synthetic yarn production and processing plant for the purpose of keeping it in business without effecting any fundamental change.[325]

Such practice does not, however, preclude the possibility that social and regional problems may justify the grant of rescue aid.[326] According to *Commission Policy on Sectoral Aid Schemes*,[327] controlled use of rescue aid for a strictly limited

---

[318] Dec. 93/133 ([1993] OJ L55/54) concerning aid granted by the Spanish Government to Merco (an agricultural processing company).

[319] Notice ([1984] OJ C269/2) of an aid package proposed by the Italian Government for investment in connection with the restructuring of the chemical industry.

[320] Community guidelines on state aid for rescuing and restructuring firms in difficulty ([1994] OJ C368/12), para. 1.3.

[321] *Ibid.*, para. 3.2.3.

[322] Case C–305/89 *Italy* v. *EC Commission: Alfa Romeo* [1991] ECR I–1603, I–1644.

[323] See, e.g., Dec. 87/418 ([1987] OJ L227/45) concerning aid to a Belgian steel pipe and tube manufacturer.

[324] Dec. 88/174 ([1987] OJ L79/19) concerning aid which Baden–Württemberg has provided to BUG-Alutechnik GmbH, an undertaking producing semi-finished and finished aluminium products. See, earlier, Dec. 72/34 ([1971] JO L10/22) prohibiting Belgian aid to undertakings in difficulty.

[325] Dec. 86/509 ([1986] OJ L300/34) on aid granted by Germany and Bavaria to a producer of polyamide and polyester yarn situated in Deggendorf. See also Dec. 89/43 ([1989] OJ L16/52) on aids granted by the Italian Government to ENI–Lanerossi.

[326] See, e.g., the *Tenth Report on Competition Policy* (EC Commission, Brussels, 1981), 139.

[327] COM(78)221, 5.

period, to ameliorate the social and economic costs of change, could be authorized. For example, rescue aid to Short Brothers plc in Belfast was authorized because the social and economic effects of a closure would be serious and would result in a loss of confidence on the part of investors, whose presence was vital to the economic development of Northern Ireland.[328]

4.3.5 Operating Aid

In the 1979 Communication on Regional Aid Systems[329] the Commission expressed reservations about the compatibility of operating aids with the common market[330] and stated that it would specify the circumstances, if any, in which it might consider such aids to be compatible. Until then there should be no increase in the level of the existing aids, and no further aids of this type should be introduced. Their application might, however, continue until final decisions on their compatibility had been taken in the course of the Commission's review of existing aid systems under Article 93(1). Subsequently such aids were abolished or modified to eliminate their operating characteristics in Germany,[331] Greece,[332] Ireland,[333] Italy,[334] and the United Kingdom.[335]

Such aids were similarly opposed in Article 9(2) of Regulation 1787/84.[336] According to this provision, Community programmes supported by the European Regional Development Fund should not have as their object the internal reorganization of declining sectors but might, by participating in the establishment of new activities, promote the creation of alternative employment in regions or areas in a difficult situation.

Nevertheless, regional conditions may increasingly be seen as justifying the grant of operating aid.

---

[328] Bull. EC 7/8–1989, 2.1.86.

[329] [1979] OJ C31/9, para. 4, where they were described as 'aids not conditional or investment or job creation'. See, earlier, the *Third EC General Report* (EC Commission, Brussels, 1970), 81.

[330] Aid which was *essentiellement conservatoire* could not be authorized under Art. 92(3)(a) or (c). See Dec. 72/34 ([1972] JO L10/22) prohibiting Belgian aid to undertakings in difficulty. Cf., under the ECSC Treaty, Roemer AG in Joined Cases 27–29/58 *Compagnie des Hauts Fourneaux et Fonderies de Givors* v. *ECSC High Authority* [1960] ECR 241, 277.

[331] *Ninth Report on Competition Policy* (EC Commission, Brussels, 1980), 89.

[332] See the objections to Greek regional turnover tax reductions in Notice ([1985] OJ C75/4) concerning certain aspects of the system of incentives in support of regional and economic development in Greece.

[333] *Eighth Report on Competition Policy* (EC Commission, Brussels, 1979), 117 and the *Tenth Report on Competition Policy* (EC Commission, Brussels, 1981), 120–1.

[334] See, regarding operating aid in the Mezzogiorno, Bull. EC 7–1972, 45. See, regarding Commission objections to rescue aid and operating aid in Sicily, the *Eighth Report on Competition Policy* (EC Commission, Brussels, 1979), 118; and Bull. EC 3–1986, 2.1.66. See also the *Ninth Report on Competition Policy* (EC Commission, Brussels, 1980), 93; and Dec. 89/43 ([1989] OJ L16/52) on aids granted by the Italian Government to ENI–Lanerossi.

[335] *Fourteenth Report on Competition Policy* (EC Commission, Brussels, 1985), 174–5.

[336] On the European Regional Development Fund ([1984] OJ L169/1).

Social Fabric

Operating aid may be found to be justified where there is a sufficient threat to the 'social fabric'.[337] For example, exemption from rates in Northern Ireland benefited all enterprises regardless of whether they undertook an initial investment. Such aid was, in principle, incompatible with the common market. The Commission considered, however, that in the particular case of Northern Ireland, where the problem of civil unrest accentuated the grave economic difficulties, aid aimed at maintaining existing industry as well as promoting initial investment was justified.[338] Subsequently, relief from electricity prices for certain commercial and industrial consumers in Northern Ireland was authorized for a three-year period.[339] Even export aid in the form of aid for market research in the Union as well as in third countries was authorized in the case of firms in Northern Ireland under Article 92(3)(a), account being taken of the socio-economic situation there as well as the 'political difficulties'.[340]

'Traditional' Periphery

In early Commission practice operating aid might be seen as contributing to the development of peripheral regions. In one decision[341] the Commission had to consider the legality of a reduced Italian railway tariff for agricultural products originating in the Mezzogiorno. The Commission accepted that agriculture was important for the development of this region. Moreover, in view of the peripheral situation of the Mezzogiorno, it was rational for aid to concern transport charges. The reduced tariff seemed appropriate to its objectives and not to have anti-competitive effects unjustified by the needs of such an underdeveloped region. Again, a reduction in the rate of tax on profits of certain service undertakings at Shannon Airport in Ireland, which applied only to initial investments, was authorized,[342] as were subsequent extensions of the tax reduction.[343]

It tended to be only in particular sectors that the grant of operating aid in peripheral regions was opposed. For example, in 1973 the Commission authorized the prolongation of certain operating aids 'in consideration of the economic and social situation in Italy and the fact that economic recovery was

---

[337] Dec. 85/18 ([1985] OJ L11/28) on the French regional planning grant scheme (*Prime d'aménagement du territoire*).

[338] *Fourteenth Report on Competition Policy* (EC Commission, Brussels, 1985), 175–6.

[339] Bull. EC 6–1993, 1.2.75.

[340] *Ninth Report on Competition Policy* (EC Commission, Brussels, 1980), 115–6. See, later, the *Twenty-Third Report on Competition Policy* (EC Commission, Brussels, 1994), 264.

[341] Dec. of 16 Feb. 1962 ([1962] JO 1229) authorizing special tariff 201 on Italian state railways.

[342] Bull. EC 6–1981, 2.1.35.

[343] *Seventeenth Report on Competition Policy* (EC Commission, Brussels, 1988), 181; *Eighteenth Report on Competition Policy* (EC Commission, Brussels, 1989), 192; and *Nineteenth Report on Competition Policy* (EC Commission, Brussels, 1990), 177.

below expectations'. Such aid was, however, opposed in the case of the textile industry.[344] More particularly, in the *Twelfth Report on Competition Policy*[345] the Commission objected, in relation to social security reductions for employees in the textile industry, that increased output without restructuring would result. However, 'this [did] not mean that the Commission [was] opposed to the reduction of social security costs as a means of granting aid'.[346]

The rationale for authorization of operating aid was that such aid might be necessary, at least temporarily, to preserve employment in peripheral regions where alternative employment opportunities would take time to create. In 1978 the Commission initially objected to aid to pay the wage costs of firms in difficulties taken over by a regional agency in Sicily, because the aid was of operating character,[347] but the aid was subsequently authorized because of its strictly limited duration.[348] The Commission also authorized Sicilian aid to cover the operating losses of sulphur producers, though only for the time needed for setting up alternative activities with all possible speed.[349] The aid was acceptable, because the nature of the deposits was such that there was little prospect of the mines ever becoming satisfactorily competitive and because sulphur mining was the only industrial activity in the areas concerned and needed to be kept going pending the establishment of successor industries which would pay their way.[350] Likewise, aid was authorized to pay for the care and maintenance of Portuguese tungsten and tin mines during their closure, because it helped to preserve a national asset and alleviate social and economic hardship caused by the closure.[351]

At the same time, operating aid in such regions might be rendered more acceptable by reason of its limited impact on competition. In the case of a Sicilian scheme to provide firms with soft loans to finance stocks of raw materials and finished goods, Commission objections[352] were lifted after certain

---

[344] Notice concerning Italian Decree Law 286 of 1 July 1972 prolonging the reduction in the burden of social payments for craft undertakings, small and medium-sized industrial undertakings, and undertakings in the textile industry instituted by Decree Law 431 of 5 July 1971, which, with amendments, became Law 590 of 4 Aug. 1971 ([1973] OJ C40/2). Cf. Dec. 80/932 ([1980] OJ L264/28) concerning the partial taking over by the state of employers' contributions to sickness insurance schemes in Italy, where the Commission stated that such relief must apply uniformly to the whole of industry.

[345] EC Commission, Brussels, 1983.

[346] *Ibid.*, 127.

[347] Notice ([1978] OJ C207/3) regarding Bill 403 of the Autonomous Region of Sicily providing special assistance for the Ente siciliano per la promozione industriale.

[348] Bull. EC 9–1979, 2.1.31.

[349] *First Report on Competition Policy* (EC Commission, Brussels, 1972), 139. See also Bull. EC 12–1968, 32 and Bull. EC 8–1970, 70–1. See, regarding aid for the upkeep of the sulphur mines, Bull. EC 11–1987, 2.1.103.

[350] *Fourth EC General Report* (EC Commission, Brussels, 1971), 3.

[351] Bull. EC 7/8–1987, 2.1.118.

[352] Notice ([1984] OJ C96/2) concerning the Law of the Region of Sicily providing for loans to industry, commerce, crafts, fisheries, and co-operatives and soft loans for building stocks of raw materials and semi-manufactured goods.

amendments to the scheme had been agreed. The Commission took into consideration the fact that the scheme was aimed at small and medium-sized enterprises, that the rate of interest payable by recipients had been raised, that the recipients were in industries mainly working for the local market in a depressed area, and that only one award could be made per firm, which sharply reduced the effects of the aid. In this case the Commission, therefore, felt able to apply the provision in paragraph 7 of the 1979 Co-ordination Principles allowing exceptions from the ban on operating aid.[353]

The 1979 Principles provided, more generally, that in the case of the least-developed regions, from 1 January 1981 for aided investments exceeding 3 million EUA[354] a further 25 per cent of initial investment costs or 4,500 EUA per job created (that is, operating aid) could be paid over a minimum of five years.[355]

'A certain rethinking',[356] or perhaps rather a more elaborate articulation, of the Commission approach to operating aid in such regions followed the accession of Greece and then Spain and Portugal.[357] In the 1988 Commission Communication[358] it was recognized that undertakings in regions covered by Article 92(3)(a) might face additional costs attributable to their location and infrastructure difficulties and that operating aid might thus be beneficial in such regions. In the first place, disadvantages as regards costs and infrastructure might be so serious that the safeguarding of existing investment might be difficult. In order to safeguard such investment, operating aid might be necessary, in earlier stages of development, to attract new investments and to promote economic development. This was particularly so because of the very small undertakings in traditional sectors which could not expand and participate effectively in the internal market without a stimulus. Secondly, there might be serious structural problems, such as those caused by remote location. For example, island regions in peripheral locations might suffer a permanent cost disadvantage with respect to trade because of the burden of additional transportation expenses. The same went for communication costs. Hence, operating aid might be authorized, provided it was limited in time,[359] sought to promote durable and balanced economic development and would not lead to Union overcapacity in the sector concerned. The last condition

---

[353] *Fifteenth Report on Competition Policy* (EC Commission, Brussels, 1986), 186–7 and Bull. EC 7/8–1985, 2.1.57.

[354] Ireland obtained an alternative threshold of 50 jobs created (*ibid.* 165).

[355] Para. 2(i) of the 1979 Principles ([1979] OJ C31/9).

[356] *Sixteenth Report on Competition Policy* (EC Commission, Brussels, 1987), 178.

[357] For example, whereas the Commission had raised objections to aid for replacement investments in the *zonenrandgebiet* (*Eleventh Report on Competition Policy* (EC Commission, Brussels, 1982), 159–60), modernization aid was authorized in Portugal (*Sixteenth Report on Competition Policy* (EC Commission, Brussels, 1987), 179).

[358] [1988] OJ C212/2.

[359] Notice C12/92 (NN113/A/93) ([1994] OJ C113/3) concerning aid granted under Regional Laws 23/1991 and 25/1993 for orders obtained by firms operating in Sicily.

implied that Union sectoral rules and rules regarding rescue aid must be respected. Thus operating aid to companies in difficulties in Article 92(3)(a) areas had to be strictly conditional on the implementation by the beneficiaries of restructuring measures which would lead to their being truly viable.[360] Export aids were not permissible,[361] and there must be an annual report to the Commission.[362]

In Decision 88/318[363] the Commission found that operating aid in the Mezzogiorno fulfilled these criteria and could, therefore, be authorized as 'assisting development' under Article 92(3)(a). This authorization applied, in particular, to the relief from social security contributions; tax concessions; state guarantees; and assistance with transport costs for firms located in Sardinia. Additional aid was prohibited,[364] and the authorized aid had to be limited in time. The Commission subsequently objected that the aid authorized by Decision 88/318 was not limited in time and that its level was increased,[365] and so continued authorization was subject to the condition that the aid was degressive.[366] Similarly, aid to assist industrial firms in Sardinia with their labour costs was authorized for 1990 and 1991 because of 'the limited period during which it was granted'.[367]

The Commission also authorized relief from corporation tax and from social charges in other Italian regions covered by Article 92(3)(a);[368] Corsican relief from corporation tax;[369] tax relief for undertakings located in the area around Shannon Airport and for financial service centres in certain areas of Dublin;[370]

[360] Dec. 91/1 ([1991] OJ L5/8) concerning aids in Spain which the central and several autonomous governments have granted to MAGEFESA, producer of articles of stainless steel and small electric appliances.

[361] Cf., however, the authorization of aid to Irish SMEs faced with problems associated with exchange rate realignments, Bull. EC 11–1992, 1.3.59.

[362] Para. I.6 of the 1988 Communication. If such reports do not materialize, aid may be objectionable because of its lack of transparency. See Notice C21/92 (NN26/92) ([1992] OJ C240/7) concerning aid granted by Italy to certain regions in the Mezzogiorno.

[363] On Law 64 of 1 Mar. 1986 on aid to the Mezzogiorno ([1988] OJ L143/37).

[364] Dec. 90/215 ([1990] OJ L114/25) on aid granted by the Italian Government to the newsprint industry; and Dec. 92/296 ([1992] OJ L159/46) concerning aid granted by the Italian Government to Nuova Cartiera di Arbatax.

[365] Notice C34/92 (N615/92) ([1994] OJ C99/3) regarding aid which Italy had decided to grant under the form of reductions in and taking over by the state of social security contributions paid by firms in the Mezzogiorno. See also Notice C21/92 (NN26/92) ([1992] OJ C240/7) concerning aid granted by Italy to certain regions of the Mezzogiorno.

[366] Dec. 95/455 ([1995] OJ L265/23) on the arrangements for reducing the social security contributions paid by firms in the Mezzogiorno and for assigning to the state some of the contributions.

[367] Bull. EC 6–1993, 1.2.74. The aid may also be expected to be 'degressive'. See Bull. EU 3–1995, 1.3.44.

[368] Decision 91/500 ([1991] OJ L262/29) concerning aid granted to enterprises in the Friuli–Venezia Giulia region.

[369] *Twentieth Report on Competition Policy* (EC Commission, Brussels, 1991), 187.

[370] H. Morch, 'Summary of the Most Important Recent Developments' (1994) 3 *Competition Policy Newsletter* 61–6, 63.

and soft loans for Sicilian undertakings.[371] Similar authorizations have been granted in respect of operating aid to Sicilian undertakings;[372] operating aid in Ireland;[373] operating aid in Portugal (Madeira) and Spain (Andalusia);[374] and operating aid to the French overseas departments of Saint-Pierre-et-Miguelon and Mayotte.[375]

Such practice apparently has the support of the European Parliament, which considers that tax incentive schemes may be desirable in the least developed regions of the Union.[376] According to the Parliament, the enormity of their problems, which stem not only from historical and geographical factors but also from insufficient productivity, should be recognized. Low productivity results from inadequate infrastructures, higher service costs, especially those connected with the use of information technologies, and a lack of professional expertise, which prevent production costs falling to offset these disadvantages.[377] In such circumstances, schemes to encourage employers to take on additional (and not replacement) employees through selective cuts in fiscal, parafiscal, and tariff charges and to reduce pay-roll taxes in less-favoured regions may assist the regions concerned.[378] However, such schemes should:

—have as their primary objective the creation of new and lasting employment opportunities, particularly in rural areas and areas which have experienced the greatest industrial decline;
—be restricted to the Union's least-advantaged regions, these regions being determined on the basis of a revised and improved 'synthetic index' comparable to Table 7.11 in the *Second Periodic Report on the Social and Economic Situation and Development of the Regions of the Community*;[379]
—be temporary in nature, in so far as such a scheme could be operated for a given period (possibly ten years) and renewed, subject to review at the end of that period, or withdrawn when regions attained a given cut-off level on the synthetic index;

[371] *Twenty-Fourth Report on Competition Policy* (EC Commission, Brussels, 1995), 499.
[372] Notice C11/92 (ex NN134/91) ([1993] OJ C59/7) concerning aid which Italy had decided to introduce by Law 34/1991 of the Sicilian Region concerning the marketing and sale of Sicilian products.
[373] *Twenty-Fourth Report on Competition Policy* (EC Commission, Brussels, 1995), 188–9.
[374] H. Morch, 'Summary of the Most Important Recent Developments' (1995) 4 *Competition Policy Newsletter* 47–51, 49.
[375] Bull. EC 3–1988, 2.1.76.
[376] Resolution of 13 Sept. 1985 ([1985] OJ C262/125) on a regional incentive scheme for the development of less-favoured regions of the EC. It was suggested in H. Clout, *A Rural Policy for the EEC?* (Methuen, London, 1984), 178, that to encourage new enterprises to develop and vulnerable ones to survive in rural areas, there should be exemption from taxation over a specified number of years in order to cushion delicate firms during particularly difficult phases of their existence.
[377] Para. 8 of the Resolution.
[378] *Ibid.*, para. 9.
[379] COM(84)569.

—give priority to industries and sectors which exploit the natural resources and potentials of any given region.[380]

According to the Committee on Regional Policy and Regional Planning,[381] the reduction in unit labour costs implied by such schemes would act as a powerful counter-incentive to the disincentives in infrastructural services. Since employees in the less developed regions were entitled, as of right, to aspire to a similar standard of living as those living in more 'fortunate' regions and the Member States, for practical reasons, had to adhere to a similar personal taxation system regardless of the geographical location of its citizens, the only apparent means of reducing such costs was to ease the tax liability of employers per employee.

However, some kinds of operating aid may still be opposed by the Commission, even in the peripheral regions.[382] According to the Commission, the concept of regional development in Article 92(3)(a) is based essentially on the provision of aid for new investment or major expansions or conversions of undertakings involving large-scale investments of a physical nature and the costs associated with these. Aid to restore the balance sheets of companies which have fallen into financial difficulties[383] or for a company going into liquidation may not be authorized.[384] Similarly, aid which serves only to relieve a basically healthy company of its financial burden may not be authorized.[385] If operating aid is to be authorized, it must have some link with the promotion of economic development.

For example, the Commission decided that aid to promote beet production through grants of 80,000 lire per hectare sown with sugar beet in Campania could not be authorized under Article 92(3)(a).[386] Such aid did not promote the development of the activity or the region in question, as the situation of the region and the activity would not have been permanently changed by the time that the aid was to be discontinued. According to the Commission, instead of encouraging beet producers in Campania to make a real effort to reorganize or convert their holdings, the aid would lead them to increase, or at least to maintain, the cultivation of beet and hence the manufacture of sugar, a product

---

[380] Para. 13 of the Resolution.

[381] Report on a regional incentive scheme for the development of less-favoured regions of the EC, EP Doc. A2–79/85, 10.

[382] Cf. Commission objections to aid for industrial estates and free zones in Cyprus in its *Opinion on the Application by the Republic of Cyprus for Membership*, COM(93)313, A/14.

[383] Dec. 88/167 ([1988] OJ L76/18) concerning Law 1386/1983 by which the Greek Government granted aid to Greek industry. In fact, Greek aid seems to have been far from successful. See *OECD Economic Surveys 1989–90: Greece* (OECD, Paris, 1990), 61.

[384] Dec. 94/343 ([1994] OJ L154/37) concerning aid granted by the Spanish Government to Merco.

[385] Notice C2/88 (NN128/87) ([1996] OJ C84/3) regarding aid which the Greek authorities had decided to grant to Heracles General Cement Company.

[386] Dec. 77/83 ([1977] OJ L24/37) concerning the measures provided for in the draft law of the Region of Campania (Italy) supplementing and amending Regional Law 29 of 22 July 1974 on measures to promote beet production.

of which there was currently a surplus in the Union. Similarly, the Commission objected to aid to the transport of agricultural goods from the Mezzogiorno and reductions in social security contributions paid by agri-foodstuffs firms in the Mezzogiorno,[387] and to aid in Sicily for wine[388] and fruit,[389] particularly mandarins.[390] The Commission considered that such aid did not in any way constitute measures for encouraging the development of the island or the agricultural products concerned but amounted to operating aid with no structural impact. There would be no lasting change in the situation of Sicily or of the products concerned after the aid ceased.[391]

Aid may thus be ineligible for authorization under Article 92(3)(a), because it is 'merely a sectorally-aimed operating aid'.[392] The same thinking led to the prohibition of aid to reduce charges for water for irrigation purposes in Sardinia[393] and to the prohibition of other operating aid in Sardinia[394] and Greece.[395]

Opposition to such aid is not confined to the agricultural sector.[396] For example, reduced railway tariffs for the carriage of bulk ores and products from Sicily and Sardinia have been prohibited, because such aid does not promote structural development.[397] For the same reason, continued public investment in loss-making companies in a sector suffering from overcapacity and without a restructuring plan may be prohibited, even in Article 92(3)(a) regions.[398] This practice is supported by the Court of Justice.[399]

---

[387] *Seventeenth Report on Competition Policy* (EC Commission, Brussels, 1988), 181–2.

[388] Dec. 82/401 ([1982] OJ L173/20) concerning aid granted in Sicily in the wine and fruit and vegetables sector.

[389] Dec. 82/651 ([1982] OJ L274/34) on the aids granted in Sicily in the citrus fruit, fruit and vegetables sector.

[390] Dec. 89/204 ([1989] OJ L76/48) on regional aid for mandarin growers in Sicily.

[391] This is the same reasoning as that applied to support the prohibition of operating aid in more developed regions. See, e.g., Dec. 93/155 ([1993] OJ L61/55) concerning an aid measure proposed by the German authorities (Rhineland-Palatinate) for the distillation of wine.

[392] Communic. C1/94 (E2/93) ([1994] OJ C94/13) concerning aid which Ireland granted to mushroom growers.

[393] Communic. C5/93 (487/A/90) ([1993] OJ C140/3) concerning aid which the region of Sardinia decided to grant for health, transport, and other activities.

[394] Dec. 95/366 ([1995] OJ L218/20) on aid granted by Italy (Sardinia) in the agricultural sector.

[395] Notice C46/91 (ex NN21/91) ([1991] OJ C296/2) concerning aid which the Greek Government proposed to grant to the fertilizer industry.

[396] See, e.g., Communic. C52/89 ([1990] OJ C32/3) concerning aid which Italy had decided to establish under the Law of the Region of Sicily on aid for regional development.

[397] Dec. 91/523 ([1991] OJ L283/20) abolishing the support tariffs applied by the Italian railways to the carriage of bulk ores and products produced and processed in Sicily and Sardinia.

[398] See, most recently, Dec. 94/374 ([1994] OJ L170/36) on Sicilian Regional Law 23/1991 concerning extraordinary aid for industry and Art. 5 of Sicilian Regional Law 8/1991 concerning, in particular financing for Sitas.

[399] Case C–303/88 *Italy* v. *EC Commission: Lanerossi* [1991] ECR I–1433, I–1481. See, similarly, Case C–305/89 *Italy* v. *EC Commission: Alfa Romeo* [1991] ECR I–1603, I–1644.

Transformation

Established principles of Commission practice regarding state aid have been
extended to cover the former German Democratic Republic,[400] and have been
applied, for example, in the case of aid to Opel,[401] Mercedes-Benz,[402] and
Volkswagen.[403] However, doubt has been expressed whether Article 92, devised
for a 'normal situation', will prove flexible enough to cope with the economic
problems there[404] and to facilitate the transition towards a market economy.

To take account of such problems, some flexibility has been introduced by
the Commission in the application of this provision. In particular, 'with a view
to the unprecedented transformation of a planned economy into a market
economy inside the Community', the Commission accepts that operating aid
may be granted to East German companies to enable them to maintain
production which may become viable after restructuring,[406] though the likelihood of future viability must be established.[407] More particularly, aid to secure
the existence of companies until privatization may be authorized,[408] provided
that the aid is limited to the absolute minimum necessary for this purpose.[409]
The aid must not, however, be used to cover losses resulting from the sale of
products below the prevailing market price or for continued manufacture of
products for which no profitability can be expected at that price because of
general overcapacity.[410] Aid may also be authorized for rationalization,[411]

[400] *The European Community and German Unification*, Bull. EC, Supp. 4/90, 74–5.
[401] Communic. C60/91 (NN73/91 & 76/91) ([1992] OJ C68/2) concerning the proposal by
the German Government to award state aid to the Opel group in support of its investment plans
in the new *Länder*.
[402] Communic. C61/91 (NN74/91 & 80/91) ([1992] OJ C68/8) concerning the proposal by
the German Government to award state aid to Mercedes-Benz in support of its investment plans
in the new *Länder*.
[403] Communic. C62/91 (NN75, 77, 78, 79/91) ([1992] OJ C68/14) concerning the proposal
by the German Government to award state aid to the Volkswagen group in support of its
investment plans in the new *Länder*.
[404] 'The general argument of the special situation in the new *Länder*' may be unimpressive to
the Commission. See the *Twenty-Third Report on Competition Policy* (EC Commission, Brussels,
1994), 319.
[405] K. Hailbronner, 'Legal Aspects of the Unification of the Two German States' [1991] *EJIL*
18–41, 40.
[406] Notice C14/93 (ex NN36/93) ([1994] OJ C162/4) concerning aid, which Germany planned
to grant to Leuna AG for the production and sale of caprolactam—closure of procedure.
[407] Communic. C4/94 (ex NN103/93) ([1994] OJ C206/10) concerning aid decided by the
German Government in favour of Leuna AG, Sachsen Anhalt.
[408] Notice C4/94, C61/94, C62/94, NN2/95, NN3/95 & N467/95 ([1995] OJ C203/6)
concerning aid the German Government intended to grant to Sächsische Olefinwerke GmbH,
Leuna-Werke GmbH, and Buna GmbH.
[409] See, e.g., Notice C16/95 (NN50/94) ([1995] OJ C215/8) concerning aid the German
Government intended to grant to SKET Schwermaschinenbau Magdeburg GmbH.
[410] Notice C43/92 (NN131/92) ([1993] OJ C35/2) concerning aid granted by Germany to
Buna AG.
[411] Notice NN56/94 & C4/94 (ex NN103/93) ([1995] OJ C227/8) concerning aid the Germany
Government intended to grant to Leuna-Werke GmbH, Leuna/Merseburg.

modernization, given 'the omissions of the former system to invest in necessary equipment, neglected maintenance and repair and outdated equipment',[412] or to permit the adaptation of an undertaking to the market necessary for privatization to be possible.[413]

However, care may be taken to ensure that Western owners of aid recipients do not benefit from such aid.[414] Moreover, aid should not be used to continue production that cannot be expected to become profitable in a reasonable period of time. If, even in the case of the more modern and most efficient European producers, a certain production is not and cannot be profitable and will have to be reduced in scale, continued loss-compensation aid must be stopped. Therefore, even if an installation in the former German Democratic Republic is 'fundamentally competitive', poor sectoral prospects may mean that such aid is unacceptable.[415] Again, if appropriate restructuring is not entailed, aid may be prohibited, even though the future of other companies in the region may depend on the survival of the aid recipient.[416]

At the same time, steps may be taken to control the aid available to competitors from third states engaged in transformation. For example, Article 63(1)(iii) of the Europe Agreement with Poland provides that aid which distorts or threatens to distort competition by favouring certain undertakings or the production of certain goods shall be incompatible with the proper functioning of the Agreement, in so far as trade between Poland and the Union may be affected. Article 63(2) provides that any practices contrary to this Article shall be assessed on the basis of criteria arising from the application of the rules of Article 92 of the EC Treaty.

However, in Article 63(4)(a) of the Agreement the Parties recognize that during the first five years after the entry into force of the Agreement aid granted by Poland shall be assessed taking into account the fact that Poland shall be regarded as an area identical to those of the Union described in Article 92(3)(a) of the EC Treaty. The Joint Committee established by the Agreement shall, taking into account the economic situation of Poland, decide whether that period should be extended by further periods of five years.

Products covered by the ECSC Treaty are not subject to the competition provisions of the Polish Agreement itself, but to Protocol 2 to the Agreement.[417]

---

[412] Cf. the account taken of the 'burden of the past' in Dec. 92/321 ([1992] OJ L176/57) concerning aid awarded by Spain to Intelhorce SA, a state-owned producer of cotton textiles.

[413] Notice C61/94 (N375/94) ([1995] OJ C113/5) concerning aid which the German Government intended to grant to Buna GmbH. See also Notice C62/94 (N376/94) ([1995] OJ C113/13) concerning aid which the German Government intended to grant to Sächsische Olefinwerke GmbH, Böhlen.

[414] *Twenty-Third Report on Competition Policy* (EC Commission, Brussels, 1994), 258.

[415] Notice C43/92 (NN131/92) ([1994] OJ C16/6) concerning aid awarded by the German Government to Buna AG; and Communic. C15/93 (ex N59/93) ([1994] OJ C159/12) concerning aids which Germany had decided to grant to modernize grain mills in Saxony.

[416] Communic. C4/94 (ex NN103/93) ([1994] OJ C206/10) concerning aid decided by the German Government in favour of Leuna AG, Sachsen Anhalt.

[417] Art. 63(8) of the Agreement.

Article 8(2) of the Protocol provides that practices contrary to Article 8(1)(iii), the equivalent of Article 63(1)(iii) of the Agreement itself, shall be assessed on the basis of the criteria arising from Union rules on state aid, including secondary legislation.

Nordic Periphery

Challenges to established practice regarding regional aid are entailed by the fourth enlargement of the Union.[418] In the agricultural sector Article 142 of the Accession Agreement with Austria, Finland, and Sweden[419] provides for the Commission to authorize operating aid in 'specific regions . . . north of the sixty-second Parallel', with a view to ensuring that agricultural activity is maintained in these regions.[420] Moreover, in Sweden operating aid is granted in the form of transport subsidies for manufacturers in the North,[421] and reductions are made in the social charges payable by employers in certain municipalities of Norrbotten, Västerbotten, and Jämtland.[422] The Commission, like the EFTA Surveillance Authority,[423] may authorize some such aid. Its willingness to do so is based on recognition of regional handicaps specific to the Nordic countries, namely the extra costs to firms caused by very long distances and harsh weather conditions. These handicaps may induce firms to relocate to less remote areas or dissuade them from locating in remote areas. Hence, partial compensation for the additional transport costs of undertakings in such areas, provided that their population density is less than 12.5 per square kilometre, may be authorized.[424]

Central Regions

Commission objections to operating aid in the central regions are well established. For example, in Decision 64/651[425] the Commission found that the

---

[418] *European Report* 1931 (5 Mar. 1994).

[419] See also Annex XV, VIIC, and D of the Accession Agreement, regarding aid which may be granted during transitional periods in the new Member States.

[420] See, e.g., Dec. 95/196 ([1995] OJ L126/35) on the long-term national aid scheme for agriculture in the northern regions of Finland; and Dec. 96/228 ([1996] OJ L76/29) on a long-term national aid scheme to assist farmers in northern areas of Sweden. See also Dec. 96/152 ([1996] OJ L34/48) on Finnish aid in the cereal seed sector. See, regarding aid to reduce the financing costs of loans contracted by Finnish farmers before accession to the Union, Bull. EU 11–1995, 1.3.167.

[421] *Reg.* (1980:803) on Regional Policy Transport Aid.

[422] *Law* (1990:912) on the Reduction of Social Charges and General Wage Charges.

[423] Dec. 88/94/COL ([1994] OJ L240/33) on the second amendment of the procedural and substantive rules in the field of state aid.

[424] Changes to the method for the application of Art. 92(3)(c) EC to regional aid ([1994] OJ C364/8), para. 6. According to the Swedish Government, the Commission also agreed in Accession negotiations that a reduction in employers' social security charges might be authorized in such areas as 'indirect' transport aid (*Sveriges Medlemskap i Europeiska Unionen*, prop. 1994/95:19, 363) or as aid 'fulfilling the same conditions' (*ibid.* 370).

[425] Concerning the prohibition of Belgian aid granted to Ford Tractors (Belgium) Ltd, in Anvers ([1964] JO 3257).

reimbursement of 50 per cent of transport charges to the French border for certain fruits for export was prohibited by Article 92(1), because the prices at which the fruit could be offered for sale at the frontier were lower than they would otherwise have been.[426]

Within the central regions aid must be linked with an initial investment or job creation.[427] Initial investment is defined in paragraph 18(1) of the 1979 Principles[428] as 'investment in fixed assets in the creation of a new establishment, the extension of an existing establishment or in engaging in an activity involving a fundamental change in the product or production process of an existing establishment (by means of rationalization, restructuring or modernization) . . . or by way of takeover of an establishment which has closed or which would have closed had such takeover not taken place'. This definition is not treated as covering restructuring aid to firms in difficulty[429] or aid granted for the acquisition of an undertaking which is not in economic difficulties and would not have closed down without the takeover.[430] Only aid to initial investment covered by the definition or for job creation is regarded as promoting regional development within the meaning of Article 92(3)(c).[431]

For example, Dutch employers taking on people unemployed for three years or more in jobs additional to those of the existing workforce before 31 December 1987 benefited from a reduction in social security charges equivalent to 15 per cent of the salaries of the new employees for four years. This aid scheme was authorized by the Commission.[432] The Commission also authorized a Belgian scheme which exempted from corporation tax for ten years new undertakings in six areas facing serious regional problems. Beneficiaries might not employ more than 200 persons and must be engaged in a high-technology industry included in a list of seven such sectors approved by the Commission.[433]

On the other hand, in Decision 87/48[434] the Commission considered an aid scheme for the cauldrons industry and, more particularly, the brewery materials industry. According to this scheme, the Belgian authorities took shares in enterprises in this sector and granted them assistance in the technological,

---

[426] See also Dec. 76/649 ([1976] OJ L229/24) on aid from the Belgian Government to the Société nationale des chemins de fer belges (SNCB) for through international railway tariffs for coal and steel.

[427] *Eighteenth Report on Competition Policy* (EC Commission, Brussels, 1989), 147. See, more particularly, Dec. 86/366 ([1986] OJ L223/30) concerning aid which the Belgian Government has granted to a ceramic sanitary ware and crockery manufacturer.

[428] [1979] OJ C31/9.

[429] Notice C24/95 (ex N682/93) ([1995] OJ C294/13) concerning Saarland's scheme of state guarantees.

[430] H. Morch, 'Summary of the Most Important Recent Developments' (1994) 3 *Competition Policy Newsletter* 61–6, 64.

[431] *Eleventh Report on Competition Policy* (EC Commission, Brussels, 1982), 161.

[432] *Sixteenth Report on Competition Policy* (EC Commission, Brussels, 1987), 173–4.

[433] Bull. EC 7/8–1989, 2.1.73.

[434] Concerning aid in Belgium in favour of the brewery equipment industry ([1987] OJ L20/30).

commercial, and managerial fields. The scheme was found not to be covered by Article 92(3)(c), because it was not conditional on initial investment or job creation. For the same reasons, in Decision 88/174[435] the Commission rejected a plan by Baden–Würrtemberg to aid a producer of aluminium products.

However, operating aid in such regions may be authorized on sectoral grounds under Article 92(3)(c).[436] Minor operating aid may also be granted on an exceptional, temporary basis in regions which have ceased to be covered by Article 92(3)(a), are covered by Article 92(3)(c), and are still badly affected by development problems.[437]

4.4 Conclusion

The Commission considers that regional aid, properly and carefully applied, constitutes an essential instrument of regional development and enables a greater balance to be achieved in the growth of the various regions, which is a Treaty objective[438] and a prior condition for greater and more thorough integration.[439] More particularly, regional aid may have the positive externalities of countering over-concentration in certain highly-developed regions,[440] reducing unemployment costs and enabling society to make better use of under-used social infrastructure in recipient regions.[441] Hence, the operation of Article 92(3)(a) and (c) may be portrayed as embodying underlying Treaty requirements concerning reduced regional disparities, growth in the Union generally through utilization of resources which might otherwise lie idle, and furtherance of integration.

In practice, however, difficulties of reconciling competition policy requirements with regional development requirements are suggested by differences in the coverage of Article 92(3)(a) and (c) and that of the ERDF (European Regional Development Fund) Objectives.[442] Regions included in the lists drawn

---

[435] Concerning aid which Baden–Württemberg has provided to BUG—Alutechnik GmbH, an undertaking producing semi-finished and finished aluminium products ([1988] OJ L79/29).

[436] Dec. 95/452 ([1995] OJ L264/30) on state aid in the form of tax concessions to undertakings operating in the Centro di Servizi Finanziari ed Assicurativi di Trieste pursuant to Art. 3 of Italian Law 19 of 9 Jan. 1991.

[437] Dec. 88/318 ([1988] OJ L143/37) on Law 64 of 1 Mar. 1986 on aid to the Mezzogiorno. See also Dec. 95/455 ([1995] OJ L265/23) on the arrangements for reducing the social security contributions paid by firms in the Mezzogiorno and for assigning to the state some of the contributions. The regions concerned in the latter Dec. were also covered by Objective 1 of the Structural Funds.

[438] In the original version of the Treaty the only explicit reference to this objective was in the fifth recital in the Preamble to the Treaty, though it might have been implicit in ideas of 'harmonious development' and 'balanced expansion' in Art. 2. See now the references to economic and social cohesion in Arts. 2, 3(j), and 130a.

[439] *First Report on Competition Policy* (EC Commission, Brussels, 1972), 116–7.

[440] *EC Seventh General Report* (EC Commission, Brussels, 1974), 195.

[441] *The Effect of Different State Aid Measures on Intra-Community Competition* (EC Commission, Brussels, 1990), 103.

[442] It has been argued, however, that the criterion laid down in Reg. 2052/88 for determining

up for the implementation of these Objectives but not eligible for regional aid from national sources at the time these lists were originally compiled covered approximately 4 per cent of the Union population.[443] More particularly, amendment of the German regional aid scheme meant that for the period 1991 to 1993 only 27 per cent of the population of the Federal Republic, as opposed to 39 per cent of this population previously, was covered by this scheme. As a result, some regions covered by Objective 2 (converting regions seriously affected by industrial decline)[444] or Objective 5b (facilitating the development and structural adjustment of rural areas)[445] became ineligible for national regional aid.[446]

The conclusion drawn by Directorate General IV is that in such regions Union aid should concentrate on infrastructure[447] and training measures which do not offend against Article 92(1). However, Directorate General XVI, which is responsible for regional policy, takes the view that application of Article 92(3)(a) and (c) should be adapted so as to allow for implementation of Community Support Frameworks governing use of ERDF aid.[448] Thus eligibility of a region under Objective 1 should be an adequate criterion for authorization of aid to that region under Article 92(3)(a). Similarly, Objectives 2 and 5b regions should be covered by Article 92(3)(c). Some support for this view may be found in the case law. According to the Advocate General in *Lanerossi*,[449] which concerned Italian aid to textiles, the possibility of granting aid with the framework of a Community programme of the ERDF does not authorize the

---

Objective 1 regions is 'virtually identical' with that applied for determining the scope of Art. 92(3)(a). Hence, 'there is a perfect compatibility between competition policy and the policy pursued through the Structural Funds when it comes to defining the objective towards which Community action leading to cohesion must ultimately be directed.' See A. Marques, 'Community Competition Policy and Economic and Social Cohesion' [1992] *Regional Studies* 404–7, 404.

[443] *Fourth Periodic Report on the Social and Economic Situation and Development of the Regions of Europe*, COM(90)609, 61.

[444] Art. 1.2 of Reg. 2052/88 on the tasks of the Structural Funds and their effectiveness and on co-ordination of their activities between themselves and with the operations of the European Investment Bank and the other existing financial instruments, as amended by Reg. 2081/93 ([1993] OJ L193/5).

[445] *Ibid.*, Art. 1.5. [446] *Europe* 5644 (11 Jan. 1992).

[447] The UK Government and the Confederation of British Industry also favour infrastructure projects as giving better value for money. See *EEC Regional Development Policy*, House of Lords Select Committee on the European Communities, HL(1991–92) 20, 14.

[448] Cf. the account taken of the coverage of the Poseidon programme, when the Commission accepted aid for Réunion in the *Twentieth Report on Competition Policy* (EC Commission, Brussels, 1991), 188. Cf. also, regarding parts of the provinces of Sondrio and Novara, which failed clearly to meet the thresholds for regional aid to be permissible, but which benefited under Objective 2, Notice C31/92 (N454/91) ([1992] OJ C324/3) concerning aid granted by Italy for the reconstruction of the Vallettina. A review of the treatment of Abruzzi was envisaged before the end of 1990 (Dec. 88/318 ([1988] OJ L143/37) on Law 64 of 1 Mar. 1986 on aid to the Mezzogiorno), but it was reclassified as an Objective 1 region. See also, regarding the aid authorized in areas of Navarre, Notice N463/94 ([1996] OJ C25/3) regarding the new map of assisted areas in Spain.

[449] Case C–303/88 *Italy v. EC Commission: Lanerossi* [1991] ECR I–1433.

Member States to grant aid outside the scope of that programme on their own initiative and without prior notification.[450] The implication is that state aid falling within such a programme is to be authorized under Article 92(3)(a) or (c).

In the event, it has been agreed that in Objective 2 regions or Objective 5b regions which are not covered by national regional aid schemes state aid will only be authorized for infrastructures, training, tourism, arts and crafts, advisory activities, and productive investments by small and medium-sized enterprises with up to 250 employees and a turnover which is, in principle, less than ECU 20 million.[451] In the case of aid to productive investments by such enterprises, the levels of aid intensity are discussed with the Member State concerned.[452]

However, such compromises may be inadequate to resolve underlying problems. In particular, it is argued that at the operational level an overly rigid distinction between infrastructure investments and productive investments— leading to a breakdown between the scope of application of regional policy or of competition policy—may not be justified in the face of the reality of disparities in development which competition policy is attempting to reduce in the long term.[453]

Moreover, as conditions change, the grant of state aid to a region covered by a Community Support Framework may become objectionable from a competition policy perspective. For example, improvement in the situation of a region, such as the creation of a large number of new jobs, may mean that regional aid is no longer seen to be justified.[454]

Directorate General XVI, possibly taking account of Article 130b of the Treaty, considers that the applicability of Article 92(3)(a) and (c) should be determined when Community Support Frameworks are agreed. In other words, the timetable for approval of state-aid schemes should follow that for agreeing these Frameworks.[455] Directorate General IV, however, perhaps reflecting

---

[450] *Ibid.*, I–1460.

[451] See, e.g., Dec. 93/353 ([1993] OJ L145/25) concerning the application of the national regional aid scheme in an area in the north of the Province of Madrid. See, however, regarding municipalities in Lazio eligible under Objective 5b but not for state regional aid, Notice C39/92 (NN 129/92) ([1993] OJ C46/3) concerning aid granted by Italy to the ceramics industry in Lazio.

[452] Notice C35/92 (ex N172/A/91) ([1994] OJ C78/2) concerning aid granted by the Region of Friuli–Venezia Giulia.

[453] *Europe* 5644 (11 Jan. 1992).

[454] Dec. 71/121 ([1971] OJ L57/19) on aid granted under art. 32 of the Law on the Adaptation of German Coal-mining Undertakings and Coal-mining Areas.

[455] According to the Committee on Economic and Monetary Affairs and Industrial Policy, competition policy should be adjusted to meet the requirements of cohesion. See the Report on the Twentieth Report on Competition Policy, EP Doc. A3–0338/91, 12. Complications may also arise in connection with Union rules designed to liberalize public procurement. Hence, the Commission adopted Notice C(88)2510 ([1989] OJ C22/3) to the Member States on monitoring compliance with public procurement rules in the case of projects and programmes financed by the Structural Funds and financial instruments.

general concerns about permanent subsidies to certain regions,[456] considers that once a region ceases to qualify under these sub-paragraphs, state aid should be prohibited.[457] Thus Directorate General IV sought elimination of state aid in the Asturias,[458] Lavienne, and Twente[459] during the life of the Community Support Frameworks for these regions,[460] because they had reached such a level of development that aid was no longer permissible under Article 92(3)(c).[461]

It has now been agreed that decisions on the eligibility of the regions for Structural Fund support on the one hand and state aid on the other will follow the same timetable, so as to guarantee the long-term stability which is indispensable to action by public authorities and economic operators, thus facilitating the achievement of cohesion.[462]

As a result of such compromises, it has been asserted that the reconciliation and even integration of Union competition policy with Union regional policy are, in general, adequate and that there is no reason to fear the occurrence of serious anomalies.[463] Even so, at the internal level in the work of the Commission, maintaining two distinct ways of thinking—exclusive responsibility of DG IV for competition, and partnership through the Community Support Frameworks for cohesion—is admitted to be problematic, the Commission as a whole bearing responsibility for guaranteeing the political and institutional coherence of policies and decisions.[464]

One suggested solution would be for the Commission to establish an independent tribunal to decide competition questions, which could be overruled by the Commission as a whole in exceptional cases, so as to give priority to regional policy.[465] Failing such reform, it has been argued that a case-by-case

---

[456] See, e.g., R. E. Baldwin, 'Assessing the Fair Trade and Safeguards Laws in Terms of Modern Trade and Political Economy Analysis' (1992) 15 *The World Economy* 185–202, 198.

[457] *European Report* 1706 (25 Sept. 1991).

[458] The Asturias failed to meet the thresholds to qualify under Art. 92(3)(c). Nevertheless, since the rate of structural unemployment had risen in recent years and the Structural Funds provided assistance there in pursuit of Objective 1 until 1993, and taking into account the restructuring of the mining industry there, the Commission decided as an exception not to raise an objection to a ceiling of 45% until 1 June 1993, i.e., until the end of the then current CSF. See Communic. E8/90 ([1991] OJ C32/5) concerning the review of the national scheme of regional aid in the areas of Madrid and the Asturias.

[459] Bull. EC 11–1992, 1.3.63. Aid to Twente was objectionable after 1 July 1991 because of the considerable improvement in unemployment and the level of GDP in the region. See, regarding earlier objections to aid to Twente, Bull. EC 5–1982, 2.1.18.

[460] *European Report* 1697 (27 July 1991).

[461] *Twentieth Report on Competition Policy* (EC Commission, Brussels, 1991), 190–1. Similar issues arose in connection with aid to Abruzzi. See *European Report* 1707 (28 Sept. 1991). Cf., regarding differences between the scope of Integrated Mediterranean Programmes and Art. 92(3)(a), A. Pappalardo, 'Aiuti regionali e controlli comunitari' in F. Cuocolo, *Istituti Comunitarie Regioni* (Edizione Scientifiche Italiane, Naples, 1990), 113–8.

[462] *Europe* 5644 (11 Jan. 1992).

[463] 'Fair Competition in the Internal Market: Community State Aid Policy' (1991) 48 *European Economy* 67.

[464] *Europe* 5644 (11 Jan. 1992).   [465] *Financial Times*, 17 June 1992.

approach to application of competition policy is inadequate and that agreement should be reached as to the cases in which cohesion should be given priority over competition policy.[466] The underlying assumption is that ERDF arrangements are well adapted to the needs of cohesion.

However, the basic criterion for the grant of ERDF aid and, more particularly, for selection of Objective 1 regions is *per capita* gross domestic product relative to the Union average. Application of this criterion has the advantage of apparent objectivity[467] and also enables ERDF aid to be concentrated on regions in those Member States seeking a 'side-payment' for acceptance of the deepening of integration envisaged in the Single European Act and the Treaty on European Union. More generally, in determining geographical eligibility for ERDF aid, the Council and Commission have been concerned to use figures which are available throughout the Union on as nearly as possible a comparable basis. Figures are available, unreliable as they are admitted to be, for gross domestic product and for employment and unemployment.[468] Hence, such figures have played a central role in determining aid eligibility, though the need for flexibility in their use is increasingly recognized.[469]

The disadvantage of these criteria is that they do not enable account to be taken of the diversity of the most serious regional problems in the Union. From the start, therefore, application of the gross domestic product criterion had to be compromised in the case of Northern Ireland and Teruel. Northern Ireland had a *per capita* gross domestic product[470] of around 80 per cent of the Union average in 1986,[471] and the 'special reasons' for its original classification as an Objective 1 region essentially concerned its recent history of civil unrest.[472] The 1993 reforms of the Structural Funds entail further relaxation in relation to Hainaut and Merseyside and in the case of the Highlands and Islands of Scotland.[473] The introduction of Objective 6 in the context of the fourth enlargement of the Union seems to be more a recognition of a symptom rather than a solution to the underlying problem.

---

[466] Report of the Committee on Economic and Monetary Affairs and Industrial Policy on the *Twentieth Report on Competition Policy*, EP Doc. A3–0338/91, 11–2.

[467] Note the objections of the French Government that Hainaut in Belgium was classified as an Objective 1 region, whereas neighbouring Hainaut-Cambresis in France, which was little better off, remained as an Objective 2 region (*European Report* 1842 (10 Mar. 1993)).

[468] *EEC Regional Development Policy*, House of Lords Select Committee on the European Communities, HL(1991–2), 20, Evidence, 7.

[469] See, e.g., *The Community's Structural Fund Operations*, COM(93)67, 4.

[470] Its unemployment rate was 1.7 times the Union average in 1986.

[471] It has now fallen to around 75% of the Union average.

[472] *EEC Regional Development Policy*, House of Lords Select Committee on the European Communities, HL(1991–2), 20, 19.

[473] These three 'are not areas of lagging development in the traditional sense but regions where the decline from relative prosperity based on industrial activity has been particularly acute. East Berlin and the new *Länder* . . . also represent a new type of problem—one of transition from a centrally planned to a market economy', *Fifth Periodic Report on the Situation and Socio-Economic Development of the Regions of the Community*, COM(94)322, 130.

On the other hand, it might be argued that the operation of Article 92(3)(a) and (c) is too dominated by concerns related to market unification to be ideally adapted to the needs of regional policy. These concerns entail that their operation chiefly depends on the volume of investment aided, its sectoral distribution, the intensity of the aid, and the regional disadvantages for which the aid is supposed to compensate.[474] The conclusion is sometimes drawn that their operation has a disruptive effect on regional development efforts.[475]

In reality, Union practice regarding regional aid granted by Member States may not so much be harmful to regional development as ineffective to ensure that aid is directed towards regional development. Such practice may mean that aid patterns do not fully reflect the relative seriousness of regional problems within the Union as a whole. For example, during the period 1986–8 the average annual expenditure on regional aid in Germany,[476] Italy (Centre-North), France, and the United Kingdom was ECU 90 *per capita*. In Greece, Ireland, Portugal, and the less favoured regions of Spain the corresponding figure was ECU 16. In 1991 annual German regional aid was ECU 4.5 billion, whereas it was only ECU 105 million in Spain and ECU 120 million in Ireland and Portugal.[477] According to the *Fourth Survey on State Aids in the European Community in the Manufacturing and Certain Other Sectors*,[478] the relative importance of industrial support in the more central Member States is rising. Such aid patterns work more to the advantage of the wealthiest countries.[479]

More particularly, because of their lack of resources aid intensities in the less developed Member States tend to be 20–25 per cent—little higher than those authorized in the central regions.[480] Thus aid in the former is unlikely to compensate for regional handicaps as effectively as aid in the latter, and so investment is likely to be attracted to the latter.[481] This possibility may be exaggerated to the extent that areas within which Member States are authorized to grant aid are extended to cover those in which ERDF aid is available.

Besides, regional aid may constitute only a small part of total state aid. The

---

[474] *Fifteenth Report on Competition Policy* (EC Commission, Brussels, 1986), 185.

[475] *Report of the Committee on Regional Policy and Regional Planning on A Concerted Regional Planning Policy*, EP Doc. A3–245/90, 4. See, earlier, the call in the European Parliamentary Resolution of 15 Dec. 1983 ([1984] OJ C10/110) on the seventh annual report on the ERDF, para. 30, for a study of the 'regional dimension' of competition policy.

[476] See, regarding Commission objections to the amount of regional aid granted in Germany, T. W. Eser, 'Die Kontrolle regionaler Beihilfen im Rahmen der Wettbewerbspolitik der Europäischen Gemeinschaften' [1989] *Raumforschung und Raumordnung* 202–16.

[477] *Europe Doc.* 1651 (9 Feb. 1991).

[478] COM(95)365, 13.

[479] A. Marques, 'Community Competition Policy and Economic and Social Cohesion' [1992] *Regional Studies* 404–7, 405–6.

[480] A. Petersen, 'State Aid and European Union: State Aid in the Light of Trade, Competition, Industrial and Cohesion Policies' in I. Harden (ed.), *State Aid: Community Law and Policy* (Bundesanzeiger, Trier, 1993), 20–5, 25.

[481] 'Fair Competition in the Internal Market: Community State Aid Policy' (1991) 48 *European Economy* 72.

bulk of state aid is devoted to sectoral and horizontal policies.[482] The position of the Commission may be that productive investment aid for large enterprises should be authorized only in assisted regions under Article 92(3)(a) or (c).[483] However, this position may be affected by requirements of sectoral and horizontal policy rules. As the Commission admits, such policies may lead to the grant of aid which tends 'to maintain and even reinforce the existing pattern of inequalities in the Community'.[484] This tendency is recognized to be 'at variance with the objective of cohesion'.[485]

[482] *Second Survey on State Aids in the European Community in the Manufacturing and Certain Other Sectors* (EC Commission, Luxembourg, 1990).

[483] Notice C24/95 (ex N682/93) ([1995] OJ C294/13) concerning Saarland's scheme of state guarantees.

[484] *Fourth Periodic Report on the Social and Economic Situation and the Development of the Regions of the Community*, COM(90)609, 71. See, similarly, the ESC Opinion of 22 Nov. 1995 ([1996] OJ C39/1) on an industrial competitiveness policy for the EU, para. 3.3.5.12–3.

[485] *Fourth Survey on State Aids in the European Community in the Manufacturing and Certain Other Sectors*, COM(95)365, 46.

5

Sectoral Aid

5.1 INTRODUCTION

Article 92(3)(c) provides that aid to facilitate the development of certain economic activities, that is, sectoral aid, may be authorized, provided that trading conditions are not adversely affected to an extent contrary to the common interest. The general approach of the Commission towards such aid was formulated in a Communication of 1978.[1] According to this Communication, Article 3(f) of the Treaty embodied the principle that competition in the common market should not be distorted. Application of the principle was justified because the customs union would founder if Member States could unilaterally circumvent its requirements by granting aid; the common market would make little sense, unless undertakings tackled the market on the strength of their own resources without any aid to distort competition between them; and a system which left the field open to competition provided for optimum distribution of production factors and ensured the most rapid economic progress.

However, market conditions might:

—obstruct progress towards certain economic and social objectives;
—permit these objectives to be achieved only within unacceptable time-limits or with unacceptable social repercussions;
—or intensify competition to such an extent that it risked destroying itself.

Hence, aid would be authorized when it was needed to correct serious regional imbalances, to encourage or speed up necessary changes or developments in certain sectors to facilitate for social reasons a smooth adjustment of certain sectors[2] or to neutralize, at least temporarily, distortions of competition

---

[1] *Commission Policy on Sectoral Aid Schemes*, COM(78)221. This Communic. followed a declaration of the European Council at Copenhagen of 7 and 8 Apr. 1978, which emphasized the need to overcome problems of structural overcapacity and to promote an industrial structure which could face up to worldwide competition (para. 6 of the conclusions of the Presidency (Bull. EC 4–1978, 1.2.2)). Cf., earlier, the *First Report on Competition Policy* (EC Commission, Brussels, 1972), 130, and *Industrial Policy in the European Community* (EC Commission, Brussels, 1970). According to the latter (at 266), aid might be justified to assist industry to overcome preliminary handicaps or external competition; to promote rationalization and the effective use of the factors of production by undertakings; and to neutralize distortions of competition due to actions of third states likely to cause difficulties to Union industries.

[2] Adam Smith recognized that 'humanity' might require gradual 'restoration' of free trade (*An Inquiry into the Nature and Causes of the Wealth of Nations*, iv. ii. 40).

due to action outside the Union.[3] Such authorization could extend to rescue aid or even controlled operating aid for a strictly limited period.[4] The level of aid which might be authorized had to be sufficient to attain the objective pursued and thereby to contribute to development of the particular sector in the Union as a whole. At the same time, the aid had to remain strictly limited to what was necessary, so that it did not affect trading conditions to an extent contrary to the common interest.[5]

Treatment of the aid concerned might be complicated by cumulation problems. For example, if regional aid were authorized, sectoral aid to the same investment might be prohibited.[6] Conversely, once a sectoral aid scheme had been authorized by the Commission and put into operation, enterprises in that sector might be ineligible for any other specific, regional, or general aid.[7]

The 1971 Principles for the Co-ordination of Regional Aid[8] had simply stated: 'the double cumulation of aids, i.e., applying simultaneously to a sectorial or regional problem regional aids and sectorial aids which overlap is prohibited'.[9] However, a modified approach was adopted in the 1979 Principles.[10] According to paragraph 12 thereof, 'when an investment benefits both from regional aids and from other types of aid on a regionally differentiated basis, the regional aid may be given only in so far as when the regional aid and the regional component of the other types of aid are cumulated, the ceilings [for regional aid] are not exceeded'. Cumulation questions would be examined with experts from the Member States.

This examination led to the Commission Communication of 1985 on the Cumulation of Aids for Different Purposes.[11] Paragraph I of this Communication introduced the requirement that 'significant' cases of cumulation[12] should be notified to the Commission and provides in Paragraph II that Member States must remain within the ceiling for each individual scheme.[13] Paragraph

---

[3] COM(78)221, 2.   [4] *Ibid.*, 5.

[5] See also Notice C47/91 (ex NN3/91) ([1992] OJ C1/5) concerning aid which Portugal had granted to the CNP and EPSI, public enterprises operating in the chemical industry. Account may be taken of the importance of the aid recipient for the national and regional economy.

[6] Dec. 81/797 ([1981] OJ L296/41) on a proposal by the Netherlands Government to grant aid for the creation of new production capacity by an undertaking in the chemical industry (magnesium oxide).

[7] Dec. 84/111 ([1984] OJ L62/18) on the proposal of the Belgian Government to grant aid to a synthetic fibre producer.

[8] [1971] JO C111/1.   [9] *Ibid.*, para. 6.

[10] [1979] OJ C31/9.   [11] [1985] OJ C3/2.

[12] Advance notification is required of the application of more than one aid scheme to a given investment project, where the investment exceeds ECU 12 million or where the cumulative intensity exceeds 25% net grant equivalent. Notification is unnecessary where the investment does not exceed ECU 3 million, the cumulative intensity does not exceed 10%, or where the investment is below the ceiling for any one of the aid schemes involved. The exemption from notification may, however, be withdrawn by the Commission where evidence of distortion of competition is found.

[13] In the case of Denmark and France, the Commission requested confirmation that cumulation would not lead to the ceiling for regional aid being exceeded (*Seventh Report on Competition*

IV lists the main types of aid schemes affected. They are: general aids, regional aids, sectoral aids, aids to small and medium-sized enterprises, research and development aid, and aid for energy conservation and environmental protection. Where investment is supported by aid for staff training directly linked with the investment, the latter aid is also taken into account. Where notification is made, the Commission is to be informed of all other aids, including rescue aid, job-creation aid, and aid for marketing, though these aids do not count towards the notification thresholds. To reach a decision on regional aid when combined with other types of aid, the Commission will take into account the overall situation of the region concerned, the intensity of the cumulative aid, and the effect on competition and upbidding of levels of aid.[14]

More particularly, treatment of sectoral aid may be affected by rules deriving from a common policy, such as that for coal,[15] steel,[16] agriculture, fisheries, or transport, for which the Treaties provide a specific legal basis. Here the acceptability of aid may be determined by the requirements of the common policy concerned.[17] Thus, in the *First Report on Competition Policy*[18] the Commission stated that 'quite important Commission positions on [aid to] agriculture or transport could not be separated from the context of the common policies specific to these sectors and within which the purpose aimed at could be more clearly understood'.[19] Indeed, the common agricultural policy entails the establishment of rules governing the distribution of Union aid to agriculture, and these rules are applied by analogy to the grant of state aid in this sector.[20] Thus, for example, the Commission had to raise the level of agricultural aid authorized in Sicily following adoption of Regulation 355/77[21] on common measures to improve the conditions under which agricultural products are

Policy (EC Commission, Brussels, 1978), 130 and 133) and obtained an assurance from the UK that amendments to its regional aid system would not have such an effect (*ibid.* 138). See, more particularly, Communic. C22/91 (NN7/89) ([1991] OJ C189/3) concerning tax aid for investment in the Basque country. Art. 93(2) procedures were initiated against France and Greece, because the Commission considered them not to have accepted the Communic. See Notice regarding cumulation of aids for different purposes in France and Greece ([1987] OJ C300/4).

[14] *Fourteenth Report on Competition Policy* (EC Commission, Brussels, 1985), 126.

[15] Note the concern that state aid should not jeopardize Union efforts under initiatives such as Resider II in the Resolution of the European Parliament of 3 May 1994 ([1994] OJ C205/108) on the draft notice to the Member States laying down guidelines for operational programmes or global grants which they are invited to establish in the framework of a Community initiative concerning the economic conversion of steel areas (Resider II), para. 2.

[16] Special rules for aid to this sector are envisaged even after expiry of the ECSC Treaty. See the Reply by Mr Santer to Written Question E-27295 ([1996] OJ C66/26) by Christoph Konrad.

[17] See, regarding aid to agriculture, the *Twenty-Third Report on Competition Policy* (EC Commission, Brussels, 1994), 316.

[18] N. 1 above.

[19] *Ibid.*, 132. See also the *Second Survey on State Aids in the European Community in the Manufacturing and Certain Other Sectors* (EC Commission, Brussels, 1990), 17.

[20] See, e.g., Notice C6/93 (610/92) ([1993] OJ C179/3) concerning aid which Germany had decided to grant to the modernization of a grain mill in Dresden. See, earlier, E. Wautrequin, 'Competition Policy in Agriculture' (1987) 221 *Green Europe* 1.

[21] [1977] OJ L51/1.

processed and marketed.[22] In the case of fishing, 'state aid may be granted only if it is consistent with the objectives of the common policy'.[23] In relation to transport, a decisive question may be whether aid is justified by reference to the 'public service' obligations which the transport policy allows Member States to impose on transporters.[24]

However, it is not only in relation to sectors for which the Treaties envisage a common policy that the use of aid may attract special Union interest. In its aid control practice the Commission may take account of the specific features of each sector.[25] According to paragraph 11 of the 1979 Co-ordination Principles for Regional Aid,[26] the Commission would examine to what extent appropriate restrictions should be applied to regional aid when such restrictions were justified by the situation in the sector concerned.

Hence, aid to 'sensitive sectors' such as the motor industry may attract special interest, because the high degree of competitive pressure[27] and high capital intensity and importance for the Union economy of the industry,[28] may be perceived as rendering aid more disruptive of competition. Deregulation and market integration may, as in the case of air transport, be perceived as having the same effect.[29] The rationale is that liberalization greatly increases the scope for competition.[30] 'Unless state aid rules are adequately applied, any increase in competition between airlines could result in the financing of such

[22] Dec. 87/302 ([1987] OJ L152/25) amending Decs 84/557, 84/562, 84/563, and 85/11 relating to laws of the region of Sicily concerning national aids in the agricultural sector regarded as incompatible with the common market.

[23] Guidelines for the examination of state aid to fisheries and aquaculture ([1994] OJ C260/3), para. 1.3.

[24] Art. 77 EC.

[25] H. Morch, 'Summary of the Most Important Recent Developments' (1995) 5 *Competition Policy Newsletter* 43–9, 48.

[26] [1979] OJ C31/9.

[27] i.e. the sensitivity of a sector may justify a special aid framework. See Communic. E4/89 ([1989] OJ C281/6) concerning the refusal of the German Government to apply the Community framework on state aid to the motor vehicle industry.

[28] Notice ([1988] OJ C39/3) regarding the proposal of the French Government to repay FF 1200 million in debts that Renault has outstanding with Crédit National; Dec. 90/381 ([1990] OJ L188/55) amending German aid schemes for the motor vehicles industry; and Notice C44/95 (E16/95) ([1995] OJ C304/14) regarding the refusal of the Spanish authorities of the Commission's proposal for reintroduction of the EC framework on state aid to the motor vehicle sector. Cf., regarding the 'growing sensitivity' of this sector, the *Seventeenth Report on Competition Policy* (EC Commission, Brussels, 1988), 145–6 and the *Eighteenth Report on Competition Policy* (EC Commission, Brussels, 1989), 165–6. See also, regarding the significance of completion of the internal market for this sector, Communic. N497/88 ([1989] OJ C281/3) concerning the proposal of the Dutch Government to revise the aid arrangements in favour of Volvo Car BV.

[29] See, regarding electricity, the Explanatory Memorandum to the Commission Proposal of 21 Feb. 1992 for a Council Dir. concerning common rules for the internal market in electricity, COM(91)548, 11.

[30] Dec. 95/466 ([1995] OJ L267/49) concerning aid granted by the Flemish region to the Belgian airline Vlaamse Luchttransportmaatschappij NV. Such thinking echoes that in Dec. 64/651 ([1964] JO 3257) concerning the prohibition of Belgian aid granted to Ford Tractors (Belgium) Ltd., in Anvers.

competition out of state aid; in short, a subsidy race'.[31] In other words, a strict policy of control of state aid is necessary to avoid any effects which would be contrary to the common interest.[32]

The Union may also take a special interest in a sector because it is in crisis. 'Crisis sectors' usually concern labour-intensive products, with low intensity of research and development, such as textiles and shipbuilding, characterized by growing import penetration by the developing countries. In such sectors it is argued that international trade is close to the Hecksher-Ohlin paradigm of comparative advantage based on different factor endowments.[33] The need for a strict aid policy may be implied.

According to the 1978 Communication,[34] aid should not exacerbate existing problems in crisis sectors[35] or transfer them from one Member State to another.[36] In such sectors overcapacity and the resulting narrowness of profit margins entailed an increased risk that aid would distort competition[37] and lead to an aid war.[38] Hence, aid should not be given where its sole effect would be to maintain the *status quo*. In particular, operating aid was inadmissible, unless it was conditional on restructuring and limited in time. Moreover, rescue aid, so as not to frustrate any necessary capacity reductions, had to be limited to cases where it was required to cope with acute social problems. Finally, investment·aid must not lead to capacity increases.[39] Where a point of extreme overcapacity had been reached in a particular sector, even regional aid which would lead to capacity-increasing investments was prohibited.[40]

At the same time, aid to 'growth' sectors may attract special Union interest, because the sectors concerned are those where Union undertakings are failing to develop so as to exploit the market opportunities available.[41] Such failure may, it is thought, result from the fact that costs at the stage of innovation and

---

[31] *Civil Aviation Memorandum No 2: Progress Towards the Development of a Community Air Transport Policy*, COM(84)72, 36.

[32] Communic. C15/94 (N122/94, NN22/94 & E3/93) ([1994] OJ C93/12) concerning the existing tax exemption and planned recapitalization of TAP. See also Communic. C41/93 (E4/93 & N640/93) ([1994] OJ C16/3) on fiscal aid given to German airlines in the form of a depreciation allowance.

[33] A. Jacquemin and A. Sapir, 'European Integration World Integration?' [1988] *Weltwirtschaftliches Archiv* 127–39 and 'La Perspective 1992 et l'après Uruguay Round' [1990] *Economie Prospective Internationale* 47–67.

[34] *Commission Policy on Sectoral Aid Schemes*, COM(78)221, 5.

[35] See, e.g., Dec. 89/373 ([1989] OJ L166/60) on aid decided by the Italian Government for investments in the public flat-glass industry (Veneziana Vetro).

[36] See, e.g., Dec. 88/283 ([1988] OJ L121/57) on French Government aid to Pechiney, a company producing mainly aluminium; and Dec. 91/555 ([1991] OJ L300/48) on aid to be granted by the Belgian Government in favour of Sabena.

[37] *Eleventh Report on Competition Policy* (EC Commission, Brussels, 1982), 126–7.

[38] *Seventeenth Report on Competition Policy* (EC Commission, Brussels, 1988), 147.

[39] COM(78)221, 8.

[40] *Ibid*.

[41] *Ibid.*, 6–8. Favourable treatment of aid to the creation of SMEs and new enterprises was considered to be related.

development may be too great for many undertakings.[42] Some products have a high research and development content, large economies of scale, and learning curves. Examples are found in telecommunications, consumer electronics, and office equipment, where the steady loss of market shares by European producers is due to competition from the United States and Japan. Strategic trade theories may favour the grant of aid in such sectors.[43]

Accordingly, the Commission may adopt a favourable attitude towards aid for computer technology,[44] electronics,[45] aeronautics,[46] and even machine tools,[47] which may be characterized as sectors of 'strategic importance'.[48] The main concern of Commission practice is to avoid wasteful duplication of efforts by different Member States.[49] For example, Germany was required to keep the Commission informed of projects it intended to support, so as to enable the Commission to take steps to ensure adequate co-ordination of the efforts made by Member States in this field.[50]

However, such practice may be more a reflection of a generally favourable attitude towards aid for research and development, which is considered in Chapter 6,[51] than a response to sectoral conditions. Hence, where research and development are not involved, aid to, for example, the 'prosperous business orientated data processing sector' may be opposed because of its anti-

---

[42] *Eleventh Report on Competition Policy* (EC Commission, Brussels, 1981), 127.

[43] L. Tsoukalis, *The New European Economy: The Politics and Economics of European Integration* (Oxford University Press, Oxford, 1991), 266.

[44] See, e.g., the *Second Report on Competition Policy* (EC Commission, Brussels, 1973), 93–4 and the *Sixth Report on Competition Policy* (EC Commission, Brussels, 1977), 120–2. Cf. the Council Resolution of 15 July 1974 ([1974] OJ C86/1) on a Community policy on data processing.

[45] See, e.g., the *Fifth Report on Competition Policy* (EC Commission, Brussels, 1976), 85 and the *Eighth Report on Competition Policy* (EC Commission, Brussels, 1979), 145–6. A framework for such aid was once proposed by the Commission. See the Report of the Committee on Economic and Monetary Affairs on the second Commission report on competition policy, EP Doc. 264/73, 21.

[46] See, e.g., the *First Report on Competition Policy*, n. 1 above, 106–9; the *Second Report on Competition Policy* (EC Commission, Brussels, 1973), 138–9; and the *Eighth Report on Competition Policy* (EC Commission, Brussels, 1979), 152. See also the Council Resolution of 4 Mar. 1975 ([1975] OJ C59/1) on concerted action and consultation between the Member States on industrial policy in the aeronautical sector, para. II.

[47] Restructuring aid to this industry may be consistent with the communication on the machine tool industry (Bull. EC 2–1983, 2.1.26) and *Advanced Manufacturing Equipment in the Community* (Bull. EC, Supp. 6/85) and may, for this reason, be authorized. See Bull. EC 7/8–1986, 2.1.78.

[48] Dec. 92/328 ([1992] OJ L182/94) concerning aid granted by the French Government for the disposal of the assets of the MFL Group (Machines français lourdes), producer of heavy-duty machine tools.

[49] See, regarding aid to aircraft production, the *Fifth Report on Competition Policy* (EC Commission, Brussels, 1976), 82.

[50] *Sixth Report on Competition Policy* (EC Commission, Brussels, 1977), 122. Cf. in the case of shipbuilding, *Policy guidelines for Restructuring the Shipbuilding Industry*, COM(83)65, 23–4.

[51] Sect. 6.3.

competitive effects.[52] At the same time, aid may not be authorized to weak undertakings in a sector which is itself healthy.[53]

To the extent that sectoral conditions do determine whether or not aid is permissible, naturally developments in such conditions are capable of affecting this determination. For example, in 1973 the United Kingdom notified the Commission of a scheme to assist its off-shore supplies industry by making interest relief grants to purchasers of such supplies. The Commission did not then object to the scheme because it was designed to promote development of new technology in a field where there was little or no intra-Union trade. By 1976, however, sales on the United Kingdom market had increased so much that the Commission found the aid likely to distort competition. Moreover, the Union off-shore supplies industry had developed to such an extent that the aid could not be authorized under Article 92(3)(c).[54]

The effects of such practice on implementation of regional policy were contested in Decision 90/381,[55] which concerned German aid to the motor vehicles sector. The German Government argued that the Commission, in its structural funds policy,[56] acknowledged the independence of Member States with regard to regional and general aid schemes as long as they were not contrary to the common interest. Moreover, the German aid schemes were based on Article 92(3)(c),[57] and pursued generally acknowledged objectives (regional and environmental policy) which were not contrary to the common interest as defined, for example, in relation to the structural funds. In the view of the Government, therefore, the Commission was not justified in introducing new restrictions, in form and substance, to aid schemes which had existed unchallenged for years.

The Commission replied that it would maintain its *a priori* favourable attitude as regards regional aid and recognized the valuable contribution that the motor industry could make to regional development. However, given the

---

[52] Notice C64/94 (NN2/93) ([1995] OJ C113/17) regarding aid which Germany has decided to grant to Grundstücksverwaltungsgesellschaft Fort Malakoff Mainz mbH & Co. KG, a subsidiary of Siemens AG/Siemens Nixdorf Informationssysteme AG.

[53] Case 84/82 *Germany* v. *EC Commission: aid to textiles and clothing* [1984] ECR 1451, 1505.

[54] Dec. 79/496 ([1979] OJ L127/50) on the UK scheme of assistance in the form of interest-relief grants in favour of the offshore-supplies industry. See also Notice concerning a proposal by the French Government to grant aid to the steel companies Usinor/Sacilor for non-steel activities carried out by a number of its subsidiaries ([1988] OJ C297/7). Cf. Dec. 93/625 ([1993] OJ L300/15) concerning aid granted by the French Government to the Pari Mutuel Urbain and to the racecourse undertakings.

[55] Amending German aid schemes for the motor vehicle industry ([1990] OJ L188/55). See also Notice C44/95 (E16/95) ([1995] OJ C304/14) regarding the refusal of the Spanish authorities of the Commission's proposal for reintroduction of the EC framework on state aid to the motor vehicle sector.

[56] In particular, the use of the European Regional Development Fund.

[57] During negotiation of the Treaty Germany had approved the wording of Art. 92(3)(c) on the understanding that it permitted the *Länder* to pursue regional-development policies within their own competence, subject to the proviso therein. See S. Neri and H. Sperl, *Traité Instituant la Communauté Economique Européenne* (European Court of Justice, Luxembourg, 1960), 231.

importance of the sector, its growing sensitivity to competition, and the very significant trade flows, the Commission sought to ensure that aid would indeed have a significant and long-standing effect on regional development which would outweigh any possible adverse effects on the sector as a whole. It appears, therefore, that policy regarding particular sectors will continue to affect the acceptability of aid. In particular, regional aid will be treated as adversely affecting trading conditions to an extent contrary to the common interest, where it conflicts with such policy.[58]

5.2 AGRICULTURE

Articles 38 to 47 of the EC Treaty deal with agriculture. Article 38(1) defines agricultural products as 'the products of the soil, of stockfarming . . . and products of first-stage processing directly related to these products'. They are listed in Annex II to the Treaty. Article 38(4) requires the establishment of a common agricultural policy (CAP) for such products.

According to Article 39(1),[59] the objectives of the common agricultural policy are: to increase agricultural productivity by promoting technical progress and by ensuring the rational development of agricultural production and the optimum utilization of the factors of production, in particular labour; to ensure a fair standard of living for the agricultural community;[60] to stabilize markets; and to ensure that supplies reach consumers at reasonable prices. These objectives mean that differential treatment of competing products is in principle precluded, but preferential treatment of certain categories of producers who are in a less favourable position than others may, if objectively justified, be permitted.[61]

In the elaboration of this policy and the special methods for its application Article 39(2) provides that account shall be taken of the particular nature of agricultural activity, which results from the social structure of agriculture and from structural and natural disparities between the various agricultural regions; the need to effect the appropriate adjustment by degrees; and the fact that in the Member States agriculture constitutes a sector closely linked with the economy as a whole. Accordingly, Article 42 provides that competition rules

[58] See, e.g., Notice C42/93 (N624/93) ([1994] OJ C79/8) regarding the UK Government's proposal to award aid to Abingdon Carpets plc, Gwent.

[59] Italy had proposed adding reduction of structural unemployment to the objectives set out in Art. 39(1)(a), but during Treaty negotiations the Dutch position that such a reduction would be associated with increased productivity was accepted. See S. Neri and H. Sperl, n. 57 above, 114.

[60] Italy had proposed that the aim should be to increase agricultural incomes, while the Netherlands and Germany had originally proposed that this provision should only apply to farmers who were *'normalement productive'* (*ibid.* 115).

[61] Capotorti AG in Joined Cases 117/76 & 16/77 *Ruckdeschel* v. *Hauptzollamt Hamburg-St Annen* [1977] ECR 1753, 1783.

only apply to production of, and trade in, agricultural products to the extent determined by the Council within the framework of Article 43(2) and (3) (which concerns establishment of common organizations of agricultural markets), account being taken of the objectives set out in Article 39. The Council may, in particular, authorize the grant of aid:

(a) for the protection of enterprises handicapped by structural or natural conditions;[62]

(b) within the framework of economic development programmes.[63]

Thus the primacy of the common agricultural policy over competition rules is established,[64] and harmonization, rather than elimination, of aid to agriculture is envisaged.[65] However, many factors affect the competitive position of farmers. The climate, soil types, rainfall, and proximity to population centres can be an advantage or disadvantage to particular farms or regions. Farmers may also be affected by economic conditions, as the price of labour, land, or other inputs into the farming process may differ on a regional basis.[66] According to the Commission, such differences cannot be considered a distortion of competition.[67] Indeed, they are the means of fuelling the competitive process and give rise to the benefits that society gains from specialization and trade.[68] The common agricultural policy is designed to secure the necessary adjustments and rationalization in order to overcome any competitive disadvantages.[69] Hence, aid cannot be authorized simply to compensate for such disadvantages, and its use has to be controlled.

Regulation 26/62[70] provided only a limited basis for such control. According to Article 4 of the Regulation, Article 93(1) and the first sentence of Article 93(3) of the Treaty were applicable to products listed in Annex II to the

[62] This para. was originally proposed by the Netherlands. See S. Neri and H. Sperl, n. 57 above, 127–8.

[63] This para. was originally proposed by France (*ibid.*).

[64] Case C–280/93 *Germany* v. *EC Council: bananas* [1994] ECR I–4793, I–5061; Case 139/79 *Maizena* v. *EC Council* [1980] ECR 3393, 3421; Cosmas AG in Case C–122/94 *EC Commission* v. *EU Council: aid to wine producers* [1996] ECR I–881, I–886.

[65] Comité Intergouvernemental créé par la Conférence de Messine, *Rapport des Chefs de Délégation aux Ministres des Affaires Etrangères* (Secretariat of the Comité, Brussels, 1956), 44 ff. According to the Resolution of the Agriculture Conference of the Member States of 11 July 1958 ([1958] JO 281), para. III. 6, elimination of agricultural aid contrary to the spirit of the Treaty was essential.

[66] The Commission is reluctant to accept that aid to an undertaking operating in such unfavourable conditions can be treated as aid to a public service under Art. 90(2) EC. See Communic. C30/94 (ex NN107/93) ([1994] OJ C271/11) concerning aids which Italy (region of Sardinia) had decided to grant to slaughter companies.

[67] *Distortions of Competition in Hothouse Agriculture*, COM(80)306, 32.

[68] *State Aids to Agriculture*, House of Lords Select Committee on the European Community, HL(1981–2) 90, vi–vii.

[69] N. 67 above.

[70] Applying certain competition rules to production and trade in agricultural products ([1962] JO 993).

Treaty. Under Article 93(1) the Commission may only 'propose' measures regarding existing aid schemes, and the first sentence of Article 93(3) merely requires that the Commission be informed of new aid.[71] Hence, the Commission carried out general studies of aid to agriculture,[72] drew up the aid inventory envisaged in the Preamble to the Regulation,[73] and made recommendations regarding aid to agricultural processing.[74] The Member States were also invited to abolish certain agricultural aids, such as those for isoglucose,[75] fruit,[76] livestock,[77] and horticulture,[78] which were linked to quantities produced or marketed or to prices or units of production.[79]

It has been argued that after the end of the transitional period for establishment of the customs union Articles 92 to 93 have applied fully to all agricultural products,[80] but this argument is not supported by judgments of the Court of Justice[81] concerning Article 46 of the Treaty[82] or by Commission practice.[83] For example, aid for the purchase and storage of alcohol obtained by distillation of fruit and potatoes was, being an aid to the production and marketing of the

[71] See sects 7.5.1 and 7.5.2 below.

[72] Aid measures to agriculture, COM(63)243; Report and Inventory on Agricultural Aids, SEC(66)920; Criterion for the Establishment of a Common Policy on Agricultural Aids, COM(66)60. The last publication included a draft proposal to modify Reg. 26 and apply Arts. 92–94 EC fully to agriculture. Unpublished guidelines regarding particular types of aid were subsequently adopted. See *State Aids to Agriculture*, n. 68 above, 150–3.

[73] *Sixth EEC General Report* (EEC Commission, Brussels, 1963), 153. Aid inventories were also compiled during the 1970s. The Commission allowed the Agriculture Committee of the European Parliament access to the 1974 inventories on the understanding that the information would be treated as 'secret'. See *State Aids to Agriculture*, n. 68 above, xv–xvii.

[74] *Eighth EEC General Report* (EEC Commission, Brussels, 1965), 84.

[75] Letter of 29 Mar. 1977 prohibiting investment aid for isoglucose. See Commission Reply by Mr Gundelach to Written Question 1110/80 by Mr Kirk ([1980] OJ C345/4).

[76] Letter of 26 Sept. 1970 concerning the application of Art. 93(1) and (3) to certain aids to the fruit sector. See, more particularly, Dec. 72/251 ([1972] JO L163/19) on the grant of aid for the creation of a reserve fund to cover risks-damage caused by hail to producers of apples and pears in the Netherlands.

[77] Letter of 19 Sept. 1975 proposing under Art. 93(1) harmonization of national aid for the stockfarming sector (unpublished).

[78] Letters of 25 June 1974 and 30 Apr. 1975 regarding aid to assist horticulture under glass and inshore fisheries to adjust to energy market developments.

[79] *Second EC General Report* (EC Commission, Brussels, 1968), 222.

[80] Capotorti AG in Case 91/78 *Hansen GmbH & Co.* v. *Hauptzollamt Flensburg* [1979] ECR 935, 964.

[81] Case 337/82 *St Nikolaus Brennerei und Likörfabriek, Gustav Kniepf-Milde GmbH* v. *Hauptzollamt Krefeld* [1984] ECR 1051; Case 181/85 *EC Commission* v. *France: compensatory taxes on imports of ethyl alcohol* [1987] ECR 689. See also Case 232/78 *EC Commission* v. *France: mutton and lamb* [1979] ECR 2729.

[82] Art. 46 provides that where in a Member State a product is subject to a national market organization or to internal rules having equivalent effect which affect the competitive position of similar production in another Member State, a countervailing charge shall be applied by Member States to imports of this product coming from the Member State where such an organization or rules exist, unless that Member State applies a countervailing charge on exports.

[83] The Commission was 'actively considering the options open to it to regularize the position in this area, particularly in the run-up to 1992'. See the *Twentieth Report on Competition Policy* (EC Commission, Brussels, 1991), 195.

alcohol in question, 'in theory' an operating aid incompatible with the common market.[84] However, in the absence of a common organization of the market in ethyl alcohol obtained from agricultural products, the Commission raised no objection to the aid under Articles 92 to 93. Instead, the Commission reserved the right to review the position when the common organization came into force.[85]

True, 'where the conditions for the grant of aid contain restrictions either on the raw material from which such a product is obtained or on the outlets for the product, the Commission takes the view that the impact of the aid can no longer be considered to be limited to the product for which the aid is granted'.[86] However, this view seeks to protect common organizations against the consequences of the absence of a common organization for interdependent markets rather than fully to subject the latter to aid control.

Hence, Commission policy regarding agricultural aid is essentially dependent on the establishment of common organizations. For example, in 1968 the Commission indicated that it was examining levy systems operating in conjunction with the grant of aid in the various Member States. In the case of agricultural products, the particular provisions of common organizations, which amounted to derogations from Articles 92 to 94, rendered a case-by-case examination necessary.[87]

In the basic regulations establishing such organizations provision is usually made for the full application of Articles 92 to 94 to the production of, and trade in, the products concerned, 'save as otherwise provided'. Thus the compatibility of state aid for such products is to be assessed in the light of the applicable regulation.[88] It is also lawful in regulations establishing common organizations for the Council to prohibit, partly or completely, certain forms of aid to the product concerned.[89]

In other words, in the case of products covered by a common organization,[90] the application of Article 92 is subordinate to the rules of the common

---

[84] See, similarly, regarding aid liable to increase alcohol production capacity, Dec. 91/474 ([1991] OJ L254/14) concerning aids granted by the Italian Government to Italgrani SpA for the setting up of an agri–foodstuffs complex in the Mezzogiorno.

[85] Notice C25/92 (N99/92) ([1992] OJ C283/6) on the AIMA programme for 1992 under which Italy planned to grant aid for the private short-term storage of table-wine and grape must.

[86] Communic. C51/94 (NN/A/92, NN/B/92, NN51/94, E18/94) ([1995] OJ C143/8) concerning aid which France had decided to grant in the biofuels sector.

[87] Reply to Written Question 227 ([1968] JO C20/2) by Mr Deringer.

[88] Case 114/83 *Stc Initiatives et Co-opération Agricole* v. *EC Commission* [1984] ECR 2589.

[89] Case 72/79 *EC Commission* v. *Italy: storage costs for sugar* [1980] ECR 1411.

[90] Products not so covered are essentially alcohol and apples. The establishment of a common organization for potatoes was proposed in 1992. See the Proposal of 25 Nov. 1992 ([1992] OJ C333/19) for a reg. on the common organization of the market in potatoes. Art. 8 provides that Arts. 92–94 of the Treaty are applicable. Pending adoption of the proposal, the Commission may only act under Art. 93(1) of the Treaty. See, e.g., Commission recommendation pursuant to Art. 93(1) and the first sentence of Art. 93(3) EC ([1994] OJ C30/10) and Commission recommendation pursuant to the first sentence of Art. 93(3) EC ([1994] OJ C42/17).

organization.[91] Express provision to this effect has been made, for example, in the case of pigmeat,[92] pork,[93] poultry meat,[94] milk and milk products[95], seeds,[96] cereals,[97] fruit and vegetables,[98] bananas,[99] processed fruit and vegetables,[100] and wine.[101]

Particularly when the organization is based on a common price system, Member States may be prohibited from unilaterally granting aid, such as aid relating to farm incomes,[102] because it would interfere with the mechanism of price formation entailed by the organization.[103] Market support is supposed to be regulated exclusively by Union law and financed exclusively from the Guarantee Section of the European Agricultural Guidance and Guarantee Fund. Hence, state aid may be prohibited, even if it supports the common agricultural policy[104] or the common organization in question does not provide any aid for the product concerned,[105] as being contrary to the equality

[91] Case 177/78 *Pigs and Bacon Commission* v. *McCarren and Company Ltd* [1979] ECR 2161, 2186–7. See also Rozès AG in Case 222/82 *Apple and Pear Development Council* v. *K. J. Lewis Ltd* [1983] ECR 4083, 4133.

[92] Art. 21 of Reg. 2759/75 ([1975] OJ L282/1) on the common organization of the market in pigmeat. This provision was cited in Communic. C8/94 (ex NN31/93) ([1994] OJ C107/2) concerning aids which France had decided to grant in the pigmeat sector.

[93] Art. 31 of Reg. 1035/72 ([1972] JO L118/1) on the common organization of the market in pigmeat.

[94] Art. 19 of Reg. 2777/75 ([1975] OJ L282/77) on the common organization of the market in poultry meat.

[95] Art. 24 of Reg. 805/68 ([1968] JO L148/24) on the common organization of the market in milk and milk products.

[96] Art. 23 of Reg. 804/68 ([1968] JO L148/13) on the common organization of the market in seeds.

[97] Art. 44 of Reg. 1785/81 ([1981] OJ L177/4) on the common organization of the market in cereals, and Art. 19 of Reg. 1766/92 ([1992] OJ L181/21) on the common organization in cereals.

[98] Art. 8 of Reg. 2358/71 ([1971] JO L246/1) on the common organization of the market in fruit and vegetables.

[99] Art. 24 of Reg. 404/93 ([1993] OJ L47/1) on the common organization in bananas.

[100] Art. 19 of Reg. 426/86 ([1986] OJ L49/1) on the common organization of the market in products processed from fruit and vegetables.

[101] Art. 76 of Reg. 822/87 ([1987] OJ L84/1) on the common organization of the market in wine.

[102] See, e.g., regarding aid to olive oil production, Communic. C7/92 (N713/91) ([1992] OJ C164/2) regarding aid which Italy had decided to grant to olive oil producers' organizations and their associations.

[103] Case 169/82 *EC Commission* v. *Italy: agricultural aid for Sicily* [1984] ECR 1603, 1617; Case C–281/87 *EC Commission* v. *Greece: national intervention scheme for inferior-quality durum wheat* [1989] ECR I–4015, I–4032; Case C–35/88 *EC Commission* v. *Greece: market in feed grain* [1990] ECR I–3125, I–3157; and Dec. 82/743 ([1982] OJ L315/21) on the aids provided for in Campania to help producers of plums. A distinction may be made between aid applying to production and wholesale trade and aid applying to subsequent stages of distribution. See Joined Cases 16–20/79 *Openbaar Ministerie* v. *Joseph Danis* [1979] ECR 3327, 3340.

[104] Case C–86/89 *Italy* v. *EC Commission: aid for the use of concentrated wine must* [1990] ECR I–3891, I–3910.

[105] Dec. 93/154 ([1993] OJ L61/52) concerning an AIMA national programme on aid which Italy planned to grant for the private storage of carrots.

principle.[106] Such aid is objectionable, because it would compromise the equality of treatment of traders throughout the Union and thus distort competition between Member States.[107] For example, Italian aid for carrots[108] and nuts[109] was objectionable because of the common organization for fruit and vegetables[110] and the rules concerning specific measures for nuts;[111] Italian aid for table wine and grape must[112] was objectionable because of Regulation 822/87[113] on the common organization of the market in wine; and French aid for the sheepmeat and goatmeat sectors was prohibited[114] because of the common organization of the market in these sectors.[115] However, aid may exceptionally be authorized by the Council under Article 93(2).[116]

According to the *Sixteenth Report on Competition Policy*,[117] the main objectives of the aid control policy of the Commission:

—to underpin the effective operation of the market organizations by preventing the payment of national aids supplementing or differing from those provided for under the relevant market organization;[118]

—to support the policy on farm structures pursued by the Union, by authorizing aids which contributed to implementation of this policy;

—to step up modernization of processing and marketing facilities in close relation with the requirements of the policy on markets and prices, while facilitating the development of this sector in regions where there were deficits and to reduce and rationalize the capacity for production of surplus products; and

—to avoid hampering the national policies supporting schemes for the

---

[106] Case 11/76 *Netherlands* v. *EC Commission: EAGGF export refunds* [1979] ECR 245, 279.

[107] Joined Cases 15 & 16/76 *France* v. *EC Commission: EAGGF* [1979] ECR 321, 340.

[108] Dec. 93/154 ([1993] OJ L61/52) concerning an AIMA national programme on aid which Italy planned to grant for the private storage of carrots.

[109] Notice C26/92 (755/91) ([1992] OJ C288/7) concerning projected Italian aid for nuts.

[110] Reg. 1035/72 ([1972] JO L118/1) on the common organization of the market in fruit and vegetables.

[111] Reg. 789/89 ([1989] OJ L85/3) instituting specific measures for nuts and locust beans.

[112] Notice C25/92 (N99/92) ([1992] OJ C283/6) on the AIMA programme for 1992 under which Italy planned to grant aid for the private short-term storage of table wine and grape must. See also, regarding aid for the preventive distillation of wine, Communic. C40/93 (655/93) ([1994] OJ C19/3) concerning aids which France had decided to grant to rationalize the market in table wines.

[113] [1987] OJ L84/1.

[114] Dec. 82/261 ([1982] OJ L113/22) concerning aid granted by the French Government in the sheepmeat and goatmeat sectors.

[115] At the time Reg. 1837/80 ([1980] OJ L183/1) on the common organization of the market in sheepmeat and goatmeat.

[116] Case 122/94 *EC Commission* v. *EU Council: aid to wine producers* [1996] ECR I–881.

[117] (EC Commission, Brussels, 1987), 190–1.

[118] 'Because of the common financial responsibility that the Member States have assumed for CAP-supported products, a state-aid induced expansion of production in one Member State will lead to increased budgetary burdens in other Member States'. See *State Aids to Agriculture*, n. 68 above, viii. According to the Report on the Mandate of 30 May 1980, COM(81)300, 13, stricter aid disciplines were necessary to prevent Union policies from being undermined.

improvement of the quality of products, technical progress,[119] and the conservation of the environment and the rescue of farms which faced short-term difficulties.

Hence, generally aid should help to:

—bring about a steady reduction in the output of certain surplus products and curb the cost to the taxpayer;
—encourage a switch to alternative forms of production and an improvement in quality, while taking into account market requirements in the Union and consumer demand;
—preserve agriculture in areas where it was indispensable in terms of land development, social balance or the protection of the countryside;
—foster, among farmers, a greater awareness of environmental issues; and
—assist the development, within the Union, of agricultural processing plants and thereby give farmers 'a stake' in agricultural change.[120]

However, policy implementation in this sector may be more problematic than its formulation.[121] For example, in 1977 the Commission expressed the view that advantages in the form of specific tax exemptions for farmers constituted aid within the meaning of Articles 92 and 93. On the other hand, it was difficult to take appropriate measures under Article 93(1) in respect of such aid systems, which existed in most Member States, as their limits could not easily be determined.[122]

Such difficulties might be exacerbated by internal Commission organization. Any aid which directly affected products listed in Annex II to the Treaty would be examined by Directorate General VI (the Directorate General for Agriculture) even if the aid were being granted not on agricultural, but on regional-policy, criteria. Directorate General IV (the Directorate General for Competition) would merely be consulted. Aid which did not directly affect products listed in Annex II to the Treaty, even if granted to the food industries, would be dealt with by Directorate General IV. However, it was said that, rather than taking an independent line in relation to such aid, Directorate General IV was

---

[119] See, e.g., Notice C60/94 (NN29/93) ([1995] OJ C278/4) concerning an aid scheme applied in Greece to cotton by the Greek Cotton Board.
[120] *Seventeenth Report on Competition Policy* (EC Commission, Brussels, 1988), 187–8. See also the framework for national aids for agricultural products and certain products not listed in Annex II ([1987] OJ C302/6).
[121] Practical difficulties arising in Commission efforts to control aid to agriculture were indicated in its Reply to Written Question 1110/80 ([1980] OJ C345/4) by Mr Kirk. A Working Party on Conditions of Competition in Agriculture, consisting of representatives of the Governments of Member States and chaired by the Commission, met only twice between Nov. 1977 and July 1981. See *State Aids to Agriculture*, n. 68 above, xix.
[122] Reply to Written Question 755/77 ([1978] OJ C150/3) by Mr Pisoni. The Commission later claimed to be acting more vigorously. See the Reply to Written Question 2356/82 ([1983] OJ C231/1) by Mr James Provan, though practical difficulties continued to be stressed. See, e.g., *The Agricultural Situation in the Community 1985* (EC Commission, Brussels, 1986), 158–9.

'tending to dance to the tune of Directorate General VI'.[123] While questions are begged why Directorate General IV should exhibit such a tendency, the result was emphasis on harmonization rather than elimination of aids.[124]

The reason may, at least partly, lie in the legislative background. The existence of the special procedure laid down in Article 93 for appraising the compatibility of aid systems with the common market cannot affect the necessity for Member States to observe the rules laid down in regulations establishing the common organization of the relevant market.[125] Proceedings for failure to observe such rules are to be taken under Article 169.[126]

According to the Commission and the Court of Justice,[127] infringement of the rules of such an organization makes it impossible to grant an authorization under Article 92(2) or (3),[128] even in critical market situations.[129] Thus an aid scheme which is permissible in relation to other products may be prohibited in relation to a product covered by a common organization.[130] In particular, aid may be found to be contrary to the common interest within the meaning of Article 92(3)(c) on the ground that it is contrary to the common organization for the relevant products.[131] Likewise, aid cannot be regarded as promoting a project of common European interest under Article 92(3)(b), if it is contrary to the rules of the common organization concerned.[132] The very fact that the aid may lead to an increase in EAGGF expenditure may mean that it is contrary to the common interest for the purposes of Article 92(3).[133] The essential consequence is that aid authorization by the Commission depends on the applica-

---

[123] *State Aids to Agriculture*, n. 68 above, xviii–xix.

[124] See, e.g., *The Agricultural Situation in the Community 1980* (EC Commission, Brussels, 1980), 81.

[125] Case 72/79 *EC Commission* v. *Italy: storage costs for sugar* [1980] ECR 1411, 1425–6.

[126] *Ibid.* and Case C–35/88 *EC Commission* v. *Greece: market in grain* [1990] ECR I–3125, I–3154. Where the Art. 93 procedure is employed, aid may be condemned as violating Art. 92 rather than the principle of *exhaustivité* of market organizations. See Case C–86/89 *Italy* v. *EC Commission: aid for the use of concentrated wine must* [1990] ECR I–3891, I–3910.

[127] Case 177/78 *Pigs and Bacon Commission* v. *McCarren* [1979] ECR 2161, 2191; and Case 72/79 *EC Commission* v. *Italy: storage costs for sugar* [1980] ECR 1411, 1425.

[128] Dec. 81/601 ([1981] OJ L220/39) on aid to maintain farm incomes in 1980 granted by the French Government. See also Dec. 89/217 ([1988] OJ L85/48) on a national aid scheme for beef in Italy.

[129] Dec. 93/255 ([1993] OJ L117/28) concerning aid which Italy had decided to grant through AIMA for the private storage of hazelnuts.

[130] See, in relation to mushrooms, the *Twenty-Third Report on Competition Policy* (EC Commission, Brussels, 1994), 317.

[131] Dec. 89/204 ([1989] OJ L76/48) on regional aid for mandarin growers in Sicily; Dec. 89/229 ([1989] OJ L94/43) on a national scheme to encourage the use of milk for feeding calves. See also Dec. 88/39 ([1988] OJ L23/18) concerning a state aid consisting of a reduction in the social charges imposed in respect of the employment of casual labour and of persons seeking employment in six agricultural sectors in France; and Dec. 89/660 ([1989] OJ L394/5) prohibiting the aid planned by the Italian Government for the storage and marketing of olive oil.

[132] Dec. 85/592 ([1985] OJ L373/1) concerning aids granted by the French Government in the beef and veal sector.

[133] Dec. 88/605 ([1988] OJ L334/22) on the draft Sicilian Law on the setting up of a regional fund to encourage exports.

tion of special rules to the general distinction between restructuring aid and operating aid.

In contrast, Council powers under Article 93(2) of the Treaty are, according to the Court of Justice, unaffected by the rules of a common organization.[134] Such powers may be exercised to tackle the 'conjunctural dysfunctioning' of a common organization, that is, problems which cannot be addressed by the common organization. Otherwise, there would be discrimination contrary to Article 42 of the Treaty.[135]

5.2.1 Restructuring Aid

Restructuring aid may be authorized, provided it does not prejudice the relevant common organization. For example, although aid for producer groups in the nuts sector was provided for in the common organization concerned, additional Italian aid was authorized, because it involved improved marketing arrangements and was thus of a structural character, and the provisions of the common organization were not exhaustive in relation to producer groups.[136] Moreover, aid for training, market development, product promotion, aid to reduce financial charges on previous investment loans in the course of repayment,[137] aid to assist farmers in joining co-operatives,[138] aid towards the financing of compensation, subsidies, and other benefits connected with combating animal diseases and improving animal hygiene and health,[139] and aid for low-interest loans may be authorized, at least in the case of small and medium-sized producers in the least-developed regions having to adapt to fluctuations in exchange rates.[140]

In addition to considering the relationship between restructuring aid and the common organization concerned, the Commission also assesses such aid in the light of rules concerning farm structures and the processing and marketing of agricultural products.[141] Such rules are regarded by the Commission as constituting 'an integration of the common organizations of the markets concerned'. Hence, aid in the field covered by such rules may be

---

[134] Case C–122/94 *EC Commission* v. *EU Council: aid to wine producers* [1996] ECR I–881.

[135] *Ibid.*, I–908.

[136] *Twenty-Second Report on Competition Policy* (EC Commission, Brussels, 1993), 503.

[137] However, aid for past investment projects may be objectionable. See Notice C44/94 (NN94/93) ([1994] OJ C347/5) concerning an aid scheme whereby France had granted assistance towards the cost of renovating vineyards in southern France.

[138] Communic. C34/94 (N124/94) ([1994] OJ C293/10) on aid which Spain had decided to grant to agricultural co-operatives.

[139] Dec. 91/538 ([1991] OJ L294/43) on the animal health and production fund in Belgium.

[140] Commission Reply by Mr Steichen to Written Question 3013/92 ([1993] OJ C145/12) by Lord O'Hagan.

[141] The Council Resolution of 25 May 1971 ([1971] JO C52/1) concerning the new orientation of the common agricultural policy envisaged harmonization of investment aids, para. VI.B. See, e.g., Art. 14 of Dir. 72/159 ([1972] JO L96/1) on the modernization of farms.

prohibited where it is incompatible with the 'exhaustive system' established thereby.[142]

Farm Structures

Rules governing aid for investment to improve farm structures are laid down by Regulation 2328/91.[143] Aid is limited to farms where the labour income per man-work unit is not more than 1.2 times the average gross wage of non-agricultural workers in the region concerned.[144] Aid not meeting the conditions laid down in this Regulation is either prohibited or subject to Article 92 of the Treaty.[145]

Particular restrictions apply to investment aid for the production of milk,[146] pork,[147] beef,[148] and eggs and poultry,[149] though aid for the protection of the environment is not affected by these restrictions. Where aid may be granted, ceilings of 35 per cent (45 per cent in Directive 75/268 areas[150]) in respect of investments in fixed assets and of 20 per cent (35 per cent in Directive 75/268 areas) in respect of other types of investment apply.[151] These ceilings do not apply to aid to encourage early retirement from farming[152] or to aid for vocational training of farmers, which is authorized up to 100 per cent of permissible expenditure.[153]

Processing and Marketing

To ensure that the processing and marketing of agricultural products develops in accordance with Union policies,[154] aid for the processing and marketing of agricultural products is not usually authorized in the case of investments

---

[142] Communic. C50/94 (ex NN85/93) ([1995] OJ C200/10) concerning aid which France had granted in the biofuels sector. See, more particularly, regarding aid incompatible with set-aside arrangements in Regs. 1765/92 and 2078/92, Communic. C25/95 (ex NN101/94) ([1995] OJ C294/17) concerning aids which Italy had granted for kenaf growing on land set aside under the Community set-aside scheme.

[143] On improving the efficiency of agricultural structures ([1991] OJ L218/1), Arts. 7 and 12, as amended by Reg. 3669/93 ([1993] OJ L398/26) and Reg. 2843/94 ([1994] OJ L302/1). See, earlier, Art. 8 of Reg. 797/85 ([1985] OJ L93/1) on improving the efficiency of agricultural structures.

[144] Art. 5 of Reg. 2328/91 ([1991] OJ L218/1).

[145] Communic. C35/95 (ex NN139/94) ([1995] OJ C294/19) concerning aid granted by Italy (Region of Sardinia) for organic farming.

[146] Art. 6(3) of Reg. 2328/91 ([1991] OJ L218/1).   [147] *Ibid.*, Art. 6(4).

[148] *Ibid.*, Art. 6(5).   [149] *Ibid.*, Art. 6(6).

[150] Sect. 5.2.2 below.

[151] Art. 7 of Reg. 2328/91 ([1991] OJ L218/1). In general, higher levels of aid are authorized. See Dec. 94/725 ([1994] OJ L289/26) on measures adopted by the French Government concerning pigmeat.

[152] Reg. 2079/92 ([1992] OJ L215/91) instituting a Community aid scheme for early retirement from farming.

[153] Dec. 94/172 ([1994] OJ L79/24) concerning Italian Law 102 providing for the reconstruction and regeneration of the Valtellina.

[154] Communic. C59/95 (ex NN79/95) ([1996] OJ C92/3) concerning aid which Italy had decided to grant to the Ostellato sugar refinery.

ineligible for Union financing[155] under Regulation 866/90.[156] Decision 94/173,[157] which replaced Decision 90/342,[158] lays down selection criteria for the grant of Union aid. Paragraph 2 of the annex to the new Decision, like paragraph 2 of the Annex to Decision 90/342 before it, excludes the grant of such aid for some or all kinds of investment in various sectors. These exclusions are applied by analogy to aid granted by Member States.

Although Decision 90/342 has been replaced by Decision 94/173, for 'reasons of legal certainty' the Commission continues to apply the sectoral restrictions set out in paragraph 2 of the Annex to Decision 90/342,[159] except when the new measure is more permissive of aid.[160]

If no exclusion applies, state aid may be authorized under Article 92(3)(c) of the Treaty.[161] Moreover, according to the Preamble to Decision 94/173, provision should be made for certain criteria specific to Objective 1 regions, that is, regions whose development is 'lagging behind',[162] and for the possibility of *ad hoc* derogations for the remotest regions to take account of the special conditions in these regions. Hence, whereas the Annex generally excludes the grant of Union aid to investments in the cereals and rice,[163] cow's milk and cow's milk products,[164] oil seeds,[165] sugar and isoglucose,[166] meat, and egg sectors,[167] the Annex also stipulates that some such aid may still be granted to these sectors in some or all Objective 1 regions. To the same extent, state aid may be authorized.

Aid was originally limited to 50 per cent for projects forming part of national programmes accepted by the Commission under Regulation 355/77[168] and

---

[155] *Twenty-Second Report on Competition Policy* (EC Commission, Brussels, 1993), 291.

[156] On improving the processing and marketing conditions for agricultural products ([1990] OJ L91/1).

[157] On the selection criteria to be adopted for investments for improving the processing and marketing conditions for agricultural and forestry products ([1994] OJ L79/29).

[158] [1990] OJ L163/71.

[159] Communic. regarding state aid for investments in the processing and marketing of agricultural products ([1994] OJ C189/5).

[160] Communic. regarding state aid for investments in the processing and marketing of agricultural products ([1995] OJ C71/6). See also Bull. EU 7/8–1995, 1.3.153.

[161] See, e.g., Communic. C35/95 (ex NN139/94) ([1995] OJ C294/19) concerning aid granted by Italy (Region of Sardinia) for organic farming. Cf., regarding aid to support a marketing programme for Italian grapes in third states, Notice ([1984] OJ C7/3) concerning Law 129/82 of the Italian Government.

[162] Art. 1.1 of Reg. 2052/88 ([1988] OJ L185/9) on the tasks of the structural funds and their effectiveness and on the co-ordination of their activities between themselves and with the operations of the EIB and the other existing financial instruments, as amended by Reg. 2081/93 ([1993] OJ L193/1).

[163] Para. 2.1 of the Annex to Dec. 90/342 ([1990] OJ L218/1).

[164] *Ibid.*, para. 2.3.

[165] *Ibid.*, para. 2.5.

[166] *Ibid.*, para. 2.7.

[167] *Ibid.*, para. 2.10.

[168] On common measures to improve the conditions under which agricultural products are processed and marketed ([1977] OJ L51/1), Art. 17(2). See also criteria for the choice of projects to be financed under Reg. 355/77 ([1983] OJ C152/2).

35 per cent in other cases.[169] However, when this Regulation was replaced by Regulation 866/90, new ceilings were established. They were 55 per cent (75 per cent in Objective 1 areas) for projects consistent with the objectives of Article 1 of Regulation 866/90 and sectoral programmes drawn up under this Regulation. In the case of other projects, the ceiling was 25 per cent (50 per cent in Objective 1 areas).[170]

Such practice has now been embodied in the Guidelines for state aid in connection with investments in the processing and marketing of agricultural products.[171] The Guidelines are designed to maintain the Commission practice of seeking to ensure consistency between the common agricultural policy and state-aid policy. In particular, the aim is to avoid encouraging investment where, for structural reasons, it is contrary to the common interest. If Decision 94/173 is subsequently amended or replaced so that the field currently covered by the second and third indents of paragraph 1.2 and paragraph 2 of the Annex to the Decision is affected, the amendment will also apply to these Guidelines.[172]

In principle, no state aid granted in connection with any of the investments referred to in the second and third indents of paragraph 1.2 of the Annex to Decision 94/173 or excluded unconditionally by paragraph 2 of the Annex may be considered compatible with the common market.[173] Moreover, the maximum permissible rates of aid which may be considered compatible are set out in the Annex to the Guidelines. They are 75 per cent for investments in Objective 1 regions and 55 per cent for investments outside such regions.

However, the Commission considers, on a case-by-case basis,[174] any aid measure which should be rejected under these Guidelines but which would in principle be eligible for Union part-financing under Regulation 2328/91.[175] Moreover, aid which complies with the terms of the Community guidelines on state aid for environmental protection is authorized, even if it is granted in respect of a product sector or activity where aid is otherwise restricted or excluded under the 1996 Guidelines. The maximum permissible rate of aid is 55 per cent (75 per cent in Objective 1 regions), except for investments on agricultural holdings, where the maximum rates are those specified in the environmental aid guidelines.[176] A similar approach is adopted in relation to aid for research and development.[177]

---

[169] Letter to Member States of 30 Oct. 1985, which was replaced by the 1996 guidelines (para. 3(e)). See, e.g., the Communic. concerning a Luxembourg draft law encouraging the development of agriculture ([1987] OJ C302/3).

[170] Dec. 94/725 ([1994] OJ L289/26) on measures adopted by the French Government concerning pigmeat; and Communic. C43/95 (ex NN73/94) ([1995] OJ C327/9) concerning aids which Italy had decided to grant to co-operatives and farms in difficulty.

[171] [1996] OJ C29/4.   [172] Para. 2 of the guidelines.

[173] *Ibid.*, para. 3(b).   [174] *Ibid.*, para. 3(d).

[175] On improving the efficiency of agricultural structures ([1991] OJ L218/1).

[176] Para. 4(a) of the 1996 guidelines and para. 3.2.3, n. 14, of the environmental aid guidelines (see sect. 6.5.5 below).   [177] Para. 4(a) of the 1996 guidelines.

Otherwise, the Guidelines relating to aid to small and medium-sized enterprises,[178] regional aid,[179] and cumulation of aid[180] are not to affect operation of the 1996 Guidelines.[181] More particularly, the Framework for investment aids relating to the manufacture and marketing of certain dairy products,[182] established in 1987,[183] has been 'cancelled and replaced' by these Guidelines.[184]

Overcapacity

Overcapacity may affect the acceptability of restructuring aid in various agricultural sectors.[185] For example, the starch sector is considered extremely vulnerable and sensitive because of, *inter alia*, excess production capacity and growing international competition. Accordingly, aid to increased capacity in this sector has been prohibited in the Mezzogiorno, because such aid cannot provide a lasting solution to the development problems of such a region.[186] Aid in the isoglucose sector[187] has also been prohibited since 1977,[188] and aid for the planting of wine-growing areas has been prohibited, in principle, from 1 September 1988. The latter prohibition, however, is subject to exceptions in favour of areas covered by specific Union provisions and in favour of aid which is allowed under Articles 92 to 93 of the Treaty and enables production to be reduced or quality to be improved without increased production.[189]

---

[178] Sect. 6.4.2 below. [179] Ch. 4.

[180] Sect. 5.1 above. [181] Para. 4(b) of the 1996 guidelines.

[182] [1987] OJ C302/4. Para. III.1 of the framework was applied in Notification NC277/89 and N278/89 ([1990] OJ C135/4) in regard to aid that the Spanish authorities had decided to grant Nestlé and Davidos Lacticus Alementicos in Castile-la Mancha. See also Notification C31/89 (39/89) ([1990] OJ C111/3) concerning aids that the Spanish authorities had decided to grant to the dairy Mantequerias Arias SA in Asturias, where restructuring aid was authorized because there would be no capacity increases.

[183] Cf. the Proposal of 5 Jan. 1984 ([1984] OJ C18/6) for a reg. on suspension of aids for investments in the field of dairy production.

[184] Para. 3(e) of the 1996 guidelines.

[185] Aid to beer producers was prohibited because beer consumption was stagnating or falling. See Bull. EC 1–1987, 2.1.45. Cf., regarding the surplus in the pigmeat sector, Dec. 77/172 ([1977] OJ L54/39) concerning an aid for the pigmeat sector in the UK; and regarding the surplus in calf production, Dec. 89/229 ([1989] OJ L94/43) on a national scheme to encourage the use of milk for feeding calves.

[186] Dec. 91/474 ([1991] OJ L254/14) concerning aids granted by the Italian Government to Italgrani SpA for the setting up of an agri–foodstuffs complex in the Mezzogiorno.

[187] The common organization for sugar is governed by Reg. 1785/81 ([1981] OJ L177/4) on the common organization of the markets in the sugar sector.

[188] Letter SG(77) D/3832 of 29 Mar. 1977; Dec. 77/83 ([1977] OJ L24/37) concerning the measures provided for in the draft law of the Region of Campania (Italy) supplementing and amending Regional Law 29 of 22 July 1974 on measures to promote beet production. Thus, e.g., the Commission prohibited the grant of Belgian investment aid for a sugar refinery by Dec. 90/379 ([1990] OJ L186/21) on state aid to SA Sucrerie Couplet, Brunehaut-Wez, Belgium. The letter has now been replaced by the guidelines for state aid in connection with investments in the processing and marketing of agricultural products ([1996] OJ C29/4).

[189] Art. 14 of Reg. 822/87 ([1987] OJ L84/1) on the common organization of the market in wine, as amended by Reg. 2253/88 ([1988] OJ L198/35) and implemented by Reg. 2741/89 ([1989] OJ L264/5). See also Dec. 89/228 ([1989] OJ L94/38) on Decree–Law 370/87 of the Italian Government subsequently converted into Law 460 of 4 Nov. 1987 on production and

5.2.2 Operating Aid

Early restrictions were imposed on operating aid which took the form of reduced transport tariffs to the frontier[190] or applied to particular sectors. In letters to the Member States of 12 January 1968 and 9 February 1970 the Commission stated that aid the level of which was based on prices or quantities, production units (unit of area, head of livestock), or purchase of production factors in the cereals, oleagenous plants, fruit and vegetables, pigmeat, eggs, and poultrymeat sectors was prohibited by Article 92(1).[191] Legislative prohibitions might also be introduced. For example, Regulation 804/68[192] provided that, subject to the provisions of Article 92(2) of the Treaty, aids the amount of which was fixed on the basis of the price or quantity were prohibited for milk and milk products.[193]

More generally, according to a Council Resolution of 25 May 1971,[194] aid affecting production costs, except aid to investment, should be eliminated.[195] Thus, for example, the Commission objected to the following aids[196] based on the units of area being farmed:

—Belgian aid per hectare of land where lucerne was cultivated, which did not encourage durable rationalization of lucerne production;[197]
—aid to horticulturalists proportional to the area under crop;[198]

marketing, including new standards for the production and marketing of wine sector products. Cf. Dec. 93/155 ([1993] OJ L61/55) concerning an aid measure proposed by the German authorities (Rhineland–Palatinate) for the distillation of wine.

[190] Dec. 63/641 ([1963] JO 2800) prohibiting French transport aid to certain products in the fruit and vegetables sector.

[191] However, certain aids for production of pigs for breeding and for selected seeds were authorized.

[192] On the common organization of the market in milk and milk products ([1968] JO L148/3), Art. 24(1).

[193] On the other hand, specific legislative authorization might be introduced. See, e.g., Art. 46 of Reg. 1785/81 ([1981] OJ L177/4) on the common organization of the markets in the sugar sector, regarding aid to sugar production. See, regarding other legislative authorizations of aid in this sector, the Reply by Mr Fischler to Written Question E–624/95 ([1995] OJ C222/9) by Robert Sturdy.

[194] Concerning the new orientation of the common agricultural policy ([1971] JO C52/1), para. VI. B.

[195] See, e.g., Dec. 77/75 ([1976] OJ L17/25) relating to the granting of aid for horticulture under glass in the Netherlands in order to offset the increase in fuel oil prices.

[196] See also Dec. 72/253 ([1972] JO L164/22) on the grant of aid to encourage the rationalization of the growing and processing of fodder plants as well as co-operation between agricultural operators in the Netherlands.

[197] Dec. 72/248 ([1972] JO L156/18) on the grant of aid in Belgium for the production of lucerne.

[198] Communic. relating to the aid granted to horticulture in Germany ([1973] OJ C13/4).

—aid to flax producers proportional to the area under crop;[199] and
—a premium per hectare of vines producing table wines.[200]

The Commission also objected to the following aids based on quantities produced:

—aid per kilogramme of dead weight to pig producers;[201]
—aid per kilogramme of cherries produced;[202]
—aid per litre of wine distilled;[203]
—aid for each calf fattened up;[204]
—aid for each breeding sow on the farm;[205]
—aid to a German stabilization fund for poultry for fattening;[206]
—aid for each bird slaughtered;[207]
—a slaughter premium granted for each sow slaughtered;[208]
—aid per 100 kilogrammes of potatoes produced;[209]
—aid for each calf fed for three months on milk produced on the holding;[210] and
—aid for the operation of wine-producer groups.[211]

---

[199] Notice ([1987] OJ C183/2) concerning a draft aid measure for the promotion of flax production.

[200] Communic. concerning the draft French aid for improving the quality of table wine ([1981] OJ C335/2).

[201] Dec. 77/172 ([1977] OJ L54/39) concerning an aid for the pigmeat sector in the UK.

[202] Notice concerning the French Government's proposal to grant aid in the fruit and vegetables sector of agriculture—aid to French groups of (hard) cherry producers ([1984] OJ C219/2).

[203] Dec. 93/155 ([1993] OJ L61/55) concerning an aid measure proposed by the German authorities (Rhineland–Palatinate) for the distillation of wine. See also, regarding aid for the preventive distillation of wine, Communic. C40/93 (655/93) ([1994] OJ C19/3) concerning aids which France had decided to grant to rationalize the market in table wines.

[204] Communic. on certain aid which is provided in the region of Latium (Italy) ([1974] OJ C91/3). See, similarly, Communic. with regard to certain aid measures proposed in Italy at regional or provincial level (Latium, Lombardy, Veneto, Trentino, Apulia, Tuscany, Sicily, Calabria, Liguria, Campania) to assist stock-farming ([1975] OJ C1/1); and Communic. on certain measures envisaged in Italy at national or regional level (Region of Friuli–Venezia Giulia, the Marches, Piedmont, Lombardy, Latium, Campania, Abruzzi, Valle d'Aosta, Emilia–Romagna, Molise) ([1974] OJ C96/2).

[205] Communic. on the aid granted by France to the stockfarming sector ([1974] OJ C92/12).

[206] Communic. on the aid which the German Government proposed to grant to the poultry sector ([1974] OJ C94/1).

[207] Communic. on a premium projected in the Netherlands for 'parent birds' of slaughtering ([1974] OJ C94/2).

[208] Communic. concerning a slaughter premium for cows which the Belgian Government had decided to grant ([1974] OJ C100/1). See also the Communic. regarding the flat-rate premium for cattle and pig farmers decided on by the Luxembourg Government ([1974] OJ C103/1).

[209] Communic. 67/192 ([1967] JO 790) on the grant of aid in the Netherlands in the form of rebates for the production of potato flour.

[210] Notice ([1988] OJ C57/4) concerning a draft aid measure of the French Government to encourage the use of milk as feed for calves.

[211] Notice with regard to the aid granted by the French Government via Onivins for the operation of producers' groups in the table wine sector ([1984] OJ C311/3).

Aid to reduce the cost of production factors might also be objectionable, as in the case of:

—aid in the form of a reduction in irrigation charges;[212]

—aid to reduce social security costs for employers of agricultural labour in France;[213]

—aid to offset the effects of interest rate variations for Italian producers of sugar beet;[214]

—aid to reduce the interest rate on operating credit for farmers in Ireland;[215]

—aid to provide a low interest rate for the purchase of store cattle in Trento;[216]

—aid to reduce milk transport costs in Trento;[217]

—aid for each calf fed for three months on milk produced on the holding on which it was kept;[218]

—reimbursement of the charges paid on cereals corresponding to the amount of products of the same type contained in feedingstuffs purchased for their holding by livestock farmers;[219]

—interest-rate subsidies and aid to administrative costs of agricultural co-operatives and associations thereof in Bolzano and Trento;[220] and

—interest-free loans for pig producers.[221]

Such aid cannot normally be authorized under Article 92(3)(c),[222] because it does not durably improve conditions in the sector in which it is granted[223] or

---

[212] Communic. C/90 (ex NN91/89) ([1994] OJ C19/4) concerning aid granted by the Region of Sardinia (reduction of irrigation tariffs).

[213] The Commission 'adopted . . . a set of measures' regarding state aids relating to welfare contributions on 13 Nov. 1985. See Notice ([1987] OJ C259/2) regarding aid planned by the Italian Government for the Mezzogiorno.

[214] Notice C33/92 (316/92) ([1992] OJ C343/5) concerning aid which Italy planned to grant for sugar.

[215] *Sixteenth Report on Competition Policy* (EC Commission, Brussels, 1987), 192–3.

[216] *Ibid.*

[217] *Ibid.*

[218] Dec. 89/229 ([1989] OJ L94/43) on a national scheme to encourage the use of milk for feeding calves.

[219] Dec. 90/197 ([1990] OJ L105/15) on an aid granted in France to cereal farmers and producers, financed by the reimbursement of specific fiscal and parafiscal charges.

[220] Dec. 82/744 ([1982] OJ L315/23) concerning Italian national Law 423/81 on measures for agriculture.

[221] Communic. concerning the granting of loans to the equalization funds responsible for regulating the market in pigs and piglets ([1977] OJ C129/3).

[222] Dec. 82/744 ([1982] OJ L315/23) concerning Italian national Law 423/81 on measures for agriculture. See, similarly, *Greece: Report on state aid measures*, COM(80)855, 13. Cf. 'State Aids and the Common Agricultural Policy' (1982) 191 *Green Europe* 7. Cf. also Communic. concerning proposed aid measures in Italy (Calabrian Regional Law 21/80) ([1986] OJ C96/4), regarding loans for purchase of livestock and farming equipment.

[223] See, e.g., Dec. 93/255 ([1993] OJ L117/28) concerning aid which Italy had decided to grant through AIMA for the private storage of hazelnuts.

under Article 92(3)(b) because of its effects on trade.[224] Moreover, in possibly bringing about an increase in the deliveries to intervention, the aid may also entail an increase in expenditure by the European Agricultural Guidance and Guarantee Fund. On that account it must be considered as against the common interest.[225]

However, certain categories of operating aid may be permissible. The aid concerned may be 'defensive' or, in the case of advertising aid or aid linked with restructuring, 'offensive'.[226]

Environmentally Friendly Farming

Regulation 2078/92[227] on agricultural production methods compatible with the requirements of environmental protection and the maintenance of the countryside allows for the granting of operating aid. Such aid may be granted up to ceilings fixed by hectare of land on which the practices are adopted. However, aid merely for the growing of crops in sensitive areas is not authorized thereunder.[228]

Natural Phenomena

Natural phenomena, such as the size of the harvest or adverse weather conditions,[229] may lead the Council to authorize aid under Article 93(2)[230] or Article 42. For example, the Council has acted under Article 42 to authorize operating aid for producers affected by drought.[231] The Commission, supported by the Court of Justice,[232] may feel less able to authorize such aid.[233]

---

[224] Dec. 94/814 ([1994] OJ L335/90) on aid in respect of exports of mushrooms, granted in connection with the Market Development Fund in Ireland.

[225] Dec. 90/197 ([1990] OJ L105/15) on an aid granted in France to cereal farmers and producers, financed by the reimbursement of specific fiscal and parafiscal charges.

[226] See, regarding 'promotional aid' paid by reference to each feed unit produced, which was authorized for a limited period, Dec. 87/417 ([1987] OJ L227/41) prohibiting an aid consisting of a subsidy on the sale of animal feed granted by the region of Abruzzi.

[227] [1992] OJ L215/85.

[228] Communic. C30/95 (ex NN113/B/93) and E7/95 ([1995] OJ C295/8) concerning aid which Italy (Sicily) had granted in the agricultural sector.

[229] The European Parliament considers that an insurance scheme against such conditions should be established at Union level. See the Resolution of 11 Dec. 1991 ([1992] OJ C13/86) on the development and the future of the common agricultural policy, para. 5.3.

[230] See Ch. 1.

[231] Reg. 3311/92 ([1992] OJ L332/1) on special measures for farmers affected by the 1991-2 drought in Portugal. Aid was also authorized for the control of harmful organisms in plants which did not form part of normal production risks (letter 72/021188 of 9 Feb. 1972).

[232] See, regarding operating aid to wine production, Case C-86/89 *Italy* v. *EC Commission: aid for the use of concentrated wine must* [1990] ECR I-3891, I-3909-10.

[233] Dec. 63/641 ([1963] JO 2800) prohibiting French transport aid to certain products in the fruit and vegetables sector; Dec. 82/744 ([1982] OJ L315/23) concerning Italian national Law 423/81 on measures for agriculture, regarding the prohibition of aid in the form of interest-rate subsidies on loans taken out for the preservation and storage of wine.

Credit Problems

The Commission recognizes that the seasonality of agricultural production and the structure of farm businesses may put farmers at a relative disadvantage to operators elsewhere in the economy in terms of their need for, and ability to finance, short-term loans. Therefore, operating aid in the form of subsidized short-term loans may be authorized. However, the aid must not be directed towards particular farmers or particular activities;[234] and the amount of subsidized loans to any beneficiary must not exceed the cash-flow requirements arising from the fact that production costs are incurred before income from output sales is received.[235]

Effects of the Common Agricultural Policy

Aid to counter the effects of the common agricultural policy is generally prohibited,[236] though it may be authorized in certain circumstances.[237] For example, national aid cannot be authorized because the market organization does not provide aid measures for the product concerned. The absence of such measures reflects the intention of the Union legislature to limit itself to the rules laid down by the market organization, judging them to be sufficient to regulate the market in question.[238] More particularly, the Commission has maintained that the method of calculating monetary compensatory amounts, which accords with the Union rules in force, cannot be regarded as a reason for a Member State to grant operating aid.[239]

Even so, Union legislation[240] has permitted VAT reductions to compensate German farmers, by way of production-linked aid, for the dismantlement of such amounts.[241] In the *Twenty-Second Report on Competition Policy*[242] the Com-

[234] Thus it may not be limited to processors engaged in ageing or refining products. See Notice C4/96 (ex N360/95) ([1996] OJ C104/13) concerning aid which Emilia–Romagna plans to grant to facilitate access to credit for certain operators in the agricultural sector.

[235] Communic. on subsidized short-term loans in agriculture ([1996] OJ C44/2). An aid ceiling of 35% may apply. See, e.g., the Recommendation pursuant to Art. 93(3) EC ([1993] OJ C336/8) and Communic. C35/93 (N520/90) ([1993] OJ C338/3) concerning aids which France had decided to grant to sheep farmers.

[236] Cf., regarding aid to counter the effects of intra-Union integration, Case 153/73 *Holtz & Willemsen GmbH* v. *EC Council and EC Commission* [1974] ECR 675, 694.

[237] See the aid authorized by the Council in Dec. 70/355 ([1970] JO L157/27) on the application of compensatory measures in favour of cereal producers.

[238] Dec. 93/154 ([1993] OJ L61/52) concerning an AIMA national programme on aid which Italy plans to grant for the private storage of carrots.

[239] Dec. 77/172 ([1977] OJ L54/39) concerning an aid for the pigmeat sector in the UK.

[240] Dir. 85/361 ([1985] OJ L192/18) on the harmonization of the laws of the Member States relating to turnover taxes—common system of value added tax: derogations in connection with the special aids granted to certain farmers to compensate for the dismantlement of monetary compensatory amounts applying to certain agricultural products.

[241] See, e.g., Dec. 92/392 ([1992] OJ L215/100) on temporary national compensation for farmers in Germany and Dec. 92/458 ([1992] OJ L257/43) on transitional national compensation for farmers in Germany for 1992.

[242] (EC Commission, Brussels, 1993), 276.

mission noted that agricultural prices and trends in Germany had been in line with those in other Member States, and there was no evidence that the aid had affected the functioning of Union agricultural markets. More particularly, aid has been authorized to compensate farmers disadvantaged as a result of an error in the distribution of Union sheep and beef premiums.[243]

Regulation 2611/95[244] establishing the possibility of national aid being granted in compensation for losses of agricultural income caused by monetary movements in other Member States has now been enacted under Article 42 of the EC Treaty.[245] Moreover, the Court of Justice accepts that devaluation in other Member States may constitute 'exceptional circumstances' such as to justify an aid authorization by the Council under Article 93(2).[246]

At the same time, common agricultural policy reform might be seen as rendering the grant of operating aid necessary for the survival of certain farms. The latter might face a number of constraints: mounting interests rates just as they were undergoing modernization, more expensive input costs (largely a matter of inflation), the freezing of their revenues because of the administrative restriction of production (milk quotas), and the freezing of agricultural prices imposed by budgetary restrictions. Hence, transitional aid to assist farmers in the least developed parts of the Union to cope with the switch from a price-protection scheme to a free market system might be authorized under Article 92(3)(c).[247]

More generally, a regulation establishing a framework for aid to agricultural income was proposed by the Commission in 1987,[248] because of fears that such aid might run out of control and cause distortions of competition.[249] The framework was embodied in Regulation 768/89,[250] and authorized aid to support farmers adjusting to reform of the common agricultural policy.

In relation to the former German Democratic Republic, transitional measures were adopted under Regulation 3577/90.[251] According to the Preamble to this Regulation, to facilitate structural change in the agricultural sector in the new *Länder*, involving both the creation of family farms and the reorganization of co-operative farms, provision had to be made for some temporary

---

[243] Bull. EU 10–1995, 1.3.193.

[244] [1995] OJ L268/3.

[245] See, earlier, Bull EU 11–1995, 1.3.168, regarding French aid to cattle farmers.

[246] Cosmas AG in Case C–122/94 *EC Commission* v. *EU Council: aid to wine producers* [1996] ECR I–881, I–913–4.

[247] Notice C42/91 (ex NN94/91) ([1994] OJ C73/10) concerning aid granted by Greece for the transport of maize to less-favoured areas. Cf. Reg. 1346/90 ([1990] OJ L134/10) instituting aid for small producers of certain arable crops and Reg. 1983/86 ([1986] OJ L171/1) laying down general rules for the system of direct aid for small producers in the cereals sector.

[248] Proposal of 15 Apr. 1987 ([1987] OJ C236/8) for a reg. establishing a framework system for national aids to agriculture.

[249] *Seventeenth Report on Competition Policy* (EC Commission, Brussels, 1988), 191.

[250] Establishing a system of transitional aids to agricultural income ([1989] OJ L84/8).

[251] On the transitional measures and adjustments required in the agricultural sector as a result of German unification ([1990] OJ L353/23).

adjustments to the rules on the acceleration of structural adjustment in the context of common agricultural policy reform. In particular, the measures for improving the efficiency of agricultural structures would in some cases have to be adopted gradually in order to prevent sudden conflicts relating both to social issues and employment and to rural and regional imbalance. Moreover, special measures were required not only to reorganize the co-operatives but also to facilitate access by farmers to ownership of the means of production. These measures were to be based as far as possible on Union concepts and criteria so as to encourage competition and prevent the creation of monopolies. At the same time, the adoption of the principles of the common agricultural policy had the effect of reducing sharply and severely the incomes of the producers concerned.[252] Hence, Article 4 of the Regulation provided that the Commission could authorize Germany to introduce in the former German Democratic Republic a system of aid to compensate for agricultural income losses in that territory as a result of the changeover to the common agricultural policy.[253] The aid had to be degressive, limited in time,[254] and eliminated not later than 31 December 1993.[255]

Developments in Other Sectors

Operating aid may be permissible because agricultural activity is adversely affected by developments in other sectors. For example, Germany introduced for 1980 aid of 12 per cent for light fuel oil used in horticulture during 1978. This aid was authorized under Article 92(3)(c)[256] to enable horticulturalists to adapt to the new situation prevailing on the energy market, to remain in activity during the period concerned, and to change over to less costly forms of energy. The aid had to be accompanied by other structural measures at national or regional level for changing over to alternative heating systems, had to be limited to one year, and could not amount to more than 30 per cent of the increase recorded between January 1978 and 1980 in the prices (excluding tax) of the fuels used. However, the Commission remained firmly attached to the principle that the price of energy must be fully reflected in the costs of

---

[252] Reg. 768/89 ([1989] OJ L84/8) establishing a system of transitional aids to agricultural income was designed to compensate for the adverse consequences of CAP reform and was thus ill-adapted to the problems of agriculture in the former GDR.

[253] Other kinds of aid might be prohibited. See Communic. C4/92 (520/91) ([1992] OJ C161/9) concerning aids which Germany decided to grant to agricultural drying enterprises in Brandenburg.

[254] Art. 93(3) EC was applicable to such aid. In appraising such aid, the Commission was to ensure that its effect on trade was as little as possible and that a harmonious transition to the CAP was assured.

[255] See, e.g., Reg. 3783/90 ([1990] OJ L364/19) on transitional measures in the seed sector after the unification of Germany. See, generally, J. Heine, 'Les Mesures prises dans le secteur agricole pour l'intégration de la RDA dans la Communauté' [1991] RMC 199–217.

[256] *Distortions of Competition in Hothouse Agriculture*, COM(80)306, 36.

production. Hence, a preferential energy tariff for horticulturalists not dictated by commercial promotion considerations might be prohibited.[257]

Regional-policy Considerations

The prohibition of discrimination in Article 40(3) of the Treaty has sometimes demanded articulation of Union approaches to agricultural aid. According to the Court of Justice,[258] various elements of a common organization, such as protective measures and aids, may have differentiated application by reference to the areas and other conditions of production or consumption in terms of criteria of an objective nature[259] which ensure a proportionate distribution of advantages and disadvantages for those concerned without distinguishing between the territory of Member States.[260] Similarly, differentiation of intervention prices as between one region and another may be justified.[261]

More particularly, operating aid may be authorized to support farming in areas where natural conditions are particularly unfavourable[262] or where farming is a vital aspect of regional development or the maintenance of social equilibrium.[263] Hence, cash aids may be authorized where farmers cannot realize assets or draw on reserves without encroaching on the profitability of their farms. This may be the case where there is a need to maintain the farm as a basis of subsistence for the family of the farmer and to safeguard employment, or where the aim is to avoid recourse to public welfare facilities.[264]

Such aid may also be authorized in individual sectors. For example, a premium payable to producers of potato starch under Union legislation[265] was designed to maintain the profitability of this industrial branch and thereby, indirectly, to ensure an outlet for an agricultural product, the importance of which for the economic development of certain Union regions was evident.[266]

---

[257] *Ibid.*, 36. Cf. the Reply to Written Question 755/77 ([1978] OJ C150/3) by Mr Pisoni, regarding tax concessions for German farmers.

[258] Case 153/73 *Holtz and Willemsen GmbH* v. *EC Council and EC Commission* [1974] ECR 675.

[259] Unjustified distinctions are prohibited. Cf., in connection with Art. 4(b) ECSC, Case C–99/92 *Terni SpA and Italsider SpA* v. *Cassa Conguaglio per il Settore Elettrico* [1994] ECR I–541.

[260] Case 153/73 *Holtz and Willemsen GmbH* v. *EC Council and EC Commission* [1974] ECR 675, 695. See also Capotorti AG in Joined Cases 117/76 & 16/77 *Albert Ruckdeschel & Co. and Hansa-Lagerhaus Ströh & Co.* v. *Hauptzollamt Hamburg–St Annen* [1977] ECR 1753, 1780.

[261] Case 167/88 *Association Générale des Producteurs de Blé et Autres Céréales (AGPB)* v. *Office national interprofessionnel des céréales (ONIC)* [1989] ECR 1653, 1684. In Case 92/78 *Simmenthal* v. *EC Commission* [1979] ECR 777, 827, Reischl AG considered that variations in the minimum selling price for meat were necessary to avoid 'regional imbalance'. Hence, there was no discrimination contrary to the Treaty.

[262] Dir. 75/268 ([1975] OJ L128/1) on mountain and hill farming and farming in less favoured areas.

[263] *Sixteenth Report on Competition Policy* (EC Commission, Brussels, 1987), 194–5.

[264] *Ibid.*, 192.

[265] Reg. 1125/78 ([1978] OJ L142/21) amending Reg. 2727/75 on the common organization of the market in cereals; and Reg. 1127/78 ([1978] OJ L142/24) amending Reg. 2742/75 on production refunds in the cereals and rice sectors.

[266] Case 166/78 *Italy* v. *EC Council: premiums for potato starch* [1979] ECR 2575, 2600.

Hence, this aid was permissible as being compatible with Article 39 of the Treaty.

In relation to the Azores, special legislative arrangements are made by Regulation 1600/92.[267] It provides for the grant, subject to certain conditions, of aid at a flat rate per hectare for the development of sugar-beet production in the Azores and special aid for the processing into white sugar of sugar-beet harvested there.

Third-country Competition

Third-country competition may justify operating aid. For example, because of the special rules affecting the Union market in tinned pineapples, and in particular because of the need for the industry to maintain prices that were competitive in relation to the prices fixed by the main third-country producers, a system of production aid was considered necessary, so that tinned pineapples could be produced at a lower price than that which would result if the producers of tinned pineapples were paid a remunerative price. Accordingly, Article 4(1) of Regulation 525/77[268] provided for aid to offset the difference between the Union offer price for tinned pineapples and the prices charged by third country suppliers of these products.[269]

Advertising

Advertising aid is covered by an aid framework.[270] According to this framework, advertising aid:

—must not infringe Article 30 of the Treaty, for example by encouraging purchase of national products only;[271]
—must not relate to products of one or more specific undertakings;
—must encourage:
    the disposal of surplus agricultural products;
    the disposal of new or substitute products not in surplus;
    the development of the least-favoured regions of the Union;[272]
    the development of small businesses manufacturing the products in question; or

---

[267] Concerning specific measures for the Azores and Madeira relating to certain agricultural products ([1992] OJ L173/1).

[268] Establishing a system of production aid for tinned pineapples ([1977] OJ L73/46).

[269] Cf. Reg. 1117/78 ([1978] OJ L142/1) on the common organization of the market in dried fodder.

[270] Framework for national aids for the advertising of agricultural products and certain products not listed in Annex II to the EC Treaty, excluding fishery products ([1987] OJ C302/6).

[271] See, e.g., Notice C18/95 (NN103/94) ([1995] OJ C289/12) concerning aid for promotional measures which France had decided to grant to the sheepmeat industry. Cf. the Communic. concerning state involvement in the promotion of agricultural and fisheries products ([1986] OJ C272/3), regarding the applicability of Art. 30 EC.

[272] i.e., those 'qualifying under Community policy on agricultural structures for preferential treatment under Art. 92(3)(a) or (c)'. See para. 3.3.2 of the framework.

the manufacture of products of high quality and part of a healthy diet; and

—must not exceed 50 per cent of the expenditure,[273] though higher levels may be permitted in certain regions or in the case of small and medium-sized enterprises.

Aid meeting these conditions may be authorized under Article 92(3)(c) as aid to facilitate the development of certain economic activities.[274]

Link with Restructuring

The Commission authorizes operating aid for agricultural undertakings where it is intended to promote the spread of certain practices which are likely to encourage the development of the sector concerned, provided the aid is confined to the period strictly necessary for making undertakings aware of the benefits of the new practices and provided the amount is gradually reduced over this period.[275]

Low-interest loans to Sicilian farmers, to consolidate earlier loans, cancel liabilities arising from outstanding loans and wipe out liabilities recorded at 31 December 1985, were also authorized by the Commission, because the Italian authorities agreed that to qualify for the aid, recipients must build up sufficient financial resources to deal with non-structural financial difficulties and submit a financial improvement plan.[276]

Moreover, a link with restructuring may mean that operating aid is exceptionally authorized by the Council. In Decision 85/213[277] the Council considered Italian aid to wine producers. In view of the large surplus on the Union table-wine market, taken together with the fact that the aid in question was accompanied by measures of structural reform, the exceptional circumstances existed which permitted a declaration to be made under Article 93(2) that the aid was compatible with the common market.

---

[273] However, aid otherwise complying with the framework will be prohibited where it is funded, at least partly, by charges contrary to Art. 12 EC. See Dec. 89/216 ([1989] OJ L85/45) on the Belgian funds for the promotion of the farming of poultry and other small animals and of fruit and vegetable growing.

[274] Notice C11/92 (ex NN134/91) ([1993] OJ C59/7) concerning aid which Italy had decided to introduce by Law 34/1991 of the Sicilian Region concerning the marketing and sale of Sicilian products.

[275] See, e.g., regarding aid to promote use of organized intermodal transport of agricultural products, Communic. C30/95 (ex NN113/B/93) & E7/95 ([1995] OJ C295/8) concerning aid which Italy (Sicily) had granted in the agricultural sector.

[276] *Seventeenth Report on Competition Policy* (EC Commission, Brussels, 1978), 195.

[277] On the granting of aid for the distillation of wines obtained from table grapes in Sicily ([1985] OJ L96/34). See also Dec. 85/272 ([1985] OJ L151/49) on the granting of aid for the short-term private storage of table wine and must in Greece, France, and Italy.

5.3 FISHING

Article 38(1) of the EC Treaty refers to 'the products of . . . fisheries and products of first-stage processing directly related to these products'. They are listed in Annex II to the Treaty. Article 38(4) requires the establishment of a common policy for such products.

In early proposals to establish a common fisheries policy (CFP)—a report of 1966[278] and draft regulations of 1968[279]—the Commission called for harmonization of certain types of aid to fishing and the prohibition of other types. In the event, the acceptability of aid has depended on the requirements of the common organization of the market in fishery products, and so Articles 92 to 94 apply to aid to fishing,[280] subject to provisions to the contrary adopted under Articles 42 to 43 of the Treaty. Hence, Member States must refrain from any action liable to entail exceptions to the common organization or to hamper its operation,[281] having due regard not only to the express provisions but also to the objectives of the regulation establishing the common organization. Aid which jeopardizes the proper functioning of, and runs counter to, the objectives of the common organization is prohibited and cannot be authorized under Article 92(3).[282] Arguments to the effect that aid provided for in the common organization is inadequate for the objectives of the organization and neglects regional considerations may be rejected.[283] The acceptability of aid has been affected, more particularly, by Council measures enacted in pursuit of the structural policy for fishing[284] and by Commission guidelines. The latter were

[278] *Basic principles of a common fisheries policy* ([1967] JO 862), para. E.I.1.

[279] Art. 11 of the Proposal of 6 June 1968 ([1968] JO C91/1) for a reg. on the establishment of a common structural policy in the fisheries sector envisaged harmonization of investment aid, and Art. 26(2) of the Proposal of 6 June 1968 ([1968] JO C91/1) for a reg. on the common organization of the market in fishery products envisaged the prohibition of operating aid.

[280] Regs 2142/70 ([1970] JO L236/5); 100/76 ([1976] OJ L20/1); 3796/81 ([1981] OJ L379/1); 3687/91 ([1991] OJ L354/1) on the common organization of the market in fishery products; and Reg. 3759/92 ([1992] OJ L388/1) on the common organization of the market in fishery and aquaculture products.

[281] See, e.g., Notice ([1984] OJ C269/5) concerning the activities of the FIOM (Intervention and Market Organization Fund for Sea Fishery and Mariculture Products) in France, where a withdrawal price support system for species for which there was no Union intervention mechanism was considered to be contrary to Reg. 3796/81.

[282] Dec. 86/561 ([1986] OJ L327/44) on an aid to fish producers' organizations granted by the German Government.

[283] Dec. 86/186 ([1986] OJ L136/55) on aids granted by the French Government to producers' organizations in the fisheries sector. See also the objections to aid additional to that provided for by Reg. 1360/78 in a Communic. ([1985] OJ C329/7) concerning Regional Law 60 of 17 Sept. 1984 implementing Reg. 1360/78 on producer groups and associations thereof in the Region of Lazio.

[284] See now Reg. 3699/93 ([1993] OJ L346/1) laying down the criteria and arrangements regarding Community structural assistance in the fisheries and aquaculture sector and the processing and marketing of its products.

first drawn up in 1980[285] and were revised in 1985,[286] 1988,[287] 1992,[288] and 1994.[289]

Those aspects of the common fisheries policy that cannot be considered to have been 'thoroughly resolved', in particular as regards structural policy, may still warrant aid,[290] provided that such aid complies with the objectives of the common rules and does not jeopardize or risk distorting the full effect of these rules. Hence, the aid must, where appropriate, form part of guidance programmes provided for under Union rules.[291]

5.3.1 Restructuring Aid

Articles 9 and 10 of Regulation 2141/70,[292] which established a common structural policy for the fisheries sector, provided that Member States might grant aid to operations which contributed to the achievement of increased productivity through the restructuring of fishing fleets and other means of production, adaptation of production and marketing conditions to market requirements or improved living standards for those dependent on fishing for their livelihood. Article 9(2) of the same Regulation provided that common rules fixing the conditions for the grant of such aid were to be laid down by the Council. The Commission forwarded a draft Regulation to the Council in 1973 laying down such rules,[293] which would have specified the types of aid permissible and the conditions under which they could be granted, but this proposal was not adopted by the Council.[294] Similar aid was authorized by Regulation 101/76,[295] which replaced Regulation 2141/70.

[285] Proposals relating to structural policy in the fisheries sector, COM(80)240, 112–6.

[286] [1985] OJ C268/2. These revisions were adopted in response to Reg. 2908/83 ([1983] OJ L290/1) on a common measure for restructuring, modernizing, and developing the fishing industry and for developing aquaculture.

[287] [1988] OJ C313/21.

[288] [1992] OJ C152/2. These guidelines dealt for the first time with aid for improving stock conservation and management (para. 2.2.10) and aid to workers in the sector as part of socio-economic back-up measures designed to deal with difficulties linked to the adjustment or reduction of capacity (para. 2.6.3).

[289] Guidelines for the examination of state aid to fisheries and aquaculture ([1994] OJ C260/3). Para. 1.2 of the guidelines states that they do not apply to subsidies which are partly funded by the Union.

[290] The failure of state aid to resolve the problems of the fishing industry has been noted by the European Parliament in its Resolution of 19 June 1987 ([1987] OJ C190/171) on national aids in the fishing sector, para. 4.

[291] Para. I.3 of the 1988 guidelines.

[292] On the establishment of a common structural policy in the fisheries sector ([1970] JO L236/1).

[293] Proposal of 5 Nov. 1973 ([1973] OJ C110/64) for a reg. laying down conditions for granting national aid under the common structural policy for seafishing.

[294] See, more particularly, the Proposal of 19 July 1980 for a reg. to encourage exploratory fishing and co-operation through joint ventures in the fishing sector, COM(80)420.

[295] Laying down a common structural policy for the fishing industry ([1976] OJ L20/19). Art. 8(2) thereof also followed Art. 9(2) of the 1970 reg.

More particularly, rules governing aid to producer organizations were adopted by Regulation 3796/81,[296] and rules governing aid for the construction and modernization of fishing boats[297] were introduced by Regulation 2908/83.[298] Moreover, Directive 83/515[299] also introduced a Union scheme to support the laying up of fishing vessels, and state aid was expected to be consistent with the scheme. Cessation aid to processors might also be authorized, provided that it was compatible with Regulation 4028/86 and limited to unprofitable processing plants, and its level did not exceed half of the current value of the movable and unmovable assets excluding land.[300]

The Commission objected to Greek scrapping aid[301] and to Sicilian aid for temporary laying up which differed too much from the Union scheme, particularly because of the excessively high premiums.[302] Sardinian aid of the same kind was prohibited, because it differed from arrangements in Regulation 4028/86. According to the Commission, the aid was covered by a Union legal framework which laid down precise parameters for, in particular, the amounts that could be paid. Any financial assistance which was not in accordance with those parameters strengthened the position of certain operators compared with their competitors in the Union. Therefore, the aid distorted competition contrary to Article 92(1) and could not be authorized under Article 92(2) or (3).[303]

---

[296] On the common organization of the market in fishery products ([1981] OJ L379/1). See, earlier, Art. 6(2) of Reg. 100/76 ([1976] OJ L20/1). See now Art. 12 of Reg. 3759/92 ([1992] OJ L388/1).

[297] Cf., regarding aid for projects involving investments in the provision of facilities at fishing ports, Art. 27 of Reg. 4028/86; Notice C65/91 (ex 614/91) ([1992] OJ C205/4) concerning certain aids which the Region of Sardinia had decided to grant in the fisheries sector; and Communic. C9/92 ([1993] OJ C59/8) on aid for the equipment for a fishing port in the region of Poitou-Charentes. See now para. 2.4 of the 1994 guidelines.

[298] On a common measure for restructuring, modernizing and developing the fishing industry and for developing aquaculture ([1983] OJ L290/1). Italian aid within the framework of this measure was accepted, as extension of the aid provided for in Dir. 83/515 (see below) to cover the laying up of vessels less than 12 metres in length and technical modifications for temporary laying up. See the *Fifteenth Report on Competition Policy* (EC Commission, Brussels, 1986), 198.

[299] Concerning certain measures to adjust capacity in the fisheries sector ([1983] OJ L290/15). The earlier Proposal of 21 Oct. 1977 ([1977] OJ C278/15) for a regulation on certain immediate measures to adjust capacity in the fisheries sector had not been approved by the Council. In practice, however, the Commission authorized Member States to take the kind of aid measures envisaged therein. See proposals relating to structural policy in the fisheries sector, COM(80)420, 2–3; *EC Twelfth General Report* (EC Commission, Brussels, 1979), 190–1.

[300] Para. 2.3.1 of the 1992 guidelines. Cf., regarding aid for improvement of product quality, para. 2.6 of the 1994 guidelines and, regarding other aid to investment by undertakings engaged in processing or marketing, para. 2.3 (*ibid.*).

[301] Communic. ([1985] OJ C306/14) concerning the aid that the Greek Government intended to grant to the fishing industry in 1985.

[302] *Fifteenth Report on Competition Policy* (EC Commission, Brussels, 1986), 199.

[303] Dec. 95/195 ([1995] OJ L126/32) concerning aid granted by the Region of Sardinia in the fisheries sector (temporary withdrawal of vessels).

Restructuring aid must, according to Regulation 4028/86,[304] now be included within the framework of a Multiannual Guidance Programme (MGP). Current MGPs were published in December 1992.[305] Such programmes authorize state aid, *inter alia*, for the purchase or construction of certain vessels[306] for the Union fleet[307] up to a ceiling laid down in Annex IV.2 to Regulation 3699/93.[308] Aid for modernization must not exceed 50 per cent of the value of a new vessel of the same type as the vessel concerned.[309] Article 92 of the Treaty applies to state aid other than that covered by this legislation.[310] In practice, the consequence is that aid for investments in the fleet will only be authorized if the conditions laid down in the legislation are met.[311]

The thinking implicit in the legislation is embodied in the 1994 guidelines. According to the latter, aid must provide incentives for development and adaptation which cannot be undertaken under normal market circumstances because of insufficient flexibility in the sector and the limited financial capacity of those engaged in it.[312] Lasting improvements must result from aid, so that the industry can continue to develop solely on the basis of market earnings. The aid must not impede application of the common fisheries policy, and so it may not be granted for export of, or trade in, fishery products. Aid filling gaps in the policy as regards restructuring may only be authorized, if it is not contrary to the objectives of common rules.[313]

For example, in 1992 the Commission objected to planned French aid,

[304] On Community measures to improve and adapt structures in the fisheries and aquaculture sector ([1986] OJ L276/7).

[305] Decs 92/588 to 92/598 ([1992] OJ L403/3).

[306] According to the 1988 guidelines, so as not to jeopardize attainment of CFP objectives, particularly given the problem of overcapacity of fleets, no aid might be granted under the Sixth Dir. on shipbuilding (see sect. 5.8 below) for fishing vessels intended for the Union fleet. As regards aid for investment in the fleet, rules regarding aid for the purchase of used vessels were introduced (para. II.B.3). See now para. 2.2.3.3 of the 1994 guidelines.

[307] See also, regarding aid to experimental fishing campaigns, para. 2.2.4 of the 1992 guidelines, regarding aid for redeployment operations, para. 2.2.5 (*ibid.*), regarding aid for joint ventures, para. 2.2.6 (*ibid.*), regarding aid to joint enterprises, para. 2.2.7 (*ibid.*), and regarding aid for improving stock conservation and management, para. 2.2.10 (*ibid.*). Redeployment aid must cease as soon as the objective of redeployment has been attained or has proved to be unattainable. See Notice ([1984] OJ C218/25) concerning the aid measures proposed by Germany for the redeployment of the fishing fleet.

[308] Laying down the criteria and arrangements regarding Community structural assistance in the fisheries and aquaculture sector and the processing and marketing of its products ([1993] OJ L290/15).

[309] Art. 9(e) of Reg. 4028/86, as amended by Reg. 3944/90 ([1990] OJ L380/1). See, e.g., Communic. C57/61 (193/91, 194/91 & 195/91) ([1992] OJ C63/13) concerning aid which the authorities of the Department of Nord had decided to grant in the fisheries sector.

[310] Art. 16(2) of Reg. 4028/86.

[311] See, e.g., Communic. C10/95 (ex N286/B/94) ([1995] OJ C157/8) concerning aids which the Italian authorities had decided to grant to assist fisheries.

[312] Para. 1.3 of the 1994 guidelines.

[313] See, regarding R & D aid, para. 2.1.2 (*ibid.*), regarding advertising aid, para. 2.1.3 (*ibid.*), and regarding training and advisory aid, para. 2.1.1 (*ibid.*). See, more particularly, regarding aid in the form of advice to small and medium-sized enterprises, para 2.1.4 (*ibid.*).

because it was not clear whether the aid would be consistent with the MGP for France;[314] whether the effectiveness of aid for permanent withdrawal of ships would be secured by scrapping,[315] as required by Article 24(1) of Regulation 4028/86, as amended by Regulation 3944/90,[316] or by definitive transfer to a third country or definitive assignment to purposes other than fishing;[317] or whether the ceiling on investment aid for the modernization of vessels was respected. The Commission also objected to Italian aid for the temporary withdrawal of fishing vessels exceeding the level fixed by Regulation 4028/86[318] and to aid for the construction of a fishing vessel for an Irish shipowner, when the capacity of the Irish fleet already exceeded that set by the MGP.[319]

5.3.2 Operating Aid

Operating aid may be granted to producer organizations under Article 7 of Regulation 3759/92.[320] However, for the state to forego repayment of loans made to such organizations on favourable terms involves the grant of unauthorized operating aid.[321] The basic rationale is that aid provided for in this Regulation is 'exhaustive in nature'.[322]

Aid in the form of fuel subsidies was also once authorized. In June 1974 the Commission published a report stating that aid designed to alleviate the adjustment of fishing vessels to increased fuel costs was permissible if such aid was for a strictly limited period and ended at the latest by 30 June 1975 (a deadline which was later extended to 31 December 1975). Such aid was not to exceed 50 per cent of the increase in fuel prices in the Member State concerned.[323]

---

[314] Communic. C54/91 (175/91, 177/91 and 178/91) ([1992] OJ C63/9) concerning aids which the authorities of the region of Lower Normandy had decided to grant in the fisheries sector.

[315] Communic. C55/91 (609/90) ([1992] OJ C63/10) concerning aids which the authorities of Provence–Alpes–Cote d'Azur had decided to grant in the fisheries sector.

[316] [1990] OJ L380/1.

[317] Communic. C56/91 (190/91) ([1992] OJ C63/11) concerning aids which the authorities of Languedoc–Roussillion had decided to grant in the fisheries sector.

[318] Notice C65/91 (ex 614/91) ([1992] OJ C205/4) concerning certain aids which the Region of Sardinia had decided to grant in the fisheries sector.

[319] Notice ([1988] OJ C336/2) as regards contract-related production aid proposed by the Dutch and German Governments in support of a particular shipbuilding contract.

[320] On the common organization of the market in fishery and aquaculture products ([1992] OJ L388/1). See, earlier, Art. 6 of Reg. 100/76 ([1976] OJ L20/1) on the common organization of the markets in fishery products and Reg. 3796/81 ([1981] OJ L379/1) on the common organization of the market in fishery products.

[321] Dec. 86/561 ([1986] OJ L327/44) on an aid to fish producers' organizations granted by the German Government and the *Sixteenth Report on Competition Policy* (EC Commission, Brussels, 1982), 197.

[322] Notice C48/94 (NN104/94 (ex N514/92)) ([1995] OJ C161/5) regarding aid which the French Government had decided to grant to 'Institut Français du Pétrole'.

[323] Bull. EC 6–1974, 2253; *Twelfth General Report* (EC Commission, Brussels, 1979), 190–1.

However, in the Proposals relating to Structural Policy in the Fisheries Sector[324] the Commission announced that it would adopt a stricter approach. Only temporary aid to cushion the impact of a sharp rise in fuel costs remained acceptable, given that such costs were not mitigated by structural measures, which could only have an effect in the longer term.[325] Accordingly, the Commission later prohibited fuel subsidies granted by Belgium,[326] France,[327] and Italy;[328] Italian aid for the purchase of fuel and ice;[329] aid granted by the United Kingdom in 1980 and 1981 to fishing vessel owners to help tide them through the crisis facing the fishing industry;[330] aid granted by the United Kingdom to producer organizations to enable them to maintain their autonomous system of withdrawal prices;[331] Sicilian aid to fishermen's co-operatives;[332] Sicilian aid in the form of subsidized loans for the storage of fishery products;[333] French aid for storage of surpluses and for price support arrangements not provided for in the common organization;[334] Greek aid for the purchase of spat, young fish, and fish feed for fresh-water aquaculture, mariculture, and cage culture;[335] and German aid in the form of low rent to a fishery-products processing factory.[336] The Commission also objected to German aid in the form of a stand-by allowance; suspension of rent payments; security for the financing of exceptional stocks; and interest subsidies on loans.[337]

---

[324] COM(80)240, 112–6.

[325] Dec. 86/561 ([1986] OJ L327/44) on an aid to fish producers' organizations granted by the German Government.

[326] Dec. 83/314 ([1983] OJ L169/35) concerning aid for fuel granted to fishermen by the Belgian Government.

[327] Dec. 83/313 ([1983] OJ L169/32) concerning aid to maintain maritime employment granted to fishing undertakings by the French Government; Case 93/84 *EC Commission* v. *France: aid to fishing undertakings* [1985] ECR 829. See, later, the *Sixteenth Report on Competition Policy* (EC Commission, Brussels, 1987), 197–8.

[328] Dec. 83/312 ([1983] OJ L169/29) concerning aid for fuel granted by the Italian Government to fishermen operating in the Mediterranean. See also Dec. 83/246 ([1983] OJ L137/28) concerning aid for fuel granted by the Italian Government to Sicilian fishermen.

[329] Communic. C15/91 (ex NN109/90) ([1992] OJ C44/9) concerning aids which the Italian authorities had decided to grant in the fisheries sector.

[330] Dec. 83/315 ([1983] OJ L137/38) concerning a subsidy granted by the UK Government in 1980 and 1981 to owners of fishing vessels.

[331] Dec. 85/425 ([1985] OJ L241/20) on an aid to producers' organizations granted by the UK Government.

[332] Communic. ([1985] OJ C105/11) concerning the aid measures proposed by the Region of Sicily in the draft law on the budget for 1984 and the multiannual budget for 1984.

[333] *Seventeenth Report on Competition Policy* (EC Commission, Brussels, 1988), 202–3.

[334] Dec. 86/186 ([1986] OJ L136/55) on aids granted by the French Government to producers' organizations in the fisheries sector.

[335] Communic. ([1985] OJ C306/14) concerning the aid that the Greek Government intended to grant to the fishing industry in 1985.

[336] Dec. 87/515 ([1987] OJ L295/25) on aid granted by Germany for the purchase and lease of the Seeadler factory manufacturing fish products in Cuxham, Lower Saxony.

[337] Communic. ([1988] OJ C334/3) concerning the aid which Bremen, Lower Saxony, and Hamburg decided to grant in the fisheries sector following the fall in consumption which occurred during the second half of 1987.

Paragraph 1.3 of the 1994 guidelines now states that aid must not be 'protective in its effect',[338] and operating aid is, in principle, prohibited.[339] Unless it is directly linked to a restructuring plan,[340] such aid is considered unlikely to facilitate economic development.[341]

In general, this prohibition seems to be strictly applied. For example, aid to cover up to 75 per cent of the costs of logistic-support vessels was prohibited as operating aid. Although paragraph 2.2.8 of the guidelines envisages aid for technical assistance at sea, it can only be authorized in really exceptional circumstances.[342] However, direct-income aid to workers in the fisheries and aquaculture sector and to workers employed in the processing and marketing of fishery and aquaculture products may be authorized, provided it forms part of socio-economic back-up measures designed to deal with difficulties linked to the adjustment or reduction of capacity.[343] Moreover, aid may be authorized to offset the loss of income suffered by fishermen as a result of a temporary cessation of fishing activities caused by 'natural disasters' at sea.[344]

5.4 FORESTRY

Standing trees are included in Annex II to the EC Treaty, though forestry products, with the exception of cork, are excluded from this Annex. Consequently, the application of Articles 92 to 93 is independent of the establishment of a common organization of the market for such products.

The forestry industry is said by the Commission to make a decisive contribution to maintaining economic balance between different regions, since it is located in all areas of the Union. However, it is most firmly established in the vicinity of extensive forests, which are often located in less-favoured regions. Hence, the development of this industry, which enables use to be made of local resources and helps to improve the employment situation and at the same time to stem the drift away from the land, should play a positive role in the reduction

---

[338] The 1992 guidelines provided that aid might not be conservative in its effect (para. 1.3).

[339] However, aid to the operation of ports and aid to reduce the port charges borne by fishermen is examined case by case. See para. 2.2.7 of the 1994 guidelines.

[340] According to para. I.3 of the 1988 guidelines, the Commission would examine operating aids 'on a case-by-case basis where they [were] directly linked to a restructuring plan considered to be compatible with the common market'.

[341] Dec. 86/592 ([1986] OJ L340/22) on the system of ceilings on the price of diesel fuel for fishermen introduced by the French Government.

[342] Dec. 90/554 ([1990] OJ L314/13) on the Spanish draft ministerial order on logistic support for the fishing fleet in 1988.

[343] Para. 2.10.3 of the 1994 guidelines.

[344] Para. 2.2.2 of the 1994 guidelines and Art. 14 of Reg. 3699/93. See, e.g., Communic. C21/94 (ex N415/93) ([1996] OJ C42/3) concerning aid that Italy had decided to grant in the fisheries sector (Region of Abruzzi).

of regional disparities.[345] The implication is that restructuring aid to this sector should not be precluded.

5.4.1 Restructuring Aid

Restructuring aid may be treated favourably by the Union legislature. Article 20 of Regulation 797/85,[346] on improving the efficiency of agricultural structures, authorized aid for the afforestation of agricultural land and for investments in woodland improvements involving the provision of shelter belts, firebreaks, and water-points and for forest roads. Similar aid is now authorized by Regulation 2328/91.[347] The same ceilings apply as in the case of restructuring aid to agriculture.[348] In the case of processing and marketing, state-aid policy is based on Regulation 867/90[349] on improving the processing and marketing conditions for forestry products.

In Commission practice aid to development of the forestry industry generally,[350] and to research and development in particular,[351] such as technological development in the use of waste water to produce newsprint,[352] may also be authorized, as is aid to afforestation and collective activities in the cellulose, paper, and board industry.[353] Similarly, aid for restructuring, involving reductions in the workforce and in production capacity, may be authorized,[354] though a 'significant' capacity reduction may be required.[355] In this connection, account may be taken of international competition. For example, to remain competitive, the Union paper and board industry must orient its production increasingly towards special papers[356] and towards lower-quality paper and board produced largely from waste paper. Therefore, aid to encourage use of

[345] Community Action Programme regarding Forestry and Forest-Based Industries, COM(83)222, 12.

[346] [1985] OJ L93/1.

[347] On improving the efficiency of agricultural structures ([1991] OJ L218/1), as amended by Reg. 2080/92 ([1992] OJ L215/96) instituting a Community aid scheme for forestry products in agriculture, regarding aid to promote afforestation as an alternative use of agricultural land and the development of forestry activities on agricultural land (Art. 1).

[348] Sect. 5.2.1 above.

[349] [1990] OJ L91/7.

[350] Bull. EC 1/2–1990, 1.1.53.

[351] *Second Report on Competition Policy* (EC Commission, Brussels, 1973), 96–9.

[352] Notice C27/92 (N295/92) ([1993] OJ C46/5) on aid to SCA Aylesford, a manufacturer of newsprint.

[353] Dec. 92/129 ([1992] OJ L47/19) on aid granted by the Italian Government to the forestry, pulp, paper, and board industry and financed by means of levies on paper, board, and cellulose. The means by which the aid was financed was more problematic. See, earlier, Dec. 76/574 ([1976] OJ L185/32) concerning the Italian scheme of assistance for the press and the paper-manufacturing industry granted through the Ente Nazionale per la Cellulosa e per la Carta.

[354] Bull. EC 12–1986, 2.1.68. See, earlier, Bull. EC 9–1982, 2.1.21.

[355] *Sixteenth Report on Competition Policy* (EC Commission, Brussels, 1987), 163.

[356] Cf. Notice C40/95 (ex N353/95) ([1995] OJ C295/20) concerning aid which Germany intended to grant to Glunz AG, a wood-processing firm.

waste paper may be authorized.[357] Relatively high rates of such aid may be authorized under Article 92(3)(c).[358]

However, aid may be regarded as adversely affecting trade to an extent contrary to the common interest where it is granted to subsectors, such as coated paper, suffering from overcapacity.[359] Aid may also be regarded as unable to facilitate the development of the sector, where it concerns investment which the recipient would be in a position to undertake using its own resources, or at least those of its parent company.[360]

Particular account may be taken of regional-policy considerations.[361] For example, restructuring aid to the solid-board industry in the Netherlands was authorized because the industry's capacity would be significantly reduced and because there were regional problems in the area where the industry was principally located.[362]

5.4.2 Operating Aid

Operating aid is less acceptable than restructuring aid.[363] Thus, in the absence of any agreed strategy for making the industry viable, long-term aid for newsprint production has been prohibited.[364] Rescue aid in the form of 'equity

---

[357] *Sixth Report on Competition Policy* (EC Commission, Brussels, 1977), 118–9.

[358] Reply by Mr Fischler to Written Question E-3200/95 ([1996] OJ C91/43) by Karl von Wogau.

[359] Notice C1/93 (N724/92) ([1993] OJ C75/7) concerning aid granted by the Italian Government (autonomous province of Trento) to Cartiere del Garda.

[360] Dec. 91/305 ([1991] OJ L156/39) concerning investment aid which the Belgian Government planned to grant to Mactac SA, Soignies.

[361] Aid to investments that create new capacity may be prohibited in areas not covered by Art. 92(3)(a) or (c). See Dec. 91/305 ([1991] OJ L156/39) concerning investment aid which the Belgian Government planned to grant to Mactac SA, Soignies. No reference to regional considerations is made in Point 2.13 of Dec. 94/173 ([1994] OJ L79/29) on the selection criteria to be adopted for investments for improving the processing and marketing conditions for agricultural and forestry products and repealing Dec. 90/342, which excluded Union aid for certain types of investment in the forestry sector. However, Dec. 90/342 continues to apply by analogy in relation to state aid in this sector (see sect. 5.2.1 above) and contains no similar clause.

[362] *Eighth Report on Competition Policy* (EC Commission, Brussels, 1979), 149–50. See also, regarding investment grants for felling and logging in Thuringia (Eastern Germany), Bull. EU 1/2–1995, 1.3.40.

[363] *Second Report on Competition Policy* (EC Commission, Brussels, 1973), 96–9. See, similarly, the *Eighteenth Report on Competition Policy* (EC Commission, Brussels, 1989), 181. Such aid was exceptionally authorized by the Council in the Decision of 19 Dec. 1960 ([1960] JO 1972) on the French aid system in favour of certain types of paper pulp, as amended by Dec. 68/160 ([1968] JO L76/12).

[364] *Eighth Report on Competition Policy* (EC Commission, Brussels, 1979), 147–9. See also Dec. 90/215 ([1989] OJ L114/25) on aid granted by the Italian Government to the newsprint industry; and Dec. 92/296 ([1992] OJ L159/46) concerning aid granted by the Italian Government to Nuova Cartiera di Arbatax. Such aid was prohibited in Dec. 82/670 ([1982] OJ L280/30) on aid granted by the Belgian Government to a paper-manufacturing undertaking, which was annulled for lack of reasoning in Case 323/82 *Intermills SA* v. *EC Commission* [1984] ECR 3809,

loans' may also be prohibited.[365] The Commission is said to have adopted a strict approach to such aid, because it regards the crisis in the paper industry as structural rather than conjunctural.[366]

Objections to operating aid may outweigh regional policy considerations.[367] In Decision 88/282,[368] which concerned French aid to the wood-processing sector, the Commission noted that part of the aid scheme complied with the principles of co-ordination of regional aid. That part of the scheme could, therefore, be regarded as permissible under Article 92(3)(c). On the other hand, since the Community Action Programme regarding Forestry and Forest-Based Industries[369] did not express a favourable view of operating aid, it could not affect the applicability of Article 92.[370] The part of the scheme which involved the grant of operating aid was, therefore, prohibited.

Such practice has been criticized as being insufficiently restrictive of aid. While aid to forestry in remote areas may be considered as a means of promoting regional development, aid directed specifically towards forestry activities may entail a potential misuse of land, which may not benefit the overall efficiency of the forestry sector. Such aid permits marketing of timber below cost and increased supply, thus reducing profitability and willingness to invest. Such willingness is any case already affected by inadequate information in the market. Hence, it has been argued that intervention in forestry should be primarily directed towards the protection of non-marketed benefits, such as the diversity of plant and animal species, recreational services, and so on. In short, the grant of aid should be based on externality considerations. However, in some cases, such as in the case of forest wetlands, there may be a conflict between externalities such as environmental protection and sectoral considerations.[371]

---

and in Dec. 82/653 ([1982] OJ L277/15) on aid granted by the Netherlands Government to a paperboard-processing firm, which was similarly annulled in Joined Cases 296 & 318/82 *Netherlands and Leeuwaarder Papierenfabriek BV* v. *EC Commission* [1985] ECR 809. In particular, the ECJ observed that there was no indication that the Commission took into consideration an essential fact—that the aid was accompanied by a restructuring of the recipient which, by diverting its production to high-quality products, led to a reduction in its production capacity and in its market share (*ibid.*, 825).

[365] Dec. 84/489 ([1984] OJ L273/26) on the FF 200 million of aid in the form of equity loans which the French Government granted to a newsprint producer in 1981 and 1982.

[366] VerLoren van Themaat AG in Case 323/82 *Intermills SA* v. *EC Commission* [1984] ECR 3809, 3847.

[367] Notice C29/92 (NN12/92) ([1993] OJ C123/7) concerning aid granted in the Basque country to La Papelera Espanola.

[368] On aid from the French Government to the wood-processing sector (Isoroy and Pinault) ([1987] OJ L119/38).

[369] COM(83)222.

[370] See also Dec. 72/436 ([1972] JO L297/32) on the French aid system for the production of paper pulp and paper forestry research and reafforestation.

[371] S. Wibe, 'Policy Failures in Managing Forests' in *Market and Government Failures in Environmental Management: Wetlands and Forests* (OECD Paris 1992) 45–82, 78.

5.5 COAL

Article 11 of the Convention on the Transitional Provisions, which was concluded with the ECSC Treaty, required the gradual elimination of aid to the coal industry[372] not authorized by the Commission. Special arrangements, including the grant of operating aid in Belgium, to avoid 'fundamental disturbances in the Belgian economy',[373] as well as aid in France[374] and Sardinia,[375] were permitted.

Article 4(c) of the ECSC Treaty itself states that 'subsidies or aids granted by states . . . in any form whatsoever' are incompatible with the common market for coal and shall, accordingly, be abolished and prohibited. More particularly, if under Article 54 of the Treaty the Commission finds that the financing of an investment programme or the operation of installations therein planned will involve aid, the undertaking is prohibited from drawing on resources other than its own funds to carry out the programme. The prohibition covers both aid specifically intended for the coal industry and the application of general, regional, or other schemes to this industry. For example, compensation to electricity generators using Union coal is treated as entailing aid to the coal industry.[376] Earlier, the view had been taken that Article 4(c) was inapplicable to 'non-specific' aid,[377] and the Commission considered that only Article 67 ECSC covered 'non-specific' aid.[378] Decision 2064/86[379] was the first legislative measure to cover such aid.[380]

However, Article 88 of the ECSC Treaty provides that where a Member State is in violation of the Treaty, the Commission may authorize 'measures, by way of derogation from the provisions of Article 4, in order to correct the effects of the infringement'. More particularly, Article 56 envisages readaptation aid for workers affected by restructuring in the coal and steel industries. Article 53 also implies that some aid may be permitted. It provides for the Commission to make recommendations to Member States where financial

---

[372] For the purposes of the ECSC Treaty, 'coal' is defined in Annex I.

[373] Art. 26(4) of the Convention. See, regarding Belgian aid which was accepted subject to reorganization requirements and respect for a production ceiling, Dec. 40/59 ([1957] JO 876) on the grant of subsidies to the coal industry by the Belgian Government.

[374] Art. 28(2) of the Convention. See also Dec. 26/53 ([1953] JO CECA 84) on the reduction of the subsidies of the French Government to coal supplied to undertakings not engaged in mining.

[375] Art. 27(1) of the Convention. See also the *ECSC Third General Report* (ECSC High Authority Luxembourg 1955), 95–6.

[376] See, e.g., Dec. 90/633 ([1990] OJ L346/20) concerning a financial measure taken by Germany in respect of the coal industry in 1990.

[377] Roemer AG in Case 59/70 *Netherlands* v. *EC Commission: aids to the iron and steel industry* [1971] ECR 639, 663.

[378] *Second Report on Competition Policy* (EC Commission, Brussels, 1973), 110.

[379] Establishing Community rules for state aid to the coal industry ([1986] OJ L177/1).

[380] *Ibid.*, Art. 1.

arrangements common to several undertakings are inconsistent with the application of the Treaty.[381]

Moreover, there was concern to avoid applying the ECSC Treaty in such a way as to put this industry in an unfavourable position in comparison with other industries which might receive aid under Article 92 of the EC Treaty.[382] Thus Article 4(c) of the ECSC Treaty was interpreted as only prohibiting the unilateral grant of aid by a Member State[383] and as permitting Commission authorization of aid to the coal industry, in view of Article 2, in order to safeguard the continuity of employment.[384] According to this provision, the ECSC was to promote rational distribution of production and productivity with continuity of employment, while taking care not to provoke fundamental and persistent disturbances in the economies of Member States. Moreover, in an Agreement of 21 April 1964, the Member States expressed the desire to establish and implement a common energy policy, particularly in relation to state aid.[385] Since then a series of decisions authorizing aid to the coal industry[386] has been enacted under Article 95 of the ECSC Treaty, which provides for enactment of measures necessary for attainment of ECSC objectives.

5.5.1 Restructuring Aid

According to the Preamble[387] to Decision 3/65,[388] Article 4(c) of the ECSC Treaty did not preclude 'a Community regime in pursuit of Community

---

[381] See, regarding this provision, Case 12/57 *Syndicat de la Sidérurgie du Centre-Midi* v. *ECSC High Authority* [1957–8] ECR 375.

[382] The High Authority apparently only regarded operating aid to the coal industry as a subsidy for the purposes of Art. 4(c) ECSC; even then there was considered to be no subsidy where state financing could be assimilated to the behaviour of a private owner. See Reply to Written Question 170 by Mr Nederhorst ([1963] JO 973).

[383] Case 30/59 *De Gezamenlijke Steenkolenmijnen in Limburg* v. *ECSC High Authority* [1961] ECR 1, 22.

[384] *Ibid.*, 30. See, regarding transitional aid to coal and steel producers, Dec. 71/293 ([1971] JO L179/33) authorizing special tariffs on the Deutsche Bundesbahn in favour of coal or steel producers established in the Saar.. Regional employment surveys in the coal and steel industries began to be produced in 1958. See the *Sixth ECSC General Report* (ECSC High Authority, Luxembourg, 1958), 180–3. See the authorization of restructuring aid by Dec. 27/58 ([1958] JO 486) on the grant of financial aid to tackle the situation in the coal industry resulting from the exceptional accumulation of stocks, which jeopardized the continuity of employment.

[385] Protocol on Energy Problems, agreed by the governments of the Member States at the 94th meeting of the Special Council of Ministers of the ECSC of 21 Apr. 1964, in Luxembourg ([1964] JO 1099), paras 5 and 11.

[386] According to C.–D. Ehlermann, 'State Aid Control in the European Union: Success or Failure?' (1995) 18 *Fordham Intl LJ* 1212–29, Art. 4(c) ECSC suffered from 'years of total disregard'.

[387] Para. 4.

[388] On the Community system of interventions by Member States in favour of the coal industry ([1965] JO 480). Its application was prolonged by Dec. 27/67 ([1967] JO 261).

objectives'. Hence, aid for the 'positive rationalization' of coal undertakings[389] and aid related to closures[390] were authorized by this Decision. Moreover, Article 5(1) of the Decision[391] provided that if the adjustment of undertakings to new coal market conditions was such as to entail serious problems, such as 'insufficient equilibrium'[392] or reconversion associated with 'polarization' around the mining industry,[393] in the economic and social life of a region because development possibilities there were limited, aid could be authorized to permit an appropriate pace of rationalization.[394]

In addition, in 1974 aid for the use of coal for electricity generation was authorized partly because it would promote diversity of Union energy supplies.[395] Such aid was later authorized, because electricity producers using coal gained no advantage over those using fuel oil or natural gas.[396]

In Decision 528/76[397] greater stress, which reflected the requirement of orderly supply in Article 3(a) of the ECSC Treaty, was placed on the need to ensure the long-term security of the Union's energy supplies.[398] Accordingly, maintenance of Union coal production, taking into account the natural and technical situation in the individual fields under satisfactory economic conditions, was sought as well as increased competitiveness in this industry.[399] For such purposes, closure aid was to be considered compatible with the common market,[400] and investment aid might be so considered.[401] Provision for authorization of training and recruitment aid was also introduced.[402]

However, there was growing concern to achieve viability in the coal industry and to reduce the volume of aid, even if this meant that substantial reductions

---

[389] Art. 3 of Dec. 3/65. See, e.g., Dec. 1991/68 ([1968] JO L298/12) authorizing Belgian aids in 1968 to undertakings in the coal industry. See, for the two previous years, Dec. 17/67 ([1967] JO 2525) and Dec. 29/67 ([1967] JO 284/5).

[390] Art. 4 of Dec. 3/65. See, e.g., Dec. 1992/68 ([1968] JO L298/14) authorizing aids granted by Germany in 1968 to undertakings in the coal industry.

[391] It was replaced by Art. 9(1) of Dec. 3/71 [1971] JO L3/7 on the Community system of interventions by Member States in favour of the coal industry.

[392] Dec. 1993/68 ([1968] JO L298/17) authorizing aids granted by the Netherlands in 1968 to undertakings in the coal industry.

[393] Dec. 1994/68 ([1968] JO L298/18) authorizing aids granted by France in 1968 to undertakings in the coal industry.

[394] See, e.g., Dec. 1991/68 ([1968] JO L298/12) authorizing aids granted by Belgium in 1968 to undertakings in the coal industry and Dec. 6/66 ([1966] JO 792) authorizing aids granted in 1965 by Belgium to undertakings in the coal industry.

[395] *Fourth Report on Competition Policy* (EC Commission, Brussels, 1975), 96.

[396] *Seventh Report on Competition Policy* (EC Commission, Brussels, 1978), 180.

[397] Regarding the Community system of measures taken by the Member States to assist the coal-mining industry ([1976] OJ L63/1), Art. 8.

[398] Roemer AG in Joined Cases 27–29/58 *Compagnie des Hauts Fourneaux et Fonderies de Givors* v. *ECSC High Authority* [1960] ECR 241, 275. The Commission continues to stress the importance of security of supply, as well as a related public-service obligation of universal, uninterrupted provision. See Art. 13(2) of the Proposal for a Dir. on common rules for the internal market in energy, COM(91)549.

[399] Part I of the Preamble to Dec. 528/76 [1976] OJ L63/1.   [400] *Ibid.*, Art. 5.

[401] *Ibid.*, Art. 7.   [402] *Ibid.*, Art. 8.

in uneconomic capacity would be entailed.[403] The maintenance of an immutable volume of coal production in the Union could no longer be a priority objective, when Union coal could only match the price of imported coal through heavy subsidies. Thus while aid could be granted to deal with the social repercussions of contraction and to promote security of supply,[404] it should be reduced as far as possible. However, German aid to encourage the use of coal for generation of electricity and Dutch aid for the conversion of natural gas-fired installations to coal firing were authorized because they were consistent with Union energy policy.[405] At the same time, conversion to solid fuel was to be encouraged.[406]

Viability concerns gained increased prominence in Decision 2064/86.[407] The Preamble stressed the need to make the coal industry competitive through restructuring, though this process was to take place in an ordered and socially acceptable fashion. In addition to helping the industry to raise its competitiveness and adjust to the new market conditions, which should reduce the level of aid for current production, satisfactory arrangements were envisaged for cushioning the effects of necessary rationalization on miners and mining communities.[408]

Accordingly, Article 2(1) of the Decision provided that aid might be permissible, if it contributed to the achievement of the following aims:

—improvement of competitiveness of the coal industry, which contributed to assuring a better security of supply;
—creating new capacities provided that they were economically viable;
—solving the social and regional problems related to developments in the coal industry.

The basic condition for authorization under this heading seems to have been that there should be a capacity reduction.[409] However, environmental aid might also be authorized under this heading,[410] without such a reduction being entailed.

In deciding whether the financial measures proposed by Member States were compatible with the common market, the Commission was also required by Article 13 to give due consideration to any aid which might be granted to

---

[403] See also the *Fourteenth Report on Competition Policy* (EC Commission, Brussels, 1985), 163.

[404] *Eleventh Report on Competition Policy* (EC Commission, Brussels, 1982), 154–5. See, regarding German and British aid, *ibid.*, 155–7. See also the *Twelfth Report on Competition Policy* (EC Commission, Brussels, 1983), 132.

[405] *Thirteenth Report on Competition Policy* (EC Commission, Brussels, 1984), 170.

[406] Rec. 83/250 ([1983] OJ L140/25) to the Member States concerning the encouragement of investment in the use of solid fuel in industry.

[407] Establishing Community rules for state aid to the coal industry ([1986] OJ L177/1).

[408] *Fifteenth Report on Competition Policy* (EC Commission, Brussels, 1986), 153–4.

[409] See, e.g., Dec. 93/147 ([1993] OJ L58/60) concerning the authorization of financial measures by Germany in respect of the coal industry in 1993.

[410] Dec. 93/146 ([1993] OJ L57/29) on a financial measure by Spain in respect of the coal industry in 1992 and 1993 and additional financial measures in respect of that industry in 1991.

Union coal producers to supply the Union steel industry under Decision 759/84[411] and Decision 3612/85[412] concerning coal and coke for the Community iron and steel industry. These measures authorized Member States to grant aid to coal undertakings which supplied coking-coal and blast-furnace coke to the Union iron and steel industry. Such aid might take the form of production aid or sales aid applicable to deliveries to areas remote from the coalfield or effected by way of trade between Member States.[413]

Aid up to 50 per cent of investment costs might be considered compatible with the common market, if the investment helped to improve competitiveness and any new capacity created was economically viable.[414] Aid to cover costs arising from restructuring which would not be viable and related to current production ('inherited liabilities', as defined in Annex I to the Decision) might be similarly treated.[415] However, the aid was not to exceed what was absolutely necessary,[416] and in practice the Commission sought to secure gradual reduction of the aid which it authorized.[417]

The 'degressive' principle is now emphasized in Decision 3632/93.[418] Article 2(1) thereof provides that aid may be authorized:

—to make, in the light of coal prices on international markets, further progress towards economic viability with the aim of achieving degression of aid;[419]

—to solve the social and regional problems created by total or partial reductions in the activity of production units;[420]

—to help the coal industry adjust to environmental protection standards.[421]

Accordingly, until expiry of Decision 3632/93 in 2002, aid may be granted pursuant to a restructuring plan to improve the economic viability of the recipients by reducing production costs.[422] In the case of undertakings incap-

---

[411] [1984] OJ L80/14.   [412] [1985] OJ L344/33.

[413] See, earlier, Dec. 1/67 ([1967] JO 562) on coking coal and coke for the Community steel industry and Dec. 1/70 ([1970] JO L2/10) on coking coal and coke.

[414] Art. 5 of Dec. 2064/86.

[415] *Ibid.*, Art. 8.   [416] *Ibid.*, s. III in the Preamble.

[417] See, e.g., Dec. 89/296 ([1989] OJ L116/52) ruling on a financial measure taken by Germany in respect of the coal industry during 1988 and a supplementary financial measure in respect of the coal industry during 1987; and Dec. 90/633 ([1990] OJ L346/20) concerning a financial measure taken by Germany in respect of the coal industry in 1990.

[418] Establishing Community rules for state aid to the coal industry ([1993] OJ L329/12).

[419] Art. 5(2) provides that aid to cover the costs arising from the modernization, rationalization, or restructuring of the coal industry which are not related to current production may be authorized. The aid must not exceed such costs. See, e.g., Dec. 94/573 ([1994] OJ L220/10) authorizing the granting of aid by Germany to the coal industry in 1994. See, regarding aid to facilitate privatization in the UK, Dec. 94/995 ([1994] OJ L379/6) ruling on measures by the UK in respect of the coal industry in the 1994/95 and 1995/96 financial years.

[420] See, e.g., Dec. 94/994 ([1994] OJ L379/3) authorizing the granting of aid by Portugal to the coal industry in 1994.

[421] Arts. 6 and 7 of Dec. 3632/93 respectively permit aid for R & D and environmental aid.

[422] *Ibid.*, Art. 3(2).

able of achieving viability, closure aid may be granted until the same deadline. Thereafter closure aid must be justified by exceptional social and regional circumstances.

5.5.2 Operating Aid

Article 2(2) of Decision 3/65[423] provided for authorization of aid in respect of social charges. Such aid was, according to Part 3 of the Preamble, necessary to re-establish the competitive conditions required by Article 4 of the ECSC Treaty. Operating aid, where it was justified by regional policy considerations or security of supply concerns, was also authorized by Decision 528/76.[424] Similarly, aid for building up stocks,[425] aid for stabilizing in the long term the sale of Union steam coal for power stations,[426] and aid for bringing the ratio between the burden per miner in employment and the benefits per person in receipt of benefit into line with the corresponding ratio in other sectors[427] were authorized by Decision 528/76.

Decision 2064/86[428] sought rather more closely to define permissible operating aid. According to the Preamble to this Decision, in view of the weak competitive position of, and the losses made by, coal undertakings in the Union, it would be necessary to close down a large proportion of pits in the short term if these losses were not covered. In addition to supply difficulties, such closure would give rise to considerable regional and employment problems. Hence, Article 6 of the Decision provided that aid granted under existing schemes to maintain the underground labour force in deep mines might be authorized.[429] Article 4 allowed for aid for supplying coal and coke to the Union's iron and steel industry and Article 7 for aid to finance social grants specific to the coal industry. Account might be taken of the inadequacy of employment opportunities for redundant miners.[430]

Moreover, Article 3(1) of Decision 2064/86 permitted 'deficit aid grants' not

---

[423] On the Community system of interventions by Member States in favour of the coal industry ([1965] JO 480).

[424] Regarding the Community system of measures taken by the Member States to assist the coal-mining industry ([1976] OJ L63/1), Art. 12. See, e.g., Dec. 89/176 ([1989] OJ L64/15) approving aid from Spain for the coal-mining industry during 1986.

[425] Arts. 9 and 10.

[426] Art. 11.

[427] Art. 4. Belgian aid bringing the ratio between the burden per mineworker in employment and the benefits for persons in receipt of benefit below the corresponding ratio in other industries exceeded the limits of Art. 7. However, the aid was authorized, because it met the objectives of the third indent of Art. 3(1). See Dec. 91/405 ([1991] OJ L226/27) ruling on the granting of aid by Belgium to the coal industry during 1991.

[428] Establishing Community rules for state aid to the coal industry ([1986] OJ L177/1).

[429] For examples of the operation of this provision see *Application of the Community Rules for State Aid to the Coal Industry in 1989*, COM(91)1240.

[430] See, e.g., Dec. 89/177 ([1989] OJ L64/17) approving aid from Portugal to the coal-mining industry during 1986.

exceeding, for each tonne produced and for each individual coal region or undertaking, the difference between foreseeable average costs and the foreseeable average returns in the following financial year (coal production year).[431] However, according to Article 3(2), if the Commission found that the difference between the average costs of coal production and the average returns achievable was due to changes in the situation of coal undertakings which were out of keeping with satisfactory economic conditions, it might fix a maximum amount for aid covering losses. For example, Spanish deficit aid was authorized for 1989, but the Commission asked Spain to produce a plan for reducing the compensation payments and for restructuring, modernizing, and rationalizing the coal industry.[432] Thus operating aid linked with restructuring might be authorized.[433] Aid was not to be used to enable undertakings to charge excessively low prices, and progressive reduction of aid would be 'welcomed' by the Commission.[434] In practice, however, a lenient view might be taken of aid of this kind.[435] For example, if the difference between the world market price and production costs turned out to be greater than originally estimated, increased aid might be authorized.[436]

The Commission favoured further efforts to bring down production costs[437] and proposed that a ceiling should be introduced on the basis of a reference price for Union coal.[438] Thus the aid should bridge the gap between the world price and average Union production costs rather than whatever the local costs were.[439]

---

[431] See, e.g., Dec. 89/102 ([1989] OJ L38/39) approving aid from Spain to the coal industry during 1986.

[432] Dec. 90/198 ([1990] OJ L105/19) ruling on a financial measure taken by Spain in respect of the coal industry during 1989 and a supplementing financial measure in respect of the coal industry in 1988 and 1987. Aid for 1990 was pegged at the 1989 level. See Dec. 91/3 ([1991] OJ L5/27) ruling on financial measures by Spain in respect of the coal industry in 1988, 1989 and 1990.

[433] See, e.g., Dec. 93/429 ([1993] OJ L198/33) ruling on the granting of aid by France to the coal industry in 1993.

[434] Dec. 91/406 ([1991] OJ L226/28) on financial aid by Germany to the coal industry in 1990 and supplementary aid to the coal industry for 1989. Aid covering only 57% of the difference was authorized in Dec. 93/429 ([1993] OJ L198/33) ruling on the granting of aid by France to the coal industry in 1993.

[435] See, e.g., Dec. 93/66 ([1993] OJ L21/33) concerning financial measures by Germany in respect of the coal industry in 1990, 1991, and 1992 and additional financial aid for the coal industry in 1989 and 1990.

[436] Dec. 89/161 ([1989] OJ L61/46) approving supplementary aid from Germany to the coal industry during 1988. See also Dec. 89/175 ([1989] OJ L64/14) approving supplementary aid from the UK to the coal industry in the 1987 financial year.

[437] *Financial Times*, 30 July 1992.

[438] *Application of the Community Rules for State Aid to the Coal Industry in 1991*, COM(93)116, 24.

[439] The Commission aims to limit the protection of indigenous fuels in the Member States to 20% of final electricity demand (*Twenty-Second Report on Competition Policy* (EC Commission, Brussels, 1993), 245; see also the Explanatory Memorandum to the Proposal for a Dir. concerning common rules for the internal market in electricity and Art. 13(5) of the Proposal, COM(91)548, 11–2). The principle was applied in Dec. 93/126 ([1993] OJ L50/14) relating to a proceeding under Art. 85 EC and Art. 65 ECSC (IV/33.151—Jahrhundertvertrag) (IV/33/997—VIK-GVSt). Ceilings imposed by individual Member States may be 'welcomed' by the

Aid authorization would also be dependent on plans for reduction of the costs of high-cost producers.[440]

Such thinking is partly reflected in Article 3(1) of Decision 3632/93,[441] which stipulates that the amount of operating aid per tonne must not cause delivered prices for Union coal to be lower than those for coal of a similar quality from third countries. Article 3(2) of this Decision requires Member States which intend to grant such aid to submit to the Commission in advance a modernization, rationalization, and restructuring plan designed to improve the economic viability of the undertakings concerned by reducing production costs. Article 5 also allows for aid to cover inherited liabilities, indicated in the Annex,[442] but Article 3 requires that the aid should not exceed costs.[443] Otherwise, such aid may only be granted within the framework of a closure plan, though the Commission does not seem very demanding as to evidence that this condition will be met,[444] and aid authorizations may be adjusted upwards because of currency fluctuations.[445] Such aid may only be granted after expiry of the Decision, that is, 23 July 2002,[446] if it is justified on exceptional social and regional grounds and is part of a progressive and continuous activity-reduction plan entailing a significant reduction in capacity before the expiry of this Decision.[447]

In this way the Union legislature apparently seeks to reconcile its commitment to economic and social cohesion, as expressed in the Preamble to the Decision, and the concern, also expressed therein, that reductions of costs and capacity should be concentrated primarily on those areas of production receiving the highest level of aid. The Preamble to the Decision also asserts that 'the Community must progressively bring about conditions which will of themselves ensure the most rational distribution of coal production'. In addition, 'it has been recognized that, in cases of early closure of installations with no prospect of future viability, aid should be granted, as deemed necessary by the Member State, for regional industrial development, to the extent compatible with the

Commission. See Dec. 95/464 ([1995] OJ L267/42) on German aid to the coal industry for 1995.

[440] *Second Progress Report on the Internal Energy Market*, COM(93) 261, 11.

[441] Establishing Community rules for state aid to the coal industry ([1993] OJ L329/12).

[442] See, regarding aid to compensate miners for industrial injury and damage to health, Dec. 96/274 ([1996] OJ L102/42) concerning additional financial aid by the United Kingdom in respect of the coal industry in the 1995–6 financial year.

[443] Dec. 95/465 ([1995] OJ L267/46) authorizing France to grant aid for the coal industry for 1994.

[444] See, e.g., Dec. 94/574 ([1994] OJ L220/12) authorizing the grant by the UK of aid to the coal industry for the last quarter of the 1993–4 financial year and for the 1994–5 financial year.

[445] Dec. 95/499 ([1995] OJ L287/53) authorizing additional aid by Germany to the coal industry for 1994.

[446] The Commission envisages that aid should be permissible 'at least' until 2002. See the Reply by Mr Matutes to Written Question E–1804/93 ([1994] OJ C255/10) by Christian de la Malène and Alain Pompidou.

[447] Art. 4 of Dec. 3632/93 [1993] OJ L329/12.

Treaties'. Article 5(2) also provides that aid to finance social grant schemes specific to the coal industry may be considered compatible with the common market provided that, for coal undertakings, it brings the ratio between the burden per mineworker in employment and the benefits per person in receipt of benefit into line with the corresponding ratio in other industries.

5.6 STEEL

The Convention on Transitional Provisions, which was concluded with the ECSC Treaty, was less permissive of aid to the steel industry than of aid to the coal industry. It merely provided that the ECSC might provide Luxembourg with assistance to deal with any repercussions for its steel industry of the special arrangements for the Belgian coal industry.[448] Article 4(c) of the ECSC Treaty itself states that 'subsidies or aids granted by states . . . in any form whatsoever' are incompatible with the common market for steel and shall, accordingly, be abolished and prohibited. The prohibition covers both aid specifically intended for the steel industry and the application of general, regional, or other schemes to this industry. However, there was concern to avoid applying the ECSC Treaty in such a way as to put this industry in an unfavourable position in comparison with other industries which might be permitted to receive aid under Article 92 of the EC Treaty.[449]

Principles regarding aid to the steel sector were originally introduced by a Commission letter to the Member States of April 1977.[450] However, 'legal considerations' were felt to necessitate legislation regarding steel producers covered by the ECSC Treaty.[451] In the case of steel producers not so covered, the acceptability of aid has remained dependent on Article 92 of the EC Treaty. According to practice under this provision, restructuring aid may be authorized under Article 92(3)(c) thereof, where there are capacity reductions or there is specialization in profitable market segments in which supply does not exceed demand.[452]

5.6.1 Restructuring Aid

According to the 1977 Principles, restructuring aid to the steel sector should not lead to capacity increases in subsectors where there was manifest over-

---

[448] Art. 31 of the Convention.

[449] See the argument of the Commission in Case 59/70 *Netherlands* v. *EC Commission: aids to the iron and steel industry* [1971] ECR 639, 646. See also Roemer AG (*ibid.*, 664), regarding the desirability of putting the various sectors of the national economy 'in an equal material position'.

[450] See, earlier, the objections of the Commission to French steel aid in the *Twelfth ECSC General Report* (ECSC High Authority, Luxembourg, 1964), 176–7.

[451] *Eighth Report on Competition Policy* (EC Commission, Brussels, 1978), 136. See also the *Eleventh EC General Report* (EC Commission, Brussels, 1977), 148 ff.

[452] Dec. 87/506 ([1987] OJ L290/21) concerning aid granted by the French Government to two steel groups.

capacity, and the form and intensity of the aid should be appropriate to the objectives sought and the problems which the aid was intended to resolve.[453]

However, the Commission considered that ECSC Treaty provisions did not offer the necessary flexibility for appraisal of aid in a period of crisis[454] and in May 1978 submitted a draft decision to the Council under Article 95 of the ECSC Treaty. The Council accepted that legislation should be adopted regarding specific aid to the steel industry, which was prohibited by this Treaty, except in the rare case where an action by a Member State damaged its own steel industry.[455] On the other hand, the Council considered that non-specific aid to the steel industry should continue to be assessed under Article 92.[456]

As a result, Decision 257/80[457] dealt only with specific aid to the steel industry.[458] It authorized such aid for investment, provided that the amount and intensity were justified by the extent of the restructuring involved, account being taken of the structural problems of the region where the investment was to be undertaken, and that the aid was limited to what was necessary for the restructuring.[459] Closure aid was also permitted.[460]

However, the deepening of the steel crisis meant that Decision 2320/81[461] had to be enacted. This measure was designed to ensure, by the phasing out of aid by the end of 1985, that restructuring was carried through with the greater rapidity which the situation now demanded. It covered specific and non-specific aid.[462] Hence, the Commission was to be informed of plans to grant aid to the steel industry under schemes which it had already authorized under the EC Treaty.[463]

The requirement was also introduced by Decision 2320/81 that aid recipients must be engaged in a restructuring programme which would result in capacity reductions,[464] and aid was not to be paid after 31 December 1985.[465] The Court of Justice accepted the introduction of the former requirement. According to the Court, 'in a situation of crisis there is a close link, for the

---

[453] *Seventh Report on Competition Policy* (EC Commission, Brussels, 1978), 181.

[454] *Eighth Report on Competition Policy* (EC Commission, Brussels, 1979), 136. See also the *Ninth Report on Competition Policy* (EC Commission, Brussels, 1980), 101–4.

[455] Art. 67(2) ECSC. See, e.g., Dec. 914/68 ([1968] JO L159/4) authorizing the French Government to grant certain aids to the steel industry.

[456] *Eighth Report on Competition Policy* (EC Commission, Brussels, 1979), 138.

[457] Establishing Community rules for specific aids to the steel industry ([1980] OJ L29/5).

[458] *Ibid.*, Art. 1(1).

[459] *Ibid.*, Art. 2.

[460] *Ibid.*, Art. 3. In Denmark restructuring aid to a steel company was acceptable, because the closure of one of its mills was involved (*Tenth Report on Competition Policy* (EC Commission, Brussels, 1981), 137).

[461] Establishing Community rules for aids to the steel industry ([1981] OJ L228/14).

[462] *Ibid.*, Art. 1(1).

[463] See, e.g., Dec. 91/547 ([1991] OJ L298/1) concerning aid granted by the Autonomous Region of Sardinia to Ferriere Acciaierie Sarde.

[464] *Ibid.*, Art. 2(1).

[465] Art. 2(1) of Dec. 2320/81 [1981] OJ L228/14. See, more particularly, the treatment of investment aid (Art. 3), closure aid (Art. 4), and R & D aid (Art. 7).

purposes of the implementation of the ECSC Treaty, between the granting of aid to the steel industry and the restructuring which that industry is required to undertake'.[466]

Thus, for example, Belgian aid was objectionable, because capacity reductions were insufficient and the recipient would not be rendered viable.[467] Similarly, aid for replacement or modernization investment was unacceptable.[468] Even where it was authorized, aid was to be progressively reduced,[469] though in practice the 'degressivity' principle proved difficult to implement.[470] However, since the restructuring effort was many-faceted, the intensity of different forms of aid varied and there were other criteria to be respected (for example, more aid than was needed should not be authorized), the Commission did not at the time accept that it should establish a fixed ceiling in monetary terms for aids per tonne of capacity reduction.[471]

Hence, an exact quantitative ratio was not established or intended between the amount of the aid and the required cuts in production capacity. In particular, the capacity cuts required by the Commission did not have to be in a fixed ratio, in all Member States, to the total amount of aid to be granted. Other factors to be taken into account included the restructuring effort made before 1980 and the regional and social problems occasioned by the crisis.[472]

Particular account was to be taken of the special situation of Member States having only one steel undertaking.[473] Thus aid for the financial restructuring of the sole Danish undertaking in this sector was accepted, even though it was not expected to lead to viability, provided that a plan to secure viability was adopted.[474] Viability was treated as requiring sales margins sufficient to cover all costs, including depreciation and capital charges, and to remunerate the capital at a minimum level.[475]

Decision 3484/85[476] was more restrictive. It permitted only research and development aid,[477] environmental aid,[478] closure aid,[479] and regional aid which

---

[466] Case 214/83 *Germany* v. *EC Commission: aid to the steel industry* [1985] ECR 3053, 3090.

[467] *Eleventh Report on Competition Policy* (EC Commission, Brussels, 1982), 134–5; Dec. 82/951 ([1982] OJ L386/27) on the aid which the Belgian Government proposed to grant to the steel firm Laminoirs de Jemappes SA.

[468] *Twelfth Report on Competition Policy* (EC Commission, Brussels, 1983), 146–7.

[469] Art. 5(1) of Dec. 2320/81 ([1981] OJ L228/14).

[470] VerLoren van Themaat AG in Case 214/83 *Germany* v. *EC Commission: aid to the steel industry* [1985] ECR 3053, 3075–6.

[471] *Twelfth Report on Competition Policy* (EC Commission, Brussels, 1983), 118–9.

[472] [1985] ECR 3053, 3091.

[473] Art. 2(3) of Dec. 2320/81 ([1981] OJ L228/14).

[474] *Eleventh Report on Competition Policy* (EC Commission, Brussels, 1982), 131–3.

[475] *Fourteenth Report on Competition Policy* (EC Commission, Brussels, 1985), 135.

[476] Establishing Community rules for aid to the steel industry ([1985] OJ L340/1).

[477] *Ibid.*, Art. 2.

[478] *Ibid.*, Art. 3.

[479] *Ibid.*, Art. 4. See, regarding authorization of closure aid for a Bavarian steel company, Bull. EC 11–1987, 2.1.100.

did not increase production capacity and was confined to Member States where restructuring aid had not been granted under Decision 2320/81.[480] The rationale for a more restrictive approach to aid was that, without the closure of inefficient plants, the continued operation of such plants could depress the market to the detriment of all undertakings in the sector. This restrictiveness reflected the Commission view that restructuring had increased capacity utilization to a level of 70 per cent, which should allow the industry to pursue further restructuring without aid.[481]

Similarly, Decision 322/89[482] authorized research and development aid,[483] environmental aid,[484] and certain forms of closure aid.[485] Environmental aid must be designed to comply with statutory environmental standards and meet the 15 per cent limit laid down by the guidelines for such aid.[486] Aid to energy conservation or improved product quality did not qualify for authorization.[487] Regional aid for steel investments which did not increase production capacity might be acceptable under Article 5. However, such aid might only be granted where the recipient undertaking was established on the territory of a Member State, that is, Greece, in which aid had not been authorized under Decision 257/80 or Decision 2320/81 and which had joined the Union during the period of validity of these measures.[488]

Since Article 5 of Decision 322/89 did not benefit Italy, the Commission found that no regional aid could be granted to steel firms in Sardinia. The fact that Sardinia might have special geographic or socio-economic features did not justify the grant of such aid to one of its steel firms.[489]

Article 5 of Decision 3855/91[490] subsequently provided that regional aid to

---

[480] Art. 5 of Dec. 3484/85 ([1985] OJ L340/1). See, however, regarding Commission objections to Portuguese regional investment aid to a steel producer, Bull. EC 7/8–1988, 2.1.74. Spanish aid was objectionable, even though the investment to be aided had been authorized under Art. 54 ECSC. See Bull. EC 7/8–1988, 2.1.72.

[481] *Fourteenth Report on Competition Policy* (EC Commission, Brussels, 1985), 134. According to Dec. 89/218 ([1988] OJ L86/76) concerning aid that the Italian Government proposed to grant to the public steel sector, since the steel market was 'cyclically in a boom situation', the capacity cuts necessary for authorization of the full amount of the aid could not be required. Hence two-thirds of the aid was authorized as a counterpart for certain reductions.

[482] Establishing Community rules for aid to the steel industry ([1989] OJ L38/8).

[483] *Ibid.*, Art. 2.   [484] *Ibid.*, Art. 3.

[485] *Ibid.*, Art. 4. These kinds of aid are compatible with the US–EC Steel Consensus ([1989] OJ L368/185). However, exceptions were permitted in relation to existing Italian aid under Dec. 89/218 ([1989] OJ L86/76) concerning aid that the Italian Government proposed to grant to the public steel sector.

[486] *Twentieth Report on Competition Policy* (EC Commission, Brussels, 1991), 153.

[487] Dec. 91/176 ([1991] OJ L86/28) on aid granted by the province of Bolzano to the Bolzano steelworks; Dec. 90/555 ([1990] OJ L314/17) concerning aid which the Italian authorities planned to grant to the Tirreno and Siderpotenza steel works.

[488] Dec. 91/176 ([1991] OJ L86/28) on aid granted by the province of Bolzano to the Bolzano steelworks.

[489] Dec. 91/547 ([1991] OJ L298/1) concerning aid granted by the Autonomous Region of Sardinia to Ferriere Acciaierie Sarde.

[490] Establishing Community rules for aid to the steel industry ([1991] OJ L362/57).

steel undertakings had to cease by 31 December 1994[491] and might only be authorized in three Member States. First, regional aid might be authorized in the case of steel undertakings in Greece, provided that the aided investment did not lead to an increase in production capacity. On the same condition regional aid might be authorized for small and medium-sized steel undertakings in Portugal. This possibility took account of the fact that Protocol 20 to the Act of Accession[492] prevented such undertakings from receiving aid for restructuring for a period of five years after accession.

Thirdly, aid might be authorized for undertakings in the territory of the former German Democratic Republic,[493] provided that the aid was accompanied by a reduction in the overall production capacity of that territory. This waiver of the prohibition of the aided investment itself leading to an increase in production capacity[494] was considered justified by reference to the effects on the steel industry in the former German Democratic Republic of 'the structural shortcomings of the planned economy system at its entry into the Community'.[495] The Commission considered that the steel industry in the former German Democratic Republic would have to undergo substantial restructuring, if its viability and its integration into the common market were to be ensured.[496] Thus investment aid to small and medium-sized steel undertakings being set up or having their capital increased in the former German Democratic Republic was accepted until the end of 1994.[497] The Commission also authorized extension of the German 'tax allowance for investment' scheme to the steel industry in the former German Democratic Republic, though each individual application of the scheme would be evaluated for compatibility with Decision 3855/91.[498] However, there must be a restructuring plan such as to lead to viability.[499] There must also be some connection

---

[491] The Commission seems to be seeking to secure respect for this deadline. See, regarding Greek aid, Bull. EU 5–1995, 1.3.44 and, regarding aid to the former GDR, Notice C11/95 (ex N777/94) ([1995] OJ C289/11) concerning aid which Germany was proposing to grant to Walzwerk Ilsenburg GmbH (Saxony-Anhalt) and Notice C2/95 (ex N775/94 & N776/94) ([1995] OJ C271/5) concerning aid which Germany was proposing to grant to Reinwald Recycling GmbH and Hansa Chemie Abbruch und Recycling GmbH (Saxony-Anhalt).

[492] On the restructuring of the Portuguese iron and steel industry.

[493] See also Notice ([1993] OJ C181/4), regarding the former GDR.

[494] The ECSC Consultative Committee considers that aid should be conditional on capacity reductions that will allow unsubsidized undertakings an opportunity to reduce costs by increasing their production. See the Resolution of 2 June 1992 ([1992] OJ C161/3) concerning a fresh policy for the future of the Community steel industry.

[495] Dec. 94/256 ([1994] OJ L112/45) concerning aid to be granted to the steel company EKO Stahl AG, Eisenhüttenstadt.

[496] *The European Community and German Unification*, Bull. EC, Supp. 4/90, 74–5.

[497] Bull. EC 6–1993, 1.2.57.

[498] Commission Communic. ([1993] OJ C163/4).

[499] *Twenty-Fourth Report on Competition Policy* (EC Commission, Brussels, 1995), 502.

between the aid and restructuring and capacity reduction,[500] and aid for a capacity-increasing investment may still be objectionable.[501]

Research and development aid[502] and environmental protection aid[503] may still be authorized under Decision 3855/91. Closure aid may also be authorized, under Article 4(2) of the same Decision,[504] and aid in respect of associated social costs may be authorized under Article 4(1) thereof.[505]

In addition, aid may be authorized by the Council under Article 95 of the ECSC Treaty.[506] Such authorization may be made subject to the condition that the ratio between the proposed aid and the reduction in capacity is sufficient.[507] The required ratios may vary from Member State to Member State, but they must not lead to discrimination.[508] Account may be taken of whether there is only one 'significant' steel producer, with plants in areas of high unemployment.[509]

It is also recognized that aid for non-ECSC steel activities may be granted to subsidiaries of steel groups and may ultimately benefit ECSC activities of the same group. Hence, a code for the former activities has been introduced.[510] In such sectors restructuring aid under regional aid schemes may be authorized

---

[500] Notice C35/94 (ex N397/94) ([1994] OJ C303/4) concerning aid which Germany intended to grant to EKO Stahl GmbH, Eisenhüttenstadt/Brandenburg.

[501] Notice C3/95 (ex 137/94) ([1995] OJ C283/5) concerning aid which Germany had granted to Werkstaff-Union GmbH, Lippendorf (Saxony).

[502] Art. 2 of Dec. 3855/91 ([1991] OJ L362/57).

[503] *Ibid.*, Art. 3.

[504] The recipients must have been 'regular' producers of steel. See Notice C54/95 (ex N777/95, N780/95, N790/95, N793/95, N794/95) ([1996] OJ C101/4) concerning aid granted by Italy to Ferriera Acciaieria Casilina SpA, Acciaierie del Sud SpA, Officine Laminatoi Sebino SpA, Montifer SRL, Moccia Irme SpA and Mini Acciaieria Odolese SpA. Undertakings belonging to the same group as the closed undertaking must not benefit indirectly from the aid. See Notice C1/96 (ex N977, N978 & N979/95) ([1996] OJ C121/3) concerning aid that Italy had decided to grant to Prolafer Srl, Dora Srl and Acciaierie San Gabriele SpA.

[505] Even if a capacity increase is entailed. See, in the case of restructuring aid for Irish Steel, *European Report* 2082 (8 Nov. 1995).

[506] Such authorization may affect ongoing Commission proceedings under Dec. 3855/91. See, e.g., Notice C29/94 (ex NN52/94) ([1995] OJ C294/9) concerning aid which Germany had granted to EKO Stahl GmbH, Eisenhüttenstadt. Such action may be 'legally legitimate, but highly unsatisfactory from other perspectives'. See C.–D. Ehlermann, n. 386 above, 1216.

[507] Bull. EC 11–1993, 1.2.60; and the *Twenty-Third Report on Competition Policy* (EC Commission, Brussels, 1994), 285.

[508] Joined Cases 172 & 226/83 *Hoogovens Groep BV* v. *EC Commission* [1985] ECR 2831.

[509] Dec. 94/257 ([1994] OJ L112/52) concerning aid to be granted by Portugal to the steel company Siderurgia Nacional. See also 'State Aid Control in the Context of Other Community Policies' [1994] *European Economy*, Supp. A, No. 4, 10, Table 7.

[510] Framework concerning notification of aid to certain steel sectors not covered by the ECSC Treaty ([1988] OJ C320/3). See, e.g., the *Nineteenth Report on Competition Policy* (EC Commission, Brussels, 1990), 151. See also Dec. 90/70 ([1990] OJ L47/28) concerning aid provided by France to certain primary processing steel undertakings, where restructuring aid was authorized under Art. 92(3)(c).

under Article 92(3)(a)[511] or (c)[512] of the EC Treaty, provided that there is no increase in the overall production capacity of the aid recipient.[513] Where no restructuring likely to lead to profitability is involved, aid will be prohibited.[514]

5.6.2 Rescue Aid

According to the 1977 Principles, rescue aid to permit orderly adaptation to the new market situation could be authorized. However, such aid should be of strictly limited duration and take account of the requisite structural modifications.[515] Thus, for example, the Commission accepted Belgian rescue aid to enable recipients to survive while a restructuring plan was prepared. To qualify for such aid, recipients had to agree to postpone any investment decisions which would lead to an increase in production capacity and any decisions on mass redundancies.[516]

A further condition was added by Decision 257/80. Aid intended for the rescue of an undertaking pending a definitive solution of its problems was permitted by this measure, provided that it was necessary to cope with acute social problems.[517]

Similarly, aid intended as a temporary solution for the rescue of an undertaking pending a restructuring programme or the closure of an undertaking might only be accepted under Decision 2320/81 where and to the extent to which, having regard to its scope and nature, it was required to cope with acute social problems.[518] Such aid could have a maximum duration of six months and must not affect trading conditions to an extent contrary to the common interest. No reference to rescue aid was made in subsequent legislation.

However, rescue aid may still be authorized under Article 95 of the ECSC Treaty. Under this provision account may be taken of unemployment levels in the region concerned and the fact that the recipient is the only steelmaker in the Member State concerned;[519] the need to avoid a sudden closure, which may have serious social and environmental consequences; and the degree of intra-Union competition in the products concerned.[520]

[511] H. Morch, 'Summary of the Most Important Recent Developments' (1995) 5 *Competition Policy Newsletter* 43–9, 46; Bull EU 6–1995,1.3.75.

[512] See, regarding Siegen, n. 513 below, and regarding Walsall in the UK, Bull. EU 10–1995, 1.3.65.

[513] See, e.g., Notice C4/93 (ex N652/92) ([1993] OJ C122/5; [1996] OJ C33/12) regarding aid which the German Government had decided to grant to Berg-Spezial-Rohr GmbH, Siegen.

[514] Dec. 87/506 ([1987] OJ L290/21) concerning aid granted by the French Government to two steel groups.

[515] *Seventh Report on Competition Policy* (EC Commission, Brussels, 1978), 181.

[516] *Ibid.*, 181–2.

[517] Art. 5 of Dec. 257/80 ([1980] OJ L29/5).

[518] Art. 6(1)(b) of Dec. 2320/81 ([1981] OJ L228/14).

[519] See, regarding aid to Irish Steel, Bull. EU 10–1995, 1.3.82.

[520] Dec. 96/269 ([1996] OJ L94/17) on aid to be granted by Austria to Voest-Alpine Erzberg Gesellschaft mbH.

5.6.3 Operating Aid

According to the 1977 Principles, aid should not be granted for the sole purpose of preserving existing structures.[521] However, conditions for authorization of operating aid were stipulated by Decision 257/80.[522] The conditions were that the aid:

—formed an integral part of a restructuring programme designed to assist the undertaking or plant in question to become competitive and able to operate without aid;

—was of limited duration or was progressively reduced at a sufficient rate for it to be eliminated within a reasonable period;

—was limited in intensity and amount to what was absolutely necessary to enable continued operation during the period of restructuring.[523]

Operating aid could also be granted under Decision 2320/81,[524] but only within the framework of a restructuring programme. Such aid was to be progressively reduced.[525] In examining the acceptability of such aid, the Commission was to take account of the problems facing the recipient and the region concerned, and of the secondary effects of the aid on competition on markets other than the steel market, for instance the transport market. Such aid could only be granted for a maximum of two years and could not lead to payments after 31 December 1984.[526] No reference to operating aid was made in subsequent legislation, though such aid may be authorized by measures adopted under Article 95 of the ECSC Treaty.[527]

5.7 TRANSPORT

Under the ECSC Treaty transport was regarded as a given fact to which undertakings had to adapt themselves. The abolition of discriminatory tariffs might involve structural alterations and the relocation of production, and all precautions had to be taken to cushion the effect of such changes which would otherwise be too disruptive. Subject to the possible need for such precautions, the Treaty sought progressively to bring about conditions which would of themselves ensure the most rational distribution of production at the highest

---

[521] *Seventh Report on Competition Policy* (EC Commission, Brussels, 1978), 181.

[522] Establishing Community rules for specific aids to the steel industry ([1980] OJ L29/5).

[523] Art. 4 of Dec. 257/80 ([1980] OJ L29/5).

[524] Establishing Community rules for aids to the steel industry ([1981] OJ L228/14).

[525] Art. 5(1) of Dec. 2320/81 ([1981] OJ L228/14). See, e.g., Dec. 83/395 ([1983] OJ L227/21) concerning the aids that the Irish Government proposed to grant to Irish Steel Limited.

[526] Art. 5(2) of Dec. 2320/81 ([1981] OJ L228/14).

[527] See, e.g., Dec. 89/218 ([1989] OJ L86/76) concerning aid that the Italian Government proposed to grant to the public steel sector; and Notice C22/95 (ex N219/95) ([1995] OJ C284/5) regarding aid which Ireland had granted to Irish Steel.

level of productivity in Article 2, that is, a real common market in the basic products existing on the European scale.[528]

Articles 74 to 84 of the EC Treaty, which apply to transport by rail, road, and inland waterway,[529] provide for a common transport policy.[530] This policy is to be implemented by decisions of the Council acting by a qualified majority after the second stage of the transitional period.[531] However, Article 77 presupposes that Articles 92 and 93 of this Treaty are applicable to the transport sector, whether or not a common transport policy has been established.[532] It provides that aid will be compatible with this Treaty if it meets the needs of coordination of transport or if it represents reimbursement for the discharge of certain obligations inherent in the concept of a public service. This provision acknowledges that aid to transport is compatible with the Treaty in well-defined cases which do not jeopardize the general interests of the Union.[533] Moreover, Article 80 provides for Commission authorization of certain aids,[534] taking account in particular of the requirements of an appropriate regional development policy,[535] the needs of underdeveloped areas, and the problems of areas seriously affected by political circumstances,[536] and also of the effects of aid on competition between different transport modes.[537]

5.7.1 Rail, Road, and Inland Waterway Transport

The Commission compiled an inventory of state aid in the transport sector in the 1960s,[538] and the Council provided in Article 9(2) of Decision 65/271[539]

---

[528] Joined Cases 3–18, 25 & 26/58 *Barbara Erzbergbau* v. *ECSC High Authority* [1960] ECR 173, 211

[529] Art. 84(1) EC.   [530] Art. 75(1) EC.

[531] *Ibid.*

[532] Joined Cases 209–213/84 *Ministère Public* v. *Lucas Asjes, Andrew Gray, Jacques Maillot and Leo Ludwig* [1986] ECR 1425, 1465.

[533] Case 156/77 *EC Commission* v. *Belgium: international railway tariffs for coal and steel* [1978] ECR 1881, 1894–5. See also Lenz AG in Case 167/73 *EC Commission* v. *France: merchant seamen* [1974] ECR 359, 378–9. Cf., regarding Art. 70 ECSC, Case 19/58 *Germany* v. *ECSC High Authority: transport tariffs for mineral fuels and oils* [1960] ECR 225, 234–5; and Joined Cases 27–29/58 *Compagnie des Hauts Fourneaux et Fonderies de Givors* v. *ECSC High Authority* [1960] ECR 241, 255.

[534] Roemer AG in Case 9/70 *Grad* v. *Finanzamt Traunstein* [1970] ECR 825, 853.

[535] Under the ECSC Treaty special transport tariffs for coal and steel could not be authorized on regional policy grounds. See the ECSC High Authority Letters of 12 Feb. 1958 to the French Government regarding special tariffs applicable to rail transport of coal for the steel industry ([1958] JOCECA 111) and regarding special tariffs applicable to the railway transport of minerals ([1958] JOCECA 127). See also Joined Cases 3–18, 25 & 26/58 *Barbara Erzbergbau* v. *ECSC High Authority* [1960] ECR 173, 191.

[536] Cf. Art. 92(2)(c) EC.

[537] Art. 80 was included in the Treaty on the initiative of France and Italy. See S. Neri and H. Sperl, *Traité Instituant la Communauté Economique Européenne* (European Court of Justice, Luxembourg, 1960), 204.

[538] J. Lemmens, 'Les Aides dans le domaine des transports' [1966] *RMC* 135–41.

[539] On the harmonization of certain provisions affecting competition in the area of transport by rail, road, and inland waterway ([1965] JO 1500).

that Article 92 of the Treaty applied to transport by rail, road, and inland waterway.[540] At the same time, Article 5 of the Decision provided that the imposition of public-service obligations implied a duty to pay compensation. More detailed legislation was subsequently adopted regarding aid to such transport.[541]

Restructuring Aid

According to the Commission, the inequality of distribution, by mode and by type of use, of infrastructure charges as well as the insufficient allocation of social costs in transport prices operates against non-road modes of transport and therefore against combined transport.[542] Hence, under Regulation 1107/70[543] aid may be granted for infrastructure costs, research and development in the field of new transport technologies, and in order to eliminate, as part of a reorganization plan, excess capacity causing serious structural problems. The last type of aid must be exceptional and temporary and should contribute towards enabling the needs of the transport market to be more effectively met.[544] Italian aid designed to improve the financial position of all undertakings in the road haulage sector without requiring any *quid pro quo* on their part did not satisfy these conditions and was objectionable.[545] Similarly, British aid for restructuring was regarded as contrary to the common interest, given the overcapacity in the bus and trucks industries.[546] On the other hand, Basque aid for road transport was authorized, because it would lead to a reduction in capacity.[547] Italian aid for the purchase of new lorries by hauliers who agreed to reduce the tonnage of their fleet was also authorized,[548] as was German research and development aid for railways,[549] and French aid to encourage small road

[540] The Member States submit to the Commission figures concerning their aid to transport by road, rail, or inland waterway under Reg. 1107/70 (see below). These figures are summarized in the annual submission of the Commission to the Consultative Committee on Aids to Transport. The Commission apparently remains unable to secure from all Member States the information regarding transport infrastructure aid required by Reg. 1108/70 ([1970] JO L130/4) introducing an accounting system for expenditure on infrastructure in respect of transport by rail, road and inland waterway. See the *Fourteenth Report on Expenditure on and Utilization of Rail, Road and Inland Waterway Structure 1984–1985–1986*, COM(91)331, 1.

[541] A section on aid to transport was introduced in the *Fifteenth Report on Competition Policy* (EC Commission, Brussels, 1986), 192–3.

[542] Explanatory Memorandum to the Proposal of 19 July 1997 for a Regulation amending Reg. 1107/70, COM(95)377, 2.

[543] On the granting of aids for transport by rail, road, and inland waterway ([1970] JO L130/1). [544] *Ibid.*, Art. 3(1).

[545] Communic. C17/91 (129/91) ([1991] OJ C137/3) and Communic. C32/92 (ex NN67/92) ([1992] OJ C316/7) on aids granted by Italy to professional road hauliers.

[546] Notice ([1987] OJ C24/7) regarding the proposal of the UK Government to provide new equity capital to an undertaking in order to facilitate the restructuring of two commercial vehicle subsidiaries.

[547] *Twentieth Report on Competition Policy* (EC Commission, Brussels, 1991), 193.

[548] *Fifteenth Report on Competition Policy* (EC Commission, Brussels, 1986), 193.

[549] Communic. C16/88 (ex N106/88) ([1990] OJ C237/2) regarding R & D aid which Germany had decided to grant in the traffic and transport sector.

transport firms to regroup either through takeovers, by joining co-operatives, or by forming economic interest groupings.[550]

Regulation 1192/69[551] allows for certain further aid to be granted to railways. In particular, aid to cover specific social costs, not borne by other undertakings and the costs of crossing facilities, as well as infrastructure costs not borne by other transport undertakings may be authorized. Again, Dutch aid to develop combined road/rail transport and to promote alternatives to road transport was unobjectionable, because it was compatible with Union transport policy, particularly with the priorities of relieving road congestion and protecting the environment.[552]

In the case of inland waterway transport, Regulation 1101/89[553] provides that aid to scrapping schemes[554] may be granted, as may aid to 'new for old' schemes,[555] on condition that an equal tonnage is scrapped or an equivalent sum is paid into the fund for scrapping aid. The same Regulation also allows for authorization of aid to encourage early retirement.[556] Further kinds of aid may be authorized under Article 92. For example, Dutch aid to reduce structural overcapacity in the inland waterway sector and to help small-scale operators to remain competitive by promoting this mode of transport was unobjectionable.[557] Moreover, a French scheme to capture a greater share of goods traffic for inland waterway transporters, through negotiating large contracts with shippers and providing aid to large owners carrying certain cargoes, was authorized.[558] On the other hand, modernization aid which does not ensure capacity reductions and differs from the arrangements in the Regulation is prohibited.[559]

Operating Aid

In order to ensure adequate transport services which, in particular, take into account social and environmental factors and town and country planning

---

[550] Bull. EU 10–1995, 1.3.142.

[551] On common rules for the normalization of the accounts of railway undertakings ([1969] JO L256/8).

[552] Bull. EU 9–1995, 1.3.80.

[553] Reg. 1101/89 ([1989] OJ L116/25) on structural improvements in inland waterway transport.

[554] *Ibid.*, Art. 5. The Commission proposed co-ordination of scrapping schemes at Union level so as to give national measures a greater impact in reducing existing excess capacity. See the *Eighteenth Report on Competition Policy* (EC Commission, Brussels, 1989), 197.

[555] Art. 8 of Reg. 1101/89 ([1989] OJ L116/25).

[556] *Ibid.*, Art. 9. See, e.g., Dec. 89/620 ([1989] OJ L356/22) concerning measures to assist the Belgian inland waterway fleet contained in the plan to restructure the fleet. A condition relating to capacity reductions may be imposed for authorization of such aid. See the *Sixteenth Report on Competition Policy* (EC Commission, Brussels, 1987), 187.

[557] Bull. EU 10–1995, 1.3.141. See also, regarding French aid to small operators, Bull. EU 11–1995, 1.3.125.

[558] *Fifteenth Report on Competition Policy* (EC Commission, Brussels, 1986), 193.

[559] Dec. 89/620 ([1989] OJ L356/22) concerning measures to assist the Belgian inland waterway fleet contained in the plan to restructure the fleet.

considerations, or with a view to offering particular fares to certain categories of passenger, the competent authorities of the Member States may conclude public service contracts with a transport undertaking.[560] The contracts may maintain or impose obligations for urban, suburban, and regional passenger transport.[561] Aid may be granted to transport undertakings by way of compensation[562] for fulfilment of such obligations.[563]

Special arrangements, including the grant of deficit aid,[564] might also have been made for railways[565] and for aid to the running costs of intra-Union combined services transiting the territory of third countries (in practice, Switzerland and States of the former Yugoslavia).[566] However, rescue aid to maintain building capacity in the inland waterway sector is contrary to the common interest under Article 92(3)(c), because there is already overcapacity in this sector.[567]

Regional policy considerations may result in authorization of further kinds of aid under Article 92. For example, transport aid to steel users in Northern Ireland, which was to be regressive and to last for only three years, to enable existing firms to adapt to new pricing conditions resulting from the accession of the United Kingdom to the Union, was authorized. Account was taken of the 'very special economic, social and political situation' in Northern Ireland.[568] On the other hand, rail tariff reductions for certain products and for an indefinite period may be objectionable, because they do not promote structural development or improve the situation in the regions concerned and may distort competition between different modes of transport.[569]

[560] Art. 1(4) of Reg. 1893/91 ([1991] OJ L169/1) amending Reg. 1191/69 [1969] JO L156/1.

[561] Art. 1(5) of Reg. 1893/91. According to the European Parliament, Member States should create a public service obligation in order to ensure good accessibility of remote regions and to compensate the operator of the transport service. See the Resolution of 18 Sept. 1992 ([1992] OJ C284/176) on transport and regional development, para. 21.

[562] See, regarding the distinction between such compensation and deficit aid, Dec. 76/649 ([1976] OJ L229/24) on aid from the Belgian Government to the Société nationale des chemins de fer belges for through international railway tariffs for coal and steel and the arguments of the Commission in Case 156/77 *EC Commission* v. *Belgium: international railway tariffs for coal and steel* [1978] ECR 1881, 1888.

[563] Art. 6 of Reg. 1191/69 ([1969] JO L156/1) on action by Member States concerning the obligations inherent in the concept of a public service in transport by rail, road, and inland waterway.

[564] Art. 5(1) of Dec. 75/327 ([1975] OJ L152/3) on the improvement of the situation of railway undertakings and the harmonization of rules governing financial relations between such undertakings and Member States. This provision has been replaced by Art. 9 of Dir. 91/440 ([1991] OJ L237/25) on the development of the Community's railways.

[565] Art. 4 of Reg. 1192/69 ([1969] JO L256/8) on common rules for the normalization of the accounts of railway undertakings.

[566] Art. 3(1)(e) of Reg. 1107/70 ([1970] JO L130/1), as amended by Reg. 3578/92 [1992] OJ L364/11.

[567] Dec. 91/306 ([1991] OJ L158/71) concerning two aid projects of the German Government in favour of a shipyard in financial difficulties.

[568] *Third Report on Competition Policy* (EC Commission, Brussels, 1974), 92–3.

[569] Dec. 91/523 ([1991] OJ L283/20) abolishing the support tariffs applied by the Italian

In some cases regional-policy considerations may be outweighed by requirements of other sectoral policies. For example, special railway tariffs for agricultural products from the south of Italy had been authorized by the Commission in 1962,[570] regard being had to Article 80 of the Treaty and the Protocol on Italy. However, this arrangement reduced production costs for the products concerned and was thus incompatible with the Council Resolution of 25 May 1971 on the new guidelines for the common agricultural policy.[571] In addition, another Member State was using the authorization as a precedent for adopting similar measures. Accordingly, in 1979 the Commission decided to insist on the gradual elimination of the Italian aid.[572]

5.7.2 Air Transport

Article 84(2) of the EC Treaty[573] excludes the automatic application of Articles 77 and 80 to air transport, and so aid to air transport remains subject to the general rules of the Treaty, including those on competition. Where the Treaty intended to remove certain activities from the ambit of the competition rules, it made an express derogation to that effect, as was done in the case of the production of, and trade in, agricultural products by Article 42.[574] Accordingly, the Commission seeks, pursuant to Articles 92 and 93, to co-ordinate aid to air transport with a view to limiting it to what is warranted in the common interest.[575] In view of the progressive liberalization of air transport, the Commission strictly controls aid in this sector.[576] The Commission also monitors implementation of restructuring plans for which aid has been authorized.[577]

Restructuring Aid

The approach of the Commission towards restructuring aid to air transport was

railways to the carriage of bulk ores and products produced and processed in Sicily and Sardinia. See, earlier, Communic. ([1984] OJ C238/4) concerning French state aid involving the granting of compensation for the cessation of transport aid.

[570] Dec. of 16 Feb. 1962 ([1962] JO 1229) authorizing special tariff 201 on Italian state railways.

[571] [1971] JO C52/1, para. VI.B(b).

[572] Dec. 79/873 ([1979] OJ L269/29) authorizing Special Tariff 201 of the Italian State Railways.

[573] It states that the Council may decide whether and to what extent and by what procedure appropriate provisions may be laid down for air transport.

[574] Joined Cases 209–213/84 *Ministère Public* v. *Lucas Asjes, Andrew Gray, Jacques Maillot and Leo Ludwig* [1986] ECR 1425, 1465.

[575] *Air Transport: a Community Approach*, Bull. EC, Supp. 5/79, 20.

[576] Dec. 94/696 ([1994] OJ L273/22) on the aid granted by Greece to Olympic Airways.

[577] Payment of the second tranche of aid in favour of Air France approved by Dec. of 27 July 1994 ([1995] OJ C295/2). Control seems to have become somewhat stricter following Dec. 91/555 ([1991] OJ L300/48) on aid to be granted by the Belgian Government in favour of Sabena. See T. Soames and A. Ryan, 'State Aid and Air Transport' [1995] *ECLR* 290–309.

outlined in 1984[578] and elaborated in 1994.[579] According to the 1984 Guidelines, the Commission would prevent the grant of aid from resulting in the transfer of the difficulties of the enterprises of one Member State to those of other Member States. Article 92(3) was considered sufficiently flexible to deal with specific cases of which it had knowledge or of which it might be notified in the future, though the matter would be kept under review.[580]

Various considerations might produce a favourable Commission attitude to the grant of aid.[581] Where carriers from third countries were subsidized or otherwise benefited from preferential treatment, the Commission would apply Article 92 in such a manner as not to put Union carriers at a competitive disadvantage, though the Commission preference came to be reliance on 'the Community's external policy towards third countries in the aviation sector'.[582]

In cases where the financial situation of an airline was particularly precarious but where real possibilities for improvement existed the Commission might also authorize aid for its recovery, provided that the aid:

—was part of a programme, to be approved by the Commission, to restore the health of the airline, so that it could, within a reasonably short period, be expected to operate without further aid;[583]

—did not transfer the difficulties from that Member State to the rest of the Union,[584] which implied that the aid must not be for expansion; and

—was structured so as to be transparent and verifiable.[585]

Further conditions are imposed by the 1994 Guidelines. First, the grant of aid must be a 'one-off' operation,[586] and no further aid may be authorized

---

[578] *Progress towards the Development of a Community Air Transport Policy*, COM(84)72, 37–9.

[579] Application of Arts. 92 and 93 EC and Art. 61 EEA to state aids in the aviation sector ([1994] OJ C350/5).

[580] *Progress towards the Development of a Community Air Transport Policy*, COM(84)72, 37. In addition, the Commission would take into account whether undertakings fell within the scope of Art. 90(2) EC.

[581] See, regarding investment aid to a pilot school in Bremen, the *Twentieth Report on Competition Policy* (EC Commission, Brussels, 1991), 194, which was authorized on regional grounds under Art. 92(3)(c).   [582] Para. 11 of the 1994 guidelines.

[583] Application of this condition may involve an issue which can also be decisive in connection with the definition of aid. According to Dec. 91/555 ([1991] OJ L300/48) on aid to be granted to the Belgian Government in favour of Sabena, only the provision of genuine risk capital sufficiently indicates the commercial viability of the restructuring concept. See, regarding application of the private investor principle, para. 28 of the 1994 guidelines.

[584] This might occur, for example, if some activities of the aid recipient were protected and the latter would be able to concentrate the anti-competitive effects of the aid on markets where it faced direct competition. See Notice C14/94 (NN133/92 & N514/93) ([1994] OJ C94/4) concerning the advantages given to Olympic Airways.

[585] *Progress towards the Development of a Community Air Transport Policy*, COM(84)72, 37–9. See, most recently, Dec. 94/653 ([1994] OJ L254/73) concerning the notified capital increase of Air France.

[586] The Commission had already sought to impose this condition in its practice. See, e.g., Dec. 91/555 ([1991] OJ L300/48) on aid to be granted to the Belgian Government in favour of Sabena. See also Dec. 94/118 ([1994] OJ L54/30) concerning aid to be provided by the Irish Government to the Aer Lingus group.

under Article 92(3)(c) 'unless under exceptional circumstances, unforeseeable and external to the company'. The definition of such circumstances was controversial from the start. For example, the Commissioner for competition policy insisted on substituting 'unforeseeable' for 'unforeseen'.[587] It is now said that only real cases of *force majeure* should be covered,[588] though controversy remains.[589]

Commission willingness to consider such circumstances is presumably designed to meet the requirement imposed by the Court of Justice in *Italy* v. *EC Commission: Aluminia*,[590] which concerned aid to aluminium undertakings in Italy, that the Commission must take account of 'any new fact' before deciding whether aid is contrary to a previous decision.[591] However, the Commission seeks narrowly to construe the circumstances covered.[592] As a result, questions may often arise whether the kind of state financing which takes place in circumstances considered by the Commission to be covered constitutes aid in the first place.[593]

Secondly, if restoration to financial viability and/or the situation of the market require capacity reductions,[594] these reductions must be provided for in the restructuring programme.

Thirdly, where the airline is a public undertaking, the government must not interfere in the management of the undertaking for reasons other than those stemming from its ownership rights and must allow the undertaking to be run according to commercial principles.[595]

Finally, the aid must be used only for the purposes of the restructuring programme and must not be disproportionate to its needs, and the recipient must for the period of its restructuring also refrain from acquiring shareholdings in other air carriers.[596] Such conditions are designed to ensure that anti-competitive effects of aid are not magnified by the maintenance of privileged or protected situations.[597] The aid may also have to be degressive.[598]

---

[587] *European Report* 1994 (19 Nov. 1994).

[588] C–D. Ehlermann, n. 386 above, 1227.

[589] See, e.g., the arguments of the Spanish Government in Dec. 96/278 ([1996] OJ L104/25) concerning the recapitalization of the Iberia company.

[590] Case C–261/89 [1991] ECR I–4437, I–4462.

[591] See also Case C–294/90 *British Aerospace and Rover Group Holdings* v. *EC Commission* [1992] ECR I–493.

[592] Notice C14/95 (N774/94) ([1995] OJ C114/7) concerning a Pta 130 billion capital injection into Iberia.

[593] See the significance attached to the Gulf War in Dec. 91/555 ([1991] OJ L300/48) on aid to be granted to the Belgian Government in favour of Sabena.

[594] The Commission does not consider the sector to suffer from overcapacity. See Dec. 94/653 ([1994] OJ L254/73) concerning the notified capital increase of Air France.

[595] See, earlier, Dec. 91/555 ([1991] OJ L300/48) on aid to be granted to the Belgian Government in favour of Sabena.	[596] Para. 38 of the 1994 guidelines.

[597] Dec. 94/696 ([1994] OJ L273/22) on the aid granted by Greece to Olympic Airways.

[598] See, earlier, Dec. 91/555 ([1991] OJ L300/48) on aid to be granted to the Belgian Government in favour of Sabena.

However, the Commission authorized payment of the second tranche of aid to Aer Lingus, even though the projected cost reductions and other conditions attached to the original authorization had not been met.[599] In the view of the Commission, the failure to secure the stipulated cost reductions was attributable to labour disputes, that is, 'circumstances which could not have been anticipated'.[600]

Where aid is provided to an airline to encourage the purchase and operation of specific aircraft, the aid is not considered as conferring a benefit on the airline, provided it merely covers the additional costs to the airline of purchasing and operating an aircraft other than the optimum in commercial terms. The aid must be linked to a special programme or project or limited to the purchase of aircraft of a particular type or with specific environmental characteristics.[601] Such aid is treated as indirect aid to the manufacturer and is assessed as such.[602]

Moreover, 'primary attention' is given to the intra-Union aspects of aid.[603] Investment aid in disadvantaged areas, such as aid for building a hangar there, may be authorized.[604] Again, aid to reorganize and increase the competitiveness of British aviation and to develop services from regional airports was authorized,[605] as was aid to a new independent airline which would operate between the United Kingdom and the Continent.[606]

Operating Aid

Aid to assist air services in underdeveloped regions of the Union may be authorized,[607] though the difficulties of the region concerned are assessed in a national and Union context.[608] In particular, compensation for maintaining a given route may be authorized on regional development grounds under Article 92(3)(c) or under Article 92(3)(a) to overcome a permanent and structural disadvantage caused by a remote location.[609] However, overcompensation of

---

[599] Payment of the second £150 million tranche of aid C34/93 approved by Dec. of 21 Dec. 1993 ([1994] OJ C399/1).

[600] Payment of the third tranche of aid in favour of Aer Lingus approved by Dec. of 21 Dec. 1993 ([1996] OJ C70/2).

[601] Communic. C41/93 (E4/93 & N640/93) ([1994] OJ C16/3) on fiscal aid given to German airlines in the form of a depreciation allowance.

[602] *Progress towards the Development of a Community Air Transport Policy*, COM(84)72, 39. Aid to aircraft production is generally treated favourably. See sect. 5.1 above.

[603] *Progress towards the Development of a Community Air Transport Policy* COM(84)72, 37.

[604] Para. 36 of the 1994 guidelines.

[605] *Sixteenth Report on Competition Policy* (EC Commission, Brussels, 1987), 189.

[606] *Seventeenth Report on Competition Policy* (EC Commission, Brussels, 1988), 186.

[607] It has been argued that a reduction in landing charges payable to a municipal airport authority granted to all air carriers using the airport could be authorized. See T. Soames and A. Ryan, n. 577 above, 299.

[608] *Progress towards the Development of a Community Air Transport Policy* COM(84)72, 38.

[609] Dec. 94/666 ([1994] OJ L260/27) concerning compensation in respect of the deficit incurred by TAP on the routes to the Autonomous Regions of the Azores and Madeira.

the deficit actually incurred may constitute aid prohibited by Article 92.[610] Moreover, the apparent Commission preference is to limit such aid to that covered by Article 92(2)(a) or that to compensate for public service obligations,[611] and only to apply Article 92(3)(c) to restructuring aid.[612]

Compensation for public-service obligations does not involve aid, provided that: the carrier has been correctly selected through a call for tender, on the basis of the limitation of access to the route to one single carrier, and the maximum level of compensation does not exceed the amount of the deficit laid down in the bid.[613] However, compensation to Italian carriers providing air services to and from Sardinia for losses incurred as a result of empty seats was prohibited.[614]

In the case of routes between Member States, account is taken of the risk of distortion of competition, the effect on trade between Member States, and the willingness of any other airline to maintain the route without aid.[615] In essence, the Commission is concerned to prevent cross-subsidization between subsidized routes and routes where aid recipients are in competition with other carriers from the European Economic Area.[616]

5.7.3 Marine Transport

Article 84(2) of the EC Treaty[617] excludes the automatic application of Articles 77 and 80 to marine transport. However, Articles 92 and 93 are applicable to aid to such transport.[618] In the light of these provisions, aid guidelines were

---

[610] Communic. C15/94 (N122/94, NN22/94 & E3/93) ([1994] OJ C93/12) concerning the existing tax exemption and planned recapitalization of TAP and Notice C14/94 (NN133/92 & N514/93) ([1994] OJ C94/4) concerning the advantages given to Olympic Airways.

[611] Communic. C63/94 (N160/94) ([1995] OJ C117/2) concerning the aid scheme for the operation of air routes provided for in the Law of the Region of Sardinia of 20 Jan. 1994. In this Communic. the Commission claims that the guidelines 'spell out quite clearly' this limitation. In fact, while para. 36 of the guidelines refers only to these grounds, it does not state that the reference is exhaustive as to the acceptable grounds for operating aid.

[612] Sect. V, n. 7 of the Communic. See, e.g., Dec. 95/466 ([1995] OJ L267/49) concerning aid granted by the Flemish region to the Belgian airline Vlaamse Luchttransportmaatschappij NV.

[613] Para. 18 of the 1994 guidelines.

[614] Dec. 96/110 ([1996] OJ L26/29) concerning aid for the operation of air routes granted under the Law of the Region of Sardinia of 20 Jan. 1994.

[615] *Evaluation des Régimes d'Aides Institués en Faveur des Transporteurs Aériens de la Communauté*, SEC(92)431, 8. See also Art. 4 of Reg. 2408/92 ([1992] OJ L240/8) on access for Community air carriers to intra-Community air routes.

[616] Para. 14 of the 1994 guidelines. See, more particularly, Communic. C63/94 (N160/94) ([1995] OJ C117/2) concerning the aid scheme for the operation of air routes provided for in the Law of the Region of Sardinia of 20 Jan. 1994.

[617] It states that the Council may decide whether and to what extent and by what procedure appropriate provisions may be laid down for marine transport.

[618] Case 167/73 *EC Commission* v. *France: merchant seamen* [1974] ECR 359, 371; Case C–49/89 *Corsica Ferries France* v. *Direction Générale des Douanes Françaises* [1989] ECR 4441; Dec. 71/295 ([1971] JO L179/37) on tax concessions under the Law of 28 Dec. 1968 on the transport of goods by road, as prolonged on 23 Dec. 1970.

adopted by the Commission in 1989.[619] These guidelines were drawn up in the context of worldwide excess capacity, high manning costs for Union companies compared with their main competitors, and a general growth in both protectionism and the use of 'flags of convenience'. They seek to prevent distortions of competition through co-ordination of national aids.

Restructuring Aid

Restructuring aid may be authorized. For example, aid to British and Italian ports to settle debts incurred by port authorities in granting redundancy or early retirement benefits to workers made surplus as a result of modernization and restructuring plans was authorized,[620] as were Dutch aid for rationalizing port handling services, in order to reduce capacity[621] and French aid to ports carrying out major infrastructure investment programmes.[622] However, such aid should lead to viability and should not provide any surplus above restructuring costs which could be used for aggressive market-distorting activities.[623]

Operating Aid

The Commission considers that the common interest within the meaning of Article 92(3)(c)[624] is served by aid to maintain ships under Union flags and to encourage the employment of Union seafarers.[625] Hence, operating aid to promote these aims may be authorized.[626] For example, aid for the British fleet for the training of seamen and for the costs of repatriating crews sailing in distant waters was authorized,[627] as was a reduction in the direct tax burden for sailors working on Dutch-flag vessels.[628] Aid to reduce social security costs may also be authorized,[629] as may training aid[630] and tax relief.[631] However, the

[619] *Financial and Fiscal Measures concerning Shipping Operations with Ships Registered in the Community*, SEC(89)921. Establishment of a Union ship register is designed to provide a transparent, common framework for state aid to Union shipowners. See the amended Proposal of 13 Dec. 1991 ([1992] OJ C19/10) for a Council Reg. establishing a Community ship register and providing for the flying of the Community flag by sea-going vessels. See also the *Twenty-Fourth Report on Competition Policy* (EC Commission, Brussels, 1995), 212.

[620] *Seventeenth Report on Competition Policy* (EC Commission, Brussels, 1988), 186. See, more recently, the *Twenty-Third Report on Competition Policy* (EC Commission, Brussels, 1994), 310.

[621] *Fifteenth Report on Competition Policy* (EC Commission, Brussels, 1986), 193.

[622] *Eighteenth Report on Competition Policy* (EC Commission, Brussels, 1989), 198.

[623] Communic. C46/95 (NN130/93) ([1996] OJ C58/4) on aid granted by France to Compagnie Générale Maritime. [624] Annex I, para. II of the 1989 Guidelines.

[625] *A Future for the Community Shipping Industry: Measures to Improve the Operating Conditions of Community Shipping*, COM(89)266, 11–2.

[626] *Twenty-Fourth Report on Competition Policy* (EC Commission, Brussels, 1995), 523.

[627] *Seventeenth Report on Competition Policy* (EC Commission, Brussels, 1988), 186.

[628] *Eighteenth Report on Competition Policy* (EC Commission, Brussels, 1989), 198. See, similarly, Communic. ([1990] OJ C239/10) regarding aid which Italy had decided to grant in order to compensate the losses of the state-owned yard Fincantieri for 1987 and 1988 and Law 234/89 providing for aid to shipbuilding in Italy.

[629] Para. III. 1 of the 1989 guidelines.

[630] *Ibid.*, para. III. [631] *Ibid.*, para. III. 4.

amount of operating aid used to secure such ends must be in proportion to the objective pursued and should, therefore, be subject to a ceiling fixed by the Commission with reference to the gap in operating costs between Union-registered ships and their main competitors. Aid must also be temporary and preferably on a declining scale. Furthermore, aid should not contribute to the creation or maintenance of excess capacity in market segments where there is 'manifest overcapacity'.

More particularly, account may be taken of regional factors. For example, in 1971 German aid to sea ports was prohibited, partly on the ground that the aid made no contribution to regional development.[632] The Commission later objected to aid to reduce the commercial deficits of Italian port companies.[633] On the other hand, Irish aid to Irish Ferries and to Swansea Cork Ferries was authorized because of the peripheral position of Ireland.[634]

5.8 SHIPBUILDING

Distortions of competition affect the shipbuilding sector in the world market and the Union shipbuilding industry cannot protect itself against outside competition by tariff measures or other measures of commercial policy without causing harm to Union shipowners who carry on their activity in an international market.[635] The EC Treaty itself recognized the special position of the shipbuilding industry only to the extent of providing in Article 92(3)(c) for the gradual reduction of aid to this industry[636] which took the place of customs duties.[637] The reduction was to be achieved under the same conditions as those which applied to the elimination of such duties, subject to Treaty provisions regarding the common commercial policy towards third countries.[638] This 'special limitation' would not make any sense if the abolition during the transitional period of all existing aid that was incompatible with the Treaty had been intended.[639] Otherwise, shipbuilding aid was fully subject to Article 92.

---

[632] Dec. 71/295 ([1971] JO L179/37) on tax concessions under the Law of 28 Dec. 1968 on the transport of goods by road, as prolonged on 23 Dec. 1970.

[633] *Twenty-Third Report on Competition Policy* (EC Commission, Brussels, 1994), 310.

[634] *Twenty-First Report on Competition Policy* (EC Commission, Brussels, 1992), 178–9. See also the EP Resolution of 19 June 1981 ([1981] OJ C174/122) on Community regional policy and Northern Ireland, para. 10(k), regarding the need for subsidies to bring the cost of travelling between Northern Ireland and Great Britain down to the cost of a journey of similar length by rail.

[635] Third recital in the Preamble to Dir. 69/262 ([1969] JO L206/25) on aids to shipbuilding; Darmon AG in Case 400/92 *Germany* v. *EC Commission: China Ocean Shipping Company* [1994] ECR I–4701, I–4710.

[636] The Commission acted under Art. 93(1) to secure such reductions. See the *Sixth EEC General Report* (EEC Commission, Brussels, 1963), 69.

[637] Art. 223 EC means that aid may be granted for the construction of military vessels. See the Reply by Mr Van Miert to Written Question E–149/95 ([1995] OJ C270/2) by Nel van Dijk.

[638] *EEC Second General Report* (EEC Commission, Brussels, 1959), 94–5.

[639] Roemer AG in Case 77/72 *Carmine Capolongo* v. *Azienda Agricola Maya* [1973] ECR 611, 630.

Apparently the concern was that the grant of such aid should not jeopardize establishment of the customs union or development of a common commercial policy.

Economic theory may provide an argument in favour of shipbuilding aid. In particular, it may be argued that the most efficient yards are the most capital-intensive. When the market is in equilibrium, they will be profitable. However, they also have the highest fixed costs, and during a recession will complete their work and thus run out of orders more quickly than other yards. Hence, they will be the most vulnerable. Operating aid to such yards during a recession may be said to be justified on such grounds.[640]

In the event, a series of directives has been enacted by the Council under Articles 92(3)(e) and 113, and a Regulation[641] has now been enacted under these provisions together with Article 94. The original proposal for the first Directive[642] was based on Articles 235 and 111 to 113 as well as Articles 92 to 94, though this proposal envisaged that the grant of aid amounting to 10 per cent of the contract price should be obligatory. The question whether it should be obligatory or discretionary was apparently controversial.[643] The Commission wanted it to be obligatory, but all Member States preferred it to be discretionary.[644] Preference for the latter arrangement was reflected in the directive adopted by the Council.[645]

These directives have, *inter alia*, permitted the Commission to authorize operating aid of a kind that it might not have been possible to authorize under Article 92(3)(a)–(d).[646] In so doing, the directives reflect a long-standing political commitment on the part of the Union institutions to the preservation of a viable shipbuilding industry within the Union. The Council Resolution of 19 September 1978[647] concerning the reorganization of the shipbuilding industry stressed the need to maintain a healthy and competitive shipbuilding industry whose scale of activity should be consistent with the size of the Union's sea-borne trade and respect its economic, social, and strategic importance.[648] The directives themselves, the last one being Directive 90/684,[649] maintained that a competitive shipbuilding industry was of vital interest to the

[640] Explanatory Memorandum to the Proposal for a Dir. amending Dir. 81/363, COM(84)73, 3.

[641] Reg. 3094/95 ([1995] OJ L332/1) on aid to shipbuilding.

[642] Proposal for a dir. establishing a Community system of aids to correct distortions of competition on the international shipbuilding market ([1965] JO 3129).

[643] *Second Medium-term Economic Policy Programme* ([1969] JO L129/6).

[644] *First EC General Report* (EC Commission, Brussels, 1968), 70.

[645] See sect. 5.8.2 below.

[646] See, regarding a UK scheme for cost-escalation insurance, the *Sixth Report on Competition Policy* (EC Commission, Brussels, 1977), 112.

[647] [1978] OJ C229/1.

[648] See, also regarding the links with shipping, the *First Report on Competition Policy* (EC Commission, Brussels, 1972), 132.

[649] On aid to shipbuilding ([1990] OJ L380/27). It was extended by Dir. 93/115 ([1993] OJ L326/62) and Dir. 94/73 ([1994] OJ L351/10).

Union and contributed to its economic and social development by providing a substantial market for a range of industries, including those using advanced technology.[650] The Preamble to this Directive also stressed that the industry contributed to the maintenance of employment in a number of regions, including some which were already suffering a high rate of unemployment.[651]

In view of such a commitment to the shipbuilding industry, a Union policy to develop this industry might have been expected to emerge. In 1966 the Commission reported that it had 'tried to work out the broad outlines of a concerted structure policy which would, in particular, make it possible to combat more effectively the growing competition from Japan'.[652] The European Parliament has long been calling for the Union institutions to work towards such a policy, while providing the necessary safeguards for the shipbuilding industry in Member States which would suffer most from changes in international market conditions.[653]

Article 9 of Directive 78/338[654] duly provided that in its appraisal of aid covered by this Directive, the Commission should take account of the common interest, as defined in common objectives for the reorganization of the industry at Union level. These objectives might be defined by the Council acting on a proposal from the Commission.[655] However, the nearest the Council came to producing such a definition was in the Resolution of 19 September 1978.[656] As a result, the European Parliament complained that no real attempt appeared to have been made to integrate Union policy on aid to shipbuilding within a wider Union strategy for the sector.[657] In the absence of such a strategy,[658] the

---

[650] The shipbuilding industry is also important for the Union fishing fleet, and so the common fisheries policy has had some impact on the treatment of shipbuilding aid. See sect. 5.8.2 below.

[651] Eighth recital in the Preamble to Dir. 90/684 [1990] OJ L380/27. The same is said to be true of ship conversion and ship repair.

[652] *EEC Ninth General Report* (EEC Commission, Brussels, 1966), 155. See, later, the Explanatory Memorandum to proposals on the shipbuilding industry, COM(73)1788.

[653] Resolution of 25 Nov. 1965 ([1965] JO 3128) on the proposal for a Dir. establishing a Community system of aids to correct distortions of competition on the international shipbuilding market, recital D; Resolution of 13 June 1974 ([1974] OJ C76/41) on the proposal for a Dir. on aid to the shipbuilding industry and on the memorandum from the Commission on procedures for action in the shipbuilding industry, para. 3; Resolution of 10 Feb. 1977 ([1977] OJ C57/57) on the Community shipbuilding industry, para. 1; Resolution of 19 Jan. 1978 ([1978] OJ C36/34) on the proposal for a Dir. on aid to shipbuilding, para. 1; Resolution of 15 Jan. 1981 ([1981] OJ C28/35) on the proposal for a Dir. on aid to shipbuilding, para. 4; Resolution of 23 Nov. 1990 ([1990] OJ C324/343) on the proposal for a Dir. on aid to shipbuilding, proposed amendment 3; and Resolution of 7 Apr. 1995 ([1995] OJ C109/302) on prospects for the future development of the shipbuilding industry, especially recital G in the Preamble.

[654] On aid to shipbuilding ([1978] OJ L98/19).

[655] Art. 8 of the proposal of 4 Nov. 1977 ([1977] OJ C294/4) had provided for account to be taken of such objectives when they had been defined by the Council.

[656] On the reorganization of the shipbuilding industry ([1978] OJ C229/1).

[657] Resolution of 12 Dec. 1986 ([1987] OJ C7/325) on the proposal for a Sixth Dir. on aid to shipbuilding, para. 11. See also the Economic and Social Committee Opinion of 19 Nov. 1987 ([1987] OJ C356/49) on the communication on shipbuilding—Industrial, social and regional aspects, paras 2.5 and 2.8.

[658] According to the Commission, the role of public authorities is to 'guide' the restructuring

Commission's aid policy had become a *de facto* sectoral policy[659] and had thus had an unfair burden placed upon it.[660]

Such reliance on aid policy for achieving sectoral policy goals is illustrated by the Preamble to Directive 90/684, according to which a tight and selective aid policy was designed to support the trend in production towards more technologically advanced ships and in order to ensure fair and uniform conditions for intra-Union trade. Such a policy was said to constitute the most appropriate approach in terms of ensuring the maintenance of a sufficient level of activity in European shipyards and, thereby, the survival of an efficient and competitive European shipbuilding industry. In particular, differentiation between restructuring aid to support desirable changes and operating aid based on a common ceiling, originally introduced by Directive 87/167,[661] was thought to remain the most appropriate way of ensuring that the industry was competitive in the long term. The legislation, maintained the Commission, on the one hand, ensured that the competitive part of the Union shipbuilding industry could maintain its activities despite abnormal competition conditions in the world market and, on the other hand, that pressure was put on less effective parts of Union shipbuilding to embark on the necessary restructuring.[662]

5.8.1 Restructuring Aid

According to the *Seventh Report on Competition Policy*,[663] major structural changes in the shipbuilding industry were necessary, involving both reduction of capacity and conversion towards the production of those types of ships for which there was still some demand. Most Member States considered that changes on the scale required could not be achieved in an orderly manner without aid.[664]

The Commission sought introduction of legislative guidelines for restructuring aid in its proposal for what became Directive 75/432.[665] This approach was supported by the Economic and Social Committee.[666] The

---

efforts of the industry and to further the creation of new jobs to compensate for those lost in shipbuilding. See the Reply to Written Question 929/79 by Mrs de Mar. *et al.* ([1980] OJ C178/4).

[659] This was implicitly admitted by the Commission in *Reorganization of the Community Shipbuilding Industry*, Bull. EC, Supp. 7/77, 12.

[660] See also the *Report of the Committee on Economic and Monetary Affairs and Industrial Policy on Community Industrial Policy in the Shipbuilding Sector*, EP Doc. A3-0278/91.

[661] On aid to shipbuilding ([1987] OJ L69/55).

[662] Explanatory Memorandum to the proposal for a dir. on aid to shipbuilding, COM(90)248, 3-4.

[663] (EC Commission, Brussels, 1978), 140.

[664] See also the proposals on the shipbuilding industry, COM(73)1788, 13.

[665] Draft guidelines were included in the Preamble to the Draft Dir. of 5 Nov. 1973 ([1974] OJ C114/23) on aids to shipbuilding.

[666] Opinion of 28 Mar. 1974 ([1974] OJ C97/43) on the proposals on the shipbuilding industry, sect. IV.

Committee on Economic and Monetary Affairs of the European Parliament favoured more thoroughgoing action, involving adoption of 'Community rules containing common provisions on when, how and to what extent investment aid should be granted in the shipbuilding sector'.[667] The Commission, however, opposed the adoption of a such rules on the grounds that it would be divesting itself of its Article 93 powers,[668] though Directive 75/432 is said to have had just this effect.[669]

Member States apparently even objected to legislative provision for general Commission evaluation of investment aid.[670] Indeed, the Commission failed in this Directive to secure Council consent to imposition on Member States of a general obligation to notify such aid in advance.[671]

As a result, the Commission relied on its powers under Article 92 of the Treaty. Article 4 of Directive 75/432 merely required Member States to inform the Commission annually of their investment aid decisions in the case of shipbuilding, ship conversion, and ship-repair yards, and Article 6 of the same Directive required investment aid to be compatible with the common market under Articles 92 to 93 of the Treaty. To this extent, the Directive sought to enable the Commission to ensure that the aid was used for restructuring.[672] The criteria which the Commission intended to employ in determining the compatibility of investment aid with the Treaty were outlined in the Proposals on the Shipbuilding Industry.[673] Aid was, as far as possible, to fit in with a general plan for the particular sector or region concerned and was to seek

---

[667] Report on the proposal for a Dir. on aid to the shipbuilding industry and the memorandum from the Commission on procedures for action in the shipbuilding industry, EP Doc. 68/74, 11. The Committee also considered that the Commission should publish market and production capacity analyses and R & D programmes so as to assist shipbuilders in making their own investment decisions (*ibid.*).

[668] Statement of Commissioner Spinelli to the European Parliament (EP Debs., No. 177, 193, 13 June 1974).

[669] Report of the Committee on Economic and Monetary Affairs on the Proposal for a dir. on aid to shipbuilding, EP Doc. 465/77, 8.

[670] *Fifth Report on Competition Policy* (EC Commission, Brussels, 1975), 76.

[671] The Draft Dir. of 5 Nov. 1973 ([1973] OJ C114/23) on aids to shipbuilding, which provided in Art. 6 for introduction of a requirement of prior notification in the case of investments exceeding 4 million u.a., was rejected by the Council. See the *Fourth Report on Competition Policy* (EC Commission, Brussels, 1975), 86. See, similarly, Art. 4 of the Proposal of 4 Nov. 1977 for a Dir. on aid to shipbuilding ([1977] OJ C294/6). Prior notification of investments over 5 million u.a. was first required by Art. 3 of Dir. 81/363. In the case of investment aid to the steel industry, such a requirement was imposed by Art. 3(1) of Dec. 2320/81 ([1981] OJ L228/14) establishing Community rules for aids to the steel industry and, in the case of investment aid to the coal industry, by Art. 5(1) of Dec. 2064/86 ([1986] OJ L177/1) establishing Community rules for state aid to the coal industry. Cf. the requirement in Dec. 22/66 ([1966] JO 3728) on information to be supplied by undertakings regarding their investments, as amended by Dec. 2237/73 ([1973] OJ L229/28), that undertakings notify the Commission of investment programmes of which the cost exceeds ECU 5 million and of programmes to reduce production capacity.

[672] *Third Report on Competition Policy* (EC Commission, Brussels, 1974), 82–4.

[673] COM(73)1788, 19.

improved international competitiveness.[674] The amount and intensity of the aid also had to be justified by the extent of the restructuring involved and limited to supporting expenditure directly related to the investment.[675]

Capacity Considerations

In practice, the Commission assessment of restructuring aid concentrated on the question of capacity reductions. For example, in 1973 the Commission authorized Italian aid to investments which came within the plan for reorganizing shipbuilding. Such reorganization was to involve: co-ordination of production and management activities in the shipyards; an effort to increase specialization and structural adaptation within the Fincantieri group; reduction of the number of production lines; and modernization of certain shipyards.[676] However, in 1976 the Commission objected to extension of the same scheme because the aid involved could lead to an increase in capacity, and the Italian Government amended the scheme accordingly.[677] Italian aid for ship repair which would have increased capacity was also opposed, while a Dutch scheme which would have had the opposite effect was authorized.[678]

Specific legislative support for such practice was supplied by Directive 78/338. Article 4(1) of this Directive expressly provided that investment aid granted under a sectoral scheme must not cause any increase in the shipbuilding capacity of the Member State concerned. The Commission had sought control of aid which would increase the capacity of the yard concerned, though account would have been taken of any offsetting capacity reductions in other yards in that Member State and of the regional context of the investment.[679] In applying general or regional aid schemes to the shipbuilding sector, Member States were also required to take all necessary steps to ensure that aided investment did not lead either to increases in sectoral capacity or to the creation of employment which was not of a stable nature. This approach was maintained in Article 3 of Directive 81/363[680] and Article 6(1) of Directive 87/167, the latter provision adding the stipulation[681] that investment aid might not be granted to ship repairers unless it was linked to a restructuring plan which resulted in an overall reduction in the ship repair capacity of the Member State concerned. In practice, however, capacity might be reduced by introduction of

---

[674] *Ibid.*, 19 and 31. See also Commission Reply to Written Question 161/77 ([1977] OJ C206/9) by Mr Müller-Hermann.

[675] Art. 6(3) of Dir. 87/167 [1987] OJ L69/55; Art. 6(2) of Dir. 90/684 [1990] OJ L380/27.

[676] *Third Report on Competition Policy* (EC Commission, Brussels, 1974), 85.

[677] *Sixth Report on Competition Policy* (EC Commission, Brussels, 1977), 110–1.

[678] *Eighth Report on Competition Policy* (EC Commission, Brussels, 1979), 135.

[679] Art. 4(1) of the Proposal of 4 Nov. 1977 for a Dir. on aid to shipbuilding ([1977] OJ C294/4).

[680] On aid to shipbuilding ([1981] OJ L137/39).

[681] In its practice under Arts. 92–93 the Commission already imposed a similar restriction on investment aid to ship repair yards. See the *Ninth Report on Competition Policy* (EC Commission, Brussels, 1980), 99.

shorter working hours rather than redundancies, and some capacity might be 'mothballed' rather than dismantled.[682] Article 6(1) of Directive 90/684 introduced a slight modification. Investment aid which was not linked to a restructuring plan involving a decrease in capacity might be permitted, provided it was directly linked to a corresponding irreversible reduction in the capacity of other yards in the same Member State over the same period.[683]

The appropriateness of such emphasis on capacity reductions has been questioned. In 1978 the Economic and Social Committee urged the Commission to exercise maximum flexibility and, in particular, to approve aid designed to boost productivity, even if a slight increase in capacity was inevitable.[684] In a subsequent opinion[685] the Committee said of the draft of what became Directive 81/363 that it was extremely limited in comparison to the scale of the problems facing the industry and criticized its failure to treat restructuring as modernization and streamlining rather than only continued capacity-shedding.[686] The Commission admitted that this Directive had achieved more in terms of quantitative than qualitative restructuring and maintained that the emphasis should be placed on the latter.[687]

Similarly, the European Parliament[688] criticized the draft for what became Directive 87/167 as being too negative and defeatist in tone and seeming to assume irreversible decline in all areas of the industry rather than decline in some areas and expansion in others. Accordingly, the Parliament favoured amendment of Article 6 of the draft to the effect that, while aid should not *normally* be granted to capacity-increasing investment, increases in capacity in Member States where restructuring had taken place should not be excluded, particularly in the long term, and in the light of changes in the world shipping situation. Such aid should be permitted for the expansion of profitable yards which would otherwise be placed at a competitive disadvantage.

In the event, Article 6(4) of Directive 87/167 merely provided, as did Article 6(4) of Directive 90/684, that in examining the acceptability of investment aid, the Commission should take account of the extent of the contribution of the

---

[682] *Policy Guidelines for Restructuring the Shipbuilding Industry*, COM(83)65, 11.

[683] See, e.g., Notice C37/90 (ex NN70/90) ([1991] OJ C148/8) regarding aid which Germany decided to grant to Flensburger Schiffbau Gesellschaft.

[684] Opinion of 2 Feb. 1978 ([1978] OJ C84/16) on the proposal for a Dir. on shipbuilding, para. 6.

[685] Of 11 Dec. 1980 ([1980] OJ C353/25) on the proposal for a Council Dir. on aid to shipbuilding, para. 3. See also the *Report of the Committee on Economic and Monetary Affairs on the Proposal for a Dir. on Aid to Shipbuilding*, EP Doc. 1–638/80, 10, and the view in the Report of the same Committee on the proposal for a Dir. on aid to shipbuilding, EP Doc. 465/77, 13 that investment aids are only defensible 'insofar as they are a means of translating a common strategy into reality'.

[686] Though this point was made in the explanatory memorandum.

[687] *Policy Guidelines for Restructuring the Shipbuilding Industry*, COM(83)65, 10.

[688] Resolution of 12 Dec. 1986 ([1987] OJ C7/320) on the proposal for a Sixth Dir. on aid to shipbuilding, para. 8.

investment programme to such Union objectives as innovation,[689] special-ization, working conditions, health, safety, and the environment.[690] This requirement apparently cumulated with the condition that investment aid should not lead to overall capacity increases in the Member State concerned.[691] The latter condition was to be strictly applied, even in the least developed regions,[692] and the only exceptions—which concerned previous reductions—were much more limited than those sought by the Economic and Social Committee and the European Parliament.

A less restrictive approach to aid for research and development in this sector is now envisaged,[693] and higher than usual ceilings may apply to the grant of such aid in this sector.[694] Other forms of investment aid are to be limited to Belgium, Portugal, and Spain during transitional periods,[695] though 'in extra-ordinary circumstances' the limitations may be relaxed.[696]

Previous Reductions

The Preamble to Directive 81/363 stated that 'in assessing the reduction of production it is appropriate to take account of the effort already made'.[697] According to the Commission, reductions of capacity and employment effected in recent years as part of restructuring programmes had brought the industry of some Member States close to size limits below which economic viability could be threatened.[698] It was not to be expected, therefore, that in proposing new aid

---

[689] Higher levels of aid than those usually accepted for R & D might be authorized. See *Implementation 1987–8 of the Sixth Council Dir. on Aid to Shipbuilding*, SEC(89)518, Annex I.

[690] Art. 8 of Dir. 90/684, which followed Art. 8 of Dir. 87/167, concerned R & D aid. Such aid had to comply with the framework for R & D aid (sect. 6.3 below). See, e.g., Notice ([1988] OJ C10/6) regarding aid planned by the UK Government partly in the form of credit facilities granted to national shipowners for construction and conversion of ships at national yards and partly by grants to new building and repair yards for research and development; and Notice ([1988] OJ C324/3) regarding a proposal by the Belgian Government to assist the shipbuilding sector.

[691] Dir. 87/167 was criticized by the Economic and Social Committee in its Opinion of 26 Sept. 1984 ([1984] OJ C307/20) on the proposal for a Dir. amending Dir. 81/363 on aid to shipbuilding, because it did 'not constitute a Community shipbuilding policy capable of putting the sector on a less precarious footing' (para. 1).

[692] e.g. the Commission objected that aid to ship repair in Sicily would lead to increased capacity. See Bull. EC 12–1987, 2.1.118.

[693] Arts. 4 and 7(2) of Reg. 3094/95 ([1995] OJ L332/1) on aid to shipbuilding.

[694] See sect. 6.3.2 below, regarding the usual ceilings.

[695] Art. 6 of Reg. 3094/95. See, e.g., Notice C56/95 (N941/95) ([1996] OJ C75/2) concerning aid that Spain planned to grant its publicly-owned shipbuilding yards.

[696] *Ibid.*, Art. 7(1). The Economic and Social Committee apparently considers that aid for 'scrap and build' programmes should be encouraged and that aid under regional programmes should be permissible. See the Opinion of 23 Nov. 1995 ([1996] OJ C39/102) on the proposal for a Reg. on aid to shipbuilding, paras 3.5.1. and 4.2.

[697] 7th recital. Art. 4 of the Commission draft of 4 Nov. 1977 ([1977] OJ C294/4) for what became Dir. 78/338 provided for the Commission to 'take particular account of any reductions in capacity in other yards in the same Member State which offset [an] increase and of the regional context of the investment'.

[698] See also *Policy Guidelines for Restructuring the Shipbuilding Industry*, COM(83)65, 11. An

schemes such Member States could offer restructuring plans of the same type and scale as in the past. In their case, the emphasis of the restructuring requirement should be shifted from simple contraction to other aspects of restructuring, such as regrouping of enterprises, modernization, rationalization of production, and so forth.[699] Hence, production aid to assist consolidation of previous restructuring efforts in Germany and the Netherlands was authorized.[700]

Article 6(2) of Directive 90/684, which followed Article 6(2) of Directive 87/167, provided that the prohibition of increases in capacity did not apply where the Member State would otherwise have no shipbuilding capacity or where the aid was granted to its only existing yard, provided that the effect of the yard in question on the Union market was minimal.[701] Accordingly, in November 1990 the Commission authorized aid for the purchase of the Damen Shipyard from Verolme Cork Dockyard, which had been closed in November 1984. This shipyard would be the only one in the Irish Republic.[702]

The European Parliament considered that Commission practice should go further. It considered that shipbuilding was one of the sectors which might be defined as being of fundamental importance, since it was 'a basic element', essential for economic development, which could not be 'delegated' outside the Union. Hence, a minimum production capacity should be maintained as part of a process of giving fresh impetus to and upgrading the sector. The Commission should examine whether there was a critical threshold below which the whole of the industry's infrastructure would begin to collapse and which would undercut any Union strategy of concentrating on specialized market niches.[703]

In fact, Union practice regarding investment aid to shipbuilding seems to have had limited impact, beyond perhaps curbing increases in capacity. In 1990 the Commission admitted that a particular problem had been the substantial delays by certain southern Member States in taking advantage of Union rules to tackle urgent structural problems in their shipbuilding industry,

---

analogy may be drawn with the ruling of the ECJ in Case 72/83 *Campus Oil Ltd* v. *Minister for Industry and Energy* [1984] ECR 2727, 2754 that it might be acceptable for Ireland to use aid to preserve the only oil refinery in the Republic.

[699] *Tenth Report on Competition Policy* (EC Commission, Brussels, 1981), 127.

[700] *Twelfth Report on Competition Policy* (EC Commission, Brussels, 1983), 125–6.

[701] In the case of aid to ship repair, the Commission might take into account capacity reductions carried out in the immediately preceding years (Art. 6(1) of Dir. 90/684 [1990] OJ L380/27).

[702] *Twentieth Report on Competition Policy* (EC Commission, Brussels, 1991), 151.

[703] Resolution of 22 Nov. 1991 ([1991] OJ C326/257) on Community industrial policy in the shipbuilding sector, para. 2. See also the *Report of the Committee on Economic and Monetary Affairs and Industrial Policy and the Opinion of the Committee on External Economic Relations*, EP Doc. A3–0278/91; and *The Shipbuilding Industry*, SEC(90)1935.

which caused a widening of the structural difference between the north and the south of the Union within this sector.[704]

Closures

Article 5 of Directive 81/363 provided that in order to deal in particular with the social and possibly regional consequences of restructuring, aid intended to cover the normal expenditure occasioned by operations for conversion to other activities or by partial or total closure of shipbuilding or ship-repair yards might be authorized. Thus, for example, the Commission authorized aid to Alsthom Atlantique of ECU 43.5 million, as this aid made it possible to implement the social aspect of the restructuring that was being undertaken.[705]

Further examples of the kind of aid which might be granted were given in Directive 87/167. According to Article 7 of this Directive, aid to defray the normal costs resulting from the partial or total closure of shipbuilding or ship-repair yards might be accepted, provided that the capacity reduction was of a genuine and irreversible nature. Such aid might cover, for example, redundancy payments, training grants, and assistance to the creation of small undertakings. The amount and intensity of the aid must take account of the structural problems of the region concerned.[706] The European Parliament had unsuccessfully proposed introduction of a requirement into this provision that the aid should be 'for the development of new economic activities in the area'.[707]

Article 7(1) of Directive 90/684 added the condition that for such aid[708] to be permissible the yards concerned had to remain closed for at least five years.[709] However, there was concern that purchasers might acquire closed yards with the main objective of reopening them after having waited out the five-year period.[710] Hence, after five years and before the tenth anniversary of closure[711] a Member State had to obtain Commission approval for reopening.[712] The decision of the Commission as to the permissibility of such aid was to be

---

[704] Explanatory Memorandum to the Proposal for a Dir. on Aid to Shipbuilding, COM(90)248, 7.

[705] *Fifteenth Report on Competition Policy* (EC Commission, Brussels, 1986), 158.

[706] Closure aid of 50% (and investment aid of 30%) was authorized in respect of the coastal *Länder* of Germany. See Communic. C18/89 (ex NN121/87–63/89) ([1991] OJ C45/3) regarding aid which Germany had decided to grant to Bremen and Niedersachsen.

[707] [1987] OJ C7/320.

[708] Such aid may include the execution of a 'security bond'. See Bull. EU 10–1995, 1.3.67.

[709] Closure aid has to be reimbursed if large-scale shipbuilding is resumed. See Commission Reply to Written Question 535/91 ([1991] OJ C199/23) by Mr Monnier-Besombes. See, regarding the reaction of the Commission to a plan to reopen a shipyard in France, the *Twentieth Report on Competition Policy* (EC Commission, Brussels, 1991), 151.

[710] Explanatory Memorandum to the Proposal of 20 June 1990 for a Dir. on aid to shipbuilding, COM(90)248, 17.

[711] The 10-year limitation period for the need to obtain Commission approval was not included in the Commission proposal of 20 July 1990 ([1990] OJ C223/4).

[712] According to the Commission, the present market situation does not suggest that such approval would be given. See the Reply by Sir Leon Brittan to Written Question 3025/91 ([1992] OJ C168/28) by Mr Frédéric Rosmini.

taken with reference both to the currently existing worldwide balance between supply and demand and to whether it was envisaged that aid would be granted for reopening the facilities.[713]

In practice, aid needed to alleviate social and regional consequences of capacity reductions was favoured.[714] For example, the Commission accepted Italian production aid of 30 per cent, because the beneficiary undertaking was restructuring with the aim of converting almost half of its workforce to non-shipbuilding activities.[715]

Such aid will continue to be authorized under Regulation 3094/95.[716] However, an express stipulation is made to the effect that the aid must be for the exclusive benefit of workers.[717]

5.8.2 Rescue Aid

Article 5 of Directive 75/432 provided that aid of a conservatory nature intended as a temporary solution for the rescue of a shipbuilding, ship-conversion, or ship-repair undertaking pending a solution to the problems confronting the undertaking concerned was to be notified individually to the Commission. Hence, the acceptability of rescue aid would depend on Commission assessment under Article 92 of the Treaty. The Commission intended to require that such aid should be designed to promote the competitiveness of the recipient undertaking.[718]

Article 5 of Directive 78/338 went further. It provided that rescue aid could be granted, pending a definitive solution to the problems of the undertaking concerned, in order to deal with acute social problems.[719] Similarly, Article 4 of Directive 81/363 provided that rescue aid intended to maintain a shipbuilding, ship-conversion, or ship-repair undertaking, pending a definite solution of its problems, in order to deal with acute social problems and the regional effects

---

[713] There is concern that 'a failure to contain the prevailing shortsighted pressure being exerted for a return of closed capacities to the market may lead to the eradication of the market improvement which has occurred'. See the Explanatory Memorandum to the proposal for a dir. on aid to shipbuilding, COM(90)248, 9.

[714] See, earlier, the Explanatory Memorandum of 7 Mar. 1984 to the Proposal for a Dir. amending Dir. 81/363, COM(84)73, 4. The need for such aid will be closely scrutinized. See Slynn AG in Case 223/85 *Rijn-Schelde-Verolme (RSV) Maschinefabrieken en Scheepswerven NV* v. *EC Commission* [1987] ECR 4617, 4651–2.

[715] *Tenth Report on Competition Policy* (EC Commission, Brussels, 1981), 130.

[716] On aid to shipbuilding ([1995] OJ L332/1).

[717] *Ibid.*, Art. 3.

[718] Proposals on the shipbuilding industry, COM(73)1788, 31.

[719] See, e.g., Notice regarding planned Italian rescue aid for the Alto Adriatico shipyard ([1981] OJ C319/3). See, earlier, Art. 7 of the proposal of 5 Nov. 1973 ([1973] OJ C114/23). The proposal for what became Dir. 78/338 ([1977] OJ C294/4) explicitly required in Art. 5 that the aid be 'warranted' by such problems. Art. 4 of the latter proposal would also have required the Commission, in assessing investment aids, to take account of the 'regional context of the investment'.

which might arise, might be authorized. The Commission was to verify that the aid did not change the terms of trade in a manner contrary to the common interest and that it did not endanger the arrangements instituted by the Directive, particularly those relating to operating aid.

Article 5(1) of Directive 90/684, following Article 5(1) of Directive 87/167, subjected rescue aid to the ceiling for operating aids discussed below.[720] Thus, for example, in 1987 rescue aid to the Lindenau yard in Germany, which amounted to operating aid of 20.5 per cent during the first half of 1987 and 21 per cent for the subsequent year and a half was authorized as being within the ceiling.[721]

Rescue aid remained permissible under Directive 90/684. However, Article 4 thereof provided that such aid could not be used, at the moment of taking the order, as a means of exceeding the limits imposed on operating aid. The primary concern of the Union may have been to ensure that aid justified by reference to social and regional policy considerations did not undermine efforts to control operating aid.[722] Under Regulation 3094/95 rescue aid will no longer be permitted.

5.8.3 Operating Aid

Controlled use of operating aid has been considered necessary to preserve a viable Union shipbuilding industry[723] within an international market where prices are not at a profitable level.[724] Commission control of such aid was designed to assist in tackling problems of fragmentation of the Union market[725] and the lack of competitiveness of Union shipyards. The former problem was addressed specifically by the prohibition of discrimination[726] and the latter by the imposition of ceilings on the amount of permissible aid.

---

[720] The European Parliament had proposed that 'supplementary rescue aid' should be permissible ([1987] OJ C7/324).

[721] *Implementation 1987–8 of the Sixth Directive*, SEC(89)518, 7. See also Communic. C38/90 (NN76/89) ([1991] OJ C3/3) regarding aid which the Netherlands had decided to grant to the shipyard van der Giessen de Noord.

[722] Cf., regarding unsuccessful attempts made in the past by Member States to have operating aid treated as rescue aid in the hope that restrictions imposed on the grant of the former could thereby be avoided, the *Tenth Report on Competition Policy* (EC Commission, Brussels, 1981), 128–31. Art. 4 of the proposal ([1980] OJ C263/1) for what became Dir. 81/363 stated that 'rescue aid may not take the form of production aid more particularly provided for in Art. 6'.

[723] Such aid is not to be authorized in the case of ship repair. See Notice C10/91, C11/91, & C12/91 (ex NN54/90, NN56/90 & NN58/90) ([1991] OJ C123/16) regarding aid which Greece had granted to shipbuilding in the period 1987 to 1990.

[724] *EC Twenty-Fourth General Report* (EC Commission, Brussels, 1990), 107.

[725] Lack of integration of national markets in this sector is a problem long recognized by the Commission. See, e.g., *The State of the Shipbuilding Industry in the Community*, COM(82)564, 13.

[726] Communic. ([1988] OJ C306/4) concerning aid which the French department of Vendee had decided to grant to the fisheries sector.

Non-discrimination

The aim of prohibiting discrimination is to ensure that, with the progress towards the full achievement of the internal market, intra-Union competition in shipbuilding takes place on an equal and equitable basis in respect of all Union yards and to provide for full aid transparency within the Union.[727]

To begin with, Member States may not grant aid which is conditional upon discriminatory practices as to products originating in other Member States. This prohibition, which was first introduced in legislative form by Article 5 of Directive 72/273[728] and is now contained in Article 2(2) of Regulation 3094/95, seeks to prevent discrimination in relation to components. In particular, it prohibits cost-escalation schemes from discriminating in favour of the use of domestically produced components. Schemes of this kind[729] in France,[730] Italy,[731] and the United Kingdom[732] have been found objectionable.[733]

Member States are also prohibited from granting aid which favours national shipbuilders in competition with shipbuilders in other Member States for a particular order.[734] Article 4(5) of Directive 90/684, which followed earlier legislation,[735] was more detailed. It provided that where there was competition between yards in different Member States for a particular contract, the Commission should require prior notification of the relevant aid proposals at the request of any Member State. In such cases the Commission should ensure

---

[727] Explanatory Memorandum to the Proposal for a Dir. on aid to shipbuilding, COM (90)248, 3.

[728] On aids to shipbuilding ([1972] JO L169/28).

[729] Generally speaking, the Commission objects to such schemes, irrespective of discriminatory elements. See the *Sixth Report on Competition Policy* (EC Commission, Brussels, 1977), 112.

[730] The Art. 169 procedure was initiated in respect of a French guarantee system against price rises in French products during the ship construction period. See Bull. EC 3–1973, 2114. France subsequently agreed to include components from other Member States in the scheme. See the *Fourth Report on Competition Policy* (EC Commission, Brussels, 1975), 87. This agreement resulted in the inclusion of Art. 2(b)(third indent) in Dir. 75/432 ([1975] OJ L192/27).

[731] See, regarding tax exemptions for Italian steel products used in shipbuilding, the *Seventh ECSC General Report* (ECSC High Authority, Luxembourg, 1959), 145.

[732] *Sixth Report on Competition Policy* (EC Commission, Brussels, 1977), 111–2 and the amendment to Art. 2(2)(b) of Dir. 75/432, introduced by Dir. 76/872 ([1976] OJ L320/27).

[733] Cf. Dec. 66/556 ([1966] JO 3141) on the aid system established by the French Government for the purchase of gliders requiring France either to abolish aid for the purchase of French gliders or extend it to cover gliders manufactured in other Member States. Cf. also, regarding discriminatory Italian aid taking the form of interest rate relief for purchasers of agricultural machinery, Bull. EC 11–1961, 48.

[734] Art. 5(3) of Reg. 3094/95. Once the order has been placed, aid may be granted. See Notice C1/91 (ex N536/90) ([1991] OJ C292/6) regarding aid which Belgium and the Netherlands had decided to grant for the benefit of the contract to build a 15000 dwt dredger for Jan de Nul.

[735] Art. 6(2) of Dir. 78/338, Art. 7(4) of Dir. 81/363, and Art. 4(5) of Dir. 87/167. See, in connection with Dir. 81/363, the Reply by Mr Andriessen to Written Question 299/82 by Ms Quin ([1982] OJ C183/11). Prior to the enactment of any specific legislative requirement the Commission exercised its powers under Arts. 92–93 EC to make compliance with such a requirement a condition for approval of aid schemes. See the *Seventh Report on Competition Policy* (EC Commission, Brussels, 1978), 142–5.

that the planned aid did not affect trading conditions to an extent contrary to the common interest. Accordingly, the Commission sought to ensure that aid to shipyards was not granted in such a way as to distort intra-Union competition for specific orders. Although this provision was inapplicable in respect of the former German Democratic Republic, the Commission applied the principle embodied therein to ensure that trade was not affected to an extent contrary to the common interest as required by Article 10(a)(3) of Directive 90/684. Thus where there was no substantial competition from third-country yards, the Commission would examine whether the price offered by the aided yard in the former German Democratic Republic was 'unjustifiably low'.[736]

In a Declaration in the Minutes of the 1136th meeting of the Council of Ministers of 22 December 1986,[737] the Commission stated that when exercising its powers under Article 4(5) of Directive 87/167, the predecessor of Article 4(5) of Directive 90/684, it would permit only the lowest level of aid unless a higher level within the ceiling appeared necessary to ensure that the contract remained within the Union. For example, in May 1990 the Commission imposed a ceiling of 5.88 per cent of the contract price where Union yards were competing for the contract to build two ferries for De Danske Statsbaner. This ceiling was set to enable a Dutch yard to compete and thus keep the order within the Union.[738] Where one Member State involved undertook to grant no aid and there was no competition from a third country, no other Member State might be authorized to grant aid.[739] In such cases the Commission usually secured by informal action an alignment downwards to the lowest aid level proposed.[740]

Occasionally, however, formal action was found necessary. For example, Decision 88/437[741] concerned aid planned by the French Government. Aid had also been offered by the Netherlands and the United Kingdom. The Commission maintained that it was necessary to limit aid to that which was strictly necessary to keep the contract available for Union yards, in order to ensure a normal play of competition undistorted by aid between yards in different Member States. The lowest level of aid had been offered by the Netherlands,

---

[736] Replies by Mr Van Miert to Written Question 2788/92 ([1993] OJ C155/17) by Mr Freddy Blak and to Written Question 1428/93 ([1994] OJ C25/33) by Mr Klaus Riskaer Pedersen.

[737] Council Doc. 4352/87 (unpublished).

[738] *Twentieth Report on Competition Policy* (EC Commission, Brussels, 1991), 146.

[739] Notice C41/91 (N305/91) ([1991] OJ C274/8) regarding the aid plans of the Dutch Government for its shipyards under its different shipbuilding aid schemes as regards the investment of the Statshavneadministrationen in Esbjerg for a trailing suction hopper dredger/ grab dredger.

[740] *Implementation 1987–8 of the Sixth Council Directive on Aid to Shipbuilding*, SEC(89)518, 12 and Annex III.

[741] Concerning aids planned by the French Government in favour of a shipbuilding contract for which there was competition between yards in several Member States ([1988] OJ L211/24). 17 previous cases had been settled by voluntary agreement between the Member States (*ibid.*).

and so France was required to abolish its aid plans or to bring the aid down to the Dutch level.

Again, Decision 90/223[742] concerned aid planned by the German Government in respect of a shipbuilding contract for which there was competition between Dutch and German yards. Although a third-country yard quoted a lower price than that of both Union yards, the application of an aid level by the German Government higher than that of the Dutch Government did not have the effect of rendering the German yard's tender price more competitive than that of the Dutch yard. Thus the higher aid level was not necessary to retain the contract within the Union.

More particularly, the difference in technical specifications of the ships offered did not mean that the Union yards concerned were not competing for the same order. The offers of the yards were both based on the same invitation to tender from the German shipowner, and it was only natural that different yards would present designs with different specifications. Such differences, together with quality, delivery time, and market-economy pricing, and not the level of aid offered, were the normal parameters on which the shipowner's choice should be based. To accept that the yards were not competing for the same contract would undermine the mechanism of Article 4(5) of Directive 87/167 and deprive the Commission of an essential instrument of pursuing the aid policy laid down by this Directive. Moreover, it was an ordinary phenomenon that the shipowner at a certain stage of the tendering procedure singled out one yard for continued detailed negotiations. This did not rule out the possibility that there was initially competition for the contract and that the aid levels proposed by the Member States involved had influenced the shipowner's choice of yard.

Consequently, the German aid had to be prohibited. The Commission would also ensure that the German Government did not grant any subsequent aid to cover losses suffered from taking the order below cost, as contracts that had been subject to the Article 4(5) procedure might not be included in the base for calculating other operating aid.

The economic rationale for such practice has been questioned. On the one hand, without aid from one Member State no purchase may occur anywhere in the Union, and in this sense no Member State can be made worse off by the capture of the order by a Member State granting aid. On the other hand, another Member State may enjoy greater benefit from the order. In other words, greater externalities may arise from the placing of the order with that Member State. Therefore, it is argued that fair competition between undertakings should not be sought without taking account of competition between

---

[742] Concerning an aid project planned by the German Government in favour of a shipbuilding contract for which there was competition between yards in different Member States ([1990] OJ L118/39).

Member States.[743] Such arguments do not seem to have influenced Commission practice.

They seem to have been no more influential in the case of aid to shipowners. Initially, Article 8 of Directive 78/338 provided that aid granted to shipowners in a Member State for the purchase of ships should not discriminate against the shipyards of other Member States. Prior to introduction of this legislative prohibition the Commission exercised its powers under Articles 92 to 93 of the Treaty to prohibit such discrimination.[744] Article 8(1) of Directive 81/363 went somewhat further and provided that such aid should not lead to distortions of competition between national shipyards and shipyards in other Member States in the placing of contracts. Directive 87/167 adopted the same approach, though Article 3(1) added a requirement of notification of aid to shipowners and third parties for building and conversion. In April 1989 the Commission objected that Greek aid to shipyards might infringe the Directive, because the aid would be granted only to Greek nationals for the construction of ships in Greek yards.[745] The same prohibition was contained in Article 3(2) of Directive 90/684 and Article 5(3) of Regulation 3094/95.[746] On the other hand, Commission ideas to the effect that Union shipowners should be required to address their calls for tenders to shipyards in Member States other than their own[747] or that a 'Home Credit Scheme' for construction of ships within the Union for Union shipowners should be introduced have not been adopted.[748] At one stage the Commission favoured the replacement of national arrangements with such a scheme, but this idea was abandoned in the face of the 'reticence' of most Member States.[749]

However, it is by no means clear that such prohibitions are effective in excluding all discrimination. The European Parliament has expressed regret that the Union policy on shipbuilding does not comprehensively cover the many different ways in which national assistance or preference may distort competition and, hence, the rational restructuring of the industry. In particular, the exclusion of military shipbuilding[750] and oilfield equipment, and the national procurement thereof, leaves ample opportunity for propping up inefficient yards and denying rewards to those that have restructured.[751] In the

---

[743] J. Atik, 'Investment Contests and Subsidy Limitations in the EC' (1992) 32 *Virginia J. of Intl Law* 837–69, 867–9.

[744] *Seventh Report on Competition Policy* (EC Commission, Brussels, 1978), 145–6.

[745] *Nineteenth Report on Competition Policy* (EC Commission, Brussels, 1990), 147.

[746] On aid to shipbuilding ([1995] OJ L332/1).

[747] Preamble to the Commission proposal of 4 Nov. 1977 ([1977] OJ C294/4).

[748] Cf. the idea of a 'Community preference' requiring Union shipowners to purchase a certain proportion of their ships from Union yards in the Resolution of the European Parliament of 10 Feb. 1977 ([1977] OJ C57/58) on the Community shipping industry, para. 3(b).

[749] *Future Aid Strategy for Shipbuilding*, COM(86)324, 11. See also *The State of the Shipbuilding Industry in the Community (Situation as at 1 Jan. 1982)*, COM(82)564, 22.

[750] By virtue of Art. 223 EC.

[751] Resolution of 15 Jan. 1981 ([1981] OJ C28/35) on the proposal for a directive on aid to shipbuilding, para. 5.

original draft of what became Directive 75/432 the Commission had proposed in Article 1 that the Directive should cover 'any civil activity carried on on a shipbuilding or ship repair yard in the Community with the object of building, converting or repairing ships or other water-borne installations to be used for navigation or other purposes of the sea'.[752] Although this proposal was not accepted by the Council, Articles 92 to 93 of the Treaty remain applicable to aid for the production of such equipment.[753]

In fact, the Union apparently became increasingly fragmented into national markets, in which shipowners usually purchased from national shipyards. Before 1976 around 20 per cent of Union production went to another Member State. By 1987 the figure had fallen to around 5 per cent.[754]

The inadequacy of specific prohibitions of discrimination seems to have been recognized, in so far as Article 3(2) of Directive 90/684, following Directive 87/167, provided that aid to shipowners should be subject to rules regarding operating aid to shipbuilders,[755] and, more particularly, such aid was covered by the ceiling for operating aid under Article 4.[756] According to the Commission, by providing that all aid granted to shipowners for construction and conversion of ships constituted another but corresponding way of granting aid to shipbuilding, the legislation eliminated previous ambiguities. The original criterion, whether such aid was being legally reserved for national yards or not, was considered inadequate, as practice had shown that such schemes would anyway almost always be used for building at national yards.[757]

---

[752] Proposals on the shipbuilding industry, COM(73)1788.

[753] Dec. 79/496 ([1979] OJ L127/50) on the UK scheme of assistance in the form of interest relief grants in favour of the offshore supplies industry and Dec. 85/351 ([1985] OJ L188/44) concerning aid granted by the Netherlands Government to an engineering undertaking. See also, regarding marine electronics, Dec. 93/412 ([1993] OJ L185/43) concerning aid awarded by the German Government to Hibeg and by Hibeg via Krupp GmbH to Bremer Vulkan AG, facilitating the sale of Krupp Atlas Elektronik GmbH from Krupp GmbH to Bremer Vulkan AG.

[754] *Shipbuilding: Industrial, Social and Regional Aspects*, COM(87)275, 16. See also *State of the Shipbuilding Industry in the Community (Situation at the Beginning of 1985)*, COM(85) 548, 19

[755] Application of OECD conditions to the grant of credit facilities is said to prevent Member States from discriminating in favour of national shipowners. See Commission Reply to Written Question 680/77 ([1978] OJ C52/9) by Mr Müller-Hermann. However, provided these conditions were respected, it was apparently unobjectionable for such facilities to be reserved for national owners purchasing from national yards. See *Aid Granted to Shipbuilding in the EEC*, COM(82)645, Annex I, 3. See also Dec. 88/437 ([1988] OJ L211/24) concerning aids planned by the French Government in favour of a shipbuilding contract for which there was competition between yards in several Member States.

[756] See below. The aim is 'to ensure complete transparency'. See Dec. 91/375 ([1991] OJ L203/105) concerning credits granted by the Belgian authorities to various shipowners for the building of nine vessels. This decision was upheld by the ECJ in Joined Cases C–356 & C–180/91 *Belgium* v. *EC Commission: aid to shipbuilding* [1993] ECR I–2323. See also Dec. 90/627 ([1990] OJ L338/21) on loans granted by the Belgian authorities to two shipowners for the purchase of a 34 000m³ LPG ship and two refrigerator ships.

[757] Explanatory Memorandum to the proposal for a directive on aid to shipbuilding, COM(90)248, 12. See also Notice C8/95 (ex NN111/93) ([1995] OJ C279/3) concerning direct and indirect aid granted by the French Government for the building of two passenger sailing ships.

As regards Italy, for example, the Commission in 1981 'noted an apparently systematic absence of invitations to yards in other Member States to tender for orders placed by Italian shipowners'.[758] In this regard at least, abolition of discrimination has apparently come to be seen as a consequence rather than a means of controlling the grant of aid.

Ceilings

Aid ceilings are a well-established means by which the Commission has sought to control the use of shipbuilding aid. The Court of Justice apparently regards the ceilings as a lawful means of balancing respect for the rules of the common market with maintenance of an efficient and competitive Union shipbuilding industry. Hence, in *Belgium* v. *EC Commission: aid to shipbuilding*,[759] where the Commission had prohibited aid in the form of credit to shipowners for the construction of ships above the aid ceiling, the Court accepted that aid above the ceiling was in itself prohibited. The view of Advocate General Roemer, that the Commission must still demonstrate its incompatibility with the common market,[760] was not apparently convincing for the Court itself.

Aid ceilings have been designed, subject to exceptions reflecting the requirements of the common fisheries policy and developments in the commercial-policy field, to be both degressive and comprehensive. The need to secure 'value-for-money from public expenditure' may be invoked to support such an approach.[761] In practice, the two qualities have not always been mutually reconcilable. More particularly, application of the degressivity principle was frustrated by the crisis in the international shipbuilding market[762] which developed in the second half of the 1970s.[763] Such crises may mean that efforts to improve competitiveness are largely 'nullified by the productivity losses incurred through longer idle periods for production facilities and work force alike'.[764] Special arrangements have also been necessitated by enlargements of the Union.

Prior to legislative intervention,[765] the Commission sought to secure the reduction of operating aid to 10 per cent of the contract price of a vessel,[766] though credit facilities for exports to third countries were unaffected.[767] In

---

[758] *Tenth Report on Competition Policy* (EC Commission, Brussels, 1981), 131.

[759] Joined Cases C–356 & C–180/91 [1993] ECR I–2323, I–2358.

[760] *Ibid.*, 2345.

[761] *Aid Granted to Shipbuilding in the EEC*, COM(83)676, 1.

[762] *Seventh Report on Competition Policy* (EC Commission, Brussels, 1978), 139.

[763] Note also the successive extensions of the period of validity of Dir. 81/363 by Dir. 82/880 ([1982] OJ L371/46) and Dir. 85/2 ([1985] OJ L2/13).

[764] *State of the Shipbuilding Industry in the Community*, COM(85)548, 22.

[765] See, regarding early efforts, the *EEC Sixth General Report* (EEC Commission, Brussels, 1963), 69.

[766] See, in the cases of France and Italy, the *EC First General Report* (EC Commission, Brussels, 1967), 71.

[767] *EEC Fifth General Report* (EEC Commission, Brussels, 1962), 82.

April 1965 the Commission proposed that the Union itself should provide such aid up to the same limit,[768] but this proposal was not accepted by the Council.

Article 2 of Directive 69/262[769] provided that aid should be no more than 10 per cent of the price contractually fixed for the purchase of new ships or for works of transformation. This figure was supposed to reflect the harm suffered as a result of distortion of competition by third countries. The structure of the sector means that 'normal trade policy measures, such as anti-dumping procedures, are ineffective for dealing with this problem'.[770] The ceiling was reduced by Directive 72/273 to 5 per cent in 1972 and 4 per cent in 1973, though credit facilities compatible with OECD conditions,[771] cost-escalation insurance,[772] Italian aid limited to restructuring, and 'indirect' aid[773] were not covered by the ceiling.[774] Directive 75/432[775] envisaged that aid for the building of ships would, with certain exceptions, be abolished by the end of 1975,[776] and aid to sales would be reduced to 5 per cent. The exceptions related to France, Ireland, and Italy, which were required progressively to reduce the level of their aid,[777] and export credit compatible with OECD conditions. Within the Union these limits applied also to aid to shipowners of the same Member State, in order to prevent discrimination against shipowners of other Member States.[778]

---

[768] Proposal for a dir. establishing a Community system of aids to correct distortions of competition on the international shipbuilding market ([1965] JO 3129). The Commission objected to French aid above 10% of the contract price. See Communic. on the aid system applied in France in favour of French shipbuilding ([1968] JO C107/1).

[769] On aids to shipbuilding ([1969] JO L206/25).

[770] 'State Aid Control in the Context of Other Community Policies' [1994] *European Economy*, Supp. A, No. 4, 12.

[771] The Commission has defined potential beneficiary countries more narrowly than the OECD Aid Committee (Letter to Member States SG(89)D/311, 3 Jan. 1989), though aid may be granted to countries excluded from the Commission list where a third country is also planning to grant assistance. See *Implementation 1987–1988 of the Sixth Council Directive on Aid to Shipbuilding*, SEC(89) 518, 14 and Annex IV. The Commission, however, considers that its OECD partners should use the Commission list and that the minimum grant element should be increased to 35%. See the Explanatory Memorandum to the proposal for a dir. on aid to shipbuilding, COM(90)248, 16.

[772] The Commission originally envisaged that account would be taken of credit facilities and guarantees against rises in costs within Union limits. See the *First Report on Competition Policy* (EC Commission, Brussels, 1972), 134.

[773] Indirect aid was apparently that which did not have 'a direct relation to the price of ships'. See the *Third Report on Competition Policy* (EC Commission, Brussels, 1974), 83.

[774] A proposal of 5 Nov. 1973 ([1973] OJ C114/23) to bring the first two categories within the ceilings was not accepted by the Council. Instead, the application of Dir. 72/273 was extended until 1975 by Dir. 74/643 ([1974] OJ L349/62).			[775] [1975] OJ L192/27.

[776] The Commission had proposed that a ceiling of 5% for 1974 and 4% for 1975 should be imposed on all 'direct aid', though credit facilities compatible with OECD conditions were not to be affected (*ibid.*).

[777] This requirement was enforced against Italy in 1976. See the *Sixth Report on Competition Policy* (EC Commission, Brussels, 1977), 110–1.

[778] Commission Reply to Written Question 680/77 ([1978] OJ C52/9) by Mr Müller-Hermann.

In the early stages the situation was 'quite erratic', with aid exceeding 30 per cent of the selling price in France and Italy, while elsewhere no aid was granted at all. After 1967 the situation tended to become more balanced, the aid figure dropping, within a few years, to around 10 per cent, with the exception of Italy where the figure was still higher. From the beginning of 1971 a downward alignment was recorded, and the average figure fluctuated around 5 per cent, again with the exception of Italy, where the figure hovered around 10 per cent. In some Member States, however, there were general aid systems which applied and which, added to the specific aid, substantially affected the prices for ships.[779]

Article 6 of Directive 78/338, which was followed by Article 6 of Directive 81/363, sought more comprehensively to control the grant of operating aid to shipbuilders.[780] All such aid, which was now treated as 'crisis' aid, should be progressively reduced. The Commission was to assess the maximum level of aid which might be granted under the various aid schemes. The extension of the scope of the ceilings and the state of the international shipbuilding market at the time meant that much higher ceilings had to be stipulated than previously. The ceiling was originally fixed by the Commission at 30 per cent of the contract price,[781] subject to exceptions which it might authorize. This figure took 'account of the average disadvantage encountered by European shipyards on the world market and should avoid unwarranted outbidding between Member States'.[782] Prior notification was also required, so that the Commission could ensure that the aid was tied to restructuring objectives and would not adversely affect yards in other Member States.[783] According to the Committee on Economic and Monetary Affairs, the Directive gave Member States *carte blanche* in the matter of production aid and only stimulated to a very minor extent the necessary restructuring.[784]

In accordance with this legislation, the Commission objected to an Italian scheme partly because of the level of aid planned. Discussions with the Italian authorities led to agreement that the level would be reduced to 30 per cent of the contract price.[785] Similarly, the British Government was prevailed upon to abandon a scheme to subsidize the supply of six bulk carriers to Poland by an amount far exceeding 30 per cent of the contract price.[786]

---

[779] *First Report on Competition Policy* (EC Commission, Brussels, 1972), 134.

[780] Art. 8(2) of the same Dir. also provided that aid to shipowners should not endanger arrangements regarding 'crisis aid' to shipbuilders.

[781] This ceiling was well above the level of aid known to be granted at that time. See *Aid Granted to Shipbuilding in the EEC*, COM(82)645, Annex I, 2.

[782] *Shipbuilding: Industrial, Social and Regional Aspects*, COM(87)275, 16.

[783] *Eighth Report on Competition Policy* (EC Commission, Brussels, 1979), 129.

[784] Report on the proposal for a Directive on aid to shipbuilding, EP Doc. 465/77, 15.

[785] *Eighth Report on Competition Policy* (EC Commission, Brussels, 1979), 131. See also the *Ninth Report on Competition Policy* (EC Commission, Brussels, 1980), 97–8.

[786] *Eighth Report on Competition Policy* (EC Commission, Brussels, 1979), 133.

However, aid within the ceiling might not necessarily be authorized.[787] As regards a United Kingdom scheme providing aid of up to 30 per cent of the contract price, the Commission considered that the criteria for selecting the yards to be aided were not sufficiently restrictive to guarantee that aid would be limited to yards with a real chance of becoming competitive in the future. Accordingly, a requirement of prior notification of grants under the scheme was imposed.[788]

Conversely, exceptions from the ceilings might be permitted by the legislation.[789] For example, although by 1980 the ceiling for France had been lowered to 25 per cent, the Commission authorized French production aid of 30 per cent, because of the restructuring already achieved and the precarious position in which the yards would be without the orders concerned.[790] The Commission also agreed to the aid it had authorized in the Netherlands in 1984 (the rate varying from 1.5 per cent to 7 per cent according to the value of the ship) being increased by an average of three percentage points because of the acute worsening of the state of the industry during 1985.[791] More generally, in 1985 the Commission accepted aid levels slightly higher than those previously authorized on account of the worsening crisis in the shipbuilding industry and of the extent of the planned restructuring.[792]

However, the importance attached to the enforcement of ceilings increased. According to the *Sixteenth Report on Competition Policy*,[793] the ever-deepening structural crisis in the shipbuilding industry could no longer appropriately be met by the aid policy embodied in Directive 81/363, if the long-term future of the industry and the jobs depending on it were to be secured. While the market outlook made further rationalization indispensable, budgetary constraints were leading most Member States to reappraise support for the industry. Further-

---

[787] Note, regarding the requirement of degressivity laid down in Art. 6(1) of Dir. 81/363, the *Thirteenth Report on Competition Policy* (EC Commission, Brussels, 1984), 160–1.

[788] *Sixth Report on Competition Policy* (EC Commission, Brussels, 1977), 141–2. A similar approach was adopted in relation to a French scheme. See the *Seventh Report on Competition Policy* (EC Commission, Brussels, 1978), 145. See also Notice regarding the UK proposal to assist shipbuilding during the period 1 July 1984 to 1 July 1986 ([1984] OJ C219/3), where the aid amounted to 35% of the contract price.

[789] Art. 6(3) of Dir. 78/338 ([1978] OJ L98/19) and Art. 6(3) of Dir. 81/363 ([1981] OJ L137/39).

[790] *Tenth Report on Competition Policy* (EC Commission, Brussels, 1981), 129. See, similarly, regarding shipyards in the Mezzogiorno, Dec. 88/281 ([1988] OJ L119/33) on aid for shipbuilding and ship repair in Italy—Art. 10 of Law 111 of 22 Mar. 1985.

[791] Notice ([1984] OJ C319/4) of the Netherlands Government's plans for aid to its shipbuilding industry between 1 Jan. and 31 Dec. 1984; and the *Fifteenth Report on Competition Policy* (EC Commission, Brussels, 1986), 157. See, generally, regarding the idea of a 'two-year moratorium on degressivity', the Explanatory Memorandum to the Proposal of 7 Mar. 1984 for a Dir. amending Dir. 81/363, COM(84)73, 4.

[792] Bull. EC 7/8–1985, 2.1.61. Cf. Notice ([1985] OJ C252/4) of a proposal by the French Government to award aid to the shipbuilding and ship repair industries from 1 Jan. 1985 to 31 Dec. 1986.

[793] (EC Commission, Brussels, 1987), 146–7.

more, the lack of transparency in the various forms of aid with which ship-building was being supported in the Member States had virtually eliminated intra-Union competition. In order to meet the situation, the Commission favoured a new selective aid strategy, designed to steer Union shipbuilding towards the market segments where it remained most competitive[794] and where the links with subcontractors and supply industries were closest, so as to spur further restructuring, provide the necessary aid transparency and revive intra-Union competition.

As the aid ceiling represented an alignment with the most efficient yards to Far Eastern prices, its application was not conditional on restructuring measures. However, according to the Commission, the ceiling should in itself constitute a built-in incentive for less competitive yards to accelerate and intensify the structural adjustments necessary in order to maintain a sufficient level of activities within this production support level.[795]

To these ends, Article 4 of Directive 87/167 provided for imposition of a common ceiling. The ceiling was to be fixed by the Commission with reference to the prevailing difference between the cost structures of the most competitive Union yards and the prices charged by their main international competitors with particular regard to the market segments in which Union yards remained relatively most competitive.[796] The Commission was to pay particular attention to ensuring that aid for the building of small specialized vessels costing less than ECU 6 million, a market segment normally served by small yards and for which the competition was mainly intra-European, was kept at the lowest level possible, allowing for the particular situation in Greece.[797] The ceiling was to be reviewed every twelve months, or sooner if warranted by exceptional circumstances, with a view to its progressive reduction.[798] In such reviews the Commission had to ensure that there were no undue concentrations of ship-building activities in specific market segments to an extent contrary to Union interests.

Similar arrangements were provided for by Article 4 of Directive 90/684, though the contract value mentioned for small specialized vessels was raised to ECU 10 million. The Preamble to Directive 90/684 stated that the reduced level of aid acceptable for such vessels and for ship conversion should be applied based on experience to the largest possible section of the market.

---

[794] Such a strategy had already been adopted in relation to ship repair. See the *Ninth Report on Competition Policy* (EC Commission, Brussels, 1980), 99.

[795] *Future Aid Strategy for Shipbuilding*, COM(86)324, 10.

[796] Details of the methodology of the Commission were given in the Reply by Sir Leon Brittan to Written Question 12/92 ([1992] OJ C209/44) by Mr Roberto Speciale.

[797] More details of the criteria which the Commission intended to employ in fixing the ceiling were given in *Future Aid Strategy for Shipbuilding*, COM(86)324, 8–10.

[798] The Commission draft ([1990] OJ C223/4) for what became Dir. 90/684 envisaged the explicit statement in Art. 4(3): 'The ceiling will be progressively reduced', but this statement was omitted from the version adopted by the Council.

Moreover, it was stipulated that, in principle, the ceiling for any particular contract could not be frozen for more than three years pending completion of the vessel concerned, though technical problems might arise, particularly in the case of more sophisticated vessels.[799]

The common ceiling covered various forms of state intervention that might have the effect of subsidizing shipbuilding,[800] including aid to shipowners,[801] and aid granted under sectoral, general or regional aid schemes. However, credit facilities[802] for the building or conversion of ships[803] as well as development assistance to developing countries[804] were not subject to the ceiling, provided that they met OECD conditions.[805] In principle these are the only kinds of operating aid which are now permissible.[806]

Aid in the form of development assistance must pursue 'a genuine development objective'.[807] For example, aid for two container vessels to be sold in Indonesia was found to be development aid, because the ships would not be operated under a flag of convenience, the owner would be resident in a developing country and the grant element in the aid was at least 20 per cent.[808]

---

[799] Opinion of the Economic and Social Committee of 19 Sept. 1990 ([1990] OJ C332/131) on the proposal for a dir. on aid to shipbuilding, para. 3.1. See also the Resolution of the European Parliament of 23 Nov. 1990 ([1990] OJ C324/343) on the proposal for a dir. on aid to shipbuilding (proposed amendment to Art. 4(3)).

[800] Art. 1(d) of Dir. 90/684 covers aid measures in the financing of nationalized yards. The *Fifteenth Report on Competition Policy* (EC Commission, Brussels, 1986), 156–7 dealt with the problem of the losses of nationalized yards being covered by the state. The practice was estimated as entailing the equivalent of 7% in production aid in the UK and 5% in Italy. The writing off of one loan and the reduction of the rate of interest on another loan by a bank in which a Member State had a majority holding was also not to exceed the ceiling. See the Communic. regarding aid which the Netherlands had decided to grant to the shipyard van der Giessen de Noord ([1991] OJ C3/3).

[801] Joined Cases C–356/90 & C–180/91 *Belgium* v. *EC Commission: aid to shipbuilding* [1993] ECR I–2323. However, aid for the purchase of vessels other than those recently built in the Union is treated as aid to sea transport. See Communic. 131/89 ([1989] OJ C302/5) in respect of the proposal of the Portuguese Government to grant subsidies to Portuguese shipowners for the purchase of vessels.

[802] At a multilateral meeting with Member States a 'common agreement' was reached that the aid equivalent of a guarantee in the shipbuilding sector would be deemed to be 10% of the amount of the loan covered by the guarantee. See Dec. 91/306 ([1991] OJ L158/71) concerning two aid projects of the German Government in favour of a shipyard in financial difficulties C54/89 (ex NN27/89, N140/89).

[803] Art. 4(6) of Dir. 90/684 [1990] OJ L380/27

[804] *Ibid.*, Art. 4(7). The grant of a guarantee to a shipyard constructing a vessel for sale to a developing country was not covered by Art. 4(7). See Dec. 91/306 ([1991] OJ L158/71) concerning two aid projects of the German Government in favour of a shipyard in financial difficulties C54/89 (ex NN27/89, N140/89).

[805] Letter to Member States SG(89)D/311 (*Competition Law in the European Communities*, Vol. II: *Rules Applicable to State Aids* (EC Commission, Brussels, 1990), 81). See also sect. 6.7.1 below.

[806] Art. 5 of Reg. 3094/95 ([1995] OJ L332/1) on aid to shipbuilding.

[807] Case C–400/92 *Germany* v. *EC Commission: aid to China Ocean Shipping Co.* [1994] ECR I–4701, I–4731.

[808] Bull. EC 1/2–1993, 1.2.79. Cf. the original Commission objections in Notice C64/91 (N726/91) ([1992] OJ C36/3) regarding development aid which Germany had decided to grant for a project to build two 1066 teu container vessels for Indonesia.

However, there is apparent concern that the ships should not be used in international traffic, thus adversely affecting the Union shipping industry.[809]

Development aid in favour of shipbuilding may be granted to countries not normally eligible for development assistance, if a third-country participant to the OECD Understanding is planning to grant development assistance to that country for a particular shipbuilding contract.[810] However, problems arose from 'the excessive use of the exemption from the ceiling in favour of shipbuilding aid granted as development assistance to developing countries'.[811] Accordingly, the Commission objected to German aid to China,[812] German aid to Israel,[813] and Spanish aid to Morocco.[814]

Aid covered by the ceiling comprised: loss compensation aid, rescue aid, and all other types of operating aid not directly supporting particular restructuring measures. Article 5 of Directive 90/684 provided that the ceiling was to be calculated by reference to the percentage of annual turnover in shipbuilding and ship conversion. In determination of whether the ceiling was respected any aid to shipowners or contract-related aid to shipbuilders would be expressed as such a percentage and cumulated with aid covered by Article 5.

The ceiling was said to be designed to secure aid transparency and fair and equitable competitive conditions between Member States, consistent with attainment of a single uniform Union market for shipbuilding. More particularly, the aim was 'to intensify and direct the structural adjustment of EC shipbuilding towards innovative specialization and a structural form which would ensure its competitiveness in the long term'. The application of the principle of degressivity to the ceiling was said to mean that 'a general impetus towards restructuring [was] ensured'[815] and that more competitive yards were favoured.[816]

---

[809] See, in the case of ships for China, Bull. EU 10–1995, 1.3.66; and Darmon AG in Case 400/92 *Germany* v. *EC Commission: aid to China Ocean Shipping Co.* [1994] ECR I–4701, I–4719.

[810] *Implementation 1987–88 of the Sixth Directive on Aid to Shipbuilding*, SEC(89)518, 14.

[811] Explanatory Memorandum to the Proposal of 20 June 1990 for a Directive on aid to shipbuilding, COM(90)248, 6.

[812] Dec. 92/569 ([1992] OJ L367/29) concerning proposed aid by Germany to the Chinese shipping company Cosco for the construction of container vessels. Here the contract prices were 20–30% below market prices, Cosco had resources to buy at the latter prices, and its operations were not directly linked to China's import or export trade.

[813] Israel was not on the OECD list of countries eligible for such assistance. See Notice ([1989] OJ C162/14) as regards development aid to Israel proposed by the German Government in support of a particular shipbuilding contract.

[814] Notice C50/91 (NN69/91) ([1992] OJ C36/2) regarding aid which Spain had decided to grant to Morocco for the purchase of a 15,345 cgt ferry by Lignes Maritimes de Detroit from the Spanish yard Hijos de J. Barreras. There were doubts whether the ferry would be 'truly Moroccan or Spanish'. Cf., regarding acceptance of aid which would develop tourism in French overseas territories, Notice C8/95 (ex NN111/93) ([1995] OJ C279/3) concerning direct and indirect aid granted by the French Government for the building of passenger sailing ships.

[815] Explanatory Memorandum to the proposal for a dir. on aid to shipbuilding, COM(90)248, 4.

[816] Dec. 88/437 ([1988] OJ L211/24) concerning aids planned by the French Government in favour of a shipbuilding contract for which there was competition between yards in several Member States.

Enforcement of compliance with such ceilings might be thought comparatively easy. However, a problem with Directive 87/167 occurred 'in relation to Commission monitoring lack of compliance by Member States with their reporting obligations under Article 11 of the Directive'.[817] Accordingly, Article 12(3) of Directive 90/684 provided that the Commission might require suspension of outstanding payments of aid which had not been reported in accordance with that provision. In such circumstances the Commission might also take the view that it was unable to authorize aid under an expired directive which was in force at the time the aid was granted.[818]

As regards the level of the ceilings, the European Parliament proposed[819] amendment of Article 4(2) of Directive 87/167 so as to require the Commission to fix differentiated ceilings from 26 per cent to 35 per cent depending on the type of ship. The Parliament also noted that the Commission had already proposed a figure of 20 per cent for the initial aid ceiling, which was said to be too low, and requested more information as to how the figure had been chosen, in view of the lack of detailed analysis as to the competitiveness of the various market segments.

In the event, a ceiling of 28 per cent was fixed from 1 January 1987. The ceiling included aid to shipowners which might, for example, be conditional on an obligation to use the national flag. Hence, there might be an element of shipping aid. For this reason, the initial ceiling was set 'a couple of points' higher than was otherwise intended.[820] In the case of small vessels costing less than ECU 6 million, the Commission stated in Council minutes that it would not allow aid exceeding 20 per cent.[821] In view of the fact that the gap between the cost structure of the most effective Union yards and world market prices widened significantly during the year,[822] the Commission decided to maintain the existing ceilings into 1988.[823] The Commission apparently considered that, in view of the widened gap, this decision was compatible with the principle of degressivity.[824] Subsequently the principle of degressivity was directly applied.

---

[817] Explanatory Memorandum to the proposal for a dir. on aid to shipbuilding, COM(90)248, 7. See, more particularly, Notice C10/89 (ex NN21/89) ([1991] OJ C58/4) regarding Greek Law 1262/82 and its amendments which apply to shipbuilding. In *Implementation 1987–88 of the Sixth Directive on Aid to Shipbuilding*, SEC(89)518, 23, the Commission threatened proceedings against Member States which failed to respect these obligations. See, more particularly, Communic. C18/89 (ex NN121/87–63/89) ([1991] OJ C45/3) regarding aid which Germany had decided to grant to Bremen and Niedersachsen.

[818] Notice C7/91 (ex N506/90) ([1991] OJ C123/14) concerning aid which Italy planned to grant to shipbuilding.

[819] [1987] OJ C7/320.

[820] Explanatory Memorandum to the proposal for a dir. on aid to shipbuilding, COM(90)248, 13. In the event, most Member States applied an aid level 'considerably' lower than the ceiling. See *Implementation 1987–88 of the Sixth Directive on Aid to Shipbuilding*, SEC(89)518, 5.

[821] Letter to Member States SG(88) D/6181 (*Competition Law in the European Communities*, Vol. II: *Rules Applicable to State Aids* (EC Commission, Brussels, 1990, 79).

[822] *Seventeenth Report on Competition Policy* (EC Commission, Brussels, 1988), 151.

[823] [1988] OJ C4/2.

[824] *Implementation 1987–88 of the Sixth Council on Aid to Shipbuilding*, SEC(89)518, 3–4.

The ceiling for 1989 was reduced to 26 per cent,[825] and from 1 January 1990 it was further reduced to 20 per cent.[826] In the case of small vessels, the ceiling was 16 per cent for 1989 and 14 per cent for 1990. For 1991 a general ceiling of 13 per cent was set with a ceiling of 9 per cent for smaller vessels.[827] The former figure reflected uncertainty regarding world shipbuilding prices because of the Gulf crisis and other factors, even though the improvement in prices and increased productivity in Union shipyards indicated a narrower gap between the costs of Union shipbuilders and world market prices.[828] Such reductions apparently reflected price increases by competitors of Union shipbuilders[829] and did not necessarily mean that the latter were becoming more competitive.

For 1992 the ceiling was fixed at 9 per cent. The ceiling for small ships of a contract price of less than ECU 10 million and for ship conversion was fixed at 4.5 per cent.[830] These ceilings were maintained for 1993, even though the difference between the costs of the most competitive Union shipyards and the prices charged by their main international competitors widened in 1992,[831] and for 1994,[832] 1995,[833] and 1996.[834]

Modifications to these arrangements were demanded by the needs of the common fisheries policy.[835] Article 1 of Directive 90/684 stated that this Directive applied to the building and repair of fishing vessels of not less than 100 GRT (gross registered tonnage). However, Regulation 4028/86[836] permits aid for construction of fishing vessels which is consistent with the Multiannual Guidance Programmes (MGPs) for individual Member States.[837] The Commission considered Regulation 4028/86 to be *lex specialis* in relation to Directive 90/684, so that the lower ceilings laid down pursuant to the latter were not applied to the construction of vessels consistent with the relevant MGP. For

---

[825] *EC Twenty-Second General Report* (EC Commission, Brussels, 1989), 203.

[826] Bull. EC 12–1989, 2.1.94.   [827] Bull. EC 12–1990, 1.3.65.

[828] Commission Reply to Written Question 400/91 ([1991] OJ C227/21) by Mr Speciale.

[829] Commission Reply to Written Question 1611/90 by Mr McMahon *et al.* ([1991] OJ C107/1).

[830] Communic. ([1992] OJ C10/3).   [831] *European Report* 1823 (24 Dec. 1992).

[832] Communic. ([1994] OJ C37/4), though the ceilings would be reviewed, with a view to their reduction, if the OECD reached an agreement to eliminate all subsidies and other obstacles to normal competition in this sector.

[833] Communic. ([1994] OJ C389/5). The lower ceiling also applied to ship conversion, but it did not apply in relation to Greece where the vessels concerned were destined for domestic use. The same ceilings were adopted by the ESA (Communic. [1995] OJ C274/13).

[834] Review of the production aid ceiling for shipbuilding ([1996] OJ C74/8).

[835] Letter to Member States SG(88)D6181 (*Competition Law in the European Communities*, ii: *Rules Applicable to State Aids* (EC Commission, Brussels, 1990), 79); and Letter to Member States SG(92)D/06981 (*Competition Law in the European Communities ii: Rules Applicable to State Aids* (EC Commission, Brussels, 1995), 289).

[836] On Community measures to improve and adapt structures in the fisheries and aquaculture sector ([1986] OJ L276/7).

[837] See, at that time, Decs 88/121, 88/122 and 88/123 ([1988] OJ L62/21) for France, Belgium and the Netherlands respectively, Decs 88/139, 88/140, 88/141, and 88/142 ([1988] OJ L67/14) for Germany, Italy, the UK, and Ireland respectively and Decs. 88/147, 88/148, 88/149, and 88/150 ([1988] OJ L70/19) for Denmark, Greece, Spain, and Portugal respectively.

the construction of vessels other than those consistent with such a plan Article 49 of the Regulation provides for the application of Articles 92 and 93 of the Treaty. In its assessment of the common interest under the terms of Article 92(3)(c) the Commission considered aid granted in such cases for the construction of ships for the Union fleet to be incompatible with the common market under the rules of Directive 90/684.[838] Thus aid proposed by Dutch and German yards for construction of a fishing vessel for an Irish shipowner was objectionable, because the Irish fishing fleet already exceeded the ceiling laid down in the MGP for Ireland.[839]

In addition to such exceptions from the common ceiling in the case of fishing vessels, certain temporary exceptions[840] applied in favour of Greece and Spain and Eastern Germany.

Article 10(2) of Directive 90/684 provided that during 1991 Greek operating aid 'not related to new contracts [might] be considered compatible with the common market if granted for the financial restructuring of yards in connection with a systematic and specific restructuring programme linked to the disposal by sale of the yards'. According to the Preamble to the Directive, a short-term financial restructuring of the Greek shipbuilding industry was necessary to enable its public owners to restore its competitiveness by selling it off to new owners.[841]

Provision for temporary exemption of Portugal and Spain from the ceiling was made by Article 9 of Directive 87/167 and for Spain alone by Article 9 of Directive 90/684. Article 9(2) of the former Directive required restructuring of the Spanish industry so as to render it competitive within four years. However, finalization, let alone implementation, of the plan was delayed.[842] The Commission later seemed to be seeking more actively to secure restructuring.[843]

In the case of East German shipyards, it was considered likely that they would need a higher level of operating aid than was permissible in the case of other Union yards. Hence, Directive 87/167 was amended by Directive 90/652.[844] According to the Preamble to the latter, the shipbuilding industry in the former German Democratic Republic would require urgent restructuring. The immediate application of the common ceiling might not facilitate this process,

---

[838] See sect. 5.4.1 above.

[839] Notice [1988] ([1988] OJ C336/2) as regards contract-related production aid proposed by the Dutch and German Governments in support of a particular shipbuilding contract.

[840] These exceptions were not provided for in the original proposal ([1990] OJ C223/4) for what became Dir. 90/684 [1990] OJ L380/27.

[841] Communic. C10/91, C11/91, C12/91 (ex NN54/90, NN56/90, & ex NN58/90), C18/90 (ex NN15/90) and NN52/90 ([1993] OJ C88/6) with regard to aid which the Greek Government had decided to grant for shipbuilding and ship repair during the period 1987 to 1990. See, later, Bull. EU 10–1995, 1.3.77.

[842] *Implementation 1987–88 of the Sixth Council Directive on Aid to Shipbuilding*, SEC(89)518, 18.

[843] Notice C26/90 (ex NN69/88) ([1991] OJ C66/10) regarding aid which Spain had decided to grant to the Spanish shipbuilding industry.

[844] [1990] OJ L353/45.

and particular arrangements should be allowed to enable the shipbuilding industry there gradually to complete restructuring and comply with the aid regime applicable to the Union as a whole. As a result of this amendment to Directive 87/187, operating aid above the common ceiling could be granted for shipbuilding and ship conversion in the former German Democratic Republic, provided that:

—the shipbuilding industry had undertaken a systematic and specific restructuring programme, including capacity reductions, which could be considered capable of allowing it to operate competitively, and

—the aid was being progressively reduced.

The inclusion of an identical clause was also envisaged in the amended version[845] of the Commission proposal[846] for Directive 90/684, though no such clause was included in the version adopted by the Council. It was recorded in the minutes of the Council[847] that, while special leniency as regards aid might be necessary during a transitional period, information was necessary as to the aid needed to adapt the shipbuilding industry in the former German Democratic Republic to operate at the same level of competitiveness as yards in the remainder of the Union.[848]

More particularly, operating aid was prohibited by the Commission in the Mecklenburg-Vorpommern shipyards, where shipbuilding provided 40 per cent of industrial employment,[849] pending the outcome of a study designed to establish the ability of these yards to compete on equal terms with other Union yards. The Commission was also concerned to ensure that such aid was not provided under the guise of development aid.[850]

Directive 90/684 was subsequently amended by Directive 92/68,[851] so that a ceiling of 36 per cent for aid to be paid by the end of December 1993 would apply to East German shipyards, provided capacity reductions of 40 per cent were made by 1995.[852]

---

[845] COM(90)400, ii, 78a. This amendment was not supported by the EP ([1990] OJ C324/343).   [846] [1990] OJ C223/4.

[847] The Parliament objected that it was not consulted regarding this minute. See the Resolution of 13 Dec. 1991 ([1992] OJ C13/472) on the *Twentieth Report on Competition Policy*, para. 25.

[848] *Twentieth Report on Competition Policy* (EC Commission, Brussels, 1991), 131. Apparently, German Government attitudes were decisive. See the Report of the Committee on Social Affairs, Employment and the Working Environment on the Community response to the problem of restructuring in Eastern Germany and the economic and social crisis, EP Doc. A3–0230/93, 25 and the Report of the Committee on Economic and Monetary Affairs and Industrial Policy on the Proposal for a Directive providing for changes to the Seventh Directive on aid to shipbuilding, EP Doc. A3–0250/92, 12.   [849] *Financial Times*, 18 June 1992.

[850] Notice C64/91 (N726/91) ([1992] OJ C36/3) regarding development aid which Germany had decided to grant for a project to build two 1,066 teu container vessels for Indonesia.

[851] Amending Dir. 90/684 ([1992] OJ L219/54).

[852] The EP favoured a requirement that production aid to East German shipyards should not exceed three times the ceiling for the rest of the Union for 1992 and twice that for 1993. It was also proposed that a capacity reduction of 55% should be required. See the Resolution of 9 July 1992 ([1992] OJ C241/184).

To the extent that the common ceiling applied, the Commission seems to have sought to secure respect for it. In April 1989 the Article 93(2)[853] procedure was opened in respect of Greek aid to shipyards[854] which, the Commission considered, might exceed the ceiling fixed under Directive 87/167. In May 1989 the Commission opened the same procedure in respect of an Italian scheme for production aid to the shipbuilding industry, indirect aid through the shipping lines, and aid to applied research in this sector.[855]

Where respect for the ceiling could not otherwise be secured, a binding decision might be adopted. In Decision 90/627[856] the Commission found that Belgium planned to award loans having a grant equivalent of 35 per cent. Accordingly, Belgium was required to revise the terms of the loans so as to reduce them to a maximum level of 26 per cent in grant equivalent terms.

The ceiling might have priority over regional policy considerations. Thus, for example, in 1989 the Commission objected that Greek regional aid could breach the ceiling for shipbuilding aid or involve operating aid to ship-repair.[857] On the other hand, in 1983 the Commission did not object to the offsetting of the losses of Harland and Wolff in Northern Ireland partly because of 'the particularly difficult conditions under which it operates'.[858]

The European Parliament apparently considers that more weight should be given to regional-policy considerations. Accordingly, it sought an amendment of Directive 90/684 so as to require that, in setting the aid ceilings, the Commission should take into account the level of economic development of the region concerned and seek to avoid contributing to the social problems which would arise from wide-scale unemployment or the threat of unemployment in the sector.[859] However, no such amendment was proposed by the Commission.[860]

Such considerations aside, the Commission might be thought to have had a degree of success in reducing the amount of aid granted to shipyards[861] and in removing some of the most obvious distortions of competition within the Union, though the Union has apparently remained fragmented into national

---

[853] See sect. 7.4.3 below.

[854] Notice C10/89 ([1989] OJ C311/3) regarding the application of Law 1262/1982 and its amendments to shipbuilding in Greece; and *Nineteenth Report on Competition Policy* (EC Commission, Brussels, 1990), 147.

[855] Notice C12/89 ([1989] OJ C293/3) regarding the Italian draft law 'Provisions concerning the shipbuilding industry and measures to foster applied research in the sector' and the loss covering aid to the group Fincantieri for 1987.

[856] On loans granted by the Belgian authorities to two shipowners for the purchase of a 34,000 m³ LPG ship and two refrigerator ships ([1990] OJ L338/12).

[857] Bull. EC 4–1989, 2.1.80.   [858] Bull. EC 2–1983, 2.1.37.

[859] Resolution of 23 Nov. 1990 ([1990] OJ C324/343).

[860] But see the reference in the 12th recital in the preamble to Dir. 90/694, regarding the importance of shipbuilding for employment in regions, some of which already had a high level of unemployment.

[861] See, generally, the *Second Survey on State Aids in the European Community in the Manufacturing and Certain Other Sectors* (EC Commission, Brussels, 1990), 20–1.

markets. The common ceiling and restrictions on investment aid leading to capacity increases may also have tended to steer aid towards assisting the development of more competitive shipyards. In 1987 the highest levels of aid, near to the ceiling for that year, were granted in respect of bulk carriers,[862] in the construction of which the lack of competitiveness of the Union shipbuilding industry was most pronounced.[863] As the ceilings were lowered and apparently enforced, specialization in the construction of more sophisticated vessels, in relation to which Union industry was more internationally competitive, might have been stimulated.[864] Certainly, a substantial reduction in Union shipbuilding capacity has been accompanied since 1987 by increases in the Union share of the world shipbuilding market.[865] This increased share has been secured despite the fact that prices are little higher now than in 1976, whereas costs, such as labour costs and steel prices, have increased, and that international efforts to manage the shipbuilding market have had little apparent impact. The implication is that the remaining Union shipyards have become more efficient[866] and more competitive internationally.[867] These developments may partly reflect Union control of state aid in this sector and, more particularly, capacity reductions.[868]

At the same time, the Committee on Economic and Monetary Affairs of the European Parliament maintains that aid control is only one instrument of industrial policy, which should not determine such policy overall. Aid control should take account of factors other than production costs and market prices,[869] and guidelines for developing production should be adopted. More fundamentally, it is considered necessary to shift policy concerns 'from competition to industry', to adapt the internal structures of the Commission, and to change (and improve) the relationship between the Union institutions and those involved in the shipbuilding industry.[870]

Such demands appear not to have been influential. In principle, operating aid is now prohibited altogether.[871] However, because of the failure of third countries to ratify the OECD Agreement governing aid to this sector,[872] the

---

[862] *Implementation 1987–88 of the Sixth Directive on Aid to Shipbuilding*, SEC(89)518, Annex I.

[863] *Future Aid Strategy for Shipbuilding*, COM(86)324, Annex I, 10.

[864] *Implementation 1987–88 of the Sixth Directive on Aid to Shipbuilding*, SEC(89)518, 11.

[865] On the other hand, the Union world market share of new orders fell from 22% in 1990 to 18.2% in 1991. See *State of the Shipbuilding Industry in the Community, Situation in 1991*, COM (93)91, 10.

[866] According to *Implementation 1987–88 of the Sixth Directive on Aid to Shipbuilding*, SEC(89)518, 11, the aid policy pursued under Dir. 87/167 had stimulated structural adjustments and specialization efforts within Union shipbuilding.

[867] Opinion of the Economic and Social Committee of 19 Sept. 1990 ([1990] OJ C332/131) on the proposal for a dir. on aid to shipbuilding, para. 1.1.

[868] *Implementation 1987–88 of the Sixth Directive on Aid to Shipbuilding*, SEC(89)518, 15 ff.

[869] Report on Community industrial policy in the shipbuilding sector, EP Doc. A3–0278/91, 7.　　　　　　　　　　　　　　　　　　　　　　　[870] *Ibid.*, 9.

[871] Reg. 3094/95 ([1995] OJ L332/1) on aid to shipbuilding, Art. 2(1).

[872] Agreement respecting normal competitive conditions in the commercial shipbuilding and repair industry ([1994] OJ C375/3).

date for entry into force of the prohibition has been postponed from 1 January 1996 to 1 October 1996.[873] The Economic and Social Committee considers that aid arrangements under Directive 90/684 should continue to apply until the Agreement is ratified by all parties, and is also concerned that the position of Union shipbuilders should not be prejudiced by shipbuilders in third States which are not parties to the Agreement at all.[874]

5.9 TEXTILES AND SYNTHETIC FIBRES

A Framework for aid to the textiles industry and a Code for aid to the synthetic-fibres industry have been introduced. Both instruments limit restructuring aid and rule out operating aid. However, demarcation between the two may sometimes be controversial.[875] There may also be questions whether aid to products covered by neither instrument indirectly supports aid to products which are so covered.[876]

5.9.1 Textiles

The Commission considers that without sufficient harmonization the use of restructuring aid in the textiles sector may escalate.[877] According to the 1971 Framework for aid to this sector,[878] which was supplemented in 1973,[879] aid was only permitted if it involved no capacity increases. It should also be designed:

—to promote research and development[880] and improved forecasting;

—to improve the structure of the industry,[881] through elimination of

---

[873] *European Report* 2082 (8 Nov. 1995).

[874] Opinion of 23 Nov. 1995 ([1996] OJ C39/102) on the proposal for a reg. on shipbuilding, paras 3.1.1.-3.1.2.

[875] Notice C20/93 (ex N29/93) ([1994] OJ C271/5) concerning aid which the UK had decided to grant to Hualon Corporation, Northern Ireland.

[876] Notice C22/94 (ex N53/94) ([1995] OJ C263/18) concerning the proposal of Belgium to award aid to DS Profil Bvba, a producer of synthetic down located in Dendermonde, Vlaandaren and Notice C27/95 (ex NN45/95) ([1995] OJ C284/8) concerning the proposal of France to award aid to the Beaulieu Group in support of the company's planned investment in new capacity for production of carpet webbing and carpets, to be located in Maubeuge, Nord-Pas-de-Calais.

[877] Dec. 70/304 ([1970] JO L128/33) on a draft Italian law for the restructuring, reorganization, and conversion of the textiles industry.

[878] SEC(71)363; *Competition Law in the European Communities*, Vol. II: *Rules Applicable to State Aids* (EC Commission, Brussels, 1990), 44–7.

[879] Bull. EC 1–1974, 2117, whereby the framework was extended to aid granted to textile companies under general or regional aid schemes.

[880] British aid for the purchase of high technology equipment by textile undertakings was objectionable, because it would have led to overcapacity. See the *Fourteenth Report on Competition Policy* (EC Commission, Brussels, 1985), 149.

[881] Cf., previously, regarding the acceptability in principle of aid for restructuring and

surplus capacity,[882] conversion to activities outside the textile industry, horizontal concentration, or vertical integration; or

—to encourage modernization and conversion within the textiles industry, provided that there were 'particularly pressing social problems'.[883]

As regards regional aid, the 'regional aspect [would] be visualized and assessed simultaneously in the light of the problems of regional development and their effects on the sector from the viewpoint of intra-Community trade'.[884]

This approach, particularly the prohibition of capacity-increasing aid, was confirmed by the 1977 Framework.[885] According to the latter, specific national aids to create additional capacity in sectors with structural excess capacity or persistent stagnation of the market must be avoided. In subsectors where excess capacity and a shrinking market had caused prices to collapse throughout the Union, aid granted to conversion outside the industry or subsector might *a priori* be given favourable consideration.

Capacity Considerations

Provided that there is no capacity increase and the results are made available to the Union as a whole on commercial terms and without discrimination, aid to improve production techniques may be given favourable treatment,[886] as may aid for applied research.[887] For example, a Dutch scheme was designed to promote the formation of larger enterprises which could compete by using modern production methods and by developing new products and markets. Aid would be granted for closures, amalgamations, modernization through investment, joint action in the fields of marketing, productivity improvement, research and development, and improvement in working conditions. Grants

---

research, Dec. 69/266 ([1969] JO L220/1) concerning the French aid system to encourage research and modernization of industrial and commercial structures in the textiles industry. No reference was then made to the need to avoid capacity increases.

[882] British aid for the purchase of new plant and machinery was objectionable, because it was not linked to restructuring or even a requirement that production capacity should not be increased. See the *Fifth Report on Competition Policy* (EC Commission, Brussels, 1976), 79. See, similarly, Dec. 83/475 ([1983] OJ L261/29) on an aid proposal in favour of two textile and clothing firms in Belgium.

[883] Para. II of the 1971 framework. Unless this proviso is met, the aid may be prohibited. See Dec. 83/486 ([1983] OJ L268/48) concerning two aid schemes in favour of the textile and clothing industry sector in France provided by means of parafiscal charges. The ECJ accepts that aid for modernization with no fundamental changes cannot be authorized under Art. 92(3)(c). See Case C–301/87 *France* v. *EC Commission: Boussac* [1990] ECR I–307, I–365.

[884] Para. I.4 of the 1971 framework.

[885] Letter to the Member States SG(77)D/1190 of 4 Feb. 1977, and annex, SEC(77)317; *Competition Law in the European Communities*, Vol. II: *Rules Applicable to State Aids* (EC Commission, Brussels, 1990), 48–51.

[886] Para. 5.1 of the 1977 framework.

[887] *Ibid.*, para. 5.3. See, regarding aid for collective training and R & D, the *Seventeenth Report on Competition Policy* (EC Commission, Brussels, 1988), 162 and, regarding aid for environmental protection and SMEs, *The Competitiveness of the European Textile and Clothing Industry*, COM(93)525, 46.

would be made for up to 20 per cent of the costs of operations begun in 1975 and 1976 and up to 7.5 per cent for those started at a later date. The Commission authorized the scheme under Article 92(3)(c).[888] Another Dutch scheme was authorized, because it would not lead to an increase in production capacity, was clearly linked with restructuring, and was to be concentrated on companies with the best prospects of viability.[889] However, the aided investment must not be such that it would result from market conditions alone,[890] or follow earlier, successful use of restructuring aid.[891]

Aid which involves an increase in capacity[892] or output[893] or which has an operating character is unlikely to be authorized. For example, a Dutch scheme was to provide interest-free loans or grants covering 20 per cent of the costs of restructuring undertaken between 1976 and 1978. However, the Commission objected to the scheme, which could have involved the grant of operating aid.[894] In response, the Dutch Government modified the scheme, so that the loans would be at non-subsidized interest rates and no capacity increases would be involved.[895] Authorization may be refused, even when job creation in an area covered by Article 92(3)(a) is entailed.[896] Thus in 1973 the Commission authorized the continued reduction of social payments for craft undertakings and small and medium-sized enterprises in Italy, but not in the textiles sector.[897] The Commission also objected to advertising aid for exporters,[898] long-term

---

[888] Bull .EC 1–1976, 2111.

[889] *Eighth Report on Competition Policy* (EC Commission, Brussels, 1979), 141–2.

[890] See, e.g., Dec. 85/380 ([1985] OJ L217/20) concerning an aid scheme in favour of the textile and clothing industry in France funded by means of parafiscal charges. The decision was upheld in Case 259/85 *France* v. *EC Commission: aid to textiles and clothing* [1987] ECR 4393.

[891] Dec. 84/564 ([1984] OJ L312/27) on the Belgian Government's proposal to prolong the textile and clothing industry aid scheme.

[892] Dec. 83/320 ([1983] OJ L171/26) in relation to a proposal for aids in the textile and clothing industry (undertakings 34 and 57).

[893] Dec. 83/507 ([1983] OJ L285/14) on a proposal of the Belgian Government to aid an undertaking (No. 156) in the textile and clothing industry. However, the portion of the aid to be used for anti-pollution measures and to centralize management was regarded as not having an effect on output and, hence, as permissible in Dec. 83/508 ([1983] OJ L285/17) on a proposal of the Belgian Government to aid an undertaking (No. 118) in the textile and clothing industry.

[894] Notice regarding the aid scheme for the cotton, rayon and linen industry notified by the Dutch Government ([1976] OJ C289/9).

[895] Bull. EC 4–1977, 2.1.29; *Seventh Report on Competition Policy* (EC Commission, Brussels, 1978), 148–9.

[896] More particularly, in 1983 the Commission prohibited operating aid to Italian clothing undertakings in the Mezzogiorno and other assisted areas whose restructuring difficulties did not appear soluble in the short or medium term. See the *Thirteenth Report on Competition Policy* (EC Commission, Brussels, 1984), 166–7.

[897] Notice ([1973] OJ C40/2) concerning Italian Decree–Law 286 of 1 July 1972 prolonging the reduction in the burden of social payments for craft undertakings and small and medium-sized industrial undertakings in the textile industry instituted by Decree–Law 431 of 5 July 1971, which, with amendments, became Law 590 of 4 Aug. 1971 .

[898] Notice ([1976] OJ C104/1) regarding assistance granted by the Italian Government to the Italian textile, clothing and footwear industries to promote sales in the other Member States.

'loss compensation' aid,[899] a partial reduction in social charges,[900] as well as to aid for industrial and commercial renovation[901] and to a scheme which had already been applicable for two years.[902] The fact that the recipient agrees to maintain or increase its levels of employment or investment[903] may not in itself render the aid acceptable. For example, a Belgian scheme comprised an interest-free loan of Bfr 20,000 in respect of every worker over a three-year period to help pay the firm's social security contributions. Firms were eligible if they agreed to maintain at least 90 per cent of their workforce for at least one year and if they agreed to help plan and carry out a reorganization of the industry. The Commission objected, however, because it was not clear how the aid would contribute to restructuring.[904]

Moreover, in subsectors where overcapacity and low demand have caused prices throughout the Union to collapse,[905] aid should only be granted for capacity reductions or to companies converting to other activities.[906] Thus, for example, Italian aid to a clothing producer to convert to medical textiles was authorized.[907] On the other hand, a Belgian scheme was objectionable, because the aid recipient was not likely to be rendered viable and no capacity reduction was involved.[908] Reductions in the production and sale of intermediate goods must not be largely offset by increases in the sale of finished products,[909] and the capacity reduction must be definitive. Temporary lay-offs, which allow for the undertaking to keep its production capacity on 'standby' for possible opportunities to expand its sales and market shares, do not meet the latter requirement.[910] Even if there is a real capacity reduction, aid may not necessarily be authorized. To a large extent, its acceptability is determined by the

[899] Dec. 89/43 ([1989] OJ L16/52) on aids granted by the Italian Government to ENI–Lanerossi.

[900] Dec. 73/274 ([1973] OJ L254/14) on Art. 20 of Italian Law 1101 of 1 Dec. 1971 on the restructuring, reorganization, and conversion of the textile industry; and Dec. 80/932 ([1980] OJ L264/28) concerning the partial taking-over by the state of employers' contributions to sickness insurance schemes in Italy.

[901] Notice ([1982] OJ C25/2) regarding the application of two existing aid schemes in favour of the textile and clothing industry in France.

[902] Notice ([1977] OJ C273/2) regarding a scheme of assistance for the benefit of the clothing industry notified by the Dutch Government .

[903] Dec. 83/245 ([1983] OJ L137/24) on an aid scheme in favour of the textile and clothing industry in France.

[904] Notice ([1978] OJ C92/4) regarding a scheme of assistance introduced by the Belgian Government for the benefit of the textile and clothing industry.

[905] In one case the Commission maintained that aid must not apply to 'sensitive subsectors' of the textile industry at all. See Bull. EC 2–1983, 2.1.39.

[906] Para. 5.2 of the 1977 framework.

[907] *Fifteenth Report on Competition Policy* (EC Commission, Brussels, 1986), 161.

[908] Bull. EC 2–1982, 2.1.25. See also Bull. EC 9–1982, 2.1.25 and, regarding French aid, Bull. EC 5–1982, 2.1.19.

[909] Dec. 92/317 ([1992] OJ L171/54) on state aid in favour of Hilaturas y Tejidos Andaluces SA and its buyer.

[910] *Ibid.*

relationship between the intensity of the aid and the capacity reduction resulting from the aided investment.[911]

Regional-policy Considerations

The Commission maintains that, given the overcapacity in the textiles sector, aid to this sector will generally not assist regional development for the purposes of Article 92(3)(a) or (c).[912] At the same time, such aid may be regarded as adversely affecting trade to an extent contrary to the common interest for the purposes of Article 92(3)(c).[913]

Regional-policy considerations may be invoked by the Commission as support for a strict approach to the control of aid to this sector. For example, in prohibiting Italian aid, the Commission took into account, *inter alia*, the precarious position of the Union textile industry generally and the concentration of the Italian textile industry in the most developed parts of the country.[914]

However, regional-policy considerations may also be invoked as a basis for a relaxation of aid control.[915] For example, in authorizing later Italian aid, the Commission took into account the fact that some recipients were located in an area heavily dependent on the textile industry in which a large number of firms had closed down, resulting in significant capacity reductions overall.[916] British aid for reorganization of the wool industry, which would prevent the emergence of social difficulties in certain less well-off regions without an overall increase in capacity, was also authorized.[917] The Commission even authorized capacity-increasing textiles aid in Northern Ireland, because it entailed 'investment and employment in a distressed area'.[918] In other words, 'regional benefits may exceptionally be weighed against the potential negative effects on overall production capacity and competition in the sector'.[919]

Such practice may be affected by Article 92(3)(b). Thus Greek aid to its largest textiles producer was authorized because of the importance for the Greek economy of the company, which accounted for a measurable percentage of total Greek manufacturing employment, production and exports, not only at

[911] Notice C15/92 (ex N469/91) ([1992] OJ C166/2) concerning aid which Italy planned to grant to the SNIA-Bpd group.

[912] See, e.g., Notice ([1983] OJ C248/4) concerning the proposal to award a regional development premium to a textile firm establishing a plant at La Chapelle St Luc (Aube).

[913] See, e.g., Notice ([1984] OJ C15/2) concerning a Dutch aid proposal in favour of a textile company situated at Helmond.

[914] Dec. 70/304 ([1970] JO L128/33) on a draft Italian law for the restructuring, reorganization, and conversion of the textiles industry.

[915] Reply by Sir Leon Brittan to Written Question 1853/91 ([1991] OJ C323/41) by Mr Diego de los Santos Lopez, regarding aid to textile producers in Andalusia.

[916] *Sixth Report on Competition Policy* (EC Commission, Brussels, 1977), 116.

[917] *Fourth Report on Competition Policy* (EC Commission, Brussels, 1975), 89.

[918] Notice C20/93 (N29/93) ([1993] OJ C269/8) regarding aid which the UK planned to grant to Hualon Corporation.

[919] *Twenty-Fourth Report on Competition Policy* (EC Commission, Brussels, 1995), 181.

sectoral level but also at national level. Such aid was treated as an important part of a remedy for a serious disturbance of the economy under this provision.[920]

5.9.2 Synthetic Fibres

A Code concerning aid to synthetic fibres was originally introduced in 1977.[921] It has successively been extended,[922] and the latest version was published in 1996.[923] It covers polyester, polyamide, acrylic, and polypropylene fibres. Even if aid concerns products not covered by the Code,[924] such aid may be treated as indirectly affecting the manufacture of products which are covered[925] because of its effect on the overall budget of the recipient, or because a 'clear and total distinction' between the aided production and manufacture of products covered by the code may be problematic.[926] Aid to activities downstream of production may also be treated as affecting production of synthetic fibres.[927] However, aid which is shown to have no effect on the production of synthetic fibres by the recipient falls outside the Code. Moreover, the Code does not apply to aid under authorized schemes for vocational training/retraining or under authorized schemes covered by the guidelines on state aid for environmental protection[928] or by the Community framework for state aid for research and development.[929]

Capacity Considerations

According to the 1977 Code, the Commission would express an *a priori* unfavourable opinion on investment aid, be it sectoral, regional, or general, which had the effect of increasing the net production capacity of companies in the synthetic-fibres sector.[930] Opposition to such aid might be all the greater

---

[920] *Seventeenth Report on Competition Policy* (EC Commission, Brussels, 1988), 149.

[921] Bull. EC 7/8–1977, 1.5.3. Its acceptance was noted in Bull. EC 11–1977, 2.1.47.

[922] [1985] OJ C171/2; [1987] OJ C183/4; [1989] OJ C173/5; [1992] OJ C346/2; [1994] OJ C224/4; [1995] OJ C142/4.

[923] Code on aid to the synthetic fibres industry ([1996] OJ C94/11).

[924] Cf. where the aid recipient could not obtain the fibres from any other producer within the EEA, Notice C22/94 (ex N53/94) ([1995] OJ C263/18) concerning the proposal of Belgium to award aid to DS Profil Bvba, a producer of synthetic down located in Dondermonde, Vlaanderen.

[925] See, regarding aid to the commercialization or transformation of fibres, H. Morch, 'Summary of the Most Important Recent Developments' (1995) 5 *Competition Policy Newsletter* 43–9, 48; Bull. EU 4–1995, 1.3.49.

[926] Notice C27/95 (ex NN45/95) ([1995] OJ C284/8) concerning the proposal of France to award aid to the Beaulieu Group in support of the company's planned investment in new capacity for production of carpet webbing and carpets, to be located at Maubeuge, Nord-Pas-de-Calais; and Communic. C14/90 concerning aids which Germany had decided to grant to Textilwerke Deggendorf GmbH ([1990] OJ C158/4).

[927] *Twenty-Fourth Report on Competition Policy* (EC Commission, Brussels, 1995), 207–8.

[928] [1994] OJ C72/3.

[929] [1986] OJ C83/2.

[930] See also Dec. 88/173 ([1988] OJ L78/44) on the Belgian Government's aid proposal in

where the recipient was profitable and could thus be expected to finance the investment itself.[931] Even aid for the purpose of solving serious social or regional problems would only be 'sympathetically considered' where it encouraged conversion to other sectors[932] or restructuring leading to reductions in capacity.[933] For example, aid to promote conversion from synthetic fibres to plastics might be authorized.[934] Aid for conversion from production of a synthetic fibre covered by the Code to one not so covered was less likely to be authorized.[935] Moreover, the fact that there might be 'basic rationalization',[936] an improvement in production techniques,[937] or the creation of new jobs would constitute insufficient development to justify authorization of the aid concerned.[938] Rather, overcapacity meant that the aid was likely to be regarded as affecting trading conditions to an extent contrary to the common interest.[939]

For example, the Commission objected to aid to a synthetic-fibre undertaking with production facilities in the Mezzogiorno, because modernization and rationalization of these facilities rather than a genuine restructuring was involved.[940] Such aid could not facilitate development,[941] because it could not render the recipient financially and economically more viable or secure the jobs concerned.[942]

favour of Roger Vanden Berghe NV, a polypropylene yarn and carpet producer located in Desselgem, Belgium. See, in relation to another Belgian scheme, Bull. EC 12–1981, 2.1.46.

[931] Dec. 91/304 ([1991] OJ L156/33) on aid granted to the producer of polyamide and polypropylene yarns, Reinhold KG, situated in Selbitz.

[932] Dec. 91/391 ([1991] OJ L215/16) on aid granted by the German Government to Deggendorf GmbH, a producer of polyamide and polyester yarns located in Deggendorf (Bavaria).

[933] The Commission also exempted under Art. 85(3) EC an agreement between producers to reduce their polyamide production capacity. See Dec. 84/380 ([1984] OJ L207/17) relating to a proceeding under Art. 85 EC (IV/30.810—Synthetic fibres).

[934] Bull. EC 10–1987, 2.1.69.

[935] Dec. 85/471 ([1985] OJ 278/26) on an aid granted by the German Government to a producer of polyamide and polypropylene yarn situated in Bergkamen.

[936] Notice ([1985] OJ C277/4) regarding two aids in favour of a producer of polyamide and polyester yarn situated in Immenstadt.

[937] Dec. 83/487 ([1983] OJ L268/51) concerning the aid that the UK Government proposed to grant for investment to expand production capacity for a polyester firm.

[938] Dec. 91/304 ([1991] OJ L156/33) on aid granted to the producer of polyamide and polypropylene yarns, Reinhold KG, situated in Selbitz.

[939] Notice ([1985] OJ C95/3) regarding an aid proposal by the Italian Government in favour of a state-owned producer of polyamide carpet yarn situated at Forlì. See also Notice ([1985] OJ C105/11) regarding an aid proposed by the Italian Government under Law 675/77 in favour of a state-owned producer of man-made fibre and yarn with production facilities in Pisticci, Ottana, and Porto Torres.

[940] *Fifteenth Report on Competition Policy* (EC Commission, Brussels, 1986), 164–5.

[941] Dec. 88/173 ([1988] OJ L78/44) on the Belgian Government's aid proposal in favour of Roger Vanden Berghe NV, a polypropylene yarn and carpet producer located at Desselgem, Belgium.

[942] Dec. 86/509 ([1986] OJ L300/34) on aid granted to a producer of polyamide and polyester yarn situated in Deggendorf. See also Dec. 84/509 ([1984] OJ L283/45) concerning assistance by the UK Government to a manufacturer of polyester yarn; and Dec. 91/304 ([1991] OJ L156/33) on aid granted to the producer of polyamide and polypropylene yarns, Reinhold KG, situated in Selbitz.

The 1992 Code[943] introduced the condition that aid would only be authorized if there was a 'significant' reduction in the production capacity of the assisted company. This condition might be strictly applied, the Commission insisting that aid which clearly facilitated the development of a region covered by Article 92(3)(c) would only be permissible where there was such a reduction.[944] For example, aid of an intensity of 28.8 per cent which would have led to a 5 per cent capacity reduction of a synthetic fibres company in Italy was questioned, and was only authorized when it was agreed that the capacity reduction would be 10 per cent.[945]

According to the present Code, aid to production will generally be prohibited, except where there is a structural shortage of supply of the relevant product. Where there is such a shortage, aid may be authorized, provided it does not result in a significant increase in the relevant capacity. Where it will result in a significant reduction in the relevant capacity, aid may also be authorized. If aid is so authorized, higher levels of aid may be accepted for small and medium-sized enterprises than for larger ones. In fixing the acceptable aid levels, the Commission will take account of the innovative character of the relevant products.[946]

Regional-policy Considerations

Given the overcapacity in this sector, aid is regarded as unlikely to assist regional development,[947] and so it may be prohibited even in regions covered by Article 92(2)(c)[948] or Article 92(3)(a). For example, in connection with proposed Irish aid of £12.9 million in favour of an investment by a producer of polyester, the Commission noted that there was to be no capacity increase, but neither was there any restructuring, capacity reduction, or conversion. The investment concerned modernization of an obsolete plant which should be carried out using the resources of the producer itself without aid, especially since a large percentage of the output from the plant was exported to other Member States. The Commission also considered that, while the standard of living in the area was very low and it suffered from serious underemployment,

---

[943] Code on aid to the synthetic fibres industry ([1992] OJ C346/2).

[944] Notice C42/93 (N624/93) ([1994] OJ C79/8) regarding the UK Government's proposal to award aid to Abingdon Carpets plc, Gwent.

[945] Notice C15/92 (ex N469/91) ([1993] OJ C43/21) concerning aid which Italy planned to grant to the SNIA-BPD group.

[946] In the case of training aid, a capacity reduction may not be required. See the *Twenty-Fourth Report on Competition Policy* (EC Commission, Brussels, 1995), 181.

[947] See, e.g., Notice ([1984] OJ C98/2) concerning the award of financial assistance by the UK for building a production unit for polyester textile yarn at Stanley (County Durham).

[948] Dec. 85/343 ([1985] OJ L181/42) on the German Government's proposal to grant an aid in favour of a producer of polyamide yarn situated in Neumünster; Dec. 86/509 ([1986] OJ L300/34) on aid granted to a producer of polyamide and polyester yarn situated in Deggendorf; and Dec. 91/304 ([1991] OJ L156/33) on aid granted to the producer of polyamide and polypropylene yarns, Reinhold KG, situated in Selbitz.

the sectoral effects of aid to polyester production had to be controlled even for the most underdeveloped areas.[949] Taking into account the situation of the polyester sector which was likely to continue in the future, the proposed aid would not promote the economic development of the region concerned but would be likely to distort competition in intra-Union trade without making a contribution to regional development sufficient to compensate for that distortion. The aid would also have the effect of further reducing capacity utilization in the industry concerned. For these reasons, it could not be authorized.[950] Similarly, aid to the clothing subsidiaries of Lanerossi in the Mezzogiorno was prohibited, because it would not lead to their viability and so, in view of the situation of the sector, would not contribute to the lasting development of the region.[951]

Even so, under the 1977 Code regional-policy considerations might lead the Commission to authorize aid which entailed no capacity reduction. For example, Luxembourg aid maintained such capacity rather than reducing it, but there were found to be compensatory benefits at Union level. The benefits took the form of product improvements and job creation, even on such a small scale as to entail only ten new jobs, in an area 'that [had] recently lost a number of industrial jobs'.[952] Accordingly, the aid was authorized. French aid which involved the development of a new product would not harm producers of other products in the Union, strengthened the technological base and competitiveness of the Union, and assisted job-creation in a declining industrial area was also authorized.[953]

Under the 1992 Code, if the project was eligible for regional aid pursuant to Article 92(3)(a) or (c), the reduction in capacity might be assessed in the light of the severity of the region's structural handicaps.[954] For example, a capacity reduction of 23 per cent in an area covered by Article 92(3)(a) might be regarded as 'significant' enough to render aid permissible.[955] In Eastern Ger-

---

[949] See also Dec. 85/471 ([1985] OJ 278/26) on an aid granted by the German Government to a producer of polyamide and polypropylene yarn situated in Bergkamen; and Dec. 95/253 ([1995] OJ L159/21) on aid awarded by the French Government to Allied Signal Fibres Europe SA, Longwy, Meurthe-et-Moselle.

[950] Dec. 84/498 ([1984] OJ L276/40) on an aid proposal by the Irish Government in favour of a producer of polyester yarn situated at Letterkenny.

[951] Dec. 89/43 ([1989] OJ L16/52) on aids granted by the Italian Government to ENI–Lanerossi. See also Dec. 85/343 ([1985] OJ L181/42) on the German Government's proposal to grant an aid in favour of a producer of polyamide yarn situated in Neumünster.

[952] Notice C44/91 (ex N470/91) ([1992] OJ C301/2) regarding aid which Luxembourg had decided to grant to Technofibres SA. [953] Bull. EC 7/8–1988, 2.1.75.

[954] Notice C42/93 (N624/93) ([1994] OJ C79/8) regarding the UK Government's proposal to award aid to Abingdon Carpets plc, Gwent; Notice C9/93 (NN22/93) ([1993] OJ C210/9) regarding aid which Germany had decided to grant to SST-Garngesellschaft mbH, Thüringen; and Notice C12/93 (NN21/93) ([1993] OJ C210/11) concerning aid which Germany proposed to grant Rhône-Poulenc GmbH. See also H. Morch, 'Summary of the Most Important Recent Developments' (1995) 4 *Competition Policy Newsletter* 47–51, 51.

[955] Notice C12/93 (NN21/93) ([1993] OJ C346/2) concerning aid which Germany had granted Rhône-Poulenc Rhotex GmbH, a synthetic-fibres producer located in Brandenburg, Germany.

many the requirement of a capacity reduction was waived altogether on grounds of 'the burden of the past' borne by the synthetic fibres industry in the new *Länder*, high levels of unemployment, and the Objective 1 status of the area concerned, and the fact that the aided investment was part of a restructuring programme which would lead to an overall capacity reduction in these *Länder*.[956]

According to the current Code, the significance of a capacity reduction is to be assessed having regard, *inter alia*, to the expected effect of the aid on the region concerned in terms of the structural handicaps of that region.

5.10 MOTOR VEHICLES

Restructuring needs and regional policy considerations have traditionally been taken into account in Commission treatment of aid to the motor vehicles sector. It is not only aid to motor vehicle manufacturers which is considered. Integration between component producers and motor vehicle manufacturers may mean that aid to the former may be found to distort competition between the latter.[957] However, such practice may entail a risk that component manufacturers which are subsidiaries of a car producer may suffer discrimination in comparison with independent component producers.[958]

5.10.1 Restructuring Aid

Early Commission practice might be favourable towards aid to the motor vehicles sector, where such aid was likely to lead recipients to become competitive or to alleviate the social costs of restructuring. In particular, restructuring aid for British Leyland was authorized because of the essential role played by the motor industry as an employer in the British economy and its contribution to the trade balance.[959] In Germany aid to create new activities for the re-employment of workers made redundant by the restructuring of Volkswagen was also authorized,[960] as was French aid to assist the merger of Citroën with Peugeot and thereby to facilitate the creation of a more profitable group.[961]

Monitoring System

The Commission established an *a priori* monitoring system in 1982 covering both specific aid to the motor industry and the use of other schemes to assist

---

[956] Dec. 94/266 ([1994] OJ L114/21) on the proposal to award aid to SST-Garngesellschaft mbH, Thüringen.

[957] Notice C29/93 (ex N431/93) ([1993] OJ C306/3) regarding aid, which Baden-Württemberg intended to grant to the Aluminium Giesserei Villingen GmbH.

[958] *Twenty-Third Report on Competition Policy* (EC Commission, Brussels, 1994), 296.

[959] *Fifth Report on Competition Policy* (EC Commission, Brussels, 1976), 84–5.

[960] *Ibid.*

[961] *Ibid.*, 83–4.

this industry. The concern of the Commission was to increase aid transparency and to avoid surplus capacity arising,[962] which could subsequently lead to protectionist measures and to aid liable to distort competition.[963]

Aid which resulted in a reduction of production capacity,[964] provided that the reduction was 'significant' and in proportion to the aid amount,[965] innovation aid which was expected to lead to improvement of technology,[966] and aid for the development of new prototypes and a radical change in the manufacturing process, such as the use of robots and flexible production systems,[967] might be authorized.

At the same time, account also continued to be taken of regional policy considerations. For example, in 1983 the Commission authorized Italian aid involving transfers to, or consolidation of, business in the Mezzogiorno by car or car components undertakings. Other aid was objectionable, because it merely assisted the normal activities of improving products and modernizing production facilities.[968] Moreover, although the motor vehicles sector in the Union was characterized by strong competition, the Commission authorized aid in the form of an investment allowance of DM 81.7 million to Daimler-Benz, which was designed to create alternative jobs in Bremen, because of the worsening of the labour market situation in this area.[969]

Aid Framework

The Commission began to adopt a stricter approach towards aid to the motor vehicles sector at the end of the 1980s.[970] An aid Framework was introduced in 1989[971] and renewed in 1991.[972]

According to the Framework, rationalization, innovation, and modernization should normally be financed by the car companies themselves. Aid for rational-

---

[962] See the objections to Spanish aid to the production of commercial vehicles (Bull. EC 2–1988, 2.1.72) and French aid to the production of trailers and semi-trailers (Bull. EC 7/8–1986, 2.1.79) because of overcapacity in these sectors.

[963] *Twelfth Report on Competition Policy* (EC Commission, Brussels, 1983), 131.

[964] *Eighteenth Report on Competition Policy* (EC Commission, Brussels, 1989), 176.

[965] Dec. 89/661 ([1989] OJ L394/9) concerning aid provided by the Italian Government to Alfa Romeo.

[966] *Eighteenth Report on Competition Policy* (EC Commission, Brussels, 1989), 177.

[967] Bull. EC 12–1984, 2.1.61.

[968] *Thirteenth Report on Competition Policy* (EC Commission, Brussels, 1984), 169. See, similarly, regarding aid to cover the extra costs involved in the relocation of plant for regional policy reasons, the *Fourteenth Report on Competition Policy* (EC Commission, Brussels, 1985), 155.

[969] *Seventeenth Report on Competition Policy* (EC Commission, Brussels, 1988), 178.

[970] Dec. 88/454 ([1988] OJ L220/30) concerning aid provided by the French Government to the Renault Group; and Dec. 89/661 ([1989] OJ L394/9) concerning aid provided by the Italian Government to Alfa Romeo.

[971] Community framework on state aid to the motor vehicle industry ([1989] OJ C123/3).

[972] [1991] OJ C81/4. The Council has called on the Commission to continue strictly to control aid in this sector and to look at the possibility of extending control to component producers. See the Resolution of 17 June 1992 ([1992] OJ C178/6) on the European motor vehicle industry, para. II.4.

ization will only be authorized when it leads to radical restructuring, and only to the extent that the financing required goes beyond that which companies should finance from their own resources. Aid for innovation must relate to genuinely innovative products,[973] as, for example, where 'exceptionally high levels of automation and productivity, world first standards of flexibility, speed in model changeover, system reliability, and product design' are involved.[974] The degree of risk involved may affect the acceptability of such aid.[975]

Even in the case of aid for research and development, a detailed technical analysis is carried out in order to distinguish between basic research and applied research and development and to distinguish these from normal modernization. More particularly, research and development aid may not be granted for the development of new engines which comply with existing legal standards, because this is a normal industrial requirement.[976] Again, account is taken of the commercial risk associated with the technical uncertainty of the research.[977]

In segments of the motor vehicles industry suffering from overcapacity aid will only be authorized if the aid recipient reduces its capacity. The reduction must be irreversible, because the effects on the industry must be lasting.[979] Such reductions may be required not only of the undertaking in receipt of aid but also of the group to which it belongs.[980]

However, the Framework acknowledges the valuable contribution to regional development which can be made by the implantation of new motor-vehicle and component production facilities and/or the expansion of such activities in disadvantaged regions. Hence, a generally positive attitude is shown towards investment aid granted in order to help overcome structural handicaps in disadvantaged parts of the Union. Even so, the Commission is concerned to prevent an 'ultimately self-defeating outbidding exercise to attract investment' into the regional development areas of individual Member States.[981]

Accordingly, prior notification of such aid is required, where the eligible cost of the project concerned is ECU 12 million or more. Even if individual projects do not reach the threshold, where such projects are carried out by the same

---

[973] Para. 3 of the 1991 framework. See, more particularly, Dec. 96/76 ([1996] OJ L15/37) concerning aid granted by the Netherlands to the truck producer, DAF.

[974] Notice C45/91 (ex NN255/91) ([1993] OJ C37/15) regarding the proposal of the Italian authorities to provide state aid to the Fiat Group in support of its second Mezzogiorno investment plan.

[975] *Twenty-Second Report on Competition Policy* (EC Commission, Brussels, 1993), 233.

[976] Summary of the decision (N657/94) ([1996] OJ C74/8) not to oppose the R & D aid which the Dutch Government intended to provide to DAF Trucks NV for the Volem project.

[977] *Ibid.*

[978] H. Morch, 'Summary of the Most Important Recent Developments' [1994] 4 *Competition Policy Newsletter* 61–6, 64.

[979] Communic. C38/87 ([1991] OJ C11/3) regarding aid granted by the French Government to the Renault Group.

[980] Bull. EU 10–1995, 1.3.76.

[981] Para. 1 of the 1991 framework.

undertaking and may thus form part of a larger investment plan, they must be notified.[982] These requirements are designed to give the Commission an opportunity to assess the regional development benefits (particularly the promotion of a lasting development of the region by creating viable jobs and linkages into the local and Union economy) against possible adverse effects on the sector as a whole (such as the creation of important overcapacity). Such an assessment does not seek to deny the central importance of regional aid for the achievement of cohesion within the Union but, rather, to ensure that other aspects of the Union interest, such as the development of the industry, are also taken into account.[983]

In Decision 90/381[984] the Commission confirmed its *a priori* favourable attitude to regional aid in this sector. However, given the sector's importance, its growing sensitivity to competition and the very significant trade flows, the Commission wanted to ensure that regional aid would indeed have a significant and long-standing effect on regional development which would outweigh any possible adverse effects on the sector as a whole. Furthermore, the Commission intended to put a stop to the widespread and highly unhealthy outbiding practice amongst Member States of granting regional aid in order to attract new industrial establishments.

For example, in relation to aid to Ford and Volkswagen to establish a car factory in Portugal, the Commission considered: the economic development of the region concerned; the particular situation of the car industry; and the specific situation of 'mono-space vehicles', for which there was growing demand. On the basis of these considerations, the Commission decided that the aid was permissible.[985]

Again, the Commission approved a French proposal to grant aid to Saab-Scania for building a new heavy-truck manufacturing plant at Angers. The Commission took account of the valuable contribution which the project would make to solving the structural problems of the region, in particular the high unemployment there. The Commission also analysed the possible effects of the aid on the industry as a whole and took particular account of the problems of declining demand and overcapacity in the Union heavy-trucks industry. However, in view of the fact that demand was expected to rise in 1993, the Commission considered that a concentration of the aid on the later stages of

---

[982] Communic. C34/95 (NN63/94 & N222/95) ([1995] OJ C237/2) concerning the proposal by the Spanish Government to award state aid to the Volkswagen group in support of its Spanish subsidiary, SEAT SA.

[983] Para. 3 of the 1991 framework. Note the Commission objection to German aid to the motor vehicles industry in the new *Länder* and Berlin in Bull. EC 12–1991, 1.2.66.

[984] Amending German aid schemes for the motor vehicle industry ([1990] OJ L188/55). See sect. 5.1 above.

[985] Summary of the dec. not to raise objections to the aid which the Portuguese Government planned to grant to the joint-venture of Ford and Volkswagen to establish a multipurpose vehicle plant in the Setubal peninsula ([1991] OJ C257/5). This decision was unsuccessfully challenged before the ECJ in Case C–225/91 *Matra SA* v. *EC Commission* [1993] ECR I–3203.

the project would reduce its distorting effect on competition and avoid exacerbating the industry's current difficulties. It would also reduce the nominal intensity of the aid from 9.85 per cent to around 8.5 per cent in 1990 prices (7 per cent net), or half the regional aid level of 17 per cent authorized for the Angers area. In the opinion of the Commission, such an aid level compensated for the structural disadvantages of the site and thus allowed the project to be undertaken in the area.[986] The Commission latter opened the Article 93(2) procedure, when it learned that the aid was to be used for purposes different from those originally agreed.[987]

The Commission even approved Luxembourg aid to General Motors for the setting-up of a new research and development centre at Bascharage. The grant satisfied the criteria for regional aid, since General Motors had chosen this disadvantaged area from among several possible sites. Moreover, the aid would not have adverse effects on the industry sufficient to outweigh the regional benefits, as the project involved a transfer of technology to which all European manufacturers would have access.[988]

In reaching such decisions, the Commission seeks as a 'constant practice'[989] to ensure that the aid is proportional to the problems of the region concerned. To this end, the Commission measures the net handicaps facing an investor in the region by making a comparison with a hypothetical greenfield project in a non-assisted area. The Commission makes the comparison even if the only practical alternative for the recipient is expansion of existing facilities in a central region. Both additional investment costs and operating costs in the first five years of operation are considered.[990] The latter costs are considered in order to test whether the aid is appropriate to overcome initial investment costs, as well as to help overcome the inevitable problems in the early years of operation arising from underdevelopment, geographical remoteness, extra transport costs and so on.[991]

An increase in a group's capacity of 3 per cent may be acceptable, at least

---

[986] Summary of the Commission decision not to raise objections to the aid which the French Government planned to grant to Saab-Scania for the construction of a heavy-goods-vehicle production facility at Angiers ([1991] OJ C160/4); *Twentieth Report on Competition Policy* (EC Commission, Brussels, 1991), 160–1.

[987] Notice C5/96 (NN138/95) ([1996] OJ C84/5) concerning aid provided by the French authorities to Saab-Scania in support of its motor vehicle plant in Angers (Maine-et-Loire).

[988] *Twentieth Report on Competition Policy* (EC Commission, Brussels, 1991), 161.

[989] Summary of the decision not to oppose the aid which the Belgian Government intended to provide to Ford Werke AG in support of an investment project in Genk ([1996] OJ C5/10). See, earlier, summary of the decision not to oppose the aid which the Navarra Regional authorities intended to provide to SEA in support of its investment plans in Arazuri (Pamplona) Spain ([1993] OJ C310/7).

[990] This method is apparently approved by the ECJ. See Van Gerven AG in Case C–225/91 *Matra SA* v. *EC Commission* [1993] ECR I–3203, I–3230.

[991] Notice C45/91 (ex N255/91) ([1993] OJ C37/15) regarding the proposal of the Italian authorities to provide state aid to the Fiat Group in support of its second Mezzogiorno investment plan.

where the aid intensity is not significantly above the net cost penalties incurred through its selection of a less developed area for new plants.[992] In the case of expansion of existing plants in disadvantaged regions, the Commission has a positive attitude towards investments that involve changes in product and production processes that are so drastic that they are considered as a mobile investment. The essential question is whether without regional aid the company would delocalize the production covered by the investment.[993] Account may be taken of the costs involved in implementing the same project at existing plants elsewhere.[994] Overcompensation, or 'top-up aid', may also be authorized, provided that aided investment will not lead to sectoral problems, as an additional incentive for the investor to move into an area covered by Article 92(3)(a) or (c).[995]

The Commission considers such practice to be justified by the characteristics of the sector and thus to be of general application throughout the sector. Therefore, no case-by-case analysis of the contribution of aid to regional development under Article 92(3)(a) or (c) is felt to be required.[996] The apparent concern of the Commission is to avoid encouragement of capacity-increasing investment without discouraging such investment in less developed regions.

The result may be, as in the case of Portuguese aid to an electronic-automotive-components manufacturer, that comparatively high levels of aid are authorized. The aid in question, amounting to ECU 16.8 million or 39 per cent of the investment costs, was regarded as likely to have a considerable impact on the economic development of the region concerned without adversely affecting the sector at Union level.[997] Aid to Opel in Eastern Germany which would lead to the creation of 2,000 jobs directly and 2,500 indirectly and would have an intensity of 28.9 per cent was also authorized.[998]

---

[992] Notice C60/91 (ex NN73/91, NN76/91) ([1993] OJ C43/14) regarding the proposal by the German Government to award state aid to the Opel Group in support of its investment plans in the new *Länder*. See also the Reply by Mr Van Miert to Written Question 177/93 ([1993] OJ C185/55) by Mr Virginio Bettini.

[993] Summary of the Commission's decision not to oppose aid which the Italian Government intended to provide to Serel SpA in support of an investment project ([1995] OJ C298/9).

[994] Communic. C61/91 (NN74/91 & 80/91) ([1992] OJ C68/8) concerning the proposal by the German Government to award state aid to Mercedes-Benz in support of its investment plans in the new *Länder*.

[995] Summary of the Commission's decision not to oppose the aid which the UK Government intended to grant to Jaguar Cars Ltd in support of an investment project ([1994] OJ C201/4). It was noted by the Commission that the alternative location for the investment was in the US. See, similarly, the summary of the ESA dec. not to raise objections to the aid which the Austrian Government planned to provide to BMW in support of an R & D and investment project in Steyr Austria ([1994] OJ C250/3).

[996] Notice C44/95 (E16/95) ([1995] OJ C304/14) regarding the refusal of the Spanish authorities of the Commission's proposal for reintroduction of the EC framework on state aid to the motor-vehicle sector.

[997] *Twentieth Report on Competition Policy* (EC Commission, Brussels, 1991), 161.

[998] *Twenty-Second Report on Competition Policy* (EC Commission, Brussels, 1993), 234.

5.10.2 Rescue Aid

In 1975 rescue aid to Chrysler was authorized 'because of the employment problems which would have been caused by plant closures in Scotland'.[999] However, according to the Framework, rescue aid may now only be authorized exceptionally. There must be a restructuring plan, and the Union interest must be best served by keeping the recipient in business and re-establishing its viability. No increase in market share may be entailed, and a capacity reduction may be required.[1000]

5.10.3 Operating Aid

A strict approach towards operating aid in the motor vehicles sector is adopted in the Framework, 'even in disadvantaged regions', because of its direct and continuing distorting effect in a sensitive sector. Accordingly, no new operating aid will be authorized in this sector and the Commission will propose, on the basis of Article 93(1), the progressive elimination of existing aid of this kind.[1001]

5.11 CONCLUSION

According to the Court of Justice, the Commission practice of examining the acceptability of aid in a given sector[1002] by reference to its general policy regarding aid to that sector is justified.[1003] Indeed, Advocate General Lenz has maintained that 'integration . . . is to take place separately according to the economic sector',[1004] though there is some (limited) recognition of the need to avoid discrimination against particular industries.[1005] Such practice means, for example, that aid to steel undertakings covered by the ECSC Treaty may be prohibited, even in the least-developed parts of the Union. In the case of steel production outside the ECSC Treaty, the positive regional impact of aid under Article 92(3)(a) may be taken to outweigh possible sectoral problems caused by aid, though care is taken to ensure that such problems do not extend to

---

[999] *Fifth Report on Competition Policy* (EC Commission, Brussels, 1977), 85. See also, regarding Dutch aid to Volvo, Bull. EC 5–1978, 2135.

[1000] Para. 3 of the 1989 framework.

[1001] *Ibid.*

[1002] It appears to be enough that aid benefits an undertaking active in a given sector, irrespective of whether the aid is for activity in that sector. See Notice C8/93 (ex N675/92) ([1993] OJ C172/2) concerning aid which Germany had decided to grant to Deggendorf GmbH.

[1003] Case 259/85 *France* v. *EC Commission: aid to textiles and clothing* [1987] ECR 4393, 4415.

[1004] Lenz AG in Case 167/73 *EC Commission* v. *France: merchant seamen* [1974] ECR 359, 378.

[1005] See, in the case of the steel industry, Dec. 90/555 ([1990] OJ L314/17) concerning aid which the Italian authorities planned to grant to the Tirreno and Siderpotenza steel works.

activities covered by the ECSC Treaty.[1006] On the other hand, in relation to coal and shipbuilding, operating aid may be authorized, even in the more developed parts of the Union. Such aid may be authorized because of world market conditions and because it reduces the social costs of adjustment.[1007]

However, aid directed towards declining industries, where vested interested are stronger, rather than to emergent industries, may have the effect of raising adjustment costs above those which would have been entailed by adjustment through market mechanisms.[1008] Not only do the cumulative costs over time tend to be higher, since relatively low-productivity sectors can remain longer in business.[1009] There may also be a penalty to efficient producers, because their market shares will grow more slowly than otherwise,[1010] and the incentive system for the maintenance of permanent efficiency and for new entrants may be undermined.[1011] In other words, such aid has the effect of altering the speeds of various sectoral adjustments,[1012] and Commission practice may 'harmonize' national degrees of slowing down adjustment.[1013] Indeed, the Commission was expressly required by Article 6(2) of Decision 81/363, on shipbuilding aid, to 'verify that the programme of adaptation of the industry [in the Member State concerned] was comparable with those carried out in the other Member States'.[1014]

Certainly, Commission practice may give the impression the principal concern is with co-ordination as such of national approaches to sectoral

[1006] Notice C17/94 (ex NN102/93) (ex N335/91 & ex N337/92) ([1995] OJ C319/4) concerning aid which Italy planned to grant to Tubificio di Terni Srl and Ilva Lamiere e Tubi Srl.

[1007] *Seventeenth Report on Competition Policy* (EC Commission, Brussels, 1988), 147.

[1008] According to the Economic and Social Committee Opinion of 29 Sept. 1977 ([1977] OJ C292/5) on the guidelines for Community regional policy, regional aid must not be used to even out cyclical fluctuations or to replace sectoral-conversion measures. It should rather be geared to creating permanent jobs that provide satisfactory working conditions and incomes, para. 1.5. For similar reasons, horizontal aid may be preferred to sectoral aid. See *Industrial Policy in an Open and Competitive Environment Guidelines for a Community Approach*, COM(90)556, 6.

[1009] Cf. the arguments as to the tendency of agricultural aid in Germany to reduce the production levels of industries where Germany has a comparative advantage in H. Dicke, J. B. Donges, E. Gerken, and G. Kirkpatrick, 'The Economic Effects of Agricultural Policy in West Germany' [1988] *Weltwirtschaftliches Archiv* 301–21.

[1010] Jacobs AG in Joined Cases C–278/92, C–279/92 & C–280/92 *Spain* v. *EC Commission: aid to textiles and footwear* [1994] ECR I–4103, I–4131.

[1011] J. Pelkmans, 'The European Community and the Newly Industrializing Countries' in W. Maihofer (ed.), *Noi si Mura* (European University Institute, Florence, 1986), 510–39. See, more particularly, Centre for International Economics, *Costs of Coal Industry Assistance in West Germany* (Centre for International Economics, Canberra, 1992).

[1012] The solution is said to be to uncouple the protection of workers and the conservation of inefficient firms. See H. Siebert, *Real Adjustment in the Transformation Process: Risk Factors in East Germany* (Kiel Working Paper No. 507, 1992), 13.

[1013] Cf. the Opinion of the Economic and Social Committee of 27 Nov. 1991 ([1992] OJ C40/31) on the Commission Communic. on industrial policy in an open and competitive environment, para. 3.2.3.

[1014] See, e.g., Dec. 88/281 ([1988] OJ L119/33) on aid to shipbuilding and ship-repair in Italy—Art. 10 of Law 111 of 22 Mar. 1985.

problems. For example, in Decision 89/204,[1015] which concerned aid to mandarin growers in Sicily, the Commission maintained that to solve the problems facing the mandarin market, the requisite measures must be taken at Union level in order to prevent the creation of even greater problems as a result of unilateral national measures which might shift problems from assisted mandarin-growing areas to non-assisted areas.[1016] Similarly, in Decision 89/43,[1017] which concerned Italian aid to the textiles industry, the Commission expressed the view that 'unco-ordinated state intervention [in the textile and clothing industry] would conflict with the Community interest'.

The justification advanced by the Commission for its practice is that the acceptability of aid may depend not only on the existence of special difficulties in the sector concerned but also on the effects of the aid for other Union policies.[1018] In particular, aid control is designed to ensure that it does not result, in a given sector, in overcompensation of regional disadvantages for the undertakings concerned.[1019]

Such practice may be criticized as being inadequate by other Union institutions. For example, the Economic and Social Committee has called for all state aid to industry to be integrated into a complete Union framework which takes account of the relative prosperity of each region.[1020] The Committee has also criticized the failure of the Commission to give sufficient consideration to the regional and social dimension of industrial policy. Increased competitiveness will not in itself suffice to develop industry in 'lagging regions' or to meet social needs. Therefore, the Commission must give greater prominence to the interests of such regions and work these interests more convincingly into its policy instruments.[1021] Possibly in response to such arguments,[1022] the Commission plans to incorporate the aid frameworks for synthetic fibres and motor vehicles within planned guidelines for regional aid for capital-intensive

---

[1015] On regional aid for mandarin growers in Sicily ([1989] OJ L76/48).

[1016] See also Dec. 89/217 ([1989] OJ L85/48) on a national aid scheme for beef in Italy and Dec. 88/605 ([1988] OJ L334/22) on the draft Sicilian Regional Law on the setting-up of a regional fund to encourage citrus exports (Italy).

[1017] On aids granted by the Italian Government to ENI–Lanerossi ([1989] OJ L16/52).

[1018] *Tenth Report on Competition Policy* (EC Commission, Brussels, 1981), 112. For example, the Commission took into account the importance of tin-mining for the development of Cornwall in authorizing aid to a tin-mining company. See Bull. EC 11–1979, 2.1.91.

[1019] *First Report on Competition Policy* (EC Commission, Brussels, 1972), 129.

[1020] Opinion of 18 Dec. 1991 ([1992] OJ C49/9) on the *Twentieth Report on Competition Policy*, para. 2.2.3.1.

[1021] Opinion of 27 Nov. 1991 ([1992] OJ C40/31) on the Commission Communic. on industrial policy in an open and competitive environment, para. 3.1.

[1022] According to the Resolution of the European Parliament of 13 Dec. 1991 ([1992] OJ C13/472) on the *Twentieth Report on Competition Policy*, para. 18, the Commission 'should bring forward proposals for a Community policy framework for investment incentives'.

investment.[1023] However, prospects for the effective realization of the plan are uncertain.[1024]

[1023] Code on aid to the synthetic fibres industry ([1996] OJ C94/11). See also the Reply by Mr Van Miert to Written Question E–2773/94 ([1995] OJ C103/36) by Hans-Gert Poettering. See, more particularly, the exemption from the requirement of prior notification of aid to the motor vehicles sector in West Berlin in Dec. 90/381 ([1990] OJ L188/55) amending German aid schemes for the motor-vehicle industry; and Notice C44/95 (E16/95) ([1995] OJ C304/14) regarding the refusal of the Spanish authorities to the Commission's proposal for reintroduction of the EC framework on state aid to the motor-vehicle sector.

[1024] See, regarding separation of the issues involved, H. Morch, 'Summary of the Most Important Recent Developments' (1995) 6 *Competition Policy Newsletter* 41–7, 47.

6

Horizontal Aid

6.1 INTRODUCTION

Horizontal aid is aid which is directed towards goals other than that of assisting particular regions or sectors. In Commission practice it is regarded as less harmful to competition than regional or sectoral aid.[1]

Such practice may be characterized simply in terms of increased readiness to allow exceptions from the basic prohibition[2] in Article 92(1). Indeed, the guidelines for environmental aid[3] are said to have transformed the environmental principles of Article 130r of the EC Treaty into 'operational exceptions' from the prohibition of state aid.[4]

Article 92(3)(b) may have particular relevance. It provides that aid to promote the execution of an important project of common European interest may be authorized. Treatment of horizontal aid may also be affected by Article 92(3)(a) and (c), in so far as development of the regions or sectors in which recipients are located is a consequence of the aid. However, other Treaty provisions, which require the Union to promote various horizontal policies, notably those concerning traininge and job creation, research and development, small and medium-sized enterprises, environmental protection and energy conservation, may have a more profound impact on the treatment of horizontal aid. These provisions take as a starting-point the desirability of aid to accomplish certain goals.[5] Hence, aid which promotes such policies may be favoured, unless it seems that the market itself is more likely to accomplish these goals.[6]

---

[1] *Eleventh Report on Competition Policy* (EC Commission, Brussels, 1982), 127–8. See, more particularly, Dec. 87/15 ([1987] OJ L12/17) on the compatibility with the common market of aid under the German Federal/*Land* Government Joint Regional Aid Programme in six labour market regions.

[2] Joint Reply by Mr Van Miert to Written Questions E–2197/93, E–2198/93, & E–2199/93 ([1994] OJ C306/9) by Nel van Dijk.   [3] See sect. 6.5 below.

[4] Though the difficulty of assessing the impact of such aid on competition, because of limited information being available about its sectoral and regional repercussions, is recognized, as is the possibility of such aid being used as an instrument of industrial policy. See the *Second Survey on State Aids in the European Community in the Manufacturing and Certain Other Sectors* (EC Commission, Brussels, 1990), 32. Cf. the *Fourth Survey on State Aids in the European Community in the Manufacturing and Certain Other Sectors*, COM(95)365, 21.

[5] Investment aid will, it is thought, do more to help industrial development if enough of the investment is directed towards new technologies and activities which tie in with Union priorities, such as R & D or environmental protection. See *A Community Strategy to Develop Europe's Industry*, COM(81)639, 11.

[6] *Eighth EC General Report* (EC Commission, Brussels, 1975), 123. See also *European Electronics and Information Technology Sector*, SEC(91)565, 16.

Ultimately, the presumption implied in the formal legal structure of Article 92,[7] established in Commission practice generally,[8] and presupposed in the case law of the European Courts[9] may be affected. Certainly, in *Tubemeuse*, which concerned Belgian aid to a producer of steel pipes, Advocate General Tesauro expressed concern to avoid the 'risk of [the Commission] failing to authorize the payment of aid meeting important objectives which were compatible with the Community interest'.[10] Rather than authorization of horizontal aid having to be justified by reference to horizontal policy requirements, its restriction may thus have to be justified by reference to competition-policy requirements.[11]

6.2 TRAINING AND JOB CREATION

Article 2 of the EC Treaty provides that achieving a high level of employment is part of the task of the Community. Accordingly, Article 118 of the Treaty provides that the Commission has the task of promoting close co-operation between Member States in the social field, particularly in matters relating to employment and vocational training. Moreover, under Article 123 the European Social Fund is to render the employment of workers easier and to increase their geographical and occupational mobility and to facilitate their adaptation to industrial changes and to changes in production systems, in particular through vocational training and retraining. Attitudes to state aid may be affected by these provisions.[12]

Training and job-creation aid is said to be difficult to treat in the same way as other kinds of aid.[13] The former aid is frequently non-specific, in the sense that

---

[7] F. Cownie, 'State Aids in the Eighties' (1986) 11 *ELRev* 247–67, 248 and 250.

[8] According to the Commission, 'on the grounds of the basic prohibition arising from Art. 92(1), state aid should only be granted where it is proven that it is necessary and is in proportion to the objectives pursued by the aid'. See Notice C44/95 (E16/95) ([1995] OJ C304/14) regarding refusal of the Spanish authorities of the Commission's proposal for re-introduction of the EC framework on state aid to the motor-vehicle sector.

[9] The presuppositions entail that Art. 92(2) and (3) are characterized as a 'derogations'. See Joined Cases C–356/90 & C–180/91 *Belgium* v. *EC Commission: aid to shipbuilding* [1993] ECR I–2323, I–2357 and Case C–400/92 *Germany* v. *EC Commission: Cosco* [1994] ECR I–4701, I–4729–30. See also Joined Cases T–244/93 & T–486/93 *TWD Textilwerke Deggendorf* v. *EC Commission* [1995] ECR II–2265, II–2288.

[10] Case C–142/87 *Belgium* v. *EC Commission: Tubemeuse* [1990] ECR I–959, I–996

[11] However, the common commercial policy may be regarded as a further horizontal policy, which may be expected to be less favourable to the use of aid.

[12] According to *The Community's Industrial Policy*, Bull. EC, Supp. 4/70, 2, aid to improve labour mobility (occupational training, redundancy pay, removal allowances, housing allowances) is an indirect aid to industry which is generally more valuable than direct aid. The latter aid is too easily diverted to the wrong purposes and lends itself too readily to escalation.

[13] The creation of employment cannot be regarded as an economic activity in itself, in the sense of Art. 92(3)(c), without considering the sectoral consequences of the employment creation. See the *Ninth Report on Competition Policy* (EC Commission, Brussels, 1980), 119.

it does not explicitly discriminate between sectors or regions. More particularly, unless training aid is heavily slanted towards the needs of the employer receiving the aid, normal labour mobility implies important externalities: the skills acquired in training may be transferred not only between firms but between sectors and Member States. At the same time, vocational-training systems vary widely between Member States; costs which in one country are borne by the employer may in another country be borne by the state as the provider of free educational and training facilities. Training aid in the first country may alone be covered by Article 92 but will not necessarily confer a clear competitive advantage in comparison with the second country's expenditure on freely available training provision.[14]

6.2.1 Training

The Commission has a generally positive attitude towards training or retraining aid,[15] especially where 'it complies with the specific objectives of the European Social Fund'.[16] However, such aid has to be examined in order to ensure that it does not simply alleviate the cost burden which companies would normally have to bear. It must, rather, reflect the externalities associated with the worker exploiting the newly acquired knowledge in the labour market.[17] Accordingly, the Commission seeks to ensure that:

—the aid does not exceed a reasonable intensity, whenever linked with productive investments; and
—the training involved corresponds to genuinely qualitative changes in the required qualifications of the labour force and relates to a significant proportion of the workers, so that it can be assumed that the training is intended to safeguard employment and develop new employment possibilities for persons at risk of unemployment.[18]

In accordance with this approach, the Youth Training Scheme in the United Kingdom, which provided aid to employers to train unemployed young people for one year, was authorized in 1983, initially for one year.[19] In authorizing the scheme, the Commission noted the extremely worrying problem of mounting unemployment among young people and that training and preparation for working life were entailed.[20]

---

[14] S. Lehner and R. Meiklejohn, 'Fair Competition in the Internal Market: Community State Aid Policy' (1991) 48 *European Economy* 7–48, 61–2.   [15] Bull. EU 6–1995, 1.3.70.
[16] Dec. 91/474 ([1991] OJ L254/14) concerning aids granted by the Italian Government to Italgrani SpA for the setting up of an agri-foodstuffs complex in the Mezzogiorno.
[17] Guidelines on aid to employment ([1995] OJ C334/4), para. 3.
[18] *Commission Policy on Sectoral Aid Schemes*, COM(78)221.
[19] Extensions of the scheme for two further years were subsequently authorized. See the *Fifteenth Report on Competition Policy* (EC Commission, Brussels, 1986), 180–1; and the *Sixteenth Report on Competition Policy* (EC Commission, Brussels, 1984), 174.
[20] *Thirteenth Report on Competition Policy* (EC Commission, Brussels, 1984), 173–4.

However, training aid should relate to workers being trained for continued employment and should not be linked to investment.[21] Thus it should be limited to direct training costs.[22] Moreover, where the incidence of the aid is sufficiently specific to a given undertaking and its level is adjudged to be excessive, the Commission may raise objections.[23] Even so, aid to pre-production courses at centres independent of the production plant of the undertaking concerned and available to other producers may be authorized.[24]

6.2.2 Job Creation

In the economics literature there is some support for job-creation aid,[25] and the Commission considers that targeted aid to reduce labour costs 'at the bottom end' offsets the difference associated with 'lower-than-average productivity'.[26] On the other hand, limiting aid to new jobs created may be problematic. Indeed, doubt has been expressed whether 'a complex marginal scheme [is] preferable to a more straightforward cut in employers' national insurance contributions'.[27] The high costs of administering and policing the former raise the possibility that such a cut would be just as effective.

According to the Commission, certain doubts exist as to the real economic and social consequences of any such aid. It may restore a certain balance between relative costs of labour and investment often affected by tax, social legislation, or investment allowances. However, it may also cause employers to bring forward recruitment in times of uncertain demand when they might otherwise postpone it. Moreover, it is likely, especially when granted for a lengthy period, to encourage firms to adopt labour-intensive methods which, in the light of the world labour market, are unlikely to ensure Union prosperity and can also artificially maintain uncompetitive production by delaying the necessary modernization.[28] Finally, it may—in certain conditions of demand—

---

[21] Dec. 92/483 ([1992] OJ L288/25) concerning aid provided by the Brussels Regional Authorities in favour of the activities of Siemens SA in the data-processing and telecommunications sectors.

[22] Notice C24/92 (N120/92) ([1992] OJ C237/6) concerning aid which Italy planned to grant for the employment of women.

[23] Leiner and Meiklejohn, n. 14 above, 61–2. See, e.g., Communic. NN83/90 ([1990] OJ C315/7) concerning aids which Italy had decided to grant to Italgrani SpA.

[24] Summary of the Commission Decision not to raise objections to the aid which the Portuguese Government planned to grant to the joint-venture of Ford and Volkswagen to establish a multipurpose vehicle plant in the Setubal peninsula ([1991] OJ C257/5).

[25] R. G. Layard and S. J. Nickell, 'The Case for Subsidising Extra Jobs' (1980) 90 *The Economic Journal* 51–73.

[26] Guidelines on aid to employment ([1995] OJ C334/4), para. 3.

[27] J. D. Whitley and R. A. Wilson, 'The Macroeconomic Merits of a Marginal Employment Subsidy' (1983) 93 *The Economic Journal* 862–80.

[28] On the other hand, aid may be unacceptable on regional grounds under Art. 92(3)(c) by very reason of its capital intensive character. See Dec. 89/456 ([1989] OJ L223/22) on the French Government's aid proposal in favour of Caulliez Frères, cotton yarn producer located in Prouvy, France.

have a displacement effect. Job creation in certain Member States, certain industries (notably those in difficulty), certain firms, or certain categories of undertakings may be offset by the disappearance of or failure to create corresponding jobs elsewhere. Therefore, the positive contribution of such aid to the employment situation is difficult to assess.[29]

Even so, although it is considered more likely than training aid to 'inadvertently create distortions' of competition,[30] job-creation aid may be favoured in Commission practice.[31] For example, in 1975 Germany introduced aid up to 66 per cent of gross wage costs for six months for newly recruited workers in areas where unemployment was 0.5 per cent higher than the national average. This aid was authorized by the Commission.[32]

However, according to *Commission Policy on Sectoral Aid Schemes*, job-creation aid had to be distinguished from aid to maintain existing jobs. If the latter kind of aid was concentrated on sectors which faced acute difficulties in all Member States and was not associated with substantial plans for reorganization, it would not lead to the solution of social and industrial difficulties but to their transfer to other Member States. Accordingly, its use had to be restricted.[33]

The general lines of Commission policy were described in the *Sixteenth Report on Competition Policy*.[34] Aid which simply had the effect of reducing labour costs without meeting special needs or furthering Union policies was, in principle, incompatible with the common market.[35] On the other hand, where the aid was temporary and would lead to the creation of new and additional jobs and/or was intimately bound up with restructuring, it might be authorized, particularly if the new jobs were to be filled by disadvantaged groups with special training needs, such as the young or long-term unemployed.

Accordingly, aid in the form of tax reliefs for companies which reduce their weekly working hours and correspondingly increase their workforce may be authorized, because it encourages employment.[36] Similarly, aid in relation to

[29] *Seventh Report on Competition Policy* (EC Commission, Brussels, 1978), 165–6.

[30] *Twenty-Second Report on Competition Policy* (EC Commission, Brussels, 1993), 257. See, more particularly, regarding aid to promote women's employment, *ibid.*, 258.

[31] See, e.g., regarding Spanish aid to co-operatives and companies whose shares are mainly held by their employees, *ibid.*, 250. The European Parliament favours employment aid, provided it is degressive and temporary. See the Resolution of 12 Oct. 1978 ([1978] OJ C261/48) on the *Seventh Report on Competition Policy*, para. 13. Cf. the consideration given to employment effects for the purposes of application of Art. 85(3) EC in Case 26/76 *Metro-SB-Großmärkte GmbH* v. *EC Commission* [1977] ECR 1875, 1916.

[32] *Fifth Report on Competition Policy* (EC Commission, Brussels, 1976), 95. See also, regarding French aid, *ibid.*, 97.

[33] COM(78)221, 8–9. See, later, in relation to agriculture, Communic. ([1986] OJ C312/3) concerning an aid which the French Government had granted for the employment of casual labour in certain agricultural sectors in order to support those vertically integrated sectors with a view to the accession of Spain and Portugal.

[34] (EC Commission, Brussels), 1987, 172.

[35] See, more recently, the *Twenty-Third Report on Competition Policy* (EC Commission, Brussels, 1994), 267.

[36] *Sixteenth Report on Competition Policy* (EC Commission, Brussels, 1987), 138.

social charges may be authorized. For example, a Dutch scheme to cover social-security charges, equivalent to 15 per cent of salaries, in the case of new employees (who had been unemployed for the last three years) for four years was authorized.[37] Such aid is regarded as assisting job creation rather than job preservation.[38] Even direct grants to employers may be authorized, as in the case of a British scheme to promote job-sharing through the division of full-time jobs. According to this scheme, employers who took on an unemployed person or a worker threatened with unemployment would receive a grant of £750 per job shared.[39]

Union Interventions

The acceptability of job-creation aid may be affected by its consistency with Union interventions, or at least with Union interventionist policy statements. For example, Spanish employment aid was accepted, because it had similar objectives to those of the European Social Fund.[40] Similarly, British aid for the recruitment of young unemployed persons was accepted,[41] as being in line with the Fourth Medium-Term Economic Policy Programme,[42] which advocated the grant of allowances for on-the-job training and measures to help unskilled young people.

Rescue Aid

Job-creation aid must not be of a purely rescue character,[43] and a link with restructuring may be required. For example, Dutch aid to tackle unemployment included the grant of Dfl 1,000 for each worker kept on the payroll throughout the year. This aid was only acceptable if it was linked with restructuring.[44] Again, Italian aid to reduce the interest rate on loans contracted by firms to carry out plans to avoid the total or partial unemployment of the workers had to be made conditional on restructuring. The aid could not be used simply to keep ailing firms alive.[45]

---

[37] Bull. EC 12–1986, 2.1.112.

[38] *Eighth Report on Competition Policy* (EC Commission, Brussels, 1979), 167.

[39] *Twelfth Report on Competition Policy* (EC Commission, Brussels, 1983), 136. On the other hand, aid related to seasonal employment may be regarded as objectionable operating aid. See Notice ([1987] OJ C98/15) concerning a draft law on aids which the Sicilian regional authorities intended to grant to fishermen.

[40] Bull. EC 1–1989, 2.1.32.

[41] Bull. EC 10–1977, 2.1.16. See, similarly, regarding an Irish scheme, Bull. EC 10–1977, 2.1.17.   [42] [1977] OJ L101/2, para. 126.

[43] However, social benefits to workers dismissed or placed on short-time working are viewed favourably. See the *Second Report on Competition Policy* (EC Commission, Brussels, 1973), 102.

[44] *Seventh Report on Competition Policy* (EC Commission, Brussels, 1978), 150. See, similarly, regarding aid to the Belgian textiles industry, the *Tenth Report on Competition Policy* (EC Commission, Brussels, 1980), 142–3. Irish aid to clothing and footwear firms facing the option of short-time working or redundancy linked with reorganization was also authorized. See Bull. EC 7/8–1978, 2.1.41.

[45] *Fourth Report on Competition Policy* (EC Commission, Brussels, 1975), 97; Bull. EC 6–1974, 2119.

Operating Aid

Aid must not normally have operating character,[46] and so the mere fact that aid may promote employment will not in itself mean that it is permissible.[47] In particular, regional aid for preserving jobs must be linked with investment and cannot be used to finance the current operations of the recipient.[48] Thus regional employment aid in the United Kingdom was only authorized because it was of a job-creation type (for six months) rather than continuing aid.[49] The rationale is that a lasting increase in employment is generally the consequence of increased investment[50] and an improvement in the competitiveness of undertakings. Accordingly, the Commission has always expressed strong reservations about schemes to assist employment as such which are in the nature of aid for continued operation, and in particular about aid to maintain existing jobs.[51] Such schemes may make no contribution to the development sought by Article 92(3)(a) and (c). At the same time, since the aid may merely transfer social and industrial difficulties to other Member States,[52] it may be contrary to the common interest.

Even where Article 92(3)(b) may be applicable, such aid is tightly controlled. For example, a temporary employment subsidy in the United Kingdom was set up as a short-term counter-cyclical instrument intended to encourage firms to keep their workers off the unemployment register[53] and was authorized under Article 92(3)(b) to remedy a serious disturbance in the economy. However, its prolongation meant that it had the effect of maintaining in production a large proportion of firms in declining industries. Since it was granted on the basis of the number of existing jobs maintained, it enabled certain industries with excess capacity to carry on with uncompetitive production. Hence, authorization could only continue if undue concentration on any one sector and purely stop-gap features of the aid were avoided.[54]

[46] See, e.g., aid for new employees which was payable for 5 years and was not linked to any investment projects: Notice C23/95 (NN59/94) ([1995] OJ C271/7) concerning aid which Italy planned to grant to the footwear industry. Aid for work on products for export to other Member States is particularly objectionable. See the *Fifteenth Report on Competition Policy* (EC Commission, Brussels, 1986), 182.

[47] See, e.g., Dec. 80/1157 ([1980] OJ L343/38) on a scheme of aid by the Belgian Government in respect of certain investments carried out by the Belgian subsidiary of an international oil group at its Antwerp refinery.

[48] Notice regarding the French scheme relating to the regional job maintenance premium ([1983] OJ C1/3). See also the *Twelfth Report on Competition Policy* (EC Commission, Brussels, 1983), 135–6.   [49] Bull. EC 4–1978, 2.1.24.

[50] However, in relation to a Danish scheme, the Commission accepted in 1985 that it was 'possible and desirable to make available, where merited, somewhat higher aid levels for more labour intensive projects'. See the *Fifteenth Report on Competition Policy* (EC Commission, Brussels, 1986), 191.

[51] Dec. 85/351 ([1985] OJ L188/44) concerning aid granted by the Netherlands Government to an engineering undertaking.

[52] *Eighth Report on Competition Policy* (EC Commission, Brussels, 1979), 127.

[53] *Fifth Report on Competition Policy* (EC Commission, Brussels, 1976), 99.

[54] *Seventh Report on Competition Policy* (EC Commission, Brussels, 1978), 168–70.

Even in the least developed regions, such aid may be objectionable. For example, in 1972 the Commission considered the increase and extension until 1980 of the abatement of welfare charges paid by small craft and industrial firms in the Mezzogiorno. The Commission could not authorize this aid, though the problems raised would be tackled in the work relating to co-ordination of regional aid in the peripheral areas of the Union. Only a one-year abatement for craft firms, small and medium-sized enterprises and all textile firms in Italy could be authorized under Article 92(3)(b) to remedy a serious disturbance in the economy.[55]

Regional-policy Considerations

Where aid is found to lack operating character, importance may be attached to regional policy considerations. Thus, for example, Belgian job-creation aid, in the form of exemption from corporation tax for ten years, was authorized. Account was taken of the fact that the aid was only to be granted in areas suffering from serious regional problems and that undertakings had to employ no more than 200 persons.[56] Again, a Dutch restructuring plan for the solid board industry included a grant to a social fund to facilitate early retirement of some workers and conversion of others. Since there were regional problems in the area where the industry was principally located, this aid was also authorized.[57]

Particular account may be taken of regional dependence on declining industries. For example, the Commission accepted a French aid scheme paying up to one-third of the wages of new employees for up to three years in Lorraine, which had been directly affected by steel redundancies. Such aid was not available in the case of industries suffering from overcapacity, and advance notice was necessary of any cases involving the creation of over 100 jobs or an investment of over ECU 6 million.[58] A similar scheme paid for three years a declining part of the wage costs associated with jobs created in areas of Nord-Pas-de-Calais most hit by the rationalization of the steel, coal, and shipbuilding industries. Industrial firms, except those in sectors suffering from overcapacity (steel, man-made fibres, textiles and clothing, shipbuilding,[59] flat-glass, the milk powder and butter sectors of the dairy industry, sugar, and isoglucose) were eligible for aid. The scheme was generally acceptable to the Commission, though not in areas where the problems of the local labour market lacked an apparent link with rationalization in declining industries.[60]

[55] *Second Report on Competition Policy* (EC Commission, Brussels, 1973), 104–5.
[56] *Thirteenth Report on Competition Policy* (EC Commission, Brussels, 1984), 174.
[57] *Eighth Report on Competition Policy* (EC Commission, Brussels, 1979), 149–50.
[58] *Fourteenth Report on Competition Policy* (EC Commission, Brussels, 1985), 172–3. See, similarly, regarding German aid in areas affected by steel restructuring, Bull. EC 6–1982, 2.1.47.
[59] See also, regarding French aid for the creation of alternative jobs in shipbuilding areas, the *Seventeenth Report on Competition Policy* (EC Commission, Brussels, 1988), 179 and, regarding German aid for the same purpose, *ibid.*, 178.
[60] *Sixteenth Report on Competition Policy* (EC Commission, Brussels, 1987), 179–80.

Equally, particular account may be taken of rural problems. For example, a French job-creation scheme was authorized as helping to counter rural depopulation.[61]

However, claims as to the effects of aid on employment are carefully scrutinized.[62] For example, the UK Off-shore Interest Relief Grants Scheme could not be authorized under Article 92(3)(a) because it had not been such as to maintain stable employment at eligible production sites. During the period of its operation about half of the sites had been closed, while others were without orders or were completing existing orders. Nor was it covered by Article 92(3)(c), because it did not help to make the industry more competitive and able to operate without aid.[63]

The Commission also seems reluctant to accept alleged 'knock-on' effects of aid in terms of job creation, and aid will not be authorized merely because it may indirectly protect employment and the pay levels of employees.[64] In one decision the Commission noted the claim of the Belgian Government that the aided investment in question would not only maintain the jobs of 336 persons, but would also lead over the next few years to the recruitment of several hundred workers in the district bordering on the Turnhout area, which qualified for regional assistance and where the rate of unemployment was particularly high. However, the Commission considered that this knock-on effect was by no means assured and so the effect of the aid on the employment situation in the Turnhout area could not be assessed.[65] Hence, the Commission decided to prohibit the aid. This decision may be regarded as reflecting general difficulties of assessing in advance the effects of aid on employment.[66]

Sectoral-policy Considerations

Sectoral-policy considerations may be decisive for the treatment of job-creation aid.[67] Thus Italian aid to female employment through the reduction of social charges was not permissible in sensitive sectors,[68] nor was the grant of French

[61] Bull. EC 5–1978, 2.1.27.

[62] Moreover, where aid has been granted in a particular region, and subsequently the employment rate there has risen to around the Union average, further aid may not be permissible. See the *Tenth Report on Competition Policy* (EC Commission, Brussels, 1981), 118.

[63] Dec. 79/496 ([1979] OJ L127/50) on the UK scheme of assistance in the form of interest-relief grants in favour of the off-shore supplies industry.

[64] Dec. 82/651 ([1982] OJ L274/34) on the aids granted in Sicily in the citrus fruit, fruit, and vegetables sector.

[65] Dec. 81/984 ([1981] OJ L361/24) on a Belgian Government proposal to aid certain investments in a refinery at Antwerp. See also the objections to figures which were 'too general' to be plausible in Communic. NN83/90 ([1990] OJ C315/7) concerning aids which Italy had decided to grant to Italgrani SpA.

[66] C. Hultin, 'The Effects of State Aid on Employment in the French Textile and Clothing Industry' (1989) 7 *International Journal of Industrial Organization* 489–501.

[67] See, regarding French job-creation aid, Bull. EC 5–1987, 2.1.71.

[68] *Twelfth Report on Competition Policy* (EC Commission, Brussels, 1983), 146. See also Dec. 80/932 ([1980] OJ L264/28) concerning the partial taking-over by the state of employers'

employment aid to industries suffering from overcapacity.[69] More recently, Italian aid to the footwear industry was found objectionable.[70] Aid may even be objectionable, simply because it is limited to a single sector.[71]

Such practice has been criticized by the European Parliament as containing inconsistencies at both national and Union level. The lack of any plan or, at the very least, of any co-ordination in this field means that the Commission's 'generally favourable attitude'[72] has virtually no effect at Union level. There is the impression that the Commission is acting on the basis of an abstract principle which conforms to the idea that competition policy is something separate. Although correct, it is inadequate to say that aid schemes for promoting employment should be 'designed not just to keep workers in employment but to encourage firms to take on new workers, and especially to create additional jobs for particular categories of workers who have special difficulty in finding employment'.[73]

1995 Guidelines

Guidelines for evaluation of employment aid were adopted by the Commission in 1995.[74] According to these Guidelines, such aid may fall outside Article 92(1), because it does not favour certain undertakings or the production of certain goods or does not affect trade between Member States. For example, a reduction of social charges or an automatic premium to all undertakings recruiting or employing certain categories of workers regardless of the size, location, or sector of those undertakings does not fall under Article 92(1). Moreover, if the advantage for an undertaking remains below the threshold of the *de minimis* rule or if assistance is given to set up purely local services, trade between Member States is not perceptibly affected.[75]

However, measures which selectively reduce labour costs in certain undertakings or in certain sectors to encourage them to increase their labour force, to recruit certain categories of workers, or to maintain the level of employment

---

contributions to sickness insurance schemes in Italy. See, earlier, the *Seventh Report on Competition Policy* (EC Commission, Brussels, 1978), 167–70 and the *Eighth Report on Competition Policy* (EC Commission, Brussels, 1979), 120–1 and 161–4, regarding job-creation aid in 'sensitive sectors'.

[69] *Fourteenth Report on Competition Policy* (EC Commission, Brussels, 1985), 172–3.

[70] Bull. EU 4–1995, 1.3.51.

[71] Notice C23/95 (NN59/94) ([1995] OJ C271/7) concerning aid which Italy planned to grant to the footwear industry.

[72] *Seventh Report on Competition Policy* (EC Commission, Brussels, 1978), 165 ff; *Nineteenth Report on Competition Policy* (EC Commission, Brussels, 1990), 170–1; and the *Twentieth Report on Competition Policy* (EC Commission, Brussels, 1991), 172.

[73] Report of the Committee on Economic and Monetary Affairs and Industrial Policy on the *Twentieth Report on Competition Policy*, EP Doc. A3–0338/91, 12.

[74] Guidelines on aid to employment ([1995] OJ C334/4). They constituted a response to the *White Paper on Growth, Competitiveness and Employment*, COM(93)700 and the Conclusions of the Essen European Council (Bull. EU 12–1994, I.3) and of the Cannes European Council (Bull. EU 6–1995, I.4). See Bull. EU 7/8–1995, 1.3.53.

[75] Para. 7 of the 1995 Guidelines.

distort competition, because they favour the beneficiaries with respect to their competitors. They may delay adjustments, result in waste of public money associated with escalating subsidies, and simply shift employment problems elsewhere. At the same time, they may be concentrated in more prosperous regions and thus be contrary to cohesion requirements.[76] Such measures constitute aid falling under Article 92(1), in so far as they affect trade between Member States. They may include: a fixed premium per job created, a subsidy as a percentage of wage costs, or relief from certain social security or tax liabilities.[77]

In respect of measures falling under Article 92(1), the Guidelines distinguish between aid for job creation, that is, aid to secure a net increase in the number of jobs in the undertaking with reference to a certain period, and aid for maintaining jobs, that is, aid to prevent an undertaking from making workers redundant.

At the same time, the Guidelines confirm the traditionally positive approach of the Commission towards aid for job creation under Article 92(3)(c).[78] Subject to certain ceilings, the Commission will normally adopt a favourable position if the aid is granted to small and medium-sized enterprises or to undertakings in regions eligible for regional aid to take on unemployed persons, provided this employment leads to a net increase in the number of jobs in the undertaking concerned.[79]

Similarly, the Commission will normally adopt a favourable position if the aid is granted to undertakings, irrespective of their location, to take on unemployed persons having particular difficulties in finding a permanent job. Although any applicable ceiling must be respected, it is not required that the employment lead to a net increase in the number of jobs in the undertaking, as long as the vacancy is due to normal departure, not redundancy.[80]

In its assessment of the aid the Commission will consider whether the unemployed person is to be employed on a contract of unlimited duration or for a period which is sufficiently long to ensure a certain stability in the job created. Moreover, the Commission will take account of possible counterparts offered by the undertaking for the aid received going beyond the employment of the unemployed, such as training. The Commission will also examine whether the intensity and the amount of aid offered to an undertaking are a necessary incentive to take on an unemployed person and verify that the aid is temporary.[81]

Even if the above conditions are met, the Commission will normally look unfavourably on aid for job creation available only to sectors which are sensitive, suffering from overcapacity, or in a crisis. The negative effects which such aid may have on competing undertakings within the same sector in other

---

[76] *Ibid.*, para. 12.   [77] *Ibid.*, para. 14.
[78] *Ibid.*, para. 20.   [79] *Ibid.*, paras. 13 and 21.
[80] *Ibid.*, para. 21.   [81] *Ibid.*, para. 20.

Member States and the risk that the aid will merely export the unemployment to other Member States prevail over the need to reduce the unemployment rate in the Member State granting the aid. However, if the aid is granted in regions with serious unemployment problems, the Commission will take this fact into account. The Commission may also adopt a more favourable position in respect of aid for job creation in sub-sectors which experience economic growth and generate many jobs.[82]

The Guidelines confirm the traditionally unfavourable approach of the Commission towards aid for maintaining jobs in an undertaking. In fact, such aid amounts to operating aid, which generally has the effect of preventing or delaying the necessary changes to render the firm/sector concerned economically viable, thereby keeping unprofitable businesses artificially alive. Therefore, the Commission will only approve aid for maintaining jobs in a limited number of cases and under strict conditions. Such aid may be authorized under Article 92(2)(b) or in regions which are faced with particularly serious socio-economic problems and for that reason are eligible for regional aid pursuant to Article 92(3)(a). Aid for maintaining jobs in the context of rescue or restructuring plans may also be approved, provided the conditions in the Guidelines for such plans are met.[83]

6.3 RESEARCH AND DEVELOPMENT

Article 130f(1) of the EC Treaty provides that the strengthening of the scientific and technological bases of Union industry is an objective of the Union. Accordingly, Article 130f(2) requires that undertakings be encouraged in their research and technological development activities, and Article 130h(1) requires that the Union and Member States co-ordinate their activities in this field. Moreover, Article 130f(3) provides that special account is to be taken of the relationship between the common research and development effort, the establishment of the internal market, and the implementation of common policies, particularly as regards competition and trade.[84] Similar concern to encourage research and development is demonstrated by the White Paper, *Growth, Competitiveness, and Employment*,[85] and by the Fourth Framework Programme in the field of research and technological development and demonstration (1994–8).[86]

Aid to research and development may be seen as remedying market imper-

---

[82] *Ibid.*, para. 23.
[83] *Ibid.*, para. 22.
[84] Art. 130f was invoked in Notice C37/91 (ex N292/91 & N316/91) ([1992] OJ C244/2) regarding aid which France had decided to grant Compagnie des Machines Bull.
[85] Bull. EC, Supp. 6/93.
[86] [1994] OJ L126/4.

fections,[87] associated with 'free riders' and inadequate information.[88] Indeed, it is argued that there is an optimum level of competition, beyond which competition has an adverse impact on innovation because of the difficulty of allocating gains and the greater risks which exist in highly competitive markets. The optimum market structure from the stand-point of innovation ought rather to promote strategic rivalry between a limited number of firms.[89] Hence, the Commission seeks to co-ordinate the grant of research and development aid, both amongst Member States and between Member States and the Union.[90]

It has been objected that most research and development aid is spent on projects that would go ahead anyway. Furthermore, research and development resources are inelastic in the short and medium term, so that aided projects may simply crowd out unaided ones without any overall benefit to the Union.[91] Hence, such aid may create serious problems for competition policy.[92] At the same time, such aid may run counter to cohesion, because aid recipients tend to be located in regions which are already well developed and urbanized.[93]

Nevertheless, the Commission 'realizes the importance of state aids in the field of research and development, that such aids may be necessary to sustain or encourage activity and is conscious that its actions must not be interpreted as restrictive or lead to a diminution of research and development in Member States'.[94] Its attitude reflects several considerations: the aims of such aid, the often considerable financing requirements for research and development, the risks attached and, given the distance from the market-place of such projects, the reduced likelihood of distortions of competition.[95]

Thus, for example, French aid to technical centres to assist small and

[87] See, e.g., the authorization of French and German aid for technological development by SMEs in the *Fourth Report on Competition Policy* (EC Commission, Brussels, 1976), 99–100. Cf. the block exemptions in Reg. 2349/84 ([1984] OJ L219/15) on the application of Art. 85(3) EC to certain categories of patent-licensing agreements; Reg. 418/85 ([1985] OJ L53/5) on the application of Art. 85(3) EC to categories of R & D agreements; and Reg. 556/89 ([1989] OJ L61/1) on the application of Art. 85(3) EC to certain categories of know-how licensing agreements. Co-operation agreements between undertakings leading to innovation are also favoured. See, e.g., Dec. 90/46 ([1990] OJ L32/19) relating to a proceeding under Art. 85 EC (IV/32.006—Alcatel Espace/ANT Nachrichtentechnik).

[88] *The Effect of Different State Aid Measures on Intra-Community Competition* (EC Commission, Brussels, 1990), 103.

[89] M. Emerson, M. Aujean, M. Catinat, P. Goybet, and A. Jacquemin, *The Economics of 1992* (Oxford University Press, Oxford 1988), 162.

[90] *Eighth Report on Competition Policy* (EC Commission, Brussels, 1979), 126.

[91] J. Gilchrist and D. Deacon, 'Curbing Subsidies' in P. Montagnon (ed.), *European Competition Policy* (Pinter, London, 1990) 31–51.

[92] Cf. the EP Resolution of 14 Nov. 1986 ([1986] OJ C322/442) on the *Fifteenth Report on Competition Policy*, para. 41.

[93] Opinion of the Economic and Social Committee of 29 Jan. 1986 ([1986] OJ C75/12) on national regional development aid, para. 4.3.

[94] *Fourteenth Report on Competition Policy* (EC Commission, Brussels, 1985), 164.

[95] Though the possibility of such distortions cannot be excluded. See, e.g., the Opinion of the Economic and Social Committee of 23 Nov. 1995 ([1996] OJ C39/102) on the proposal for a reg. on aid to shipbuilding, para. 3.1.8.

medium-sized enterprises in the clock and watch and leather industries was authorized under Article 92(3)(c),[96] because the Commission was 'usually favourably disposed towards aids which facilitate[d] industrial development by improving technical progress'.[97]

The Framework for research and development aid, which was introduced in 1986[98] and revised in 1995,[99] maintains the 'presumption' in favour of aid of this kind,[100] provided that it is not likely adversely to affect trading conditions to an extent contrary to the common interest.[101] Any such aid which is shown to be designed to promote the execution of a project of common European interest may be authorized under Article 92(3)(b).[102] This provision, according to the Commission, applies to research and development projects which are both qualitatively and quantitatively important, transnational in character, and related to the definition of industrial standards that can allow the Union's industries to benefit from all the advantages of the common market.[103] Other aid for research and development may be authorized under Article 92(3)(c).[104]

6.3.1 Authorization Conditions

Various considerations, related to Union programmes for research and development, the nature of the aid, and other Union policies, may affect the acceptability of aid for research and development.

Union Interventions

The relationship of state aid with Union programmes may be important.[105] For example, research and development aid to microelectronics was authorized,[106] because it was in line with the Commission communication on industrial and technical innovation.[107] German aid to information technology, which was 'tied

---

[96] Dec. 74/8 ([1974] OJ L14/23) on para-fiscal taxes financing the 'Technical Centres' for leather and for the clock and watch-making industry.

[97] *Third Report on Competition Policy* (EC Commission, Brussels, 1974), 88–9.

[98] Community framework for state aids to R & D ([1986] OJ C83/2). See also *Towards a European Technology Community*, COM(85)350.

[99] H. Morch, 'Summary of the Most Important Recent Developments' (1995) 6 *Competition Policy Newsletter* 41–7, 41–3.

[100] Para. 1.4.2 of the 1986 Framework. See also the *Sixteenth Report on Competition Policy* (EC Commission, Brussels, 1987), 167.

[101] Summary of the Commission's dec. not to oppose the R & D, environmental, and training aid which the Austrian Government intended to provide to Opel Austria in support of its expenditure in the Family-O-engine project ([1995] OJ C310/4).

[102] Para. 3.2 of the 1986 Framework. In practice, the operation of this paragraph may be limited to Eureka projects. See the *Twenty-Second Report on Competition Policy* (EC Commission, Brussels, 1993), 215–6.

[103] See, e.g., the *Eighteenth Report on Competition Policy* (EC Commission, Brussels, 1989), 151.

[104] Para. 3.3 of the 1986 Framework.

[105] Cf. Dec. 89/337 ([1989] OJ L142/1) on a high-definition television, Art. 2.

[106] Bull. EC 1–1982, 2.1.21.

[107] Bull. EC 12–1980, 2.1.141. See also Reg. 1996/79 ([1979] OJ L231/1) on a Community support mechanism in the field of data processing.

in with' the Esprit programme,[108] was also authorized,[109] as was aid to the computer industry,[110] the electronics industry,[111] and wind power.[112] However, the mere fact that an aided project is part of a Union project, such as Esprit, does not necessarily mean that the aid qualifies for authorization.[113]

In examining aid to Eureka[114] projects[115] the Commission applies the same favourable attitude[116] and criteria as are applied in relation to national projects, while paying particular attention to the transnational character of the former projects.[117] Five Eureka projects—HDTV,[118] DAB, ESF, Eprom, and Jessi—have been classified as Article 92(3)(b) projects,[119] though the aid may also be approved under Article 92(3)(c).[120] However, aid to such projects will not necessarily be authorized.[121] For example, German aid to Eureka projects was objectionable, because the intensity was higher than the ceilings established by the Framework for research and development aid.[122]

Incentives

Aid must have the effect of encouraging additional efforts in the research and development field over and above the normal operations[123] which firms carry out in any case[124] or respond to exceptional conditions for which their own

[108] Dec. 84/130 ([1984] OJ L67/54) concerning a European programme for research and development in information technologies (Esprit). See, earlier, the Council Resolution of 15 July 1974 ([1974] OJ C86/1) on a Community policy on data processing, para. 3.

[109] Bull. EC 5–1985, 2.1.34.   [110] Bull. EC 12–1976, 2133.

[111] Bull. EC 3–1977, 2.1.37.   [112] Bull. EC 10–1986, 2.1.70.

[113] Joined Cases 62 & 72/87 *Exécutif Régional Wallon and Glaverbel* v. *EC Commission* [1988] ECR 1573, 1594–5.   [114] European Research Co-ordination Agency.

[115] *Reinforcing Co-operation between Eureka and the European Community*, COM(88)291 emphasized synergies between Eureka and Union programmes.

[116] *Eighteenth Report on Competition Policy* (EC Commission, Brussels, 1989), 151. Subsidiaries of companies from third states may be involved. For example, ICL, the UK-based computer group, 80% owned by Fujitsu of Japan, was to work with Bull of France and Siemens-Nixdorf Informations Systems of Germany on the Sesame Project (Secure European System for Applications in a Multivendor Environment). See the *Financial Times*, 18 Mar. 1992.

[117] *Seventeenth Report on Competition Policy* (EC Commission, Brussels, 1988), 143.

[118] See, regarding the market failure of the HDTV project, the *Financial Times*, 9 Feb. 1993.

[119] *Twentieth Report on Competition Policy* (EC Commission, Brussels, 1991), 140. See, regarding German aid to German firms involved in Jessi projects, Bull. EU 3–1994, 1.2.56, and, regarding Italian aid to Italian firms participating in Jessi and Prometheus (another Eureka project), H. Morch, 'Summary of the Most Important Recent Developments' (1995) 6 *Competition Policy Newsletter* 43–9, 49; Bull. EU 5–1995, 1.3.41.

[120] *Eighteenth Report on Competition Policy* (EC Commission, Brussels, 1989), 151.

[121] Notice C53/91 (N529/91) ([1992] OJ C10/4) regarding aid which Germany had decided to grant in the laser research sector.

[122] Bull. EC 12–1991, 1.2.65. See sect. 6.3.2. below, regarding these ceilings.

[123] Thus the considerable R & D effort which had gone into the production of a new engine could not of itself justify aid for investment in its production. See Dec. 84/364 ([1984] OJ L192/35) concerning the proposal by the Italian Government to award aid to an engine and tractor manufacturer.

[124] Thus the research activities of a recipient do not justify aid for productive investment. See Dec. 91/305 ([1991] OJ L156/39) concerning investment aid which the Belgian Government planned to grant to Mactac SA, Soignies.

resources are too limited. As a result of the aid received, undertakings should thus carry out more research than they would have without the aid.[125] In cases where no such incentive effect is evident or the research and development is too close to the actual production or marketing stage, the generally positive attitude of the Commission towards research and development aid may not be applicable. Thus aid which merely enables the recipient to lower its prices and/ or increase its profits is likely to be prohibited.[126] The underlying idea is that aid should secure 'positive externalities'. They may be secured where, for example, the research is designed to meet higher environmental standards than those in existence and where without the aid the research would be less ambitious and spread over a longer period.[127] More questionable is the Commission view that the condition is met where aid leads to the incorporation of the recipient into a network concerned with research and development and to an increase in its staff dedicated to research and development activities.[128]

Dissemination

The Framework favours aid to projects the results of which will be widely disseminated,[129] and Commission practice may require that the results of aided research be made available throughout the Union without discrimination.[130] This requirement raises problems as to the economic rationale underlying the Framework. It implies that the benefits of research could otherwise be appropriated. However, to the extent that they can be appropriated, there are no 'negative externalities' attributable to market failure and likely to be corrected through aid.[131]

Innovation

Commission practice relies on a distinction between aid to 'modernization' and aid to 'genuine innovation' at Union level.[132] Aid must not cover ordinary

---

[125] Para. 8.2 of the 1986 Framework. See also the *Twenty-Second Report on Competition Policy* (EC Commission, Brussels, 1993), 215.

[126] See, e.g., Notice ([1986] OJ C181/3) regarding aid which the Belgian Government was reported to have granted to five pharmaceutical companies in 1983.

[127] Summary of the dec. N657/94 ([1996] OJ C74/8) not to oppose aid which the Dutch Government intended to provide to DAF Trucks NV for the Volem project.

[128] Summary of Dec. N538/93 ([1996] OJ C94/7) not to oppose the proposal of the Spanish authorities to provide regional aid to Ford España, SA in support of an investment project for the expansion of engine capacity in Almusafes (Valencia).

[129] Paras. 1.4 and 5.4 of the 1986 Framework.

[130] See, in the case of textiles, the *Sixth Report on Competition Policy* (EC Commission, Brussels, 1977), 115; and Letter SG(77)D1190, Annex, para. 5 (*Competition Law in the European Communities Vol. II: Rules Applicable to State Aids* (EC Commission, Brussels, 1990), 51–4).

[131] Cf. J. S. Chard and M. J. Macmillan, 'Sectoral Aids and Community Competition Policy: The Case of Textiles' [1979] *JWTL* 132–57, 145.

[132] Innovation aid helping to improve the technological standards of the French electrical engineering industry as a whole (but not modernization) was acceptable. See Bull. EC 3–1988, 2.1.87.

expenditure but should relate to particularly risky projects or to research avenues which the limited resources of the recipients would not allow them to explore.[133] The aim of the aid should not be the steady development of existing products and known production techniques, which follow automatically from the normal behaviour of undertakings and normal replacement of assets, as these wear out. Rather, the aim should be the introduction of new products or new production technologies, which have not previously existed but respond to future needs.[134] Account is taken not only of the current state of science in the relevant field but also of what is currently being done by the main competitors of the aid recipient.[135]

A project may be regarded as insufficiently innovatory where it concerns processes already in use in other Member States or where the recipient does not intend to export the resulting products to other Member States.[136] On the other hand, aid to a project which involves high risk and leads to the development of a system unique within the Union, as in the case of aid to development of a flat-square television tube[137] and to work on new-generation vaccines developed with the assistance of genetic engineering techniques,[138] may be authorized on sectoral development grounds within the meaning of Article 92(3)(c).[139] Aid for innovative application of existing technology may also be authorized.[140] Otherwise, the aid may be prohibited.

The rationale for such practice is that in many industries, such as the chemicals industry, it is 'only natural' that undertakings should devote large sums of money to research into new processes, new products, and their improvement.[141] Aid for such activity is considered unnecessary.

Strategic Considerations

Strategic considerations may be influential. For example, German aid to the development of micro-electronic technology[142] and for construction of an

[133] *Twenty-First Report on Competition Policy* (EC Commission, Brussels, 1992), 131.

[134] *Thirteenth Report on Competition Policy* (EC Commission, Brussels, 1984), 144–5. The size of the recipient and the competitive pressures on the recipient to engage in scientific development may affect the acceptability of aid. See, e.g., Dec. 89/254 ([1989] OJ L106/34) relating to aid which the Belgian Government had granted to a petrochemicals company at Ottignies/Louvain-la-Neuve (SA Belgian Shell).

[135] Notice C37/91 (ex N292/91 & N316/91) ([1992] OJ C244/2) regarding aid which France had decided to grant Compagnie des Machines Bull.

[136] Dec. 87/16 ([1987] OJ L12/27) on a proposal by the Italian Government to grant aid to a firm in the chemical industry (producing industrial auxiliaries, intermediates and pesticides).

[137] Bull. EC 11–1986, 2.1.85.

[138] Notice C46/89 ([1990] OJ C229/2) concerning aid which Belgium has decided to grant to Smith Kline Biologicals SA, a pharmaceuticals undertaking based at Rixensant.

[139] See also Dec. 89/305 ([1989] OJ L123/53) concerning aid from the French Government to an undertaking in the motor vehicle sector—Peugeot SA

[140] Dec. 91/254 ([1991] OJ L123/46) concerning the proposal by the Brussels Regional Authorities (Belgium) to provide aid in favour of Volkswagen Brussels SA.

[141] Dec. 87/16 ([1987] OJ L12/27) on a proposal by the Italian Government to grant aid to a firm in the chemical industry (producing industrial auxiliaries, intermediaries, and pesticides).

[142] *Twelfth Report on Competition Policy* (EC Commission, Brussels, 1983), 130.

electronic memories factory, which was of great importance for the future development of the Union electronics industry,[143] was authorized. Similarly, aid to the aircraft industry[144] and data processing[145] may be authorized because of the strategic concern to maintain or restore the international competitiveness of Union industry in these sectors.[146] At the same time, as in the case of data processing, the effects of aid to data processors of one Member State on other Union producers are likely to be relatively small, because competition is mainly with producers from third states.[147]

Aid may also be authorized simply because of the 'poor performance' of the industry concerned[148] or because, as in the case of biotechnology, the Union is 'significantly lagging behind'.[149] However, aid which would do no more than help the electronics industry through a difficult period was prohibited,[150] and the Commission may take care to ensure that aid recipients undertake real restructuring.[151]

Operating Aid

Aid to research and development should not become the equivalent of operating aid. For example, Decision 89/254[152] concerned a Belgian plan to aid an oil refinery at Ottignies/Louvain-la-Neuve. The aid was not intended to finance well-defined research and development projects but, rather, mainly the acquisition of the site and building costs of a laboratory.[153] Moreover, the area concerned was not included in the special regional aid zones previously accepted by the Commission. Hence, the aid was prohibited.

Similarly, aid to the costs of employing existing research and development staff is objectionable,[154] unless calculated as a sum of the total amount needed

---

[143] *Seventeenth Report on Competition Policy* (EC Commission, Brussels, 1988), 171.

[144] *First Report on Competition Policy* (EC Commission, Brussels, 1972), 138. GATT requirements and the need to reach agreement with the US have affected Commission practice in this sector. See, e.g., the *Financial Times*, 2 Apr. 1992.

[145] *Second Report on Competition Policy* (EC Commission, Brussels, 1973), 93, and *Sixth Report on Competition Policy* (EC Commission, Brussels, 1977), 120–2.

[146] *Eighth Report on Competition Policy* (EC Commission, Brussels, 1979), 126.

[147] *Sixth Report on Competition Policy* (EC Commission, Brussels, 1977), 121. Such reasoning may also take into account regional considerations. See, regarding aid for a micro-electronics plant in Saxony, Bull. EU 4–1994, 1.2.52.

[148] Bull. EC 12–1977, 2.1.60.

[149] Notice C46/89 ([1990] OJ C229/2) concerning aid which Belgium had decided to grant to Smith Kline Biologicals SA, a pharmaceuticals undertaking based at Rixensant.

[150] Bull. EC 6–1982, 2.1.47.

[151] See, regarding French aid to microelectronics, the *Thirteenth Report on Competition Policy* (EC Commission, Brussels, 1984), 168, and, regarding Italian aid to a consumer electronics firm, the *Fourteenth Report on Competition Policy* (EC Commission, Brussels, 1985), 157.

[152] Relating to aid which the Belgian Government had granted to a petrochemicals company at Ottignies/Louvain-la-Neuve (SA Belgian Shell) ([1989] OJ L106/34).

[153] See also Notice C2/96 (ex N829/95) ([1996] OJ C121/6) concerning the German aid scheme 'Investment programme for the reduction of environmental pollution'.

[154] Notice of a proposed amendment to the German aid scheme for the salaries of R & D staff ([1985] OJ C73/3). Earlier, Dutch aid to the wage costs incurred by undertakings in respect of

to carry out the aided project.[155] Particularly if given for a long period, such aid merely supports current operations rather than encouraging additional efforts.[156] Equipment costs may be aided only in so far as the equipment is used exclusively for research and development,[157] and only those additional overhead costs which are incurred directly as a result of the research and development project being promoted may be aided.[158] Thus aid for renovation is prohibited, even if technological innovation is involved.[159] More particularly, aid for the importation of scientific equipment may be prohibited, where the equipment is used for current production.[160]

Sectoral-policy Considerations

Particular account may be taken of the state of the sector in which research and development aid is granted.[161] Thus a project, though involving use of new production technology, will not be regarded as of 'common European interest' under Article 92(3)(b), where the products concerned 'have to be sold on a saturated market'.[162] Aid may not be authorized, unless it is shown that outlets can be found for the new products.[163] More particularly, in the electronics sector, where the technical characteristics and performance of products are critical, aid for product development may not be authorized.[164] Again, in the aircraft industry the high-technology element of the products, the strong international competition, and the possibility of collaboration in supported

employees engaged in R & D as well as for R & D investments was authorized (Bull. EC 4–1981, 2.1.19), but only for 5 years (*Eleventh Report on Competition Policy* (EC Commission, Brussels, 1982), 172).

[155] Annex II to the 1986 Framework.

[156] *Fifteenth Report on Competition Policy* (EC Commission, Brussels, 1987), 175–6.

[157] Dec. 72/261 ([1972] JO L166/12) on aids for the importation of scientific instruments and advanced technology goods, granted under Italian Law 471 of 14 July 1969.

[158] Annex II to the 1986 Framework. See, e.g., Communic. C46/93 (ex N425/93) ([1994] OJ C71/5) concerning aids which Germany had decided to grant to Georgsmarienhütte Gmbh in Georgsmarienhütte. See also, regarding costs of instruments and equipment, land and buildings, Notice C32/94 (N48/94) ([1994] OJ C293/6) concerning aid for the construction of a rape seed oil methylester pilot plan operated by the Raiffeisen Hauptgenossenschaft Nord AG, Kiel. However, aid for office building in Bremen for scientific and technical staff was authorized because of the high unemployment there and the importance of promoting the aerospace industry. See Bull. EC 7/8–1989, 2.1.81. See also, regarding earlier German aid, the *Ninth Report on Competition Policy* (EC Commission, Brussels, 1980), 122–3.

[159] Dec. 91/305 ([1991] OJ L156/39) concerning investment aid which the Belgian Government planned to grant to Mactac SA, Soignies.

[160] Dec. 72/261 ([1972] OJ L166/12) on aids for the importation of scientific instruments and advanced technology goods, granted under Italian Law 471 of 14 July 1969.

[161] Para. 6 of the 1986 Framework. Cf. regarding the acceptability, in principle, of such aid to the textiles industry, Roemer AG in Case 47/69 *France* v. *EC Commission: aid to textiles* [1970] ECR 487, 500.

[162] Joined Cases 62 & 72/87 *Exécutif Régional Wallon and Glaverbel* v. *EC Commission* [1988] ECR 1573, 1595.

[163] Communic. NN83/90 ([1990] OJ C315/7) concerning aids which Italy had decided to grant to Italgrani SpA.

[164] *Seventh Report on Competition Policy* (EC Commission, Brussels, 1979), 152–3.

research[165] may mean that aid is only authorized where it secures co-ordinated action between European and national research in this sector.[166]

Sectoral Legislation

Express reference to research and development aid may be made in Union legislation[167] regarding aid to particular sectors, notably shipbuilding, coal, and steel.

In the shipbuilding sector an exception from the legislative prohibition of investment aid leading to capacity increases in this sector was introduced by Directive 87/167[168] in favour of research and development aid. Article 8 of Directive 90/684[169] also allowed for aid relating to fundamental research, basic industrial research, and applied research and development, but not for aid related to industrial application and commercial exploitation of the results. Detailed rules regarding authorization conditions and ceilings for such aid in this sector are now laid down by Regulation 3094/95.[170]

In relation to the coal industry, Article 6 of Decision 3632/93[171] allows for authorization of research and development aid, provided that it complies with the Framework. In practice, the Commission may authorize aid thereunder because it contributes to an improvement of mining technology and, hence, to a reduction in production costs.[172]

In the steel industry research and development aid up to 50 per cent of the eligible costs[173] of a project is permitted under Article 7 of Decision 3855/91,[174] provided that the aid has one of the following objectives:

—a reduction in the costs of production (notably energy saving) or an improvement in productivity;

—an improvement in product quality;

—an improvement in the performance of iron and steel products or an increase in the range of uses of steel; or

---

[165] *The European Aircraft Industry: First Assessment and Possible Community Actions*, COM(92) 164, 28.

[166] Council Conclusions of 17 June 1992 ([1992] OJ C178/9) on the European Civil Aviation Industry. See, earlier, the *First Report on Competition Policy* (EC Commission, Brussels, 1972), 138–9.

[167] Cf. in the agricultural sector, Dec. 90/379 ([1990] OJ L186/21) on state aid to SA Sucrérie Couplet, Brunehaut-Wez, Belgium.

[168] On aid to shipbuilding ([1987] OJ L69/59).

[169] On aid to shipbuilding ([1990] OJ L380/27).

[170] On aid to shipbuilding ([1995] OJ L332/1), Art. 4.

[171] Establishing Community rules for aid to the coal industry ([1993] OJ L329/12).

[172] Dec. 95/519 ([1995] OJ L299/18) authorizing France to grant aid to the coal industry for 1995.

[173] Capital expenses may not be eligible. See the *Eleventh Report on Competition Policy* (EC Commission, Brussels, 1982), 136–7.

[174] Establishing Community rules for aid to the steel industry ([1991] OJ L362/57).

—an improvement in working conditions as regards health and safety.[175] The aid must also comply with the Framework.[176]

6.3.2 Ceilings

In principle, the level of aid for basic industrial research[177] should not be more than 50 per cent of the gross costs of the project or programme. A particular problem, which was to be examined according to paragraph 9.2 of the 1986 Framework, arises in measurement of the aid element of government research and development contracts. Aid may be involved, when a commercial undertaking is paid in excess of the market rate for the research and development carried out, use of the results of research and development is restricted contractually to a single business, or only one business is able to derive benefit from them. Hence, it has been argued that the Commission should issue guidelines on the appropriate way to award contracts and requiring notification of those contracts not awarded according to the guidelines.[178]

As the aided activity gets nearer to the market place, that is, as it covers the areas of applied research and development,[179] lower levels of aid will be expected.[180] In the case of applied research, the permissible level depends on the distance from the market but is typically limited to 25 per cent,[181] though exceptions may be made in 'cases of high specific risk'.[182] Aid with a possible intensity of 30 per cent for investments concerning production facilities may be prohibited.[183] A lower ceiling—of 10 per cent—may be imposed on aid for process development.[184] Costs of market introduction of the products concerned may not be supported at all by research and development aid.[185]

---

[175] See, regarding the authorization of German aid for R & D and environmental protection, the *Seventeenth Report on Competition Policy* (EC Commission, Brussels, 1988), 155.

[176] Dec. 95/437 ([1995] OJ L257/37) concerning a German proposal to grant state aid to Georgsmarienhütte GmbH.

[177] Defined in para. 3 of Annex I to the 1986 Framework.

[178] *Aid Element of Government R & D Contracts* (EC Commission, Luxembourg, 1991), 67.

[179] Defined in para. 4 of Annex I to the 1986 Framework.

[180] Para. 5.3 of the 1986 Framework.

[181] Thus the Commission requested Belgium to bring down its level of R & D aid for basic research to 50% and for successful applied research to 25%. See Bull. EC 9–1988, 2.1.51. However, German aid up to 30% for applied research was authorized. See Bull. EC 12–1988, 2.1.122. Where R & D aid is cumulated with regional aid, so that ceilings for the latter are breached, the Commission may object. See Notice ([1987] OJ C183/3) regarding the investment aid allowances which the German Government planned to alter.

[182] Dec. 95/437 ([1995] OJ L257/37) concerning a German proposal to grant state aid to Georgsmarienhütte GmbH.

[183] Notice C19/89 ([1989] OJ C272/5) regarding the German R & D schemes 'Programm Zukunftstechnologien' and 'Technologieprogramm Wissenschaft'.

[184] Summary ([1995] OJ C310/4) of the Commission's dec. not to oppose the R & D, environmental, and training aid which the Austrian Government intended to provide to Opel Austria in support of its expenditure in the Family-O-engine project ([1995] OJ C310/4).

[185] Communic. C46/93 (ex N425/93) ([1994] OJ C71/5) concerning aids which Germany had decided to grant to Georgsmarienhütte GmbH in Georgsmarienhütte.

Aid may have to be reimbursed. For example, research and development aid for aircraft production should be reimbursable from the yield on sales when the aircraft are marketed.[186] Loans entailing aid of 40 per cent (50 per cent, in the case of small and medium-sized enterprises) of the costs of applied research in the event of failure are permissible, provided the loans are repayable in the event of the project being successful, so that the actual aid level does not exceed 25 per cent.[187] In the case of failure, aid up to the same level need not be repaid.[188] The reasoning is that the effect on competition resulting from a failed research and development project is not the same as when there is a successful product on the market.[189]

Higher levels of aid are usually objectionable, particularly where intra-Union competition is 'very intense', as in the case of Italian aid to applied research in pharmaceuticals[190] and Dutch aid for producing new-crop protection agents,[191] or where large undertakings or large programmes are involved.[192] In such circumstances, aid may be treated as adversely affecting trade between Member States to an extent contrary to the common interest.[193] However, higher levels may be authorized under Article 92(3)(b)[194] where the projects are recognized to be of special economic importance,[195] are linked to important Union projects or programmes,[196] involve international co-operation,[197] are related to specific welfare services, imply a very high risk,[198] are located in the

---

[186] R & D costs should be taken to include all expenditure, including expenditure on initial production pooling, occasioned by the implementation of the programmes up to flight worthiness certification (construction of prototypes and texts). See the *Second Report on Competition Policy* (EC Commission, Brussels, 1973), 91. See later Bull. EC 2–1988, 2.1.67.

[187] *Twenty-Third Report on Competition Policy* (EC Commission, Brussels, 1994), 274.

[188] *Eighteenth Report on Competition Policy* (EC Commission, Brussels, 1989), 152.

[189] Communic. C45/94 (NN105/93) ([1995] OJ C63/4) with regard to the aid for the development of the regional aircraft (turbo-prop) CASA-3000 by Construcciones aeronautics SA.

[190] Bull. EC 7/8–1991, 1.2.70.   [191] Bull. EC 5–1988, 2.1.67.

[192] Notice C37/91 (ex N292/91 & N316/91) ([1992] OJ C244/2) regarding aid which France had decided to grant Compagnie des Machines Bull.

[193] Notice C53/91 (N529/91) ([1992] OJ C10/4) regarding aid which Germany had decided to grant in the laser research sector.

[194] See, regarding aid for research concerning the integrated manufacture of computer software, Bull EC 11–1992, 1.3.64.

[195] See, regarding applied research in computer software, which was a national and Union priority, Bull. EC 2–1988, 2.1.67.

[196] See, regarding Italian aid to an undertaking participating in a Eureka project, H. Morch, 'Summary of the Most Important Recent Developments' (1995) 4 *Competition Policy Newsletter* 47–51, 51. See also, regarding an Art. 92(3)(b) authorization of aid to a project within the scope of a Union project in the agricultural area, Communic. C32/94 (N48/94) ([1996] OJ C76/3) concerning the aid for the construction of a rape seed oil methylester pilot plan by the Raiffeisen Hauptgenossenschaft Nord AG, Kiel.

[197] French aid of 35% for applied research involving international co-operation was authorized. See the *Twentieth Report on Competition Policy* (EC Commission, Brussels, 1991), 141.

[198] i.e., a risk which is, in technical terms, higher than that usually involved in R & D projects. See Communic. C46/93 (ex N425/93) ([1994] OJ C71/5) concerning aids which Germany had decided to grant to Georgsmarienhütte GmbH in Georgsmarienhütte. See also, regarding

least-favoured areas of the Union[199] or are 'directed genuinely' at small and medium-sized enterprises. In such cases aid up to 10 per cent higher than in other cases may be authorized.[200]

For example, in the case of small and medium-sized enterprises in the Mezzogiorno, the maximum levels are 60 per cent for basic research and 35 per cent for applied research.[201] In the case of a Spanish aid scheme designed to promote research and development in the less-favoured areas of Spain and to reduce the gap between Spain and the rest of the Union in electronics and data processing, higher levels than usual are permissible in areas benefitting from regional aid.[202] In Portugal aid levels of 65 per cent for basic industrial research and 50 per cent for applied research and development, the latter level being reached only if the project fails,[203] have been authorized. Such practice reflects the 'understanding' by the Commission that Member States may want to promote projects of regional interest with other types of aid than traditional investment aid.[204] However, even in Article 92(3)(a) regions, such higher levels of aid may be objectionable because of overcapacity in the sector concerned.[205]

Considerations relating to other horizontal policies may be influential. For example, Dutch aid of 40 per cent was accepted for applied research into wind turbines and their installation, because wind energy was very attractive as an alternative, renewable, and environmentally acceptable energy source.[206] In addition, the research risks were high, and the recipients were small compared to other undertakings in the energy sector.[207] Again, in accordance with Union

German aid to aerospace R & D, the *Twenty-Second Report on Competition Policy* (EC Commission, Brussels, 1993), 217.

[199] Additional regional aid may be objectionable. See Bull. EU 9–1994, 1.2.59.

[200] Para. 5.4 of the 1986 Framework. See, e.g., Notice (N184/91) ([1991] OJ C244/4) concerning an Italian proposal to grant aid to Sigma-Tau Industrie Farmaceutiche Riunite SpA. See, in the case of Northern Ireland, the *Twenty-First Report on Competition Policy* (EC Commission, Brussels, 1992), 176. However, the Commission objected to aid for applied research of up to 50% in the new *Länder*. See Bull. EC 1/2–1992, 1.3.94.

[201] Dec. 93/254 ([1993] OJ L117/22) on Italian Decree–Law 14 of 21 Jan. 1992 relating, *inter alia*, to the overall refinancing of the aid measures provided for by Law 64 of 1 Mar. 1986 on special aid to the Mezzogiorno. Italian aid of 70% in exceptional cases had previously been authorized, though prior notification was required for investments of more than 10,000 million lire and for aid grants of over 55%. See the *Thirteenth Report on Competition Policy* (EC Commission, Brussels, 1984), 147–8 and the *Fifteenth Report on Competition Policy* (EC Commission, Brussels, 1986), 177. See, regarding R & D aid in the former GDR, the *Twenty-First Report on Competition Policy* (EC Commission, Brussels, 1992), 155.

[202] *Eighteenth Report on Competition Policy* (EC Commission, Brussels, 1989), 154.

[203] *Twentieth Report on Competition Policy* (EC Commission, Brussels, 1991), 143.

[204] Communic. C24/89 (ex NN18/89) ([1990] OJ C280/6) concerning aid awarded by the Dutch authorities to their regional programmes.

[205] Notice C45/94 (NN105/93) ([1995] OJ C63/4) with regard to the aid for the development of the regional aircraft (turbo-prop) CASA-3000 by Construcciones aeronautics SA.

[206] Aid to investment in renewable energy as well as aid for energy conservation is treated in the same way as environmental aid. See the Community Guidelines on state aid for environmental purposes ([1994] OJ C72/3), para. 2.3.

[207] *Sixteenth Report on Competition Policy* (EC Commission, Brussels, 1987), 170–1. See also, regarding operating aid for Danish windmills, *Europe* 5828 (3 Oct. 1992), and the Communic.

policy for small and medium-sized enterprises, Belgium was authorized to grant aid up to 10 per cent above the usual ceilings to independent undertakings with fewer than 200 employees and a turnover of less than ECU 15 million, if the assisted project accounted for more than half of the undertaking's annual expenditure on research and development or if the project was expressly linked to a current Union programme.[208]

6.3.3 1995 Framework

The 1995 Framework relaxes restrictions on research and development aid to take account of the importance attached to such activity and the rules contained in the Agreement on Subsidies and Countervailing Measures annexed to the Agreement establishing the World Trade Organization.

The new Framework distinguishes between 'industrial research' and 'pre-competitive development activity'. To determine whether aid provides an incentive to research and development, the Commission will look at quantitative factors, such as the number of persons employed in research and development. The Commission may presume that, in respect of research and development aid to small and medium-sized enterprises, the incentive effect exists. The Commission will be more demanding where aid is for large firms carrying out close-to-the-market research and where a significant proportion of the research and development expenditure for a given project has been made prior to the application for aid.

Ceilings will generally be 50 per cent for industrial research and 25 per cent for pre-competitive development.[209] These ceilings may be raised in the common interest: 10 per cent extra may be granted to small and medium-sized enterprises; 5 or 10 per cent extra in areas eligible for regional aid; 15 per cent extra for a project which is a priority under a Union research and development programme; and 10 per cent extra for crossborder co-operation between independent undertakings, co-operation between undertakings and universities, or when the results and industrial property rights of the project are widely disseminated. In such circumstances, or where a firm located outside the Union has received aid of such an intensity, an overall ceiling of 75 per cent for industrial research and 50 per cent for pre-competitive development activity applies. Small and medium-sized enterprises may receive aid up to the same levels for patent applications and renewals. These ceilings also apply in respect

concerning aid which Italy had decided to grant by means of the R & D scheme relating to alternative sources of energy ([1990] OJ C237/13).

[208] *Twentieth Report on Competition Policy* (EC Commission, Brussels, 1981), 138–9.

[209] See, regarding demonstration projects, Notice C2/96 (ex N829/95) ([1996] OJ C121/6) concerning the German aid scheme 'Investment programme for the reduction of environmental pollution'.

of cumulation of Union and Member State aid for the same project and in respect of projects of common European interest.[210]

6.4 SMALL AND MEDIUM-SIZED ENTERPRISES

Aid to small and medium-sized enterprises may be authorized under Article 92(3)(c),[211] Article 92(3)(a),[212] or, as aid to remedy a serious disturbance, Article 92(3)(b).[213]

The rationale for authorizing such aid may be that financial structures are regarded as ill-suited to the launching of new developments by small and medium-sized enterprises, even though such enterprises have an important role to play in the economy.[214] Moreover, completion of the internal market might, it was felt, necessitate increased support for such enterprises, which might be too small to benefit from the economies of scale expected to result for their larger competitors.[215]

Accordingly, aid to small and medium-sized enterprises may be regarded as conducive to competition,[216] or at least to improving the competitive structure of Union markets, and 'positive action' in the form of such aid may be favoured.[217] Thus the Commission does not require aid for restructuring of such enterprises to meet the same strict conditions, regarding for example capacity reductions and reporting obligations, as aid for restructuring large firms.[218]

Cyclical economic problems may add to the perceived desirability of aid to small and medium-sized enterprises. In the case of Italian aid to such enterprises, the Commission considered that they faced structural difficulties, which had become harder to cope with since the business slowdown at the end of 1970, and an increase in wage costs, which in some cases had proved hard to finance. These factors made the necessary restructuring more difficult to carry out (from the financing point of view) at a time when certain strains were already discouraging firms from embarking on new capital ventures. Without

---

[210] H. Morch, 'Summary of the Most Important Recent Developments' (1995) 6 *Competition Policy Newsletter* 41–7, 41–3.

[211] See, regarding Danish aid to SMEs for restructuring and development, Bull. EC 7/8–1976, 2128.

[212] See, in the case of aid to SMEs in Sicily, Bull. EC 2–1970, 65.

[213] *Second Report on Competition Policy* (EC Commission, Brussels, 1973), 106.

[214] Hence, German aid to a company to provide financial and management assistance to SMEs was authorized. See the *Fourth Report on Competition Policy* (EC Commission, Brussels, 1976), 99–100.

[215] Cf. *Public Procurement: Regional and Social Aspects*, COM(89)400 and, more particularly, *Promoting SME Participation in Public Procurement in the Community*, COM(90)166.

[216] *Seventeenth Report on Competition Policy* (EC Commission, Brussels, 1988), 29.

[217] *Twenty-First Report on Competition Policy* (EC Commission, Brussels, 1992), 165.

[218] Community guidelines on state aid for rescuing and restructuring firms in difficulty ([1994] OJ C368/12), para. 3.2.4.

aid to help them restructure, the enterprises concerned might have been forced to scale down operations or even, in some cases, to close down altogether; this would have been bound to worsen an economic and social climate which was already unfavourable. Hence, such aid was authorized for one year to remedy a serious disturbance under Article 92(3)(b).[219]

Such practice assumes that the effects of aid to small and medium-sized enterprises on competition are limited. According to the Commission, it is a positive trend that Member States are tending to allocate their budgets to aid schemes that are both less harmful to competition and more likely to strengthen the general efficiency and competitiveness of the Union economy. In the forefront of such schemes are those to improve the general business environment, particularly for small and medium-sized enterprises, through the use of specialized consultants, training, the dissemination of advanced technology, and the improvement of production and management methods.[220]

For example, a Sicilian aid scheme concerned mineral deposits in quarries. The object of the scheme was to solve the problem of tipping quarry waste with the help of local authorities and to encourage its use as inert filling material. The scheme was intended for very small firms which would be enabled to restore the landscape spoilt by the quarries. Given that the market for the materials was almost entirely local, that the danger of intra-Union competition being affected was remote, and that the aim of restoring the land accorded with the Union's environmental policy, the Commission authorized the scheme under Article 92(3)(c).[221]

Ideas of competitive structures and market failure, particularly in the financial market, underlie such practice. Little apparent consideration is given to the possibility that their size may, sometimes at least, render small and medium-sized enterprises inefficient and, hence, that to grant them aid may be an inefficient use of the resources involved.[222] In other words, the difficulties of small and medium-sized enterprises may often reflect the 'normal' working of the market rather than its failure.

---

[219] *Second Report on Competition Policy* (EC Commission, Brussels, 1973), 106.

[220] The favourable view the Commission takes of such aid is in line with similar action undertaken at Union level. See Dec. 89/490 ([1989] OJ L239/33) on the improvement of the business environment and the promotion of the development of enterprises, and in particular SMEs in the Community. See also the *Twentieth Report on Competition Policy* (EC Commission, Brussels, 1991), 177. In the fisheries sector see para. 2.1.4 of the Guidelines for the examination of state aid to fisheries and aquaculture ([1994] OJ C260/3).

[221] *Twentieth Report on Competition Policy* (EC Commission, Brussels, 1991), 171; Communic. ([1972] JO C120/24) on the reduction of social charges in favour of craft undertakings, small and medium-sized enterprises, and textile undertakings, though the Commission objected to this operating aid in the textiles sector.

[222] Note also the argument that the contribution of an SME to growth depends on the sector in which it operates in D. Schina, *State Aids under the EEC Treaty* (ESC, Oxford, 1987), 94.

6.4.1 1976 Guidelines

Difficulties faced by small and medium-sized enterprises were noted in a Commission memorandum of 1970,[223] and aid guidelines were produced in 1976.[224] Aid for such enterprises was seen in these guidelines as a means of assisting them to overcome their 'peculiar difficulties'. These difficulties, which might be exaggerated in the less developed regions of the Union,[225] were treated as including: limited access to markets for financial capital; small size not justified by economic need; greater difficulty adapting to technological, industrial, and commercial developments; lack of information needed to extend operations to the Union scale and beyond.[226] Aid to overcome such difficulties generally was seen as having little effect on competition, though it was not to be of a conservatory nature.

An all-purpose definition of small and medium-sized enterprises applicable to all Member States, all industries, and all their problems was considered impossible at the time. The concept of a small and medium-sized enterprise was so variable that the question whether an aid scheme concerned this type of enterprise could only be assessed in each individual case in a pragmatic fashion.[227] Thus, for example, the Commission might seek information about the definition employed for the purposes of a given aid scheme.[228]

Where aid was found to concern such enterprises, it might be permissible in the form of:

—loans at preferential rates or guarantees providing credits for investments similar to those obtained by larger enterprises;
—establishment of specialized agencies by public authorities to provide capital in the form of temporary shareholdings;
—research and development incentives in the form of grants and

---

[223] *Memorandum on Industrial Policy in the European Community*, COM(70)100. See also the Communic. on the notification on aids of minor importance (SG(85)D/2611). See, more generally, *Integrated Programme in Favour of SMEs and the Craft Sector*, COM(94)207.

[224] *Sixth Report on Competition Policy* (EC Commission, Brussels, 1977), 133–4.

[225] *Fourth Periodic Report on the Social and Economic Situation and Development of the Regions of the Community*, COM(90)609, 34.

[226] Aid is regarded as more appropriate than tariff protection in such cases. See, e.g., R.E. Baldwin, 'The Case Against Infant-Industry Tariff Protection' (1969) 77 *Journal of Political Economy* 295–305.

[227] See, e.g., Notice C52/89 (ex NN4/89) ([1991] OJ C266/3) concerning aid which Italy decided to establish under the Sicilian Regional Law on aid for industrial development; and Notice NN71/89 ([1991] OJ C266/4) concerning interest subsidies Italy had decided to grant to small and medium-sized industrial and commercial enterprises. See also the *Sixth Report on Competition Policy* (EC Commission, Brussels, 1977), 131–5; *Eighth Report on Competition Policy* (EC Commission, Brussels, 1979), 163–4 and 170; and *Eleventh Report on Competition Policy* (EC Commission, Brussels, 1982), 155 and 170–1.

[228] Notice C19/89 ([1989] OJ C272/5) regarding the German R & D schemes 'Programm Zukunftstechnologien' and 'Technologieprogramm Wissenschaft'.

establishment of technology centres to carry out research work which
they could not do alone;[229] or

—technical assistance with commercial or management policies (market
surveys) and financial incentives to encourage the use of modern
equipment (data processing equipment).[230]

Union Interventions

The acceptability of aid to small and medium-sized enterprises might be
affected by Union interventions. For example, within the framework of the Star
Programme,[231] Portugal provided aid to help such enterprises to obtain access
to telecommunications services and to assist the creation of undertakings
producing telecommunications equipment and of telecommunications centres
in Portugal. Considering the contribution of the aid to the development of the
least favoured regions of the Union, the Commission authorized the aid under
Article 92(3)(a).[232]

Regional-policy Considerations

Regional-policy considerations might be important in the treatment of aid to
small and medium-sized enterprises. For example, the Commission authorized
an Irish scheme for such enterprises which envisaged aid for outside consultancy help and related services, recruitment and training aid, equity stakes by
public authorities, research and development aid, and special terms for the sale
or rental of industrial land or buildings. In authorizing this scheme, the
Commission took account of the difficult economic and social situation in
Ireland, which was characterized by below-average living-standards and severe
unemployment levels. An assurance was secured from the Irish authorities that
implementation of the scheme would entail no discrimination between Irish
firms and those from other Member States. The Irish authorities were also
requested to provide annual reports on the scheme so as to maintain transparency.[233]

More questionably, regional-policy considerations might be taken to favour
aid to 'low tech' activities by small and medium-sized enterprises. For example,
in connection with an Irish scheme to assist undertakings in the Inner City
area of Dublin which employed fewer than 100 persons, the Commission
accepted that the area was suffering from multidimensional deprivations: high
unemployment, low incomes, poor housing, derelict sites and buildings, high

---

[229] See, earlier, regarding German aid for the launching of new products or new technologies
by SMEs, Bull. EC 6–1974, 2121.

[230] *Sixth Report on Competition Policy* (EC Commission, Brussels, 1977), 133–4.

[231] Reg. 3300/86 ([1986] OJ L305/1) instituting a Community programme for the development of certain less-favoured regions of the Community by improving access to advanced
telecommunications services.

[232] *Eighteenth Report on Competition Policy* (EC Commission, Brussels, 1989), 183.

[233] *Twentieth Report on Competition Policy* (EC Commission, Brussels, 1991), 188–9.

levels of vehicular traffic, vandalism, and crime. The high rate of unemployment was mainly due to the inability of residents to compete, because of the low level of their educational attainment, for the skilled and specialized jobs available in Dublin. The scheme was authorized in the hope that it would encourage the provision of less-skilled jobs through increased investment by small and medium-sized enterprises.[234]

Aid to craft firms might be particularly favoured. For example, the Commission authorized a scheme to improve such firms in Sardinia. The scheme had a total annual budget of approximately ECU 25 million. The maximum grant payable to an individual craft firm was about ECU 46,000, with an estimated aid intensity of 18.9 per cent and cumulation with other regional aids possible up to 33.2 per cent. The Commission, which encouraged national and regional schemes to assist craft firms and promote co-operation and partnership, especially in the more disadvantaged parts of the Union, authorized the scheme under Article 92(3)(c).[235]

Similarly, an Italian scheme for the Mezzogiorno, which gave priority, *inter alia*, to co-operatives or companies established to develop local resources and involving craft industries was authorized.[236] Also acceptable was Sicilian aid to help craft firms to adjust to technological change, to give them easier access to credit and to facilitate the setting up of new firms or associations of firms,[237] as was aid for small and medium-sized enterprises and craft firms in Sicilian sulphur-mining areas at levels above the ceiling for the Mezzogiorno.[238] Even operating aid was authorized in the case of aid to help finance stocks of raw materials and finished products held by small and medium-sized enterprises in Sicily.[239]

However, the Commission considered the implications of such aid on a case-by-case basis, to ensure that the aid was in the common interest and did not conflict with the unity of the common market.[240] An otherwise objectionable scheme would not be rendered permissible simply because it was characterized as being targeted to small and medium-sized enterprises.[241] For example, in the case of a proposed scheme for the Mezzogiorno, the Italian

[234] *Twelfth Report on Competition Policy* (EC Commission, Brussels, 1983), 145–6.

[235] *Ibid.*, 178.

[236] Bull. EC 7/8–1986, 2.1.69.

[237] Bull. EC 6–1986, 2.1.89.

[238] Bull. EC 7/8–1984, 2.1.65.

[239] Bull. EC 1/2–1990, 1.1.79. See, similarly, the *Fifteenth Report on Competition Policy* (EC Commission, Brussels, 1985), 186–7; Notice regarding aid planned by the French Government for the Nord-Pas-de Calais region ([1986] OJ C136/2); and Dec. 94/374 ([1994] OJ L170/36) on Sicilian Regional Law 23/1991 concerning extraordinary assistance for industry and Art. 5 of Sicilian Law 8/1991 concerning, in particular, the financing of Sitas. See also the Report of the Committee on Regional Policy and Regional Planning on the effects of Arts 92 and 93 EC on regional policy, EP Doc. A2–114/87, 7.

[240] *Twelfth Report on Competition Policy* (EC Commission, Brussels, 1983), 110–2.

[241] Such aid must not be used to promote exports to other Member States. See the *Eighth Report on Competition Policy* (EC Commission, Brussels, 1979), 170.

authorities had argued that the industrial base of the area consisted mainly of such enterprises in mature industries which were vulnerable to foreign competition. Without the proposed aid the process of replacing obsolete activities and introducing technological innovation and new industry would come to a halt. The Commission, however, noted that the economy of the Centre-North had such a structure. There decentralization and a swing away from vertical integration had produced a new pattern of industry based on smaller units.[242] In other words, the aid was considered unnecessary, because market forces seemed capable of preserving a place for such undertakings. The same approach was adopted in evaluation of aid to replacement investment by small and medium-sized enterprises[243] and of operating aid to such enterprises in the agricultural[244] and textiles sectors.[245]

Again, a Dutch Government scheme assisted small and medium-sized enterprises in certain regions to carry out projects in industry, tourism, agriculture, and services. These projects were partly for demonstration purposes and concerned infrastructure, particularly education and research. Nevertheless, the Commission raised objections.[246]

A Belgian aid scheme involved the establishment of special employment zones. These zones, of limited size and in areas of high structural unemployment, effectively combined aid for high technology and aid for small and medium-sized enterprises. However, the intensity of the aid, the size of the recipients, the open-ended availability of the aid, and the danger to competition for mobile investment projects were such that the Commission required substantial modifications to the scheme before authorizing it.[247]

Sectoral-policy Considerations

Aid to small and medium-sized enterprises in 'sensitive' sectors was generally opposed.[248] Thus in authorizing a Bavarian scheme to provide soft loans to small and medium-sized enterprises, the Commission checked that the aid was

---

[242] Dec. 88/318 ([1988] OJ L143/37) on Law 64 of 1 Mar. 1986 on aid to the Mezzogiorno.

[243] Notice ([1986] OJ C205/3) regarding the regional aid and one general aid scheme of Bavaria.

[244] Notice ([1985] OJ C252/3) concerning the aid measures proposed by Hessen to encourage the exploitation of pasture and to guarantee employment in small and medium-sized farms.

[245] Notice ([1984] OJ C187/4) regarding a proposal by the UK Government to assist the clothing, footwear, knitting, and textile industries by means of a scheme the declared aim of which was to enable SMEs to undertake investment in advanced technology equipment, where the Commission objected to the aid because of the aid framework for this sector, the lack of sufficiently defined general objectives and the danger of increased overall capacities.

[246] Notice C24/89 ([1989] OJ C309/2) regarding aid granted by the Netherlands Government to regional programmes; *Nineteenth Report on Competition Policy* (EC Commission, Brussels, 1990), 178.

[247] *Twelfth Report on Competition Policy* (EC Commission, Brussels, 1983), 111–2 and the *Thirteenth Report on Competition Policy* (EC Commission, Brussels, 1984), 174.

[248] Bull. EC 4–1986, 2.1.51. In Notice ([1988] OJ C124/5) regarding aid which the Italian Government planned to grant to small and medium-sized shipyards aid was considered objectionable because of the absence of a satisfactory restructuring plan for the recipients.

not for replacement investment and was not available in such sectors.[249] Again, in the case of Belgian job-creation aid to small and medium-sized enterprises, the Commission checked on the industry breakdown of the aid to prevent any concentration of aid on industries 'under pressure' throughout the Union.[250]

More particularly, in the case of aid to a sugar producer, the Commission considered in Decision 90/379[251] that the fact that the recipient undertaking was small and that the process it would be using was technologically new and advanced could not alter the opposition to investment aids in this sector which had been maintained since the Commission letter to Member States of 1 February 1972.[252] This approach was stricter than that in Decision 86/498,[253] when restructuring aid was authorized within a programme under Regulation 355/77.[254]

Such practice might accommodate compromises, in the form of aid authorizations subject to strict conditions. For example, Italian rescue aid to small and medium-sized enterprises was acceptable, if it was granted within the framework of suitable reorganization, modernization, or conversion programmes designed to ensure the rationalization of the recipients.[255] Again, British aid to innovation by small and medium-sized enterprises was authorized on condition that a restrictive definition of the concept of innovation was introduced, with overriding priority being given to a specific list of new products and technologies.[256]

6.4.2 1992 Guidelines

The 1992 Guidelines[257] are more detailed than those of 1976. The new Guidelines establish definitions of small enterprises and medium-sized enterprises. In order to ensure that the treatment of enterprises is based on common rules, whether national or Union aid is involved,[258] these definitions have been

---

[249] Bull. EC 3-1987, 2.1.72.

[250] *Eighth Report on Competition Policy* (EC Commission, Brussels, 1979), 168. Cf. Dec. 85/305 ([1985] OJ L155/55) on the UK's proposal to assist sections of the clothing, footwear, knitting and textile industries.

[251] On state aid to SA Sucrérie Couplet, Brunehaut-Wez, Belgium ([1990] OJ L186/21).

[252] No. 936/VI/72.

[253] On aid to Italian sugar producers ([1986] OJ L291/42).

[254] On common measures to improve the conditions under which agricultural products are processed and marketed ([1977] OJ L51/1).

[255] *Third Report on Competition Policy* (EC Commission, Brussels, 1974), 96–7.

[256] *Thirteenth Report on Competition Policy* (EC Commission, Brussels, 1984), 148–9.

[257] Community guidelines on state aid for small and medium-sized enterprises (SMEs) ([1992] OJ C213/2).

[258] The definition of an SME used by the European Investment Bank was an independent undertaking with fewer than 500 employees and fixed assets (net of depreciation) of less than ECU 75 million. See P. Aitken, 'SMEs, Research and Development and Technology Policies and the European Community: Issues in Implementation' in K. Dyson (ed.), *Local Authorities and New Technologies: The European Dimension* (Croom Helm, London, 1988) 59–83, 59. However, the Commission objects to national aid schemes which rely on a less strict definition of small

modified in accordance with definitions to be applied to both kinds of aid.[259] A medium-sized enterprise is now defined as an enterprise which

—has no more than 250 employees

and

—has an annual turnover not exceeding ECU 40 million or
—has a balance sheet total not exceeding ECU 27 million

and

—is not more than 25 per cent owned by one or more companies not falling within this definition, except public investment corporations, venture capital companies, or, provided no control is exercised, institutional investors.

A small enterprise is one which

—has no more than fifty employees

and

—has an annual turnover not exceeding ECU 7 million or
—has a balance sheet total not exceeding ECU 5 million

and

—is not more than 25 per cent owned by one or more companies not falling within this definition, except public investment corporations, venture capital companies, or, provided no control is exercised, institutional investors.[260]

Authorization Conditions

Besides aid that can be treated as *de minimis* and thus falling outside Article 92(1),[261] the Guidelines provide that aid for small and medium-sized enterprises up to certain intensities is generally eligible for authorization under Article 92(3)(c).[262] According to the Guidelines, there can be no doubt that aid for such enterprises facilitates the development of certain economic activities or of certain economic areas, though the nature and intensity of the aid must

enterprises than that in the Guidelines. See Notice C40/92 (ex NN132/92 & N300/92) ([1993] OJ C74/9) concerning Law 317 of 5 Oct. 1991 on aid for SMEs. It is now envisaged that a common definition will apply. See Rec. 96/280 ([1996] OJ L107/4) concerning the definition of small and medium-sized enterprises.

[259] Rec. 96/280 ([1996] OJ L107/4) concerning the definition of small and medium-sized enterprises.

[260] Para. 2.2 of the 1992 Guidelines and Art. 1 of the Annex to Rec. 96/280. For most purposes, the two categories of companies, which are termed SMEs, are treated alike, though the distinction between the two categories has some significance in relation to general investment aid. See para. 4.1 (*ibid.*). According to Art. 1(5) of the Annex, 'micro-enterprises are those having fewer than 10 employees. Craft enterprises "continue to be defined at national level" due to their specific characteristics' (28th recital in the Preamble to the Recommendation).

[261] See sect. 2.3.4 above.

[262] Para. 3.4 of the 1992 Guidelines.

not be such as to affect trading conditions to an extent contrary to the common interest.[263] In particular, soft aid related to the development of export markets, such as aid for consultancy and market research, provided the aid is a one-off operation and limited to the entry into new markets, may be authorized, as may aid for participation in trade fairs.[264] Such aid may be authorized, even if exports are aided.[265]

However, authorization of aid to small and medium-sized enterprises is far from automatic, and a circumspect approach to authorization of such aid has some support in the Court of Justice. According to Advocate General Jacobs in *Italy* v. *EC Commission*,[266] which concerned Italian aid to the Mezzogiorno, the Commission is entitled to adopt a relatively benign attitude towards aid which benefits small and medium-sized enterprises, but that does not mean that it must systematically approve schemes giving preferential treatment to such enterprises. It is equally entitled, in the exercise of its discretion, to consider that general schemes available to all undertakings are sufficiently generous and that there is no justification for granting even greater sums of aid to small and medium-sized enterprises. This view was followed by the Court itself.[267]

More particularly, in certain sectors, currently steel, shipbuilding, synthetic fibres, and motor vehicles, stricter principles than those in the Guidelines for aid to small and medium-sized enterprises apply.[268] Thus the fact that aid to an enterprise within one of these sectors may comply with the latter Guidelines will not necessarily mean that such aid will be authorized. For example, Belgian aid to a textile producer meeting the above definition of a small enterprise was objectionable because it was contrary to the principles governing aid to the textiles industry. The reasoning of the Commission was that aid contrary to the latter principles affected trade to an extent contrary to the common interest.[269]

Ceilings

The Guidelines impose ceilings, apparently designed to bring aid levels below those previously authorized.[270] In areas eligible for national regional aid the

---

[263] Cf. AG Mancini in Case C–259/85 *France* v. *EC Commission: aid to textiles and clothing* [1987] ECR 4393, 4409.

[264] H. Morch, 'Summary of the Most Important Recent Developments' (1995) 6 *Competition Policy Newsletter* 41–7, 43.

[265] See, regarding aid to SMEs in the former GDR, H. Morch, 'Summary of the Most Important Recent Developments' [1995] 4 *Competition Policy Newsletter* 47–51, 49.

[266] Case C–364/90 [1993] ECR I–2097, I–2115–6.

[267] *Ibid.* I–2126.

[268] Para. 1.6 of the 1992 Guidelines. See, e.g., Dec. 93/193 ([1993] OJ L85/22) on the aid granted for the creation of industrial enterprises in Modane, Savoy (France).

[269] Notice C22/94 (N53/94) ([1994] OJ C201/2) regarding the Belgian Government's proposal to award aid to BUBA DS Profil, Vlaanderen. See also Dec. 93/508 ([1993] OJ L238/38) concerning aid decided by the Italian Government in favour of the ceramics industry of Lazio.

[270] F. Rawlinson, 'The Role of Policy Frameworks, Codes and Guidelines in the Control of State Aid' in I. Harden (ed.), *State Aid: Community Law and Policy* (Bundesanzeiger, Trier, 1993), 52–60, 57.

ceiling fixed by the Commission for such aid applies to medium-sized enterprises. Small enterprises may receive an extra 10 per cent gross of investment aid[271] in Article 92(3)(c) areas and an extra 15 per cent in Article 92(3)(a) areas, though 'overall' ceilings of 30 per cent in the former areas and 75 per cent in the latter areas cannot be exceeded.[272]

In areas which are not eligible for national regional aid but are covered by Objective 2 of the Structural Funds, that is, converting regions seriously affected by industrial decline,[273] or Objective 5b, that is, facilitating the development and structural adjustment of rural areas,[274] the ceilings are 10 per cent and 20 per cent for medium-sized and small enterprises respectively.[275] In areas which are neither eligible for national regional aid nor covered by these Objectives general investment aid must be limited to 7.5 per cent for medium-sized enterprises and 15 per cent for small enterprises. These low levels may not only ensure that the aid does not have a perceptible impact on trade and competition between Member States[276] but are also designed to avoid frustration of the cohesion objective.[277] However, particularly because aid to small and medium-sized enterprises tends to be a greater proportion of total aid in the more developed Member States than the less developed ones, differentiation in favour of the latter may not, in practice, be secured.[278]

In the case of help and advice by outside consultants or training provided to newly established small and medium-sized enterprises and their staff, in management, financial matters, new technology (especially information technology), pollution control, protection of intellectual property rights, or similar fields, or assessment of the feasibility of new ventures, aid of up to 50 per cent is generally authorized. Each aid scheme will be judged on its merits, with particular reference to the distance of the activity from the market place, any cash limits on the aid per firm, possibilities of cumulation, and other relevant

[271] These figures are a percentage of the nominal (before-tax) value of grants and the discounted before-tax value of interest subsidies as a proportion of the investment cost.

[272] Para. 4.1 of the 1992 Guidelines. See, regarding the Mezzogiorno, Dec. 93/254 ([1993] OJ L117/22) on Italian Decree–Law 14 of 21 Jan. 1992 relating, *inter alia*, to the overall refinancing of the aid measures provided for by Law 64 of 1 Mar. 1986 on special aid to the Mezzogiorno.

[273] Art. 1.2 of Reg. 2052/88 on the tasks of the Structural Funds and their effectiveness and on co-ordination of their activities between themselves and with the operations of the European Investment Bank and the other existing financial instruments, as amended by Reg. 2081/93 ([1993] OJ L193/5).

[274] *Ibid.*, Art. 1.5.

[275] Notice C40/92 (NN132/92 & N300/92) ([1993] OJ C190/3) on Law 317 of 5 Oct. 1991 on aid for SMEs; and Dec. 93/508 ([1993] OJ L238/38) concerning aid decided by the Italian Government in favour of the ceramics industry of Lazio.

[276] Notice C31/92 (N454/91) ([1992] OJ C324/3) concerning aid granted by Italy for the reconstruction of the Valtellina.

[277] Para. 4.1 of the 1992 Guidelines. However, higher levels of R & D aid for SMEs are permitted. See sect. 6.3.2 above. A similar arrangement is entailed by the new environmental aid guidelines. See sect. 6.5.4 below.

[278] A. Marques, 'Community Competition Policy and Economic and Social Cohesion' (1992) *Regional Studies* 404–7, 406.

factors. In certain exceptional circumstances aid of more than 50 per cent may be authorized. Aid for general information campaigns in particular can be assisted up to a higher level, as the financial benefit to individual enterprises is relatively small.[279]

6.5 ENVIRONMENTAL PROTECTION

Article 2 of the EC Treaty establishes as a Union objective 'growth respecting the environment'. More particularly, Article 130r(1) of the Treaty provides that Union environmental policy shall contribute to preserving, protecting, and improving the quality of the environment. According to Article 130r(2), the policy is to be based on the precautionary principle and on the principles that preventive action should be taken,[280] that environmental damage should as a priority be rectified at source, and that the polluter should pay. This last principle means that 'the cost of measures required to reduce nuisances and pollution to an acceptable level should be borne by the firms whose activities are responsible for them'[281] or that those 'who are responsible for pollution must pay the costs of such measures as are necessary to eliminate that pollution or to reduce it so as to comply with the standards or equivalent measures' applicable.[282] The requirements entailed by these principles must, according to the same provision, be integrated into the definition and implementation of other Union policies. Article 92(3)(b) may be seen as offering a basis for their integration into competition policy. Certainly, according to the Court of Justice, 'concerted action by a number of Member States to combat a common threat such as environmental pollution' may justify the authorization of aid under this provision.[283]

6.5.1 Early Commission Practice

Early Commission practice seems to have been unsympathetic to aid allegedly favouring environmental objectives. For example, in 1964 the Commission

---

[279] Para. 4.3 of the 1992 Guidelines.

[280] Taxation of the polluter is often preferred to aid as a means of tackling the negative externalities involved. See *The Effect of Different State Aid Measures on Intra-Community Competition* (EC Commission, Brussels, 1990), 103.

[281] *Fourth Report on Competition Policy* (EC Commission, Brussels, 1975), 101.

[282] Para. 2 of Rec. 75/436 ([1975] OJ L194/1) regarding cost allocation and action by public authorities on environmental matters. An even more effective principle might be that the 'user of the resource pays'. See the Opinion of the Committee on the Environment, Public Health and Consumer Protection on the proposal for a Community Programme of Policy and Action in relation to the Environment and Sustainable Development, EP Doc. A3–0317/92, 28.

[283] Joined Cases 62 & 72/87 *Exécutif Régional Wallon and Glaverbel* v. *EC Commission* [1988] ECR 1573, 1595. See, generally, E. Grabitz and C. Zacker, 'Scope for Action by the EC Member States for the Improvement of Environmental Protection under EEC Law: The Example of Environmental Taxes and Subsidies' (1989) 26 CMLRev. 423–47.

objected to German aid for the regeneration of mineral oils and required the scheme to be terminated by 1966,[284] though it was subsequently authorized on environmental grounds.[285] Objections were also raised in the case of a German scheme to allow faster depreciation for tax purposes of company investments intended to reduce pollution. The Commission insisted that aid could only be authorized if it involved adaptation of existing companies to new or special constraints imposed on them in certain sectors or certain regions and after prior notification.[286]

The premise for such practice was the principle that undertakings should normally face the consequences of the pollution which they caused; they should only be assisted in eliminating their pollution if it was shown that there were particular difficulties, especially of a regional or industrial nature, and that those difficulties could only be overcome by enabling the industries concerned to make the necessary adaptations to their existing production plants.[287] Undertakings had to provide in each case the information to justify a waiver of that principle for their particular industry.[288]

In such practice the possibility that environmental aid might qualify for authorization as contributing to 'an important project of common European interest' under Article 92(3)(b) was not accepted.[289] Aid might, however, be authorized under Article 92(3)(c) where it had beneficial effects for the environment of a lasting nature.[290] In considering the possibility of authorizing aid under the latter provision, the Commission might treat the 'common interest' as requiring that reference be made to sectoral-policy considerations. For example, aid to reduce pollution in the paper-making industry was only authorized because it was likely to facilitate the development of this industry.[291]

---

[284] Bull. EC 6–1964, 24.

[285] *EEC Tenth General Report* (EEC Commission, Brussels, 1967), 106.

[286] Bull. EC 3–1974, 2117. However, following adoption of aid Guidelines (sect. 6.5.2 below), it was agreed that the scheme could continue until 31 Dec. 1980 (Bull. EC 5–1975, 2118).

[287] Dec. 73/293 ([1973] OJ L270/22) on aid which the Belgian Government intended to grant for extending an oil refinery at Antwerp and for setting up a new refinery at Kallo (province of East Flanders).

[288] *Third Report on Competition Policy* (EC Commission, Brussels, 1974), 100.

[289] Dec. 73/293 ([1973] OJ L270/22) on aid which the Belgian Government intended to grant for extending an oil refinery at Antwerp and for setting up a new refinery at Kallo (province of East Flanders).

[290] Dec. 72/253 ([1972] JO L164/22) on the grant of aid to encourage the rationalization of the growing and processing of fodder plants as well as co-operation between agricultural operators in the Netherlands.

[291] *Third Report on Competition Policy* (EC Commission, Brussels, 1974), 89–90.

6.5.2 1974 Guidelines

Recognition of the need for exceptions from the 'polluter-pays' principle[292] and stress placed on harmonization rather elimination of environmental aid[293] led to the adoption of Guidelines concerning such aid in November 1974.[294] According to these Guidelines, firms would normally be expected to bear the cost of investments necessary to comply with environmental laws. Environmental policies, both at the national and the Union level, should be based, not on the general grant of aid, which simply meant that the public paid in the end, but on the imposition of obligations (standards and levies) enabling the authorities to make polluters bear the cost of protecting the environment. Aid should be granted only when objectives considered essential for the environment were seriously in conflict with other social or economic objectives also of priority importance. Basically, then, aid should be limited to existing undertakings which were not in a position to support the new costs facing them and where socio-economic difficulties might arise in certain regions or industries.[295]

However, the necessary changes could not take place overnight, since all the Member States would have to overcome a considerable degree of inertia and, at the same time, try to ensure that improving the quality of the environment did not stand in the way of other priority objectives, particularly in the industrial, regional, and social fields. Accordingly, the Commission distinguished between its attitude to environmental aid which was granted during a transitional period of six years[296] and met certain conditions, and its approach generally to environmental aid.

During the transitional period aid would be authorized where it aimed at speeding up the application of regulations embodying the 'polluter-pays' principle and at adapting existing businesses to these regulations.[297] The

---

[292] Programme of Action of the European Communities on the Environment ([1973] OJ C112/3), Title II, para. 5.

[293] Agreement of the Representatives of the Governments of the Member States meeting in the Council of 5 Mar. 1973 ([1973] OJ C9/1) on information to the Commission and for the Member States with a view to the possible harmonization throughout the Communities of urgent measures concerning the protection of the environment.

[294] Letter S/74/30.807 (*Competition Law in the European Communities* Vol. II: *Rules Applicable to State Aids* (EC Commission, Brussels, 1990), 124–9). The need for temporary exceptions from the principle was confirmed in para. 6 of the Commission Communic. annexed to Rec. 75/436 ([1975] OJ L194/1) regarding cost allocation and action by public authorities on environmental matters. See also Rec. 79/3 ([1979] OJ L5/28) regarding methods of evaluating the cost of pollution control to industry.

[295] Para. II.2 of the 1974 Guidelines.

[296] The Commission felt that this period was long enough to enable all the Member States to implement measures ensuring that the polluter-pays principle was applied throughout the Union on a broadly similar basis (*ibid.*, para. III.1).

[297] In practice, 'add-on technology' rather than 'process-integrated technology' may be more readily recognized by officials as entailing environmental improvements worthy of support. See L. Reijnders, 'Subsidies and the Environment' in R. Gerritse (ed.), *Producer Subsidies* (Pinter, London, 1990) 111–21, 115.

adaptation must be necessitated by 'new major obligations . . . in relation to environmental protection' and must concern plants in operation on 1 January 1975. A ceiling, which was to be progressively lowered from 45 to 15 per cent of investment costs by the end of the period, was imposed on aid meeting these conditions.[298] Such aid could be authorized as aid to a project of common European interest within the meaning of Article 92(3)(b).[299] When existing production capacity was increased, that part of the investment corresponding to the increase was not eligible for aid.

In the case of aid granted after the transitional period or not meeting the above conditions, the Commission would declare it to be compatible with the common market only if it qualified for authorization under Article 92(3)(a) or (c).[300] Hence, such aid, including aid above the ceiling, would be authorized where the new obligations imposed on firms in the interest of environmental protection were of such a nature that, within the framework of a sector or region, difficulties would be provoked such as might disturb the equilibrium of that sector or region and which justified the aid proposed. Aid could also be granted for research and development programmes with a view to developing new products or production techniques which polluted less or the results of which could be used to promote industrial exploitation.[301]

Operating aid with the sole effect of relieving certain firms or certain product lines of all or part of the financial burden which they would normally have had to bear by reason of the pollution caused would not be authorized.[302] Investment aid would only be authorized where it was necessitated by a sudden major change in the obligations and constraints imposed by environmental rules. Normally it should be limited to existing businesses and to alterations to plant already in service. It could only be granted to new firms and new plant where international competition was such that certain of their activities would be seriously handicapped by being subject to different obligations from those imposed in third states or where such states were themselves granting similar environmental protection aid.[303]

Adoption of these Guidelines seems to have had some immediate impact on the treatment of aid. In August 1974 the Commission had initiated the Article 93(2) procedure[304] in respect of aid to assist French sugar factories in complying with environmental standards.[305] At the time, the Commission considered that

---

[298] Germany and Belgium were required to bring their aid within the ceiling. See the *Sixth Report on Competition Policy* (EC Commission, Brussels, 1977), 127–8.

[299] Para. III.1 of the 1974 Guidelines.

[300] Though such aid might lack the sectoral or regional specificity usually required for authorization thereunder.

[301] Para. III.2 of the 1974 Guidelines.　　　　　　　　　　　　　　　　　[302] *Ibid*.

[303] *Ibid*. See, regarding aid to wool washing, the *Sixth Report on Competition Policy* (EC Commission, Brussels, 1977), 129.　　　　　　　　　　[304] See sect. 7.5.3 below.

[305] Communic. on the aid granted in France under the branch agreement concluded between the French Government and the national association of French sugar manufacturers ([1974] OJ C94/2).

firms should bear the cost of such compliance, unless they were in special difficulties. However, following adoption of the Guidelines, the Commission decided to authorize the aid.[306]

Even so, in the case of German aid in the form of automatic exemption from a waste-water levy in return for constructing water-purification plants, the Commission initially objected that environmental aid could not be allowed to become the rule for the future.[307] The aid was eventually authorized, only because it would be time-limited.[308]

The necessity for the aid might also have to be demonstrated. In Decision 77/260[309] the Commission maintained that, in estimating the costs of the anti-pollution equipment to be installed by an oil refinery in Belgium at Bfrs 4,500 million, the Belgian Government had included equipment worth more than Bfrs 3,000 million to improve product quality through desulphurization and reduction of lead content. However, all refineries needed the latter equipment to meet standards required by public authorities and consumers, both in Belgium and elsewhere. Accordingly, the Commission decided that aid related to such equipment could not be authorized. Of the remaining anti-pollution equipment costs aid could only be authorized under Article 92(3)(b) in respect of that part, Bfrs 460 million, which could not be used to extend capacity.[310] In granting the authorization, the Commission recognized that the 1974 Guidelines compelled it to depart from its earlier prohibition of essentially the same aid in September 1973.[311]

Sectoral considerations might remain influential in the treatment of such aid. For example, in authorizing aid to wool-washing companies under Article 92(3)(c), the Commission noted that the aid would not cause prices of washed wool to fall or lead to undesirable overcapacity in this sector.[312] Again, British aid to encourage use of waste paper by the paper industry was authorized, because it would help to improve the supply of indigenous raw materials as well as having favourable environmental effects.[313] It was in line with Commission proposals,[314] and trade and competition between the British paper industry and those of other Member States was 'relatively slight'.[315]

---

[306] *Sixth Report on Competition Policy* (EC Commission, Brussels, 1977), 128. The Commission had also objected to Belgian and German environmental aids, but authorized them following adoption of the Guidelines. See the *Fourth Report on Competition Policy* (EC Commission, Brussels, 1975), 105–6.

[307] Bull. EC 5–1976, 2117.   [308] Bull. EC 12–1979, 2.1.51.

[309] Concerning aid planned by the Belgian Government towards the extension of capacity of an oil refinery at Antwerp ([1977] OJ L80/23).

[310] Belgian aid of 15% to a car firm in Antwerp limited to environmental improvements was also authorized. See the *Tenth Report on Competition Policy* (EC Commission, Brussels, 1981), 143.

[311] Dec. 73/293 ([1973] OJ L270/22) on aid which the Belgian Government intended to grant for extending an oil refinery at Antwerp and for setting up a new refinery at Kallo (province of East Flanders).   [312] Bull. EC 4–1975, 2113.

[313] Bull. EC 5–1976, 2116. See, similarly, regarding a Dutch scheme, Bull. EC 11–1976, 2125.   [314] Bull. EC 3–1974, 2247.

[315] *Sixth Report on Competition Policy* (EC Commission, Brussels, 1977), 118–9.

6.5.3 1980 Guidelines

Recession and the need for industry to adjust to the new international situation meant that the funds which Member States could set aside for environmental protection were limited and that attempts to regulate environmental matters were hampered. The drawing up of relevant laws and regulations, particularly at Union level, and their subsequent national application proceeded more slowly than expected, while improvements in scientific and technological knowledge created the need for new environmental legislation. There was also increasing public demand for environmental-protection measures going beyond those so far adopted by Member States. Hence, the original transitional period was extended for another six years by Guidelines adopted in 1980.[316]

The condition was introduced in the new Guidelines that aid should only be granted within the framework of legislation specifying the 'type of pollution abatement installation investments required'.[317] The ceiling remained at 15 per cent.[318] The undertakings themselves must bear the entire cost of normal replacement investment and operating expenses[319] and must have been in operation at least two years before introduction of the new standards to be met.[320]

The last condition seems to have been applied with some flexibility. As regards Danish aid, the Commission considered that when it concerned an investment aimed at the introduction of less-polluting technology which generally had an innovative character and did not correspond to specific legislative requirements, the period of two years needed for qualifying the recipient as existing should be calculated in relation to the date of the investment.[321] In other words, the recipient need only have been in existence two years before that date.

Aid above the ceiling might also be authorized. For example, Danish aid of 25 per cent of investment costs was authorized, because it was designed to encourage introduction of new technologies which made production processes less polluting than those in current use, to implement pollution-control

---

[316] Annex to Letter SG(80)D/8287 (*Competition Law in the European Communities Vol. II: Rules Applicable to State Aids* (EC Commission, Brussels, 1990), 130–3).

[317] *Ibid.*, para. 2.3.

[318] *Ibid.*, para. 3.2. However, Dutch aid to enable a telecommunications equipment manufacturer to comply with planning regulations was authorized (*Fourteenth Report on Competition Policy* (EC Commission, Brussels, 1985), 156–7).

[319] Para. 3.4 of the 1980 Guidelines. See, e.g., Dec. 84/417 ([1984] OJ L230/28) on a proposed aid for the Netherlands Government in respect of certain investments to be carried out by an oil company at its refinery in Borsele; and Dec. 84/418 ([1984] OJ L230/31) on a proposal by the Netherlands Government in respect of certain investments to be carried out by an oil company at its refinery in the area of Rotterdam-Europoort.

[320] Para. 3.3 of the 1980 Guidelines.

[321] *Tenth Report on Competition Policy* (EC Commission, Brussels, 1981), 158.

measures conforming to recent standards, and to link the recipient undertaking to a public sewerage-treatment system.[322]

Aid for production of less-polluting products was treated less favourably. For example, aid for the production of non-polluting petroleum additives entailed unacceptable distortion of competition, given that other undertakings in the sector also had plans to enter the growing market for such fuels.[323]

6.5.4 1986 Guidelines

By the end of the second transitional period the Commission had come to the conclusion that a 'purely transitional approach' was inappropriate and that 'improvement in the environment and the need to avoid distortions of competition caused by national measures in this field [would] remain a major task for an indefinite period'. Hence, further Guidelines were introduced in 1986.[324] In introducing these Guidelines, the Commission is said also to have been influenced by the fact that aid did not always comply with the 15 per cent ceiling. In any case, compliance was almost impossible to monitor owing to the scope for applying Article 92(3)(a) and (c) as well as the multitude of sectoral aids and their cumulative effect.[325]

The 1986 Guidelines confirmed that environmental aid could be authorized under Article 92(3)(b), if four conditions were fulfilled.[326] The aid had to be intended to facilitate the implementation of new environmental standards. It was not to exceed 15 per cent net grant equivalent of the aided investment and might only be granted for a limited period. Only firms having installations in operation for at least two years before entry into force of the standards in question might qualify for aid. The eligible firm must bear the entire cost of normal replacement investment and operating costs.[327]

Aid beyond these limits might be authorized under Article 92(3)(c) for specific purposes, such as to assist existing firms to undertake research and

---

[322] Bull. EC 12–1980, 2.1.38. Environmental aid of more than 15% was also authorized in special cases involving investments in the Ruhr by steel, mining, and chemical firms causing heavy pollution. See Bull. EC 12–1981, 2.1.49.

[323] Notice of a proposal by the Netherlands Government to grant aid to a Rotterdam chemical firm ([1984] OJ C15/3).

[324] *Sixteenth Report on Competition Policy* (EC Commission, Brussels, 1987), 176.

[325] L. Krämer, *EEC Treaty and Environmental Protection* (Sweet & Maxwell, London, 1990), 21.

[326] See, regarding French aid for implementation of Dir. 91/676 ([1991] OJ L375/1) concerning the protection of waters against pollution caused by nitrates from agricultural sources, Bull. EC 5–1992, 1.1.177. See, regarding German aid to compensate farmers for restrictions on the use of agricultural land, Bull. EC 7/8–1991, 1.2.236.

[327] Aid to an investment which solely concerned an increase in capacity could not be authorized under Art. 92(3)(b), since it did not comply with the polluter-pays principle. See Dec. 93/564 ([1993] OJ L273/51) concerning aid the Italian Government intended to grant to Carbiere del Garda.

development in the environmental field.[328] For example, German aid for demonstration of methods and equipment for reducing pollution was recognized as being outside the Guidelines, but it was still authorized.[329] Aid in excess of the ceiling might also be authorized. For example, environmental aid up to 20 per cent was authorized in the Mezzogiorno,[330] as was German aid covering up to 20 per cent of the additional investment costs entailed in going beyond current pollution requirements.[331] Spanish aid of between 15 per cent and 50 per cent of the investment costs to create an industrial, energy, and technology base was authorized,[332] as were Italian aid of up to 50 per cent for research and development in relation to alternative energy[333] and Dutch aid for establishment of manure processing factories.[334] In practice, where research and development was involved, a general ceiling of 35 per cent, aid above which would 'raise basic questions regarding application of the polluter pays principle',[335] seems to have emerged. Aid up to 50 per cent for demonstration projects might also be authorized.[336]

Equally, aid might be authorized where it was designed to assist firms in meeting environmental standards which had not yet become obligatory. For example, a Dutch tax reduction in relation to use of subterranean water was authorized, because it accorded with Union policy regarding the use of such water.[337] The Commission also authorized a German scheme for temporary partial exemption from road taxes of less polluting cars which met new Union emission standards before they came into force.[338] Little importance seems to have been attached to the fact that firms might have an interest in complying with such standards and that the costs of such compliance might be well within

---

[328] *Twentieth Report on Competition Policy* (EC Commission, Brussels, 1991), 173. Cf. Notice ([1987] OJ C286/5) regarding aid planned by the Dutch Government in favour of a manufacturer of plant protective agents, where the Commission objected to an aid intensity of 45%.

[329] Bull. EC 12–1984, 2.1.73. See also, regarding French aid to companies carrying out development or demonstration projects connected with the disposal or recycling of waste, Bull. EC 12–1988, 2.1.121.

[330] *Twentieth Report on Competition Policy* (EC Commission, Brussels, 1991), 170.

[331] Bull. EC 11–1986, 2.1.80.

[332] *Twentieth Report on Competition Policy* (EC Commission, Brussels, 1991), 173.

[333] Communic. C50/89 (ex NN69/89) ([1990] OJ C237/13) concerning aid which Italy has decided to grant by means of the scheme 'R & D relative to alternative sources of energy'.

[334] Notice C17/90 (ex N88/90) ([1991] OJ C82/3) regarding aid which the Netherlands had decided to grant to test projects in manure processing.

[335] Communic. 413/90 ([1991] OJ C45/7) concerning aids under the storage facilities programme in Hessen. Cf. Notice C17/90 ([1990] OJ C229/4) concerning aids which the Netherlands had decided to grant to test projects in manure processing.

[336] Bull. EC 12–1987, 2.1.108. See, similarly, Bull. EC 3–1988, 2.1.75.

[337] See the Council Resolution of 25 Feb. 1992 ([1992] OJ C59/2) on the future Community groundwater policy.

[338] *Fifteenth Report on Competition Policy* (EC Commission, Brussels, 1986), 180–1. It was noted that purchasers of cars equipped with catalytic converters would not receive a net benefit. See, similarly, regarding a Dutch scheme, *ibid.*, L.181.

their means.[339] Importance seems to have been attached to such considerations only where the aid was for companies manufacturing plant which reduced or eliminated pollution, particularly where companies in sensitive sectors might begin manufacturing the plant and thus receive the aid.[340]

Aid to action going beyond established legislative requirements might also be favoured,[341] even though such action was mentioned by the Guidelines only in connection with 'special circumstances', such as aid to support research and development in this field.[342] For example, aid covering 20 per cent of the cost of air-pollution-control measures[343] and aid of 50 per cent for innovative investment in non-productive plant, which would involve compliance with standards going beyond those required by law, were authorized.[344] A five-year reduction of a waste-collection tax paid to the City of Wiesbaden in return for a commitment to purchase from the City, at current market prices, all waste paper collected was also authorized under Article 92(3)(c). The aid was considered compatible with the common market because of this commitment.[345]

In addition, the Commission authorized: German temporary tax exemptions for purchasers of cars with diesel engines which complied with strict particle-emission standards;[346] exemption from a special vehicle-registration tax on cars fitted with anti-pollution equipment in Denmark;[347] Luxembourg aid for purchasers of cars meeting stricter emission standards;[348] Dutch reduction of a special consumption tax on new cars, so as to speed up the introduction of vehicles that met the new-car emission standards during the period pending the introduction of stricter compulsory standards;[349] and Dutch aid to low-noise lorries.[350]

More particularly, aid might be authorized, as in the case of aid to German farmers for the disposal of animal manure,[351] to assist recipients in going

---

[339] Empirical studies suggest that most aided investments designed to secure environmental improvements would have been undertaken without the aid. See L. Reijnders, 'Subsidies and the Environment' in R. Gerritse (ed.), *Producer Subsidies* (Pinter, London, 1990) 111–21, 114.

[340] Notice C2/93 (N505/92) ([1994] OJ C100/5) concerning aid schemes for environmental investment.

[341] Notice C60/91 (ex NN73/91, NN76/91) ([1993] OJ C43/14) regarding the proposal by the German Government to award state aid to the Opel group in support of its investment plans in the new *Länder*.

[342] *Sixteenth Report on Competition Policy* (EC Commission, Brussels, 1987), 176.

[343] *Ibid.*, 177.

[344] *Ibid.*, 174.

[345] *Twenty-Second Report on Competition Policy* (EC Commission, Brussels, 1993), 252.

[346] Bull. EC 3–1991, 1.2.38.

[347] Bull. EC 1/2–1990, 1.1.59.

[348] Bull. EC 10–1987, 2.1.62.

[349] Bull. EC 12–1985, 2.1.72.

[350] Bull. EC 11–1989, 2.1.67. See also Lehner and Meiklejohn, n. 14 above, 60–1.

[351] *European Report* 1850 (8 Apr. 1983). See also Dec. 92/316 ([1992] OJ L170/34) concerning aid envisaged by the Netherlands Government in favour of an environmentally sound disposal of manure.

beyond standards established by Union law.[352] The aid consisted of 1 DM per cubic metre of manure spread by a third party. The aid was acceptable, because it was an environmentally appropriate way for farmers who were not in a position to purchase spreading equipment themselves to dispose of the manure, it went beyond the level of environmental protection stipulated in Directive 91/676,[353] and it only partly covered the extra costs involved. The German authorities also intended to integrate it with other programmes which complied with the state aid rules in Regulation 2078/92.[354]

Aid might thus be used to compensate for the failure of the Union legislature to introduce sufficiently high Union-wide standards. More fundamentally, aid might be seen as aiming 'to harness its vast potential for innovation and efficient management of costs' rather than relying on subjection of the private sector to 'command and control type regulations'.[355]

Where technological development was involved, aid might be particularly favoured. For example, aid for development of gas-cleaning techniques or improvement of existing processes was authorized under Article 92(3)(c), having regard to the technological developments involved.[356]

However, aid had to be justified on environmental grounds. As regards a German aid scheme for agriculture, no details of the environmentally sensitive nature of the areas concerned or of practices particularly favourable to the environment were given. The aid was only authorized when amendments were made to the scheme.[357]

Moreover, aid to assist investment in desulphurization plant was prohibited. Although it would lead to environmental improvement, certain running costs would also be subsidized.[358] Aid to an investment concerning the setting-up of a new production line leading to a 30 per cent increase in overall capacity was also prohibited.[359] If, however, the result would be to increase demand for waste for recycling, aid might be authorized under Article 92(3)(c).[360]

---

[352] See also Notice C21/90 (ex N330/90) ([1991] OJ C73/2) concerning aid which Belgium had decided to grant to Solvay SA and Solvic SA at Jemeppes/Sambre.

[353] Concerning the protection of waters against pollution caused by nitrates from agricultural sources ([1991] OJ L375/1).

[354] On agricultural production methods compatible with the requirements of the protection of the environment and maintenance of the countryside ([1992] OJ L215/85).

[355] *Report of the Group of Independent Experts on Legislative and Administrative Simplification*, COM(95)288, 52.

[356] Communic. C22/89 ([1989] OJ C294/8) concerning environmental aid which France had decided to grant to the 'Agence pour la qualité de l'air'.

[357] *Eighteenth Report on Competition Policy* (EC Commission, Brussels, 1989), 208.

[358] Bull. EC 6–1989, 2.1.77. See also, regarding aid for the treatment and recovery of industrial waste, Dec. 94/172 ([1994] OJ L79/24) concerning Italian Law 102 of 2 May 1990 providing for the reconstruction and regeneration of the Valtellina.

[359] Dec. 91/305 ([1991] OJ L156/39) concerning investment aid which the Belgian Government planned to grant to Mactac SA, Soignies.

[360] Notice C27/92 (N295/92) ([1993] OJ C46/5) on aid to SCA Aylsford, a manufacturer of newsprint. See also, regarding the distinction between aid to cover fixed costs and aid to cover

Regional-policy Considerations

The application of the polluter-pays principle might be withheld where it would cause regional difficulties. Thus, for example, in Eastern Germany aid to enable undertakings to meet environmental requirements, given 'the former omissions' to respect these requirements, might be authorized.[361] More generally, according to the Economic and Social Committee, the polluter-pays principle should be withheld in respect of all the least-developed regions or acknowledged problem areas of the Union.[362]

Sectoral-policy Considerations

Sectoral-policy considerations might be decisive for the treatment of environmental aid. In particular, such considerations might determine whether environmental aid was treated as adversely affecting trade between Member States to an extent contrary to the common interest under Article 92(3)(c).[363]

In the agricultural sector aid might be authorized, *inter alia*, if it supported farming in areas where it was a vital aspect of the protection of the environment and the countryside.[364] In the case of projects aiming to protect the environment,[365] investment could, in principle, be aided up to a maximum of 35 per cent.[366] In areas covered by Directive 75/268[367] on mountain and hill farming and farming in less favoured areas the maximum was 45 per cent.[368] Higher rates of aid might be authorized, if additional conditions, intended to ensure that any damage to the environment was kept at the lowest possible level, were imposed on the beneficiaries concerning reduction of production intensity and reduced use of means of production.[369] The Commission, however, main-

variable costs, the *Twenty-Second Report on Competition Policy* (EC Commission, Brussels, 1993), 251–2.

[361] Notice C61/91 (N375/94) ([1995] OJ C113/5) concerning aid which the German Government intended to grant to Buna GmbH. See also Notice C62/91 (N376/94) ([1995] OJ C113/13) concerning aid which the German Government intended to grant to Sächsische Olefinwerke GmbH Böhlen.

[362] Opinion of 19 Sept. 1990 (CES(90)1052) on environmental policy and the Single European Market, 14.

[363] Communic. C22/89 ([1989] OJ C294/8) concerning environmental aid which France had decided to grant to the Agence pour la qualité de l'air.

[364] *Sixteenth Report on Competition Policy* (EC Commission, Brussels, 1987), 194–5.

[365] Art. 12(1) of Reg. 2328/91 ([1991] OJ L218/1) on improving the efficiency of agricultural structures permits higher rates of aid than the general ones laid down in Art. 7(2), where it is for environmental protection and the aid is compatible with Art. 92 EC. Aid not meeting requirements laid down therein may be objectionable. See Notice C31/995 (ex NN140/94) ([1995] OJ C292/14) concerning aid to organic farming granted by Italy (Campania Region).

[366] Art. 8(2) and (4) of Reg. 797/85 ([1985] OJ L93/1) on improving the efficiency of agricultural structures laid down this ceiling.

[367] [1975] OJ L128/1.

[368] Communic. C48/90 ([1994] OJ C23/9) concerning aids which Germany had decided to grant for manure storage.

[369] Communic. C7/90 (N336/89) ([1991] OJ C180/8) concerning aids under Dir. B of the Baden-Württemberg regional programme—assistance for installing additional equipment in

tained that the polluter-pays principle must apply to agriculture as to other activities.[370]

In the case of sectors such as coal,[371] steel, shipbuilding, textiles,[372] and motor vehicles, a more restrictive approach towards aid authorization might be adopted.

In the case of the steel industry, Decision 2320/81[373] had merely provided for account to be taken of environmental-policy considerations, where the requirements of Union policy for this industry were met. However, according to the Preamble to Decision 322/89,[374] it would be unjustified, and would be treating the steel industry differently from other industries, to prohibit aid for bringing plants into line with new environmental standards.[375] Such aid was in the public interest and, provided it satisfied the conditions laid down in the Decision, should be available to the steel industry, just as similar aid was permitted to other industries under Article 92 of the EC Treaty. Accordingly, Article 3 of the Decision, which was later replaced by Article 3 of Decision 3855/91,[376] permitted aid to bring plants operating at least two years before introduction of new standards into line with such standards. Up to 15 per cent of the investment costs directly related to the environmental measures concerned could be covered. Where the investment was associated with an increase in the capacity of the plant, the eligible costs should be proportionate to the initial capacity of the plant.[377] However, aid for the normal replacement[378] or modernization[379] of plant or for new plant[380] was prohibited.

Beyond the scope of such legislation, environmental aid to the steel sector might exceptionally be authorized. For example, the Danish and Dutch authorities introduced a specific additional tax on carbon dioxide and energy coupled with reliefs for firms.[381] The reliefs constituted aid, but they were found to be

---

existing glasshouses to protect the environment. See also Communic. N336/89 ([1990] OJ C121/9) concerning aids which the German Government had decided to grant to horticultural enterprises in water catchment areas (Baden-Württemberg).

[370] *Environment and Agriculture*, COM(88)338.

[371] Art. 7 of Dec. 3632/93 ([1993] OJ L329/12) establishing Community rules for state aid to the coal industry.

[372] *Twelfth Report on Competition Policy* (EC Commission, Brussels, 1983), 134–5.

[373] Establishing Community rules for aids to the steel industry ([1981] OJ L228/14), Art. 3(2).

[374] Establishing Community rules for aid to the steel industry ([1989] OJ L38/8).

[375] 6th recital in the Preamble (*ibid.*).

[376] Establishing Community rules for aid to the steel industry ([1991] OJ L362/57).

[377] See, regarding environmental aid to a Spanish steel undertaking, the *Twentieth Report on Competition Policy* (EC Commission, Brussels, 1991), 153.

[378] Notice C22/93 (N412/92) ([1993] OJ C278/6) concerning aid which Italy planned to grant to Acciaierie e Ferriere Leali Luigi SpA.

[379] Notice C23/93 (N414/92) ([1993] OJ C278/7) concerning aid which Italy planned to grant to Lucchini Siderurgica SpA (Casto Mura).

[380] Bull. EU 6–1994, 1.2.71.

[381] Despite these reliefs, firms subject to the tax would incur additional costs.

compatible with the common market under Article 92 of the EC Treaty.[382] Their object was to limit the loss of competitiveness of recipient firms, as a result of their being subject to the tax, as compared with their competitors in countries which had not introduced such a tax. At the same time, the positive effects which the introduction of the tax was likely to have in terms of environmental protection were not jeopardized. In the case of steel under-takings covered by the ECSC Treaty, the restrictiveness of Decision 3855/91[383] meant that aid to such firms had to be authorized under Article 95 of that Treaty.[384]

On the other hand, the Italian authorities planned to grant aid under the general aid scheme for development of the Mezzogiorno to a steelworks for an investment for environmental improvement. The aid was prohibited, because the authorities had not demonstrated the existence of new environmental protection standards, compliance with which the investment was intended to achieve, or that the ceiling of 15 per cent was respected.[385]

In the case of shipbuilding aid, Article 6(4) of Directive 90/684[386] provided that Commission assessment of the acceptability of investment aid should take account of the extent of the contribution of the investment to such Union objectives for the sector as innovation, specialization, working conditions, health, safety, and the environment. This provision added to rather than relaxed the condition that investment aid should not lead to an increase in sectoral capacity.[387]

In the motor vehicles sector, the development of less polluting and energy-saving vehicles was regarded as a standard requirement for the industry and thus to be financed from the manufacturer's own resources.[388] Only to the extent that development activities related to the introduction of genuinely

---

[382] Art. 10 of the Proposal of 2 June 1992 ([1992] OJ C196/1) for a directive introducing a tax on carbon dioxide emissions and energy provides that, in the case of undertakings with a high energy consumption that are seriously disadvantaged on account of an increase in imports from third states which have not introduced a similar tax, Member States may grant a reduction of, or exemption from, the tax.

[383] The Commission entered a statement in the Council minutes that Art. 2 of this Decision allowed for R & D aid with the objective of energy conservation or a study of run-down areas formerly occupied by steel undertakings and that Art. 3 covered, *inter alia*, investment in environmental protection which resulted in energy conservation. See Notice C24/93 (N415/92) ([1993] OJ C278/9) concerning aid which Italy planned to grant to Lucchini Siderurgica SpA (Settimo Torinese).

[384] Dec. 92/411 ([1992] OJ L223/28) on the granting of aid to steel undertakings by the Danish and Dutch Governments. See also the objections to aid for energy saving and improve-ment of product quality in Notice C39/95 (ex NN47/95) ([1995] OJ C344/8) concerning aid granted by Italy to Acciaierie di Bolzano.

[385] Dec. 90/555 ([1990] OJ L314/17) concerning aid which the Italian authorities planned to grant to the Tirreno and Siderpotenza steelworks.

[386] On aid to shipbuilding ([1990] OJ L380/13).

[387] *Ibid.*, Art 6(1).

[388] Similarly, the Commission may be unsympathetic to the grant environmental aid to equipment producers. See Bull. EC1/2–1993, 1.2.74.

innovative products at Union level could their subsidization be approved in this sector.[389] The Commission sought to prevent competition from being distorted through the grant of aid to assist manufacturers in catching up with existing technologies.[390] Aid for general pollution-control might still be authorized, but such cases had to be examined individually.[391]

The Commission expressed general satisfaction with such arrangements for the control of environmental aid and was 'not aware of a considerable extent of fiscal or financial incentives given at large scales in Member States for environmental purposes'.[392] Even so, there were calls for the Commission to adopt a stricter approach towards control of such aid. In particular, the criterion of adaptation to environmental legislation was said to be an unsuitable yardstick. Reservations were also expressed whether environmental protection really could be subsumed under the heading of a 'project of common European interest' within the meaning of Article 92(3)(b). It was, therefore, to be expected that in future years the Commission would examine aid for environmental purposes to ascertain whether it was genuinely compatible with Article 92 and the polluter-pays principle.[393]

Such calls might at least partly be reflected in the evolution of Commission practice.[394] In particular, the Commission might authorize aid under Article 92(3)(c), but reserve the right to review its decision in the event of modification of the 'polluter-pays' principle.[395]

However, the EC Treaty may set limits to aid control through the application of the polluter-pays principle. According to Article 130r(3) of the Treaty,[396] the environmental policy of the Union is to take account, *inter alia*, of the potential benefits and costs[397] of action or lack of action and the economic development of the Union as a whole and the balanced development of the regions. The implication that the polluter-pays principle is only one guiding principle for

---

[389] See, more particularly, Dec. 96/76 ([1996] OJ L15/37) concerning aid granted by the Netherlands to the truck producer, DAF.

[390] Dec. 90/381 ([1990] OJ L188/55) amending German aid schemes for the motor-vehicle industry.

[391] Community framework on state aid to the motor-vehicle industry ([1989] OJ C123/3 and [1991] OJ C81/4), para. 3.

[392] *Implementation and Enforcement of Environmental Legislation*, House of Lords Select Committee on the European Communities, HL(1991–2), 53–II, 278.

[393] L. Krämer, n. 325 above, 21.

[394] See, e.g., Communic. N336/89 ([1990] OJ C121/9) concerning aids which the German Government had decided to grant to horticultural enterprises in water catchment areas (Baden-Würrtemberg).

[395] Communic. C22/89 ([1989] OJ C294/8) concerning environmental aid which France had decided to grant to the Agence pour la qualité de l'air. But see Communic. 22/89 ([1990] OJ C172/11) concerning aid which the French Government had decided to grant through the Agence pour la qualité de l'air for investments in desulphurization, where objections were lifted on technological grounds.

[396] See also Art. 73(2) EEA.

[397] The capacity of a region to bear environmental rather than economic costs is said to be envisaged. See L. Krämer, n. 325 above, 68.

environmental policy[398] is confirmed by Article 130s(4), which provides for the Member States to finance this policy. Accordingly, Council enactments may allow for the grant of state aid to promote environmental improvements,[399] though 'fear of seeing a kind of parallel Common Agricultural Policy emerge' apparently constrains the Union in this area.[400] For example, Directive 91/441[401] authorized aid in the car sector by way of tax incentives, provided that they:

—were such as to 'meet the provisions of the Treaty';
—applied generally and aimed at early compliance with binding Union standards;[402]
—ceased when these standards became applicable;[403] and
—were significantly less than the real costs for the pollution reduction equipment and their installation.[404]

6.5.5 1994 Guidelines

The 1994 Guidelines[405] lay down the same basic conditions[406] for aid authorization as the earlier Guidelines, though increased willingness to authorize aid not meeting these conditions is apparent and thinking as to the underlying legal justification for authorization has been modified. Aid may be authorized

[398] E. Grabitz and C. Zacker, n. 283 bove, 439.
[399] See, earlier, Dir. 75/439 ([1975] OJ L194/23) on the disposal of waste oils, which permitted the grant of aid to collectors or users of waste oil in compensation for the duties of collection and disposal imposed on them. Cf. the Commission communication on the recycling of waste paper (Bull. EC 3–1974, 2247). In line with this communication, the Commission approved a UK aid scheme (*Sixth Report on Competition Policy* (EC Commission, Brussels, 1977), 118–9).
[400] Club de Bruxelles, *Packaging in the Single European Market* (Club de Bruxelles, Brussels, 1992), 175.
[401] Amending Dir. 70/220 on the approximation of the laws of the Member States relating to measures to be taken against air pollution by emissions from motor vehicles ([1991] OJ L242/1).
[402] The European Parliament considers, more generally, that aid is justified if it allows undertakings better to adapt their installations to new Union legislation in the field of environmental protection. See the Resolution of 13 Dec. 1991 ([1992] OJ C13/472) on the *Twentieth Report on Competition Policy*, para. 20.
[403] Thereafter purchase-tax incentives may be objectionable because they may 'give rise *de facto* to a proliferation of standards . . . with consequential effects on the unity of the internal market'. Circulation tax incentives may be more acceptable. See the Explanatory Memorandum to the amended proposal of 1 Dec. 1993 (COM(93)626) for a dir. amending dir. 70/220 [1970] JO L76/1.
[404] Art. 3 of Dir. 91/441. See now Art. 3 of Dir. 93/59 ([1993] OJ L186/21) and Art. 3 of Dir. 94/12 ([1994] OJ L100/42) amending Dir. 70/220. Unless the relevant legislation is more restrictive, aid covering up to 100% of the extra environmental costs can be authorized. See para. 3.5 of the 1994 Guidelines (below).
[405] Community guidelines on state aid for environmental purposes ([1994] OJ C72/3).
[406] *Ibid.*, para. 3.2. However, these conditions may be relaxed where the aid recipients are SMEs. See Bull. EU 4–1995, 1.3.43.

on sectoral grounds under Article 92(3)(c)[407] or, in areas covered by Article 92(3)(a), under the latter.[408] Article 92(3)(b) may be applied where the aid is necessary for the project to proceed, the project is specific, well defined, and qualitatively important, and makes an exemplary and clearly identifiable contribution to the common European interest. When this subparagraph is applied, higher rates of aid may be authorized than those permissible under Article 92(3)(c).[409]

Authorization Conditions

Aid must be strictly confined to the extra investment costs necessary to meet environmental objectives.[410] In the calculation of these costs any reductions in operating costs are subtracted.[411] No aid is normally authorized for investment needed to comply with mandatory standards in new plant.[412] However, firms that, instead of simply adapting existing plant more than two years old, opt to replace it by new plant meeting the new standards may receive aid in respect of that part of the investment costs which does not exceed the cost of adapting the old plant.[413]

Such practice may imply the need for amendment of sectoral legislation. For example, the Commission has authorized aid in the case of a Luxembourg steel company in view of the principle in section II of the Preamble to Decision 3855/91[414] that aid for environmental purposes should be available to steel undertakings on conditions and terms equivalent to applying to undertakings in other sectors.[415] Presumably to establish a clearer legislative basis for authorization, the Commission has proposed that Article 3(1) of the Decision[416] should be amended and provide expressly for authorization of aid in the steel sector for replacement of existing installations with new ones meeting new environmental requirements.[417]

---

[407] Authorization may cover aid to initial investment, where a special effort is required of recipients to exceed environmental standards in force. See Notice C2/93 (ex N505/92) ([1996] OJ C33/7) concerning environmental aid that Belgium had decided to grant under two decrees of the Walloon Regional Council.

[408] Para. 3.6 of the 1994 Guidelines.

[409] *Ibid.*, para. 3.7.

[410] *Ibid.*, para. 3.2.1.

[411] Notice C33/94 (N654/93) ([1994] OJ C271/17) concerning aid the Italian Government (autonomous province of Trento) intended to grant to Cartiere del Garda.

[412] Cf., regarding production methods, Communic. C43/94 (NN49/93) ([1994] OJ C365/3) concerning aids which Italy had decided to grant to producers and processors of oil-seeds with a view to encouraging the production of biofuels.

[413] Para. 3.2.3.A of the 1994 Guidelines.

[414] Establishing Community rules for aid to the steel industry ([1991] OJ L362/57).

[415] H. Morch, 'Summary of the Most Important Recent Developments' (1995) 4 *Competition Policy Newsletter* 47–51, 50.

[416] In its current version this provision refers only to aid for 'bringing into line with new statutory environmental standards plants which entered into service at least two years before the introduction of the standards'.

[417] H. Morch, n. 415 above, 50.

Moreover, aid for investment that allows significantly higher levels of environmental protection to be attained than those required by mandatory standards may be authorized in proportion to the improvement of the environment that is achieved and to the investment necessary for achieving the improvement.[418] In fields where there are no mandatory standards or other legal obligations on firms to protect the environment, aid may be granted to investments which will enable undertakings significantly to improve their environmental performance or match that of firms in other Member States in which mandatory standards apply. The same conditions operate as in the case of aid enabling undertakings to go beyond mandatory standards.[419] Aid authorization is limited to users of environmentally friendly equipment and products, though it is admitted that manufacturers of such equipment and products may indirectly benefit.[420]

Even operating aid may be authorized in certain well-defined circumstances.[421] Such aid must only compensate for extra production costs by comparison with traditional costs and should be temporary and, in principle, degressive, so as to provide an incentive for reducing pollution or introducing more efficient uses of resources more quickly. More particularly, the public financing of the additional costs of selective collection, recovery, and treatment of municipal waste for the benefit of businesses as well as consumers may be authorized, provided that businesses are charged in proportion to their use of the system or to the amount of waste they produce in their enterprises. Temporary relief from new environmental taxes may also be authorized where it is necessary to offset losses in competitiveness, particularly at international level.[422] Without such relief the competitiveness of firms in certain sectors might be so damaged that introduction of the taxes would be 'politically impracticable', though the relief must, in principle, be degressive.[423] For example, the Commission authorized Dutch relief for certain firms from environmental taxes on the consumption of groundwater and on waste[424] and Italian relief from a tax on the production of plastic bags in Italy to the benefit of plastic bags for export.[425]

---

[418] Para. 3.2.3.B of the 1994 Guidelines.   [419] *Ibid.*, para. 3.2.3.C.

[420] H. Morch, 'Summary of the Most Important Recent Developments' (1994) 3 *Competition Policy Newsletter* 61–6, 65.

[421] See the authorization under Art. 93(2)(c) of aid for management of waste oil, the *Twenty-Fourth Report on Competition Policy* (EC Commission, Brussels, 1995), 533.

[422] Para. 3.4 of the 1994 Guidelines.

[423] H. Morch, 'Summary of the Most Important Recent Developments' (1995) 6 *Competition Policy Newsletter* 41–7, 46.

[424] H. Morch, 'Summary of the Most Important Recent Developments' (1995) 5 *Competition Policy Newsletter* 43–9, 49.

[425] Notice C29/95 (NN93/94) ([1995] OJ C290/5) concerning aid granted by Italy for polyethylene recycling. Cf. the view of the ESA that a tax from which exports were exempted could not affect the international competitiveness of a national producer in Notice 95–002 ([1995] OJ C212/6) concerning aid which Norway proposed to grant in the form of a tax exemption for glass packaging from a basic tax on non-reusable beverage packaging.

Ceilings

The new Guidelines seek to bring down aid levels.[426] No general aid ceiling is imposed by these Guidelines, though only in the case of small and medium-sized enterprises may aid above 15 per cent be granted for compliance with new standards.[427] Aid for investment that allows significantly higher levels of environmental protection to be attained than those required by mandatory standards or where there are no standards may be authorized up to a maximum of 30 per cent gross of the eligible costs.[428]

For small and medium-sized enterprises an extra 10 per cent may be authorized.[429] In an area covered by a national regional development scheme aid may be granted up to the prevailing rate of regional aid authorized by the Commission for the area. If, however, the aid available for environmental investment in a non-assisted area under the Guidelines exceeds the prevailing rate of regional aid authorized in an Article 92(3)(c) area in the same Member State, the rate of aid in the latter area can be raised to that available in the non-assisted area.[430] For small and medium-sized enterprises a further 10 per cent in Article 92(3)(c) areas and 15 per cent in Article 92(3)(a) areas may be authorized. Thus, for example, aid up to 50 per cent was authorized in Brandenburg.[431] In areas not covered by such a scheme, but eligible under Objective 1, 2, or 5b of the Structural Funds, the level of aid will be decided in each case.[432]

For agricultural investments covered by Article 12(1) and (5) of Regulation 2328/91,[433] on improving the efficiency of agricultural structures, the maximum level is 35 per cent or 45 per cent[434] in areas referred to in Directive 75/268.[435] In Objective 1 or 5b areas the Commission may also, on a case-by-case basis, accept higher levels,[436] where the Member State concerned demonstrates that they are justified.

6.6 ENERGY CONSERVATION

Aid to encourage energy saving is favoured in Union practice. For example, in the interests of better energy use, Council Recommendation 77/713[437] envis-

---

[426] Reply by Mr Van Miert to Written Question E–3208/95 ([1996] OJ C91/44) by James Fitzsimons.

[427] Para. 3.2.A of the 1994 Guidelines.   [428] *Ibid.*, paras. 3.2.3 B–C.

[429] *Ibid.*, para. 3.2.3 A.   [430] *Ibid.*, n. 18.

[431] Bull. EU 6–1994, 1.2.64.   [432] N. 17 in the 1994 Guidelines.

[433] [1991] OJ L218/1.   [434] Para. 3.2.3, n. 14, of the 1994 Guidelines.

[435] On mountain and hill farming and farming in less-favoured areas ([1975] OJ L128/1).

[436] See, regarding Greek aid for the relocation of livestock holdings and the construction of slurry facilities, Bull. EU 7/8–1995, 1.3.158. Account was also taken of the particularly high market cost of capital in Greece.

[437] Concerning the rational use of energy in industrial undertakings ([1977] OJ L295/3), para. 1.

aged that Member States would take measures, in accordance with Article 92 of the Treaty, to encourage energy saving.[438] The Commission considered that increased energy prices might not in themselves be sufficient to stimulate adequate energy-saving measures and that 'the state must offer financial incentives to encourage firms to take the necessary steps without too much delay'.[439] For example, in relation to hothouse agriculture, the Commission stated in 1980 that transitional aid for up to a year to assist the changeover to new sources of energy and a more rational use of energy was acceptable,[440] though the ultimate objective was that the costs of production should reflect the price of energy.[441] More recently, the Commission approved a Dutch aid programme which aimed to stimulate investments in heating appliances. The appliances had to comply with energy-efficiency norms and with reduced nitrogen oxide emission levels to qualify for aid. The aid covered 15.5 per cent to 60 per cent of the extra costs of the investments.[442] Similarly, aid of up to 20 per cent from the Brussels Region to investment with the sole object of the rational use of energy was authorized.[443]

Such aid may be authorized under Article 92(3)(b) as promoting a project of common European interest[444] or Article 92(3)(c) as facilitating sectoral development. It cannot be authorized under the former provision where it is granted to one undertaking alone,[445] though it may be authorized under the latter provision because of its contribution to wider Union objectives.[446]

The possibility that market forces may lead firms to take energy-conservation measures and that benefits may accrue to firms which do so are recognized. The Commission takes the view that industry itself is the first to gain from any reduction in its energy and, hence, production costs. It is only natural and in the producer's own interest that it should use the most efficient technology and materials permitting a reduction in overheads, including energy consumption.[447] Even so, it is felt that in the absence of a general harmonization of rules

---

[438] See also Rec. 82/604 ([1982] OJ L247/9) concerning the encouragement of investments in the field of the rational use of energy. More particularly, aid for 'renewable-generated electricity' is not counted towards the limit of 20% of electricity demand which the Commission applies to aid for indigenous fuels. See *Twenty-Third Report on Competition Policy* (EC Commission, Brussels, 1994), 306.

[439] *Seventh Report on Competition Policy* (EC Commission, Brussels, 1978), 175–6.

[440] *Distortions of Competition in Hothouse Agriculture*, COM(80)306, 2. See, earlier, the *Memorandum on the Changed Conditions of Competition in Certain Sectors of Agriculture Resulting from the New Situation on the Energy Market*, SEC(74)2200.

[441] *Distortions of Competition in Hothouse Agriculture*, COM(80)306, 37.

[442] Commission Press Release, 13 Mar. 1991.

[443] Notice C52/91 ([1992] OJ C22/8) concerning a draft order of the Brussels region on economic growth and scientific research.

[444] *Seventh Report on Competition Policy* (EC Commission, Brussels, 1978), 176; *Ninth Report on Competition Policy* (EC Commission, Brussels, 1980), 113–4.

[445] Dec. 89/254 relating to aid which the Belgian Government had granted to a petrochemicals company at Ottignies/Louvain-la-Neuve (SA Belgian Shell) ([1989] OJ L106/34).

[446] *Twentieth Report on Competition Policy* (EC Commission, Brussels, 1991), 175–6.

[447] Dec. 87/194 ([1987] OJ L77/43) on a FIM loan to a mineral-water and glass-bottle

and obligations,[448] such as, for example, the adoption of a general tax on carbon dioxide, aid will always be necessary to mitigate the imperfections of a market in which energy prices do not take account of the real costs of environmental protection.[449]

Aid to producers of energy-saving equipment[450] may be treated more strictly. According to the Commission, market conditions, together with state measures to encourage conservation in the form of aid to consumers, may mean that the industry can develop in a normal fashion using its own resources and without such aid.[451] Sectoral legislation may also preclude the authorization of aid for energy conservation.[452]

6.6.1 Union Interventions

Compatibility with Union interventions may be an important consideration in the treatment of aid for energy conservation. For example, Danish energy-saving aid was authorized under Article 92(3)(b),[453] as being in accordance with the Commission Communication *Towards a New Energy Policy Strategy for the Community*[454] and the Council Resolution of 17 December 1974 on a Community action programme on the rational utilization of energy.[455] Dutch aid to promote demonstration projects relating to new energy-saving techniques was compatible with a Commission proposal for a Regulation on the granting of financial aids to demonstration projects in the field of energy-saving,[456] and was also authorized.[457] Likewise, Italian aid to promote utilization of solar energy,[458] Italian motor vehicle aid to assist energy conservation,[459] and British

---

manufacturer. See also Notice ([1986] OJ C284/7) regarding a scheme of support for investment aimed at achieving energy savings under which the French Government planned to award, through the Agence française pour la maîtresse de l'energie, a grant to Société Papetière Cartonnerie Maurice Franck.

[448] *Specific Actions for Greater Penetration for Renewable Energy Sources Altener*, COM(92)180; Proposal for a dec. for a monitoring mechanism of Community CO_2 and other greenhouse gas emissions, COM(92)181; Proposal for a dir. to limit carbon dioxide emissions by improving energy efficiency (SAVE programme), COM(92)182; and Proposal for a dir. introducing a tax on carbon dioxide emissions and energy, COM(92)226.

[449] *Twenty-First Report on Competition Policy* (EC Commission, Brussels, 1992), 164.

[450] *Twenty-Third Report on Competition Policy* (EC Commission, Brussels, 1994), 263; *Twenty-Fourth Report on Competition Policy* (EC Commission, Brussels, 1995), 532.

[451] Dec. 81/523 ([1981] OJ L196/1) on a proposal by the Netherlands Government to grant aid for certain investments by a manufacturer of insulating material (Rockwell).

[452] See, in the case of the steel industry, Dec. 90/555 ([1990] OJ L314/17) concerning aid which the Italian authorities planned to grant to the Tirreno and Siderpotenza steelworks; Communic. 26/90 (N389/90) ([1990] OJ C318/3) regarding aid which Italy had decided to grant to Bolzano.

[453] Bull. EC 12–1976, 2131.　　　　　　　　　　　　　　[454] Bull. EC, Supp. 4/74.

[455] [1975] OJ C153/5.　　　　　　　　　[456] Proposal of 25 May 1977, COM(77)187.

[457] *Seventh Report on Competition Policy* (EC Commission, Brussels, 1978), 177.

[458] *Ibid.*, 178.

[459] *Fourteenth Report on Competition Policy* (EC Commission, Brussels, 1986), 155. Energy-saving aid to the automobile sector is now assessed under the Framework for aid to this sector.

aid to keep nuclear power stations operating until the end of their useful life[460] were authorized, as was a Dutch scheme offering investment grants for energy conservation in existing buildings. The Dutch scheme promoted better insulation and improved installation techniques and was thus found to be consistent with the objectives of Union energy policy.[461] More particularly, Portuguese aid for energy conservation was authorized[462] as being in line with the Valoren programme.[463]

6.6.2 Operating Aid

Energy-saving investments undertaken at the time of the periodic renovation of a production plant should, according to the Commission, normally be effected without the need for incentives in the form of aid.[464] It is usual for undertakings to install equipment which is more advanced and thus reduces energy consumption. Hence, the energy-saving involved cannot in itself justify aid.[465] Aid may only be authorized where recipients make a special effort, for example, to introduce processes that use renewable sources of energy,[466] an objective encouraged by Commission policy.[467] In the absence of any such effort, the aid has operating character and cannot be authorized as promoting a project of common European interest under Article 92(3)(b), because it conflicts with the objective of energy saving and more rational use of energy,[468] or as facilitating sectoral development under Article 92(3)(c).[469]

A fortiori, aid simply to reduce the costs of consuming energy is objectionable. Thus, for example, the Commission objected to German aid to reduce energy

See, e.g., Communic. C45/91 (ex N255/91) ([1991] OJ C299/4) concerning the proposal by the Italian Government to award state aid to the Fiat group in support of its Second Mezzogiorno Investment Plan.

[460] The low marginal cost of electricity produced by such power stations and the nuclear sector's contribution to the security and diversity of energy supplies were stressed. See the *Twentieth Report on Competition Policy* (EC Commission, Brussels, 1991), 176.

[461] *Ibid.*, 175–6.   [462] Bull. EC 1–1988, 2.1.39.

[463] Reg. 3301/86 ([1986] OJ L305/6) instituting a Community programme for the development of certain less-favoured regions of the Community by exploiting endogenous energy potential.

[464] Dec. 86/593 ([1986] OJ L342/32) on a proposal by the Belgian Government to grant aid for investments by a flat-glass producer at Auvelais.

[465] Dec. 87/303 ([1987] OJ L152/27) on an FIM (Industrial Modernization Fund) loan to a brewery.

[466] Notice C3/93 (ex N506/92) ([1994] OJ C100/7) concerning aid that Belgium had decided to grant in Wallonia in respect of two investment aid schemes for renewable sources of energy.

[467] *Energy and the Environment*, COM(89)369, 24–6.

[468] Cf., regarding reduced electricity prices to industries located in a remote region of France, Notice C13/92 (NN167/91) ([1992] OJ C149/4) concerning French aid towards the creation of industrial enterprises in Modane.

[469] Dec. 86/60 ([1986] OJ L72/30) on the aid which Rheinland-Pfalz had provided to an undertaking producing primary aluminium, situated in Ludwigshafen. See, similarly, Dec. 82/175 ([1982] OJ L80/40) on a direct aid for the purchase of oil-based fuels for heating glasshouses granted by the Belgian Government to commercial horticulturalists subject to the special value-added tax scheme.

costs during and after the restructuring of chemical companies;[470] German aid
to offset fuel price increases for fodder producers;[471] Italian aid to reduce the
annual electricity expenditure of flour-millers and pasta producers;[472] and
French aid to hydro-electric power.[473]

Again, a reduced rate for natural gas charged to growers of greenhouse
vegetables could not be treated as a measure intended to promote the execution
of an important project of common European interest within the meaning of
Article 92(3)(b); this reduction ran counter to the objectives of the common
energy policy, which aimed at energy-saving and at a rational use of energy.
Since the aid was based on quantities produced and involved no restructuring,[474] energy saving, or regional development, it was prohibited as operating
aid.[475] However, following adoption of 'the broad lines of a Community energy
policy',[476] this particular prohibition was lifted.[477]

Moreover, in the guidelines for the granting of national aid with a view to the
adaptation of horticulture under glass and inshore fisheries to developments
on the energy markets[478] the Commission decided to authorize aid to offset the
increase in the price of oil products used in horticulture between 1 July 1975
and 30 June 1976, provided that it did not exceed one-third of the price
increase for these products recorded between 1 September 1973 and the date
on which the aid measure was introduced. Such aid was authorized so as to
alleviate the effects of the increase in the price of oil products and to enable
undertakings engaged in horticulture under glass to remain operative during a
certain period of adjustment to the new situation, likely to be a lasting one,
created by this increase, thereby avoiding social and regional problems. The
maximum rate fixed by the guidelines constituted the limit within which aid
could be considered as intended to facilitate the development of horticulture

---

[470] Bull. EU 11–1995, 1.3.57.

[471] Communic. concerning the aid which Baden-Württemberg proposed to grant in the
dehydrated fodder sector in order to offset the rise in fuel oil prices ([1974] OJ C87/1).

[472] Bull. EC 1–1987, 2.1.44. The scheme was later withdrawn. See Bull. EC 6–1987, 2.1.77.

[473] Dec. 93/193 ([1993] OJ L85/22) on the aid granted for the creation of industrial
enterprises in Modane, Savoy (France).

[474] Payment by the state of part of the energy costs of undertakings may only be acceptable as
part of a restructuring programme involving capacity reductions. See Dec. 83/396 ([1983] OJ
L227/24) concerning the aids that the Italian Government proposed to grant to certain steel
undertakings.

[475] Dec. 82/73 ([1982] OJ L37/29) on the preferential tariff charged to glasshouse growers for
natural gas in the Netherlands. See, similarly, Notice C31/92 (N454/91) ([1992] OJ C324/3)
concerning aid granted by Italy for the reconstruction of the Valtellina.

[476] See, e.g., Rec. 82/604 ([1982] OJ L247/9) concerning the encouragement of investment in
the rational use of energy.

[477] Dec. 82/73 was repealed by Dec. 82/518 ([1982] OJ L229/38). See also Dec. 85/215
([1985] OJ L97/49) on the preferential tariff charged to glasshouse growers for natural gas in the
Netherlands. Cf. Dec. 86/60 ([1986] OJ L72/30) on the aid which Rheinland-Pfalz had provided
to an undertaking producing primary aluminium, situated in Ludwigshafen.

[478] Unpublished, but see Dec. 77/75 ([1977] OJ L17/25) relating to the granting of aid for
horticulture under glass in the Netherlands in order to offset the increase in fuel oil prices.

within the meaning of Article 92(3)(c). This rate enabled Member States to grant sufficient aid to ensure the adjustment of healthy and viable undertakings to the increase in the price of oil products. At the same time, it maintained the need for an effort on the part of the undertakings themselves to cover two-thirds of this increase. Aid in excess of this rate would reduce the effort required of the undertakings, would enable less profitable undertakings to remain operative and would impair trade patterns to a degree contrary to the common interest.

6.6.3 Ceilings

No general ceiling has been introduced for aid to energy conservation. However, the Commission may raise objections to high intensities or large volumes of aid to energy saving,[479] though account may be taken of regional and sectoral policy considerations. For example, Italian aid covering between 20 per cent and 40 per cent of the costs of constructing or converting buildings and equipment so as to conserve energy was authorized. Cumulation with other kinds of aid would only be permissible in the Mezzogiorno, and special sectoral rules would be applicable.[480] German aid for the restructuring of heating networks in the new *Länder* was also authorized up to the level of 35 per cent, because it was granted to heating and accommodation companies which did not play a significant role in intra-Union trade.[481]

6.7 COMMERCIAL POLICY

Article 110 of the EC Treaty provides that the customs union aims to contribute to harmonized development of world trade, progressive abolition of restrictions on international trade, and the lowering of customs barriers.[482] Article 113 provides, in turn, that the common commercial policy is to be based on uniform principles, particularly in regard to changes in tariff rates, conclusion of tariff and trade agreements, achievement of uniformity in measures of liberalization, export policy, and measures to protect trade, such as those to be taken in the event of dumping or subsidies. More particularly, according to Article 112(1), Member States are required to harmonize aid systems for exports to third countries, to the extent necessary to ensure that competition between Union undertakings is not distorted.[483]

---

[479] *Twelfth Report on Competition Policy* (EC Commission, Brussels, 1983), 111.

[480] *Twenty-First Report on Competition Policy* (EC Commission, Brussels, 1992), 164.

[481] *Ibid.*, 165.

[482] Art. 229 requires the Commission to ensure maintenance of all appropriate relations with the organs of GATT, and Art. 231 provides for the Community to establish close co-operation with the OECD.

[483] See, regarding development aid, the Reply by Sir Leon Brittan to Written Question 1140/91 ([1991] OJ C259/41) by Stephen Hughes.

The position of Article 112(1) within Title VII, which is headed 'Common Commercial Policy', of Part Three of the Treaty may be significant. The implication is that the Treaty seeks to separate commercial-policy issues from state-aid issues under Article 92. In practice, however, it may be problematic to seek to insulate pursuit of this policy from issues arising under Article 92.[484]

On the one hand, aid may be seen as 'undermining' the common commercial policy.[485] On the other hand, aid for exports to third states may distort competition between undertakings in the various Member States in external markets.[486]

6.7.1 International Aid Rules

In pursuit of the common commercial policy the Union may undertake obligations regarding international trade, that is, trade between the Union and third states. Such obligations as those in the Agreement on Subsidies and Countervailing Measures,[487] annexed to the Agreement establishing the World Trade Organization, may have implications for aid control within the Union.[488] Implications for aid control may also arise from bilateral agreements between the Union and third states and from application of 'autonomous' rules by the Union in response to the grant of aid by third states.

Trade Liberalization

Aid control within the Union is seen by the Commission as a means of demonstrating Union commitment to free trade and GATT.[489] At the same time, there may be concern that third states may 'benefit gratuitously from the EU's internal control mechanism' for state aid.[490] Hence, limitations to disclosure of information regarding authorized aid may be justified on the ground

---

[484] Cf. Darmon AG in Joined Cases 72 & 73/91 *Sloman Neptun Schiffahrts AG* v. *Seebetriebsrat Bodo Ziesemer der Sloman Neptun Schiffahrts AG* [1993] ECR I–887, I–913; and Case C–142/87 *Belgium* v. *EC Commission: Tubemeuse* [1990] ECR I–959, I–1000.

[485] Darmon AG in Case C–400/92 *Germany* v. *EC Commission: Cosco* [1994] ECR I–4701, I–4718. At the same time, constitutional problems relating to the 'prerogatives' of the European Parliament may arise from the conclusion of international agreements. See the Resolution of 7 Apr. 1995 ([1995] OJ C109/302) on prospects for the future development of the shipbuilding industry, para. 5.

[486] Opinion 1/75 *Understanding on a Local Cost Standard* [1975] ECR 1355, 1364.

[487] [1994] OJ L336/156. There is a 'joint procedure' for notification under the EC Treaty and under this Agreement (Letter D20506).

[488] Though Reg. 3284/94 ([1994] OJ L349/22) on protection against subsidized imports from countries not members of the EC, which was introduced to implement the results of the Uruguay Round, may seem less permissive of aid than practice under Arts. 92–93 EC.

[489] *Second Survey on State Aids in the European Community in the Manufacturing and Certain Other Sectors* (EC Commission, Brussels, 1990), 51.

[490] C-D. Ehlermann, 'State Aid Control in the European Union: Success or Failure?' (1995) 18 *Fordham Int. LJ* 1212–29, 1219–20.

that the Union should not 'give possible ammunition to its trading partners in international trading disputes'.[491] However, the preferred solution of the Commission is to seek reciprocity in aid control. If reciprocity is achieved, it is hoped that aid will become less a cause of dispute than at present and that 'all the main actors on the world trade scene' will benefit.[492]

Thus, for example, the Preamble to Decision 3855/91,[493] which deals with aid to the steel industry, refers to the 'consensus' reached with the United States concerning trade in certain steel products,[494] and application of the Decision is to be consistent with current or future international obligations of the Union concerning aid to this sector.[495] Similarly, legislation concerning aid to shipbuilding has been enacted 'without prejudice to any amendments that may be necessary in order to comply with international obligations entered into by the Community'.[496]

However, international negotiations may not necessarily provide the solution to international market distortions which the Union seeks.[497] For example, in 1974 the European Parliament urged the Commission to draw up a timetable for the abolition of aid to shipbuilding, including investment aid; to insist, in the 1975 OECD negotiations, on the complete abolition at world level of all existing aid constituting a source of distortion to competition; and to ensure, by agreements with Japan and other countries, that no world surplus production capacity arose.[498] The only result was the adoption on 4 May 1976 of non-binding guidelines, according to which a remedy to the serious structural disequilibrium existing in this industry depended on efforts by ship-

---

[491] C-D. Ehlermann, 'State Aids under European Community Law' (1994) 18 *Fordham Intl LJ* 410–36, 431.

[492] *Second Survey on State Aids in the European Community in the Manufacturing and Certain Other Sectors* (EC Commission, Brussels, 1990), 51.

[493] Establishing Community rules for aid to the steel industry ([1991] OJ L362/57).

[494] [1989] OJ L368/185. Cf. the Agreement between the EC and the US Government concerning the application of the GATT Agreement on Trade in Civil Aircraft ([1992] OJ L301/32).

[495] In 1991 the Commission had examined R & D aid for a Luxembourg steel producer for compatibility with Dec. 322/89 ([1989] OJ L38/8) establishing Community rules for aid to the steel industry, which preceded Dec. 3855/91 ([1991] OJ L362/57) establishing Community rules for aid to the steel industry, and with the Consensus. See the *Twenty-First Report on Competition Policy* (EC Commission, Brussels, 1992), 144. See, generally, M. F. Dominick, 'Countervailing State Aids to Steel: A Case for International Consensus' (1984) 21 *CMLRev*. 355–403. An underlying Union concern is apparently to reduce the risk of anti-dumping proceedings by the United States. See, e.g., the *Financial Times*, 2 Apr. 1992.

[496] 7th recital in the Preamble to Dir. 93/115 ([1993] OJ L326/62) amending Dir. 90/684 [1990] OJ L380/27.

[497] The Commission appeared somewhat optimistic as to the prospects of such negotiations in relation to shipbuilding aid. See the *First Report on Competition Policy* (EC Commission, Brussels, 1972), 134. See also the *Second Report on Competition Policy* (EC Commission, Brussels, 1973), 85.

[498] Resolution of 13 June 1974 ([1974] OJ C76/41) on the proposal for a dir. on aid to the shipbuilding industry and on the memorandum on procedures for action in the shipbuilding industry, para. 4.

building countries to reduce world shipbuilding capacity in the least damaging and most equitable way possible.[499]

The Commission has continued to seek an international agreement entailing that all forms of aid and other trade obstacles are removed and that the main shipbuilding countries agree on fair prices for ships, so that normal competition is restored to the shipbuilding industry.[500] The Preamble to Directive 90/ 684,[501] which was designed partly to protect Union industry against unfair competitive conditions on the international market,[502] referred to the importance of a multilateral agreement being concluded between these countries.[503] Such an agreement should, it was said, ensure fair competition at an international level among shipyards through a balanced and equitable elimination of all existing impediments to normal competitive conditions and should provide a suitable instrument for counteracting all illegal practices and forms of assistance incompatible with the agreement.[504] However, the extension of Directive 90/684 was considered necessary, so as to leave the Union with sufficient flexibility to adapt its shipbuilding aid policy in the light of developments.[505]

The European Parliament considered that the Commission and all the competent bodies should take a firm and rigorous stand in international negotiations in order to obtain from international competitors, in particular Japan, Korea, and the United States:

—greater transparency in the systems for direct and indirect support of shipbuilding;

—a correct attitude in competition practices in parallel with the policies implemented by the Union in this sector; and

—a common code of practice in the management of registers in which social factors, safety and environmental protection were of prime importance.[506]

---

[499] *Seventh Report on Competition Policy* (EC Commission, Brussels, 1978), 139.

[500] Reply by Mr Andriessen to Written Question 853/91 ([1992] OJ C102/4) by Mr Ben Visser.

[501] 5th recital in the Preamble.

[502] Explanatory Memorandum to the Proposal for a Dir. on aid to shipbuilding, COM(90)248, 2. See also *Implementation 1987–88 of the Sixth Directive on Aid to Shipbuilding*, SEC(89)518, 21.

[503] In the absence of such an agreement, the Economic and Social Committee considers that Union legislation served as a deterrent to unfair competition from the major shipbuilding nations. See the Opinion of 19 Sept. 1990 ([1990] OJ C332/131) on the proposal for a dir. on aid to shipbuilding, para. 2.1.

[504] The nature of the shipbuilding market means that an instrument such as the GATT Multifibre Agreement (BISD, 21st Suppl. 3) or a 'voluntary export restraint' agreement of the kind secured by the Union in relation to textiles, such as that with Poland ([1987] OJ L156/41), cannot be employed as a solution to such problems.

[505] Explanatory Memorandum to the Proposal of 20 Apr. 1993 for a dir. amending Dir. 90/ 684 on aid to shipbuilding, COM(93)160, 4. See also the Explanatory Memorandum to the Proposal of 20 June 1990 for a dir. on aid to shipbuilding, COM(90)248, 10.

[506] Resolution of 22 Nov. 1991 ([1991] OJ C326/257) on Community policy in the shipbuilding sector, para. 3.

Agreement has finally been reached within the OECD on the elimination in principle of operating aid to shipbuilding from 1 January 1996.[507] In implementation of the Agreement, Regulation 3094/95 has been adopted.[508] Even so, the European Parliament considers that such aid should still be authorized by the Commission, if the Agreement is not respected by other parties.[509]

Underlying problems of negotiating and enforcing international agreements may be problems of reconciling sectoral policy with commercial policy. For example, the Commission takes the view that 'duty exemptions which are common in all Member States and therefore . . . constitute a part of the economic environment in the Community' are an acceptable form of shipbuilding aid.[510] Moreover, efforts to compensate for international distortions of competition through aid for Union shipbuilders are well established.[511] Even more fundamental problems arise in reconciling a defensive response to international overcapacity, exaggerated by distortions of competition by third states, with achievement of 'a level playing field so far as intra-Community competition in shipbuilding is concerned'.[512]

If pursuant to sectoral-policy considerations, the Commission is willing to permit aid to increase the international competitiveness of Union shipbuilding, attempts within the context of the commercial policy to negotiate elimination of international distortions of competition in this sector may be impeded.[513] An analogy might be drawn with the difficulties caused for the Union by the proposal of Australia and the United States that the Uruguay Round GATT negotiations should cover distortions of competition, including those associated with state aid, in the energy sector.[514]

On the other hand, it might equally be said that unilateral elimination of aid within the Union would leave the latter with little to offer in a multilateral framework in exchange for agreed aid reductions by others.[515] Hence, to the

---

[507] Agreement respecting normal competitive conditions in the commercial shipbuilding and repair industry ([1994] OJ C375/3).

[508] On aid to shipbuilding ([1995] OJ L332/1).

[509] Resolution of 7 Apr. 1995 ([1995] OJ C109/302) on prospects for the future development of the shipbuilding industry, para. 11.

[510] Notice C10/91, C11/91 & C12/91 (ex NN54/90, NN56/90 & NN58/90) ([1991] OJ C123/16) regarding aid which Greece had granted to shipbuilding in the period 1987 to 1990.

[511] See, e.g., *Second programme de politique economique à moyen terme*, (EC Commission, Brussels, 1969), App. I, 21.

[512] Explanatory Memorandum to the Proposal of 26 July 1995 for a reg. on aid to shipbuilding, COM(95)410, 1.

[513] The Commission proposed that the criteria for setting the aid ceiling under Dir. 90/684 [1990] OJ L380/27 should be expressly stated to be without prejudice to future international agreements requiring a lower level ([1990] OJ C223/4). However, this part of the proposal was not apparently acceptable to the Council.

[514] Information Report of the Section for External Relations, Trade and Development Policy of the Economic and Social Committee of 18 Dec. 1989 on the GATT/Uruguay Round negotiations 1989/90, CES(89)1415, 7.

[515] The US suspended proceedings under s. 301 of the Trade Act 1974 against German

extent that international agreements can be reached, the practical effect may be, as in the case of OECD agreements concerning credit facilities and development assistance in the shipbuilding sector, to set limits to aid control within the Union. Conclusion of the Agreement on Subsidies and Countervailing Measures, annexed to the Agreement establishing the World Trade Organization, was also taken by the Commission to necessitate some relaxation in control of research and development aid within the Union.[516]

Trade Management

The emphasis in Union practice may be on management rather than liberalization of international trade. Although Article XVI of GATT prohibits export aid, OECD agreements harmonizing export credits[517] have been concluded. Such harmonization may be portrayed as 'an effective instrument of international discipline, assisting in lowering subsidies and reducing counter-productive competition' in this field.[518] Its effect has been to allow credit at international rates comparable to those of competing industries in third states.[519]

In the shipbuilding sector particular agreements have been concluded and implemented in Union legislation. Directive 72/273[520] applied conditions (a minimum interest rate of 7.5 per cent, a minimum deposit of 20 per cent of the contract price, and a maximum of eight years' credit) established by an OECD Council Resolution of 16 December 1970[521] to aid in the form of export credits.[522] Directive 75/432[523] imposed the new conditions (a minimum interest rate of 8 per cent, a minimum deposit of 30 per cent, and a maximum duration of seven years) established by an OECD Council Resolution of 18 July 1974.[524] Directive 81/363[525] applied the conditions of a minimum interest rate of 8 per

shipbuilders allegedly in receipt of unfair subsidies in the hope that a multilateral solution to problems of unfair competition could be reached within the OECD. See the Explanatory Memorandum to the Proposal for a dir. on aid to shipbuilding, COM(90)248, 10.

[516] H. Morch, 'Summary of the Most Important Recent Developments' (1995) 6 *Competition Policy Newsletter* 41–7, 41.

[517] Dec. of 4 Apr. 1978 (Bull. EC 4–1978, 2.2.46) acceding to the OECD Arrangement on Guidelines for Officially Supported Export Credits; Dec. 93/112 ([1993] OJ L44/1) extending the Decision of 4 Apr. 1978 on the application of certain guidelines in the field of officially supported export credits; and the proposed amendment of 12 July 1995 (COM(95)185). Cf. Dec. 73/391 ([1973] OJ L346/1) on consultation and information procedures in matters of credit insurance, credit guarantees and financial credits.

[518] 8th recital in the Preamble to Dec. 93/112, n. 517 above.

[519] *First Report on Competition Policy* (EC Commission, Brussels, 1972), 138.

[520] On aids to shipbuilding ([1972] JO L169/28), Art. 3(1).   [521] C(70)204.

[522] Since market interest rates varied from Member State to Member State, the 7.5% rate would give a varying degree of assistance depending on the Member State concerned. The Commission, therefore, considered that the difference beween the subsidized rate and the market rate should not exceed 5%. See the *Third Report on Competition Policy* (EC Commission, Brussels, 1974), 84. See also Proposals on the Shipbuilding Industry, COM(73)1788.

[523] On aid to shipbuilding ([1975] OJ L192/27), Art. 3.

[524] C(74)88.   [525] On aid to shipbuilding ([1981] OJ L137/39), Art. 2.

cent, a minimum deposit of 20 per cent, and a maximum credit period of eight and a half years, which were established by an OECD Council Resolution of 30 January 1980.[526] Article 4(6) of Directive 87/167[527] permitted the grant of similar credit facilities in accordance with the OECD Resolution of 3 August 1981.[528] Directive 90/684[529] provided in Article 4(6) that credit facilities for the building of ships would be permitted provided that they were compatible with that Resolution or any agreements that might replace it.[530] Although the granting of such credits on terms below those prevailing in the national market constituted aid, the fact that they represented negotiated general international terms meant, in accordance with an 'alignment strategy', that this aid might be disregarded by the Commission within the ceiling applied to shipbuilding aid.[531]

Initially at least, the Commission was apparently prepared to allow minor divergences from OECD conditions. Thus the Commission accepted a Danish scheme at 8 per cent interest, covering up to 80 per cent of the contract price for twelve years (with a two-year grace period).[532] Extension of the period of the loan to fourteen years (with a four-year grace period) was accepted two years later.[533] However, in Decision 82/47[534] the Commission, noting that there was no competing offer from a third country, prohibited a UK scheme for granting credit for the exportation of two ships to Panama, which would have been provided at 9 per cent interest and for 95 per cent of the contract value of the two ships.

Even so, the general tendency in such practice seems to be to seek 'management' of international trade. According to the Commission, the Union should insist that third states match its own contribution to the smooth functioning of the international trading system according to GATT principles. Measures may have to be taken together with such states along the lines of the OECD agreement on steel, which guarantees 'solidarity' between the Union and the other producer countries in restructuring the industry,[535] and the Multifibre Arrangement for textiles.[536] The implication is that treatment of aid within the

---

[526] C(79)232.

[527] On aid to shipbuilding ([1987] OJ L69/55).

[528] C(81)103; C(81)110. See now Annex II to the Arrangement on guidelines for officially supported export credits ([1993] OJ L44/1).

[529] On aid to shipbuilding ([1990] OJ L380/27).

[530] See now Reg. 3094/95 ([1995] OJ L332/1) on aid to shipbuilding.

[531] *Future Aid Strategy for Shipbuilding*, COM(86)324, 9.

[532] *Thirteenth Report on Competition Policy* (EC Commission, Brussels, 1984), 160.

[533] *Fifteenth Report on Competition Policy* (EC Commission, Brussels, 1986), 158–9. See, however, the *Seventeenth Report on Competition Policy* (EC Commission, Brussels, 1988), 154 and *Implementation 1987–88 of the Sixth Directive on Aid to Shipbuilding*, SEC(89)518, Annex I.

[534] On a proposal by the UK Government to grant aid for the export of two ships to Panama ([1982] OJ L20/43).

[535] Arrangement in the form of an exchange of letters with the US concerning trade in steel pipes and tubes, [1985] OJ L9/2.

[536] *A Community Strategy to Develop Europe's Industry*, COM(81)639, 9.

Union may thus be affected by perceived 'management' needs reflected in multilateral agreements.

Bilateral agreements with third states, such as the Free Trade Agreements with EFTA States,[537] may also be concluded. Such agreements may contain rules regarding aid which affects trade between the parties.[538] Pursuant to such agreements, the Commission may seek harmonization in line with Union practice. For example, Article 23(1)(iii) of the Free Trade Agreement with Austria, according to which aid affecting trade between the Parties was incompatible with the Agreement, was invoked against Austrian aid to General Motors. The grounds were that the aid breached Union 'principles', which were to be embodied in the EEA Agreement, regarding regional aid and regarding aid to the motor vehicles sector.[539] In the absence of Austrian acceptance of the Commission position, safeguard measures were adopted which took the form of reintroduction of the Common Customs Tariff in respect of the products concerned.[540] In the case of aid to Grundig, tariffs were reintroduced,[541] but then lifted following repayment of the aid to which the Commission objected.[542] The Commission secured a 'compromise' concerning aid for a Chrysler car plant in Graz, which entailed a reduction of aid intensity from 33 per cent to 14.4 per cent.[543] Similarly, it was agreed that aid to Steyr Nutzfahrzeuge AG would be 'reduced to a level which the Commission considered reasonable for a comparable area in the Community'.[544] However, following Austrian accession to the Union, the Commission authorized aid to General Motors for research and development, environmental and training expenditure in Austria.[545]

Where no such agreement is applicable 'voluntary export restraints' (VERs)

---

[537] *Commission Policy on Sectoral Aid Schemes*, COM(78)221, 4. The Commission also took proceedings under Art. 85 against third-country wood suppliers as well as anti-dumping proceedings, and there were exceptional arrangements in the Free Trade Agreements made to limit imports of certain types of paper from EFTA States until 1984 (*ibid*).

[538] The European Parliament called for inclusion of 'a shipbuilding clause' in trade agreements with state-trading countries because of their anti-competitive practices. See the Resolution of 10 Feb. 1977 ([1977] OJ C57/57) on the Community shipping industry, para. 6.

[539] Annex XIV to the EEA Agreement. More 'traditional' association agreements may also require third states to adapt their aids to 'the rules laid down in the relevant Community frameworks and guidelines'. See, e.g., Art. 39(2)(c) and (d) of Dec. 1/95 of the EC–Turkey Association Council ([1996] OJ L35/1) on implementing the final phase of the Customs Union.

[540] Reg. 3697/93 ([1993] OJ L343/1) withdrawing tariff concessions in accordance with Art. 23(2) and Art. 27(3)(a) of the Free Trade Agreement between the Community and Austria (General Motors Austria).

[541] Reg. 317/94 ([1994] OJ L41/18) withdrawing tariff concessions in accordance with Art. 23(2) and Art. 27(3)(a) of the Free Trade Agreement between the Community and Austria (Grundig Austria GmbH).

[542] Reg. 318/94 ([1994] OJ L41/20) repealing Reg. 317/94, n. 541 above.

[543] *Twenty-Second Report on Competition Policy* (EC Commission, Brussels, 1993), 210.

[544] *Twenty-Third Report on Competition Policy* (EC Commission, Brussels, 1994), 294.

[545] H. Morch, 'Summary of the Most Important Recent Developments' (1995) 6 *Competition Policy Newsletter* 41–7, 45.

may be sought. For example, as regards alleged Austrian aid to beef and veal production, the Commission saw the solution as being to conclude an agreement with Austria, which would require the latter, *inter alia*, to ensure that the prices applied by its exporters to these products would not 'cause problems' on the Union market.[546]

Such regulatory protection may, as in the case of air transport,[547] motor vehicles[548] and wood, be regarded as the most appropriate response to problems allegedly arising from the grant of aid by third states.[549] For example, in Decision 88/282[550] the French Government stated that one of the aims of the aid in question was to enable the recipient, a wood processor, to cope with fierce competition from imports from third states. It referred in particular to the number of Indonesian imports and to cases of dumping by Eastern European countries. However, the Commission considered that any problems involving trade with third states should be settled in compliance with the common commercial policy[551] and not by having recourse to unilateral national measures, such as the grant of state aid. To allow such aid because it was also allegedly granted by third states 'would have constituted a precedent and enabled Member States to outbid each other under the pretext of counteracting the measures' of third states.[552]

The common commercial policy may allow for certain 'autonomous' measures to be taken by the Union against the grant of aid by third states under Regulation 2641/84.[553] For example, the Commission acted under this Regulation when Japan introduced port charges to finance the creation of a Harbour Management Fund.[554]

In the past, Article 115 authorizations might also permit restriction of intra-

---

[546] Reply by Mr MacSharry to Written Question 581/91 ([1992] OJ C2/6) by Mr Bocklet. Cf., regarding hazel nuts, the Reply by Mr Steichen to Written Question E–2255/93 ([1994] OJ C240/15) by Mr Giuseppe Mottola *et al*.

[547] See, regarding aid to third-country airlines, Application of Arts. 92 and 93 EC and Art. 61 EEA to state aids in the aviation sector ([1994] OJ C350/5), para. 11.

[548] See, regarding aid to motor vehicle producers in third states, Notice C44/95 (E16/95) ([1995] OJ C304/14) regarding refusal of the Spanish authorities of the Commission's proposal for reintroduction of the EC framework on state aid to the motor vehicle sector.

[549] The Proposal of 18 Oct. 1995 on protection against injurious pricing of vessels (COM(95)473) is seen as 'the counterpart for the stricter disciplines, in particular on subsidies, imposed on the EU shipbuilding industry' (Explanatory Memorandum, 1).

[550] On aid from the French Government to the wood-processing sector (Isoroy and Pinault) ([1988] OJ L119/38).

[551] In the context of plans for cumulation of rules of origin for Central and East European countries which have concluded Europe Agreements the Commission is studying the impact on particularly sensitive sectors, including textiles and electronics, and contemplates limited sectoral exceptions to cumulation. See *Follow Up to the Communication on 'The Europe Agreements and Beyond: A Strategy to Prepare the Countries of Central and Eastern Europe for Accession'*, COM(94)361, 8.

[552] *Sixth Report on Competition Policy* (EC Commission, Brussels, 1977), 126.

[553] On the strengthening of the common commercial policy with regard in particular to protection against illicit commercial practices ([1984] OJ L252/1). The kinds of action which may be taken are specified in Art. 10(3).

[554] Dec. 92/169 ([1992] OJ L74/47) suspending the examination procedure concerning illicit

Union trade in products from third states. Member States might be authorized to adopt protective measures thereunder, in order to ensure that the execution of measures of commercial policy taken in accordance with the EC Treaty by any Member State was not obstructed by deflection of trade or where differences between such measures led to economic difficulties in one or more Member States. For example, according to Regulation 1087/84,[555] the substantial injury suffered by the French industry producing assembled watches, seen against the background of the poor general economic situation in Franche-Comté, where watchmaking was the main source of employment, made safeguard measures for the French market indispensable in the interest of the Union, in order to enable the current switch in production to be achieved under optimum conditions. In spite of completion of the internal market, certain such measures may remain permissible.[556]

Such measures may sometimes be presented as being compatible with the restructuring of Union industry[557] and, more particularly, with the use of restructuring aid. For example, according to the Commission, VERs are designed to protect the Union textile and clothing industry from excessive imports from low-wage countries.[558] The industry should use this period of protection to adapt its structures to current world market conditions and thereby facilitate a return to competitiveness. The policy of the Commission regarding aid to the textile industry is, therefore, aimed at cutting back overcapacity and preventing aid which would shift difficulties from one Member State to another.[559]

In other words, regulatory protection and the controlled use of aid may be

---

commercial practices within the meaning of Reg. 2641/84 [1984] OJ L252/1 consisting of the imposition in Japan of a port charge or fee used for the creation of a Harbour Management Fund.

[555] Introducing protective measures in respect of certain electronic piezo-electric quartz watches with digital display ([1984] OJ L106/31).

[556] See, e.g., Art. 11 of Reg. 3030/93 ([1993] OJ L275/1) on common rules for imports of certain textile products from third countries and Art. 16 of Reg. 517/94 ([1994] OJ L67/1) on common rules for imports of textile products from certain third countries not covered by bilateral agreements, protocols or other arrangements, or by other specific Community import rules.

[557] Though antitrust problems may arise. For example, in Case T–7/92 *SA Asia Motor France* v. *EC Commission* [1993] ECR II–669 the CFI found unlawful the failure of the Commission to act against a state-sponsored cartel to restrict imports of Japanese cars into France. See also Case T–37/92 *Bureau Européen des Consommateurs and National Consumer Council* v. *EC Commission* [1994] ECR II–285.

[558] According to the Economic and Social Committee, 'a coordinated external trade policy based on voluntary action which must promote fair trade and eliminate unfair competition and abuse of trade (e.g. social dumping, counterfeit products, pirated trade marks, subsidies)' will be necessary. See the Opinion of 29 Apr. 1992 ([1992] OJ C169/25) on the draft notice laying down guidelines for operational programmes which Member States are invited to establish within the framework of the Community initiative for regions heavily dependent on the textiles and clothing sector (Retex), para. 2.1.3.

[559] *Twelfth Report on Competition Policy* (EC Commission, Brussels, 1983), 126.

seen as mutually supportive. Thus, according to the Committee on Economic and Monetary Affairs and Industrial Policy, a 'determined commercial strategy' for the textiles industry is a necessary accompaniment[560] to the restructuring aid envisaged by Retex.[561] Indeed, regulatory protection may be considered necessary to avoid jeopardy to aid measures,[562] even where the aid has been granted by a Member State without authorization.[563]

The Commission sought to pursue such an approach in relation to the steel sector. It is claimed that the aid had 'no injurious effect on competition'.[564] However, although regulatory protection kept import flows stable and thereby helped to facilitate the internal restructuring of the industry, adverse side effects arose from the very fact that the Union industry concentrated on short-term rather than long-term trade objectives. In particular, some Union firms did not adjust sufficiently to the new marketing techniques applied by international competitors on the common market.[565] In other words, the effects of regulatory protection under the common commercial policy and efforts to ensure that aid leads to restructuring may be contradictory.

6.7.2 Compensatory Aid

To the extent that international trade liberalization is secured, the Commission is generally opposed to compensatory aid for Union industries adversely affected by increased competition. In fact, the Commission maintains that reduction in aid levels will lead to increased trade within the Union and with third states and thus to a general increase in economic prosperity for all Member States.[566] Thus, for example, in a decision concerning Belgian aid to a paper manufacturer[567] the Commission refused to accept that every time the Union made changes in the common customs tariff (CCT), the industries which suffered thereby should expect sympathetic consideration to be given to the grant of state aid. However, the Commission may face pressures from other Union institutions to modify its position. For example, the Economic and Social Committee considers that the exceptional circumstances faced by some

---

[560] Report on restructuring the textile and clothing industry in the Community, EP Doc. A3–0257/91, 20–1.

[561] Notice laying down guidelines for operational programmes which Member States are invited to establish within the framework of a Community initiative for regions heavily dependent on the textiles and clothing sector ([1992] OJ C142/5).

[562] See, regarding the Poseidom programme, Joined Cases T–480/93 & T–483/93 *Antillean Rice Mills NV* (not yet reported).

[563] Slynn AG in Case 291/86 *Central-Import Munster GmbH & Co. KG* v. *Hauptzollamt Munster* [1988] ECR 3679, 3697.

[564] Petersen, n. 270 above, 20–5, 24.

[565] *External Commercial Policy in the Steel Sector: Stocktaking and Prospects*, COM(86)585, 10.

[566] *Fourth Survey on State Aids in the European Community in the Manufacturing and Certain Other Sectors*, COM(95)365, 46–7.

[567] Dec. 82/670 ([1982] OJ L280/30) on aid granted by the Belgian Government to a paper-manufacturing undertaking.

sectors mean that a 'forward-looking, realistic evaluation of state aid' is needed.[568]

Such pressures may not be without their impact. The Commission claims that it examines aid requests in the light of problems which the industrial situation and the abolition of intra-Union border controls under Article 115 of the Treaty pose for certain products and sectors.[569] Recognition of such problems may lead to the authorization of restructuring or even operating aid.

Restructuring Aid

Restructuring aid may be authorized in response to problems arising from international trade liberalization.[570] For example, the Commission considered that the abolition of CCT duties on paper imports from EFTA States after 1984[571] would render structural adjustments necessary in the Union paper industry. Hence, aid could not be granted simply to rescue firms facing difficulties. However, aid granted to firms which could eventually become viable and designed to facilitate their efforts to switch to products with better market prospects, particularly having regard to the 1984 deadline, would receive sympathetic consideration under Article 92(3)(c).[572] Accordingly, the Commission authorized Dutch aid designed to facilitate the reduction of production in a field (the manufacture of printing and writing paper) in which the paper industry would have to face increased competition after 1984.[573]

In relation to the textiles sector, the Commission acknowledged that Member States were likely to respond to international trade liberalization by granting aid.[574] Such aid would be authorized if it sought to improve production techniques or to encourage applied research, provided that the results were made available on commercial terms and without discrimination throughout the Union.[575] The Union itself might also grant aid to regions which might otherwise suffer from increased competition in this sector.[576]

Trade liberalization with Central and Eastern European countries is now

---

[568] The Committee has complained that the 'persistence of the worldwide recession afflicting the maritime economy, combined with pressure from a competition policy conceived virtually exclusively in terms of the internal market, has caused the maritime industries within the EC to withdraw into their shells'. See the Opinion of 26 May 1992 ([1992] OJ C223/36) on the Communication on 'New Challenges for Maritime Industries', para. 2.5.

[569] *Implementation of the Reform of the Structural Funds 1989*, COM(90)516, 11.

[570] See, e.g., regarding hazel nuts, Commission Reply by Mr Steichen to Written Question E–2255/93 ([1994] OJ C240/15) by Giuseppe Mattola *et al*.

[571] See, e.g., Art. 1 of Prot. 1, concerning the treatment applicable to certain products, to the Swedish Free Trade Agreement ([1972] JO L300/97).

[572] *Twelfth Report on Competition Policy* (EC Commission, Brussels, 1983), 128–9. See, more particularly, Dec. 82/670 ([1982] OJ L280/30) on aid granted by the Belgian Government to a paper-manufacturing undertaking.

[573] *Twelfth Report on Competition Policy* (EC Commission, Brussels, 1983), 129.

[574] Community framework for state aids to the textile industry, SEC(71)363, para. I.3.

[575] Community framework for state aids to the textile industry, SEC(77)317, para. 5.3.

[576] *Improving the Competitiveness of the Community's Textile and Clothing Industry*, COM(91)399, 5.

considered likely to entail increased competition for Union industry, particularly the agricultural and textiles sectors, which are important for the economies of the weaker regions within the Union. There are also fears of increasing diversion of investment from such regions to Central and Eastern Europe.[577] To secure national approval of Europe Agreements with these countries, the Commission has offered various forms of compensation for the Member States and regions likely to be adversely affected by the liberalization envisaged in these Agreements.

Such compensation has included a large increase in the sums available to the Structural Funds for the period up to 1997.[578] More particularly, on 30 September 1991, within the framework of negotiations for Europe Agreements between the Union and the then Czechoslovakia, Hungary, and Poland, consensus was reached regarding liberalization of trade in textiles. At the same time, the Commission undertook to adopt measures to improve and modernize the textile industry within the Union and to promote its competitiveness, particularly in the regions most affected by such liberalization.[579] On 23 October 1991 the Commission produced the draft of its Retex programme,[580] pursuant to which the Union grants aid to textile-producing regions. Such Union aid is to be complementary to state aid, and so authorization of the latter is implied.[581]

Operating Aid

Operating aid may sometimes be authorized to deal with problems arising from international trade liberalization. For example, when the Common Customs Tariff was drawn up for List G products,[582] France stated that it could accept the tariff in relation to certain paper products because of its aid system. Accordingly, the Council decided to authorize this aid under Article 93(2) of

---

[577] R. Hall and D. van der Wee, 'Community Regional Policies for the 1990s' (1992) *Regional Studies* 399–404. At the same time, there may be new export opportunities for the regions including those outside the main development areas of the Union.

[578] Reply by Mr Millan to Written Question 24/92 ([1992] OJ C285/7) by Mr Gary Titley *et al*.

[579] *European Report* 1708 (2 Oct. 1991). Cf. the special textile initiative for Portugal, which was negotiated in the Council of Ministers in Dec. 1993 in return for Portuguese acceptance of the GATT Uruguay Round (*European Report* 1921 (29 Jan. 1994)).

[580] Notice to the Member States laying down guidelines for operational programmes which Member States are invited to establish within the framework of a Community initiative for regions heavily dependent on the textiles and clothing sector ([1992] OJ C142/5).

[581] See, regarding the desirability of granting Union aid and allowing Member States to grant aid to assist the 'lagging regions' to adjust generally to competition from Central and Eastern Europe, National Economic Research Associates, *Trade and Foreign Investment in the Community's Regions: The Impact of Economic Reform in Central and Eastern Europe* (European Commission, Regional Development Studies No. 7, Brussels, 1993).

[582] i.e., products in List G of Annex I to the EC Treaty, in relation to which special arrangements were made in Art. 20 EC.

the Treaty.[583] Under Article 42 of the Treaty the Council also authorized aid in the form of indemnities for tuna producers 'disadvantaged' by suspension of CCT duties.[584]

Moreover, at least where measures of regulatory protection may be unavailable or ineffective, the Commission may be willing to authorize aid to Union undertakings competing with third-country undertakings in receipt of aid from their own authorities. Such willingness is supported by the Economic and Social Committee. According to this Committee, while 'rigorously respecting' the rules of the Treaty, Commission evaluation of state aid must take account of the fact that in many sectors, third-country competitors enjoy state support in various guises.[585]

For example, aircraft producers in third states received aid in the form of very favourable credit terms for their sales abroad.[586] They could thus offer financing terms well below the lowest rates in the Union. Moreover, the suspension of CCT duties[587] meant that Union undertakings faced the same conditions for Union sales as for those on external markets and had a less favourable position than third-state producers in their domestic markets. Hence, aid, including production aid and export aid in intra-Union trade, to place Union undertakings in a situation as favourable as that enjoyed by competitors in third states[588] might be authorized under Article 92(3)(b) as promoting the execution of projects of common European interest.[589] Authorization of such aid, provided that it took 'precise account' of aid granted to non-Union competitors, was supported by the European Parliament.[590]

In relation to shipbuilding, the Commission stated in the *EEC Seventh General Report*[591] that it would have liked to see aid distorting competition between the Member States abolished where it could not be justified by

---

[583] Dec. of 19 Dec. 1960 ([1960] JO 1972) on the French aid system in favour of certain types of paper pulp, as prolonged by Dec. 67/146 ([1967] JO 548) and Dec. 68/160 ([1968] JO L76/12). The Commission had hoped for a solution through GATT (*Eighth EEC General Report* (EC Commission, Brussels, 1965), 83).

[584] Reg. 3687/91 ([1991] OJ L354/1) on the common organization of the market in fishery products, Art. 20 and recital 39 in the Preamble.

[585] Opinion of 19 Dec. 1990 ([1991] OJ C60/19) on the *Nineteenth Report on Competition Policy*, para. 2.4. See sect. 6.5. above, regarding environmental aid.

[586] Enforcement of bilateral agreements to control aid may be problematic. See the Resolution of the EP of 14 July 1995 ([1995] OJ C249/230) on the bilateral negotiations between the EU and the US on civil aircraft, paras. 4–7.

[587] See, currently, Sect. II, para. B, of the preliminary provisions in Annex I to Reg. 3115/94 ([1994] OJ L345/1) amending Annexes I and II to Reg. 2658/87 [1987] OJ L256/1 on the tariff and statistical nomenclature and on the CCT.

[588] *Second Report on Competition Policy* (EC Commission, Brussels, 1973), 91–2.

[589] *Memorandum on Industrial and Technological Policy Measures to be Adopted in the Aircraft Industry* (EC Commission, Brussels, 1973), 89–93.

[590] Resolution of 20 Apr. 1993 ([1993] OJ C150/34) on the Commission's report on the evaluation of aid schemes established in favour of Community air carriers, para. 14.

[591] (EEC Commission, Brussels, 1964), 82–3.

exceptional social or regional circumstances. However, German measures to encourage the export of ships to third countries were authorized in 1965.[592] The Commission realized the need for effective measures to offset distortions of competition in non-member countries or to provide a defence against them.[593] In this connection, due allowance had to be made for the fact that shipbuilding was a homogeneous market with no distinction between the internal and the export market.[594] Hence, the Preamble to Directive 69/262[595] stated that aid to compensate for the harm attributable to distortions of international competition could be authorized, provided it did not modify conditions of competition to a degree greater than that strictly required for such compensation.[596] The distortions were estimated as amounting to 10 per cent of the contract price,[597] and so Article 2(2) of the Directive provided that aid up to this limit was permissible. The Commission continued to take the view that a need for aid arises from the reluctance of major shipbuilding countries outside the Union to 'undertake wholeheartedly the structural adjustments necessary to restore normal market conditions to this industry'.[598]

6.7.3 Defensive Aid

Treatment of aid may be affected by international market conditions, such as 'economic repercussions of the crisis in Yugoslavia'[599] or the loss of markets in Central and Eastern Europe.[600] In such circumstances, aid may be authorized not specifically because of the effects of trade liberalization, but more generally because of the unfavourable market position of Union undertakings.

---

[592] *EEC Ninth General Report* (EEC Commission, Brussels, 1966), 86–7.

[593] See also the Opinion of the Economic and Social Committee of 19 Nov. 1987 on shipbuilding—industrial, social, and regional aspects, CES(87)1074, 4. See, most recently, regarding below-cost pricing, Reply by Mr Van Miert to Written Question E–1690/94 ([1995] OJ C42/2) by Jaak Vandemeulebroucke.

[594] Opinion of the Economic and Social Committee of 28 Mar. 1974 ([1974] OJ C97/41) on the proposals from the Commission on the shipbuilding industry, sect. I.

[595] On the grant of aids to shipbuilding to correct distortions of competition on the international shipbuilding market ([1969] JO L206/25).

[596] See, later, Commission Reply to Written Question 680/77 ([1978] OJ C52/9) by Mr Müller-Hermann.

[597] Or at least those which could be quantified were so estimated. See the *Second Medium-term Economic Policy Programme* (EC Commission, Brussels, 1969), App. I, 21. In the *First Report on Competition Policy* (EC Commission, Brussels, 1972), 132, the Commission maintained: 'thanks to aid, some non-member countries have been able to build up an important, and in one particular case, a dominating position on the world market'.

[598] *Seventeenth Report on Competition Policy* (EC Commission, Brussels, 1988), 152.

[599] Notice C35/92 (ex N172/A/91) ([1994] OJ C78/2) concerning aid granted by the Region of Friuli–Venezia Giulia.

[600] See, regarding the authorization of restructuring aid to a machine tool manufacturer in Hanover which had been badly affected by the loss of such markets, the *Twenty-Third Report on Competition Policy* (EC Commission, Brussels, 1994), 270.

Restructuring Aid

The Court of Justice does not rule out the possibility that aid specifically designed to strengthen the competitiveness of the undertakings of a Member State in the face of imports from third states with low labour costs may be authorized.[601] In practice, the Commission may authorize aid, irrespective of whether the lack of competitiveness of Union producers is attributable to differences in such costs. In the case of shipbuilders in the Netherlands and the United Kingdom, the Commission authorized aid linked with restructuring to enable them to align their prices with those of non-Union competitors.[602] Again, Belgian aid to a chemical manufacturer was authorized under Article 92(3)(c), because it enabled the recipient to switch to higher value-added products less sensitive to trends in international competition.[603] In authorizing aid to the Italian steel industry, the Commission took account of 'pressure from imports and . . . a trade dispute with the United States' on the financial position of Union steel companies.[604] More generally, aid which may result in replacement of imports predominantly from third states with domestic products is less likely than other aid to be treated as distorting competition to an extent contrary to the common interest for the purposes of Article 92(3)(c).[605]

Operating Aid

In considering the acceptability of operating aid, the Commission may take account of 'particularly heavy pressure' from imports from third countries, as in the case of the ship-repair industry in the Mediterranean.[606] Where the volume of such imports increases 'to an abnormal degree', they may be treated as liable to hinder restructuring of the relevant Union industry.[607] The implications of such language have become clear in the case of the shipbuilding industry. The mere fact that third-country producers capture a sufficiently large share of the market at the expense of Union producers may be regarded as an 'abnormality' liable to hinder such restructuring.[608]

More particularly, the Commission has admitted that owing to the unshakeable advantages of certain competing shipbuilders, at least in the short term,

---

[601] Case 259/85 *France* v. *EC Commission: aid to textiles and clothing* [1987] ECR 4393, 4419.

[602] Reply to Written Question 680/77 ([1978] OJ C52/9) by Mr Müller-Hermann.

[603] *Seventeenth Report on Competition Policy* (EC Commission, Brussels, 1988), 171.

[604] Dec. 94/259 ([1994] OJ L112/65) concerning aid to be granted by Italy to the public steel sector (Ilva group).

[605] Notice C27/92 (N295/92) ([1993] OJ C46/5) on aid to SCA Aylesford, a manufacturer of newsprint.

[606] *First EC General Report* (EC Commission, Brussels, 1968), 71.

[607] Case 13/63 *Italy* v. *EEC Commission: Italian refrigerators* [1963] ECR 165, 178.

[608] Several reasons for the situation have been mentioned from time to time, such as disparities in interest rates and variations in exchange rates. See, e.g., *The State of the Shipbuilding Industry (Situation as at 1 Jan. 1980)*, COM(80)443, 6 and *The State of the Shipbuilding Industry (Situation as at 1 Jan. 1982)*, COM(82)564, 3. Shipbuilding is also sensitive to changes in the sea transport sector (*ibid.*, 4).

market forces will not ensure that certain types of Union-built ships are internationally competitive.[609] In particular, Union shipbuilding is handicapped by unsuitable structures and by uncompetitive operating costs—the large number of yards in the Union prevent large-scale production as in the Japanese yards, which are virtually new and form part of integrated industrial groups, enabling them to withstand the hazards of the economic cycle. The need for structural adjustment is all the more urgent since Union yards have no hope of reducing social-security charges which, in comparison with certain countries with a recently developed shipbuilding industry, are a handicap.[610]

Hence, the controlled use of operating aid within the Union has been seen as necessitated by international market conditions. According to the preamble to a Commission proposal of 1984,[611] the structural crisis in the shipbuilding industry had led to an increasingly marked loss of competitiveness in Union shipbuilding compared with that in some third countries. While some small and medium-sized yards which had specialized in certain types of high-value-added products were managing to hold their own in such segments of the market, the overall state of the market was such that it was virtually impossible for the majority of Union shipbuilders to win orders for standard types of vessels at prices covering their production costs against the low-price competition from newly industrialized countries.[612] The overcapacity in the industry and the extra cost of preserving it were preventing the investment necessary to modernize production facilities, which was essential if the industry was to be able to face competition from third countries. The system of aid control set up by Directive 81/363[613] had helped to reduce distortions of competition between Member States. The Directive had also enabled the Union to speak with a common voice in talks with non-member shipbuilding nations. However, the restructuring measures had, owing to the considerable delay in implementing them and the worsening of the industry's difficulties, the severity of which exceeded expectations, so far proved inadequate to achieve the restoration of the industry's competitiveness and to allow for withdrawal of all operating aid.

Such thinking was elaborated in the Preamble to Directive 87/167.[614] World overcapacity in shipbuilding had caused prices to fall to a level which was often below the fixed costs of European shipyards. The price problem had been aggravated by the development of very cost-competitive capacity in third countries, particularly in the production of standardized vessels in series.[615] In view of the cost differences which existed for most categories of ships in

---

[609] *Reorganization of the Community Shipbuilding Industry*, Bull. EC, Supp. 7/77, 10.

[610] *Ibid.*, 5. See also *Policy Guidelines for Restructuring the Shipbuilding Industry*, COM(83)65, 7–8; and *Shipbuilding: Industrial, Social and Regional Aspects*, COM(87)275, 9–10.

[611] Proposal of 14 Mar. 1984 ([1984] OJ C86/5) for a dir. amending Dir. 81/363 [1981] OJ L137/39 on aid to shipbuilding, 5th recital in the preamble.

[612] *Fourteenth Report on Competition Policy* (EC Commission, Brussels, 1985), 145.

[613] On aid to shipbuilding ([1981] OJ L137/39).

[614] On aid to shipbuilding ([1987] OJ L69/55).

[615] 2nd recital in the Preamble (*ibid.*).

comparison to shipyards in some third countries, operating aid could not immediately be abolished.[616] However, aid should be geared towards supporting production where the Union's cost disadvantage was lowest and where there was a real possibility of restoring long-term competitiveness.[617] More particularly, the Preamble to Directive 90/684[618] treated aid as a means 'to support the present trend in production towards more technologically advanced ships'.

In the view of the European Parliament,[619] a 'shift of emphasis' was involved. Operating aids were no longer to be judged merely in terms of their impact within the Union. Rather, they were to be judged more in terms of facing up to worldwide market conditions, and, in particular, competition from Far Eastern yards.

However, the use of aid to respond to international market conditions is controversial and may be less acceptable in certain sectors than it has been in the shipbuilding sector. For example, over-reliance on aid to solve problems of industrial adjustment *vis-à-vis* third-country producers is said to have undermined the competitiveness of Union car manufacturers by hindering the economically healthy influence of market forces.[620] Hence, the Commission has sought to implement a stricter approach to aid in this sector.

6.7.4 Strategic Aid

Aid to enable Union undertakings to capture or recapture markets from third-country competitors may be favoured, as in the case of aid to the Italian chemicals industry;[621] Dutch aid to 'offset the current shift in pilot training to countries outside the EEA';[622] British aid for import substitution, to counter 'delocalization', to enable recipients to 'occupy a niche' and to counter the consequences of high exchange rates entailed by monetary policy;[623] and aid to the shipping industry generally.[624] In the case of shipbuilding, aid may be advocated because of concern over 'the strategic dependence of the world's No. 1 trading area on means of transport which are going to be built more and more by some of its competitors'.[625]

---

[616] 6th recital (*ibid.*).   [617] 7th recital (*ibid.*).
[618] On aid to shipbuilding ([1990] OJ L380/27), 9th recital.
[619] Resolution of 12 Dec. 1986 ([1987] OJ C7/325) on the proposal for a Sixth Dir. on aid to shipbuilding, para. 4.
[620] *Eighteenth Report on Competition Policy* (EC Commission, Brussels, 1989), 145.
[621] *Sixteenth Report on Competition Policy* (EC Commission, Brussels, 1987), 169.
[622] Dec. 94/996 ([1994] OJ L379/13) concerning the transfer by the Netherlands of a pilot school to the Royal Dutch Airline.
[623] Notice C20/93 (N29/93) ([1993] OJ C269/8) regarding aid which the UK planned to grant to Hualon Corp.
[624] Annex I, para. II to *Financial and Fiscal Measures Concerning Shipping Operations with Ships Registered in the Community*, SEC(89)921.
[625] Opinion of the Economic and Social Committee of 19 Nov. 1987 on shipbuilding—industrial, social, and regional aspects, CES(87)1074, para. 2.4.

More particularly, aid to assist penetration of East European (though not other European) markets may be authorized,[626] as was Italian aid to investment and lending operations in Eastern Europe.[627] Authorization of aid to stimulate investment in Eastern Europe is 'very much in line with an important aspect of external relations policy'.[628] In general, the Commission recognizes the importance of direct investment in third states, both for strengthening links with those states and for diversifying and internationalizing European industry.[629]

Authorization of such aid is all the more likely where technological development or exploitation of natural resources is involved.

Technological Development

To encourage increased productivity and competitiveness with imports from third states, aid may be granted to research and development[630] as well as for improvement of production techniques and for applied research, provided that the results are made available on commercial terms and without discrimination throughout the Union.[631] For example, the French authorities loaned FF 86 million to La Radiotechnique, a company mainly producing television sets. The authorities had explained that the loan, with a net grant equivalent of 5 per cent, was for development of genuinely innovative products, such as flat TV tubes, which would replace Japanese imports into the Union. The Commission authorized the aid under Article 92(3)(c).[632] In view of the Union interest in having a viable high-technology industry, electronics aid was similarly authorized.[633] Aid of this kind may also be authorized, as in the case of the Airbus project, under Article 92(3)(b).[634]

In relation to data processing, the Commission considered that the Union industry must be able to compete on the world market. Since this market was dominated by undertakings from third states and Union undertakings were technologically backward and lacked funds, aid might be justified to help solve

---

[626] Notice C35/92 (ex N172/A/91) ([1994] OJ C78/2) concerning aid granted by the Region of Friuli–Venezia Giulia.

[627] Bull. EU 4–1995, 1.3.41.

[628] Dec. 95/45 ([1995] OJ L264/30) on state aid in the form of tax concessions to undertakings operating in the Centro Finanziari ed Assicurativi di Trieste pursuant to Art. 3 of Italian Law 19 of 9 Jan. 1991.

[629] Though such considerations do not necessarily mean that aid will be authorized. See Notice C49/95 (ex N76/95) ([1996] OJ C71/4) concerning aid which Germany intended to grant to Brandenburg for investment projects in Poland; Notice C50/95 (ex N317/95) ([1996] OJ C71/6) concerning aid which Austria intended to grant to the ERP programme for the internationalization of Austrian firms; and Notice C51/95 (ex N320/95) ([1996] OJ C71/9) concerning aid which Austria intended to grant to the ERP programme for investments in Eastern Europe.

[630] *First Report on Competition Policy* (EC Commission, Brussels, 1972), 138.

[631] *Sixth Report on Competition Policy* (EC Commission, Brussels, 1977), 138.

[632] *Sixteenth Report on Competition Policy* (EC Commission, Brussels, 1987), 158.

[633] *Ibid.*, 157.

[634] Bull. EC 4–1974, 2112; and Bull. EC 3–1989, 2.1.73.

the difficulties which the latter faced in their efforts to mobilize private capital.[635]

In relation to electronic components, a significant Union presence in this industry was considered desirable in order to maintain security of supply. Without aid the Union industry would not be able to overcome its competitive handicap.[636] Thus, for example, German aid to this industry was authorized, in view of the need to strengthen Union structures in the face of competition from the undertakings of certain third states and the fact that research and development expenditure had to be on a scale that most Union undertakings would not be able to afford.[637]

In relation to telecommunications, Italian research and development aid was authorized partly because of the need to improve the Union's international competitiveness in this sector.[638] Spanish research and development aid was also authorized, because it contributed to achieving Union objectives in the telecommunications field, strengthened 'Europe's' competitive position in the field, and reduced the technology gap between Spain and the rest of the Union.[639]

Exploitation of Natural Resources

In relation to exploitation of natural resources, strategic aid may be treated favourably, particularly where Member States are dependent on imports from third states.[640] For example, a considerable shortfall in Union production of bauxite was one consideration leading to approval of aid for a Greek bauxite producer.[641] This consideration, combined with the very limited Union competition in bauxite production, meant that the aid could not adversely affect trade between Member States to an extent contrary to the common interest for the purposes of Article 92(3)(c).[642] On the same grounds aid for the production of magnesite was authorized.[643] Aid for the modernization of Cornish tin mines was also authorized because of the Union interest in maintaining the last tin mines in the Union and the possibility of higher tin prices within five years when the company would have to start repaying the aid.[644]

---

[635] However, aid should not help to maintain fragmentation of the market, since only the grouping of operations of Union industry would enable it to solve its current problems. See the *Second Report on Competition Policy* (EC Commission, Brussels, 1973), 93.

[636] *Eighth Report on Competition Policy* (EC Commission, Brussels, 1979), 145–6.

[637] *Fifth Report on Competition Policy* (EC Commission, Brussels, 1976), 87. See, more recently, the *Twenty-Fourth Report on Competition Policy* (EC Commission, Brussels, 1995), 515 and 528.

[638] Bull. EC 6–1988, 2.1.113.   [639] Bull. EC 11–1988, 2.1.95.

[640] See, e.g., Notice C27/92 (N295/92) ([1993] OJ C46/5) on aid to SCA Aylsford, a manufacturer of newsprint.

[641] Bull. EC 12–1989, 2.1.102.

[642] Communic. C44/88 (ex NN130/87) ([1991] OJ C143/5) concerning aids which Greece had decided to grant to the Eleusis Bauxite Mines.

[643] Notice C7/89 (ex NN129/87) ([1991] OJ C58/3) concerning aid which Greece decided to grant to Fimisco.

[644] *Sixteenth Report on Competition Policy* (EC Commission, Brussels, 1987), 156.

More particularly, aid to the exploitation of local energy sources tends to be favoured, as for example in the case of aid to a company extracting and enriching peat for power stations in Uppsala.[645] British aid to assist its offshore oil and gas supplies industry by making interest relief grants to purchasers of such supplies was also authorized, given that this industry was underdeveloped within the Union. However, subsequent development of this industry meant that the aid ceased to be permissible.[646] Aid to German firms to explore for and exploit oil reserves on parts of the Continental Shelf under the sovereignty of other Member States initially seemed more problematic, because of Union rules on the right of establishment, and in 1968 the Commission requested the German Government to cease granting it. However, the amount of the aid was small relative to the cost of exploration and development on the Continental Shelf, and the German companies concerned were competing against oil groups from other countries which might well grant other incentives, notably tax concessions. Hence, the Commission decided to drop its request.[647]

However, a strategic interest in authorizing aid to Union industry is not always recognized. In *Glaverbel*,[648] which concerned Belgian aid to a flat-glass producer in Namur, it was argued that the aid at issue merely served to strengthen the position of the Union on export markets and to ensure its independence with regard to imports. In other words, it served an important project of common European interest within the meaning of Article 92(3)(b) and could thus be authorized thereunder. Such thinking was said to have influenced the Union approach to the grant of aid to the coal industry.[649] Advocate General Lenz responded by arguing that, according to Article 3(b) of the Treaty, the principles of the Union included the establishment of a common commercial policy towards third countries and, according to Article 110, the same policy served to contribute to the harmonious development of world trade. Hence, the attempt to achieve self-sufficiency and to conquer world markets could not be regarded as a project covered by Article 92(3)(b).[650] Indeed, the inadequate information possessed by public authorities leads some economists to doubt whether 'strategic trade policies' can ever be economically justified.[651]

---

[645] Bull. EU 9–1995, 1.3.35

[646] Dec. 79/496 ([1979] OJ L127/50) on the UK scheme of assistance in the form of interest-relief grants in favour of the offshore supplies industry.

[647] *Fifth Report on Competition Policy* (EC Commission, Brussels, 1976), 87–9.

[648] Joined Cases 62 & 72/87 *Exécutif Régional Wallon and Glaverbel* v. *EC Commission* [1988] ECR 1573.

[649] Sect. 5.5 above.

[650] [1988] ECR 1573, 1588.

[651] A. Winters, 'Goals and Own Goals in European Trade Policy' (1992) 15 *The World Economy* 557–74, 570.

6.8 CONCLUSION

Horizontal policies may lead to relaxation of the aid prohibition in Article 92(1) of the Treaty. Union practice in this regard reflects a general tendency in OECD countries to move from 'defensive' to 'offensive' support policies.[652] Such policies are seen as correcting market imperfections. However, just as the market has imperfections, so may the efforts of political processes to correct such imperfections.[653] In other words, it cannot be assumed that horizontal aid is innocuous to competition or, indeed, that it is always effective in contributing to achievement of the objectives of the horizontal policy concerned. Certainly, practice within the commercial policy field suggests that such policies may be captured by narrow sectoral interests and thus rendered harmful to competition.

[652] *Investment Incentives and Disincentives: Effects on International Direct Investment* (OECD, Paris, 1989).

[653] W. F. Schwartz and E. W. Harper, 'The Regulation of Subsidies Affecting International Trade' (1972) 70 *Michigan Law Review* 831–58.

7

Procedures

7.1 INTRODUCTION

Aid control may be affected by procedures taking various forms, including adoption of intergovernmental acts, legislation, 'soft legislation', administrative decision-making, and judicial decision-making. With the possible exception of the last one, these forms have in common that Commission negotiation[1] with Member States, or at least their representatives in the Council of the Union, may be involved, in some cases the negotiation being multilateral and in other cases bilateral.[2]

7.2 ADOPTION OF INTERGOVERNMENTAL ACTS

Adoption of intergovernmental acts may be associated with the 'deepening' of integration, as for example when the Single European Act and the Treaty on European Union were adopted. Their adoption may also be associated with the 'broadening' of integration, as when accession acts are adopted. Such acts, and particularly protocols[3] or declarations[4] annexed thereto, may have significant implications for aid control.

Formally, Protocols annexed to the Treaty by common accord of the Member States are, according to Article 239, an integral part thereof,[5] and declarations can, in turn, be used to interpret the Treaty.[6] However, the real effect of such instruments on state aid control may not depend solely on their formal status.

---

[1] The Commission apparently finds such negotiation 'difficult'. See F. Andriessen, 'The Role of Anti-Trust in the Face of Economic Recession: State Aids in the EEC' [1983] *ECLR* 340–50, 347.

[2] Such negotiation may even be important in individual aid cases. See, e.g., Dec. 73/274 ([1973] OJ L254/14) on Art. 20 of Italian Law 1101 of 1 Dec. 1971 on the restructuring, reorganization, and conversion of the textile industry.

[3] A Protocol to the EC Treaty envisaged support for the economic development of Italy. In addition, a Protocol on certain provisions relating to France concerned export aids.

[4] A Joint Declaration of the original Six regarding measures to ease the economic and social situation of Berlin, to promote its development and to ensure its economic stability was annexed to the EC Treaty itself. Reference was made to this declaration in Dec. 92/465 ([1992] OJ L263/15) concerning aid granted by Berlin to Daimler-Benz.

[5] See, e.g., Case C–57/93 *Anna Adriaantje Vroege* v. *NCIV Instituut voor Volkshuisvestering BV and Stichting Pensioenfonds NCIV* [1994] ECR I–4541; Case 260/86 *EC Commission* v. *Belgium: Protocol on Privileges and Immunities* [1988] ECR 955.

[6] *R.* v. *Secretary of State for the Home Dept, ex p. Donald Walter Flynn* [1995] 3 CMLR 397, 404.

[*See p. 402 for n. 6 cont.*]

7.2.1 First Accession Act

A Declaration on hill farming in the United Kingdom was attached to the First Accession Act.[7] The Declaration recognized that the special conditions obtaining in certain areas of the enlarged Union might require action with a view to attempting to resolve the problems raised by these conditions and, in particular, to maintain reasonable incomes for farmers in such areas. The result was the enactment of Directive 75/268,[8] which allowed for the grant of aid, to be partly reimbursable by the European Agricultural Guidance and Guarantee Fund, to hill farmers and farmers in less favoured areas.[9]

Moreover, Protocol 30 to the Accession Act concerned Ireland. According to this Protocol, the High Contracting Parties recognized that in the application of Articles 92 and 93 of the Treaty account must be taken of the objectives of economic expansion and the raising of the standard of living of the population. Article 154 of the Accession Act itself provided that the co-ordination principles governing regional aid,[10] supplemented to take account of enlargement,[11] would apply to the new Member States. Pursuant to this provision, the Commission designated the central regions in the new Member States, where regional aid was subject to a ceiling.[12] Consistently with the Protocol, no part of Ireland was designated as such a region.

7.2.2 Second Accession Act

The Greek Association Agreement[13] had entailed application of substantially the same derogation as in Article 92(3)(a) of the EC Treaty to the whole of Greece. According to Article 52(2) of the Association Agreement, initially for a transitional period of ten years, which was renewable, state aid to promote Greek economic development was to be considered compatible with the association if it did not alter conditions of trade to an extent inconsistent with the mutual interests of association. Greece sought continuation of such

See also Jacobs AG in Case C–297/92 *Istituto Nazionale della Previdenza Sociale (INPS)* v. *Corradina Baglieri* [1993] ECR I–5211, I–5225. Cf. Case 43/75 *Gabrielle Defrenne* v. *Société Anonyme Belge de Navigation Aérienne (Sabena)* [1976] ECR 455, 478, where the ECJ ruled that a resolution of Member States cannot 'modify' the Treaty. According to Trabucchi AG, such a 'political resolution' cannot 'constitute an independent source of obligations for the states' (*ibid.*, 488).

[7] Prot. 17, on the import of sugar by the UK from the exporting countries and territories referred to in the Commonwealth Sugar Agreement, also influenced the acceptability of aid to British sugar refineries. See Dec. 73/209 ([1973] OJ L207/47) concerning the present system of aid in the UK for the refining of raw sugar.

[8] On mountain and hill farming and farming in less favoured areas ([1975] OJ L128/1).

[9] It was preceded by a Council Resolution of 15 May 1973 ([1973] OJ C33/1) on farming in certain less-favoured areas.

[10] Principles for the co-ordination of regional aid ([1971] JO C111/1).

[11] 'So that all Member States [would be] in the same position with regard to them'.

[12] *General Regional Aid Schemes*, COM(73)1110.

[13] [1963] JO 293.

arrangements under the Second Accession Act.[14] The Commission, however, considered that a Protocol to the Act should deal with the matter.[15] Consequently, Protocol 7, which followed the precedent provided by the Irish Protocol, was adopted.

According to a Greek Government memorandum,[16] which was designed to ensure that effect was given to the substance of Protocol 7, the Union institutions should recognize, for a sufficiently long period, the need for derogations from Union competition rules. The derogations should concern development incentives, provisional and regulated protection of newly created industries, export aid for small and medium-sized enterprises, and exemption from production limits.

Commission practice does seem to have been influenced by the Protocol. For example, Greek rescue aid, primarily in the form of debt recapitalization, was authorized, because restructuring and reductions in capacity and workforce were entailed, sectoral rules would be respected, and there was a disturbance in the Greek economy within the meaning of Article 92(3)(b) and Protocol 7.[17] When one recipient, a cement producer, failed to restructure, the Commission initially raised objections.[18] The development requirement in Article 92(3)(a) meant that aid for new investment or major expansions or conversions of undertakings involving large-scale investments of a physical nature and the costs associated with these was envisaged by this subparagraph. Article 92(3)(c), in turn, required restructuring if rescue aid was to be authorized thereunder. However, in view of the economic crisis and 'particularly in view of Protocol 7', the Commission concluded that application of Article 92(3)(b), which would underline that it was dealing with an unprecedented situation, was appropriate.[19]

Such practice is not without judicial support. According to the Court of First Instance, Protocol 7 'does not constitute an exception to Articles 92 and 93 of the Treaty but merely requires the Commission to take into consideration, when assessing the effects of aid to a Greek undertaking, the objectives

[14] Permission was also sought for certain tax concessions to continue to be granted to its industries. See Point 6 of the Statements by the Head of the Greek Delegation (Bull. EC 7/8–1976, 1204).

[15] *Opinion on the Greek Application for Membership*, Bull. EC, Supp. 2/76, 15. At the negotiating session of 28 Feb. 1977 Greece did not ask for any specific adjustment or transitional arrangements in relation to state aid. See Dec. 82/364 ([1982] OJ L159/44) concerning the subsidizing of interest rates on credits for exports from France to Greece after the accession of that country to the EEC.

[16] *Position of the Greek Government on Greece's Relations with the EC*, which was submitted to the Council Foreign Affairs meeting of 22 Mar. 1982 (Bull. EC 3–1982, 3.4.1).

[17] Bull. EC 7/8–1988, 2.1.77; *Eighteenth Report on Competition Policy* (EC Commission, Brussels, 1989), 170. The Commission was to be notified of aid to companies with over 300 employees (or 100 in certain sensitive industries). See Bull. EC 10–1987, 2.1.61.

[18] Bull. EC 2–1988, 2.1.65.

[19] Dec. 88/167 ([1988] OJ L76/18) concerning Law 1386/1983 by which the Greek Government granted aid to industry.

set forth in that Protocol'.[20] The Commission must still examine the anti-competitive effects of the aid.[21]

7.2.3 Third Accession Act

In the case of the Third Accession Act, Protocol 12, on Spain, and Protocol 21, on Portugal, followed the precedents provided by the Irish and Greek Protocols. Protocol 12 at least seems to have influenced Commission practice. In the case of the two outlying areas and the central mining area of the Asturias region and the Sierra Norte of the Madrid region, the Commission decided to permit, as an exception and for a period of three years followed by a review, the grant of regional aid with an intensity ceiling of 45 per cent.[22] A ceiling of 30 per cent to 45 per cent was accepted for Campóo (Cantabria) because of the highly unfavourable socio-economic situation of the area, both in a Union and a national context.[23] An increase in the ceiling from 30 per cent to 40 per cent was also accepted in certain parts of the Basque country.[24] In all these cases the Commission expressly claimed to have taken account of the Protocol.

However, lower levels of aid in the Asturias and Sierra Norte were imposed by Decision 93/353.[25] Moreover, where the aid is of a kind, such as rescue aid, which is not justified under Article 92(3)(a) or on regional grounds under Article 92(3)(c), the Protocol may apparently be disregarded.[26]

The Commission preference may be to take account of the 'burden of the past' rather than the formal terms of Protocol 12. In Decision 92/318[27] the Spanish Government referred to the Protocol. The Commission, however, focussed on the fact that pre-accession industrial policy in Spain, in respect of public companies, had sometimes been based on principles radically different from those employed in formulating the competition policy rules of the EC Treaty. At that time certain loss-making public companies were maintained on poor managerial principles and were kept in business artificially by state aid.

[20] According to the ECJ in Case 258/81 *Metallurgiki Halyps A.E.* v. *EC Commission* [1982] ECR 4261, 4279, the Protocol is 'a declaration addressed to the Community institutions' and does not provide a derogation from the steel production quotas. However, VerLoren van Themaat AG thought it 'possible to argue that [because of Prot. 7] the Community's steel policy . . . should not run counter to the recognized development needs of Greece' (*ibid.*, 4284–5). Cf. Jacobs AG in Case C–173/91 *EC Commission* v. *Belgium: redundant female employees* [1993] ECR I–673, I–688.

[21] Joined Cases T–447/93, T–448/93 & T–449/93 *Associazione Italiana Tecnico Economica del Cemento, British Cement Association, Titan Cement Company SA* v. *EC Commission* [1995] ECR II–1971.

[22] Bull. EC 7/8–1989, 2.1.83.

[23] Bull. EC 12–1987, 2.1.115.

[24] Bull. EC 7/8–1989, 2.1.83; *Nineteenth Report on Competition Policy* (EC Commission, Brussels, 1990), 174.

[25] Concerning the application of the national regional aid scheme in an area in the north of the Province of Madrid ([1993] OJ L145/25).

[26] Dec. 93/627 ([1993] OJ L309/21) concerning aid granted by the Spanish authorities on the occasion of the sale by Cenemesa/Cadmesa/Conelec of certain selected assets to Asea-Brown Boveri.

[27] On aid granted by Spain to Industrias Mediterraneas de la Piel SA ([1992] OJ L172/76).

After accession these companies were forced to adapt to an environment of fair competition. In these circumstances, aid mainly aimed at facilitating such adaptation and representing a significant effort to create a basis for the definitive restructuring of the company concerned could be considered compatible with the common market under Article 92(3)(c).[28]

7.2.4 Fourth Accession Act and the EEA Agreement

Closer integration with EFTA States has implications for aid control. Such implications, which won some recognition in negotiations both for the European Economic Area (EEA) Agreement and for the Fourth Accession Act,[29] were discussed in Chapter 4.[30]

7.3 LEGISLATION

Article 94[31] of the EC Treaty empowers the Council, acting on a Commission proposal,[32] to enact any appropriate regulations for the application of Articles 92 and 93.[33] In particular, the Council may[34] enact regulations determining the conditions in which Article 93(3) shall apply and the categories of aid exempted from the notification obligation in Article 93(3).[35] Provision in Article 94 for regulations rather than directives, which would have left Member States more freedom regarding the form and means of attaining the required results, implies an intention on the part of the Treaty authors to reserve for the Union institutions the task of aid control.

The Commission, it is said, has sought to preserve its discretion in assessment of aid by insisting that only procedural rules can be adopted pursuant to Article 94.[36] However, the Court of Justice does not apparently regard the

---

[28] See, similarly, Dec. 92/317 ([1992] OJ L171/54) on state aid in favour of Hilaturas y Tejidos Andaluces SA and its buyer.

[29] See, generally, A. Evans, *European Community Law, including the EEA Agreement* (Kluwer, Deventer, 1994). [30] See sects. 4.2.1 and 4.3.5 above.

[31] The ECJ accepted in Joined Cases 188–190/80 *France, Italy, and the UK* v. *EC Commission* [1982] ECR 2545, 2575, that the Commission may also enact dirs. concerning aid to public undertakings under Art. 90(3) EC.

[32] The TEU introduced a requirement that the EP should be consulted.

[33] It has been suggested that the Commission should consider proposing under Art. 94 the introduction of transparency obligations regarding state aid generally along the lines of Dir. 80/723 ([1980] OJ L195/35) on the transparency of financial relations between Member States and public undertakings. See the Opinion of the Committee on Legal Affairs and Citizens' Rights in the Report of the Committee on Economic and Monetary Affairs and Industrial Policy on the *Eighteenth Report on Competition Policy*, EP Doc. A3–108/89, 16.

[34] Cf. the obligation to act in Art. 87 EC.

[35] See sect. 7.5.2 below, regarding this obligation.

[36] M. Melchior, 'Les Communications de la Commission' in *Mélanges en Honneur de Fernand Dehousse* (Labov, Brussels, 1979), ii, 243–58, 248.

scope of this provision as being so limited.[37] Moreover, in *France, Italy, and the UK* v. *EC Commission: transparency Directive* the Commission admitted that measures under Article 94 could define aid, or aid incompatible with the common market, as well as making procedural arrangements.[38] This view was followed by Advocate General Reischl.[39] The Court itself drew a distinction between measures for application of Articles 92 and 93,[40] which could be adopted under Article 94, and mere surveillance arrangements.[41]

The Commission duly proposed legislative action in 1965,[42] but the proposal has never been approved by the Council.[43] Instead, the Commission has merely issued communications on notification of aid schemes of minor importance.[44]

More particularly, in February 1973, the Commission produced a draft regulation to control regional aid in the central regions.[45] The proposal apparently had the support of the European Parliament,[46] which called for the early replacement of existing control measures by a regulation under which the scale of the aid would be geared to the economic and social backwardness of a given region.[47] Member States may have been unwilling to see their use of aid circumscribed by such a regulation, and this proposal also failed to secure Council approval.

However, attitudes are by no means static. Commission practice under

---

[37] Case 77/72 *Carmine Capolongo* v. *Azienda Agricola Maya* [1973] ECR 611, 621–2.

[38] Joined Cases 188–190/80 [1982] ECR 2545, 2565.

[39] *Ibid.*, 2591.

[40] According to Van Gerven AG in Case 225/91 *Matra SA* v. *EC Commission* [1993] ECR I–3203, I–3258, an Art. 94 reeg. could establish rules governing the question whether or the Art. 93(2) procedure should be opened.

[41] *Ibid.*, 2575. However, Art. 92(2) can only be amended by action under Art. N TEU.

[42] Bull. EC 6–1966, 11; *Tenth EEC General Report* (EEC Commission, Brussels, 1967), 100–1. According to the *Sixth EEC General Report* (EEC Commission, Brussels, 1963), 71, 'a modification of the obligations flowing from Art. 93(3)' in the case of aid measures covered by Art. 92(2)(b) and (c) was 'under consideration'. Pursuant to Art. 112 EC, the Commission also envisaged harmonization of export aid to third states in the *Action Programme in Relation to the Common Commercial Policy* ([1962] JO 2354), para. B.1. Similarly, in the *Guidelines for European Agriculture* the Commission stated that in order to give a clearer picture of the rules governing national aid to agriculture it would propose to the Council a regulation specifying which aids were to be notified, which were prohibited and which were authorized (COM(81)608, para. 50). However, no such measure was adopted.

[43] According to the Commission, there was a general consensus of opinion within the Council Working Party concerned in favour of the proposal. See the *Third Report on Competition Policy* (EC Commission, Brussels, 1974), 77.

[44] SG(85)D/2611. See, later, Notification of an aid scheme of minor importance ([1990] OJ C40/2). See now the Communication on the accelerated clearance of aid schemes for SMEs and of amendments of existing schemes ([1992] OJ C213/10). The Commission is once again considering a proposal for legislation under Art. 94 in this area. See the *Twenty-Second Report on Competition Policy* (EC Commission, Brussels, 1993), 277.

[45] Bull. EC 2–1973, 2109; *Second Report on Competition Policy* (EC Commission, Brussels, 1973), 78.

[46] Resolution of 12 Feb. 1973 ([1973] OJ C14/8) on the first report on competition policy, para. 9.

[47] Resolution of 15 Jan. 1974 ([1974] OJ C11/8) on the second report from the Commission on the implementation of the principles of co-ordination of regional aid in 1972, para. 9.

Articles 92 and 93 apparently so affected perceptions of the likely consequences of legislating in this area that legislation came to be advocated by some Member States as a means of controlling the Commission. Thus in 1990 the Italian Government, with the support of Belgium, France, and Spain,[48] urged the formalization of Commission powers through enactment of legislation under Article 94.[49] Legislation would, it was envisaged, render Commission policy regarding state aid more transparent and give Member States a say in deciding the criteria to be applied by the Commission in individual aid cases. However, the majority of Member States opposed such legislation.[50] The Commission itself was also opposed, since it had come to prefer to maintain a clear separation between its powers and those of the Council and to rely on 'dialogue and consultation' with Member States.[51] Apparently, the Commission was influenced by the lax approach to aid control adopted in successive legislative measures regarding aid to the shipbuilding and coal industries. Even in relation to steel aid, 'it took a united and very determined Commission and a situation in the industry widely regarded as catastrophic and needing strong medicine to obtain the necessary tight control'.[52]

As a result, Article 94 has had limited use.[53] It has been used only to exempt major categories of aid to inland transport from notification requirements[54] and as a basis (along with Articles 92(3)(e) and 113 of the Treaty) for a Regulation on aid to shipbuilding.[55]

On the other hand, in some cases, such as agriculture, steel, and shipbuilding, aid rules may be embodied in sectoral legislation. Such legislation, it

---

[48] Spain, and Portugal also, apparently favoured the idea of adopting a reg. under Art. 94 to require differential treatment of aid as between poorer and richer Member States. See *Europe* 5350 (15/16 Oct. 1990).

[49] See also, regarding aid financed by means of quasi-fiscal measures, Communic. C24/90 (E9/89) ([1990] OJ C304/3) regarding aids to forestry, pulp, and paper production in Italy financed by means of quasi-fiscal levies.

[50] *Twentieth Report on Competition Policy* (EC Commission, Brussels, 1991), 127.

[51] *Europe* 1656 (19 Oct. 1990). The arrangements for dialogue and consultation were agreed with the Commission in the Industry Council meeting of 15 Oct. 1990 (*ibid.*). See also P. J. Slot, 'Procedural Aspects of State Aids: The Guardian of Competition versus the Subsidy Villains?' (1990) 27 *CMLRev.* 741–60.

[52] F. Rawlinson, 'The Role of Policy Frameworks, Codes and Guidelines in the Control of State Aid' in I. Harden (ed.), *State Aid: Community Law and Policy* (Bundesanzeiger, Trier, 1993), 52–60, 60.

[53] Case 84/82 *Germany* v. *EC Commission: aid to textiles and clothing* [1984] ECR 1451, 1487; and Case 301/87 *France* v. *EC Commission: Boussac* [1990] ECR I–307, I–355.

[54] Reg. 1191/69 ([1969] JO L156/1) on action by Member States concerning the obligations inherent in the concept of a public service in transport by rail, road, and inland waterway; Reg. 1192/69 ([1969] JO L156/8) on common rules for the normalization of the accounts of railway undertakings; and Reg. 1107/70 ([1970] JO L130/1) on the granting of aids for transport by rail, road, and inland waterway. In the Resolution of 20 Apr. 1993 ([1993] OJ C150/34) on the Commission's report on the evaluation of aid schemes established in favour of Community air carriers, para. 18, the European Parliament also called for action under Art. 94 in relation to aid to air transport.

[55] Reg. 3094/95 ([1995] OJ L332/1).

is thought, may 'reduce the danger of worsening interpretation of the competition rules and even of contradictions in the process of applying these rules in their entirety'.[56] While such thinking may be justified in formal terms, the substantial implications for the acceptability of aid may be considerable. Inconsistency of national legislation with Union legislation governing aid to this sector may be sufficient to render aid incompatible with the common market, even if distortion of competition is not established.[57] In effect, a legislative vacuum may be partly filled by measures approaching aid control issues from sectoral policy perspectives.[58]

7.4 'SOFT LEGISLATION'

'Soft law' may be defined 'as rules of conduct which, in principle, have no legally binding force but which nevertheless may have practical effect'.[59] A possible problem with this definition is that rules having practical effects may not be readily distinguishable from those having binding legal force.[60] For present purposes, the expression 'soft legislation' is used to indicate instruments which may have effects of legislation without being adopted according to formal legislative procedures.

The Commission usually describes such legislation as 'co-ordination principles', 'guidelines', 'codes', or 'frameworks'. It plays an important role in aid control within the Union, and may serve 'as a reference when establishing the Union's position on state aid cases in countries with whom the Community has entered into free-trade agreements'.[61] The instruments concerned may 'elaborate' rules contained in more formal Union legislation,[62] but more usually they elaborate rules contained in the Treaty itself. Their adoption may be justified by reference to the fact that 'Member States face problems of a similar nature or intensity, for example regional aid and aid for the environment'.[63]

At first sight, the legal context might seem unfavourable to the development of soft legislation. As the Commission admits, the acceptability of an aid must

---

[56] G. Bernini, 'The Rules on Competition' in *Thirty Years of Community Law* (EC Commission, Luxembourg, 1981) 323–73, 373.

[57] Case C–400/92 *Germany* v. *EC Commission: Cosco* [1994] ECR I–4701, I–4733.

[58] See Ch. 5.

[59] F. Snyder, 'The Effectiveness of European Community Law: Institutions, Processes, Tools and Techniques' (1993) 56 *MLR* 19–54, 32.

[60] See, generally, K. C. Wellens and G. M. Borchardt, 'Soft Law in European Community Law' (1989) 14 *ELRev.* 267–321. Cf., regarding the use of such law by national administrations, G. Ganz, *Quasi-Legislation* (Sweet & Maxwell, London, 1987).

[61] *European Union Automobile Industry*, COM(94)49, 15.

[62] Cf., regarding public procurement, Notice C(88)2510 ([1989] OJ C22/3) on monitoring compliance with public-procurement rules in the case of projects and programmes financed by the Structural Funds and financial instruments.

[63] *Commission Policy on Sectoral Aid Schemes*, COM(78)221, 6.

be judged in isolation, on the basis of Article 92, and not on the basis of previous Commission decisions concerning aid to other companies.[64] Even so, the Commission considers that such legislation may 'clarify the application of Community regulations and ensure greater legal certainty for Member States and companies', though it may be argued that the importance of legal certainty implies the need for resort to Article 94.[65] At the same time, the 'details of the aid are left to the discretion of the national authorities', and a 'flexible approach' is followed by the Commission. As a result, a contribution to implementation of the subsidiarity principle in Article 3b of the EC Treaty[66] is said to be involved.[67]

The Commission recognizes the danger that adoption of such legislation for a given industry may lead to the generalized grant of aid to that industry, even when aid is not strictly necessary. Inflexibility may also result, in the sense that account cannot be taken of the specific characteristics of the industry concerned in each Member State.[68] However, in cases where it becomes evident that an industry faces, or will face, a situation of particular difficulty throughout the Union, the Commission may develop principles which indicate the policy it will pursue regarding aid to this industry.[69] Apparently, such action may be welcomed by Member States generally and by sectoral interests, as in steel and shipbuilding, which 'have had bad experience of "beggar-thy-neighbour" subsidies'.[70]

7.4.1 Forms

The Commission may seek merely to formulate 'criteria' for particular types of aid, such as aid regimes financed by parafiscal charges[71] or 'management loans';[72] to follow 'constant practice'[73] or a single precedent,[74] though attempts

---

[64] Dec. 93/564 ([1993] OJ L273/51) concerning aid the Italian Government intended to grant to Cartiere del Garda.

[65] K. Hellingman, 'State Participation as State Aid under Article 92 of the EEC Treaty: the Commission Guidelines' (1986) 23 *CMLRev.* 111–31, 127–8.

[66] It states: 'in areas which do not fall within its exclusive competence, the Community shall take action, in accordance with the principle of subsidiarity, only if and in so far as the objectives of the proposed action cannot be sufficiently achieved by the Member States and can therefore, by reason of the scale or effects of the proposed action, be better achieved by the Community'.

[67] *Application of the Subsidiarity Principle 1994*, COM(94)533, 22–3.

[68] Cf. the reference to the possibility of 'an effective co-ordination of national measures' in Case 171/83R *EC Commission* v. *France: aid to textiles and clothing* [1983] ECR 2621, 2630.

[69] *First Report on Competition Policy* (EC Commission, Brussels, 1972), 131.

[70] F. Rawlinson, n. 52 above, 57.

[71] Notice C48/94 (NN104/94 (ex N514/92)) ([1995] OJ C161/5) regarding aid which the French Government had decided to grant to Institut Français du Pétrole.

[72] Notice C57/94 (ex NN108/94) ([1995] OJ C184/5) regarding aid which the French Government intended granting in the fisheries sector.

[73] Notice C45/91 (ex N255/91) ([1993] OJ C37/15) regarding the proposal of the Italian authorities to provide state aid to the Fiat Group in support of its Mezzogiorno investment plan.

[74] Dec. 88/468 ([1988] OJ L229/37) on aids granted by the French Government to a farm

by Member States to invoke such precedents in proceedings before the Commission may be cursorily rejected;[75] to implement a 'global sectoral approach', as for example in relation to aluminium producers;[76] or to develop a 'consistent policy' regarding aid to a particular sector, which has been applied in previous decisions,[77] or regarding aid of a particular type[78] or form.[79] The Commission has done so in relation to synthetic fibres,[80] motor vehicles,[81] and various other sectors.

For example, in Decision 87/194,[82] which concerned planned aid to a Belgian producer of mineral water, the Commission noted that aid planned by the Belgian Government for similar investments in this sector had previously been found incompatible with the common market and, hence, had been prohibited.[83] As the situation in the sector had not changed, the Commission felt that it must be guided by the same considerations. Only where the facts are sufficiently different to exclude 'parallelism' will the Commission depart from

machinery manufacturer at St Dizier, Angers, and Croix; and Notice C66/91 (NN154/91) ([1992] OJ C48/3) regarding aid which Germany had decided to grant to Sony GmbH.

[75] Notice C7/95 (N412/94) ([1995] OJ C262/16) concerning aid the German Government intended to grant to Maschinenfabrik Sangerhausen, GmbH i K, Sachsen-Anhalt.

[76] Dec. 88/174 ([1988] OJ L79/29) concerning aid which Baden-Württemberg had provided to BUG-Alutechnik GmbH, an undertaking producing semi-finished and finished aluminium products.

[77] See, regarding the flat-glass sector, Dec. 89/373 ([1989] OJ L166/60) on aid decided by the Italian Government for investments at the public flat-glass industry (Veneziana Vetro).

[78] See, regarding aid for exports to other Member States, Dec. 92/129 ([1992] OJ L47/19) on aid granted by the Italian Government to the forestry, pulp, paper, and board industry and financed by means of levies on paper, board and cellulose.

[79] See, regarding preferential tariffs, Dec. 86/592 ([1986] OJ L340/22) on the system of ceilings on the price of diesel fuel for fishermen introduced by the French Government.

[80] Dec. 88/173 ([1988] OJ L78/44) on the Belgian Government's aid proposal in favour of Roger Vanden Berghe NV, a polypropylene yarn and carpet producer located in Desselgem, Belgium.

[81] Dec. 89/633 ([1989] OJ L367/62) concerning aid provided or to be provided by the Spanish Government to Enasa, an undertaking producing commercial vehicles under the brand 'Pegasus' and Dec. 89/661 ([1989] OJ L394/9) concerning aid provided by the Italian Government to Alfa Romeo. Cf., in relation to decisions concerning successive aid grants under the same scheme, Dec. 89/348 ([1989] OJ L143/44) on aid granted by the French Government to an undertaking manufacturing equipment for the motor vehicle industry—Valéo, n. 1.

[82] On a FIM loan to a mineral-water and glass-bottle manufacturer ([1987] OJ L77/43). The Commission also referred to earlier decisions in Dec. 84/417 ([1984] OJ L230/28) on a proposed aid by the Netherlands Government in respect of certain investments to be carried out by an oil company at its refinery in Borsele and in Dec. 84/418 ([1984] OJ L230/31) on a proposal by the Netherlands Government in respect of certain investments to be carried out by an oil company at its refinery in the area of Rotterdam-Europoort.

[83] Dec. 82/774 ([1982] OJ L323/31) on a Belgian Government aid scheme concerning the setting-up of a new factory by a soft drinks manufacturer; Dec. 82/775 ([1982] OJ L323/34) on a Belgian Government aid scheme concerning the expansion of the production capacity of an undertaking manufacturing mineral water and soft drinks; and Dec. 82/776 ([1982] OJ L323/37) on a Belgian Government aid scheme concerning the expansion of the production capacity of an undertaking manufacturing mineral water, hot-spring water, and soft drinks.

an earlier decision.[84] The principle of equal treatment may be invoked by the Commission as the legal basis for such practice,[85] and consistency of Commission practice may be expected by the European Courts.[86] The Commission is also willing to be consulted by national courts regarding 'its customary practice'.[87]

Policy statements in the annual reports on competition policy are sometimes included within the field of soft legislation.[88] According to Advocate General VerLoren van Themaat in *Intermills*, 'certain guidelines as to the Commission's policy may be deduced from those reports'.[89] The Commission itself considers that such statements promote transparency,[90] and may 'assist' national courts in examining individual cases.[91]

The Commission may seek to rely on unpublished guidelines, as in the case of the 'rules governing national aids in the event of damage to agricultural production or the means of agricultural production, and national aids comprising payment of a proportion of the cost of insuring against such risks'[92] or the 'set of measures' regarding aid relating to welfare contributions in agriculture,[93] or letters to Member States. For example, principles regarding state guarantees were communicated to Member States by letters dated 5 April and 20 June 1989.[94] Principles restricting investment aid to the sugar sector were contained in a Commission letter to Member States of 1 February 1972 and

[84] Dec. 93/627 ([1993] OJ L309/21) concerning aid granted by the Spanish authorities on the occasion of the sale by Cenemesa/Cadmesa/Conelec of certain selected assets to Asea-Brown Boveri.

[85] Case C–313/90 *Comité International de la Rayonne et des Fibres Synthétiques (Cirfs)* v. *EC Commission* [1993] ECR I–1125, I–1187.

[86] Case T–459/93 *Siemens SA* v. *EC Commission* (not yet reported). See, similarly, regarding 'internal directives', Case 148/73 *Raymond Louwage and Marie-Thérèse Louwage, née Moriame* v. *EC Commission* [1974] ECR 81, 89.

[87] Notice regarding co-operation between national courts and the Commission in the state-aid field ([1995] OJ C312/8), para. 29.

[88] C. Blumann, 'Régime des aides d'état: jurisprudence récente de la Cour de justice' (1992) *RMC* 721–39, 731.

[89] Case 323/82 *SA Intermills* v. *EC Commission* [1984] ECR 3809, 3835.

[90] *Twenty-Third Report on Competition Policy* (EC Commission, Brussels, 1994), 255.

[91] Notice on co-operation between national courts and the Commission in applying Arts. 85 and 86 EC ([1993] OJ C39/6), para. 36. Cf., however, M. G. Santiago, 'Las "comunicaciones interpretativas" de la Comission: concepto y valor normativo' (1992) *Revista de Instituciones Europeas* 933–49, 936, regarding the inadequate details usually provided in such statements.

[92] They were referred to in a Communic. ([1987] OJ C96/3) concerning the application of aid measures for fruit growers covering a proportion of the cost of insuring against hail.

[93] Of 13 Nov. 1985. See Notice regarding aid planned by the Italian Government for the Mezzogiorno ([1987] OJ C259/2).

[94] Notice C28/93 (N446/93) ([1993] OJ C286/2) concerning aid which Germany intended to grant to NINO Textil AG, Nordhorn. By letter dated 4 Mar. 1991 to the Member States concerning the procedures for the notification of aid plans and procedures applicable when aid is provided in breach of the rules of Art. 93(3) the Commission also stated that, in the absence of an undertaking not to grant aid until the Art. 93(2) procedure was completed, it reserved the right to take a decision requiring the suspension of payments (*Competition Law in the European Communities ii: Rules Applicable to State Aids* (EC Commission, Brussels, 1995), 71–6).

another letter, regarding isoglucose, of 28 January 1977. On the apparent assumption that responses by Member States might affect the force of such instruments, the Commission observed that 'the Member States did not contest the Commission's position' in the letters.[95] Such letters may be accompanied by published communications.[96] It is argued that to be 'effective', they must concern matters within the sphere of competence of the Commission, be published in the Official Journal and be clearly written and informative.[97]

In some cases a 'common agreement' may be reached at a multilateral meeting of Member States, though the terms of the agreement may remain unpublished.[98] In other cases, as in the case of privatization, the Commission may 'agree' certain principles with several Member States[99] or even with a single Member State.[100]

While Commission officials apparently believe that it makes no practical difference whether principles are embodied in formal legislation or in 'simple notices or statements by the Commission which may or may not be immediately published',[101] the Commission may prefer embodiment of its principles in forms expressly approved by Member States. Indeed, the Commission secured approval of its original co-ordination principles for regional aid in a Resolution of the Representatives of the Governments of the Member States meeting in the Council.[102] In general, however, communications in the Official Journal seem to have become the favoured form for introduction of such instruments. Such practice does not in itself meet the demand of the European Parliament

---

[95] Dec. 90/379 ([1990] OJ L186/21) on state aid to SA Sucrerie Couplet, Brunehaut-Wez, Belgium. See also Dec. 86/509 ([1986] OJ L300/34) on aid granted by Germany and Bavaria to a producer of polyamide and polyester yarn situated in Deggendorf.

[96] Letter to the Member States of 3 Nov. 1983 (see Communic. C34/93 (N557/93) ([1993] OJ C291/4) on equity injections by the Irish Government in favour of Aer Lingus) and the Communic. of 24 Nov. 1983 ([1983] OJ C318/3) regarding unnotified aid. Cf., regarding the use of communications and the elimination of unjustified trade barriers, *Completing the Internal Market*, COM(85)310, 39.

[97] A. Mattera, *Le Marché Unique Européen: Ses Règles, Son Fonctionnement* (2nd edn., Jupiter, Paris, 1990), 45. See, generally, M. Melchior, n. 36 above.

[98] Dec. 91/306 ([1991] OJ L158/71) concerning two aid projects of the German Government in favour of a shipyard in financial difficulties.

[99] See Reply by Mr Van Miert to Written Question 423/93 ([1993] OJ C288/7) by Mrs Cristiana Muscardini, regarding privatization guidelines agreed with Greece, Germany, and Portugal.

[100] The 'Andreatta–Van Miert Agreement' between the Italian Government and the Commission of July 1993 concerning certain public undertakings in Italy, which deals with reduction of the debt of public undertakings in Italy, was published in Annex 3 to Communic. C38/92 (ex NN128/92) regarding aid which Italy had decided to grant to EFIM ([1993] OJ C349/2). Individual aid grants must still be examined for compatibility with Art. 92, but they will apparently be authorized if they are not 'additional' to aid approved under the Agreement and help to achieve the objectives of that aid. See Bull. EU 3–1995, 1.3.42.

[101] F. Rawlinson, n. 52 above, 59.

[102] Of 20 Oct. 1971 ([1971] JO C111/1) on general systems of regional aid.

that the Parliament should 'contribute to reaching some kind of agreement with those at whom such measures are aimed'.[103]

7.4.2 Creation

Article 93(1) of the EC Treaty,[104] which provides for the Commission to propose 'appropriate measures' to the Member States, may be regarded as offering a legal basis for the adoption of soft legislation. According to the terms of this provision, such proposals may only relate to existing aid.[105] This limitation may be recognized in the instrument concerned[106] or in individual decisions,[107] though the Commission apparently considers that for these purposes the distinction between new aid and continuation of existing aid schemes is unclear.[108] Moreover, if such proposals constitute only recommendations for the purposes of Article 189 of the Treaty,[109] they need not be followed by Member States.[110] Hence, the Commission seeks to obtain the consent of Member States to instruments containing the proposals.

Consensus

According to the Court of Justice, Article 93(1) 'involves an obligation of regular, periodic co-operation on the part of the Commission and the Member States, from which neither the Commission nor a Member State can release itself for an indefinite period depending on the unilateral will of either of them'.[111] Obligations on the Commission to obtain acceptance from the Member States of measures proposed under this provision, periodically to review them[112] and to amend them only with such acceptance[113] are implied.

In fact, the creation of soft legislation, like more formal legislation,[114] may be

[103] Report of the Committee on Economic and Monetary Affairs and Industrial Policy on the *Twentieth Report on Competition Policy*, EP Doc. A3–0338/91, 17.

[104] See sect. 7.5.1 below.

[105] Lenz AG in Case C–313/90 *Comité International de la Rayonne et des Fibres Synthétiques (Cirfs)* v. *EC Commission* [1993] ECR I–1125, I–1154, n. 13.

[106] In the introduction to the Guidelines for the examination of state aid to fisheries and aquaculture ([1994] OJ C260/3) the Commission 'proposes' under Art. 93(1) that Member States apply criteria laid down in the Guidelines to their existing schemes.

[107] The Community framework on state aid to the motor vehicle industry ([1989] OJ C123/3) is expressly limited to existing aid, though it was described as being so limited in Dec. 90/381 ([1990] OJ L188/55) amending German aid schemes for the motor-vehicle industry.

[108] Intervention by F. Rawlinson in I. Harden (ed.), n. 52 above, 86.

[109] According to Lenz, AG in Case C–135/93 *Spain* v. *EC Commission: framework for aid to the motor vehicle industry* [1995] ECR I–1651, I–1661, they may be so classified.

[110] According to this provision, recommendations lack binding force. See also Mayras AG in Case 70/72 *EC Commission* v. *Germany; investment grants for mining* [1973] ECR 813, 834.

[111] Case C–135/93 *Spain* v. *EC Commission: framework for aid to the motor vehicle industry* [1995] ECR I–1651, I–1680.

[112] *Ibid.*, I–1681.   [113] Lenz AG, *ibid.*

[114] J. Biancarelli, 'Le contrôle de la Cour de Justice des Communautés européennes en matière d'aides publiques' [1993] *AJDA* 412–36, 423 refers to the Commission as exercising a *quasi normatif* power.

regarded by the Commission as conditional on information to, and negotiation with, Member States. There may also be more formal similarities with legislation. Whereas principles regarding aid to textiles[115] and synthetic fibres[116] and state financing of public undertakings were originally published as a 'paper' in the Bulletin of the European Communities,[117] they may now be reasoned and published in the Official Journal.[118] More particularly, it is argued that, to be binding, the instruments concerned must be reasoned in accordance with Article 190 of the Treaty.[119] However, reasoning requirements in the instruments themselves are reduced if Member States have already been informed.[120] More fundamentally, institutions such as the European Parliament do not play the same role in adoption of soft legislation as in adoption of formal legislation.

Adoption procedures may include those proposed by the Commission in 1990. The Commission proposed:[121]

—the annual report on competition policy would be discussed in the Council each year:

—twice a year multilateral meetings at expert level under Commission Presidency on state aid issues would be organized:[122] and

—a collection of procedures, general texts in application and judgments of the Court of Justice concerning state aid would be published.

In the course of the contacts entailed, which may be complemented by contacts with sectoral interest groups,[123] the Commission may seek to secure consent for the instruments concerned,[124] and the reactions of Member States may be decisive. In the case of a sectoral code, particular importance may be attached to reactions of Member States whose economies 'depend heavily' on the sector concerned.[125] Apparently, the Commission fears that soft legislation

---

[115] Bull. EC 1–1974, 37.   [116] Bull. EC 7/8–1977, 1.5.3.
[117] Bull. EC 9–1984, 3.5.1.   [118] M. Melchior, n. 36 above, 252.
[119] Lenz AG in Case C–135/93 *Spain* v. *EC Commission: framework for aid to the motor vehicle industry* [1995] ECR I–1651, I–1669–70.
[120] *Ibid.*   [121] *Europe* 5350 (15/16 Oct. 1990).
[122] Such meetings are held to enable the Commission to take account of the comments and suggestions of the Member States and to help national administrations to gain a better understanding of its principles and, thereby, to promote legal certainty. See the *Twenty-Second Report on Competition Policy* (EC Commission, Brussels, 1993), 76–7. The ESA may attend such meetings as an observer. See the *Twenty-Third Report on Competition Policy* (EC Commission, Brussels, 1994), 241.
[123] See, regarding aid to the textiles sector, Case C–313/90 *Comité International de la Rayonne et des Fibres Synthétiques (Cirfs)* v. *EC Commission* [1993] ECR I–1125, I–1185.
[124] See, regarding those for aid towards capital-intensive investment, aid for rescuing and restructuring firms in difficulty, aid in connection with export credit insurance, aid towards environmental protection measures, and aid to the tourist industry, the *Twenty-Second Report on Competition Policy* (EC Commission, Brussels, 1993), 27. However, subsequent challenges to the code on public undertakings and the aid framework for the motor industry imply that the Commission may be satisfied with less than unanimous consent.
[125] Dec. 90/381 ([1990] OJ L188/55) amending German aid schemes for the motor vehicle industry.

may be unworkable if 'strongly opposed' by Member States and its implementation may be likely to be delayed by proceedings before the Court of Justice.[126] Thus, for example, the aid framework for the motor vehicles sector 'took into account the principal observations made by the representatives of the Member States at a multilateral meeting on 27 October 1988'.[127] On the other hand, since the reactions of Member States to the draft principles regarding export aid were 'mixed', the Commission favoured leaving the matter to a Council directive under Article 113 of the Treaty.[128] Planned frameworks may also be abandoned because of opposition within the Commission.[129] In other cases, as in the case of new guidelines for environmental aid[130] and aid to undertakings in difficulty because of a recession or because they were in the process of restructuring,[131] disagreements may merely lead to postponed introduction of the guidelines concerned. In contrast, 'broad support' led the Commission to adopt a revised code for aid to synthetic fibres.[132]

Once such an instrument has been adopted by the Commission, the latter seeks to secure its acceptance by Member States. For example, Member States were 'asked' to signify their agreement to the code for aid to the synthetic fibres industry, both as to the notification procedure and to powers of assessment under Article 92, within fourteen days.[133] In the absence of such agreement, the Commission has taken the position that the instrument concerned may in any case 'enter into force' by whatever deadline is set by the Commission.[134] It is uncertain whether this position would be supported by the European Courts.[135]

---

[126] F. Rawlinson, n. 52 above, 60.

[127] Case C–135/93 *Spain* v. *EC Commission: framework for aid to the motor vehicle industry* [1995] ECR I–1651, I–1675.

[128] *Twenty-Second Report on Competition Policy* (EC Commission, Brussels, 1993), 207–8.

[129] F. Rawlinson, n. 52 above, 55, regarding aid to the audio-visual industry.

[130] *Twenty-Second Report on Competition Policy* (EC Commission, Brussels, 1993), 208. Earlier work on a framework for aid in the energy sector led to nothing. See the *Thirteenth Report on Competition Policy* (EC Commission, Brussels, 1984), 139. See also, regarding revision of the 1979 Principles for regional aid, the *Thirteenth Report on Competition Policy* (EC Commission, Brussels, 1984), 175, and, regarding the draft code on state guarantees, which envisaged that financial institutions lending money on the basis of a guarantee might also be treated as aid recipients, T. Soames and A. Ryan, 'State Aid and Air Transport' [1995] *ECLR* 290–309, 295.

[131] *European Report* 1837 (20 Feb. 1993). Community Guidelines on state aid for rescuing and restructuring firms in difficulty ([1994] OJ C368/12) were later adopted.

[132] *Twenty-Second Report on Competition Policy* (EC Commission, Brussels, 1993), 208.

[133] Code on aid to the synthetic fibres industry ([1992] OJ C346/2). In the case of aid to fishing, Member States 'will confirm to the Commission before 31 Dec. 1994 that they will comply with the criteria laid down in these guidelines' (Guidelines for the examination of state aid to fisheries and aquaculture ([1994] OJ C260/3), para. 3.1).

[134] See, regarding aid to the automobiles sector, H. Morch, 'Summary of the Most Important Recent Developments' [1995] 5 *Competition Policy Newsletter* 43–9, 47.

[135] According to Lenz AG in Case C–135/93 *Spain* v. *EC Commission: framework for aid to the motor vehicle industry* [1995] ECR I–1651, I–1661, for the purposes of Art. 93(1), consultation of Member States is not sufficient, unless their consent is also obtained.

Unilateralism

Soft legislation may be perceived by the Commission as entailing greater flexibility for continued negotiation and elaboration[136] and for adaptation to market changes[137] than formal legislation. For example, the Commission stated that it would follow its guidelines on environmental aid[138] until the end of 1999. Before the end of 1996 it would review their operation.[139] It might amend them at any time, should it prove appropriate to make changes for reasons connected with competition policy, environmental policy, and regional policy or to take account of other Union policies and of international commitments.[140] The apparent implication is that the need for flexibility may lead to unilateral amendment or, in other words, may be perceived to override the need to obtain consent.

The implication may be supported by earlier Commission practice in the field of regional aid. In May 1973 the Commission organized a multilateral meeting with senior national officials responsible for aid to discuss implementing the principles regarding regional aid in the three new Member States (Denmark, Ireland, and the United Kingdom) and, more particularly, the definition of central and peripheral regions there. In contrast to the situation in 1971, 'no general agreement was to be found'.[141] Therefore, the Commission unilaterally extended the principles to these Member States.[142]

Subsequently the Commission informed the Council that, in accordance with the powers vested in it by Articles 92 to 93 of the Treaty, it would, as from 1 January 1975 apply new principles to general regional-aid systems already in force or to be established in the regions of the Union. The Commission considered it desirable that the governments of the Member States modify their resolution of 20 October 1971 to take account of the new principles.[143]

In 1981 the Commission also discussed with Member States the possibility

---

[136] The instruments concerned are systematic rather than piecemeal and thus resemble legislation rather than litigation. They enable the Commission, without securing the consent of the legislature or the European Courts, to present its interpretation and seek to develop its policy. They circumscribe the arena for debate and define the agenda for negotiation and, if necessary, litigation. See M. Melchior, n. 36 above, 250. Thus they may assist Commission efforts to become 'head of the river' (F. Andriessen, n. 1 above, 350).

[137] Code on aid to the synthetic fibres industry ([1992] JO C346/2).

[138] Community guidelines on state aid for environmental purposes ([1994] OJ C72/3).

[139] Such a review cannot justify renewal of principles indefinitely. See Case C–135/93 *Spain* v. *EC Commission: framework for aid to the motor vehicle industry* [1995] ECR I–1651, I–1683–4.

[140] Community guidelines on state aid for environmental purposes ([1994] OJ C72/3), para 4.3. See, similarly, regarding 'amplification' or 'modification' of the Guidelines for the examination of state aid to fisheries and aquaculture ([1994] OJ C260/3) 'in the light of the gradual development of the common fisheries policy', para. 1.7 thereof. See also Application of Arts. 92 and 93 EC and Art. 61 EEA to state aids in the aviation sector ([1994] OJ C350/5), para. 51.

[141] *Third Report on Competition Policy* (EC Commission, Brussels, 1974), 76.

[142] COM(73)1110, para. III.

[143] COM(75)77, para. II.

of lowering the aid ceiling of 20 per cent for the central regions, but the majority of Member States where such regions were located was opposed.[144] Again, the response of the Commission was unilaterally to impose ceilings of 15 per cent of investment or ECU 2,500 per job created up to 20 per cent of investment costs in parts of Belgium;[145] 15 per cent of investment costs other than for the setting up of firms in parts of Denmark;[146] 17 per cent in parts of France,[147] and 10 per cent in parts of the Netherlands,[148] though exceptionally these ceilings could be exceeded.[149]

Such practice may be problematic. It is not clear that the European Courts would accept that Article 93(1) supported examination of aid according to 'rules established or agreed . . . depending on the unilateral will of either the Commission or the Member States'.[150] These Courts may take the view that instruments which only apply by virtue of the consent of the Member States cannot be amended unilaterally by the Commission.[151]

Coercion

If consent to its soft legislation is not forthcoming, the Commission may resort to coercive measures. For example, the Commission requested Member States to notify their acceptance of the framework regarding automobiles aid, adopted on 22 December 1988, within one month. The Article 93(2) procedure was opened against all approved aid schemes in Spain[152] and Germany[153] which could benefit the motor vehicle industry, since these two Member States initially withheld their consent. In the case of Spain, the procedure was closed, when the Spanish Government agreed 'to accept unconditionally the application of the framework as from 1 January 1990'.[154] In the case of Germany, the framework came into force following a negative decision under Article 93(2).[155]

---

[144] *Twelfth Report on Competition Policy* (EC Commission, Brussels, 1983), 139.

[145] *Ibid.*, 143. [146] *Ibid.*, 143–4.

[147] *Ibid.*, 145. [148] *Ibid.*, 147–8.

[149] *Fourteenth Report on Competition Policy* (EC Commission, Brussels, 1985), 172.

[150] Case C–135/93 *Spain* v. *EC Commission: framework for aid to the motor vehicle industry* [1995] ECR I–1651, I–1685. According to Lenz AG, the Commission may not unilaterally amend principles adopted under Art. 93(1) (*ibid.*, I.–1660–1).

[151] Lenz AG in Case C–313/90 *Comité International de la Rayonne et des Fibres Synthétiques (Cirfs)* v. *EC Commission* [1993] ECR I–1125, I–1175.

[152] Communic. E5/89 ([1989] OJ C281/1) concerning the refusal of the Spanish Government to apply the Community framework on state aid to the motor vehicles industry.

[153] Communic. E4/89 ([1989] OJ C281/6) concerning the refusal of the German Government to apply the Community framework on state aid to the motor vehicles industry.

[154] Communic. C33/90 ([1990] OJ C159/13) concerning the application by the Spanish Government of the Community framework on state aids in the motor vehicle industry.

[155] Communic. C62/91 (NN75, 77, 78, 79/91) ([1992] OJ C68/14) concerning the proposal by the German Government to award state aid to the Volkswagen group in support of its investment plans in the new *Länder*, n. 1. See, similarly, Communic. 60/91 (N73/91 & 76/91) ([1992] OJ C68/2) concerning the proposal by the German Government to award state aid to the Opel group in support of its investment plans in the new *Länder*, n. 1; and Communic. C61/91 (NN74/91 & 80/91) ([1992] OJ C68/8) concerning the proposal by the German Government to award state aid to Mercedes-Benz in support of its investment plans in the new *Länder*, n. 1.

The Commission later decided, on 23 December 1992, that the framework should remain in force, until the situation was reviewed.[156] Spain challenged this decision before the Court of Justice, which annulled the decision in 1995.[157] To fill the legal vacuum created by the judgment, the Commission decided as an emergency provisional measure[158] to extend the validity of the original framework, with retroactive effect from 1 January 1995, for a maximum period of one year. Thus an aid notification of 27 June 1995 was treated as being 'subject to the provisions of the Community framework'.[159] The Commission also proposed to reintroduce a new framework with slight changes for a period of two years and to seek agreement from Member States on its reintroduction.[160] According to the Commission, reintroduction was a proposal, whereas the retroactive prolongation was a 'decision'.[161]

The Commission admitted that this prolongation constituted an exception from the principle of legal certainty. It was considered justified because of the objective to be attained—undistorted competition in the motor vehicles sector —and the need to ensure that legitimate expectations of the parties were respected. The presumption that the Commission 'decision' of 23 December 1992 was valid prevented the creation of legitimate expectations on the part of the parties concerned; the Member States and undertakings had, moreover, considered that the framework was in force. However, the German Government argued that the framework could only legally be renewed upon formal acceptance of that prolongation by the Government or pursuant to an Article 93(2) procedure.[162]

The Spanish Government also rejected reintroduction of the framework, and so the Commission opened the Article 93(2) procedure regarding the various Spanish aid schemes allowing for the grant of aid to motor manufacturers from 1 January 1996.[163] The Commission did not accept that the

---

[156] [1993] OJ C36/17.

[157] Case C–135/93 *Spain* v. *EC Commission: framework for aid to the motor vehicle industry* [1995] ECR I–1651.

[158] i.e., only until the Art. 93(1) procedure was completed. See Notice C44/95 (E16/95) ([1995] OJ C304/14) regarding refusal of the Spanish authorities of the Commission's proposal for reintroduction of the EC framework on state aid to the motor vehicle industry. The Commission maintained in this Notice that the opening of the Art. 93(2) procedure was necessary to secure equality of treatment between Member States.

[159] Notice C34/95 ([1995] OJ C237/12) regarding aid provided in favour of the restructuring plan of Seat SA following a re-notification of the aid by the Spanish authorities.

[160] Bull. EU 7/8–1995, I.3.52.

[161] *Corrigendum* to 'Framework for state aid in the motor vehicle sector' ([1995] OJ C307/22).

[162] Communic. C62/91 (NN75, 77, 78, 79/91) ([1992] OJ C68/14) concerning the proposal by the German Government to award state aid to the Volkswagen group in support of its investment plans in the new *Länder*. See, similarly, Communic. 60/91 (N73/91 & 76/91) ([1992] OJ C68/2) concerning the proposal by the German Government to award state aid to the Opel group in support of its investment plans in the new *Länder*; and Communic. C61/91 (NN74/91 & 80/91) ([1992] OJ C68/8) concerning the proposal by the German Government to award state aid to Mercedes-Benz in support of its investment plans in the new *Länder*.

[163] Bull. EU 9–1995, 1.3.38.

condition to which the Spanish Government made dependent the application of the framework—the prior adoption of a Union-wide industrial policy in the sector—justified a specific derogation for Spain not to apply the framework in contrast to all other Member States. Only in exceptional circumstances in a Member State could the Commission accept the non-application of the framework to a single Member State.[164]

7.4.3 Legal Effects

In the absence of soft legislation, inconsistency as between Commission decisions may be treated simply as indicating an 'irregularity' in a previous decision which does not affect the validity of a later inconsistent decision.[165] According to the Court of Justice, the compatibility of aid with the common market should be based on an individual analysis of the aid in question and not on previous state interventions the legality of which has not been challenged.[166] The aim of introducing such legislation, however, may be to secure simultaneous modification in all Member States of existing aid systems or to provide policy statements regarding future treatment of such systems.[167]

The Commission considers that the instruments concerned not only make for transparency and legal certainty for undertakings. They also promote consistency of application and interpretation by the Commission[168] and improved levels of compliance and discipline on the part of the Member States.[169] Even if not binding in the strict sense,[170] they have authority, in that they publicly set out the policy which the Commission intends to follow.[171] Member States and all the others concerned are entitled to expect[172] by virtue of the principles of legal certainty and legitimate expectations,[173] that the policy will be followed.[174] With the policy of the Commission becoming increasingly well

---

[164] H. Morch, 'Summary of the Most Important Recent Developments' (1995) 6 *Competition Policy Newsletter* 41–7, 44.

[165] Darmon AG in Joined Cases C–324/90 & C–342/90 *Germany and Pleuger Worthington GmbH* v. *EC Commission* [1994] ECR I–1173, I–1191.

[166] Joined Cases C–278/92, C–279/92, & C–280/92 *Spain* v. *EC Commission* [1994] ECR I–4103, I–4168.

[167] *Competition Law in the European Communities ii: Rules Applicable to State Aids* (EC Commission, Brussels, 1995), 42–3.

[168] *Twenty-Third Report on Competition Policy* (EC Commission, Brussels, 1994), 239–40.

[169] Reply by Mr Van Miert to Written Question 365/93 ([1993] OJ C288/5) by Mrs Christine Oddy.

[170] In Joined Cases 188–190/80 *France, Italy, and the UK* v. *EC Commission* [1982] ECR 2545, 2565, the Commission maintained that the 'institutional balance' within the Union would alter if it were to 'adopt rules on the application of Arts 92 and 93'.

[171] The Commission stated that the Community guidelines on state aid for rescuing and restructuring firms in difficulty ([1994] OJ C368/12) would apply for three years from their date of publication (para. 4.4).

[172] See, regarding a presumption to this effect, C. Blumann, n. 88 above, 731.

[173] Cf., regarding estoppel, M. Melchior, n. 36 above, 254.

[174] See the submission of the Commission in Joined Cases 166 & 220/86 *Irish Cement Limited*

known, it is anticipated that Member States will seek to restrict, and hence structure, their granting of aids, so that they are in line with the policy.[175] On the other hand, the possibility is not ruled out that individual Commission decisions may depart from, though 'without prejudice to', any such instruments.[176] However, in the absence of 'completely new and unforeseen circumstances',[177] such departures may entail violation of the equality principle.[178]

Formal Legal Effects

The Court of Justice accepts that soft legislation has 'legal effects' for the purposes of judicial review of its legality and treats it as 'secondary Community law'.[179] However, the requirements of legal certainty may set limits to the formal legal effects of the instruments concerned. According to Advocate General Darmon in *Deufil*,[180] such instruments 'constitute a frame of reference, reinforcing, in particular, the obligation of notice laid down in Article 93(3), but they cannot be regarded as legally binding and thus capable of forming the basis of a negative decision'.

According to the Court itself, new obligations can only be introduced or existing obligations amended by Union acts which expressly indicate their legal basis in a provision of Union law which prescribes the legal form which the act must take.[181] The implication, it may be imagined, is that the prescribed legal form must be that of a binding act. Thus although the Commission may derive powers under Articles 5[182] and 155[183] of the Treaty, these provisions cannot be

---

v. *EC Commission* [1988] ECR 6473, 6482. For such reasons, the Economic and Social Committee had urged the introduction of such guidelines in its Opinion of 25 Oct. 1984 ([1984] OJ C343/5) on the *Thirteenth Report on Competition Policy*, para. 12.

[175] *Seventeenth Report on Competition Policy* (EC Commission, Brussels, 1988), 141. See also the importance attached to publication in *Competition Law in the European Communities ii: Rules Applicable to State Aids* (EC Commission, Brussels, 1995), 55.

[176] Dec. 94/266 ([1994] OJ L114/21) on the proposal to award aid to SST–Garngesellschaft mbH, Thüringen.   [177] M.G. Santiago, n. 91 above, 945.

[178] Cf., regarding the need to give reasons for departures from internal guidelines of the Commission, Case 148/73 *Raymond Louwage and Marie-Thérèse Louwage, née Moriame* v. *EC Commission* [1974] ECR 81, 89.

[179] Case C–135/93 *Spain* v. *EC Commission: framework for aid to the motor vehicle industry* [1995] ECR I–1651. I–1666.

[180] Case 310/85 *Deufil GmbH & Co. KG* v. *EC Commission* [1987] ECR 901, 914. See sect. 5.1 above.

[181] Case C–325/91 *France* v. *EC Commission: communication on aid to public undertakings* [1993] ECR I–3283, I–3311–2. Note also the objections of Warner AG to resort to unpublished documents for interpretation of binding measures in Case 28/76 *Milac GmbH Groß- und Aussenhandel* v. *Hauptzollamt Freibourg* [1976] ECR 1639, 1664. But cf. where a binding measure itself is not published, Case 299/82 *Horst W. Steinfort* v. *EC Commission* [1983] ECR 3141, 3146.

[182] Art. 5 does not entail that Commission memoranda have binding force. See Case 229/86 *Brother Industries* v. *EC Commission* [1987] ECR 3757, 3763. Cf., however, regarding this provision and the effects of notification requirements imposed by the Commission in its co-ordination principles, K. Hellingman, n. 65 above, 125.

[183] The power in Art. 155 to formulate recommendations or opinions does not provide a basis for the adoption of binding measures. See Case C–303/90 *France* v. *EC Commission: code of conduct*

used to create new obligations.[184] An extreme position is that even a 'negotiated act' must be empowered.[185] Thus the Commission maintains that its assessment of aid granted will always be 'based' on Article 92.[186]

It appears, however, that obligations may arise from acceptance by the Member State concerned of an otherwise non-binding act,[187] though mere acquiescence may be insufficient for this purpose.[188] In other words, the relevant instruments may not have original binding force, but the possibility cannot be ruled out that they subsequently acquire such force. Indeed, Article 154 of the first Accession Act provided that the principles for regional aid would apply to the new Member States, as *acquis communautaire*, from 1 July 1973.[189] They may also acquire binding legal force by agreement with third states,[190] and there may be calls for their incorporation in the domestic law of Member States.[191]

---

on use of the Structural Funds [1991] ECR I–5315, I–5348. However, in Case C–135/93 *Spain* v. *EC Commission: framework for aid to the motor vehicle industry* [1995] ECR I–1651, I–1663, Lenz AG did not apparently rule out the possibility that Art. 155 could play a role in relation to binding principles.

[184] See, however, H. Morch, 'Summary of the Most Important Recent Developments' (1995) 5 *Competition Policy Newsletter* 43–9, 47. See also, regarding a Commission request by reference to Art. 155 for Member States to adopt legislation on the *de minimis* rule (Explanatory note on use of the *de minimis* rule provided for by the Community Framework on aids to SMEs, letter of 23 Mar. 1993 (*Competition Law in the Europen Communities ii: Rules Applicable to State Aids* (EC Commission, Brussels, 1995), 68.

[185] Case C–325/91 *France* v. *EC Commission: communication on aid to public undertakings* [1993] ECR I–3283, I–3312.

[186] Dec. 90/381 ([1990] OJ L188/55) amending German aid schemes for the motor vehicle industry. The objectives in the Community interest to which aid to the textile and clothing industry must contribute were 'further specified' by the Commission in the Community framework for aid to the industry laid down in 1977. See Dec. 84/351 ([1984] OJ L186/45) on a proposal by the Italian Government to award aid to an undertaking in the textile and clothing industry.

[187] Lenz AG in Case C–313/90 *Comité International de la Rayonne et des Fibres Synthétiques (Cirfs)* v. *EC Commission* [1993] ECR I–1125, I–1154–6.

[188] Lenz AG in Case C–135/93 *Spain* v. *EC Commission: framework for aid to the motor vehicle industry* [1995] ECR I–1651, I–1660, and in Case C–313/90 *Comité International de la Rayonne et des Fibres Synthétiques (Cirfs)* v. *EC Commission* [1993] ECR I–1125, I–1175.

[189] Cf. the requirements in Annexes to the EEA Agreement, including Annex XIV, on State Aid, that 'due account' is taken of such principles; ESA Dec. 4/94/COL ([1994] OJ L231/1) on the adoption and issuing of the procedural and substantive rules in the field of state aid (guidelines on the application and interpretation of Arts 61 and 62 EEA and Art. 1 of Prot. 3 to the Surveillance and Court Agreement); and, more particularly, the Summary of the ESA dec. not to raise objections to the aid which the Austrian Government planned to provide to BMW Motoren Gesellschaft mbH in support of an R & D and investment project in Steyr Austria ([1994] OJ C250/3).

[190] See, e.g., Art. 39 of Dec. 1/95 of the EC–Turkey Association Council ([1996] OJ L35/1).

[191] C. Pourre, 'Le Cumul d'aides' [1993] *AJDA* 444–50, 451. See, earlier, regarding Belgian incorporation, M. Melchior, n. 36 above, 256.

Interpretative Significance

Whether or not binding force is formally acquired, soft legislation may be of interpretative significance.[192] An analogy may be drawn with the holding of the Court of Justice that national courts must take account of recommendations designed to 'supplement' binding Union provisions.[193] At the same time, such legislation must be 'understood in a manner consistent with the Treaty provision it is intended to implement'.[194] In practice, however, it may be difficult to maintain a distinction between instruments which 'make more explicit' a binding rule[195] and those which 'add to the text' of the provision containing that rule[195] or 'add new obligations'.[196] In other words, the distinction between the interpretation and modification of a rule may be difficult to maintain.

Formally, the obligations in Articles 92 and 93 may not be affected by soft legislation,[197] and the assessment of aid measures may be based on the former provisions.[198] For example, the fact that an aid code applicable to a given sector does not cover a particular product within that sector does not entail that aid in relation to that product is permissible.[199] In practice, however, soft legislation may effectively have binding force as an interpretation of Articles 92 and 93,[200] and the Commission may simply refer to 'objective criteria' in such principles, without having to set out its assessment.

As a result, the burden of the reasoning requirements otherwise imposed on the Commission may be eased.[201] Moreover, since the processing of aid schemes covered by soft legislation is simplified, the Commission is enabled to concentrate its scarce resources[202] on cases that involve the most serious distortions of competition.[203]

---

[192] Cf., regarding 'position statements of the Commission', *R.* v. *Secretary of State for the Home Dept, ex p. Donald Walter Flynn* [1995] 3 CMLR 397, 409. Cf. also, regarding the interpretative function of declarations, Case C–292/89 *R.* v. *Immigration Appeal Tribunal, ex p. Gustaff Desiderius Antonissen* [1991] ECR I–745, I–778.

[193] Case C–322/88 *Salvatore Grimaldi* v. *Fonds des Maladies Professionnelles* [1989] ECR I–4407, I–4421.

[194] Case C–135/93 *Spain* v. *EC Commission: framework for aid to the motor vehicle industry* [1995] ECR I–1651, I–1683.

[195] Case C–366/88 *France* v. *EC Commission: internal instructions on use of the EAGGF* [1990] ECR I–3571, I–3601.

[196] Case C–325/91 *France* v. *EC Commission: communication on aid to public undertakings* [1993] ECR I–3283, I–3311.

[197] Case 310/85 *Deufil GmbH & Co. KG* v. *EC Commission* [1987] ECR 901, 927.

[198] Dec. 90/381 ([1990] OJ L188/55) regarding German aid schemes for the motor-vehicle industry.

[199] Case 310/85 *Deufil GmbH & Co. KG* v. *EC Commission* [1987] ECR 901, 928.

[200] Case C–313/90 *Comité International de la Rayonne et des Fibres Synthétiques (Cirfs)* v. *EC Commission* [1993] ECR I–1125, I–1186.

[201] Darmon AG in Joined Cases C–324/90 & C–342/90 *Germany and Pleuger Worthington GmbH* v. *EC Commission* [1994] ECR I–1173, I–1189.

[202] *Twenty-Third Report on Competition Policy* (EC Commission, Brussels, 1994), 239–40. Such scarcity may lead the Commission to put aid investigations out to tender. See, regarding aid to privatized companies in the former GDR, Call for tenders (IV G5PSI/01) ([1996] OJ C36/8).

[*See opposite page for n. 202 cont. and n. 203*].

The convenience entailed may be of substantive as well as procedural significance. For example, the Commission may find aid to be prohibited merely because it is contrary to the relevant instrument.[204] Moreover, inconsistency of aid with such an instrument may be decisive for a finding by the Court of Justice that aid is prohibited.[205] Equally, the fact that a Commission decision is found to have been taken on the basis of a misinterpretation of the instrument may lead the decision to be annulled by the Court.[206] The Commission may also be obliged to comply with procedures laid down in such instruments.[207]

Where they go beyond mere 'interpretation' of Articles 92 and 93, however, their effects may depend on the consensus of Member States not to challenge them. If such a challenge takes the form of proceedings before the Court of Justice, the result may be that the relevant instrument is annulled.[208] The Commission may respond to,[209] or possibly seek to pre-empt, such proceedings by embodying the principles in a more formal legal act. The latter has been done, for example, in relation to the framework for aid to automobiles,[210] the 'rules' regarding aid cumulation,[211] and, more particularly, following failure of

See, regarding the staffing constraints on the Commission, J. Gilchrist and D. Deacon, 'Curbing Subsidies' in P. Montagnon (ed.), *European Competition Policy* (Pinter, London, 1990), 31–51. Cf., regarding the concern of regulatory agencies to utilize their resources efficiently through securing successful 'prosecutions', R. A. Posner, 'The Behaviour of Administrative Agencies' [1972] 1 *The Journal of Legal Studies* 305–47.

[203] Reply by Mr Van Miert to Written Question 365/93 ([1993] OJ C288/5) by Mrs Christine Oddy.

[204] See, e.g., Dec. 83/245 ([1983] OJ L137/24) on an aid scheme in favour of the textile and clothing industry in France. See also Dec. 95/253 ([1995] OJ L159/21) on aid awarded by the French Government to Allied Signal Fibres Europe SA, Longwy, Meurthe-et-Moselle.

[205] Case C–301/87 *France* v. *EC Commission: Boussac* [1990] ECR I–307, I–364–5 and Case C–303/88 *Italy* v. *EC Commission* [1991] ECR I–1433, I–1480.

[206] Case C–313/90 *Comité International de la Rayonne et des Fibres Synthétiques (Cirfs)* v. *EC Commission* [1993] ECR I–1125, I–1189. The Commission responded by re-opening the procedure. See Notice C16/93 (NN42/93) ([1993] OJ C215/7) concerning aid which France planned to grant to Allied Signal.

[207] Lenz AG in Case C–135/93 *Spain* v. *EC Commission: framework for aid to the motor vehicle industry* [1995] I–1651, I–1667.

[206] Cf., regarding a Communic. on the sampling and analysis of products to benefit from aid from the EAGGF, Case C–366/88 *France* v. *EC Commission: internal instructions on use of the EAGGF* [1990] ECR I–3571.

[209] Following annulment by the Court in Case C–325/91 *France* v. *EC Commission: communication on aid to public undertakings* [1993] ECR I–3283 of the Communic. concerning the application of Arts. 92. and 93 of the EEC Treaty and of Art. 5 of Commission Dir. 80/723 [1980] OJ L195/35 to public undertakings in the manufacturing sector, the Commission embodied in Dir. 93/84 ([1993] OJ L254/16) amending Dir. 80/723 the obligation for Member States to provide the Commission with financial data on an annual basis. At the same time, the Commission readopted the Communic. omitting the reporting requirement in paras 45–53 and the references thereto in paras. 2, 27, 29, 31, and 54 (application of Arts. 92 and 93 EC and Art. 5 of Dir. 80/723 to public undertakings in the manufacturing sector ([1993] OJ C307/3)).

[210] Dec. 90/381 ([1990] OJ L188/55) amending German aid schemes for the motor-vehicle industry.

[211] Notice ([1987] OJ C300/4) regarding cumulation of aids for different purposes in France and Greece.

the Belgian authorities to comply with an 'informal agreement' previously reached with the Commission.[212]

7.4.4 Implementation

The most developed arrangements regarding implementation of soft legislation are those made in relation to the co-ordination principles for regional aid. While the Commission had originally envisaged a case-by-case 'pragmatic' approach to the control of such aid, various Member States pressed for the introduction of more systematic procedures.[213] Accordingly, the 1971 Principles[214] established the following procedures:

— imposition of ceilings for the amount of aid;
— introduction of aid transparency;
— regional specification of aid;
— consideration for the sectoral consequences.

Ceilings

The Commission proposed in 1969 the introduction of maximum and minimum limits for aid in three types of region: 'industrialized', 'semi-industrialized', or 'predominantly agricultural' regions.[215] However, by 1971 agreement with Member States had apparently been reached only on a single ceiling of 20 per cent for the 'central regions'.[216]

The ceiling was extended to the new Member States by revised Principles in 1973,[217] and refinements were envisaged so as to take account of 'the diversity of the regional situations in the enlarged Community' and 'the relative seriousness of the problems in each of the regions not designated as "central"'.[218] Furthermore, the terms 'central' and 'peripheral' would cease to be used to classify regions, and the principles, especially those regarding aid ceilings, would be differentiated more widely in the light of the 'nature and seriousness of the problems besetting other regions'.[219] The 1975 Principles[220] duly divided all Union regions into four groups with different aid ceilings.[221]

---

[212] Dec. 75/397 ([1975] OJ L177/13) on the aids granted by the Belgian Government pursuant to the Law of 17 July 1959 introducing and co-ordinating measures to encourage economic expansion and the creation of new industries.

[213] *First Report on Competition Policy* (EC Commission, Brussels, 1972), 116–8.

[214] Principles of co-ordination of general systems of regional aid ([1971] JO C111/8).

[215] *Memorandum on Regional Policy in the Community*, Bull EC, Supp. 12/69, 49.

[216] Para. 4 of the Annex to the 1971 Co-ordination Principles ([1971] JO C111/1).

[217] *Third Report on Competition Policy* (EC Commission, Brussels, 1974), 77–8. The Union institutions may act unlawfully if they do not adapt their practice to take account of different conditions in acceding Member States. See Case 192/83 *Greece* v. *EC Commission: aid for tomatoes and peaches* [1985] ECR 2971, 2811.

[218] *Fourth Report on Competition Policy* (EC Commission, Brussels, 1975), 85.

[219] *Ibid.*, 86.

[220] COM(75)77.   [221] *Ibid.*, para. I.3.

This extension of ceilings throughout the Union seems to have had some effect. For example, after bilateral consultations the Italian authorities decided 'to base themselves to a certain extent on the Commission's guidelines' on regional aid when preparing legislation to reframe the aid system in the Mezzogiorno for the period 1976–80.[222]

However, modifications were found necessary in the 1979 Principles,[223] when aid ceilings were expressed in two ways: either as a percentage of the amount of initial investment or in terms of aid per job created.[224] Moreover, successive enlargements of the Union have required more differentiated ceilings.

More fundamentally, the ceilings as such seem to have proved inadequate for Commission control of regional aid. In practice, the aid levels approved by the Commission when it takes individual decisions are often lower and even much lower than the relevant ceiling.[225] Thus it is said that 'maximum intensities' fixed by individual decisions are effectively replacing the ceilings set in the principles.[226]

Transparency

The 1971 Principles applied only to the central regions, where most aids were already transparent, that is, their amount could be measured. Where it was lacking, Member States were required to achieve transparency during a transitional period.[227] More problematic was to extend the principles to the peripheral regions, where 'opaque' operating aids,[228] particularly those relating directly or indirectly to the creation or maintenance of jobs, were much more prevalent.[229] If a ceiling was to apply to these regions, a method of measuring such aids had to be found.[230] Pending introduction of such a method, the 1973 Principles stated that no new aids of this kind were to be introduced.[231] The

---

[222] *Fifth Report on Competition Policy* (EC Commission, Brussels, 1976), 73.

[223] Communic. of 21 Dec. 1978 ([1979] OJ C31/9), para. 2.

[224] Problems might arise from fixing ceilings in terms of the amount of aid per job created. In the first place, the amount would vary depending on labour costs in the region concerned. More aid might, therefore, be available in regions where labour costs were highest. Moreover, in the case of labour-intensive projects, the amount of aid permitted might be greater than the total cost of the investment. See *Les Régimes d'aide régionale dans la Communauté européenne—Etude comparative* (Regional Policy Series 15, EC Commission, Brussels, 1979).

[226] See, e.g., Dec. 91/500 ([1991] OJ L262/29) concerning aid granted to enterprises in the Friuli-Venezia Giulia region.

[226] Report of the Committee on Regional Policy and Regional Planning on the Effects of Arts. 92 and 93 EC on Regional Policy, EP Doc. A2–114/87, 10.

[227] Annex to the 1971 Co-ordination Principles ([1971] C111/8), para. 6.

[228] Around 50% of national aid to the regions was regarded as opaque. See the *Sixth Report on Competition Policy* (EC Commission, Brussels, 1977), 100.

[229] *Fifth Report on Competition Policy* (EC Commission, Brussels, 1976), 68–9.

[230] *Sixth Report on Competition Policy* (EC Commission, Brussels, 1977), 100.

[231] *Third Report on Competition Policy* (EC Commission, Brussels, 1974), 77–8. Such aid could be authorized exceptionally, pursuant to paras. 4 and 7 of the 1979 Co-ordination Principles ([1979] OJ C31/9).

1975 Principles subsequently acknowledged that aid authorization should not be prejudiced by the presence or absence of transparency.[232]

In the central regions at least the Commission seems to have had some success in securing the transparency sought. For example, lengthy discussions, both bilateral (at different levels between the Commission and the British authorities) and multilateral, led the United Kingdom to agree to amend the Regional Development Grant scheme, so as to bring it into line with Union law. Under this scheme aid was granted automatically for any investment (including the renewal of capital goods) and was introduced for an unlimited period.[233]

However, the argument that the transparency requirement could distort regional aid schemes[234] seems to have had an impact. In several cases, particularly those concerning the least developed regions, the Commission has abandoned the requirement that aids be transparent. In other words, it has become more tolerant of operating aid.[235]

Regional Specificity

Regional specification means that: regional aids must not cover the whole national territory,[236] that is, general aids must not be granted under the heading of regional aids; aid regimes must clearly specify, either in geographical terms or by quantitative criteria, the limits of aided regions or, within these, the limits of aided areas; except in the case of growth points, regional aids must not be granted in a pin-point manner, that is, not to isolated geographical points having virtually no influence on the development of a region; where problems which are different in kind, intensity, or urgency occur, the aid intensity must be adapted accordingly; and the graduation and variation of rates across different areas and regions must be clearly indicated.[237]

Application of this principle presupposes definition of regions, a process which is by no means unproblematic.[238] Moreover, without modification the principle might preclude differentiated treatment of parts of the same region where local conditions varied significantly or the population was sparse, or might preclude authorization of aid to projects outside the region which might have direct beneficial effects for that region. Such problems are likely to be increased by accession to the Union of countries such as Finland and Sweden, with their sparsely populated northern regions.[239]

---

[232] COM(75)77, para. I.4.

[233] *Tenth Report on Competition Policy* (EC Commission, Brussels, 1981), 115.

[234] Report of the Committee on Regional Policy and Regional Planning on the Effects of Arts. 92 and 93 EC on Regional Policy, EP Doc. A2–114/87, *addendum*, 2.

[235] Sect. 4.3.5 above.

[236] Para. 7 of the Annex to the 1971 Co-ordination Principles ([1971] JO C111/1). However, Ireland and Luxembourg are each treated as one region (para. 9, n. of the 1979 Co-ordination Principles ([1979] OJ C31/9)).   [237] *Ibid.*, para. 9.

[238] See sect. 4.2.2 above   [239] See sect. 4.3.1 above.

Sectoral Consequences

The 1971 Principles noted that lack of sectoral specificity was a basic feature of most regional aid schemes, since such aid was often granted to all industrial sectors without distinction. Therefore, a procedure was envisaged to enable its consequences for various sectors to be assessed.[240]

According to the *Second Report on Competition Policy*,[241] the following was required:

—identification of Union industries in which regional aid schemes were most extensive;

—identification, among those industries, of cases where aid posed the greatest risk to Union trade and competition;

—identification of Member States in which regional aid was most likely to cause problems in these industries; and, finally,

—analysis of the causes of the situation so identified.

Significant cases were to be notified to the Commission in advance.[242] There would be a quantitative assessment of such cases, based on statistical analysis, and a qualitative assessment, based on a number of currently non-quantifiable criteria for adjusting and clarifying the statistics.[243] The results were to be implemented through contact between Directorate General IV, the Directorate General for Competition, Directorate General XVI, the Directorate General for Regional Policy, and the Directorate General responsible for the sectoral policy concerned. In practice, little more seems to have been achieved than application of a general principle that regional aid should not give rise to sectoral overcapacity at the Union level.[244]

Problems in the implementation of the co-ordination principles have led to claims that the Commission enjoys too much discretionary power in relation to state aid, which can hamper pursuit of regional policy at national level. The conclusion drawn is that a clearly defined framework, as provided for in Article 94, should be established.[245] However, it is not clear that the implementation problems which have arisen would necessarily be any more amenable to resolution through formal legislation than through soft legislation.

---

[240] Para. 8 of the Annex to the 1971 Co-ordination Principles ([1971] JO C111/1).

[241] (EC Commission, Brussels, 1973), 79–80.

[242] Where an investment benefited from regionally differentiated sectoral aid, regional aid could not be granted to the same investment (COM(75)77, para. I.6).

[243] Bull. EC 4–1973, 2109. According to para. 11 of the 1979 Co-ordination Principles ([1979] OJ C31/9), the Commission would examine to what extent appropriate restrictions should be applied when awarding regional aids where such restrictions were justified by the situation in a sector.

[244] Communic. on the method for the application of Art. 92(3)(a) and (c) ([1988] OJ C212/2), para. I. 6. See, earlier, *Commission Policy on Sectoral Aid Schemes*, COM(78)221.

[245] Report of the Committee on Economic and Monetary Affairs and Industrial Policy on the *Twentieth Report on Competition Policy*, EP Doc. A3–0338/91, 16.

7.5 ADMINISTRATIVE DECISION-MAKING BY THE COMMISSION

Article 93 of the Treaty grants decision-making powers to the Commission in individual aid cases.[246] Such decisions may generate new rules or principles[247] or, to the extent that a decision entails interpretation of a rule contained in the Treaty or a soft law principle, modify existing ones.[248] In the latter case the translation which is entailed from one legal form to another may be accompanied by effective alteration in the content of the rule or principle concerned.

7.5.1 Article 93(1) Review

Article 93(1) provides that the Commission shall, in co-operation with Member States, keep under constant review all[249] systems of aid existing in those Member States. This procedure 'assumes constant co-operation between states and the Commission',[250] and is said by the Commission to allow account to be taken of changed conditions.[251]

Aid in operation when the EC Treaty came into force or, in the case of Member States other than the original Six, on accession, is existing aid, as is aid subsequently put into operation with the express consent of the Commission.[252] Aid granted pursuant to a scheme already approved by the Commission and meeting the conditions laid down in the decision of approval also constitutes existing aid.[253] Particular cases of the implementation of an approved

---

[246] See, generally, J. A. Winter, 'Supervision of State Aid: Article 93 in the Court of Justice' (1993) 30 *CMLRev*. 311–29.

[247] To the extent that actors cán induce 'general principles' from such decisions, they may 'spontaneously' modify their conduct accordingly. See M. Melchior, n. 36 above, 246. Moreover, according to the Commission, national courts 'can always be guided . . . by the existing decisions of the Commission'. See Notice on co-operation between national courts and the Commission in applying Arts. 85 and 86 EC ([1993] OJ C39/6), para. 21.

[248] Thus the Commission stated, in connection with its assessment of significant cases of application of a Dutch general aid scheme, that it 'would assess each case on its own merits in the light of the rules contained in Art. 92 ff or rules developed during the administration of those provisions'. See Dec. 81/523 ([1981] OJ L196/1) on a proposal by the Netherlands Government to grant aid for certain investments by a manufacturer of insulating material (Rockwool). See, however, Case C–313/90 *Comité International de la Rayonne et des Fibres Synthétiques (Cirfs)* v. *EC Commission* [1993] ECR I–1125, I–1186, where the effect of the code was to withdraw previous authorization, so that existing aids became new aids and had to be notified.

[248] There is no express requirement that the aid be incompatible with the common market.

[250] Case 173/73 *Italy* v. *EC Commission: aids to the textile industry* [1974] ECR 709, 716 and Lenz AG in Case 40/85 *Belgium* v. *EC Commission: Boch* [1986] ECR 2321, 2332.

[251] Joint Reply by Mr Van Miert to Written Questions E-2197–2199/93 ([1994] OJ C306/9) by Nel van Dijk. See, regarding annual reports on existing schemes requested by the Commission, annex 2 to the Letter of 22 Feb. 1994 (*Competition Law in the European Communities ii: Rules Applicable to State Aids* (EC Commission, Brussels, 1995), 73).

[252] Warner AG in Case 173/73 *Italy* v. *EC Commission: aids to the textile industry* [1974] ECR 709, 723.

[253] Case C–47/91 *Italy* v. *EC Commission: Italgrani* [1994] ECR 4635, 4655. See also Case C–44/93 *Namur—Les Assurances du Crédit SA* v. *Office National du Ducroire and Belgium* [1994] ECR I–3829, I–3876–7.

scheme are not systematically examined by the Commission, unless they concern areas governed by special aid rules.[254]

In the case of existing aid, the Commission is to propose to the Member States any appropriate measures required by the progressive development or the functioning of the common market.[255] The proposals are 'simple recommendations' within the meaning of Article 189,[256] though they must be reasoned.[257] They may, in particular, envisage amendment of previously authorized schemes to bring them into line with soft legislation.[258]

The proposals may be made in discussions between the Commission and national officials concerning general state-aid issues and the annual Report of the Commission on Competition Policy,[259] where a specific legal obligation may merely be one element in negotiations.[160] If, however, the Member State concerned does not undertake to follow the proposal, the Commission may initiate the Article 93(2) procedure,[261] which is considered below.[262] The Commission may combine Article 93(1) proposals regarding an existing scheme with adoption of a decision under Article 93(2) regarding changes to the scheme.[263] However, the Commission accepts that such a decision does not entail retroactive effect for the proposal and may limit the decision to procedural arrangements embodied in the proposal.[264]

[254] Reply by Sir Leon Brittan to Written Question 2317/92 ([1993] OJ C47/29) by Mr Francesco Speroni.

[255] e.g., by letter of 19 May 1993 ([1993] OJ C163/5) the Commission proposed that the Portuguese Government abolish the taxation exemption enjoyed by the national airline, TAP.

[256] Darmon AG in Joined Cases 166 & 220/86 *Irish Cement Limited* v. *EC Commission* [1988] ECR 6473, 6492.

[257] Case 78/76 *Firma Steinike und Weinlig* v. *Germany* [1977] ECR 595, 609.

[258] See, regarding German guarantee schemes in Baden-Württemberg and Hamburg, Bull. EU 3–1995, 1.3.50 and the Guidelines on state aid for rescuing and restructuring firms in difficulty ([1994] OJ C368/12). See also Notice C19/95 ([1995] OJ C242/5) concerning the state guarantee schemes of the *Länder* of Saxony–Anhalt, North Rhine–Westphalia, Rhineland–Palatinate, Bavaria, Bremen, Mecklenburg–Western Pomerania, Schleswig–Holstein and Saxony.

[259] *Europe* 5350 (15/16 Oct. 1990).

[260] F. Snyder, 'The Effectiveness of European Community Law: Institutions, Processes, Tools and Techniques' (1993) 56 MLR 19–54, 30.

[261] See, e.g., Letter to the German Government ([1993] OJ C289/2) proposing action to be taken in respect of Case E/93 (fiscal aid given to German airlines in the form of a depreciation facility). See also, regarding German guarantees, Bull. EU 5–1995, 1.3.51.

[262] Sect. 7.5.3.

[263] See, regarding aid for the rationalization of vineyards in Rhineland–Palatinate, Bull. EU 3–1995, 1.3.127.

[264] Dec. 90/381 ([1990] OJ L188/55) amending German aid schemes for the motor-vehicle industry.

7.5.2 Article 93(3) Notifications

Article 93(3) provides that the Commission shall be informed,[265] in sufficient time to enable it to submit its comments,[266] of any plans to grant or alter aid.[267] The role of the Commission is principally to react to the initiatives thus notified by Member States.[268] Detailed requirements as to the content of the notifications were first laid down by the Commission in a letter to Member States of 5 January 1977.[269]

As well as planned aid schemes, 'non-negligible',[270] 'substantial',[271] or 'material'[272] modifications of existing aid are to be notified. In so far as aid is granted within the rules of an existing system, it does not become notifiable simply because its amount increases.[273] For example, amendments to already authorized schemes need not be notified where the only change is a budget increase not exceeding 20 per cent of the budget initially approved.[274] In the case of an aid scheme for research and development, increases of 100 per cent in the annual budget or prolongation of the scheme for five years[275] need not be notified.[276] Moreover, *de minimis* aid to an undertaking which does not exceed

---

[265] See Bull. EC 3–1993, 1.2.39 and the *Twenty-Third Report on Competition Policy* (EC Commission, Brussels, 1994), 243–4, regarding standardized notifications.

[266] See, regarding 'the distinction between the observations of the Commission provided for in Art. 93(3) and the opinions in Art. 93(1)', Capotorti AG in Joined Cases 142–143/80 *Amministrazione delle Finanze dello Stato* v. *Essevi SpA and Carlo Salengo* [1981] ECR 1413, 1443.

[267] See, generally, S. W. Venceslai, 'Progetti di aiuti e communicazioni nel quadro dell'esame preventivo di cui all' art. 93(3) del Trattato di Roma' [1969] *Rivista di Diritto Europeo* 257–84.

[268] *Commission Policy on Sectoral Aid Schemes*, COM(78)221, 5.

[269] SG(77)D122 and SG(81)12740 (*Competition Law in the European Communities ii. Rules Applicable to State Aids* (EC Commission, Brussels, 1995), 89).

[270] Case 177/78 *Pigs and Bacon Commission* v. *McCarren & Co. Ltd* [1979] ECR 2161, 2204; and Joined Cases 91 & 127/83 *Heineken Brouwereijen BV* v. *Inspecteurs der Vennootschapsbelasting, Amsterdam and Utrecht* [1984] ECR 3435, 3453–4.

[271] Trabucchi AG in Case 51/74 *Hulst/Produktschap voor Siergewassen* [1975] ECR 79, 104–5.

[272] Lenz AG in Case C–44/93 *Namur—Les Assurances du Crédit SA* v. *Office National du Ducroire and Belgium* [1994] ECR I–3829, I–3850.

[273] *Ibid.*, I–3874–5. If an existing aid is altered without prior notification, the Commission may initiate the Art. 93(2) procedure and require the recovery of the aid. See Joined Cases 91 & 127/83 *Heineken Brouwereijen BV* v. *Inspecteurs der Vennootschapsbelasting, Amsterdam and Utrecht* [1984] ECR 3435, 3454.

[274] Communic. to the Member States on the accelerated clearance of aid schemes for SMEs and of amendments of existing schemes ([1992] OJ C213/10), para. 2 and Letter to Member States of 22 Feb. 1994 (*Competition Law in the European Communities ii: Rules Applicable to State Aids* (EC Commission, Brussels, 1995), 73).

[275] Extension for two years of an originally 'provisional' scheme would usually be treated as non-negligible and have to be notified. See Mayras AG in Case 70/72 *EC Commission* v. *Germany: investment grants for mining* [1973] ECR 813, 840. Cf., in connection with sectoral legislation requiring notification of aid plans, Case 214/83 *Germany* v. *EC Commission: aid to the steel industry* [1985] ECR 3053, 3094.

[276] Community Framework for state aids on R & D ([1986] OJ C83/2); H. Morch, 'Summary of the Most Important Recent Developments' (1995) 6 *Competition Policy Newsletter* 41–7, 41–3.

ECU 100,000 over three years does not need to be notified,[277] though Member States must establish national machinery enabling them to answer 'any questions the Commission might wish to ask'.[278] In the case of general aid schemes, individual aid measures have to be notified if they reach certain thresholds.[279] Aid to a particular sector may also have to be notified where the scheme concerned has been authorized without prejudice to the application of the principles applicable to that sector.[280]

More specific notification obligations may be contained in individual decisions.[281] Soft legislation may also be involved. For example, in 1972 Member States agreed to notify the Commission of all specific aid to the textiles industry as well applications of general aid schemes and regional aid schemes to this industry.[282]

Not only measures which 'unquestionably constitute aid' have to be notified but also 'measures whose very character as aid may appear to be in doubt'.[283] According to the Commission, notification is obligatory where there is a sufficient likelihood, in the light of the case law of the Court of Justice and Commission practice, that aid is involved.[284] Financial transfers to public undertakings must be notified if they can constitute aid.[285] Thus, for example, all financial measures which relate to public undertakings and are only suspected of being aid must be notified.[286]

Moreover, notification obligations do not apply only in relation to 'effective payment' of aid.[287] Aid is deemed to have been put into effect as soon as the

---

[277] Community Guidelines on aid for small and medium-sized enterprises ([1992] OJ C213/2), para. 3.2; and Notice on the *de minimis* rule for state aid ([1996] OJ C68/9).

[278] *Ibid.*

[279] Joined Cases 166/86 & 226/86 *Irish Cement Ltd* v. *EC Commission* [1988] ECR 6473, 6502 (which concerned aid within the regional aid ceiling); and Case C–47/91 *Italy* v. *EC Commission: Italgrani* [1994] ECR 4635, 4653 (which concerned the possibility of reservations being made by the Commission in an approval decision).

[280] Case C–313/90 *Comité International de la Rayonne et des Fibres Synthétiques (Cirfs)* v. *EC Commission* [1993] ECR I–1125.

[281] See, e.g., Dec. 75/397 ([1975] OJ L177/13) on the aids granted by the Belgian Government pursuant to the Law of 17 July 1959 introducing and co-ordinating measures to encourage economic expansion and the creation of new industries.

[282] *Second Report on Competition Policy* (EC Commission, Brussels, 1973), 87. Proposals as to notification procedures may also be made under Art. 93(1). See, regarding an Italian rescue aid scheme, Bull. EU 12–1994, 1.2.80.

[283] Lenz AG in Case 40/85 *Belgium* v. *EC Commission: Boch* [1986] ECR 2321, 2332.

[284] *Competition Law in the European Communities ii: Rules Applicable to State Aids* (EC Commission, Brussels, 1995), 27.

[285] Paras 4.3 and 4.4, Bull. EC 9–1984, 3.5.1, and paras. 27–31 of Application of Arts. 92 and 93 EC and Art. 5 of Dir. 80/723 to public undertakings in the manufacturing sector ([1993] OJ C307/3).

[286] *Ibid.*

[287] Notice C37/93 (NN 63/93) ([1994] OJ C170/5) concerning Art. 29*ter* of the Walloon decree of 25 June 1992 on support for Walloon firms participating in Community industrial programmes which are the subject of specific international agreements.

legislative machinery enabling it to be granted has been set up.[288] Thus legislative provision for aid and any draft laws granting aid[289] must be notified, even if the authorities say that the legislation will only become operative after Commission approval.[290] More particularly, a decision to award a guarantee, even if not actually awarded, must also be notified prior to the award being made public.[291] Apparently, the rationale for requiring notification of such arrangements is that, if notifications are made at a later stage and the Commission finds the aid in question to be contrary to Article 92, the Member State concerned would face otherwise unnecessary difficulties in complying with the Commission decision. Not only might positions in favour of the aid have become 'well entrenched' but also recipients might have acquired rights to the aid under national law.[292]

Notifications must be made at least two months before adoption of such arrangements.[293] If this obligation is not respected, Article 169 proceedings may be taken for breach of Article 93(3).[294] Such proceedings have been threatened in the event of a Member State tending systematically or flagrantly to violate notification requirements in Article 93(3).[295]

To add to the effectiveness of the obligations, the Commission has recommended Member States to include a clause in their national legislation to the

---

[288] Dec. 93/627 ([1993] OJ L309/21) concerning aid granted by the Spanish authorities on the occasion of the sale by Cenemesa/Cadmesa/Conelec of certain selected assets to Asea-Brown Boveri. Cf. the Letter to Member States of 27 Apr. 1989 (SG(89)D/5521) in *Competition Law in the European Communities: Rules Applicable to State Aids* (EC Commission, Brussels, 1990), 19 and *Twenty-First Report on Competition Policy* (EC Commission, Brussels, 1992), 154–5. But see where the development plans which would establish the details of aid measures and thus govern the granting of aid provided for in unnotified legislation had not been adopted, Notice C31/92 (N454/91) ([1992] OJ C324/3) concerning aid granted by Italy for the reconstruction of the Valtellina.

[289] Case 169/82 *EC Commission* v. *Italy: agricultural aid for Sicily* [1984] ECR 1603, 1615.

[290] Dec. 93/508 ([1993] OJ L238/38) concerning aid granted by the Italian Government in favour of the ceramics industry of Lazio.

[291] Communic. C29/92 (NN12/92) ([1992] OJ C234/8) concerning aid decided by the Basque country in favour of La Papelera Española.

[292] Cf., in connection with Art. 37 Euratom, which requires Member States to inform the Commission of plans for the disposal of radioactive waste, Case 187/87 *Saarland* v. *Minister for Industry, Post and Telecommunications and Tourism* [1988] ECR 5013, 5041–2. See also Slynn AG (*ibid.*, 5034).

[293] This period was determined by the Court in Case 120/73 *Gebr. Lorenz GmbH* v. *Germany* [1973] ECR 1471, 1481.

[294] Case 169/82 *EC Commission* v. *Italy: agricultural aid for Sicily* [1984] ECR 1603; Case C–35/88 *EC Commission* v. *Greece: Kydep I* [1990] ECR I–3125, I–3159; and Case C–61/90 *EC Commission* v. *Greece: Kydep II* [1992] ECR I–2407, I–2453.

[295] Notification of State Aids to the Commission pursuant to Art. 93(3) EC: the failure of Member States to respect their obligations ([1980] OJ C252/2). This Communic. contained the 'essence' of the letter sent to Member States. See Communic. ([1983] OJ C318/3). On 2 Oct. 1974 the Governments had declared in the Council of Ministers that 'the rules of the EEC Treaty regarding aids (Arts. 92 and 93) shall be strictly observed both with respect to existing and future aid measures'.

effect that aid can only be paid after it has been cleared by the Commission.[296] In the absence of such a clause in the legal basis for the grant of aid, creation of the basis without prior notification will be treated as contrary to Article 93(3).[297]

Notified Aid

In the case of aid which is duly notified, the Commission must act within two months of the notification, and an accelerated procedure may apply to certain aid.[298] The Commission considers that the relevant period does not start to run until it has full information.[299] Internal Commission rules require that the appropriate service must examine the dossier within fifteen days of its receipt to decide whether or not the dossier is complete.[300] The Commission may issue an interim order requiring the Member State to supply the necessary information. If the Member State does not comply, the Commission may conclude the procedure and issue a decision on the basis of the information received.[301]

Any modifications to the original proposal must also be notified.[302] Where the Commission raises initial objections and a radically new and different proposal with different objectives and legally and economically incompatible with the basis of the original proposal is produced, the new proposal will not be considered until the original one is either formally withdrawn or has been the subject of a negative decision.[303] Information arriving after closure of the procedure need not be taken into account by the Commission.[304]

[296] *Twenty-Third Report on Competition Policy* (EC Commission, Brussels, 1994), 250. See, earlier, in the case of a general aid scheme, Dec. 81/738 ([1981] OJ L262/22) on a proposal by the Netherlands Government to grant aid for the creation of new production capacity by an undertaking in the petro-chemical industry (aromatic solvents).

[297] Communic. C45/94 (NN105/93) ([1995] OJ C63/4) with regard to the aid for the development of the regional aircraft (turbo-prop) CASA-3000 by Construcciones Aeronautics SA. See also, regarding aid agreements and loan contracts, Communic. C34/95 (NN63/94 & NN222/95) ([1995] OJ C237/2) concerning the proposal by the Spanish Government to award state aid to the Volkswagen group in support of its Spanish subsidiary Seat SA.

[298] Community Guidelines on aid for small and medium-sized enterprises ([1992] OJ C213/2), para. 5; Guidelines on aid to employment ([1995] OJ C334/4), para. 26.

[299] Communic. N340/89 ([1990] OJ C103/9) concerning aid which the Netherlands Government had decided to grant to glasshouse growers in the form of a preferential tariff for natural gas. Commission submission in Case 84/82 *Germany* v. *EC Commission: aid to textiles and clothing* [1984] ECR 1451, 1463, though the ECJ did not squarely address the issue.

[300] *Europe* 5367 (9 Nov. 1990).

[301] Case C–301/87 *France* v. *EC Commission: Boussac* [1990] ECR I–307, I–356, and Case 142/87 *Belgium* v. *EC Commission: Tubemeuse* [1990] ECR I–959, I–1009.

[302] Joined Cases 91 & 127/83 *Heineken Brouwereijen BV* v. *Inspecteurs der Vennootschapsbelasting, Amsterdam and Utrecht* [1984] ECR 3435.

[303] Dec. 84/417 ([1984] OJ L230/28) on a proposed aid by the Netherlands Government in respect of certain investments to be carried out by an oil company at its refinery in Borsele; Dec. 84/418 ([1984] OJ L230/31) on a proposal by the Netherlands Government in respect of certain investments to be carried out by an oil company at its refinery in the area of Rotterdamn-Europoort.

[304] Case 234/84 *Belgium* v. *EC Commission* [1986] ECR 2263, 2288; Darmon AG in Joined Cases C–324 & C342/90 *Germany and Pleuger Worthington GmbH* v. *EC Commission* [1994] ECR I–1173, I–1195–6.

At this stage the Commission does not grant the right to be heard by third parties. The Commission claims support for this practice in the case law of the Court of Justice.[305] However, in *Sytraval*[306] the Court of First Instance imposed on the Commission the obligation, in certain circumstances, to initiate a contradictory procedure with complainants in cases involving difficult questions as to the qualification of a measure as an aid.[307]

The Commission may decide to raise no objections under Article 93(3), though current Commission practice is to approve new aid schemes only for limited periods. After expiry of such a period, the aid will have to be notified again under Article 93(3).[308]

If the Commission decides to raise no objections, it is not required to take a formal decision within the meaning of Article 189 or to inform other Member States or third parties.[309] However, in the interests of good administration, it should inform the Member State concerned.[310] In practice, such decisions are usually listed in the Official Journal, and some further information may be published in the Bulletin of the European Union.[311] Interested third parties may normally obtain no more information than is contained in the letter addressed to the Member State concerned.[312]

It is assumed by the Court of Justice that a decision to raise no objections may constitute an act subject to judicial review under Article 173.[313] If the decision is annulled by one of the European Courts and the aid is subsequently found to be incompatible with the common market, the Commission may require its repayment.[314]

If a Member State implements the aid without waiting for the outcome of the procedure, the Commission may issue an interim order suspending the implementation of the aid.[315] The order has the effect of confirming the standstill clause in Article 93(3).

If, however, the Commission does not act within the two-month period, the

---

[305] Case 84/82 *Germany* v. *EC Commission: aid to textiles and clothing* [1984] ECR 1451.

[306] Case T–95/94 *Chambre Nationale des Entreprises de Transport de Fonds et Valeurs (Sytraval) and Brink's France SARL* v. *EC Commission* [1995] ECR II–2651.

[307] The Commission, however, intends to appeal against this judgment.

[308] S. Lehner and R. Meiklejohn, 'Fair Competition in the Internal Market: Community State Aid Policy' (1991) 48 *European Economy* 7–148.

[309] Case C–225/91 *Matra SA* v. *EC Commission* [1993] ECR I–3203, I–3254–5 and I–3263.

[310] Case 120/73 *Gebr. Lorenz GmbH* v. *Germany* [1973] ECR 1471, 1482.

[311] Letter to Member States of 11 Oct. 1990 (*Competition Law in the European Communities ii: Rules Applicable to State Aids* (EC Commission, Brussels, 1995), 98).

[312] Case 236/86 *Dillinger Huttenwerke* v. *EC Commission* [1988] ECR 3761, 3784; Case C–180/88 *Wirtschaftsvereinigung Eisen- und Stahlindustrie* v. *EC Commission* [1990] ECR I–4413, I–4440–1.

[313] Case 84/82 *Germany* v. *EC Commission: aid to textiles and clothing* [1984] ECR 1451, 1459, and 1486.

[314] H. Morch, 'Summary of the Most Important Recent Developments' (1995) 4 *Competition Policy Newsletter* 47–51, 48.

[315] Case 301/87 *France* v. *EC Commission: Boussac* [1990] ECR I–307, I–356; Case 142/87 *Belgium* v. *EC Commission: Tubemeuse* [1990] ECR I–959, I–1009; Case 173/73 *Italy* v. *EC Commission: aids to the textile industry* [1974] ECR 709, 717.

aid concerned may be implemented, provided the Member State concerned has informed the Commission that it intends to do so.[316] The aid thus becomes existing aid for the purposes of Article 93(1).[317] What is involved is not 'authorizations *en bloc*' but the logical consequence of the fact that aid systems 'crystallize' under Article 93(1).[318]

Unnotified Aid

In the five years up to 1995 18 per cent of the aid cases examined by the Commission were registered as involving non-notified aid.[319] Such cases may come to light because of complaints from competitors of aid recipients as well as from individuals concerned about waste of taxpayers' money.[320] Complaints of this kind are said to be increasing, as lawyers discover the potential offered by state aid rules.[321] After an examination the Commission replies to all complainants.[322] If it takes a decision, the complainant is sent a copy of the letter announcing the decision to the Member State concerned.[323]

Where aid has not been notified, the Commission does not have to close its preliminary examination within two months, though it must act with diligence,[324] and tries to reach a decision within two months.[325] Delay by the Commission in reaching a decision cannot transform unnotified aid into existing aid.[326]

Interim decisions requiring production of 'all such documentation, information and data as are necessary in order that it may examine the compatibility of the aid with the single market'[327] or 'all appropriate information,

---

[316] According to *Competition Law in the European Communities ii: Rules Applicable to State Aids* (EC Commission, Brussels, 1995), 41, n. 3, this proviso means that it still has a reasonable period (2 weeks) within which to initiate the Art. 93(2) procedure.

[317] Case 120/73 *Gebr. Lorenz GmbH* v. *Germany* [1973] ECR 1471, 1481–2; and Case 84/82 *Germany* v. *EC Commission: aid to textiles and clothing* [1984] ECR 1451, 1488. See also Cases 31/77R & 53/77R *EC Commission* v. *UK* and *UK* v. *EC Commission: aid to pig producers* [1977] ECR 921, 923; Case 171/83R *EC Commission* v. *France: aid to textiles and clothing* [1983] ECR 2621, 2628; and Joined Cases 91 & 127/83 *Heineken Brouwerijen BV* v. *Inspecteurs der Vennootschapsbelasting, Amsterdam and Utrecht* [1984] ECR 3435, 3454.

[318] Darmon AG in Joined Cases 166 & 220/86 *Irish Cement Limited* v. *EC Commission* [1988] ECR 6473, 6492–3.

[319] Reply by Mr Van Miert to Written Question E–2872/95 ([1996] OJ C79/31) by Winifred Ewing.

[320] A standard form for making complaints has been published ([1989] OJ C26/6).

[321] F. Rawlinson, n. 52 above, 56.

[322] Communic. ([1989] OJ C26/7).

[323] *Competition Law in the European Communities ii: Rules Applicable to State Aids* (EC Commission, Brussels, 1995), 45.

[324] See, e.g., Van Gerven AG in Case C–312/90 *Spain* v. *EC Commission: Cenemesa* [1992] ECR I–4117, I–4131

[325] *Competition Law in the European Communities ii: Rules Applicable to State Aids* (EC Commission, Brussels, 1995), 39.

[326] Jacobs AG in Case C–39/94 *Syndicat Français de l'Express International (SFEI)* v. *La Poste*, Opinion of 14 Dec. 1995.

[327] Communic. C52/95 (N184/B/93) ([1996] OJ C2/3) concerning aid in favour of transport undertakings in the Friuli–Venezia Giulia region.

documentation and data allowing the Commission to assess the compatibility with Article 92 of the aid'[328] may be adopted by the Commission.[329] According to the Commission, Articles 92–94 'lay down procedures which imply that the Commission is in a position to determine, on the basis of the material at its disposal, whether the disputed financial assistance constitutes aid'.[330] A six-week deadline for receipt of the information may be set.[331] If the Member State does not provide the necessary information, the Commission may reach a decision on the basis of the information in its possession.[332]

The Commission can also require the suspension of unnotified aid.[333] If the Member State does not suspend the aid, the Commission may bring the violation of Article 93(3) or a decision requiring suspension before the Court of Justice.[334] However, the Commission may not require suspension simply because it has doubts whether the aid falls within a previous approval.[335]

Advocate General Jacobs in *Spain* v. *EC Commission*[336] expressed the view that the Commission should also be able to require immediate repayment of the aid. Consistently with this view, the Commission 'intends in appropriate cases to adopt, by decision, interim measures designed to neutralize the aid and charge interest, so as to cancel out any advantage illegally conferred on the recipient, regardless of whatever final decision it takes on the compatibility of the aid with the common market'.[337] In particular, provisional decisions requiring recovery are envisaged in a 1995 Communication to the Member States.[338] Such action is considered necessary, because a decision requiring recovery after a finding of incompatibility with the common market, even with interest, may not eliminate the advantages to the recipient of having had the use of the aid. The advantages may include factors such as the positive tax

---

[328] Dec. 96/179 ([1996] OJ L53/50) enjoining the German Government to provide all documentation, information, and data on the new investment projects of the Volkswagen Group in the new *Länder* and on the aid that was to be granted to them.

[329] The Commission claims similar powers under Art. 88 ECSC. See Notice C22/A/92 (NN53/93) ([1993] OJ C213/6) regarding aid which Italy planned to grant to Ilva SpA.

[330] Communic. C34/95(NN63/94 & NN222/95) ([1995] OJ C237/2) concerning the proposal by the Spanish Government to award state aid to the Volkswagen group in support of its Spanish subsidiary Seat SA.   [331] *Ibid.*

[332] Case C–301/87 *France* v. *EC Commission: Boussac* [1990] ECR I–307.

[333] SG(91)D/4577 (*Competition Law in the European Communities ii: Rules Applicable to State Aids* (EC Commission, Brussels, 1995), 63); Case 171/83R *EC Commission* v. *France: aid to textiles and clothing* [1983] ECR 2261 (interim order granted by the ECJ, so as to suspend aid implemented before expiry of the two-month period under Art. 93(3)); Case 142/87 *Belgium* v. *EC Commission: Tubemeuse* [1990] ECR I–959, I–1009; Case C–301/87 *France* v. *EC Commission: Boussac* [1990] ECR I–307, I–356.

[334] Case C–301/87 *France* v. *EC Commission: Boussac* [1990] ECR I–307, I–357. See, e.g., Dec. 94/220 ([1994] OJ L107/61) requiring France to suspend the payment to Groupe Bull of aid granted in breach of Art. 93(3) EC.

[335] Case 47/91 *Italy* v. *EC Commission: Italgrani* [1994] ECR I–4635, I–4658.

[336] Case C–42/93 *Merco* [1994] ECR I–4175, I–4186.

[337] *Twenty-Fourth Report on Competition Policy* (EC Commission, Brussels, 1995), 32.

[338] [1995] OJ C156/5.

implications, the increase in available cash funds, the substantive advantages deriving from the aid, the intermediate investments, the possibilities of obtaining supplementary loans, and the interest thereon.[339] The Member State concerned will be given twenty days to submit its comments and will have the opportunity to consider the alternative of granting rescue aid.[340] The decision will remain in force until the Commission reaches a final decision as to the compatibility of the aid with the common market. Failure of the Member State concerned to comply with the decision may result in the matter being referred to the Court of Justice.

7.5.3 Article 93(2) Procedure

The Commission describes the procedure in Article 93(2) as 'formal'.[341] According to this provision, if, after giving notice to the parties concerned to submit their comments, the Commission finds that aid is not compatible with the common market having regard to Article 92, or that such aid is being misused, it shall decide that the Member State concerned shall abolish or alter such aid within a period of time to be determined by the Commission. If the Member State concerned does not comply with the decision within the prescribed time, the Commission or any other interested Member State may, in derogation from Articles 169 and 170, refer the matter to the Court of Justice direct.[342] States which are not 'interested' may only proceed under Article 170. Where the Commission considers an aid system to be contrary to Union law rules other than Article 92, it may bring proceedings under Article 169.[343]

Article 93(2) requires a more elaborate examination than Article 93(3),[344] and the Commission has a reasonable time to complete the procedure.[345] In practice, however, the Commission 'aims to close proceedings within six months of their being commenced'.[346] For non-notified aid measures, no deadline exists for the decision-making process of the Commission, though the Commission undertakes to act as speedily as possible.[347] In the event of

---

[339] Joined Cases T–244/93 & T–486/93 *TWD Textilwerke Deggendorf GmbH* v. *EC Commission* [1995] ECR II–2265, II–2296–9. [340] Bull. EU 5–1995, 1.3.32.

[341] *Competition Law in the European Communities ii. Rules Applicable to State Aids* (EC Commission, Brussels, 1995). Art. 93(3) is 'informal'. See also Van Gerven AG in C–225/91 *Matra SA* v. *EC Commission* [1993] ECR I–3203, I–3238.

[342] i.e., there is no need for a reasoned opinion. Cf. Art. 88 ECSC.

[343] Case C–35/88 *EC Commission* v. *Greece: Kydep I* [1990] ECR I–3125, I–3154.

[344] Mayras AG in Case 70/72 *EC Commission* v. *Germany; investment grants for mining* [1973] ECR 813, 834.

[345] Case 59/79 *Fédération Nationale des Producteurs de Vins de Table* v. *EC Commission* [1979] ECR 2425, 2428.

[346] *Twenty-Fourth Report on Competition Policy* (EC Commission, Brussels, 1995), 197, n. 1. Dec. 3855/91 ([1991] OJ L362/57) establishing Community rules for aid to the steel industry refers in Art. 6(4) to a maximum period of 3 months.

[347] Notice on co-operation between national courts and the Commission in the state-aid field ([1995] OJ C312/8), para. 18.

indefinite delay, there is the possibility that proceedings for failure to act might be brought against the Commission under Article 175.[348]

Initiation

If the Commission has any reason to think that aid could be incompatible with the common market,[349] has serious difficulties in determining whether aid is compatible with the common market,[350] is unable to satisfy itself after a preliminary examination that aid is compatible, or is not convinced that the aid is compatible,[351] it must initiate the Article 93(2) procedure without delay.[352] Delay may, however, be acceptable, where the delay results from the failure of the Member State concerned to notify the aid in the first place and its failure subsequently to provide the Commission with information requested.[353] The Commission must also open the procedure where the terms of an earlier authorization have not been respected or aid additional to that authorized has been granted.[354] In the former case the Commission may also refer the matter directly to the Court of Justice.[355] If the aid is unnotified, the Commission requests the Member State, in the letter opening the procedure, to confirm within ten working days the suspension of all aid payments. If such confirmation is not provided, suspension may be ordered.[356]

There is nothing inherently contentious in resort to this procedure.[357] Its use became more automatic after the judgment in *Germany* v. *EC Commission: Belgian aid to textiles*.[358] Here 'extensive' negotiations between the Commission and Belgium had taken place over a period of sixteen months concerning a Belgian aid scheme to the textiles industry. These negotiations led to 'substantial amendments' to the scheme. The latter was then authorized by the Commission, though only for one year, without the Article 93(2) procedure being opened. The Court of Justice annulled the authorization.

When the procedure is opened, Member States are invited to comment by a

---

[348] Mayras AG in Case 70/72 *EC Commission* v. *Germany: investment grants for mining* [1973] ECR 813, 836.

[349] Case C–198/91 *William Cook PLC* v. *EC Commission* [1993] ECR I–2487, I–2529.

[350] Case 84/82 *Germany* v. *EC Commission: aid to textiles and clothing* [1984] ECR 1451, 1488.

[351] Case T–49/93 *Société Internationale de Diffusion et de l'Édition* v. *EC Commission* [1995] ECR II–2501, II–2523.

[352] A corresponding procedure is contained in Art. 6(4) of Dec. 3855/91 ([1991] OJ L362/57) establishing Community rules for the aid to the steel industry and Art. 8 of Dec. 3632/93 ([1993] OJ L329/12) establishing Community rules for state aid to the coal industry

[353] Case 169/82 *EC Commission* v. *Italy: agricultural aid for Sicily* [1984] ECR 1603, 1642.

[354] C–294/90 *British Aerospace and Rover Group Holdings* v. *EC Commission* [1992] ECR I–493.

[355] *Ibid.*, I–522.

[356] *Competition Law in the European Communities ii. Rules Applicable to State Aids* (EC Commission, Brussels, 1995), 39.

[357] J. Flynn, 'State Aid and Self-help' (1983) 8 *ELRev.* 297–312, 299, n. 15.

[358] Case 84/82 *Germany* v. *EC Commission: aid to textiles and clothing* [1984] ECR 1451, 1490.

letter addressed to them.[359] Other interested parties are invited to comment by a notice published in the C section of the Official Journal.[360] In the *Fifteenth Report on Competition Policy*[361] the Commission stated that it would in future provide considerably more information in the notices. The aim of the notices is to obtain from all the information required for the guidance of the Commission with regard to its future action.[362]

Interested parties include customers, employees, and trade associations.[363] According to the Court of Justice, it is 'an indeterminate group', including 'the persons, undertakings or associations whose interests might be affected by the grant of the aid'.[364] Unlike the Article 169 procedure, the Article 93(2) procedure is said to guarantee the other Member States and the sectors concerned[365] an opportunity to make their views known and allows the Commission to be fully informed of all the facts of the case before making its decision.[366]

Once the procedure is opened, aid may not be granted until the Commission has reached a positive decision. Aid granted before the Commission has reached a final decision under Article 93(2) may be subject to a recovery procedure.[367] However, aid may be permitted where the investments to be aided are 'compellingly urgent'.[368]

If the Member State does not reply to the initiation of the procedure, the Commission may adopt a decision on the basis of the information it has.[369] If the Commission does not have sufficient information, it must order the Member State concerned to supply the missing information.[370]

---

[359] 'Doubtless in connection with the joint review of existing systems of aid provided for in Art. 93(1)'. See VerLoren van Themaat AG in Case 323/82 *Intermills SA* v. *EC Commission* [1984] ECR 3809, 3837.

[360] Case 323/82 *Intermills SA* v. *EC Commission* [1984] ECR 3809, 3837.

[361] (EC Commission, Brussels, 1985), 140.

[362] Case 70/72 *EC Commission* v. *Germany; investment grants for mining* [1973] ECR 813, 830.

[363] VerLoren van Themaat AG in Case 323/82 *Intermills SA* v. *EC Commission* [1984] ECR 3809, 3837.

[364] *Ibid.*, 3827.

[365] Or all interested parties (Mischo AG in Case C–35/88 *EC Commission* v. *Greece: Kydep I* [1990] ECR I–3125, I–3139).

[366] Case 290/83 *EC Commission* v. *France* [1985] ECR 439, 449.

[367] Communic. of 24 Nov. 1983 ([1983] OJ C318/3). According to Communic. N340/89 ([1990] OJ C103/9) concerning aid which the Netherlands Government had decided to grant to glasshouse growers in the form of a preferential tariff for natural gas, the period does not start to run until the Commission considers it has 'received all the necessary information'.

[368] Notice C4/94, C61/94, C62/94, NN2/95, NN3/95 & N467/95 ([1995] OJ C203/6) concerning aid the German Government intended to grant to Sächsische Olefinwerke GmbH, Leuna-Werke GmbH, and Buna GmbH.

[369] Letter to Member States, 30 April 1987 (*Competition Law in the European Communities ii. Rules Applicable to State Aids* (EC Commission, Brussels, 1995), 91); Case 234/84 *Belgium* v. *EC Commission: Meura* [1986] ECR 2263, 2286; Case 142/87 *Belgium* v. *EC Commission: Tubemeuse* [1990] ECR I–959, I–1010.

[370] Joined Cases C–324/90 & C–342/90 *Germany and Pleuger Worthington GmbH* v. *EC Commission* [1994] ECR I–1173, I–1206.

However, if an aid measure falls under a scheme previously approved by the Commission and is compatible with the decision approving the scheme, the Commission cannot assess the compatibility of the measure with Article 92.[371] On the other hand, the Commission may act under Article 93(2) to secure modification of approved schemes, where Article 93(1) recommendations have not been followed.[372]

Closure

Decisions to close proceedings under Article 93(2) may be negative or positive. A positive decision may be conditional, as to the type of aid, its amount, the recipients, its duration, and so on. The Commission may also approve an aid scheme subject to notification requirements in the case of 'significant' individual grants of aid above certain thresholds. It must then assess the compatibility of any such grants with the common market and not merely with the conditions stipulated in the earlier decision.[373]

If the Commission adopts a negative decision, finding that the aid is incompatible with the common market, it may decide that the Member State concerned shall abolish or alter the aid. A decision prohibiting existing aid is constitutive, and so the aid need only be eliminated by the future date specified in the decision.[374] A reasonable period for elimination must be allowed.[375] A decision prohibiting unnotified aid is declaratory, and the aid is *ab initio*[376] incompatible with the common market.[377]

The Commission must indicate those aspects of the aid which it finds incompatible with the common market and which require elimination or modification.[378] The Commission fixes the date by which the aid has to be discontinued. Where the Member State is obliged to inform the Commission of action to comply with the decision by a given date, that date constitutes the deadline for discontinuation of the aid.[379]

---

[371] Case T–435/93 *Association of Sorbitol Producers in the EC (ASPEC)* v. *EC Commission* [1995] ECR II–1281, II–1320.

[372] Case C–312/90 *Spain* v. *EC Commission: Cenemesa* [1992] ECR I–4117, I–4141; and Case C–47/91 *Italy* v. *EC Commission: Italgrani* [1992] ECR 4145, 4159. See, e.g., Dec. 90/381 ([1990] OJ L188/55) amending German aid schemes for the motor-vehicle industry.

[373] Joined Cases T–447/93, T–448/93 & T–449/93 *Associazione Italiana Tecnico Economica del Cemento, British Cement Association, Titan Cement Company SA* v. *EC Commission* [1995] ECR II–1971.

[374] Case 70/72 *EC Commission* v. *Germany: investment grants for mining* [1973] ECR 813, 831.

[375] Case 173/73 *Italy* v. *EC Commission: aids to the textile industry* [1974] ECR 709, 716–7.

[376] Dec. 94/725 ([1994] OJ L289/26) on measures adopted by the French Government concerning pigmeat.

[377] It has been argued that Art. 93(2) is inapplicable to improperly introduced aid and that the Art. 169 procedure is less cumbersome. See Warner AG in Case 173/73 *Italy* v. *EC Commission: aids to the textile industry* [1974] ECR 709, 724. Cf. Lagrange AG in Case 6/64 *Flaminio Costa* v. *ENEL* [1964] ECR 585, 609.

[378] Case 70/72 *EC Commission* v. *Germany: investment grants for mining* [1973] ECR 813, 831.

[379] Case 213/85 *EC Commission* v. *Netherlands: preferential gas tariff for horticulturalists* [1988] ECR 281, 299–300.

If the Member State concerned objects to such a decision, it can challenge the legality of the decision by means of an application for annulment under Article 173 of the Treaty. An order may also be sought for the suspension of a Commission decision prohibiting aid. However, the recipient may be denied such an order on the grounds that it may have adequate remedies under national law,[380] and the Member State concerned may be denied an order, because it is unable to show that it risks serious harm which is irreparable.[381] Unless such a remedy is obtained, the only defence for a Member State failing to abolish aid in accordance with the decision is impossibility. This defence is not established merely by the difficulties which would arise for undertakings from abolition of the aid.[382]

The Commission also considers that it may order suspension of aid compatible with the common market, where aid incompatible with the common market has previously been granted to the same recipient and has not been recovered pursuant to an earlier Commission decision.[383] This practice was approved by the Court of First Instance in *Deggendorf*,[384] on the ground that the power to require the 'alteration' of aid may entail imposition of conditions to ensure that authorized aid does not affect trading conditions to an extent contrary to the common interest. However, if the value of the later aid exceeds that of the earlier aid, such a decision may be void for breach of the principle of proportionality.[385] The Commission even considers that it may order suspension of aid compatible with the common market where the earlier decision was adopted against a different Member State.[386] Conversely, a set-off of part of the sum required to be repaid against aid payable subsequently under a plan found compatible with the common market may be permissible.[387]

In accordance with Article 191 of the Treaty,[388] the full text of the decision is communicated to the Member State concerned, where the decision is negative,

---

[380] Case 310/85R *Deufil* v. *EC Commission* [1986] ECR 537, 542–3.

[381] Case 142/87R *Belgium* v. *EC Commission: Tubemeuse* [1987] ECR 2589, 2597.

[382] Case 63/87 *EC Commission* v. *Greece: aid to exports* [1988] ECR 2875, 2892.

[383] Dec. 92/330 ([1992] OJ L183/36) on aid by Germany to the Deggendorf textile works. See, similarly, Dec. 91/391 ([1991] OJ L215/16) on aid granted by Germany to Deggendorf GmbH, a producer of polyamide and polyester yarns located in Deggendorf (Bavaria). See also the *Twenty-Fourth Report on Competition Policy* (EC Commission, Brussels, 1995), 511–2.

[384] Joined Cases T–244/93 & T–486/93 *TWD Textilwerke Deggendorf GmbH* v. *EC Commission* [1995] ECR II–2265.

[385] *Ibid.*, II–2300.

[386] See, regarding French aid to the Beaulieu group, which followed previous Belgian aid to the same group, Notice C27/95 (ex NN45/95) ([1995] OJ C284/8) concerning the proposal of France to award aid to the Beaulieu Group in support of the company's planned investment in new capacity for production of carpet webbing and carpets, to be located in Maubeuge, Nord-Pas-de-Calais.

[387] Jacobs AG in Case 354/90 *Fédération Nationale du Commerce Extérieur des Produits Alimentaires et Syndicat National des Négociants et Transformateurs de Saumon* v. *France* [1991] ECR I–5505, I–5520.

[388] This provision merely required decisions to be notified to those to whom they were addressed. See now Art. 191(3), as amended by the TEU.

partly negative, or conditional. Such decisions are published in full in the L section of the Official Journal. Where the decision is positive, the Member State is informed by letter, and a communication reproducing the letter is reproduced in the C section.[389] In the *Fifteenth Report on Competition Policy* of 1985[390] the Commission stated that it would publish such decisions in more detail where the original proposal was accepted after substantial modification. It would also send a copy of the decision to interested third parties who had intervened in the Article 93(2) procedure.

At the same time, Article 17(2) of Regulation 17/64[391] provides that intervention by the European Agricultural Guidance and Guarantee Fund must not alter the conditions of competition in such a way as to be incompatible with the principles contained in the relevant provisions of the Treaty. At the stage of the clearing of accounts the Commission may, in accordance with this provision, refuse EAGGF reimbursement of state aid granted contrary to the rules of a common organization. Reimbursement may also be refused at the stage of payment of advances.[392] Such practice has been approved by the Court of Justice.[393]

In practice, however, the influence of Commission policy is said to be reflected in the large number of decisions in which restrictions or further criteria have been applied to bring the schemes into line with Union objectives and to restrict adverse effects on intra-Union trade rather than in the relatively small number of negative final decisions.[394]

Recovery

Unnotified aid which is found to be incompatible with the common market may have to be recovered by the Member State concerned,[395] so as to 'restore the *status quo*'.[396] The Commission also once claimed the power to order the

---

[389] Letter to Member States of 27 June 1989 (*Competition Law in the European Communities ii. Rules Applicable to State Aids* (EC Commission, Brussels, 1995), 97).

[390] (EC Commission, Brussels, 1986), 140.

[391] On the conditions for granting aid from the EAGGF ([1964] JO 586).

[392] Communic. ([1983] OJ C318/3).

[393] Joined Cases 15 & 16/76 *France* v. *EC Commission: clearance of EAGGF accounts* [1979] ECR 321, 337.   [394] F. Andriessen (n. 1 above), 348.

[395] Cf. Case 70/72 *EC Commission* v. *Germany: investment grants for mining* [1973] ECR 813, 829; and Case 310/85 *Deufil GmbH & Co. KG* v. *EC Commission* [1987] ECR 901, 927. See also Communication ([1983] OJ C318/3). But note the early reticence of the Commission to publicize the fact and its *corrigendum* ([1982] OJ L289/35) to Dec. 82/312 ([1982] OJ L138/18) concerning the aid granted by the Belgian Government to an industrial and commercial group manufacturing wall coverings, which replaced recovery demands with a declaration of incompatibility.

[396] Notice C33/B/93 (NN12/94) ([1994] OJ C80/4) regarding aid which France had decided to grant to Groupe Bull. Jacobs AG in Case C–301/87 *France* v. *EC Commission: Boussac* [1990] ECR I–307, I–341 considered that the Commission had power to order recovery for breach of Art. 93(3) alone. In support of this view he cited Tesauro AG in Case 142/87 *Belgium* v. *EC Commission: Tubemeuse* [1990] ECR I–959, I–997. The latter, however, only had in mind provisional orders. The deterrent effect has been doubted. See H.-J. Priess, 'Recovery of Illegal State Aid: An Overview of Recent Developments in the Case Law' (1996) 33 *CMLRev.* 69–91, 71.

recovery of aid solely because it had been granted without the notification required by Article 93(3).[397] However, this power was denied to the Commission in *Boussac*.[398] Where a decision not to object is annulled, the Commission may also feel that recovery should not be sought.[399]

Although Article 93(2) refers only to the abolition or alteration of aid,[400] recovery may be considered necessary to give practical effect to either.[401] The withdrawal by recovery of illegal aid is a logical consequence of the finding that the aid is illegal and cannot, in principle, be held to be disproportionate with regard to the aims of the Treaty provisions concerning state aid.[402] Rather, it is considered necessary to deprive the aid recipient of any advantages on the market relative to its competitors.[403] However, recovery will not be required of aid exceeding the undue financial advantage received.[404] Where the aid granted has been taxed, the recipient will be able to assert a claim against the competent national authorities in respect of any financial disadvantage or discrimination arising from the reimbursement of the nominal amount of the aid granted.[405]

The aid is to be repaid with interest from the date it was granted.[406] Interest used to be charged at a 'legal rate', which was sometimes much lower than the commercial rate. It is now to be calculated on the basis of the rates charged on bank loans to firms.[407] Payment of interest is necessary to prevent the recipient from retaining financial advantages resulting from the grant of the illegal aid, in the form of an interest-free loan.[408] However, interest may only be recovered in

---

[397] *Sixteenth Report on Competition Policy* (EC Commission, Brussels, 1987), 135.

[398] Case C–301/87 *France* v. *EC Commission: Boussac* [1990] ECR I–307. But see above, regarding 'provisional recovery'.

[399] *Fourteenth Report on Competition Policy* (EC Commission, Brussels, 1985), 127.

[400] Darmon AG in Joined Cases C–324/90 & C–342/90 *Germany and Pleuger Worthington GmbH* v. *EC Commission* [1994] ECR I–1173, I–1194.

[401] Case T–459/93 *Siemens SA* v. *EC Commission* [1995] ECR II–1675, II–1712.

[402] Case C–142/87 *Belgium* v. *EC Commission: Tubemeuse* [1990] ECR I–959, I–1020. However, in Dec. 92/328 ([1992] OJ L182/94) concerning aid granted by the French Government for the disposal of the assets of the MFL Group (Machines françaises lourdes) the Commission decided that certain aid did not need to be abolished, because the initial beneficiary had gone bankrupt and its assets were not taken over by the final beneficiary. In Dec. 92/329 ([1992] OJ L183/30) on aid granted by the Italian Government to a manufacturer of ophthalmic products (Industrie Ottiche Riunite) no recovery was required because of the time (more than 2 years) between the date when the aid became known to the Commission and the date of the Decision.

[403] See, e.g., Case C–350/93 *EC Commission* v. *Italy: Lanerossi II* [1995] ECR I–699, I–716; and Case C–348/93 *EC Commission* v. *Italy: Alfa Romeo II* [1995] ECR I–673, I–696.

[404] Dec. 96/236 ([1996] OJ L78/31) concerning state aid granted by Hamburg to the ECSC undertaking Hamburger Stahlwerke GmbH, Hamburg.

[405] Case T–459/93 *Siemens SA* v. *EC Commission* [1995] ECR II–1675, II–1708.

[406] Communic. to the Member States supplementing Letter SG(91)D/4577 concerning the procedures for the notification of aid plans and procedures applicable when aid is provided in breach of the rules of Art. 93(3). See, e.g., Dec. 93/349 ([1993] OJ L143/7) concerning aid provided by the UK Government to British Aerospace for its purchase of Rover Group Holdings over and above those authorized in Dec. 89/58 authorizing a maximum aid to this operation subject to certain conditions.   [407] Bull. EU 1/2–1995, 1.3.34.

[408] Case T–459/93 *Siemens SA* v. *EC Commission* [1995] ECR II–1675, II–1712. See also Case C–350/93 *EC Commission* v. *Italy: Lanerossi II* [1995] ECR I–699, I–716.

order to offset the financial advantages actually arising from the allocation of
aid to the recipient and must be in proportion to the aid. In particular, interest
may only start to run from the date on which the recipient actually had the aid
at its disposal.[409]

Even if an aid recipient is declared insolvent as a result of the obligation to
repay unnotified aid, the Commission considers that a Member State may not
have the bankruptcy proceedings suspended and provide a guarantee in respect
of the debt arising from that obligation.[410] If the direct recipient has gone into
liquidation, recovery may have to be sought from indirect beneficiaries.[411]

Similarly, a clause in a privatization contract providing that any important
financial events occurring in consequence of acts prior to the sale of the
company are to be borne by the seller would allow the Member State to
indemnify the buyer for any reimbursement of aid required by the Commission.
Such a clause is, therefore, prohibited by Article 92(1) and may not be
applied.[412]

Recovery procedures depend on national law,[413] 'in the absence of Community rules',[414] though the scope and effectiveness of Union law must not be
affected. Hence, recovery must not be rendered impossible in practice, and
there must be no discrimination in relation to comparable cases governed
solely by national legislation.[415] In particular, a provision laying down a time-
limit for the revocation of an administrative act creating rights must be applied
in such a way that the recovery required by Union law is not rendered
practically impossible and the interests of the Union are taken fully into
consideration.[416]

The legitimate expectations of aid recipients are recognized by Union law,[417]
though undertakings are responsible for verifying that aid to be received is
lawful.[418] Such expectations may be relied on in proceedings before a national

---

[409] Case T–459/93 *Siemens* v. *EC Commission* [1995] ECR II–1675, II–1713–4.

[410] Notice C59/94 (NN125/94) ([1995] OJ C220/2) concerning the extraordinary administration of enterprises in a state of insolvency resulting from the obligation to repay aid
incompatible with Arts 92 and 93 EC.

[411] Dec. 89/661 ([1989] OJ L394/9) concerning aid provided by the Italian Government to
Alpha Romeo.

[412] Dec. 92/317 ([1992] OJ L171/54) on state aid in favour of Hilaturas y Tejidos Andaluces
SA and its buyer.

[413] Case C–94/87 *EC Commission* v. *Germany: Alcan* [1989] ECR 175, 192, and Case C–5/89 *EC
Commission* v. *Germany: Alutechnik* [1990] ECR I–3437, I–3458.

[414] Joined Cases 205–215/82 *Deutsche Milchkontor* v. *Germany* [1983] 2633, 2665.

[415] Case T–459/93 *Siemens SA* v. *EC Commission* [1995] ECR II–1675, II–1708.

[416] Case C–5/89 *EC Commission* v. *Germany: Alutechnik* [1990] ECR I–3437, I–3458; Joined
Cases T–244/93 & T–486/93 *TWD Textilwerke Deggendorf GmbH* v. *EC Commission* [1995] EC II–
2265, II–2293.

[417] Case 223/85 *Rijn-Schelde-Verolme (RSV) Maschinenfabrieken en Scheepswerven NV* v. *EC Commission* [1987] ECR 4617, 4659.

[418] Slynn AG *ibid.*, 4652; Case C–5/89 *EC Commission* v. *Germany: Alutechnik* [1990] ECR I–3437,
I–3457. See also Case 94/87 *EC Commission* v. *Germany: Alcan* [1989] ECR 175, 186 (Darmon AG);
Case C–102/92 *Ferriere Acciairie Sarde* v. *EC Commission* [1993] ECR I–801, I–806.

court[419] and in 'exceptional circumstances'.[420] The Court of Justice has not explained what such circumstances might be, but Advocate General Darmon has referred to doubts which some undertakings might have as to whether 'atypical' forms of aid were subject to notification requirements.[421] A delay of twenty-six months by the Commission in reaching a final decision may also establish such an expectation.[422] Moreover, the recipient's good faith, and the difficulties caused by the sharing of powers between the local and central authorities may dissuade the Commission from requiring recovery of the aid.[423]

Where recovery is required and the Member State concerned fails to respect the requirement, the Commission may bring proceedings before the Court of Justice. The only defence to such proceedings is absolute impossibility[424] or, presumably imprecision in the recovery requirements.[425] The former condition is not met by bankruptcy rules,[426] intangibility of capital,[427] or where recovery would entail liquidation of the recipient.[428] However, recovery is only required 'within the limits of the possibilities afforded by the firm's liquidation'.[429]

Where proceedings are pending before the European Courts and immediate repayment would preclude the possibility of re-establishing the *status quo ante* in the event of the decision being annulled, a compromise solution, such as the deposit by the aid recipient of the sum concerned in a blocked bank account, may be accepted by the Commission.[430] Merely to make a provision in the balance sheet would be inadequate. The sum remains indirectly available to the undertaking, and its tax charges are reduced.[431]

---

[419] Case T–459/93 *Siemens SA* v. *EC Commission* [1995] ECR II–1675, II–1714.

[420] Case C–5/89 *EC Commission* v. *Germany: Alutechnik* [1990] ECR I–3437, 3456–7.

[421] *Ibid.*, I–3449.

[422] Case 223/85 *Rijn-Schelde-Verolme (RSV) Maschinenfabrieken en Scheepswerven NV* v. *EC Commission* [1987] ECR 4617, 4659; Dec. 95/195 ([1995] OJ L126/32) concerning aid granted by the Region of Sardinia (Italy) in the fisheries sector (temporary withdrawal of vessels).

[423] Notice C39/95 (ex NN47/95) ([1995] OJ C344/8) concerning aid granted by Italy to Acciaierie di Bolzano.

[424] Case 52/84 *EC Commission* v. *Belgium: Boch* [1986] ECR 89, 104.

[425] Case 70/72 *EC Commission* v. *Germany: investment grants for mining* [1973] ECR 813.

[426] Case C–142/87 *Belgium* v. *EC Commission: Tubemeuse* [1990] ECR I–959, I–1019–20.

[427] Case 52/84 *EC Commission* v. *Belgium: Boch* [1986] ECR 89, 104; Case 5/86 *EC Commission* v. *Belgium: aid to synthetic fibres* [1987] ECR 1773.

[428] Case 52/84 *EC Commission* v. *Belgium: Boch* [1986] ECR 89, 104.

[429] Dec. 86/366 ([1986] JO L223/30) concerning aid which the Belgian Government had granted to a ceramic sanitary ware and crockery manufacturer.

[430] Dec. 95/367 ([1995] OJ L219/34) amending the Dec. of 27 July 1994 concerning the subscription by CDC–Participations to bonds issued by Air France.

[431] Joined Cases T–244/93 & T–486/93 *TWD Textilwerke Deggendorf GmbH* v. *EC Commission* [1995] ECR II–2265, II–2296–7.

7.6 JUDICIAL DECISION-MAKING

The plenary jurisdiction of the European Courts is limited to review of the legality of Commission decisions.[432] The lack of direct effectiveness of Article 92 of the Treaty means that the role of preliminary rulings by the Court of Justice and the role of national courts may also be limited. Even so, the contribution of the judiciary to both the formulation and implementation of Commission policy in relation to aid control may not be without significance.

7.6.1 *Locus Standi*

The Commission or any interested Member State may apply to the Court of Justice under Article 93(2) if the Member State concerned does not comply with a Commission decision prohibiting aid. Application may also be made for interim measures under Article 186.[433] At the same time, the Member State concerned, including regional authorities which have granted the aid at issue,[434] may challenge the legality of the decision under Article 173. Such a challenge does not in itself have suspensive effect.[435] It must be brought within the period of two months laid down by Article 173,[436] unless the alleged defect in the decision is so serious that, if substantiated, the decision 'would lack any legal foundation in the context of the Community'.[437]

A natural or legal person may also challenge before the Court of First Instance the legality of a decision under Article 173 which, although in the form of a regulation or decision addressed to another person, is of direct and individual concern to the former. Such persons may only claim to be individually concerned if that decision affects them by reason of certain attributes peculiar to them or by reason of circumstances differentiating them from all other persons and distinguishing them individually just as in the case of the person addressed.[438] Hence, a decision under Article 93(2) may be

---

[432] Darmon AG in Case 248/84 *Germany* v. *EC Commission: regional aid* [1987] ECR 4013, 4033.

[433] Cases 31/77R & 53/77R *EC Commission* v. *UK: aid to pig producers* [1977] ECR 921; Case 171/83R *EC Commission* v. *France: aid to textiles and clothing* [1983] ECR 2621.

[434] Joined Cases 62 & 72/87 *Exécutif Régional Wallon and SA Glaverbel* v. *EC Commission* [1988] EC 1573.

[435] Art. 185 EC. See, e.g., Case 63/87 *EC Commission* v. *Greece: aid to exports* [1988] ECR 2875, 2891.

[436] Cf. Case 156/77 *EC Commission* v. *Belgium: aid for railway transport* [1978] ECR 1881, 1897; Case 52/83 *EC Commission* v. *France: aid to textiles* [1983] ECR 3707, 3715; and Case 183/91 *EC Commission* v. *Greece: tax concessions for exports* [1993] ECR I–3131, I–3149.

[437] Joined Cases 6 & 11/69 *EC Commission* v. *France: export aid* [1969] ECR 523, 539.

[438] Case 25/62 *Plaumann* v. *EEC Commission* [1963] ECR 95, 107; Joined Cases T–447/93, T–448/93 & T–449/93 *Associazione Italiana Tecnico Economica del Cemento, British Cement Association, Titan Cement Company SA* v. *EC Commission* [1995] ECR II–1971.

challenged by the recipient or intended recipient of the aid,[439] though problems may occur where the recipients are various.[440]

Competitors

A competitor of the aid recipient may challenge the legality of a Commission decision under Article 173,[441] where its market position has been 'significantly affected' by the aid which is subject to the decision.[442] Account may be taken of such factors as the limited number of producers of the product concerned and the substantial increase in production capacity entailed by the aided investment;[443] and whether the competitor has participated in the proceedings leading to the adoption of the decision in question.

Locus standi requirements are easier to fulfil when a decision pursuant to Article 93(3) rather than Article 93(2) is being challenged. Because of lack of transparency and the absence of a defined role for third parties under the former provision, there is no requirement regarding previous participation in the administrative procedure. Moreover, an effect on the market position of the applicant need not be established. A third party need only show that it is a party concerned.[444]

Such requirements may also be easier to fulfil under Article 33 of the ECSC Treaty. According to this provision, undertakings may challenge 'decisions . . . concerning them which are individual in character'. An undertaking is concerned by a Commission decision which permits benefits to be granted to one or more undertakings which are in competition with it.[445]

For a competitor to challenge a Commission failure to act against a Member State under Article 175 may be more problematic.[446] Such challenges may only be brought where the Commission has failed to address to that person an act

---

[439] Case 730/79 *Philip Morris Holland B.V.* v. *EC Commission* [1980] ECR 2671, 2687.

[440] Joined Cases 67, 68, & 70/85 *Kwekereij Gebroeders van der Kooy* [1988] ECR 219, 267–8.

[441] Case 169/84 *Cie Française de l'Azote (COFAZ) SA* v. *EC Commission* [1986] ECR 391, 415–6; Case C–198/91 *William Cook PLC* v. *EC Commission* [1993] ECR I–2487, I–2528.

[442] Case 169/84 *Cie Française de l'Azote (COFAZ) SA* v. *EC Commission* [1986] ECR 391, 415; and Joined Cases T–447/93, T–448/93, & T–449/93 *Associazione Italiana Tecnico Economica del Cemento, British Cement Association, Titan Cement Company SA* v. *EC Commission* [1995] ECR II–1971.

[443] Case T–435/93 *Association of Sorbitol Producers in the EC (ASPEC)* v. *EC Commission* [1995] ECR II–1281, II–1309.

[444] Case C–198/91 *William Cook PLC* v. *EC Commission* [1993] ECR I–2487; Case C–225/91 *Matra SA* v. *EC Commission* [1993] ECR I–3203.

[445] Joined Cases 24 & 34/58 *Chambre Syndicale de la Sidérurgie de l'Est de la France* v. *ECSC High Authority* [1960] ECR 281, 292; and Joined Cases 172 & 226/83 *Hoogovens Groep BV* v. *EC Commission* [1985] ECR 2831, 2847.

[446] See, regarding a failure to open the Art. 93(2) procedure, Case T–49/93 *Société Internationale de Diffusion et d'Édition* v. *EC Commission* [1995] ECR II–2501.

other than a recommendation or opinion.[447] However, damages may be claimed for unlawful inaction under Article 215(2).[448]

Trade Associations

The 'administration of justice' may imply that trade associations should be entitled to bring proceedings, given the 'valuable role' they may play in administrative procedures under Article 93. They are in a better position than their individual members to put the sector's case to the Commission.[449] The Court of Justice may be sympathetic to such thinking, at least where the interests of such an association are shown to be distinct from the interests of the Member State granting the aid in the modernization and restructuring of a broad sector of the national economy.[450]

However, conceptions of aid control essentially as an instrument of competition policy may imply limitations to recognition of *locus standi*. According to Advocate General Mancini in *DEFI*,[451] a distinction may be made between a decision declaring aid compatible with the common market and a decision declaring it incompatible. Persons who consider themselves adversely affected by a decision of the former type are fully entitled to judicial protection, because the Treaty guarantees them protection against aid which distorts competition. It is not so with persons, including trade associations,[452] complaining of a decision of the second type, because the Treaty does not guarantee, but at most tolerates, state aid. In other words, the aid has its source not in the Treaty but in the will of the Member State concerned. Where the Commission takes the view that it is unlawful, the Member State may or may not challenge the Commission's decision. If it brings a challenge, the interests of the recipients are indirectly protected by this challenge. If the Member State does not bring a challenge, either because it considers the decision well founded or because its own policy has changed, no one can remedy its *volonté défaillante*.

Opportunities to intervene in proceedings before the European Courts may also be available, though an intervener must accept the case as he finds it at the

---

[447] Case 60/79 *Fédération Nationale des Producteurs de Vins de Table et Vin de Pays* v. *EC Commission* [1979] ECR 2425, 2428. See also Case 84/82 *Germany* v. *EC Commission: aid to textiles and clothing* [1984] ECR 1451, 1491.

[448] Case 40/75 *Société des Produits Bertrand SA* v. *EC Commission* [1976] ECR 1, but see Reischl AG *ibid.*, 12, regarding the problems involved.

[449] Slynn AG in Joined Cases 67, 68, & 70/85 *Kwekerij Gebroeders van der Kooy* [1988] ECR 219, 246. See also the view of the EFTA Court in Case E-2/94 *Scottish Salmon Growers Association Ltd* v. *ESA* [1995] 1 CMLR 851, 862.

[450] Case 282/85 *Comité de Développement et de Promotion du Textile et de l'Habillement (DEFI)* v. *EC Commission* [1986] ECR 2469, 2474.

[451] *Ibid.*, 2481.

[452] A body created by the state, subject to state control, in administering textiles aid had no standing.

time of his intervention.[453] Thus, for example, if the parties do not dispute that aid was granted contrary pleas by an intervener are inadmissible.[454]

7.6.2 Substantive Legality

According to Article 173, Commission decisions may be annulled on grounds of lack of competence, infringement of the Treaty or of any rule of law relating to its application, or misuse of powers.

However, the wording of Article 92(2) appears to leave the Commission with a considerable margin of appreciation even under this paragraph, and Article 92(3) expressly confers a discretionary power upon the Commission. For example, the Commission may reasonably take account of regional disparities which investment faces and for which aid is designed to compensate, and may reasonably decide not to act under Article 93(2) where regional aid is below the ceiling fixed in its approval of the regional aid scheme concerned.[455] More generally, as a body which supervises compliance with the competition rules and has specialized departments for that purpose, the Commission has many years of experience with the result that its findings carry a degree of authority.[456] At the same time, the Commission is responsible for the implementation and orientation of competition policy. The performance of this task necessarily entails complex economic assessments.[457] As *Philip Morris Holland*[458] illustrates, the Court of Justice will only question such assessments in extreme cases.[459]

Such an assessment may be overturned where there is found to have been an *erreur manifeste d'appréciation* (clear error of assessment) contrary to the Treaty. For example, in *Cook*[460] the Commission had decided not to open the Article 93(2) procedure on the ground that the sector concerned did not suffer from overcapacity. However, the Court of Justice ruled that the Commission had failed to substantiate its finding that the sector was not in a state of overcapacity. Hence, the decision was annulled for manifest error.[461]

---

[453] Art. 93(4) of the Rules of Procedure of the ECJ ([1991] OJ L176/7).

[454] Joined Cases T–447/93, T–448/93 & T–449/93 *Associazione Italiana Tecnico Economica del Cemento, British Cement Association, Titan Cement Company SA* v. *EC Commission* [1995] ECR II–1971.

[455] Case C–225/91 *Matra SA* v. *EC Commission* [1993] ECR I–3203, I–3257.

[456] Van Gerven AG in Case C–128/92 *H. J. Banks & Co. Ltd* v. *British Coal Corpn.* [1994] ECR I–1209, I–1265.

[457] Case C–234/89 *Stergios Delimitis* v. *Heninger Bräu AG* [1991] ECR I–935, I–991.

[458] Case 730/79 *Philip Morris Holland B.V.* v. *EC Commission* [1980] ECR 2671, 2691. See sect. 3.3.2 above.

[459] See also VerLoren van Themaat AG in Case 169/84 *Cie Française de l'Azote (COFAZ) SA* v. *EC Commission* [1986] ECR 391, 405, regarding the comparison between Commission discretion under Art. 85 and under Art. 92.

[460] Case 198/91 *William Cook PLC* v. *EC Commission* [1993] ECR I–2487, I–2531 (Tesauro AG, I–2520).

[461] See also Case 84/82 *Germany* v. *EC Commission: aid to textiles and clothing* [1984] ECR 1451, 1501, where Slynn AG considered that the Commission had wrongly classified a capital injection as aid.

Overestimation of the costs saving associated with a preferential tariff charged by a publicly controlled supplier of natural gas has also been found to constitute such an error.[462]

A Commission decision may also be annulled because an *erreur de droit* (error of law) renders it contrary to the Treaty. Such an error may be present where the Commission reaches its decision without examining whether the aid distorts competition and affects trade between Member States[463] or on the basis of irrelevant or incorrect facts.[464]

Finally, a decision may be annulled for a misuse of powers.[465] A decision is vitiated on this ground where it appears, on the basis of objective, relevant, and consistent factors, to have been taken with the purpose of achieving ends other than those stated.[466]

7.6.3 Procedural Legality

The European Courts may, according to Article 173, intervene on grounds of procedural illegality, that is, infringement of an essential procedural requirement. Such an infringement may take the form of a failure by the Commission to grant a hearing to the Member State concerned or to give adequate reasons for its decisions.

Fair Hearing

According to the Court of Justice, the Member State must be enabled to make known its views on the observations which interested third parties have submitted under Article 93(2) and on which the Commission proposes to base its decision. In so far as the Member State has not been afforded the opportunity to comment on these observations, the Commission may not use them in its decision against that Member State. However, for such an infringement of the right to a fair hearing to result in annulment of the decision concerned, it must be established that had it not been for that irregularity, the outcome of the procedure might have been different.[467]

---

[462] Case C–169/84 *Société CdF Chimie Azote et Fertilisants SA et Société Chimique de la Grande Paroisse SA v. EC Commission* [1990] ECR I–3083. The Commission procedure against the aid in question was reopened. See Notice C50/83 ([1992] OJ C10/3).

[463] Joined Cases T–447/93, T–448/93 & T–449/93 *Associazione Italiana Tecnico Economica del Cemento, British Cement Association, Titan Cement Company SA v. EC Commission* [1995] ECR II–1971.

[464] Case T–471/93 *Tierce Ladbroke SA v. EC Commission* [1995] ECR II–2531, II–2561.

[465] Joined Cases T–244/93 & T–486/93 *TWD Textilwerke Deggendorf GmbH v. EC Commission* [1995] ECR II–2265, II–2290.

[466] *Ibid.*

[467] Case 259/85 *France v. EC Commission: aid to textiles and clothing* [1987] ECR 4393, 4415. See also Case C–142/87 *Belgium v. EC Commission: Tubemeuse* [1990] ECR I–959, I–1016 and Case C–301/87 *France v. EC Commission: Boussac* [1990] ECR I–307, I–359.

Reasons

Article 190 requires that regulations, directives, and decisions 'state the reasons on which they are based'. The European Courts are entitled to review, even of their own motion, the statement of reasons for Commission decisions challenged before them.[468] The statement must be appropriate to the act at issue and must not be contradictory;[469] it must disclose in a clear and unequivocal fashion the reasoning of the Commission in such a way as to enable the persons concerned to ascertain the reasons for the decision and to enable the European Courts to carry out their review; and sufficient detail must be given to alert the Courts and individuals to the elements of the Commission's reasoning.[470] The statement need not, however, go into all the relevant facts and points of law, since the question whether it meets the requirements of Article 190 must be assessed with regard not only to its wording but also to its context and to all the rules governing the matter in question.[471]

In practice, the effect of reasoning requirements may not be greatly different from a review of the grounds for a decision which examines the *exactitude* (accuracy) and *qualification* (relevance) of the facts but otherwise avoids consideration of the *opportunité* (reasonableness) of the decision. As Advocate General Mancini put it in *France* v. *EC Commission*, which concerned French aid to the textile and clothing industry, 'provided that they are supported by a logical and adequate statement of reasons, decisions taken by the Commission cannot be challenged from the point of view of expediency'.[472]

While these reasoning requirements seem limited, the Commission may sometimes fail to satisfy them. For example, in *Leeuwarder*[473] a decision prohibiting aid to a Dutch wood processor was challenged.[474] Here the Court of Justice ruled that even if in certain cases the very circumstances in which the aid was granted were sufficient to show that it was capable of affecting trade between Member States and of distorting or threatening to distort competition for the purposes of Article 92(1),[475] the Commission must at least set out those

---

[468] Case T–471/93 *Tierce Ladbroke SA* v. *EC Commission* [[1995] ECR II–2537, II–2549.

[469] Joined Cases T–447/93, T–448/93, & T–449/93 *Associazione Italiana Tecnico Economica del Cemento, British Cement Association, Titan Cement Company SA* v. *EC Commission* [1995] ECR II–1971. Cf., regarding reasoning requirements under the EEA Agreement, Case E–2/94 *Scottish Salmon Growers Association Ltd* v. *ESA* [1995] 1 CMLR 851.

[470] Fennelly AG in Case C–56/93 *Belgium* v. *EC Commission: natural gas tariffs* (not yet reported).

[471] Case C–56/93 *Belgium* v. *EC Commission: natural gas tariffs* [1996] I–723, I–792; Case T–471/93 *Tierce Ladbroke SA* v. *EC Commission* [1995] ECR II–2537, II–2551.

[472] Case 259/85 *Aid to Textiles and Clothing* [1987] ECR 4393, 4440.

[473] Joined Cases 296 & 318/82 *Netherlands and Leeuwarder Papierwarenfabriek B.V.* v. *EC Commission* [1985] ECR 809.

[474] Dec. 82/653 ([1982] OJ L277/15) on aid granted by the Netherlands Government to a paperboard processing firm.

[475] The Commission draws the implication that the 'actual nature of the aid and the reason for its award' may in themselves be sufficient to show that aid is so capable. See Dec. 89/659 ([1989] OJ L394/1) relating to Ministerial Dec. E3789/128 of the Greek Government establishing a special single tax on undertakings.

circumstances in the statement of reasons for its decision.[476] In this case it had failed to do so, since the decision in question did not contain the slightest information concerning the situation of the relevant market, the place of the aid recipient in that market,[477] the pattern of trade between Member States in the products in question, or the exports of the aid recipient.[478]

The Commission had also failed to explain why the aid could not be authorized under Article 92(3)(c). According to the Court, there was no indication whatsoever in the decision in question that the Commission had taken into account the essential fact, which might have caused it to make a different assessment, that the aid was accompanied by a restructuring of the recipient undertaking. This restructuring entailed diversion of its production to high-quality products and reductions in its production capacity and its market share.[479]

On these grounds, the Court annulled the decision. The duty of confidentiality imposed on the Commission by Article 214 of the Treaty[480] was found to offer no defence. This provision could not be interpreted so broadly that the duty to give reasons was 'deprived of its essential content'. In any case, some relevant facts, especially those relating to the structure of the market, were manifestly not of a confidential nature. At the same time, since publication of the decision was not required under Article 191 of the Treaty, information which was confidential could have been omitted from the published text.

In another case, where the Commission had imposed ceilings on investment loans, the Commission had failed to explain why an increase in the nominal amount of already authorized aid, only to offset inflation, could be regarded as a further grant of aid.[481] On this ground the decision was annulled for inadequate reasoning.

The significance of such rulings might have been lessened if the view previously expressed by Advocate General Capotorti in *Philip Morris Holland*

---

[476] See also Case 57/86 *Greece* v. *EC Commission: export aid* [1988] ECR 2855, 2873. Cf. Case 52/76 *Luigi Benedetti* v. *Munari Flli s.a.s.* [1977] ECR 163, 181, where the Court ruled that 'details of the effects' of 'conduct' were necessary to determine whether trade between Member States was affected.

[477] Slynn AG criticized the Commission for referring only to allegations of third parties and for not explaining why aid to keep afloat a company having 10% of its domestic market affected trade between Member States ([1985] ECR 809, 814). See, similarly, the Court itself in Case 323/82 *Intermills SA* v. *EC Commission* [1984] ECR 3809, 3832. In Case 223/85 *Rijn-Schelde-Verolme (RSV) Maschinenfabrieken en Scheepswerven NV* v. *EC Commission* [1987] ECR 4617, 4648–9 Slynn AG criticized another Commission decision for saying 'practically nothing' about such matters.

[478] [1985] ECR 809, 824.

[479] *Ibid.*, 825.

[480] According to this provision, the Commission must not 'disclose information of the kind covered by the obligation of professional secrecy, in particular, information about undertakings, their business relations or their cost components'.

[481] Case C–364/90 *Italy* v. *EC Commission: aid to areas in the Mezzogiorno affected by natural disasters* [1993] ECR I–2097, I–2130.

regarding the onus of proof under Article 92(3) had been adopted by the Court. According to the Advocate General, the onus of proof was on the applicant for an aid authorization.[482] The same view was expressed by Advocate General Darmon in *Germany* v. *EC Commission: regional aid*,[483] who also stated that the Commission was not obliged to go beyond the information supplied to it by the Member State seeking the authorization of aid under Article 92(3). These views were not adopted by the Court itself.

On the other hand, reasoning requirements might be limited because of information available to a Member State by virtue of its involvement under proceedings under Article 93.[484] For example, in *Intermills* Advocate General VerLoren van Themaat noted that the decision in question made no reference to the position of Intermills in intra-Union trade, but in his view this position was sufficiently known to the government addressee and to the applicant.[485]

Such views seem questionable. It may be that the Commission is not obliged 'to adopt a position on all the arguments relied on by the parties concerned'.[486] Even so, Article 92(2) and (3) are concerned with action by Member States favourable to attainment of Union objectives, which the Commission is also obliged to seek to promote in accordance with the principles in Articles 4[487] and 155[488] of the Treaty. A possible implication is that the Commission should not simply give reasons for rejecting claims made by the Member State concerned but should ensure that its reasons also show why the aid is not justified by reference to such objectives. More particularly, if such views were followed, aid recipients, their competitors, and others might be denied the information needed to ascertain whether the decision was well founded. Such considerations may underlie the position of the Court of First Instance that Article 190 requires an opportunity for 'all interested parties of ascertaining the circumstances in which the Commission has applied the Treaty'.[489] Such a requirement may be thought to have the effect of opening up Commission decision-making in this area and thus to imply the possibility of increased pluralism in such decision-making.

Formal Commission practice, particularly its use of reports from consultants,[490] certainly seems to have been affected by the case law. The Commission

---

[482] Case 730/79 *Philip Morris Holland B.V.* v. *EC Commission* [1980] ECR 2671, 2702.

[483] Case 248/84 [1987] ECR 4013, 4032.

[484] Case 102/87 *France* v. *EC Commission: a brewery loan* [1988] ECR 4067, 4090.

[485] Case 323/82 *Intermills S.A.* v. *EC Commission* [1984] ECR 3809, 3843.

[486] Case T–459/93 *Siemens SA* v. *EC Commission* [1995] ECR II–1675, II–1691.

[487] According to Art. 4, the Commission is to 'carry out' Community tasks.

[488] Art. 155 provides that, in order to ensure the proper functioning and developing of the common market, the Commission shall, *inter alia*, ensure that the provisions of this Treaty are applied.

[489] Case T–459/93 *Siemens SA* v. *EC Commission* [1995] ECR II–1675, II–1690.

[490] Compare the annulment of the Commission decision in Case C–198/91 *William Cook PLC* v. *EC Commission* [1993] ECR I–2487 for lack of supporting figures or statistics with the acceptance of the decision in Case C–225/91 *Matra SA* v. *EC Commission* [1993] ECR I–3203, where such a report had been obtained.

no longer feels able simply to cite its previous decisions[491] or simply to refer to the general difficulties of beneficiary industries[492] as sufficient to show that trade between Member States is likely to be affected and competition distorted by aid. Commission decisions now routinely contain market and trade statistics to support conclusions concerning the impact of aid on competition and on trade between Member States. In particular, they may contain statistics, such as those regarding the proportion of the production of an aided undertaking which is exported to other Member States[493] as well as the share in Union production of the Member State where it is based. The rationale for considering statistics relating to the latter is that if a Member State is involved in intra-Union trade in the product concerned, the recipient must also be in competition on its domestic market with imports from other Member States.[494]

Whether there has been any impact on the substance of Commission decisions is another matter.[495] For example, according to Advocate General Lenz in *Belgium* v. *EC Commission: Meura*,[496] which concerned capital subscriptions in a Belgian producer of equipment for the food industry, the Commission considered it proven that the undertaking in question exported 40 per cent of its products to other Member States. As a result, it was entitled to assume that artificially keeping this undertaking in existence was in itself bound to distort competition and affect trade between Member States. The Commission's decision would certainly have been clearer and plainer had it included particulars of the volume of business conducted by the undertaking in absolute terms and of its market share in Belgium and in the Community. However, the Advocate General did not consider such particulars to have been absolutely essential in order to reach the finding made in the contested decision. The Commission did at least set out in the decision the proportion of the undertaking's production exported to other Member States. Where an undertaking participating in intra-Union trade received aid denied to competitors, it was possible to conclude that such trade was affected and competition distorted by that aid.[497]

The Court itself ruled that despite its concise nature—which was due in part

---

[491] Dec. 82/829 ([1982] OJ L350/36) on a proposed aid by the Belgian Government in respect of certain investments carried out by an oil company at its Antwerp refinery.

[492] Dec. 80/932 ([1980] OJ L264/28) concerning the partial taking-over by the State of employers' contributions to sickness insurance schemes in Italy.

[493] Details of the domestic sales of an undertaking may also be relevant. See Dec. 87/98 ([1987] OJ L40/17) on aid proposed by Rheinland-Pfalz for a metalworking firm in Betzdorf.

[494] Dec. 87/98 ([1987] OJ L40/17) on aid proposed by Rheinland-Pfalz for a metalworking firm in Betzdorf.

[495] See regarding the failure of the Commission to give reasons for not permitting the index-linking of authorized aid, Jacobs AG in Case C–364/90 *Italy* v. *EC Commission: aid to areas of the Mezzogiorno affected by natural disasters* [1993] ECR I–2097, I–2118, and for finding a preferential tariff not to constitute aid, Case T–95/94 *Chambre Nationale des Entreprises de Transport de Fonds et Valeurs (Sytraval) and Brink's France SARL* v. *EC Commission* [1995] ECR II–2651.

[496] Case 234/84 [1986] ECR 2263, 2273–4.   [497] *Ibid.*, 2274–5.

to lack of co-operation by the Belgian Government—the statement of reasons made it clear that the Commission took into account that the undertaking concerned exported about 40 per cent of its output to other Member States, that excess production capacity existed in the market in question and that, in those circumstances, the aid granted to the undertaking had the effect of reducing its financial costs by comparison with those of its competitors. In the absence of any information to the contrary, those findings entitled the Commission to conclude that the aid in question affected trade between Member States and distorted, or threatened to distort, competition within the meaning of Article 92(1). The figures provided by the Belgian Government during the proceedings before the Court showed that the Commission's assessment was by no means invalidated by the fact that the undertaking in question was small and was endeavouring to direct its products towards new markets and its exports to third countries.[498]

In another case the considerable proportion of the recipient's production accounted for by exports suggested, in conjunction with the total volume of its production (which had to be disclosed pursuant to Directive 68/151[499]), that the recipient was substantially involved in intra-Union trade. Moreover, the volume of business in absolute terms could be calculated from the losses and percentages of turnover mentioned in the decision being challenged.[500]

In short, the reluctance of the Court of Justice to question economic assessments of the Commission may imply limits to the reasoning requirements imposed on the latter.[501]

7.6.4 Court of First Instance

Decision 93/350[502] means that the jurisdiction of the Court of First Instance is no longer limited to the implementation of competition rules applicable to undertakings. Rather, it now covers proceedings brought by private persons generally under Articles 173 and 175. This reform is designed, particularly in respect of actions requiring close examination of complex facts, to improve the judicial protection of individual rights and to maintain the quality and effectiveness of judicial review in the Union legal order by enabling the Court of Justice to concentrate on its fundamental task, of ensuring uniform interpretation of Union law.[503] However, the Court of Justice retains jurisdiction in relation to

---

[498] *Ibid.*, 2287–8.

[499] On co-ordination of safeguards which, for the protection of the interests of members and others, are required by Member States of companies within the meaning of the second para. of Art. 58 EC, with a view to making such safeguards equivalent throughout the Union ([1968] JO L65/8).

[500] Lenz AG in Case 40/85 *Belgium* v. *EC Commission: Boch* [1986] ECR 2321, 2334.

[501] See, most recently, Van Gerven AG in Case C–347/87 *Triveneto Zuccheri SpA* v. *EC Commission* [1990] ECR I–1083, I–1099–1100.

[502] Amending Dec. 88/59 establishing a CFI ([1993] OJ L144/21).

[503] *Ibid.*, 8th recital in the Preamble.

actions brought by Member States, Union institutions or in relation to references for preliminary rulings. There is also a right of appeal for private persons from the Court of First Instance to the Court of Justice on points of law.[504] Generally, the position of private persons is said to have been improved,[505] and it is anticipated that a more critical appraisal of Commission policy concerning aid control may be stimulated.[506]

For example, in *Sytraval*[507] the Court of First Instance annulled a Commission decision rejecting a complaint of alleged aid in favour of Securipost, a subsidiary of the French Post Office. The Court made clear that the Commission must examine impartially and exhaustively all allegations by complainants and cannot impose on the complainant the burden of proof concerning the existence and incompatibility of aid. Otherwise, complainants would be required to obtain information in support of their allegations which in most cases they would be unable to obtain without the Commission as an intermediary. Therefore, the Commission could not justify the lack of sufficient reasoning by referring to the scarce information provided by the complainant.[508]

Complications may arise where actions brought by individuals and actions brought by Member States against the same decision may be pending before different courts. In such circumstances, the Court of First Instance may decline jurisdiction and refer the matter to the Court of Justice under Article 47(3) of the Statute, in order to enable the individuals to put their case to the latter court.[509]

7.6.5 National Courts

National courts may play a limited role in relation to the interpretation of Union law regarding aid control. They may play a somewhat greater role in protecting lawful interests of private persons when Member States implement Commission decisions. However, particularly from the perspective of the Commission, the main role of national courts is in securing compliance with the aid control requirements of Union law.

Interpretation

Unlike Article 4(c) of the ECSC Treaty,[510] Article 92 of the EC Treaty has been interpreted by the Court of Justice as lacking direct effects. Only decisions

---

[504] Art. 49 of the Statute of the ECJ.   [505] H.-J. Priess, n. 396 above, 86.

[506] L. Hancher, T. Ottervanger and P. J. Slot, *EC State Aids* (Chancery Law Publishing, London, 1993), 15; F. Y. Jenny, 'Competition and State Aid Policy in the European Community' (1994) 18 *Fordham Int. LJ* 525–54.

[507] Case T–95/94 *Chambre Nationale des Entreprises de Transport de Fonds et Valeurs (Sytraval) and Brink's France SARL* v. *EC Commission* [1995] ECR II–2651.

[508] See also Case T–49/93 *Société Internationale de Diffusion et de l'Édition* v. *EC Commission* [1995] ECR II–2501, II–2527–8.

[509] Case T–490/93 *Bremer Vulkan Verbund AG* v. *EC Commission* [1995] ECR II–477.

[510] Joined Cases 7 & 9/54 *Groupement des Industries Sidérurgiques Luxembourgeoises* v. *ECSC High Authority* [1954–6] ECR 175, 218.

applying the latter provision[511] or regulations or directives regarding state-aid matters[512] may produce effects which may be invoked before national courts. In any case, the Commission may be reluctant to 'attach great importance' to national court judgments in this area, at least in relation to applications for interim measures, given the complexity of the issues raised.[513]

True, Article 93(3) is directly effective,[514] and so national courts may have to determine whether there has been a violation of notification requirements. However, to make this determination, such courts must only decide whether aid within the meaning of Article 92(1) has been granted and not whether it distorts competition and affects trade between Member States.[515] In other words, they are not to decide whether or not the aid is compatible with the common market.[516]

Under Article 177 national courts may request preliminary rulings from the Court of Justice on the question whether measures are 'capable of constituting aid within the meaning of Article 92(1)'. They should only give judgment where they conclude that the measures 'clearly' do or do not constitute aid.[517] Difficulties may still arise, however, where the Commission subsequently finds a measure not to constitute aid and the national court has already ordered its repayment for breach of Article 93(3).

Validity

Aid recipients may take proceedings before national courts against national measures implementing Commission decisions. Such courts may refer questions of the validity of the decision being implemented to the Court of Justice under Article 177. There is no requirement of direct and individual concern under this provision. However, where the recipient of illegal aid has had actual knowledge of a Commission decision ordering recovery and of the ability to take action against that decision under Article 173 but has failed to do so within the prescribed period, he is precluded from bringing an indirect challenge under Article 177.[518]

---

[511] Case 77/72 *Carmine Capolongo* v. *Azienda Agricola Maya* [1973] ECR 611, 621.

[512] Lenz AG in Case C–44/93 *Namur—Les Assurances du Crédit SA* v. *Office National du Ducroire and Belgium* [1994] ECR I–3829, I–3850.

[513] Dec. 94/996 ([1994] OJ L379/13) concerning the transfer by the Netherlands of a pilot school to the Royal Dutch Airlines. Cf. Dec. 76/649 ([1976] OJ L229/24) on aid from the Belgian Government to the Société nationale des chemins de fer belges for through international railway tariffs for coal and steel.

[514] Case 74/76 *Iannelli and Volpi S.p.A.* v. *Meroni* [1977] ECR 557, 575; Joined Cases C–78–83/90 *Compagnie Commerciale de l'Ouest E.A.* [1992] ECR I–1847, I–1883.

[515] Lenz AG in Case C–44/93 *Namur—Les Assurances du crédit SA* v. *Office National du Ducroire and Belgium* [1994] ECR I–3829, I–3847–8.

[516] The Court, *ibid.*, I–3871.

[517] Jacobs AG in Case C–39/94 *Syndicat Français de l'Express International (SFEI)* v. *La Poste*, Opinion of 14 Dec. 1995.

[518] Case C–188/92 *TWD Textilwerke Deggendorf GmbH* v. *Germany* [1994] ECR I–833, I–855; Case 52/84 *EC Commission* v. *Belgium: Boch* [1986] ECR 89, 104.

Enforcement

A role for national courts in enforcing state-aid control is foreseen by the Commission and the European Courts, though the Commission in particular seeks to maintain a clear distinction between its role and that of national courts. The Commission describes itself as the administrative authority responsible for the implementation and development of competition policy in the Community's public interest. National courts are said to be responsible for the protection of rights and the enforcement of duties, usually at the behest of private parties.[519]

Hence, it is the Commission which examines the compatibility of the proposed aid with the common market, even where the Member State has acted in breach of the prohibition on giving effect to aid. The Commission's final decision cannot have the effect of regularizing implementing measures which are invalid for having been effected in breach of Article 93(3).[520] National courts, in turn, have to ensure that individuals are in a position to enforce rights of action in respect of any disregard of this provision, from which all the proper consequences follow, in accordance with their national law, both regarding the validity of acts involving the implementation of aid measures and the recovery of financial support granted in breach of that provision or of any provisional measures. Such courts are thus to preserve, until the final decision of the Commission, the rights of individuals faced with a possible breach by state authorities of the prohibition laid down in the last sentence of Article 93(3).[521] In particular, they may find acts implementing aid measures to be invalid,[522] suspend the implementation of unnotified aid,[523] order its repayment,[524] or award damages against the state to competitors.[525]

[519] Notice on co-operation between national courts and the Commission in the state aid field ([1995] OJ C312/8), para. 4. Cf. the dismissal by the French *Cour de Cassation* of a negligence action regarding the failure to apply for aid in good time on the ground that the Commission had found the aid to be contrary to Art. 92. The defendant had been negligent, but no reparable loss had been caused to the plaintiff, since the aid was unlawful anyway (*Lener Ignace SA* v. *Beauvois* [1994] 2 CMLR 419).

[520] Case C–354/90 *Fédération Nationale du Commerce Extérieur des Produits Alimentaires et Syndicat National des Négociants et Transformateurs de Saumon* v. *France* [1991] ECR I–5505, I–5528. See also Jacobs AG in Case 301/87 *France* v. *EC Commission: Boussac* [1990] ECR I–307, I–339; and Wolf J in *R.* v. *Att.-Gen, ex p. ICI* [1985] 1 CMLR 588, 608.

[521] Case C–354/90 *Fédération Nationale du Commerce Extérieur des Produits Alimentaires et Syndicat National des Négociants et Transformateurs de Saumon* v. *France* [1991] ECR I–5505, I–5528. A remedy before national courts may remove the need for counter aid. See I. Harden 'State Aids and the Economic Constitution of the Community' in I. Harden (ed.), n. 52 above, 12–8, 17.

[522] Case C–17/91 *Georges Lornoy en Zonen NV* v. *Belgium* [1992] ECR I–6523, I–6545.

[523] M. Dony, 'Les Aides aux entreprises et le droit communautaire de la concurrence' (1991) 1316 *Courrier Hebdomadaire de la centre de recherche et d'information socio-politiques* 26.

[524] Para. 10 of the Notice on co-operation between national courts and the Commission in the state aid field ([1995] OJ C312/8); Case C–354/90 *Fédération Nationale du Commerce Extérieur des Produits Alimentaires et Syndicat National des Négociants et Transformateurs de Saumon* v. *France* [1991] ECR I–5505, I–5528; Jacobs AG in Case C–39/94 *Syndicat Français de l'Express International (SFEI)* v. *La Poste*, Opinion of 14 Dec. 1995.   [525] Jacobs AG, *ibid.*.

7.7 CONCLUSION

The various procedures for state-aid control may be viewed in hierarchical terms. Soft legislation may be seen simply as implementing rules contained in the EC Treaty or in Council legislation, while individual decisions may be seen simply as entailing detailed application of such rules, subject to judicial review. According to such thinking, Commission guidelines may appear to violate distinctions between regulation and adjudication,[526] and to undermine the institutional balance envisaged in Article 94 of the Treaty.[527] In reality, the relationship between the different legal forms is more complicated and may be of a horizontal rather than vertical kind, with requirements established pursuant to adoption of one legal form affecting the requirements established pursuant to adoption of another such form.[528] Ultimately, successive opportunities for negotiation with Member States[529] and sometimes with sectoral interest groups[530] may be entailed. The exigencies of such negotiation as much as legal definition of its powers may impose limits on Commission discretion.[531]

The importance of such negotiation is highlighted by use of soft legislation.[532] However, given the limitations on judicial control in this area, scope for negotiation in the adoption of individual decisions may also be considerable, and negotiation in the implementation of such decisions may even have judicial encouragement. According to the Court of Justice,[533] a Member State having difficulties complying with a decision prohibiting aid should submit to the

---

[526] e.g., the Commission may act against 'misuse' of aid purporting to fall within an approved system of existing aid, and against aid purporting to be within an approved regional aid scheme but which is granted to an undertaking not in the region concerned. See the Commission submission in Joined Cases 166 & 220/86 *Irish Cement Limited* v. *EC Commission* [1988] ECR 6473, 6483.

[527] G. della Cananea, 'Administration by Guidelines: The Policy Guidelines of the Commission in the Field of State Aids', in n. 52 above, 61–75, 72–3.

[528] e.g., even if the aid recipient goes bankrupt, the Commission 'is under an obligation to pursue the [Art. 93(2)] procedure, particularly in order to avoid the continuance in future of practices incompatible with the common market'. See Dec. 82/312 ([1982] OJ L138/18) concerning the aid granted by the Belgian Government to an industrial and commercial group manufacturing wall coverings.

[529] See, e.g., K. van Miert, 'Community State Aid Policy: an Overview' (1994) 1 *Competition Policy Newsletter* 54–6.

[530] See, regarding the involvement of a delegation of semolina manufacturers, Reischl AG in Case 40/75 *Société des Produits Bertrand SA* v. *EC Commission* [1976] ECR 1, 10.

[531] C.-D. Ehlermann, 'State Aid Control in the European Union: Success or Failure?' (1995) 18 *Fordham Int. LJ* 1212–29, 1218.

[532] There has been criticism that in such legislation 'DG IV uses so-called quantitative criteria to provide a spurious 'scientific' justification for decisions which are often subjective and the net result of extensive negotiations with Member States'. See 'Regional Policy and the European Community' [1992] *Journal of Regional Policy* 557–600, 592.

[533] Case C–183/91 *EC Commission* v. *Greece* [1993] ECR I–3131, I–3151. Cf., regarding a duty of co-operation under Art. 5 EC, Case 52/84 *EC Commission* v. *Belgium: Boch* [1986] ECR 89, 105 and Case 94/87 *EC Commission* v. *Germany: Alcan* [1989] ECR 175, 192.

Commission alternative means of implementing the decision.[534] The apparent implication is that in this area at least, the Court prefers to contribute to, rather than to determine, the development of Treaty rules.

Development of Union law in this field is likely to be affected to the extent of the closure or openness of such negotiation. The strictness of the *locus standi* requirements imposed by the European Courts suggest lack of interest on their part in fully opening up the negotiation. Indeed, the case law seems essentially consistent with a conception of aid control simply as an instrument of competition policy.

---

[534] Cf. Dec. 82/466 ([1982] OJ L211/37) amending the Dec. of 31 Mar. 1982 concerning aid granted by the French Government in the sheepmeat and pigmeat sectors, where the Commission extended the deadline for the elimination of the aid. On the other hand, a 'political compromise' between the Commission and a Member State may not obviate the need for compliance with procedural requirements. See Joined Cases T–432–434/93 *Socurte Sociedade de Curtumes a Sul de Tejo, LdA* v. *EC Commission* [1995] ECR II–503, II–530.

8

Conclusions

Articles 92 to 94 of the EC Treaty provide the formal legal basis for state-aid control within the European Union. However, the operation of these provisions may be affected by various other Treaty provisions. The latter provisions, by virtue of their very generality or their place in the Treaty, may invite processes of adaptation to social demands in the application of Article 92 and articulation of such application in policy terms.[1]

These processes may be designed to give technical rationality and legitimacy to Union practice, but their consequence may be that the requirements of Article 92 are activated selectively by reference to policy needs. In other words, what the European Courts describe as 'choices of economic policy'[2] affect the application of this provision. Underlying policy conflicts in Commission practice may sometimes be obscured,[3] because the Commission, in controlling state aid, proceeds on the basis of prevailing assumptions within mixed economies.[4] Nevertheless, the operational meaning of Article 92 may still be affected by the particular policy perspective on state aid which proves dominant in a given case and ultimately by procedural rules which may have a bearing on the perspective applied.[5]

In its decisions applying Article 92 the Commission seeks to reconcile conflicting aspects of the various policies involved. The outcome must be a reconciliation which is sufficiently reasoned to satisfy the demands of the rule of law upheld by the European Courts and, furthermore, must be one which Member States are likely to accept from an institution lacking the same inherent legitimacy as a judicial body.[6] As a result, the content of these

---

[1] The very nature of aid control is said to entail that such control should be 'the responsibility of an essentially political body, such as the Commission'. See C.-D. Ehlermann, 'State Aid Control in the European Union: Success or Failure?' (1995) 18 *Fordham Int. LJ* 1212–29, 1218.

[2] Joined Cases T–480/93 & T–483/93 *Antillean Rice Mills NV* [1995] ECR II–2305.

[3] It has been argued that, in practice, substantial policy differences between Directorates General may be more limited than they appear. See S. Padgett, 'The Single European Energy Market: The Politics of Realisation' [1992] *JCMS* 53–75, 73.

[4] Cf., generally, the Opinion of the Committee on Regional Policy and Transport on the second report on competition policy and on the communication on the implementation of the principles of co-ordination of regional aid in 1972 (EP Doc. 264/73), 17.

[5] Where 'multiple criteria' issues are involved, the content of decisions cannot be separated from decision-making procedures. See M. Paruccini, *Decision Support Systems for Environmental Management* (EC Commission, Brussels, 1992).

[6] The result may be *quasi-pedagogique* reasoning. See C. Garbar, 'Aides d'état: pratique décisionnelle de la Commission de la Communauté européenne (1990–1994)' [1994] *RMC* 665–74, 671.

decisions may offer an exposure of the tendencies for aid control to be affected by variations in the dominant policy perspective.

The tendencies are particularly pronounced where the relationship between Article 92 and other Treaty provisions is treated in terms of policy conflicts. Such treatment means that the requirements of Article 92 may not be exhaustively explored, but only to the extent considered necessary to resolve the policy conflict in question.

Even where conflict between the goals of the different policies may, as in the case of competition policy and regional policy, appear to be resolved, tendencies towards selective activation of Article 92 requirements may remain pronounced, because different policies may imply different means of achieving apparently reconciled goals.[7] For example, from a competition-policy perspective strict application of the prohibition in Article 92(1) may be seen as making a vital contribution to cohesion by eliminating aid which exacerbates regional disparities. From the perspective of regional policy, however, broad interpretation of Article 92(3)(a) and (c) may be seen as making a similarly vital contribution to cohesion through ensuring that the Structural Funds,[8] particularly the European Regional Development Fund, can pursue their interventionist activities.

The implied need for policy 'integration' rather than mere reconciliation may not be unrecognized by Union institutions. For example, according to the European Parliament, substantial progress in bringing development and income levels in the Union regions closer together can be achieved only if Union regional policy goes beyond action taken by the various funds and is considered as an integral part of all Union policies and is taken into account when defining the objectives of the latter. It is, therefore, considered essential regularly to examine the compatibility of such policies with regional development.[9]

Formal legal support for such arguments may be found in the Treaty. Article 130b provides that Member States shall conduct their economic policies and shall co-ordinate them in such a way as to attain the objectives set out in Article 130a.[10] The formulation[11] and implementation of the Union's policies and actions and the implementation of the internal market shall also take into account the objectives set out in Article 130a and shall contribute to their achievement. The implications for competition policy, including state-aid

[7] See, regarding 'conflict of method', T. Frazer, 'The New Structural Funds, State Aids and Interventions on the Single Market' (1995) 20 *ELRev.* 3–19, 10.

[8] i.e., the European Regional Development Fund, the European Social Fund, and the European Agricultural Guidance and Guarantee Fund, Guidance Section.

[9] Of 18 Nov. 1988 ([1988] OJ C326/289) on Community Regional Policy and the Role of the Regions.

[10] See sect. 4.1 above.

[11] As originally introduced by the Single European Act, this provision made no reference to 'formulation'.

control, are confirmed by Article B of the Treaty on European Union. This provision apparently means that promotion of cohesion and trade liberalization are means of achieving the Union objective of economic and social progress. More particularly, Article 7c requires the Commission, in drawing up proposals for measures needed for completion of the internal market under Article 7a, to take into account the extent of the effort that certain economies showing differences in development will have to sustain. Again, Article 130r(2) requires that environmental-protection requirements must be integrated into the definition and implementation of other Union policies.[12]

Obstacles to such 'integration' are various, and may have legal form. For example, *Wuidart*[13] concerned Union legislation providing for a levy on milk production. The validity of the legislation was challenged partly on the ground that it did not require differentiation in favour of disadvantaged regions. The Court of Justice rejected the challenge, Advocate General Mischo noting that the legislation did not preclude such differentiation.[14] The apparent implication is that Union sectoral policy should allow for account to be taken of regional disparities, but need not follow regional policy. Indeed, sectoral-policy rules may be regarded as *lex specialis*,[15] such that they should have priority over regional policy requirements.

There may also be practical obstacles. It is said that Union policies to raise standards regarding, for example, environmental protection and research and development cannot be regionally differentiated. Such policies can merely be followed by actions to assist weaker regions to reach Union standards.[16] More fundamentally, there may be conflict between efficiency concerns in relation to global competition and equity concerns in relation to regional development. As a result, policies to improve the international competitiveness of Union firms may be seen as counteracting efforts to secure cohesion.

More particularly, from the competition policy perspective, aid control concentrates on market unification requirements[17] and proceeds on the basis of concern to limit distortions of competition perceived to be contrary to such requirements. Thus some distortions may be permitted, because market unification is not jeopardized. For example, infrastructure aid and aid of low intensities may be permissible in the Union generally, because of their limited

---

[12] In contrast, Art. 130v merely requires that the Community 'shall take account' of development co-operation objectives in the policies it implements that are likely to affect developing countries.

[13] Joined Cases C–267–285/88 *Gustave Wuidart* v. *Laiterie Coopérative Eupenoise, a Cooperative Society* [1990] ECR I–435, I–488.

[14] *Ibid.*, I–465.

[15] Cf., regarding the Euratom Treaty, Dec. 94/285 ([1994] OJ L122/30) relating to a procedure in application of Art. 53(2) Euratom.

[16] R. Hall and D. van der Wee, 'Community Regional Policies for the 1990s' [1992] *Regional Studies* 399–404.

[17] According to the *Twenty-Fourth Report on Competition Policy* (EC Commission, Brussels, 1995), 31, competition policy is 'an essential instrument in achieving the internal market'.

effect on such unification, even though they may not necessarily entail efficient use of resources and may harm the competitive position of weaker regions.[18]

From the perspective of regional policy, on the other hand, aid control should be designed to promote economic and social cohesion. A legal obligation so to design aid control might be said to arise from Article 130b of the Treaty. To the extent that competition policy opposes aid in the stronger regions and is tempered by regional-policy considerations so as to allow aid in the weaker regions, there may seem to be some reconciliation of the two policies. However, such reconciliation has not gone so far in Commission practice that account is taken of regional policy in all aid decisions. Rather, the general tendency in such practice seems to be for regional policy considerations merely to be 'grafted onto' other policies, as for example when higher levels of horizontal aid are permitted in less favoured regions.[19] Only in extreme cases are regional-policy requirements given overriding importance.[20] Apparently, therefore, reform of Commission practice is essential, if the obligation in Article 130b is to be fulfilled.

The relationship between state-aid control and sectoral policy perspectives, which may reflect sectoral interests[21] rather than efficiency concerns, may be at least as controversial. For example, in Decision 90/381[22] the German Government argued that efforts 'to enforce measures which are motivated by industrial policy pursuant to Articles 92 and 93 . . . would represent an abuse of these Treaty provisions.'

Controversy may be added because 'discrimination' between sectors may be entailed.[23] In some cases sectoral policy perspectives may entail a permissive approach to aid.[24] To the extent that sectoral interests are well entrenched in stronger regions, the result may be that aid is concentrated in such regions and

[18] Such a permissive approach to aid may do little to prevent the position of regions such as Northern Ireland and the Mezzogiorno and Greece from deteriorating relative to the rest of the Union. See the *Fifth Periodic Report on the Situation and Socio-Economic Development of the Regions of the Community*, COM(94)322, 12.

[19] Cf., regarding the problems of taking specific account of consumer interests in the application of competition policy, A. Evans, 'Article 85(3) Exemption: "Allowing Consumers a Fair Share of the Resulting Benefit"' in M. Goyens (ed.), *European Competition Policy and the Consumer Interest* (Bruylant, Brussels, 1985), 99–120.

[20] See, regarding the need 'on occasion' for cohesion requirements to be given priority over competition policy requirements, the Report of the Committee on Economic and Monetary Affairs and Industrial Policy on the *Twentieth Report on Competition Policy*, EP Doc. A3–0338/91, 11–2.

[21] Such interests may be represented by national officials in Commission consultation with Member States. See, e.g., Dec. 82/73 ([1982] OJ L37/29) on the preferential tariff charged to glasshouse growers for natural gas in the Netherlands.

[22] Dec. 90/381 ([1990] OJ L188/55) amending German aid schemes for the motor-vehicle industry, where the German Government argued that efforts 'to enforce measures which are motivated by industrial policy pursuant to Arts. 92 and 93 . . . would represent an abuse of these Treaty provisions'.

[23] *Ibid.*

[24] See, regarding alleged inconsistency between treatment of aid in the transport sector and treatment of aid in the steel sector, the *Financial Times*, 20 July 1991.

used inefficiently there. To the same extent, not only may resources be misallocated to relatively inefficient producers but also the economy generally may be weakened through misdirection of entrepreneurial activity into rent-seeking. Where sectoral aid does reach weaker regions, it may often have operating form. As such, it may impede their structural adjustment and thus jeopardize their development.

In other cases, to the extent that sectoral policy entails strict control of aid, its effects may also be harmful in terms of competition policy and cohesion,[25] in that aid capable of assisting weaker regions to exploit unrealized comparative advantages may be prohibited.[26] The permissibility of such aid depends on the rules contained in sectoral legislation. It has been argued, however, that in 'crisis' sectors regions with growth potential may be penalized and development of the relevant sector as a whole may be inhibited by the prohibition of aid.[27] More particularly, the European Parliament[28] and the Committee of the Regions[29] consider that prohibition of aid leading to increases in Portuguese textile-production capacity should be reviewed, since the textile industry is a strategic element in the Portuguese economy.[30]

Horizontal-policy perspectives, in turn, may mean that aid supporting achievement of various goals is favoured. In the control of such aid limited account may be taken of efficiency concerns or of considerations related to regional policy. As a result, not only may resources be inefficiently used. Since such aid tends to assist stronger regions, such as those with an established research and development capacity or dynamic small and medium-sized enterprises, regional disparities may tend to be increased.

As regards environmental policy, Article 130r(2) of the Treaty embodies the polluter-pays principle and envisages integration of environmental-protection requirements into the definition and implementation of other policies. However, application of the principle remains problematic and undeveloped in

[25] D. J. Neven and J. Vickers, 'Public Policy towards Industrial Restructuring: Some Issues Raised by the Internal Market Programme' in K. Cool, D. J. Neven, and I. Walter (eds.), *European Industrial Restructuring in the 1990s* (Macmillan, London, 1992), 162–98, 175.

[26] e.g. the mere fact that state aid to shipbuilding is permitted and even supported under the Renaval programme (Reg. 2506/88 ([1988] OJ L225/24) instituting a Community programme to assist the conversion of shipbuilding areas) does not mean that other aid to the region concerned will be permissible. See Dec. 91/389 ([1991] OJ L215/1) on aid granted by the city of Hamburg.

[27] *The Regional Impact of Community Policies* (Regional Policy and Transport Series No. 17, European Parliament, Luxembourg, 1991), 15 and 83.

[28] Resolution of 3 May 1994 ([1994] OJ C205/121) on the draft notice setting the guidelines for the modernization of the textile and clothing industry in Portugal, para. 14.

[29] Opinion of 17 May 1994 ([1994] OJ C217/14) on the Community initiative on the modernization of the textile and clothing industry of Portugal.

[30] Cf. the criticism of the lack of regional differentiation in application of the CAP to products in surplus in the Opinion of the Economic and Social Committee of 30 Apr. 1992 ([1992] OJ C169/41) on the Commission proposals on the prices for agricultural products and on related measures (1992/3), para. 1.8.

Commission practice.[31] There is no general requirement that aid may only be granted where it promotes environmental protection, or even that aid projects must not be environmentally harmful.[32] Introduction of such a requirement would seem legally legitimate. It would be consistent generally with the 'compensatory-justification' principle, which the Commission applies so as to prohibit aid which will not produce benefits from a Union perspective. More particularly, it would be consistent with the terms of Article 92. For example, aid which does not secure environmental improvements might be said to be unable to facilitate the regional or sectoral development necessary for aid to be authorized under Article 92(3)(c). At present, however, the polluter-pays principle is applied only in relation to aid which the Member State concerned seeks to justify on environmental-policy grounds. In other words, the principle is apparently invoked primarily as a justification for setting limits to the toleration of distortions of competition associated with such aid.[33]

Such problems may be exaggerated by the relationship between economic-law provisions and institutional-law provisions. This relationship may be thought to be elucidated by models of the 'input-output' kind. Models of this kind treat institutional law as denoting rules governing participation in decision-making and economic law as denoting rules contained in the decisions made. However, to the extent that the two categories of rules are thus treated as operating separately, such models may be inadequate to capture the real nature of the relationship. The latter is such that, for example, controversial public debate, in both institutionalized democratic form and the non-institutionalized media, may be expected to contribute to aid policy as much as the rapidly growing number of judicial decisions.[34]

On the one hand, economic-law provisions may have effects on the conduct of participants in decision-making. Such effects may be particularly prominent in the case of inter-institutional relations. For example, under Article 130 of the Treaty the Council legislates regarding the work of the Structural Funds, but under Article 93 it is primarily the Commission which controls the compatibility of the work of these Funds with competition requirements. Resolution of conflicts likely to result as between the legislative powers of the Council and the 'administrative' powers of the Commission may mean that operation of the institutional-law provisions conferring these powers has to be modified in accordance with reconciled requirements of the relevant economic-law provisions.

---

[31] Its application may also be misguided to the extent that it fails to acknowledge 'the infant-clean-industry' argument. See H. Verbruggen, 'Subsidies as an Instrument for Environmental Policy' in R. Gerritse (ed.), *Producer Subsidies* (Pinter, London, 1990) 122–33.

[32] Aid may exacerbate environmental problems or even, in the case of much R & D aid, create new problems. See L. Reijnders, 'Subsidies and the Environment' in R. Gerritse (ed.), n. 31 above, 111–21, 119–20.

[33] Or at least to prevent 'gross distortions' of competition (F. Cownie, 'State Aids in the Eighties'(1986) ELRev. 247).   [34] C.-D. Ehlermann, n. 1 above, 1213.

The latter provisions may have equivalent effects on intra-institutional relations. For example, Article 162(2) of the Treaty provides for the Commission to adopt rules of procedure to regulate the functioning of its departments. However, Treaty provisions regarding agricultural aid and transport aid may entail that the Directorates General concerned with these two sectors approach the requirements of economic-law provisions differently from Directorate General IV. The vertical structure of Directorates General is regarded as limiting the possibility of policies evolved in one Directorate General penetrating the thinking of others.[35] The result is that integration of the various policies into state-aid control may be impeded. Occasional Green Papers, discretionary guidelines, and joint Council meetings are considered inadequate for this purpose, since they do not form a structured programme of systematic administrative adjustment or reform.[36] Conflict-resolution may depend not only on reconciliation of the various requirements of economic-law provisions but also on the consistency of such reconciliation and the modification of the operation of institutional-law provisions.[37]

On the other hand, institutional-law provisions may affect the content of decisions. Such decisions may be said to evidence the transformation of aid control from an administrative procedure between civil servants into a system of economic law enforcement.[38] Thus aid granted by a Member State is no longer controlled exclusively or principally in the interest of other Member States, but also, and perhaps even more so, in the interests of competitors of the intended aid beneficiaries.[39] In other words, the original macroeconomic approach of the Treaty authors is being supplanted progressively by a microeconomic perspective, similar to that which has always dominated substantive and procedural anti-trust law.[40] This transformation may reflect the fact that procedures established by institutional-law provisions affect the requirements in Article 92 which are invoked[41] and, therefore, activated in state-aid decisions.

[35] The Commission is said to be divided into 'watertight compartments which do not communicate with each other'. See *The Future of Rural Society*, House of Lords Select Committee on the European Communities, HL(1989–90)80–I, 33.

[36] *Fifth Environmental Action Programme: Integration of Community Policies*, House of Lords Select Committee on the European Communities, HL(1992–3)27, 7–8.

[37] 'Concentration [of aid control] in DG IV would guarantee coherence and consistency' (C.-D. Ehlermann, n. 1 above, 1222).

[38] C.-D. Ehlermann, 'State Aids under European Community Competition Law' (1994) 18 *Fordham Int. LJ* 410–36, 436.

[39] Thus according to the Commission, 'all manufacturers are entitled to a consistent approach compatible with the Treaty.' See Community framework on state aid to the motor-vehicle industry ([1989] OJ C123/3), para. 1.   [40] C.-D. Ehlermann, n. 1 above, 1219.

[41] According to the Opinion of the Economic and Social Committee of 22 Nov. 1995 ([1996] OJ C39/79) on the *Twenty-Fourth Report on Competition Policy*, para. 6.7, 'details of the launch of formal enquiries should be passed on to the social partners and the ESC at an early stage, albeit without setting up a formal consultation procedure'. The same Committee has also called for the Commission to consider establishing a publicly accessible register of all aid granted. See the Opinion of 22 Nov. 1995 ([1996] OJ C39/1) on an industrial competitiveness policy for the European Union, para. 3.3.5.14. The demand for information may be seen as

More particularly, limits to the role of the European Courts in relation to aid control may arise from the operation of institutional-law provisions. Such provisions may mean, for example, that a regional authority may lack standing to challenge before the Court of First Instance the grant of aid in more prosperous regions.[42] Similarly, environmental groups lack standing to challenge grants on environmental grounds.[43] Such limitations on access to the Court have the consequence that the range of Article 92 requirements likely to be invoked and, hence, activated and developed in proceedings before the Court is narrowed down.[44] This consequence may at least partly explain why the issues involved tend to be pictured in simple 'state versus market' terms and, more particularly, why this provision is not treated as prohibiting all aid that is inconsistent with economic and social cohesion or with environmental protection. The failure so to treat Article 92 fits uneasily with 'establishment' of Union Citizenship by Article 8 of the Treaty on European Union. Its establishment may imply that Union Citizens should be recognized as having rights to cohesion, environmental protection, and so on which should be fully taken into account in state-aid control.

Preliminary rulings might have enabled a broader range of Article 92 requirements to be invoked before the Court of Justice, but this possibility has been excluded by the finding of the Court that this provision is not directly effective. The Court may thus have preserved the decision-making role of the Commission under this provision, but it has done so at the expense of denying itself the opportunity to make the same contribution to the development of Union law governing state aid as it has made to development of the law governing the 'four freedoms'. This self-denial might be thought simply to reflect recognition of limits on the capacity of judges to resolve state-aid issues. However, the case law governing the four freedoms regularly requires national courts to deal with essentially the same issues—the acceptability of distortions of competition—as does the Commission under Article 92. Apparently, therefore, the reluctance of the Court to tackle aid issues reflects its assumptions, based on Articles 93 to 94, as to the inter-institutional relations intended by the Treaty authors.[45]

reflecting 'the overall debate on transparency following the Maastricht Treaty negotiations' (C.-D. Ehlermann, n. 1 above, 1219).

[42] Case 222/83 *Municipality of Differdange* v. *EC Commission* [1984] ECR 2889, 2896.

[43] In Case T–461/93 *An Taisce—The National Trust for Ireland and WWF UK (World Wide Fund for Nature)* v. *EC Commission* ([1994] ECR II–733) the CFI left open the question whether such a group had standing to challenge Commission decisions regarding the grant of Union aid.

[44] The Commission is concerned that there should not be a proliferation of judicial challenges to its decision making. See Case C–312/90 *Spain* v. *EC Commission: Cenemesa* [1992] ECR I–4117, I–4122.

[45] According to Roemer AG in Case 77/72 *Carmine Capolongo* v. *Azienda Agricola Maya* [1973] ECR 611, 630, aid control was a 'preserve' of the Commission, which was to be implemented in a uniform manner throughout the Union. According to the ECJ itself, in Case 78/76 *Firma Steinike und Weinlig* v. *Germany* [1977] ECR 595, 609, the intention of the Treaty, in providing

The problems implied for the practice of aid control may be recognizable to other social sciences as being of the kind addressed by public-choice theory and even of the kind with which studies of the relationship between the economic market and the political market are concerned. From a legal perspective, they may ultimately be attributed to the undeveloped constitutionalism of the Union. Particularly given the legitimacy crisis caused by the 'very redefinition of the European polity',[46] the European Parliament may be unable to provide an effective alternative to increased judicial involvement in tackling these problems.[47] Therefore, if these problems are to be tackled effectively, actors other than Member States and Union institutions may have to be granted the right to invoke the requirements of Article 92 before the European Courts on constitutional grounds without the need to show that their competitive position in the market is affected by Commission decision-making in the state-aid field. In other words, effective pursuit of the types of equality envisaged in Article 92 and promotion of institutional equality—as, for example, between environmental interests and sectoral interests or between different regions—may be interdependent processes.

Such interdependencies might be expected to have their counterparts in national law, given that Member States also pursue a range of policies having implications for the use of aid. However, the significance of specific features of the European Union should not be underestimated. For example, the potential for contradiction between competition policy and regional policy may be latent at the national level and hence inaccessible to democratic control, where both policies are the responsibility of the state. Indeed, Member States may prefer to provide aid in the form of grants rather than tax concessions because the former are less 'costly' in terms of parliamentary procedures.[48] Although, it is true, the Belgian Audit Court disputed whether aid from the Brussels Region was compatible with the Economic Expansion Law of 17 July 1959,[49] this was an exceptional case, apparently attributable to particular institutional arrangements in Belgium.

---

through Art. 93 for aid to be kept under constant review and supervised by the Commission, was that the finding that an aid might be incompatible with the common market was to be determined, subject to review by the Court, by means of an appropriate procedure which it was the Commission's responsibility to set in motion. This part of the ruling was followed in Joined Cases C–78–83/90 *Compagnie Commerciale de l'Ouest* [1992] ECR I–1847, I–1883.

[46] J. Weiler, 'The Transformation of Europe' (1991) 100 *Yale Law Journal* 2403–83, 2473.

[47] Though the annual reports on competition were introduced following a request of the European Parliament that such reports be provided. See the Resolution of 7 June 1971 ([1971] JO C66/11) on competition and the position of European undertakings in the common market and the world economy, para. 17.

[48] *Fourth Survey on State Aid in the European Community in the Manufacturing and Certain Other Sectors*, COM(95)365, 18.

[49] See Dec. 92/483 ([1992] OJ L288/25) concerning aid provided by the Brussels Regional Authorities in favour of the activities of Siemens SA in the data-processing and telecommunications sectors.

The usual situation within Member States may be contrasted with that within the Union. On the one hand, competition policy within the Union is the responsibility of the Commission—an institution independent of national governments. According to the Commission, aid control is 'an area where, by definition, the principle of subsidiarity plays only a minor role'.[50] On the other hand, in accordance with the formulation of the subsidiarity principle in Article 3b of the Treaty, it is national governments to which the main responsibility for implementation of regional policy is attached. The potential for contradiction between the two policies, which is scarcely articulated by conventional definitions of regional policy,[51] may thus be realised in the Union context.

The impact of these differing policy perspectives on aid control may be complicated by the dual character of Union decision-making procedures. Such procedures have two aspects: the organic and the intergovernmental.[52] The form taken by organic decision-making is predominantly that of negotiation between the Commission and Member States within the framework of Articles 92 to 94. Representatives of sectoral interests may also be involved in the negotiations leading to the adoption of decisions. The accessibility of such negotiation to regional interests or interests reflecting horizontal policy concerns may be more limited.[53]

Intergovernmental decision-making takes the form of bargains between Member States, and such bargains may result in Treaty amendments, protocols to accession agreements, and so on. Such decision-making might be thought to have a negative impact on organic decision-making, in that the bargains struck between Member States limit the room for manœuvre of the Union institutions.[54] However, the relationship between the two aspects of decision-making procedures is too complex to be regarded simply as one of conflict. The relationship may also be mutually reinforcing. Thus, for example, net contributors to the Union budget may find Treaty amendments containing commitments to economic and social cohesion more acceptable because of the Commission role in applying competition policy to investments subsidized by the Structural Funds. Equally, this role may derive support from the outcome

---

[50] *Twenty-Second Report on Competition Policy* (EC Commission, Brussels, 1993), 79; and *Twenty-Fourth Report on Competition Policy* (EC Commission, Brussels, 1995), 29.

[51] See, e.g., the definition in N. Vanhove and L. H. Klaassen, *Regional Policy: A European Approach* (Avebury, London, 1980), 43.

[52] Cf. D. Gerber, 'The Transformation of European Community Competition Law' (1994) 35 *Harv. Int. LJ* 97–147, 99, who distinguishes between 'those components of the system that operate as part of the process of establishing and applying generally applicable norms (here, the juridical components) and those that are the result of the political mediation of the interests of states and Community institutions'.

[53] Cf. the view, in relation to states, that the 'various bureaucracies are . . . incompletely coordinated and, because of their deficient capacity for perceiving and planning, dependent on the influence of their clients. It is precisely this deficient rationality of governmental administration that guarantees the success of organized special interests' in J. Habermas, *Legitimation Crisis* (Polity Press, Cambridge, 1988), 60.

[54] S. Padgett, n. 3 above, 54.

of intergovernmental decision-making, as, for example, when Treaty amendments are invoked by the Commission in support of stricter control of aid to the stronger regions. The relationship between the two aspects of Union decision-making may, therefore, seem to imply a pluralist approach to state-aid control.[55]

In reality, aid control through decision-making in which participation by regional interests or interests representing horizontal policy concerns (that is, 'latent interests'[56]) is not guaranteed[57] involves only limited pluralism. The establishment of the Committee of the Regions by Article 198a of the EC Treaty, as amended by the Treaty on European Union, might be regarded as a radical reform. However, even if such centralized representation were appropriate for ensuring that aid control took account of regional diversity,[58] the establishment of the Committee fails to guarantee regional participation, since there is no legal requirement that its members should be elected representatives of their respective regions.[59] An apparent consequence is that Union decision-making procedures remain ill adapted to aid-control.

Therefore, the obstacles and, by implication, the solutions to securing reform of aid control do not fall exclusively within the field of economic law. Such control does not depend solely on the operation of rules in Article 92 distinguishing between aid which is compatible with the common market and aid which is not compatible aid but also, particularly because of the impact of differing policy perspectives, on the interaction of such rules with those rules

[55] See, regarding the opportunities for Member States to 'participate in Commission decisions', the *Twenty-Fourth Report on Competition Policy* (EC Commission, Brussels, 1995), 78.

[56] M. Teutemann, *Completion of the Internal Market: An Application of Public Choice Theory* (Economic Papers No. 83, EC Commission, Brussels, 1990), 8. The solution advocated is 'the building up of non-institutionalized counter-influences within the system', in connection with which the theory of 'externalities' may be invoked (*ibid.*, 37).

[57] The French Green Party has apparently complained to the Commission about special rates for nuclear-generated electricity charged by the French company, EDF, to large industrial users. See L. Hancher, 'State Aids and Energy' in I. Harden (ed.), *State Aid: Community Law and Policy* (Bundesanzeiger, Trier, 1993), 136–50, 149. See also Commission Reply by Sir Leon Brittan to Written Question ([1990] OJ C233/21); and D. Vaughan (ed.), *EC Environment and Planning Law* (Butterworths, London, 1991), 237.

[58] The inadequacy of such representation is implicitly recognized by the Committee of the Regions itself, which considers that it should be represented on various committees consulted by the Commission, so as to ensure that views of *individual regions* affected by Union decisions will be 'heard'. See the Opinion of this Committee of 17 May 1994 ([1994] OJ C217/26) on the Proposal for a Decision laying down a series of guidelines on trans-European energy networks, para. A.5.1.

[59] The Commission had proposed that membership of the Committee should be limited to those holding elective office at regional or local level (Art. 198a(2) of the draft Treaty prepared by the Commission (Bull. EC, Supp. 2/91, at 178). See, similarly, the position of the European Parliament in its Resolution of 18 Nov. 1993 ([1993] OJ C329/279) on the participation and representation of the regions in the process of European integration: the Committee of the Regions, para. 9. Such proposals were not adopted in the final version of the Treaty. The reason, according to the Commission, is that 'the Member States have very different institutional structures which are exclusively within their purview'. See the Reply by Mr Millan to Written Question 1405/92 ([1993] OJ C16/15) by Sotiris Kostopoulos.

which govern the presentation and resolution of issues involved. This dependence may not simply be a matter of constitutional imperative.[60] If aid-control is fully to meet Treaty requirements, it may also be an inherent necessity.

Failure to secure reform of aid-control may mean that 'transaction-cost' problems, implicit in the increased diversity likely to result from future enlargements of the Union, may be exaggerated. According to Coase, a firm will tend to expand until the costs of organizing an extra transaction within the firm become equal to the costs of carrying out the same transaction by means of an exchange on the open market.[61] Dynamic analysis would take account of the capacity of the firm internally to reorganize and thereby to reduce the relative costs of expansion. If an analogy between the expansion of a firm and the expansion of the Union is justified, it seems that Union approaches to aid control will need to be adapted to cope with future enlargements.[62] The importance of adaptation may be greater for the Union than for the firm, given that expansion, at least in relation to Central Europe, may have the characteristics of a political imperative.

[60] 'State aid control in the EU is of constitutional nature, both with respect to substance and procedure' (C.-D. Ehlermann, n. 1 above, 1214).

[61] R. H. Coase, 'The Nature of the Firm' (1937) 4 *Economica* 386–405.

[62] According to the Conclusions of the Presidency at the Copenhagen Summit of June 1993, 'the Union's capacity to absorb new members, while maintaining the momentum of European integration, is also an important consideration in the general interest of both the Union and the candidate countries' (Bull. EC 6–1993, I.13).

Bibliography

AITKEN, P., 'SMEs, Research and Development and Technology Policies and the European Community: Issues in Implementation' in K. Dyson (ed.), *Local Authorities and New Technologies: The European Dimension* (Croom Helm, London, 1988), 59–83

ALBRECHTS, L., MOULAERT, F., ROBERTS, P., and SWYNGEDOUW, E., *Regional Policy at the Crossroads* (Kingsley, London 1989)

ALDSKOGIUS, G., 'Regionalpolitikens utmaningar' [1991] 4 *Nordrevy* 7–11

ALLEN, K., 'International Forces and Regional Policy' in *Internationalisering och regional utveckling* (NordREFO 1990:2), 37–46

—— 'Requirements for an Effective Regional Policy' in L. Albrechts *et al.*, *Regional Policy at the Crossroads* (London, 1989), 107–24

ANDRIESSEN, F., 'The Role of Anti-Trust in the Face of Economic Recession: State Aids in the EEC' [1983] *European Competition Law Review* 340–50

ARMSTRONG, H.W., 'Competition Policy in the Common Market: A Comment' [1984] *Regional Studies* 69–71

ATIK, J., 'Investment Contests and Subsidy Limitations in the EC' (1992) 32 *Virginia Journal of International Law* 837–69

BALASSA, B., *European Economic Integration* (North Holland, Amsterdam, 1975)

—— 'Subsidies and Countervailing Measures: Economic Considerations' in B. Balassa (ed.), *Subsidies and Countervailing Measures: Critical Issues for the Uruguay Round* (World Bank Discussion Paper No. 55, Washington, DC, 1989), 27–46

BALDWIN, R. E., 'Assessing the Fair Trade and Safeguards Laws in Terms of Modern Trade and Political Economy Analysis' (1992) 15 *The World Economy* 185–202

—— 'The Case Against Infant-Industry Tariff Protection' [1969] *Journal of Political Economy* 295–305

BARENTS, R., 'Recente ontwikkelingen in de rechtspraak over steunmaatnegelen' [1988] *SEW* 352–64.

BATTEN, D., *Infrastructure as a Network System: Mera Revisited* (CERUM Working Paper 1989:2, Umeå)

BEGG, I., 'European Integration and Regional Policy' [1989] *Oxford Review of Economic Policy* 90–104

—— 'The Regional Dimension of the "1992" Proposals' [1989] *Regional Studies* 368–76

BERNINI, G., 'The Rules on Competition' in EC Commission, *Thirty Years of Community Law* (EC Commission, Luxembourg, 1981), 323–73

BIANCARELLI, J., 'Le Contrôle de la Cour de Justice des Communautés européennes en matière d'aides publiques' [1993] *Actualité Juridique de Droit Administratif* 412–36

BLISS, C., 'Adjustment, Compensation and Factor Mobility in Integrated Markets' in C. Bliss and J. Braga de Macedo (eds.), *Unity with Diversity in the European Economy: The Community's Southern Frontier* (Cambridge University Press, Cambridge, 1990), 18–52

BLUMANN, C., 'Régime des aides d'état: jurisprudence récente de la Cour de Justice (1989–1992)' [1992] *Revue du Marché Commun et de l'Union européenne* 721–39

BUCK, T., 'Regional Policy and European Integration' [1975] *Journal of Common Market Studies* 368–78

CARCELEN CONESA, J. M., 'Hacia una politica regional comun en el marco de la CEE' [1983] *Revista de Instituciones Europeas* 475–91

CARDIEUX, J.-L., 'Restructuration industrielle et politique communautaire vis-à-vis des aides nationales' in J. Dutheil de la Rochère and J. Vandamme (eds.), *Interventions Publiques et Droit Communautaire* (Pedone, Paris, 1988), 77–88

CASPARI, M., 'EEC Competition Law and Industrial Policy' [1989] *Fordham Corporate Law Institute* 163–78.

CAVES, R. E., 'Industrial Policy and Trade Policy: The Connections' in H. Kierzkowski (ed.), *Protection and Competition in International Trade* (Blackwell, Oxford, 1987), 68–85

CENTRE FOR INTERNATIONAL ECONOMICS, *Costs of Coal Industry Assistance in West Germany* (Canberra, 1992)

CHARD, J. S. and MACMILLAN, M. J, 'Sectoral Aids and Community Competition Rules: The Case of Textiles' [1979] *Journal of World Trade Law* 132–57

CHEROT, J.-Y., 'La Discipline des aides nationales dans la Communauté européenne' [1993] *Revue d'Economie Industrielle* 222–41

COLLIARD, C. A., 'Eureka ou une Coopération technologique européenne' [1988] *Revue Trimestrielle de Droit Européen* 5–22

COLLINS, P. and HUTCHINGS, M., 'Articles 101 and 102 of the EEC Treaty: Completing the Internal Market' [1986] *European Law Review* 191–9

COOMBES, D. and REES, N., 'Regional and Social Policy' in L. Hurwitz and C. Lequesne (eds.), *The State of the European Community* (Lynne Reinner, London, 1991), 207–28

COUSSIRAT-COUSTÈRE, V., 'Les Aides locales aux entreprises face au droit communautaire' [1985] *Actualité Juridique de Droit Administratif* 171–86

COWNIE, F., 'State Aids in the Eighties' (1986) *European Law Review* 247–67

CRAMÉR, P. and ÖSTLING, L., *Svenskt statsstöd och samhandel med EEC* (Göteborg, 1986)

CURRAN, W. J., 'On Democracy and Economics' (1988) 33 *The Antitrust Bulletin* 753–77.

CURZON PRICE, V., *1992: Europe's Last Chance? From Common Market to Single Market* (Institute of Economic Affairs, London, 1988)

DAMETTE, F., 'The Regional Framework of Monopoly Exploitation: New Problems and Trends' in J. Carney, R. Hudson, and J. Lewis (eds.), *Regions in Crisis: New Perspectives in European Regional Theory* (Croom Helm, London, 1980), 76–92

DEHOUSSE, R., 'Completing the Internal Market: Institutional Constraints and Challenges' in R. Bieber, J. Pinder, and J. H. H. Weiler, *1992: One European Market* (Nomos, Baden-Baden, 1988), 311–36.

DESTERBECQ-FOBELETS, H., 'Le Contrôle externe de l'octroi des aides étatiques aux entreprises privées en Belgique' [1979] *Administration Publique* 277–301

DIXIT, A. and KYLE, A., 'The Use of Protection and Subsidies for Entry Protection and Deterrence' (1985) 75 *American Economic Review* 139–52

DOMINICK, M. F., 'Countervailing State Aids to Steel: A Case for International Consensus' (1984) 21 *Common Market Law Review* 355–403

DONY, M., 'La Participation des pouvoirs publics au capital des entreprises et le droit de la concurrence' [1986] *Cahiers de Droit Européen* 161–84

—— 'Les Aides aux entreprises et le droit communautaire de la concurrence' (1991) 1316 *Courrier hebdomadaire de la centre de recherche et d'information socio-politiques*

EC COMMISSION, *The Measurement of the Aid Element of State Acquisition of Company Capital* (Evolution of Concentration and Competition Series: Collection: Working Papers 87)

EHLERMANN, C.-D., 'The Contribution of EC Competition Policy to the Single Market' (1992) 29 *Common Market Law Review* 257–82

—— 'Les Enterprises publiques et le contrôle des aides d'état' [1992] *RMC* 613–20.

—— 'State Aids under European Community Competition Law' (1994) 18 *Fordham International Law Journal* 410–36

—— 'State Aid Control in the European Union: Success or Failure?' (1995) 18 *Fordham International Law Journal* 1212–29

ESER, T. W., 'Die Kontrolle regionaler Beihilfen im Rahmen der Wettbewerbspolitik der Europäischen Gemeinschaften' [1989] *Raumforchung und Raumordnung* 202–16

EVANS, A., 'Freedom of Trade under the Common Law and European Community Law: The Case of the Football Bans' (1984) 102 *Law Quarterly Review* 510–42

—— 'Energy Pricing and Community Law: *Kwekerij Gebroeders van der Kooy BV, Joannes Wilhelms van Vliet, the Landbouwschap and the Netherlands: Commission v. Netherlands*' (1988/89) *Oil and Gas Law and Taxation Review* 70

—— 'Competition Policy and Regional Policy under the Europe Agreements' in A. Zielinska-Glebocka *et al.* (eds.), *Transformation and Integration in Europe* (University of Gdansk, 1994) 117–43

—— *European Community Law, including the EEA Agreement* (Kluwer, Deventer and Stockholm, 1994)

—— *The Law of EU Regional Policy* (Kluwer, Deventer, 1995)

—— and MARTIN, S., 'Socially Acceptable Distortion of Competition: EC Policy on State Aid' [1991] *European Law Review* 79–111

FLYNN, J. H., 'Legal Reasoning, Antitrust Policy and the Social "Science" of Economics' (1988) 33 *The Antitrust Bulletin* 713–43

FRAZER, T., 'The New Structural Funds, State Aids and Interventions on the Single Market' [1995] *European Law Review* 3–19

GAISFORD, J.D. and McLACHLAN, D. L., 'Domestic Subsidies and Countervail: the Treacherous Ground of the Level Playing Field' [1990] *Journal of World Trade* 55–77

GANSHOF, VAN DER MEERSCH, W. G., *Le Droit des Communautés Euuropéennes* (Larcier, Brussels, 1969)

GANZ, G. *Quasi-Legislation* (Sweet & Maxwell, London, 1987)

GARBAR, C., 'Aides d'état: pratique décisionnelle de la Commission de la Communauté européenne (1990–1994)' [1995] *Revue du Marché Commun* 36–45

GERBER, D., 'The Transformation of European Community Competition Law?' (1994) 35 *Harvard International Law Journal* 97–147

GIEGERICH, T., 'The European Dimension of German Reunification: East Germany's Integration into the European Communities' [1991] *Zeitschrift für ausländisches öffentliches Recht und Völkerrecht* 384–450

GILCHRIST, J. and DEACON, D., 'Curbing Subsidies' in P. Montagnon (ed.), *European Competition Policy* (Pinter, London, 1990), 31–51

GRABITZ, E., 'Réglementation nationale des aides aux entreprises et droit communautaire' in J. Dutheil de la Rochere and J Vandamme (eds.), *Interventions Publiques et Droit Communautaire* (Pedone, Paris, 1988), 72–6

—— and HILF, M., *Kommentar zum Europäische Union* (Beck, Munich, 1992)

—— and ZACKER C., 'Scope for Action by the EC Member States for the Improvement of Environmental Protection under EEC Law: The Example of Environmental Taxes and Subsidies' (1989) 26 *Common Market Law Review* 423–47

HABERMAS, J., *Legitimation Crisis* (Polity Press, Cambridge, 1988)

HAILBRONNER, K., 'Legal Aspects of the Unification of the Two German States' [1991] *European Journal of International Law* 18–41

HANCHER, L., 'State Aids and Judicial Control in the European Community' [1994] *European Competition Law Review* 134–50

——, OTTERVANGER, T. and SLOT, P.J., *EC State Aids* (Chancery Law Publishing, London, 1993)

HARDEN, I. (ed.), *State Aid: Community Law and Policy* (*Bundesanzeiger*, Trier, 1993)

HAWK, B., 'La Recherche et le développement en droit communautaire et en droit antitrust américain' [1987] *Revue Internationale de Droit Economique* 211–69

—— 'The American (Anti-trust) Revolution: Lessons for the EEC' [1988] *European Competition Law Review* 53–87

HEINE, J., 'Les Mesures prises dans le secteur agricole pour l'intégration de la RDA dans la Communauté' [1991] *Revue du Marché Commun* 199–217

HELLER, T. and PELKMANS, J., 'The Federal Economy: Law and Economic Integration and the Positive State—The U.S.A. and Europe Compared in an Economic Perspective' in M. Cappelletti *et al.* (eds.), *Integration Through Law* (Berlin, 1986), i, 245–412

HELLINGMAN, K., 'State Participation as State Aid under Article 92 of the EEC Treaty: The Commission Guidelines' (1986) 23 *Common Market Law Review* 111–131

HUDSON, R. and SADLER, D., *The International Steel Industry: Restructuring, State Policies and Localities* (Routledge, London, 1989)

HUGHES, G. and HARE, P., 'Competitiveness and Industrial Restructuring in Czechoslovakia, Hungary and Poland' in *European Economy* (Special Edition No. 2, 'The Path of Reform in Central and Eastern Europe'), 83–105

HULTIN, C., 'The Effects of State Aid on Employment in the French Textile and Clothing Industry' [1989] *International Journal of Industrial Organization* 489–501

JACQUEMIN, A. and SAPIR, A., 'European Integration World Integration?' [1988] *Weltwirtschaftliches Archiv* 127–39

—— 'La Perspective 1992 et l'après Uruguay Round' [1990] *Economie Prospective Internationale* 47–67

JENNY, F. J., 'Competition and State Aid Policy in the European Community' [1994] 18 *Fordham International Law Journal* 525–54

—— 'Competition and State Aid Policy in the European Union' [1994] *Fordham Corporate Law Institute* 75–98

JOHNSON, H. G. *Aspects of the Theory of Tariffs* (Allen and Unwin, London, 1971)

JOVANOVIC, M. N. *International Economic Integration* (Routledge, London, 1992)

KARSTEN, D., 'Regional Policy' in C.-C. Schweitzer and D. Karsten (eds.), *The Federal Republic of Germany and EC Membership Evaluated* (Pinter, London, 1990), 94–101

KIERZKOWSKI, H. (ed.), *Protection and Competition in International Trade* (Oxford University Press, Oxford, 1987)

KOVAR, R., 'Les Prises de participation publiques et le régime communautaire des aides d'état' [1992] *Revue Trimestrielle de Droit Européen* 109–57

KRUGMAN, P., 'Introduction: New Thinking About Trade Policy' in P. Krugman (ed.), *Strategic Trade Policy and the New International Economics* (MIT Press, Cambridge, Mass., 1986)

KRÄMER, L., *EEC Treaty and Environmental Protection* (Sweet & Maxwell, London, 1990)

KUKLINSKI, A., *Efficiency versus Equality: Old Dilemmas and New Approaches in Regional Policy* (European Policies Research Centre Research Paper No. 8, Glasgow, 1990)

LANGHAMMER, R. J., *EC Integration Widening Towards Eastern Europe* (Kiel Working Paper No. 524, 1992)

LASOK, D., 'State Aids and Remedies under the EEC Treaty' [1986] *ECLR* 53–60

LAYARD, P. R. G. and NICKELL, S. J. 'The Case for Subsidising Extra Jobs' (1980) 90 *The Economic Journal* 51–73

LE BOZEC, A., 'Les Aides nationales à la construction de navires de pêche: une specificité toujours plus affirme' [1990] *Revue du Marché Commun* 702–7

LEHNER, S. and MEIKLEJOHN, R., 'Fair Competition in the Internal Market' (1991) 48 *European Economy* 7–148

LEMMENS, J., 'Les Aides dans le domaine des transports' [1966] *Revue du Marché Commun* 135–41

LIIKANEN, E., 'Structural Changes and European Integration—A Finnish View' in *Internationalisering och regional utveckling* (NordREFO, Copenhagen, 1990), 23–7

LIPSEY, R. G. and LANCASTER, K., 'The General Theory of the Second Best' (1956) 23 *Review of Economic Studies* 11–32

LUNDBERG, L., 'Economic Integration, Inter- and Intra-Industry Trade: The Case of Sweden and the EC' [1992] *Scandinavian Journal of Economics* 393–408

LYCK, L., 'Regional Policy' in L. Lyck (ed.), *Denmark and EC Membership Evaluated* (Pinter, London, 1992) 158–64

MACCORMICK, N. and WEINBURGER, O., *An Institutinal Theory of Law* (Reidel, Dordrecht, 1986).

MARQUES, A., 'Community Competition Policy and Economic and Social Cohesion' [1992] *Regional Studies* 404–7

MARQUES MENDES, A. J., 'Economic Cohesion in Europe: The Impact of the Delors Plan' [1990] *Journal of Common Market Studies* 17–36

MARSH, J., 'Agriculture and Structural Policy' in K. Burger, M. Groot, J. Post, and V. Zachariasse (eds.), *Agricultural Economics and Policy: International Challenges for the Nineties* (Elsevier, Amsterdam, 1991), 95–118

MARTIN, J. M. F. and STEHMANN, O., 'Product Market Integration versus Regional Cohesion in the Community' [1991] *European Law Review* 216–43

MARTIN, R. C. and PELZMAN, J., 'The Regional Welfare Effects of Tariff Reductions on Textile Products' [1983] *Journal of Regional Science* 323–36

MATTERA, A., *Le Marché unique européen: ses règles, son fonctionnement* (2nd edn., Jupiter, Paris, 1990)

McINERNEY, J., 'Agricultural Policy at the Crossroads' [1986] *Countryside Planning Yearbook* 44–75

MEGRET, J., LOUIS, J.-V., VIGNES, D., WAELBROECK, M., DEWOST, J. L., BRUECKNER, P., and SACCHETTINI, A., *Le Droit des Communautés Européennes* (Université Libre de Bruxelles, Brussels, 1972)

MELCHIOR, M., 'Les communications de la Commission' in *Mélanges en honneur de Fernand Dehousse* (Labor, Brussels, 1979), ii, 243–58

MINNECI, F., 'Le Partecipazioni pubbliche al capitale di imprese' [1991] *Diritto Comunitario e degli Scambi Internazionali* 365–72

MOLLE, W. *Regional Disparity and Economic Development in the European Community* (Saxon House, London, 1980)

—— and CAPPELLIN, R. (eds.), *Regional Impact of Community Policies in Europe* (Avebury, Aldershot 1988)

MORCH, H., 'Summary of the Most Important Recent Developments' [1994] 3 *Competition Policy Newsletter* 61

—— 'Summary of the Most Important Recent Developments' [1995] 3 *Competition Policy Newsletter* 41–7

—— 'Summary of the Most Important Recent Developments' [1995] 4 *Competition Policy Newsletter* 47

—— 'Summary of the Most Important Recent Developments' [1995] 5 *Competition Policy Newsletter* 43–9

—— 'Summary of the Most Important Recent Developments' [1995] 6 *Competition Policy Newsletter* 41

—— 'Summary of the Most Important Recent Developments' [1995] 6 *Competition Policy Newsletter* 41–7

MORTELMANS, K., 'The Compensatory Justification Criterion in the Practice of the Commission in Decisions on State Aids' (1984) 21 *Common Market Law Review* 405–34

MUELLER, H. and VAN DER VEN, H., 'Perils in the Brussels-Washington Steel Pact of 1982' (1982) 5 *The World Economy* 259–78

NEVEN, D. J. and VICKERS, J., 'Public Policy towards Industrial Restructuring: Some Issues Raised by the Internal Market Programme' in K. Cool, D. J. Neven, and I. Walter (eds.), *European Industrial Restructuring in the 1990s* (Macmillan, London, 1992), 162–98

O'DONNELL, R., 'Industrial Policy' in P. Keatinge (ed.), *Ireland and EC Membership Evaluated* (Pinter, London, 1991) 96–103

PADGETT, S., 'The Single European Energy Market: The Politics of Realisation' [1992] *Journal of Common Market Studies* 53–75

PALMIERI, G. *Gli Aiuti di Stato alle attivita produttive ed il loro regime comunitario* (Rimini, 1989)

PAPPALARDO, A., 'Aiuti regionali e controlli comunitari' in F. Cuocolo *et al.*, *Istituti Comunitarie e Regioni* (Edizione Scientifiche Italiane, Naples, 1990) 113–18

PELKMANS, J., 'The European Community and the Newly Industrializing Countries' in W. Maihofer (ed.), *Noi si Mura* (European University Institute, Florence 1986), 510–39

PEMBERTON, M. *Europe's Motor Industry after 1992* (Economist Intelligence Unit, London, 1991)

PETERSEN, A., 'State Aid and European Union: State Aid in the Line of Trade, Competition, Industrial and Cohesion Policies' in I. Harden (ed.) *State Aid: Community Law and Policy* (Bundesanzeiger, Trier, 1993)

PETERSON, J., 'Technology Policy in Europe: Explaining the Framework Programme and Eureka in Theory and Practice' [1991] *Journal of Common Market Studies* 269–90

PFALLER, A., GOUGH, I., AND THERBORN, G. (eds.), 'The Issue' in A. Pfaller *et al.*, *Can the Welfare State Compete?* (Macmillan, London, 1991), 1–14

PINDER, J., 'Positive Integration and Negative Integration: Some Problems of Economic Union in the EEC' [1968] *The World Today* 88–110

POSNER, R. A. 'The Behaviour of Administrative Agencies' (1972) 1 *Journal of Legal Studies* 305–47

—— *Antitrust Law: An Economic Perspective* (University of Chicago Press, Chicago, Ill., 1976)

POURRE, C., 'Le umul d'aides' [1993] *Actualité Juridique de Droit Administratif* 444–50

QUADRI, R., MONACO. R., AND TRABUCCHI, A., *Trattato Istitutivo della Communità Europea del Carbone e dell' Acciaio: Commentario* (Giuffrè, Milan, 1970)

QUIGLEY, C., 'The Notion of State Aid in the EEC' [1988] *European Competition Law Review* 242–56

Reijnders, L., 'Subsidies and the Environment' in R. Gerritse (ed.), *Producer Subsidies* (Pinter, London, 1990), 111–21

RENGELING, H.-W., 'Das Beihilferecht der Europäischen Gemeinschaften' in B. Borner and K. Neundorfer (eds.), *Recht und Praxis der Beihilfen im Gemensamen Markt* (Heymann, Cologne, 1984), 23–54

Roberti, G. M., 'Le Contrôle de la Commission des Communautés européennes sur les aides nationales' [1993] *Actualité Juridique de Droit Administratif* 397–411

ROSENBLATT, J., MAYER, T., BARTHOLDY, K., DEMEKAS, D., GUPTA, S., and LIPSCHITZ, L., *The Common Agricultural Policy of the European Community: Principles and Consequences* (International Monetary Fund, Washington, DC, 1988)

ROSS, M., 'A Review of Developments in State Aids 1987–88' (1989) 26 *Common Market Law Review* 167–92

ROTTENBURG, S., 'Adjustment to Senility by Induced Contraction' [1964] *Journal of Political Economy* 575–83

SACLE, A., 'Les Aides d'état et la Communauté économique européene' [1965] *Revue du Marché Commun* 136–44

SANTIAGO, M. G., 'Las "comunicaciones interpretativas" de la Comission: concepto y valor normativo' [1992] *Revista de Instituciones Europeas* 933–49

SCHAUER, F. 'Formalism' (1988) 97 *Yale Law Journal* 509–48

SCHEUING, D. H., *Les aides financières publiques* (Berger-Levrault, Paris, 1974)

Schina, D. *State Aids under the EEC Treaty* (ESC, Oxford, 1987)

Schmiedling, H. *External Protection for the Emerging Market Economies?* (Kiel Working Paper No. 498, Kiel, 1991)

Schrader, J.-V., 'EC Agricultural and Regional Policy: Consistent Interventions or Cumulative Inconsistencies' [1989] *Inter-Economics* 167–73

Schütte, M., and Hix, J.-P., 'The Application of the EC State Aid Rules to Privatizations: The East German Example' (1995) 32 *Common Market Law Rev.* 215.

Schwartz, W. F. and Harper, E. W. 'The Regulation of Subsidies Affecting International Trade' (1972) 70 *Michigan Law Review* 831–58

Siebert, H., *Real Adjustment in the Transformation Process: Risk Factors in East Germany* (Kiel Working Paper No. 507, Kiel, 1992)

Slot, P. J., 'Procedural Aspects of State Aids: The Guardian of Competition versus the Subsidy Villains?' (1990) 27 *Common Market Law Review* 741–60

Slotboom, M. M., 'State Aid in Community Law: Broad or Narrow Definition?' [1995] *European Law Review* 289–301

Smit, H. and Herzog, P., *The Law of the European Economic Community: A Commentary on the EEC Treaty* (Matthew Bender, New York, 1990)

Snape, R. H., 'The Importance of Frontier Barriers' in H. Kierzkowski (ed.), *Protection and Competition in International Trade* (Oxford University Press, Oxford, 1987), 215–32

Snyder, F., 'The Effectiveness of European Community Law: Institutions, Processes, Tools and Techniques' (1993) 56 *Modern Law Review* 19–54

Soames, T., and Ryan, A., 'State Aid and Air Transport' [1995] *Eur4opean Competition Law Review* 290–309

Stammati, G., 'Disciplina degliaiuti' in A. Valsecchi and G. Stammati, *L'Integrazione Economica Europea* (Jandi Sapi, Rome, 1960), 274

Teubner, G., 'Autopoiesis in Law and Society: A Rejoinder to Blankenburg' (1984) 18 *Law and Society Review* 281–301

Tichy, G., 'Theoretical and Empirical Considerations on the Dimension of an Optimum Integration Area in Europe' [1992] *Aussenwirtschaft* 107–37

Tinbergen, J., *International Economic Integration* (Amsterdam 1954)

—— *International Economic Integration* (2nd edn., Amsterdam 1965)

Tsoukalis, L., *The New European Economy: The Politics and Economics of Integration* (Oxford University Press, Oxford, 1991)

van Empel, M., 'Technology and Common Market Law' in Aspen Institut Colloquium on European Law, *Technological Development and Cooperation in Europe—Legal Aspects* (TMC Asser Institute, The Hague, 1986), 57–71

Verbruggen, H., 'Subsidies as an Instrument for Environmental Policy' in R. Gerritse (ed.), *Producer Subsidies* (London, 1990), 122–33

von der Groeben, H., von Boeckh, H., Thiessing, J., and Ehlermann, C.-D., *Kommentar zum EWG-Vertrag* (Nomos, Baden-Baden, 1983)

Wadley, D., *Restructuring the Regions* (OECD, Paris, 1986)

Waelbroeck, J., 'The Logic of EC Commercial and Industrial Policy Making' in A. Jacquemin (ed.), *European Industry: Public Policy and Corporate Strategy* (Clarendon Press, Oxford, 1984), 99–125

Wäldchen, P., 'Industrial Change, New Technologies and EC Regional Policy' in

K. Dyson (ed.), *Local Authorities and New Technologies: The European Dimension* (London 1988) 49–58

WELLENS, K. C. and BORCHARDT, G. M., 'Soft Law in European Community Law' (1989) 14 *European Law Review* 267–321

WESTHOLM, E. *Lansbygd i EG* (ERU-rapport nr. 58, Expertgruppen for Forskning om Regional Utueckling, Stockholm, 1990)

WHITING, A. (ed.) *The Economics of Industrial Subsidies* (HMSO, London, 1976)

WHITLEY, J. D. and WILSON, R. A., 'The Macroeconomic Merits of a Marginal Employment Subsidy' (1983) 93 *The Economic Journal* 862–80

WIBE, S., 'Policy Failures in Managing Forests' in OECD, *Market and Government Failures in Environmental Management: Wetlands and Forests* (OECD, Paris, 1992), 45–82

WINTER, J. A. *Nationale Steunmaatregelen en het Gemeenschapsrecht* (Kluwer, Deventer, 1981)

—— 'Supervision of State Aid: Article 93 in the Court of Justice' (1993) 30 *Common Market Law Review* 311–29

WINTERS, A., 'Goals and Own Goals in European Trade Policy' (1992) 15 *The World Economy* 557–74

WISHLADE, F. G., 'Competition Policy, Cohesion and the Coordination of Regional Aids in the European Community' [1993] *European Competition Law Rev.* 143–50

WOHLFARTH, E., EVERLING, U., GLAESNER, H. J., and SPRUNG, R., *Die Europäische Wirtschaftsgemeinschaft, Kommentar zum Vertrag* (Vahlen, Berlin, 1960)

Index

484   *Index*